DESIGNING MOVIE CREATURES AND CHARACTERS

BEHIND THE SCENES WITH THE MOVIE MASTERS

RICHARD RICKITT

Editor: Chris Middleton
Art director: Tony Seddon
Design: Studio Tonne

Focal Press is an imprint of Elsevier
30 Corporate Drive, Suite 400, Burlington, MA 01803, USA
Linacre House, Jordan Hill, Oxford OX2 8DP, UK

RotoVision SA
Sales and Editorial Office
Sheridan House, 114 Western Road
Hove BN3 1DD, UK
Tel: +44 (0)1273 72 72 68
Fax: +44 (0)1273 72 72 69
www.rotovision.com

Library of Congress Cataloging-in-Publication Data

British Library Cataloguing-in-Publication Data
A catalogue record for this book is available from the British Library.

ISBN 13: 978-0-240-80846-8
ISBN 10: 0-240-80846-0

For information on all Focal Press publications visit our website at www.focalpress.com

06 07 08 09 10 10 9 8 7 6 5 4 3 2 1

Reprographics in Singapore by ProVision Pte.
Tel: +65 6334 7720
Fax: +65 6334 7721

Printed in Singapore by Star Standard Industries (Pte) Ltd

DESIGNING MOVIE CREATURES AND CHARACTERS

BEHIND THE SCENES WITH THE MOVIE MASTERS

ELSEVIER

Amsterdam • Boston • Heidelberg • London
New York • Oxford • Paris • San Diego
San Francisco • Singapore • Sydney • Tokyo

Focal Press is an imprint of Elsevier

Focal Press

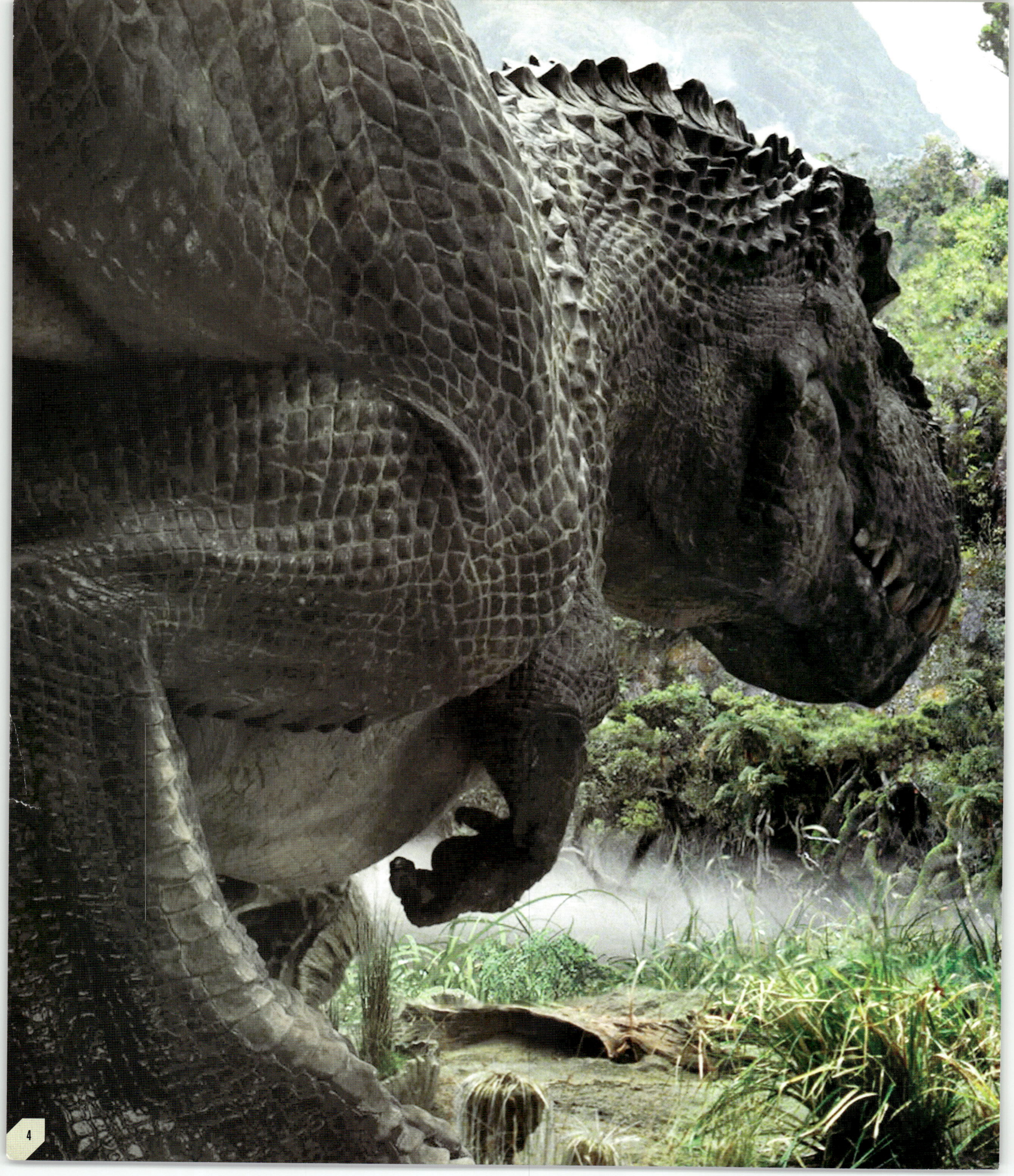

CONTENTS

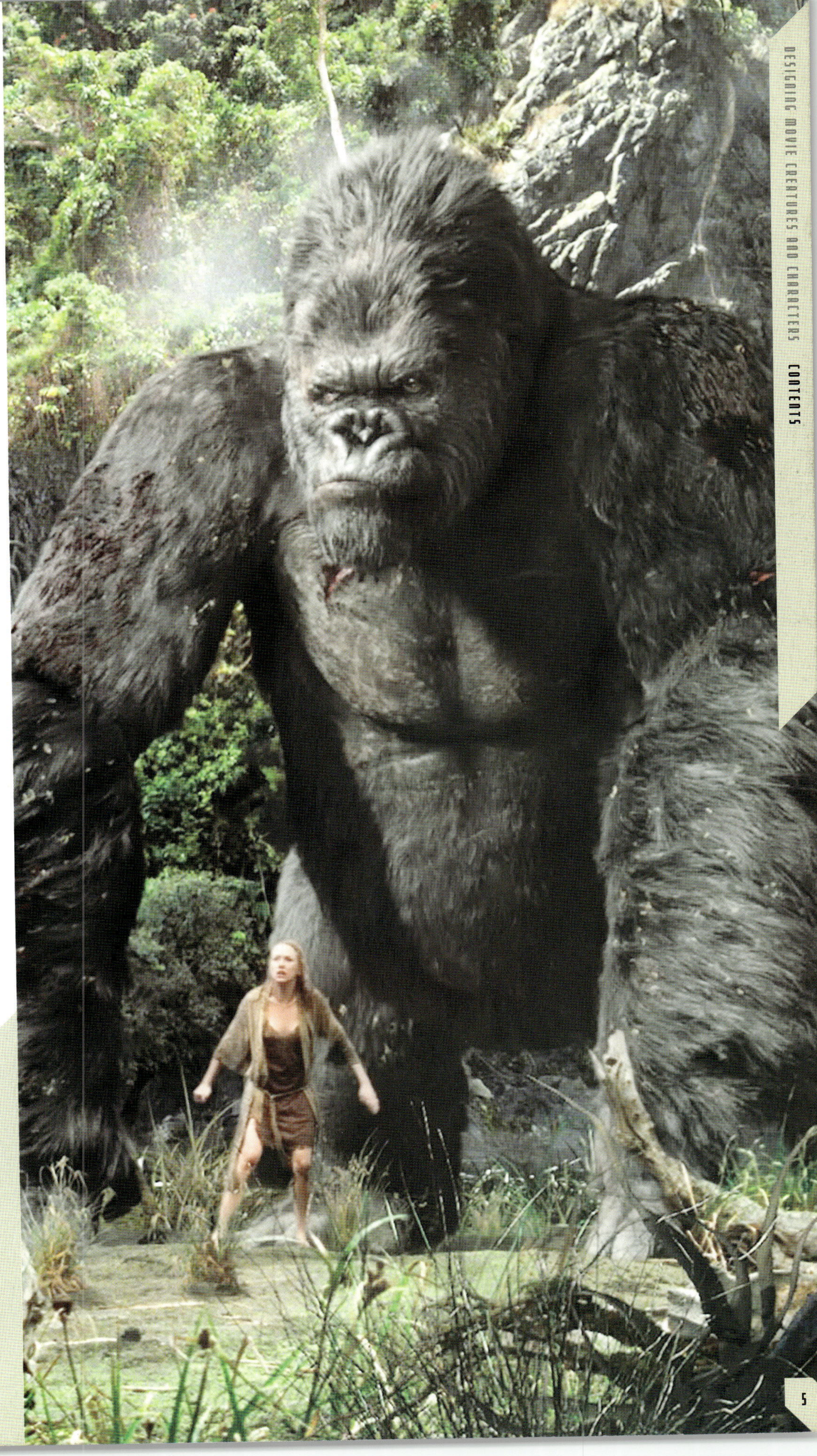

DAWN OF THE MONSTERS: 1895–CGI

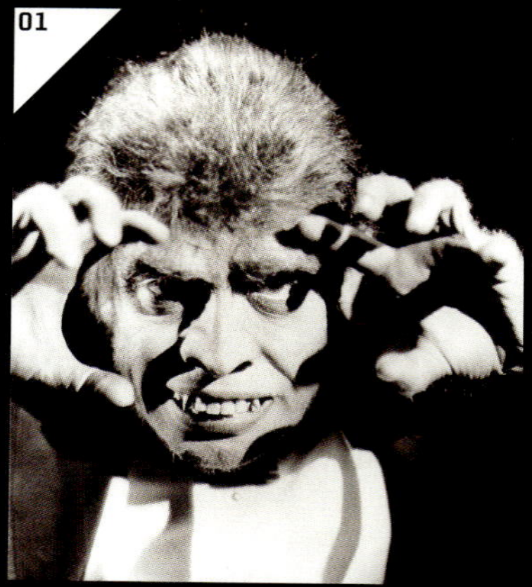

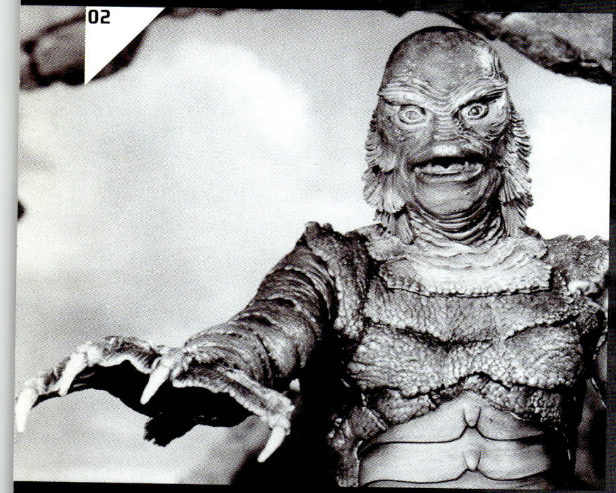

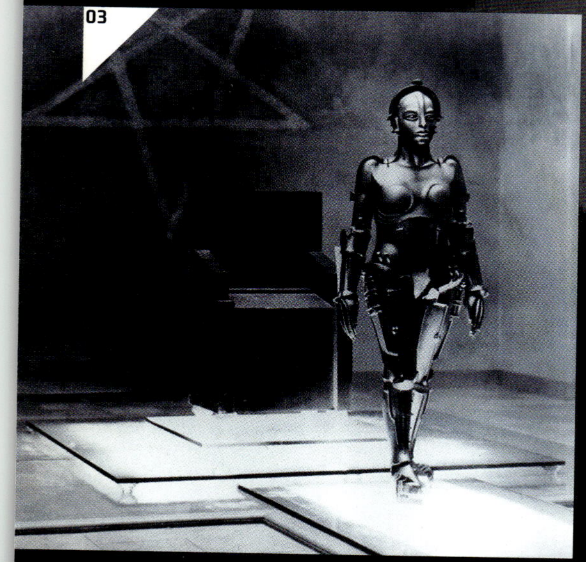

Since mankind first told stories, we have been both fascinated and frightened by monsters of the imagination, but it was only with the invention of moving pictures that showmen could begin to create fantastic creatures and characters that had true realism, flair, and sophistication.

In 1895, Parisian Georges Méliès (1861–1938) was one of the first people to see a demonstration of the Cinématographe, the miracle of moving pictures devised by brothers Auguste and Louis Lumière. Méliès saw the Cinématographe as a chance to create elaborate illusions. Building a studio in his Paris garden, Méliès produced hundreds of movies, often with a supernatural theme. By stopping and starting the camera mid-shot, and using double-exposures and fantastic makeups, audiences could watch a scientist use an X-ray machine to extract the skeleton from a living body, Satan remove his own head, and a skeletal horse pull a phantom carriage. For his spectacular adventure *Conquest of the Pole* (1912), Méliès built an enormous puppet of an Ice Giant. The 23ft-high (7m) bust, built of plaster, timber, and papier-mâché, was controlled by a large crew of puppeteers using pulleys, winches, and capstans. It was the first great mechanical movie monster.

The first iconic monster makeup was for the Edison Company's 1910 adaptation of *Frankenstein*, but the best-known example from the silent era is F.W. Murnau's *Nosferatu* (1922), an adaptation of Bram Stoker's *Dracula*. In it, actor Max Schrek wore false nose, chin, and ears, as well as claw-like finger extensions to become the first movie vampire.

In Hollywood, mechanical marvels were becoming the stars of the show. One example was the life-size brontosaurus tail built for *The Lost World* (1925). One of the most expensive movies of its day, it also premiered the animated dinosaurs of early stop-motion pioneer, Willis O'Brien.

(01) Fredric March in *Dr. Jekyll and Mr Hyde* (1931)
(02) The Gill Man from *The Creature from the Black Lagoon* (1954)
(03) The first movie robot, Maria, in Fritz Lang's *Metropolis* (1927).

04

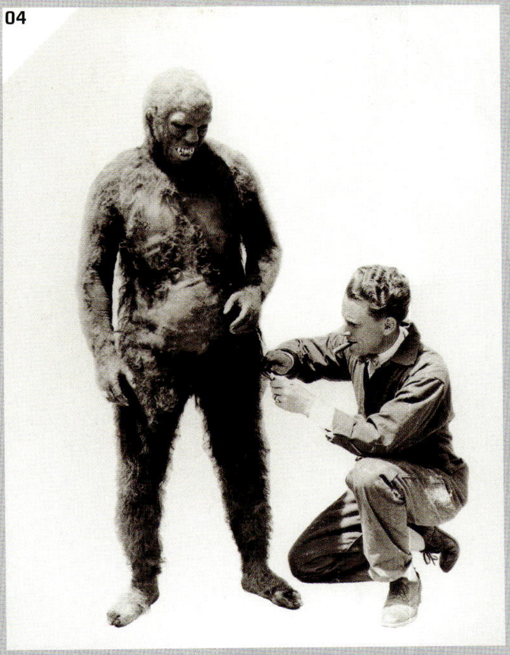

05

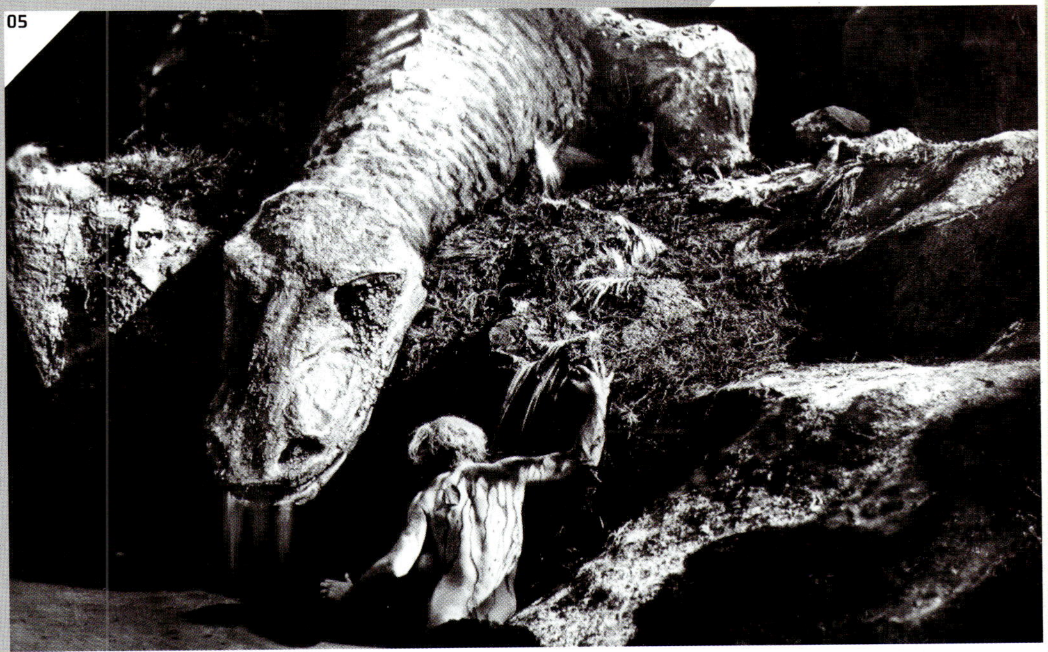

06

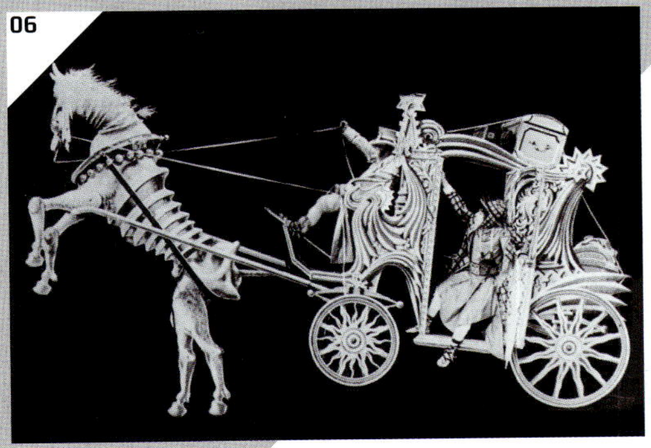

07

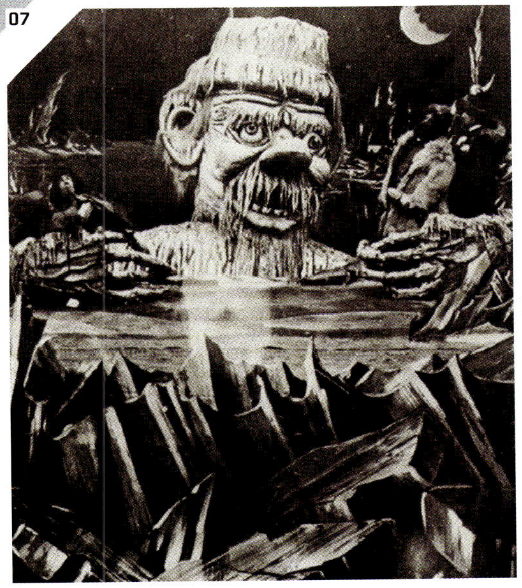

08

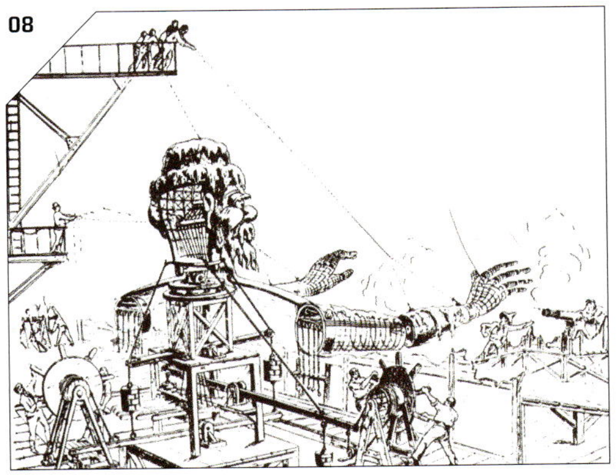

(04) Ape-man makeup applied by Cecil Holland (*The Lost World*, 1925) **(05)** Fafner, the dragon (*Die Niebelungen*, 1924) **(06)** Phantom carriage from Méliès' *The Four Hundred Tricks of the Devil* (1906) **(07–08)** Ice monster and mechanical designs for *Conquest of the Pole* (1912).

One of the 1920s' most enduring creatures was the first movie robot, Maria, in Fritz Lang's *Metropolis* (1927). Walter Schultze-Mittendorf sculpted the art deco curves of the character's outer shell, modeled on actress Brigitte Helm, using a putty-like material called plastic wood. The hugely influential design was echoed in many later movie robots, from *Star Wars*' C-3PO to Robocop.

One of the prime movers of special-effects makeup was English actor Cecil Holland (1887–1973), who later became Hollywood's first full-time makeup artist, but the true master was Lon Chaney (1883–1930). Chaney strove to find ever more extreme methods of portraying his outlandish characters, earning himself the title "Man of a Thousand Faces." His roles included Quasimodo in *The Hunchback of Notre Dame* (1923) and Erik in *The Phantom of the Opera* (1925). After his death, his son, Lon Chaney Jr, continued his work with similar success. Indeed, the 1930s was the first golden age of movie monsters, heralded in 1931 by Universal's smash-hit *Dracula*. Bela Lugosi's creepy screen presence was aided by a green makeup that gave his skin an ethereal appearance when shot in black and white. It was made by makeup artist Max Factor (1904–96), to a formulation by Universal Studios' Jack Pierce (1889–1968).

Other horrors followed. For Universal's *Frankenstein* (1931), actor Boris Karloff spent six hours a day being transformed into the monster by Pierce. The makeup included wax eyelids, metal staples, platform boots, calipers, and bolts that were glued so securely that they left scars on Karloff's neck for years afterward. Paramount released *Dr. Jekyll and Mr. Hyde* in 1931, for which Wally Westmore (1906–73) designed a system whereby makeup was applied in green for Jekyll, and in red for Hyde. When filmed through a green filter, only the red makeup was visible, and when shot through a red filter only the green makeup appeared. By switching filters during photography, actor Fredric March was transformed before the audience's eyes.

RKO's *King Kong* (1933) was one of the first features to rely solely on special effects for its star. The 18in (46cm) rabbit-fur-covered Kong model was the apotheosis of Willis O'Brien's stop-motion technique, where an articulated puppet is moved frame by frame to create the illusion of fluid movement. However, the ape was also brought to life using a number of full-sized mechanical props.

During the 1930s, studios also began using masks and prosthetics made from foam latex, which allowed the creation of multiple "appliances," pieces of premade foam that could be fixed to the face. The pioneers were the brothers George and Gordon Bau (1905–74; 1907–75), and the technology remains largely unchanged to this day. One of its first uses was in the creation of some of the most loved movie characters, those of *The Wizard of Oz* (1939), including the visages of the cowardly Lion and the wicked witch.

The Cold War and atomic age provided fertile ground for movie creatures of the 1950s. In Japan, Toho studios tapped into the spirit of unease with *Godzilla* (1954), known as *Gojira* in Japan. The giant lizard was created by filming a performer dressed in a rubber costume as he crashed his way through miniature sets.

09

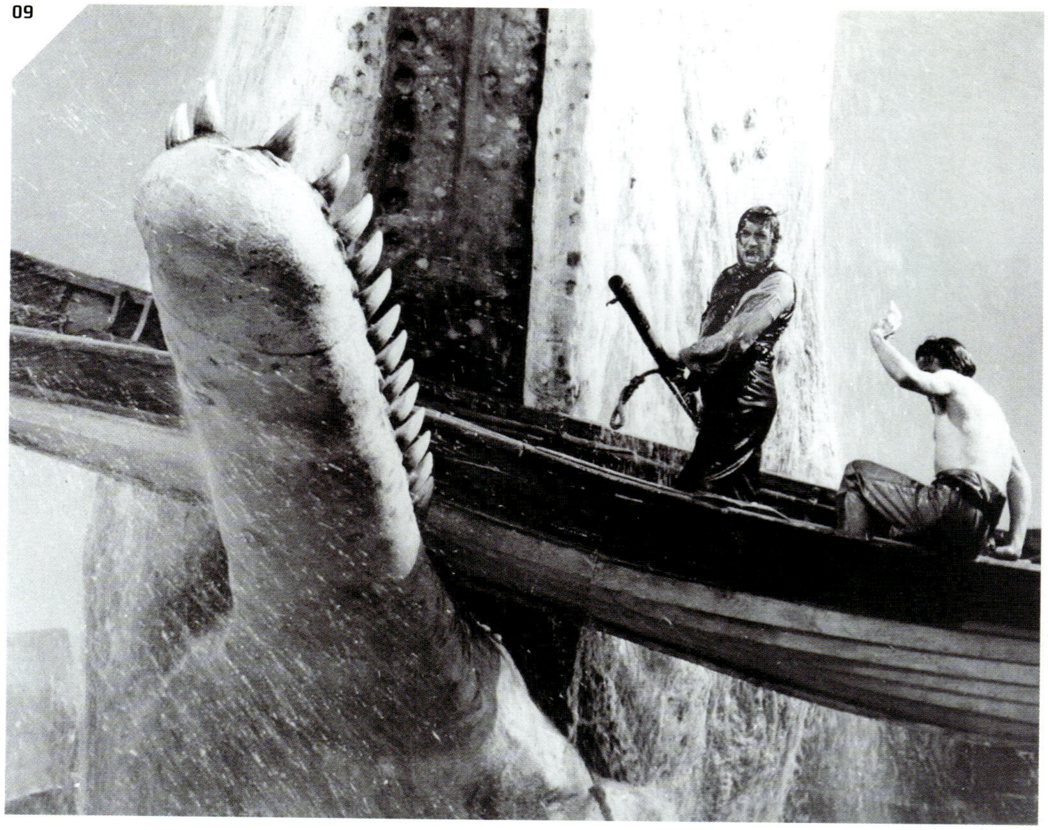

10

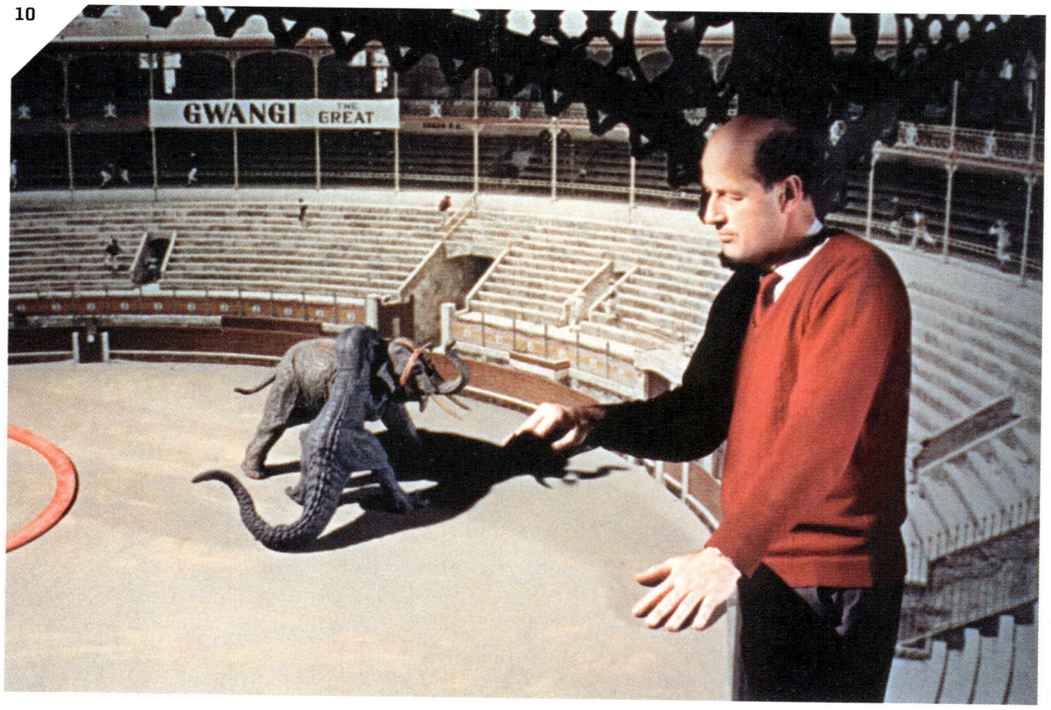

11

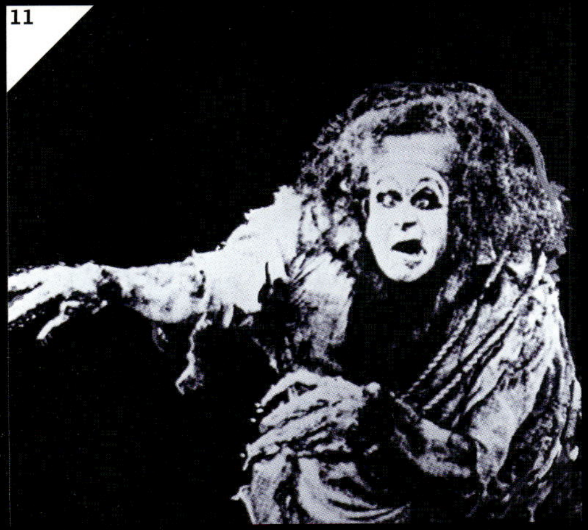

12

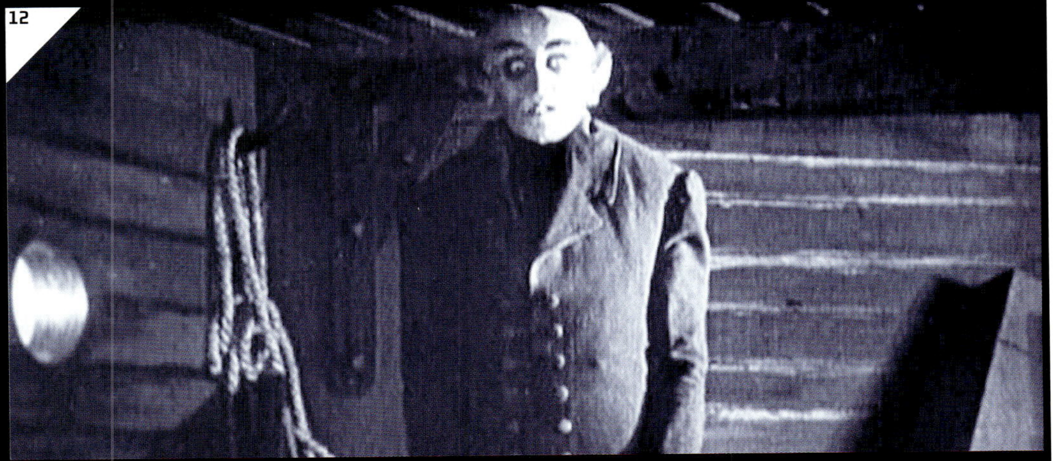

Many 1950s rubber suits and masks were made using a technique called "slush casting," whereby a sculpture was created and used to produce a mold (rather than suits being designed to fit a specific actor). This low-budget approach produced masks and suits for such B-movie classics as *The Creature from the Black Lagoon* (1954) and *The Fly* (1958). However, there was little doubt in audience's minds that these creations were men in rubber suits.

An alternative approach came with the work of legendary character designer and stop-motion animator, Ray Harryhausen (1920–). He had been inspired by *King Kong*, and later worked with Kong's creator, Willis O'Brien, on another gorilla movie, *Mighty Joe Young* (1949). Harryhausen's big break came in 1953 when he was hired to create the lizard star of *The Beast from 20,000 Fathoms*. "Willis O'Brien taught me the importance of studying the anatomy, the physiognomy of real creatures," says Harryhausen. "He made me realize that an understanding of how nature worked would help me design more believable characters. From that understanding and attention to character design came the technical ability to animate creatures that had real presence, that moved in a naturalistic way, that had weight and a sense of inner conscience." Harryhausen contributed visual effects to dozens of movies until the 1980s.

The greatest mechanical beast of the age was the giant squid built for Disney's *20,000 Leagues Under the Sea* (1954), using a combination of electronics, hydraulics, pneumatics, and overhead puppeteering to bring the two-ton contraption to life at a then-enormous cost of $200,000.

In the 1960s, one of the key makeup achievements was for *Planet of the Apes* (1968). Hundreds of simian appliances, designed by John Chambers, were cast in a new foam that drew the performers' sweat away from their skin and allowed it to emerge on the surface of the makeup. The decade also saw important developments outside the industry. In 1955 Walt Disney had opened his revolutionary theme park, Disneyland. In 1963 a new attraction called "The Enchanted Tiki Room" was added. This featured a host of singing mechanical birds operated by a tape recording that sent electrical pulses to pneumatic valves that opened or closed a beak or raised a wing. Because the techniques used to bring these exhibits to life combined sound, animation, and electronics, the method became known as "Audio Animatronics." Today the term "animatronic" is used to describe any mechanically operated character.

For *The Exorcist* (1973), a range of ghoulish makeup designs were created by one of the most admired and influential of all makeup artists, Dick Smith (1922–). He designed a scheme that would gradually transform 13-year-old actress Linda Blair into the possessed Regan—reshaping her mouth and eyebrows, and slowly changing the color of her skin. More complex tasks involved making the infamous revolving head.

13

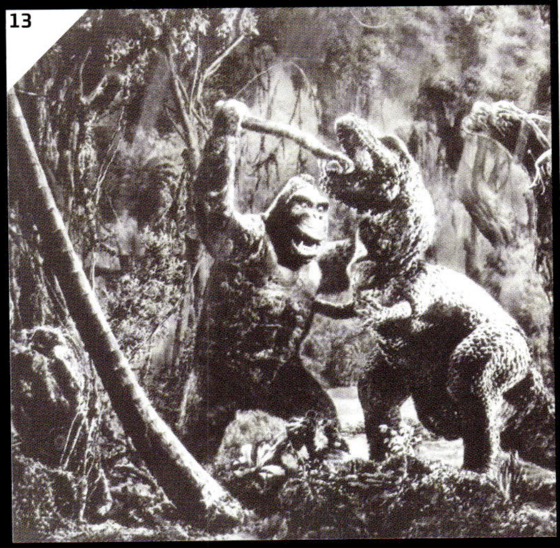

(09) Captain Ahab (Gregory Peck) battles the white whale (*Moby Dick*, 1956). The 80ft mechanical whale was created by Augie Lohman and whale expert Robert Clark **(10)** Stop-motion master Ray Harryhausen working on *The Valley of Gwangi* (1969) **(11)** Charles Ogle as the monster (*Frankenstein*, 1910) **(12)** Max Schrek as the original screen vampire (*Nosferatu*, 1922) **(13)** Kong battles a Tyrannosaur in *King Kong* (1933). Here, Kong is an 18in puppet covered in rabbit fur.

14

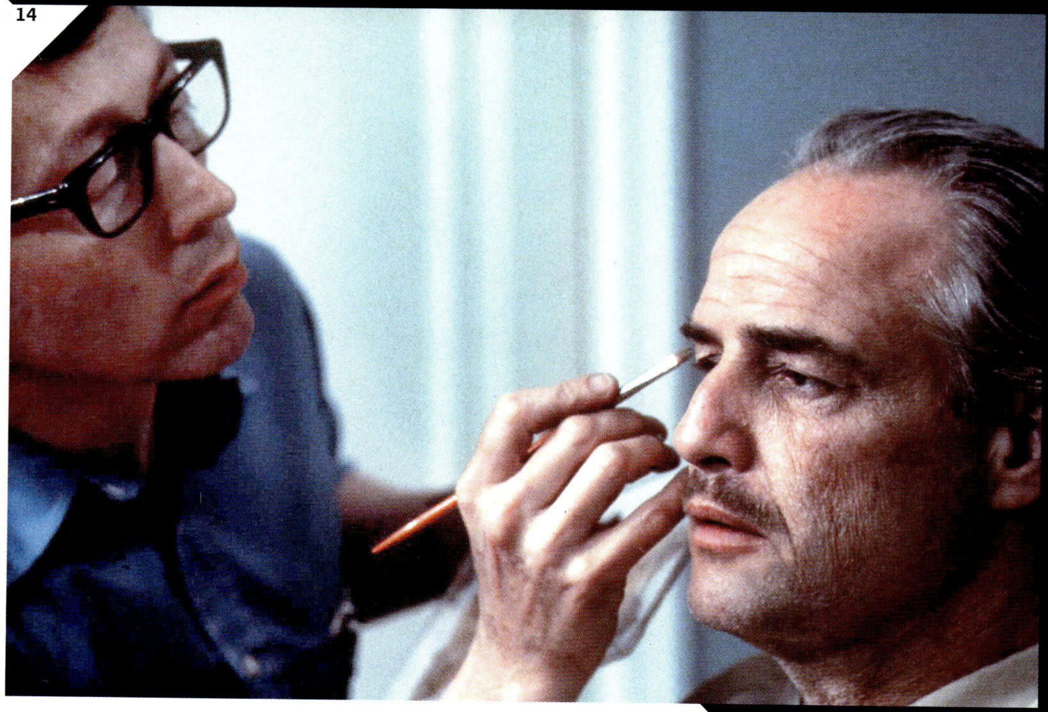

15

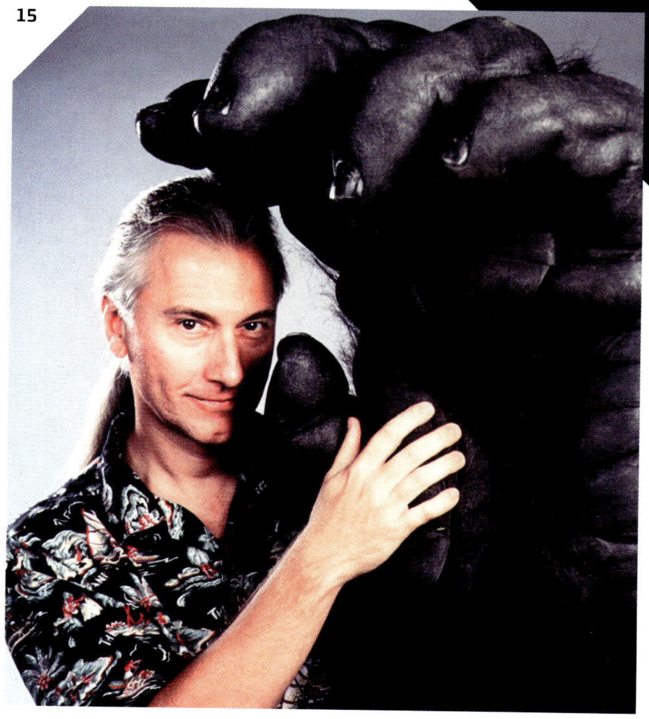

(14) Dick Smith ages Marlon Brando for *The Godfather* (1972) **(15)** Rick Baker is best known for his skill at creating artificial apes **(16)** Yoda, as brought to life by Frank Oz (*Star Wars Episode V: The Empire Strikes Back*, 1980) **(17)** Stan Winston with an animatronic velociraptor (*Jurassic Park*, 1993).

The elusive star of Steven Spielberg's *Jaws* (1975) was a mechanical shark, despite the technical difficulties that often kept it off-screen. Spielberg hired Bob Mattey, whose previous credits included the giant squid of *20,000 Leagues Under the Sea*. Using an original shark sculpture provided by production designer Joe Alves Jr., Mattey created a number of complete and partial mechanical beasts that ran on underwater rails.

Jaws' box-office records were shattered with the release of *Star Wars* (1977) and its sequels. The most complex creature was the Wookie, Chewbacca, created by Stuart Freeborn, who improved a facial performance system first created for the apes in *2001: A Space Odyssey*. Other notable creations included the iconic droids C-3PO and R2-D2, and the host of aliens in the cantina—some created by young makeup artist Rick Baker. By contrast, *Alien* (1979) featured a far more malevolent space monster—designed by Swiss fantasy painter H.R. Giger and largely realized by a performer in a foam-latex costume. It was made by Roger Dicken with an articulated head built by Carlo Rambaldi.

Movies including *E.T. The Extraterrestrial* (1982); *Gremlins* (1984); *Ghostbusters* (1984); *The Terminator* (1984); and *Legend* (1985) relied on a new generation of self-taught creature artists—Rob Bottin, Greg Cannom, Steve Johnson, Bob Keen, Chris Walas, and Stan Winston, among others—who had grown up watching late-night reruns of classic sci-fi movies. Among their number was Rick Baker (1950–). He had always been fascinated by apes, and his first shot at a great movie ape was in the 1976 *King Kong*. In 1981, Baker was the first artist to win the Academy Award in the newly created special effects makeup category for the legendary man-to-wolf transformations in *An American Werewolf in London* (1981). He was finally given the time and resources to create superb apes for *Greystoke: The Legend of Tarzan, Lord of the Apes* (1984), the bigfoot of *Harry and the Hendersons* (1987), and the naturalistic stars of *Gorillas in the Mist* (1988), which were intercut with real ape footage.

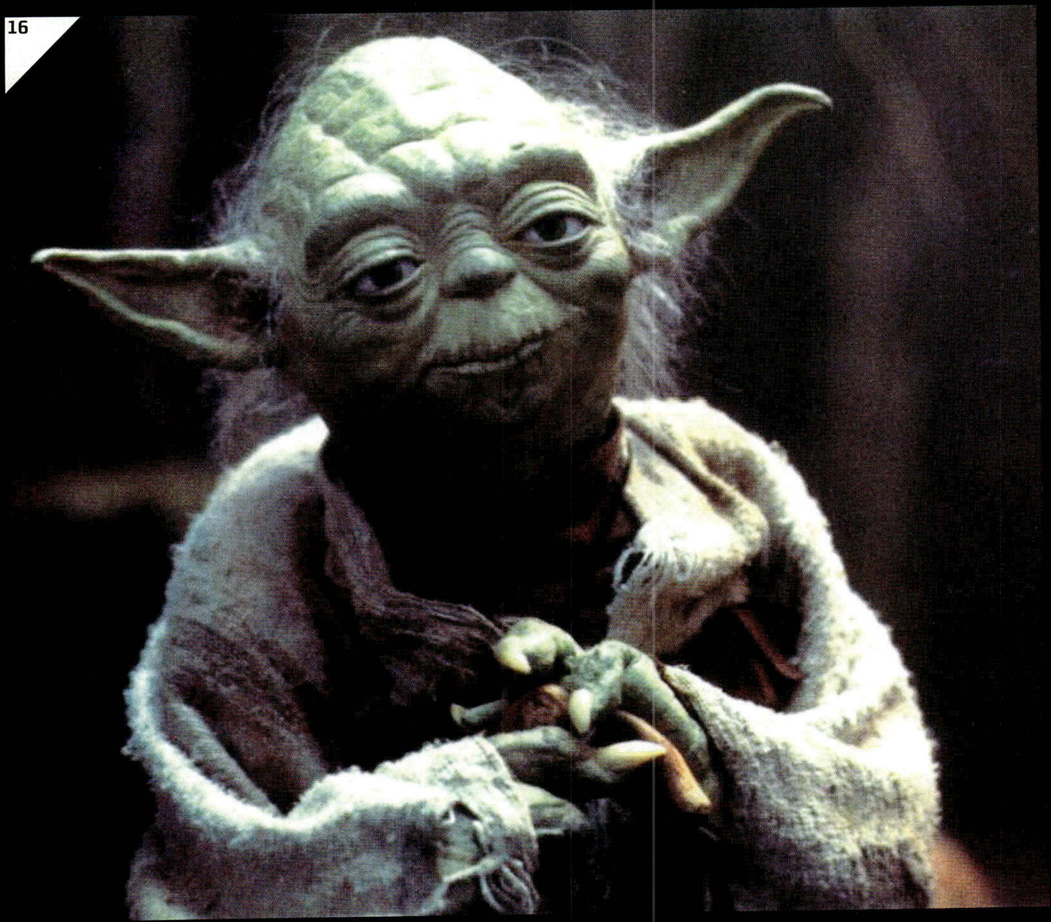

16

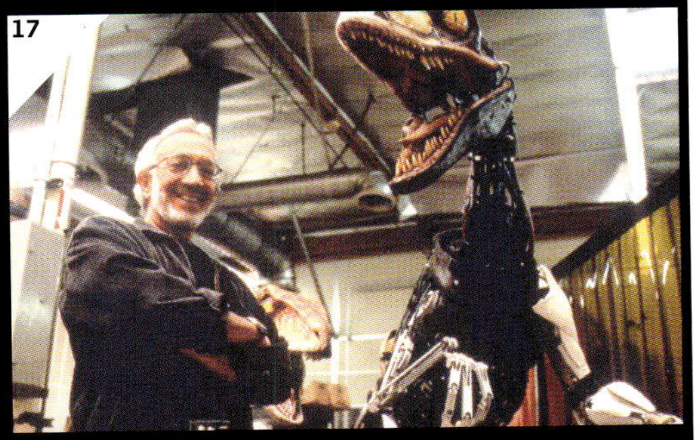

17

The creation of entirely synthetic screen characters that could give lifelike performances was perfected during the 1980s. One of the pioneers was Muppet-master Jim Henson. In 1982, Henson released *The Dark Crystal*, a movie filled with fantasy creatures of a quality and subtlety never seen before. Henson's Creature Shop was just one of a number of standalone special-effects makeup studios that emerged in the 1980s. Undoubtedly the most iconic creation was 800-year-old Jedi master Yoda for the second two movies of the original *Star Wars* trilogy. Created by Stuart Freeborn with advice from Jim Henson's Creature Shop, Yoda was voiced and puppeteered by Miss Piggy's alter-ego Frank Oz. *Return of the Jedi* (1983) also witnessed the debut of Jabba the Hutt—the most elaborate animatronic creature built by that time.

The success of movies such as *The Exorcist* and *Dawn of the Dead* in the previous decade prompted the production of more horror movies, this time more effects-based, with stomach-churning blood and gore, such as the *Halloween*, "Chucky," and *Hellraiser* franchises. Independently produced, low-budget horror features were also on the rise in the new age of video. The ring-master of 1980s gore effects was ex-combat photographer Tom Savini (1946–), who had witnessed plenty of real horror in Vietnam.

The 1990s saw the emergence of the computer as a serious rival to the special-effects makeup artist. For James Cameron's *The Abyss* (1989), George Lucas's visual effects facility, Industrial Light and Magic (ILM), created a computer-generated (CGI) water alien that would have been impossible to achieve before. For his next movie, *Terminator 2: Judgment Day* (1991), Cameron asked ILM to create a liquid metal Terminator, although the movie's other robots were largely created physically—such as the puppet Terminator endoskeleton made by Stan Winston for the first *Terminator* movie. But for Robert Zemeckis's black comedy *Death Becomes Her* (1992), ILM used digital techniques to help conjure characters that were closer to the realm of the traditional makeup artist, proving that the computer was now capable of creating more naturalistic elements and applying them to human performers.

In 1993 people queued around the block to see the digital dinosaurs unleashed by ILM for Spielberg's *Jurassic Park*. Some predicted the demise of traditional visual-effects companies and makeup studios. In fact, *Jurassic Park* was typical of many subsequent movies, using digital creatures for shots where the dinosaurs needed to perform feats impossible to shoot in any other way, while close-up shots were achieved with animatronic models and puppets. However, in 1999 George Lucas released *Star Wars Episode I: The Phantom Menace*, featuring an array of entirely digital, photorealistic characters interacting with human actors.

Whether through the use of CGI, or foam latex and greasepaint, the monsters that stalk our imaginations will continue to be created by the legions of talented and visionary artists and technicians to whom this book is dedicated.

MILES TEVES

CV

Character designer; b. Salinas, CA. Met Rob Bottin in 1982, who was impressed by his portfolio; moved to LA in 1983 to study at Art Center College of Design, Pasadena; after his money ran out was offered a job as an illustrator by Bottin; after a couple of movies, went back to college to study sculpture; returned to the movies, on Bottin's invitation, to work on *Robocop* (1987), since when he has worked on many high-profile characters.

SELECT FILMOGRAPHY

Legend (1985); *Explorers* (1985); *Robocop* (1987); *Interview with the Vampire* (1994); *Batman and Robin* (1997); *Hollow Man* (2000); *Spider-Man* (2002); *Terminator 3: Rise of the Machines* (2003); *Reign of Fire* (2002); *Van Helsing* (2004); *Pirates of the Caribbean: The Curse of the Black Pearl* (2003); *The Passion of the Christ* (2004); *Chronicles of Riddick* (2004); *King Kong* (2005)

KEY CHARACTERS

Darkness, Meg Mucklebones (*Legend*); Robocop (*Robocop*); Lestat (*Interview with the Vampire*); Robin (*Batman and Robin*); dragons (*Reign of Fire*); Jesus (*The Passion of the Christ*); Hell Hound (*Chronicles of Riddick*); Kong (*King Kong*)

TECHNIQUES

Traditional design and illustration; sculpting; Photoshop

01

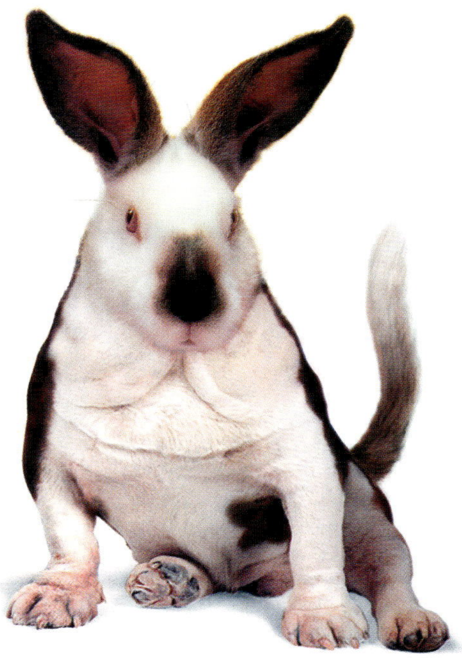

02

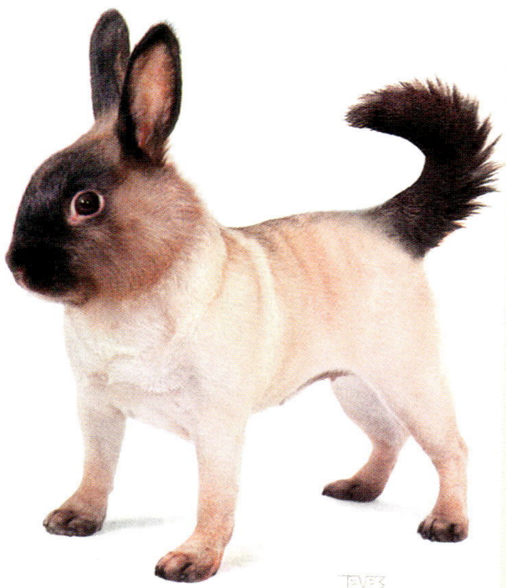

(01–02) Photographic concept hybrids for *The Shaggy Dog* (2006)
(03) Concept art for *Anaconda* (1997)
(04–05) Teves designed and sculpted Pearl the vampire in *Blade* (1998)
(06) Teves works on a sculpture of Tom Cruise as the vampire Lestat for *Interview with the Vampire* (1994).

06

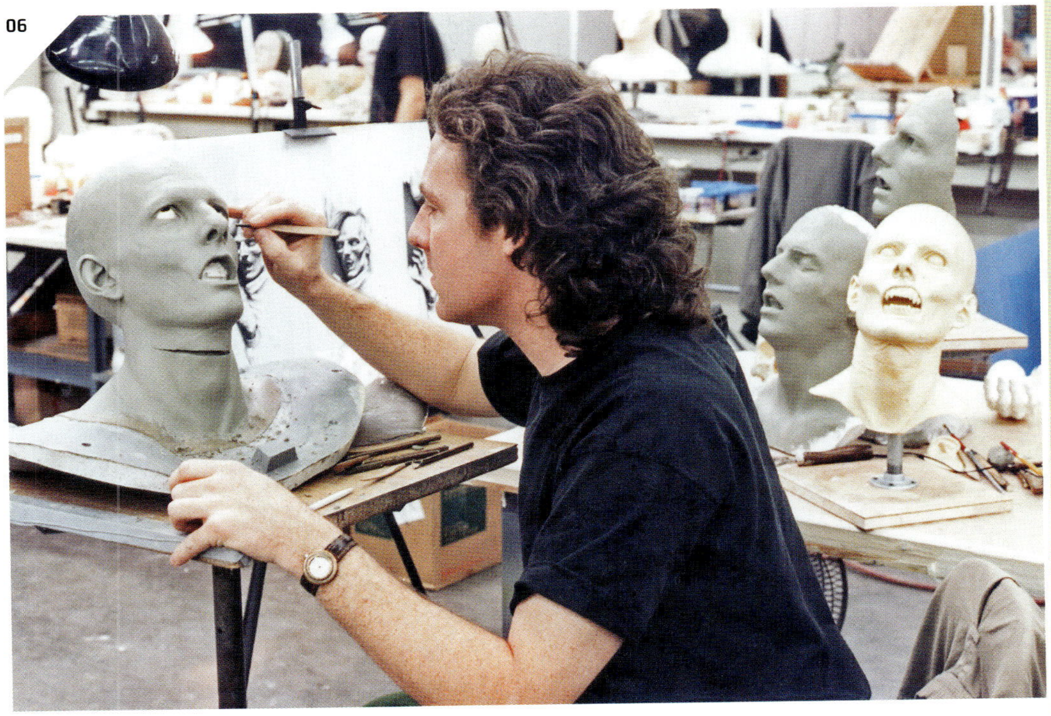

03

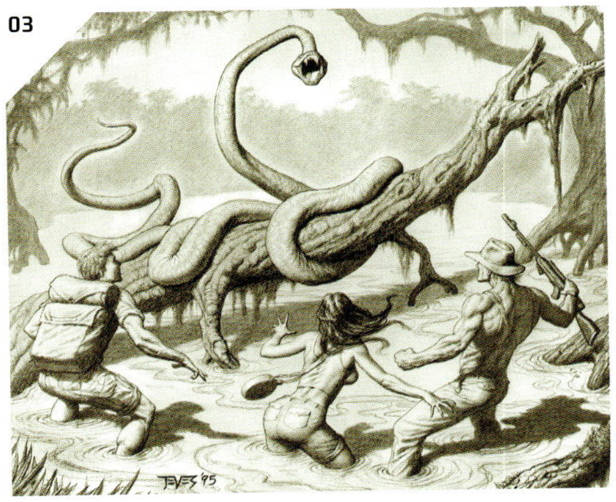

04

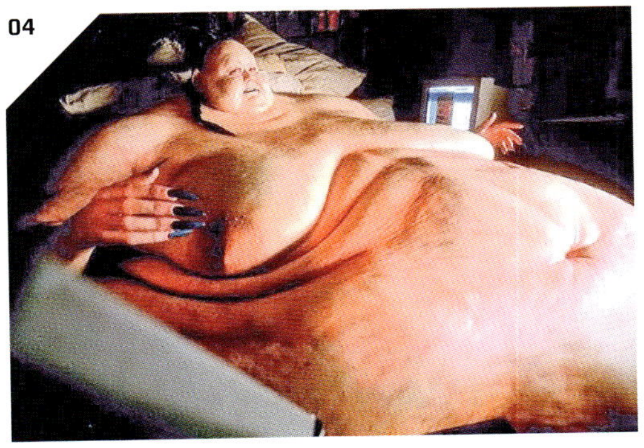

05

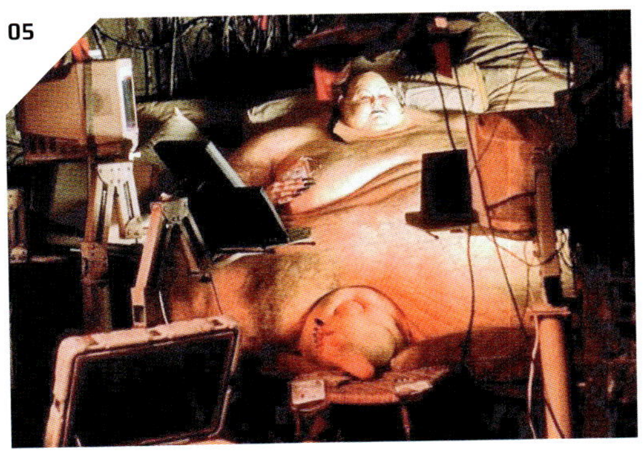

Miles Teves (1963–) was born in the small coastal Californian city of Salinas, where he grew up a keen artist and an avid fan of *Batman*, *Godzilla*, *Star Trek*, and the usual science-fiction and horror movies shown on late-night television. Inspired by these, he used the family's 8mm movie camera to make his own stop-motion monster movies. While he was in junior high school, *Star Wars* (1977) was released, becoming for Teves what he describes as a "cinematic Messiah for 13-year-old boys." At about the same time he discovered a series of Time-Life books about the great masters of European art. His passion for movies and art began to suggest that a career combining both interests might be a possibility. In 1982 he attended a science-fiction convention where he met Rob Bottin, recently responsible for the special-effects makeup in *The Thing* (1982). Teves showed Bottin his portfolio, and was encouraged to stay in touch.

In 1983 Teves moved to Los Angeles to study Illustration at Pasadena's Art Center College of Design. After a year his money ran out, and he decided to contact Bottin, who was working on *Legend* (1985). He offered the eager young artist a job as an illustrator.

Working for Bottin was a harsh introduction to the realities of the business. "I was paid very little and spent many long hours working on my own in a tiny, windowless room," says Teves. "I was isolated from the rest of the crew and discouraged from talking to anyone. This was partly due to the fact that I wasn't a member of a proper union, but there was also an effort to maintain the illusion that everything that emerged from Rob's studio was solely the creation of Rob Bottin. Of course, the truth is that nobody in this business does it all alone."

Teves's first task on *Legend* was to help design the movie's emblematic 8ft-tall (2.4m) horned-devil character, Darkness. "A lot had already been done on designing Darkness," remembers Teves. "At that time he was a very bestial character—much more like a Minotaur. It was a more elaborate design that would have required animatronics. At the same time, Rob's key sculptor, Henry Alvarez, had been quietly working away on a different design. I thought it was incredible. I'd never seen such an inspiring sculpture before!" The new Darkness concept could utilize the actor's own performance without the need for animatronics.

07

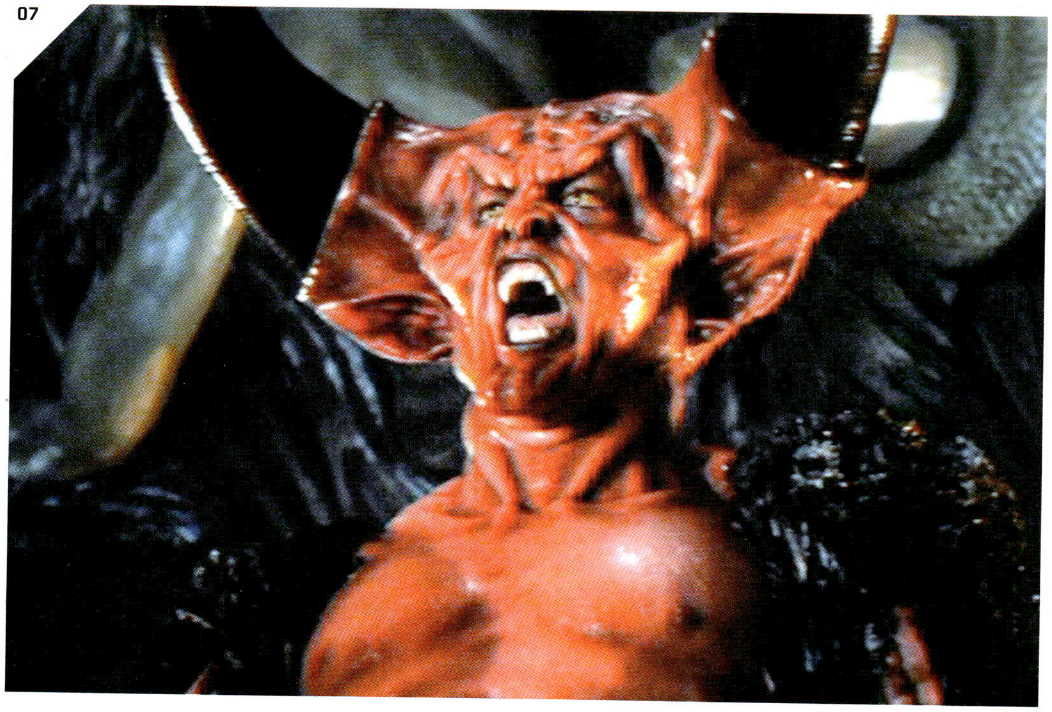

08

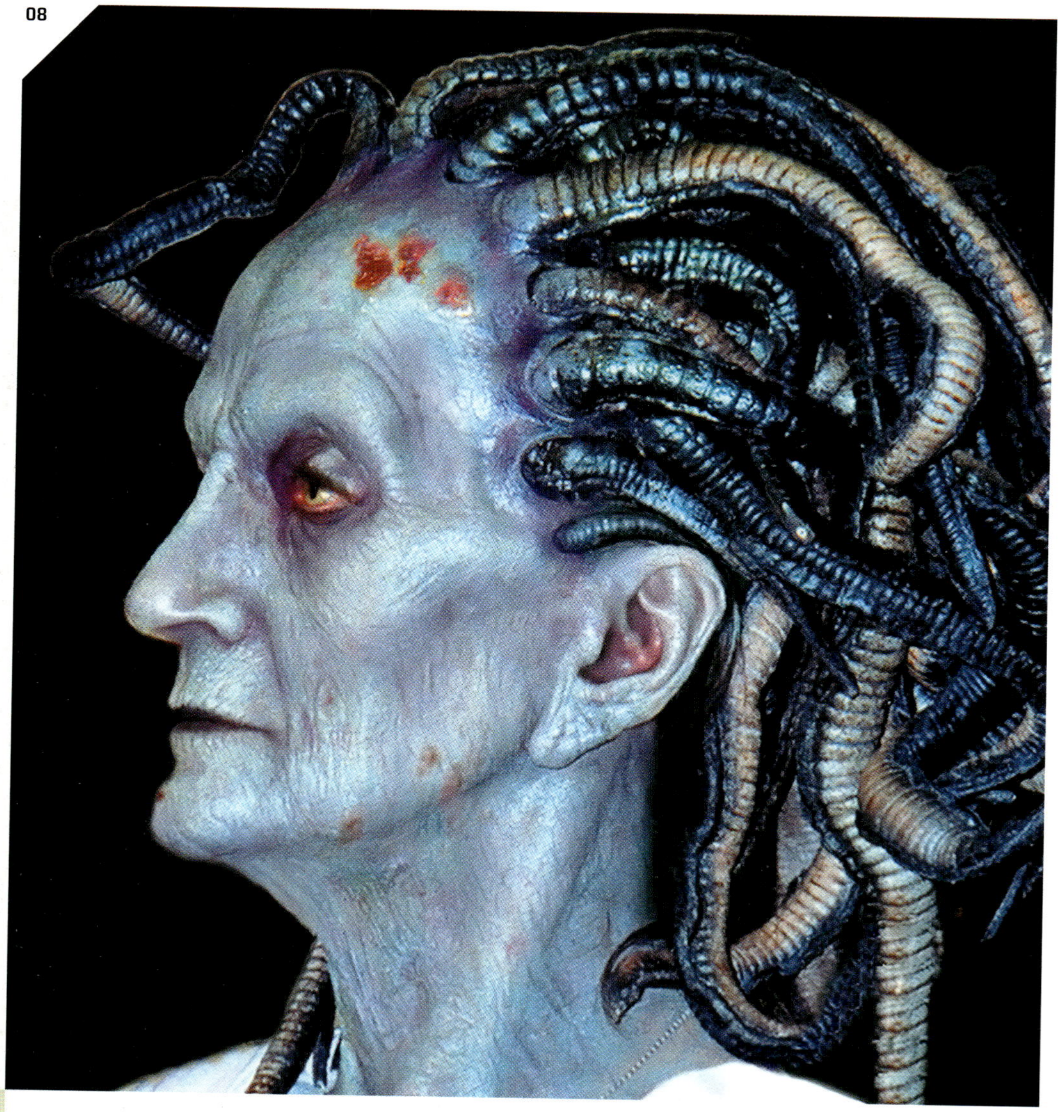

09

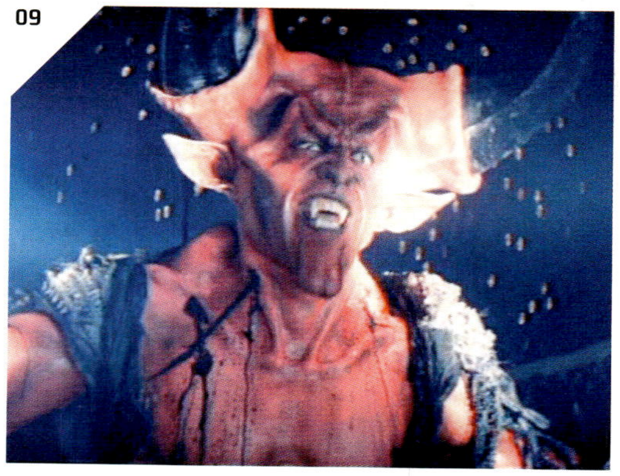

"Under the guidance of Bottin I started sketching up refinements based on Alvarez's sculpture," says Teves. "Rob called it the 'T-head,' and the quest was on to work out a design for the horns. Rob just kept saying, 'Push them further! Make them really long!' So we pushed them until they could be pushed no more. When we had finalized the overall design I created a color painting of Darkness, over which I laid transparent acetate sheets. On those I did further designs for things like the eyes and teeth."

The final design involved covering the whole of actor Tim Curry's upper body and face with numerous foam-latex appliances, a process that took up to eight hours each day. He wore 3ft-long (1m) horns that slotted into sockets.

Not all of the characters in *Legend* had so much time lavished upon them. "Because we spent so long on Darkness and some of the other characters, when it came to the witch, Meg Mucklebones, there was very little time left," explains Teves. "Rob basically brought me a picture of the witch from Disney's *Snow White*, and said, 'This is what we're going to do—only more real and more extreme.' He liked the simple lines—the little apple cheeks, the bulgy eyes, and the way the chin hooked up to meet the nose. We really pulled that one off fast."

Teves describes his time working on *Legend* as an incredible opportunity that taught him much. "Rob Bottin was a fantastic ideas man and a demanding art director, who really knew what he wanted," says Teves. "He'd hammer at you very hard to get you to do your best work.

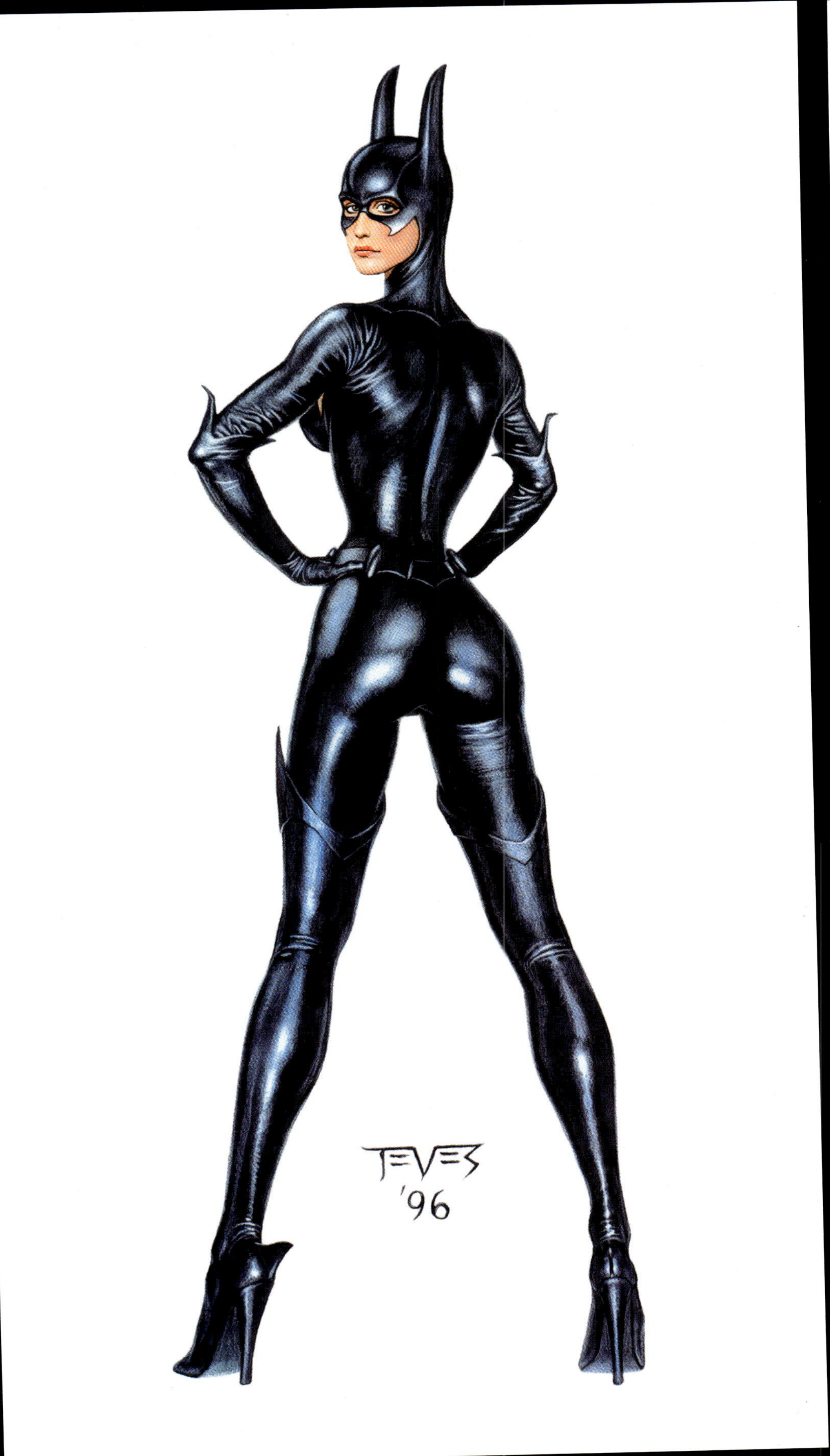

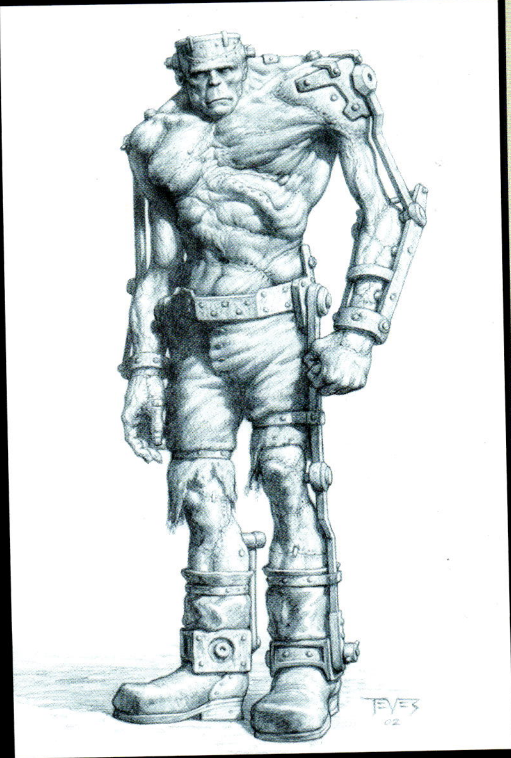

He would bring me the germ of an idea in the form of a little sketch and then ask me to take it to the next level. Then he would make you push the idea as far as it could go. To this day I still apply this basic approach to design."

(07) Darkness, the result of Teves' collaboration with mentor Rob Bottin (*Legend*, 1985) **(08)** Dana, from *Bless the Child* (2000) **(09)** Tim Curry as Darkness **(10)** Teves' vision of Alicia Silverstone as Batgirl in *Batman & Robin* (1997) **(11)** Concept artwork for Frankenstein's monster (*Van Helsing*, 2004).

After working with Bottin on his next project, *Explorers* (1985), Teves went back to college to study sculpture. Then he received a call from Bottin inviting him to work on a new movie called *Robocop* (1987). "Rob called and said, 'Have you ever drawn robots before?'"

Bottin's obsessive approach meant that a vast amount of time was spent exploring the design possibilities. "We actually came up with a concept not very far from the final version quite early on. But Rob wanted to exhaust all other possibilities, so different directions were explored, including a variety of designs where the robot was much blockier—the chest becoming a giant sphere, the arms huge and chunky—but eventually we came back to the more elegant concept."

For additional inspiration Teves looked to the work of Japanese artist Hajimi Soroyama, whose erotic images of female androids were first published in the 1983 book, *Sexy Robots*. "We tried to combine that elegant, streamlined style of line with a more masculine, law-enforcement look, and then graft all of that onto [actor] Peter Weller's physique. Peter is a relatively short actor with very wide hips—about the worst combination for designing a heroic, full-body costume! As well as everything else, the actor had to be able to perform with speed and agility. If you look at previous costume-performer robots, like C-3PO from *Star Wars*, they could barely move. We eventually came up with a design that looked both heroic and sleek. Eventually we devised a two-tone color system using silver-gray for the chest, arms, and legs, and glossy black for the hip and waist area, which helped to make things look more streamlined."

12

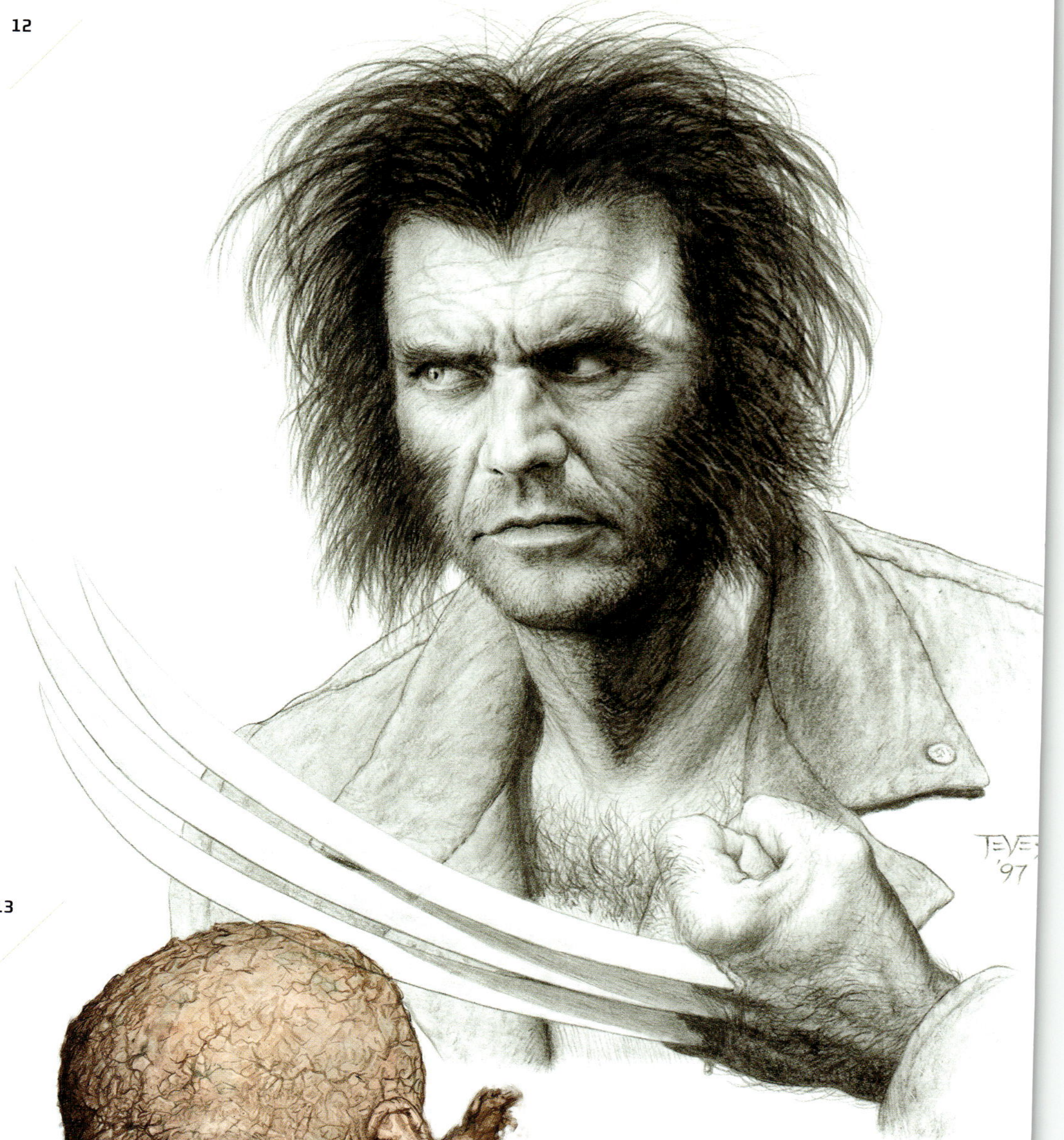

13

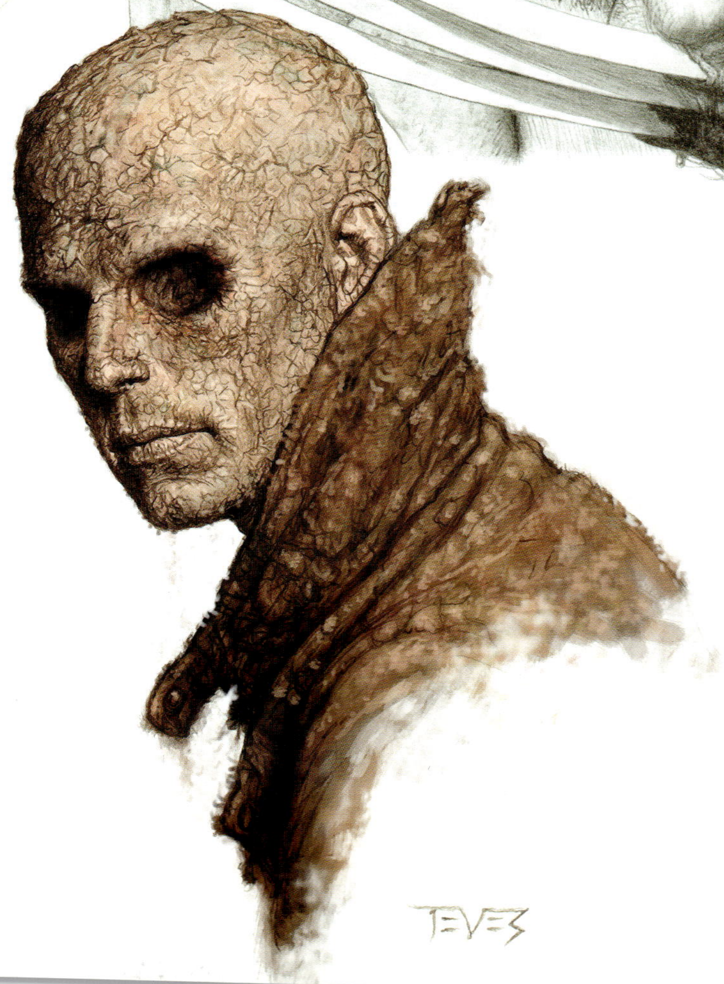

(12) Character design envisioning Mel Gibson as Wolverine (*X-Men* movie series) **(13)** Gressel, from *Ghost Rider* (2007) **(14–15)** Two versions of Hyde from *Van Helsing* (2004)

The finished design was sculpted onto a bodycast of Peter Weller using a hard styling clay traditionally used by vehicle designers, which allows sharp, clean machined-looking surfaces to be created. The outer body parts—chest, arms, legs, and backplate—were then molded in silicone rubber before being cast in semi-rigid polyurethane. The finished parts were sprayed metallic silver. The inner suit, which covered the lower chest, waist, hips, arm, and leg joints, was made from flexible foam latex. The metallic outer pieces were attached to this using snap fasteners and Velcro. The helmet was created from fiberglass.

Teves is all too aware of the exploitation of those keen to get their foot on the ladder as makeup artists. But even for established artists, working conditions and rewards can vary. "There are two ways that designers like myself get work in Hollywood," he explains. "Sometimes I'm hired by a makeup-effects workshop that has won the contract to create characters for a film. There instructions are filtered through whoever runs the shop—and that person ultimately gets all the credit. Regardless of your creative contribution, you're just a hired hand.

"Other times I'll be employed directly by the production art department, in which case I collaborate closely with the production designer or even the director. In those situations, you usually get to read the script as it's evolving. You are involved in the larger creative process—and you usually receive fairer credit for your work."

Teves finds this way of working more satisfying. "You can really bring a lot more to the movie. For example, on *Pirates of the Caribbean* [*The Curse of the Black Pearl*, 2003] there was a scripted scene in the development phase where the pirates needed to get from a cave back to the boat. In the script they were to swim, but I came up with this concept of a wall of zombie pirates lumbering slowly across the seabed toward the viewer. I painted the image and brought it in to the director, and that whole scene ended up being rewritten around it."

14

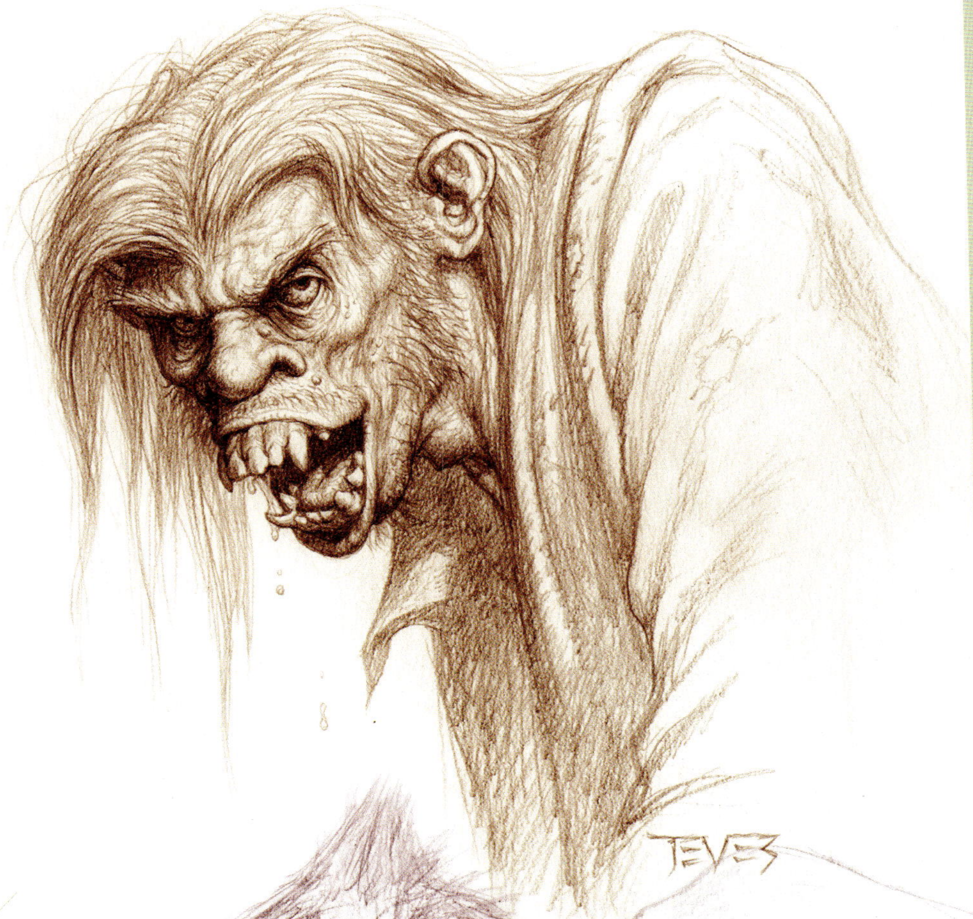

15

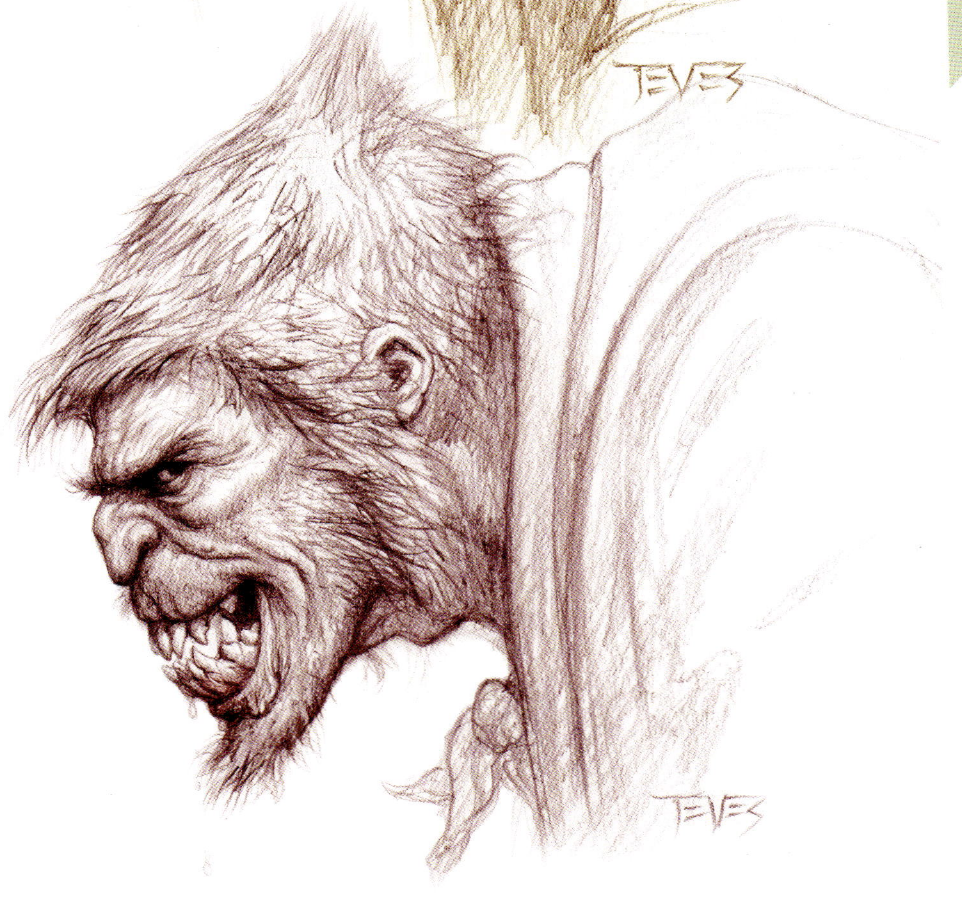

16

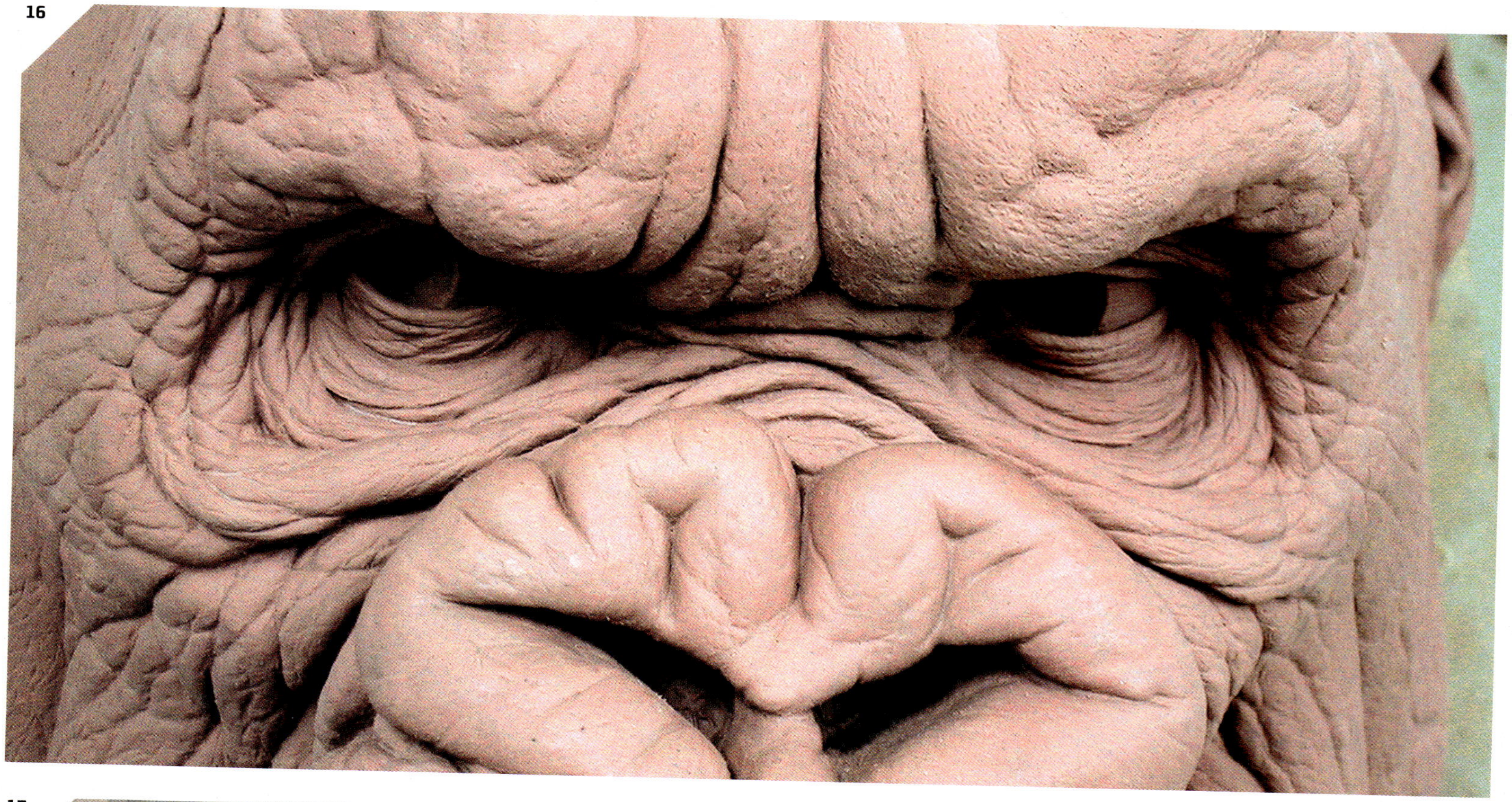

17

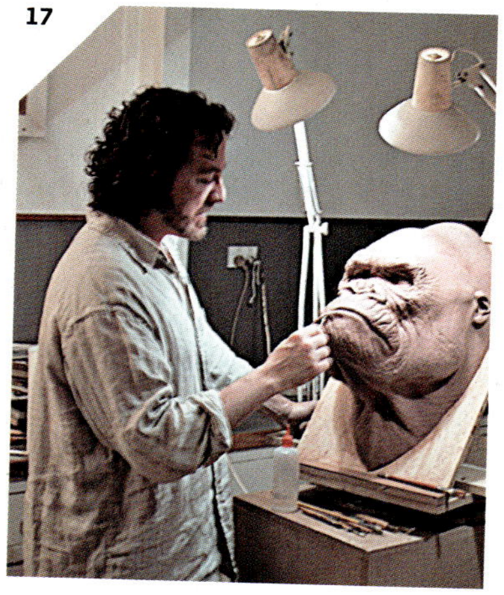

19

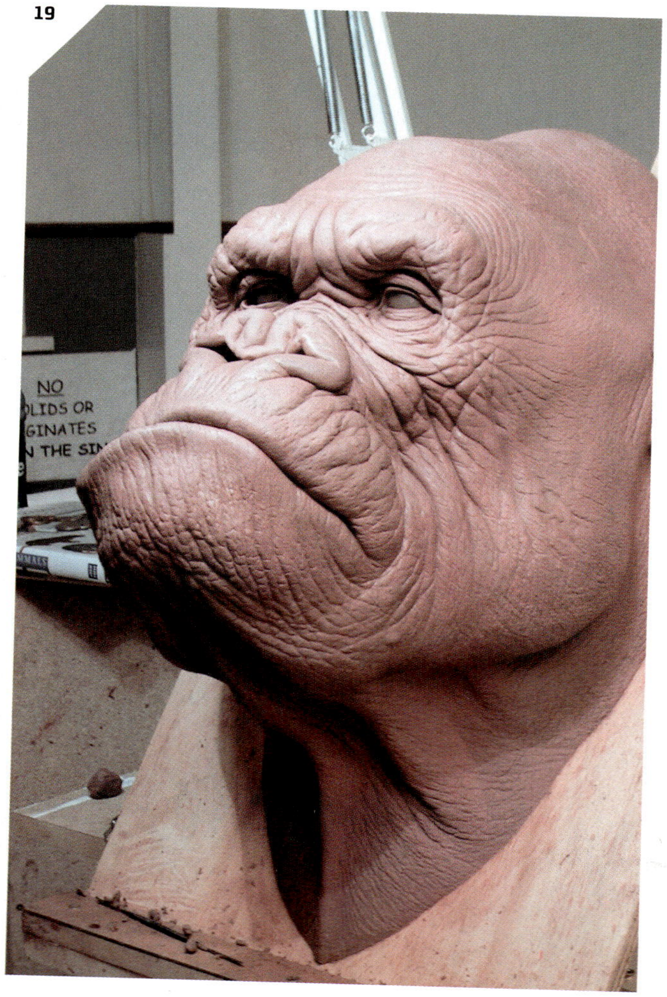

20

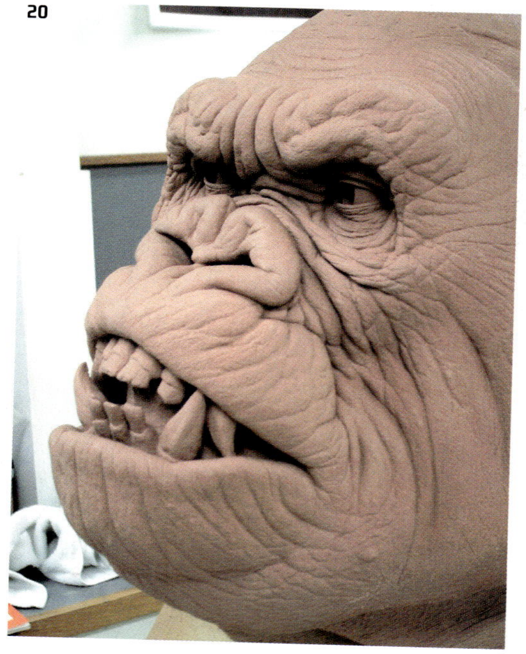

18

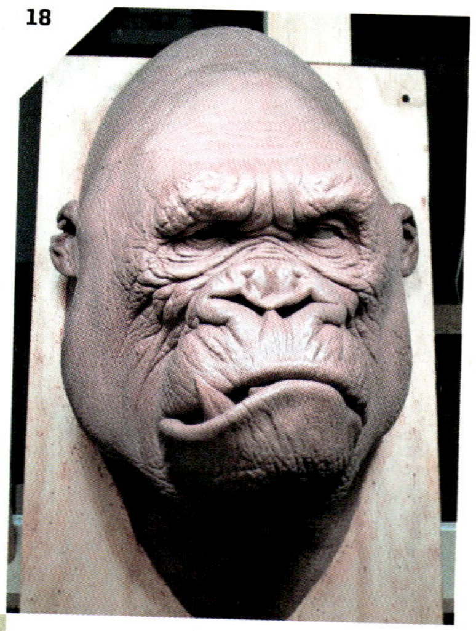

(16–20) Teves working on a sculpture of Kong for Weta, a client that prefers sculpture to illustrations on paper (*King Kong*, 2005) **(21–22)** Meg Mucklebones design (*Legend*, 1985) **(23)** The Batcostume takes shape (*Batman & Robin*, 1997)

21

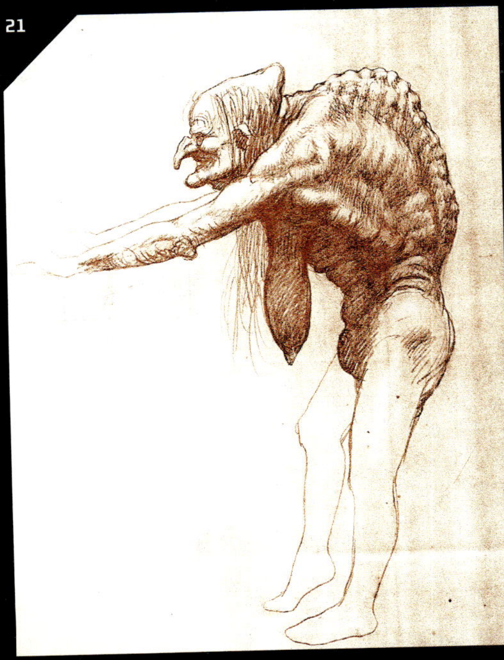

22

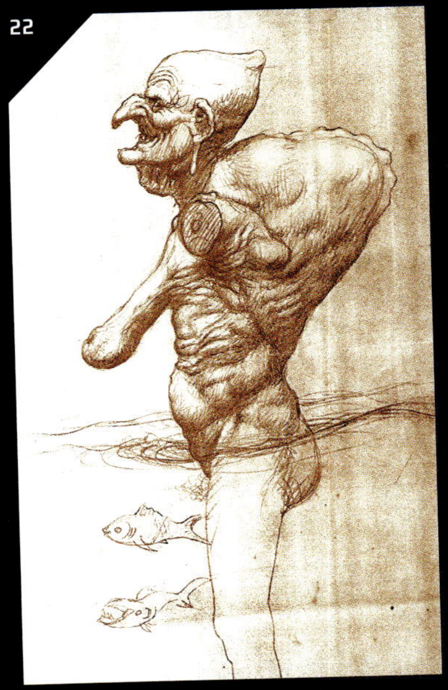

23

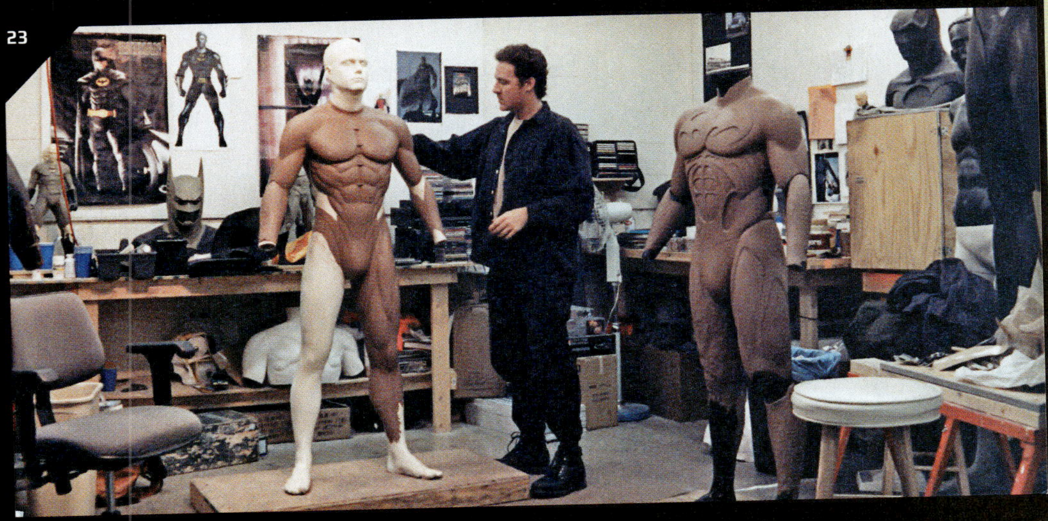

For movies such as *Hollow Man* (2000), *Spider-Man* (2002), *Terminator 3: Rise of the Machines* (2003), and *Van Helsing* (2004), Teves has been responsible for imagining some of the most high-profile modern Hollywood characters. However, he has also created some extremely subtle makeup designs. For *Interview with the Vampire* (1994), he was asked to depict Tom Cruise as the vampire, Lestat. During a difficult casting period, Teves' design did much to sell the idea of Cruise as a vampire, even reassuring the star himself, who wasn't certain if the role was for him. "I created an image of Cruise with long hair and visible veins that would be airbrushed onto his face each day to give the appearance of translucent skin," he says.

Another subtle design was for Mel Gibson's Biblical epic *The Passion of the Christ* (2004). "Mel wanted to make the actor playing Jesus, James Caviezel, look more ethnically Middle Eastern, and it was decided that we could do it best by changing the shape of his nose. I looked at photos of people from that part of the world, but in the end realized that someone in the workshop had a great nose for the part! So we took a cast of it, and I studied it and then sculpted a similar shape in clay onto a lifecast of Caviezel. The gelatin nose was very thin in most places—just a millimeter or so—but it dramatically changed his appearance. With noses, a little goes a long way!"

Like many artists Teves has come to rely on the computer as part of the design process. "I sketch in pencil—I can't draw very well on the [graphics] tablet. When I'm happy with a design, I'll scan it in and then use Photoshop to stretch things and play around with proportions. It's a quick way of making several variations, so you can give the client some options. I also design color schemes in layers, so they can be quickly changed and updated."

Research is also a vital aid when Teves is designing a new character. "I'm a reference nut. I have hundreds of books; my house is full of them. And thank God for Google! I often create montages of relevant animals or characters and tape them all around my desk for inspiration."

When asked what it takes to be a top-class character designer, Teves offers this advice: "A good foundation in life drawing is key. You need to be able to imbue your designs with a sense of realism and nuance that you can only get from studying nature directly. A lot of young people send me their designs, but they are often images of monsters and characters that are clearly two or three times removed from nature and display the heavy stylistic influence of other artists. You can see the artist grew up looking at comic books and not studying living things. I also think you have to be a bit of an actor. All the people I know who are really good are actually closet actors. They get into character and draw."

ADI

TOM WOODRUFF JR.
ALEC GILLIS

CV

ADI (Tom Woodruff Jr., Alec Gillis) formed in 1988.

SELECT FILMOGRAPHY

Alien³ (aka *Alien 3*, 1992); *Death Becomes Her* (1992); *The Santa Clause* series (1994; 2002; 2006); *Starship Troopers* (1997); *Alien Resurrection* (1997); *Bedazzled* (2000); *Hollow Man* (2000); *Spider-Man* series (2002, 2004, 2007); *AVP: Alien Vs. Predator* (2004)

KEY CHARACTERS

Michael's wings (*Michael*); Alien bugs (*Starship Troopers*); The Alien (xenomorph), Newborn, Alien Warriors, Alien Queen, Predators (*Alien* series, and *AVP: Alien Vs. Predator*); Santa Claus and reindeers Comet and Chet (*The Santa Clause* series); the devil (*Bedazzled*)

TECHNIQUES

Special effects makeup design and application; fabrication; animatronics

01

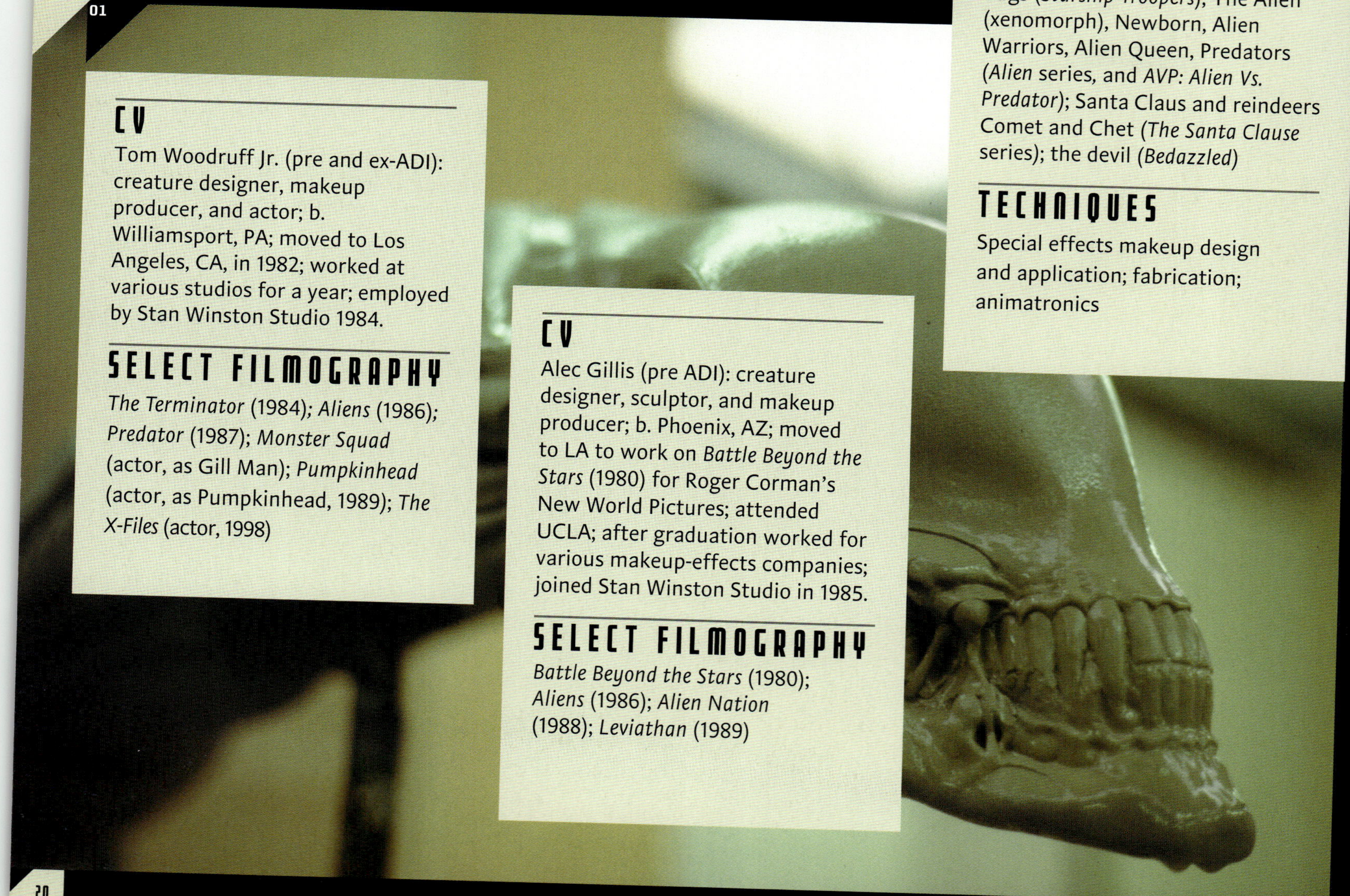

CV

Tom Woodruff Jr. (pre and ex-ADI): creature designer, makeup producer, and actor; b. Williamsport, PA; moved to Los Angeles, CA, in 1982; worked at various studios for a year; employed by Stan Winston Studio 1984.

SELECT FILMOGRAPHY

The Terminator (1984); *Aliens* (1986); *Predator* (1987); *Monster Squad* (actor, as Gill Man); *Pumpkinhead* (actor, as Pumpkinhead, 1989); *The X-Files* (actor, 1998)

CV

Alec Gillis (pre ADI): creature designer, sculptor, and makeup producer; b. Phoenix, AZ; moved to LA to work on *Battle Beyond the Stars* (1980) for Roger Corman's New World Pictures; attended UCLA; after graduation worked for various makeup-effects companies; joined Stan Winston Studio in 1985.

SELECT FILMOGRAPHY

Battle Beyond the Stars (1980); *Aliens* (1986); *Alien Nation* (1988); *Leviathan* (1989)

02

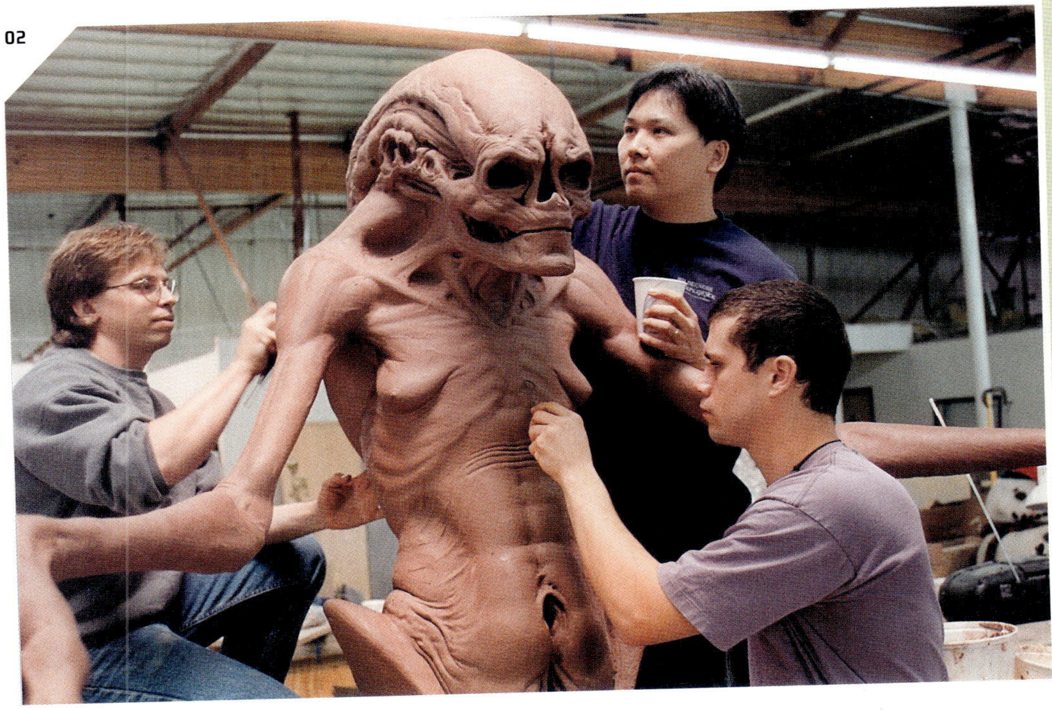

03

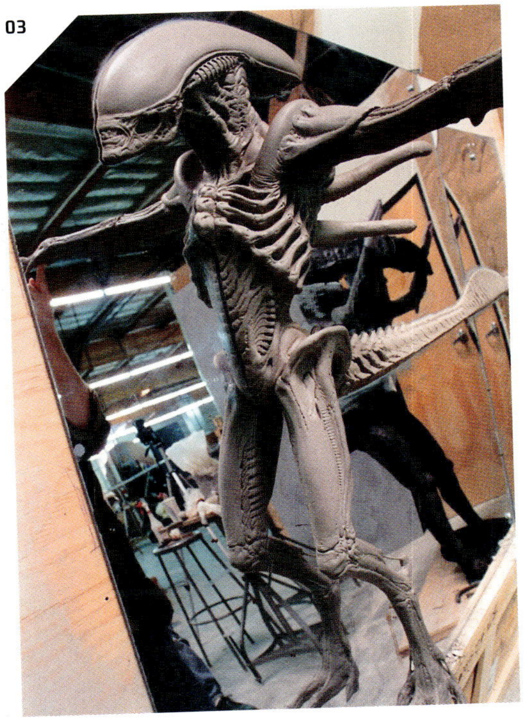

(01) Alien head sculpture for *Alien*³ **(02)** Steve Koch, Steve Wang, and Jeff Boccacio work on the full-scale Newborn creature (*Alien: Resurrection*, 1997). **(03)** This half-scale Alien from *Alien: Resurrection* was scanned to create a CG version.

Tom Woodruff Jr. grew up in Williamsport, Pennsylvania, watching late-night broadcasts of the classic Universal monster movies and the stop-motion fantasies of Ray Harryhausen. However, it was seeing one of the *Planet of the Apes* movies that set his heart on a career in pictures. Using his father's 8mm cine camera, Woodruff began creating home-movies filled with animation, special effects, and makeup, converting the family basement into a workshop and studio. Like many of his contemporaries, Woodruff also spent hours trying to figure out how makeup effects were achieved by studying behind-the-scenes shots in *Famous Monsters in Filmland* magazine.

Woodruff finally made the move to Los Angeles in 1982. After a year moving between small makeup studios he was employed by Stan Winston to work on *The Terminator* (1984). Over the next five years, Woodruff became a key coordinator at Stan Winston Studio, overseeing makeup for films including *Aliens* (1986) and *Predator* (1987). During this time Woodruff also began wearing many of the complicated creature costumes produced at the studio. His ability to perform as an actor led to his portrayal of the title characters in movies such as *Monster Squad* (1987) and *Pumpkinhead* (1989). For *Alien*³ (1992, aka *Alien* 3), Woodruff climbed into the Alien suit and has played the role in every *Alien* movie since, plus characters in *The X-Files* (aka *X-Files: The Movie,* 1998), *Hollow Man* (2000), and *Evolution* (2001).

Born in Phoenix, Arizona, and raised in Orange County, California, Alec Gillis was already an avid fan of fantasy and science-fiction movies before his tenth birthday. Influenced by films such as *King Kong* (1933) and *Jason and the Argonauts* (1963), Gillis decided that creating creatures for Hollywood would be his career. At the age of 13 he began making his own amateur movies, experimenting with increasingly sophisticated special effects in the garage.

Gillis's first professional job was with Roger Corman's New World Pictures, helping to create special effects for low-budget space epic, *Battle Beyond the Stars* (1980). Other newcomers on the same crew included future director James Cameron, future producer Gale Anne Hurd, and effects legends Robert and Dennis Skotak. Gillis next attended film school at UCLA and, after graduation, began working for some of the top names in makeup effects, including Greg Cannom and Tom Savini. In 1985 Gillis joined Stan Winston Studio as a creature designer, sculptor, and supervisor on movies including *Aliens*, *Alien Nation* (1988), and *Leviathan* (1989).

04

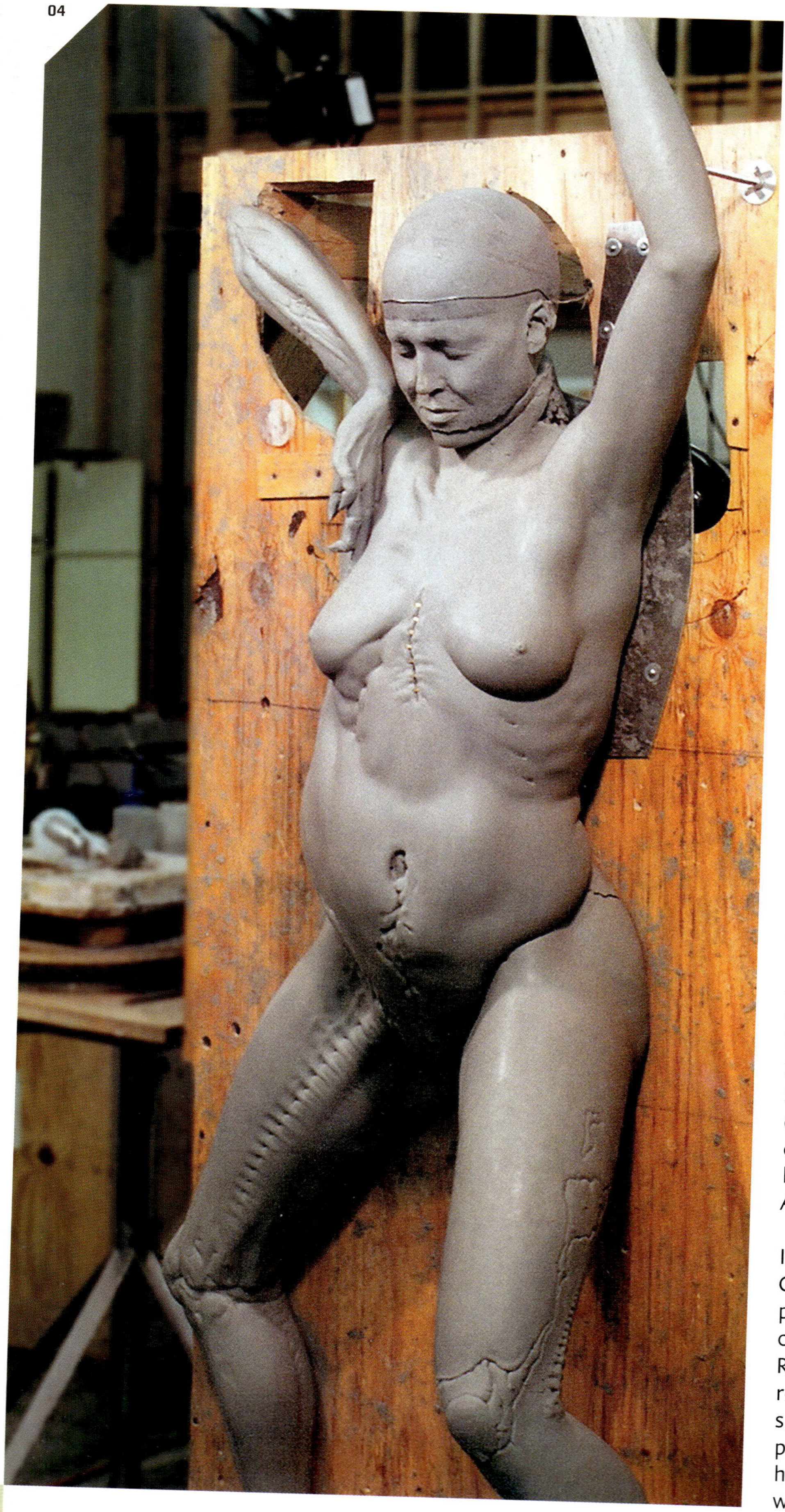

05

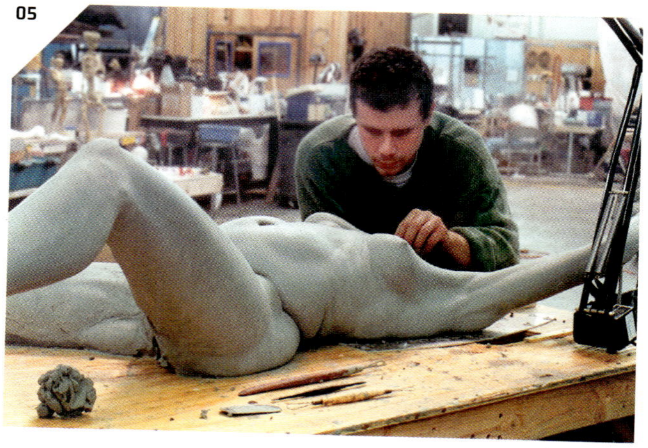

06

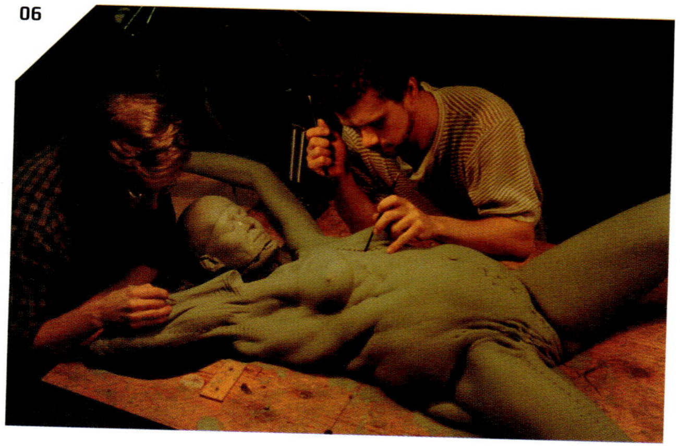

In 1988 Gillis and Woodruff teamed up to form Amalgamated Dynamics Incorporated (ADI). The company quickly became recognized as one of Hollywood's leading makeup studios, soon earning an Academy Award for the animatronic effects in *Death Becomes Her* (1992).

ADI is perhaps best known for its contributions to the *Alien* sequels. Woodruff and Gillis both worked on the second film in the series, *Aliens*, while at Stan Winston Studio. As ADI, they clinched the contract to create the alien effects for Alien^3 (1992). This was followed by work on *Alien Resurrection* (1997) and *AVP: Alien Vs. Predator* (2004).

In Ridley Scott's original *Alien* (1979), H.R. Giger's design was brought to life by a performer wearing a rubber suit and a cable-operated head constructed by Carlo Rambaldi. For *Aliens*, Stan Winston Studio replaced the rubber suits with a more supple stretch-fabric suit onto which polyurethane foam pieces were glued. The head was articulated using servo motors, while close-ups of the complex mouth

07

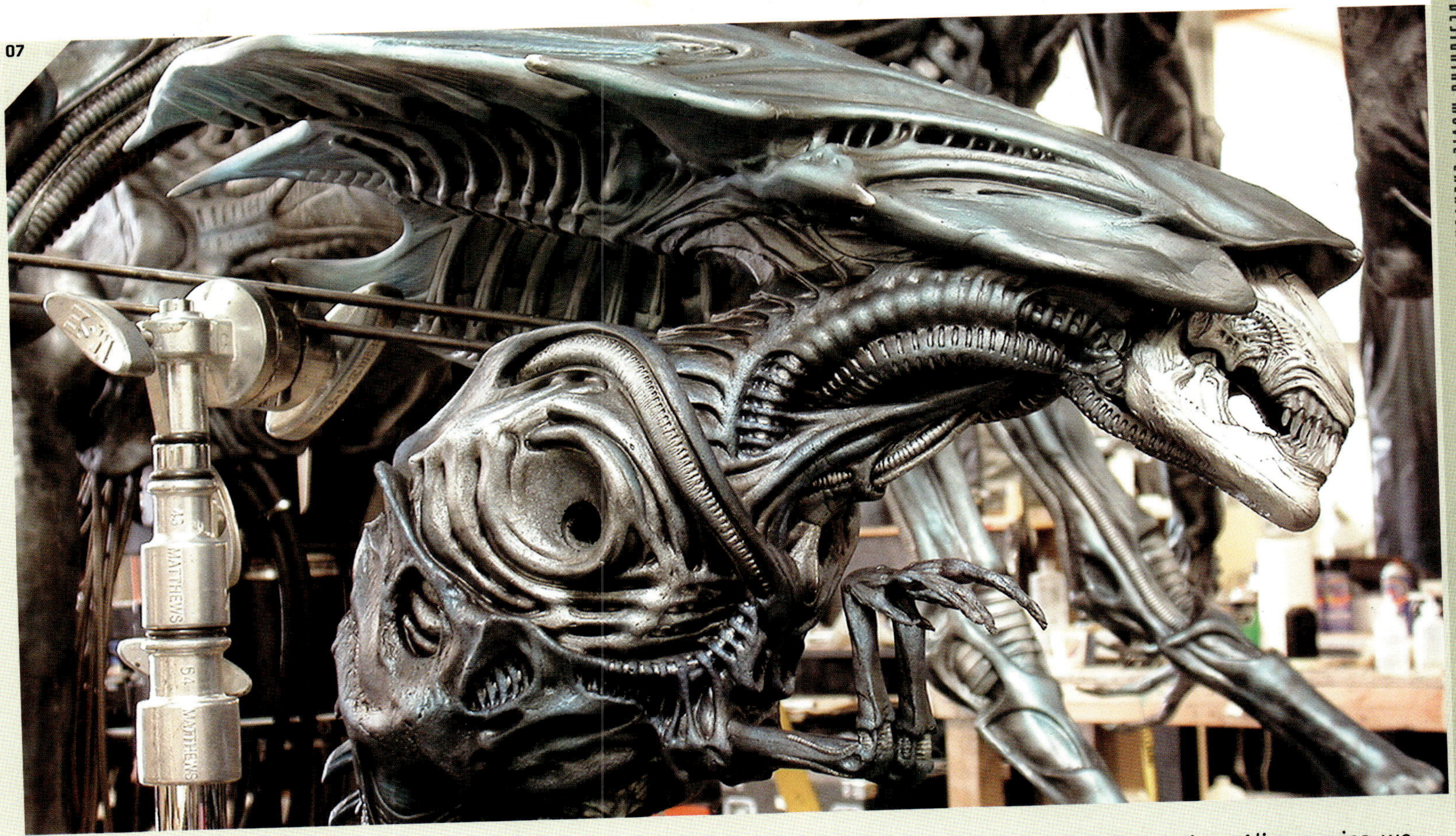

(04–06) A number of body sculpts of the Ripley clone for *Alien: Resurrection* were created at ADI. The finished animatronic bodies were headless and were attached to actress Sigourney Weaver at the neck, enabling her to provide convincing facial performances **(07)** ADI's Alien monsters were created and filmed in a range of scales according to the requirements of the script. This quarter-scale Queen was just eighteen inches long.

were shot using mechanized heads. The Queen Alien was produced as a quarter-scale, cable-controlled puppet, and as a full-size hydraulic-and-cable-operated animatronic that housed two human operators. For *Alien*^{3} the creature was largely created using Woodruff in a suit, as well as some rod-operated puppets (plus a smattering of CGI). *Alien Resurrection* introduced the Newborn, a creature designed and built as an 8ft-tall (2.5m) animatronic puppet with silicone skin. The movie also used CGI creatures.

The build list for *AVP: Alien Vs. Predator* included over 30 full-body suits—many with servo-articulated heads—five hand-puppeted "facehuggers," one animatronic facehugger, several chestbursters, articulated Alien eggs, a fully articulated, computer-controlled hydraulic Alien warrior, mechanical weaponry, a full-size, motion-controlled Queen Alien, and various Alien and Predator body pieces that could be sliced or exploded in battle. One of the greatest challenges was the limited period of time available in which to design and build everything.

"Based on the previous *Alien* movies, we estimated that we needed nine months to complete the work for *AVP*," states Alec Gillis. "Unfortunately, the movie's summer release date meant that we had just five months to get the work done and shipped to Prague for filming. Luckily the director, Paul Anderson, knew exactly what he wanted. A lot of time is often wasted waiting for decisions or producing work that is never used."

"We had made some major changes to the Alien character for the last two films," says Woodruff, "but looking at the script for the new film, we realized that a few subtle sculpture and performance changes would again be necessary for the new Alien. But it was the Predator characters that would require the bulk of original design input. For a start, we didn't have any existing Predator designs or molds, because our studio didn't work on those films. In many ways that was an advantage. Because we had to recreate everything from scratch, there was plenty of scope for updating the character design."

08

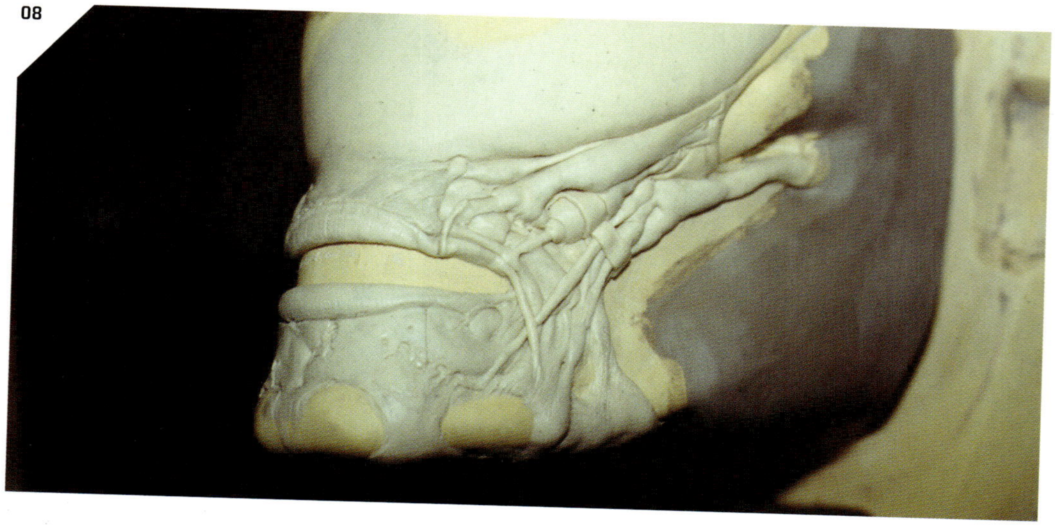

09

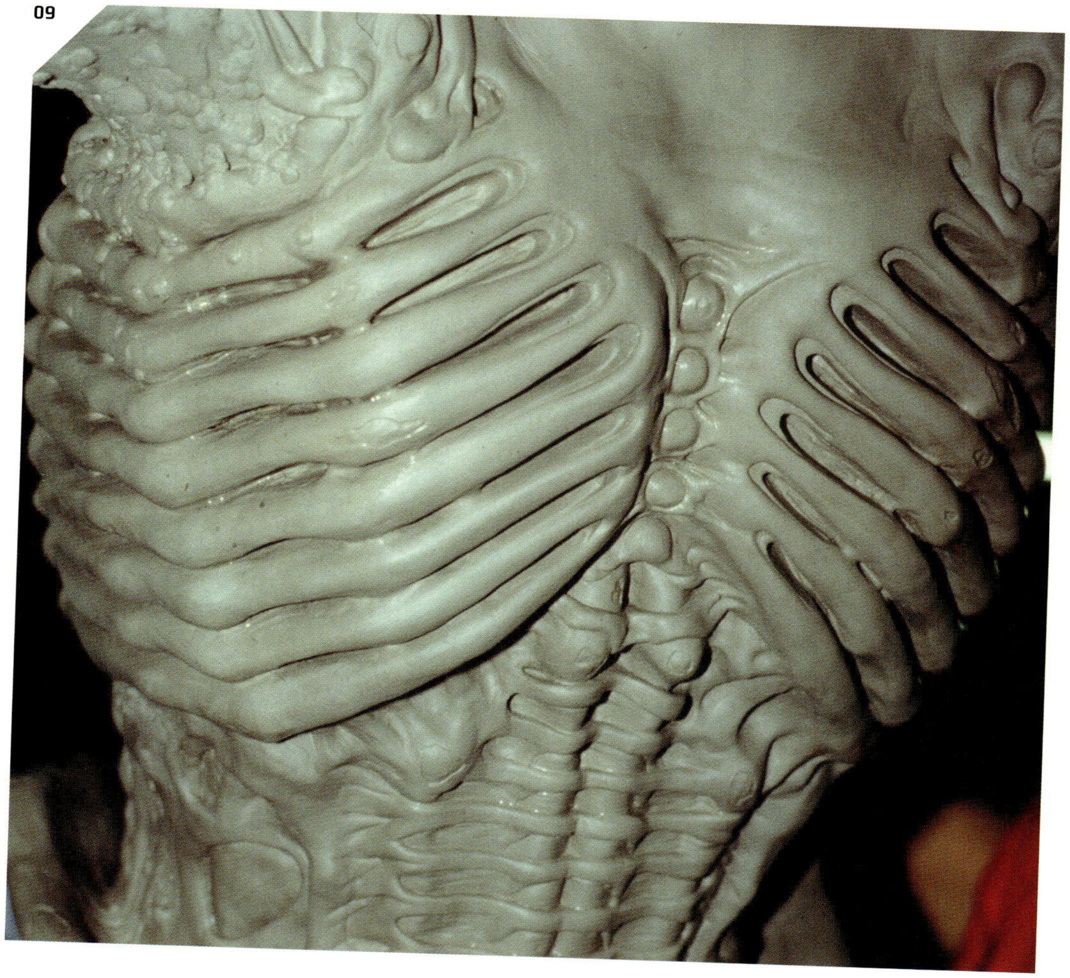

10

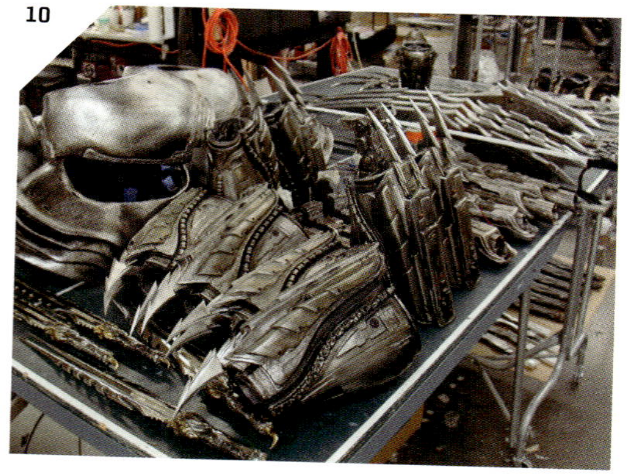

(08) This mouthpiece was sculpted to fit over the front of the Alien head for *Alien*³. **(09)** Alien torso sculpture for *Alien*³. **(10)** A range of armor and weapons created for the Predators in *AVP* (2004). **(11)** The Alien from Alien³.

"We redesigned the Predator armor based on what we gleaned from the esthetic approach in the original movies," explains Woodruff. "In the original film, the design was a mix of Asian and tribal influences, and there was a rough-hewn, artisan quality to the armor. In *Predator 2* (1990) the look was more ornate, and quite insect-like. Our job was to amalgamate these eclectic design motifs and create a new esthetic that was a combination of the previous styles, but which was also appropriate and original to the new film."

As well as drawing on the previous films, Woodruff and Gillis referred to the original source material, the *Dark Horse* comics on which the films were based. As a result, the final Predator designs for *Alien Vs. Predator* also contained shades of comic-book physiognomy, with more heroic proportions—wider shoulders, narrower waists, and smaller heads.

Gillis and Woodruff studied the screenplay, looking for aspects of the character's behavior that might provide cues for the visual design. "In the script, the Predator called Scar teams up with Lex, the film's human heroine. Of course, there was never going to be an inter-species romance going on, but the subtext was definitely there," explains Woodruff. "In addition, Scar spends a considerable amount of time with his mask off—something that rarely happened before. As a result we found we needed to create a much more rounded character, one that had to convey emotions that weren't required before, such as rage, respect, pain, surprise, and even sadness." The result was a character that drew strongly on the design work of previous films, but which was subtly refined. "We made him

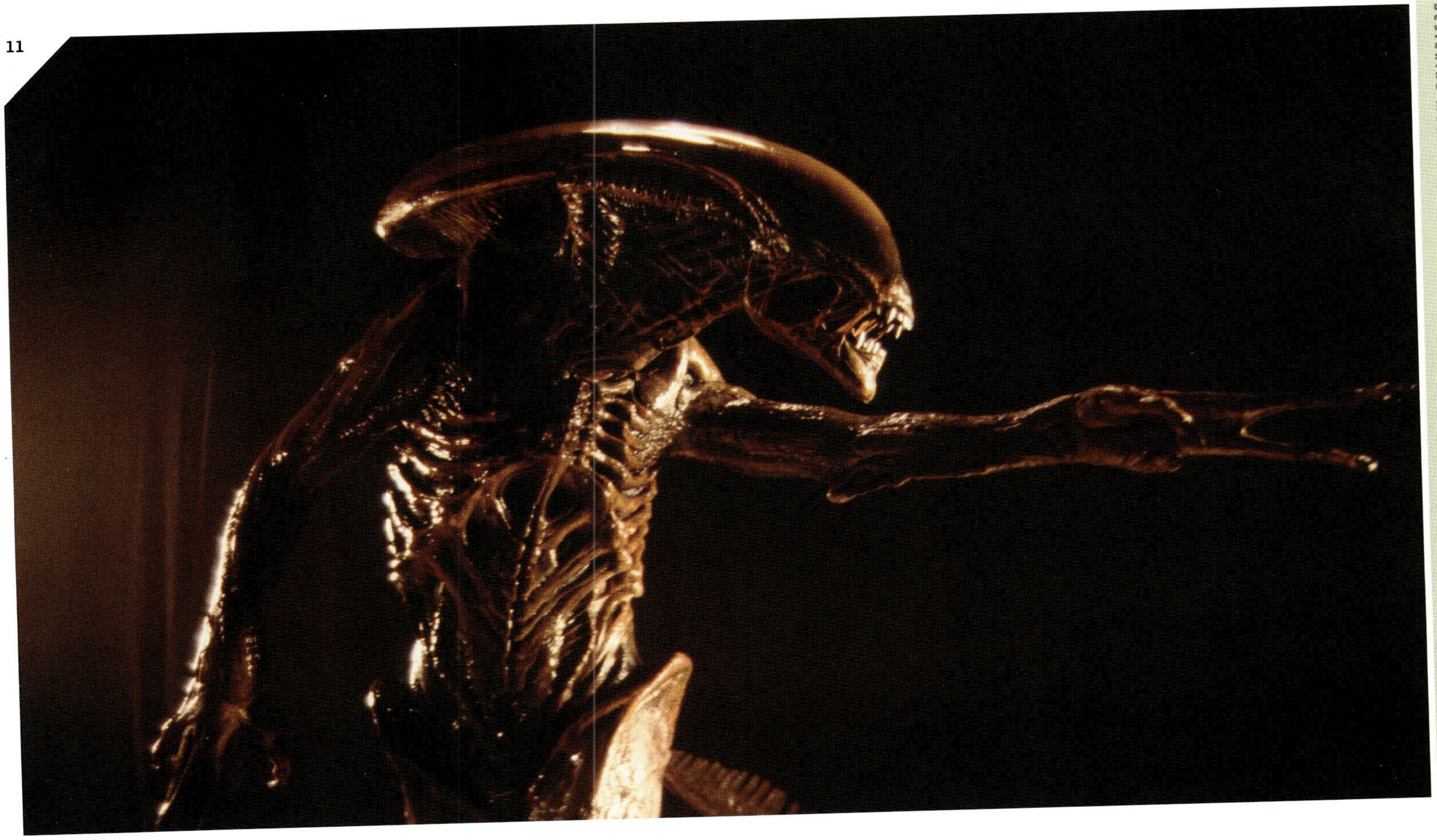

sculpturally more regal—more of a leading man," states Woodruff. "For his color scheme we opted for less pale, clammy, amphibian tones, and went for more human skin tones. We based the design of his eyes on those of a predatory cat—warm and with a large iris. We also reduced the amount of slime used on his skin to make him look a little less repulsive. The need for the character to emote more also led to a subtler facial design, which allowed for more mechanical movement of the facial muscles, brows, and mouth." The final articulated Predator masks were crammed with 27 servo motors to create a wide range of expressions when puppeteered by four operators via radio control.

In order to create a number of different Predator characters within a limited schedule and budget, ADI designed and created five basic Predator face masks. These were then supplemented with additional prosthetic appliances and color schemes in order to produce a wider variety of character designs.

A subtler design challenge was presented by the Alien Warrior characters. "The director really liked the Warriors we had produced for *Alien Resurrection*," says Gillis. "However, he wanted the color scheme from the last two films—which had used warmer brown and sepia tones—to shift back to the original *Alien* color designs of colder metallic blacks and silvers. Because the Aliens were going to be fighting Predators, it was also felt that their spindly hands were not up to the job. The hands were redesigned to be meatier, with longer talons." With these changes, ADI was able to reuse many of the molds created for the previous movie.

The Alien Warrior was brought to life using two techniques. Most shots were created by using Woodruff in a rubber suit. For *Aliens*, Stan Winston Studio had glued polyurethane-foam body pieces to a Lycra suit. But since its involvement in *Alien*^{3}, ADI has always placed the Lycra suit within the mold and cast the foam latex over it, producing a one-piece suit of foam rubber on the outside with Lycra embedded on the inside. On top of the suit the performer wore an articulated, radio-controlled Alien head created from fiberglass with a vacuformed outer dome.

A fully animatronic Warrior was constructed for the fight scenes. "Our animatronic Alien was capable of many fast, dynamic moves that a human performer in a suit would be unable to achieve," says Gillis. "We find hydraulics very responsive and powerful. They used to be large, unwieldy devices, but now you can get hydraulic rams that are only about twice the size of a pencil." The hydraulically operated Warrior was constructed from the knees up, reaching 7ft (2m) in height. The creature's performance was controlled using a motion-control system called Overdrive.

12

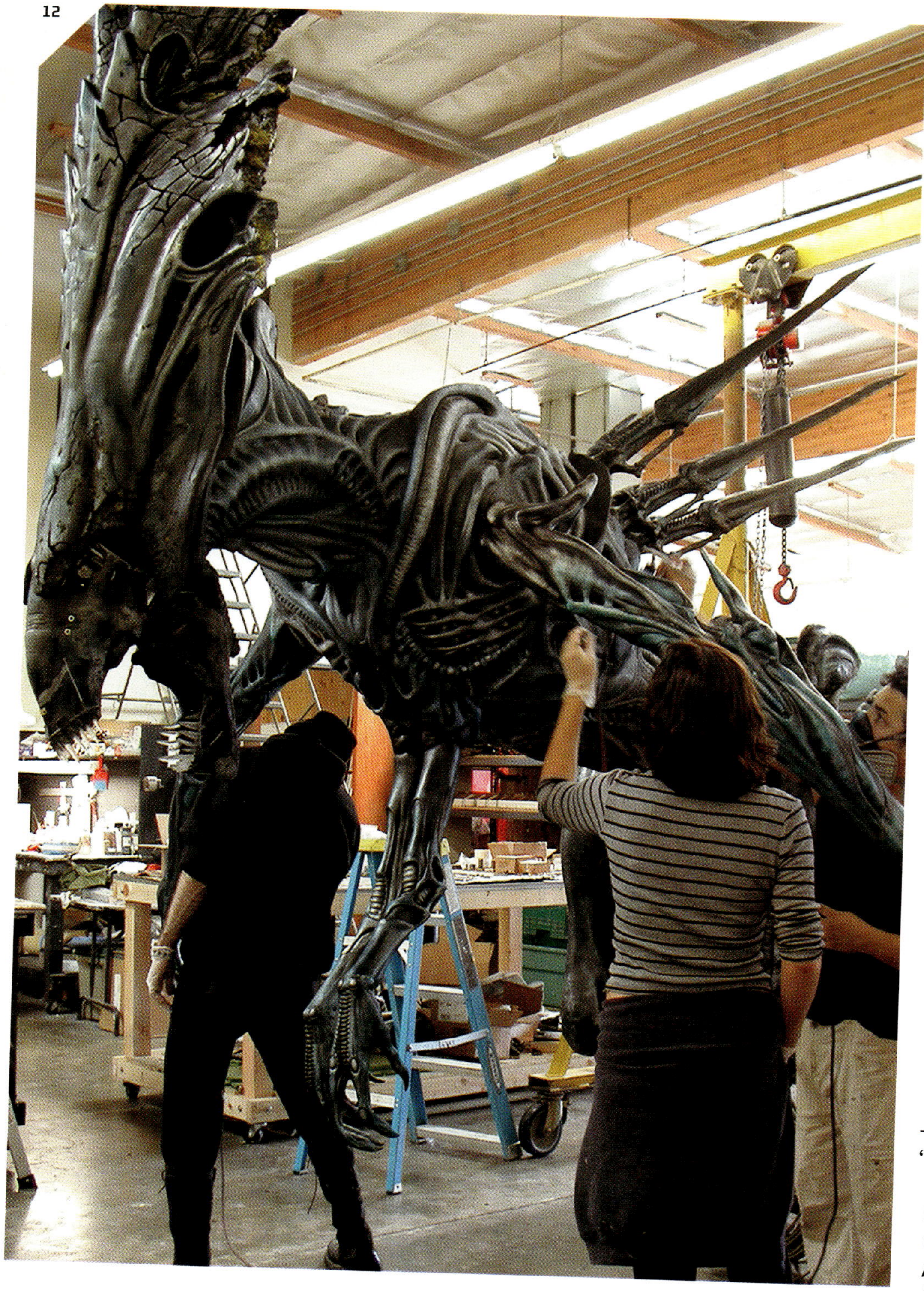

13

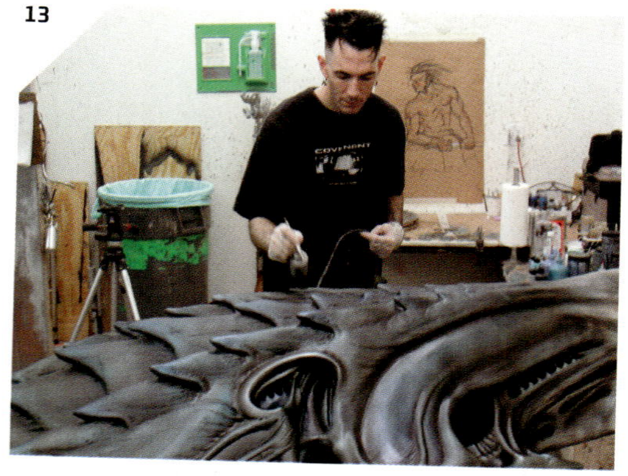

"Overdrive is based on a system we developed for *Starship Troopers* and refined on *Alien Resurrection*. It allows you to program, edit, record, and play character movements in slow motion, or even in reverse," explains Woodruff.

"In this case, we used it to program and then play back the performance of the Warrior Alien precisely and repeatedly. That was really important, because it meant that we knew exactly where the character would be at every stage, allowing actors and cameras to move around it safely during filming. This was particularly useful for the scene where an Alien attacks Lex and is impaled on her spear, thrashing about as it gradually slides down the spear and dies. It was really important that we could guarantee the safety of the performer."

The animatronic Warrior was also capable of throwing out its lashing, toothed tongue, one of the character's trademark features. "In the past the Warrior was always brought to life using a performer—usually me—in a suit," says Woodruff. "However, full-body shots could never have the tongue lashing out of the head because there wasn't room for a tongue mechanism inside the mask. Our new Alien Warrior could be filmed performing full-body moves while at the same time striking with its tongue."

ADI's other major challenge was creating the Alien Queen. "For *Aliens*, the Queen was created as a full-scale character with an animatronic head and face. However, her overall movement was very limited," recalls Gillis. "But for *AVP* the Queen was required to be much more mobile and perform very specific actions."

(12) ADI technicians assemble the full-scale animatronic Queen Alien for *AVP* **(13)** The Queen Alien has her head makeup applied by airbrush **(14)** ADI's Alec Gillis admires the powerful hydraulic Queen Alien built for *AVP*.

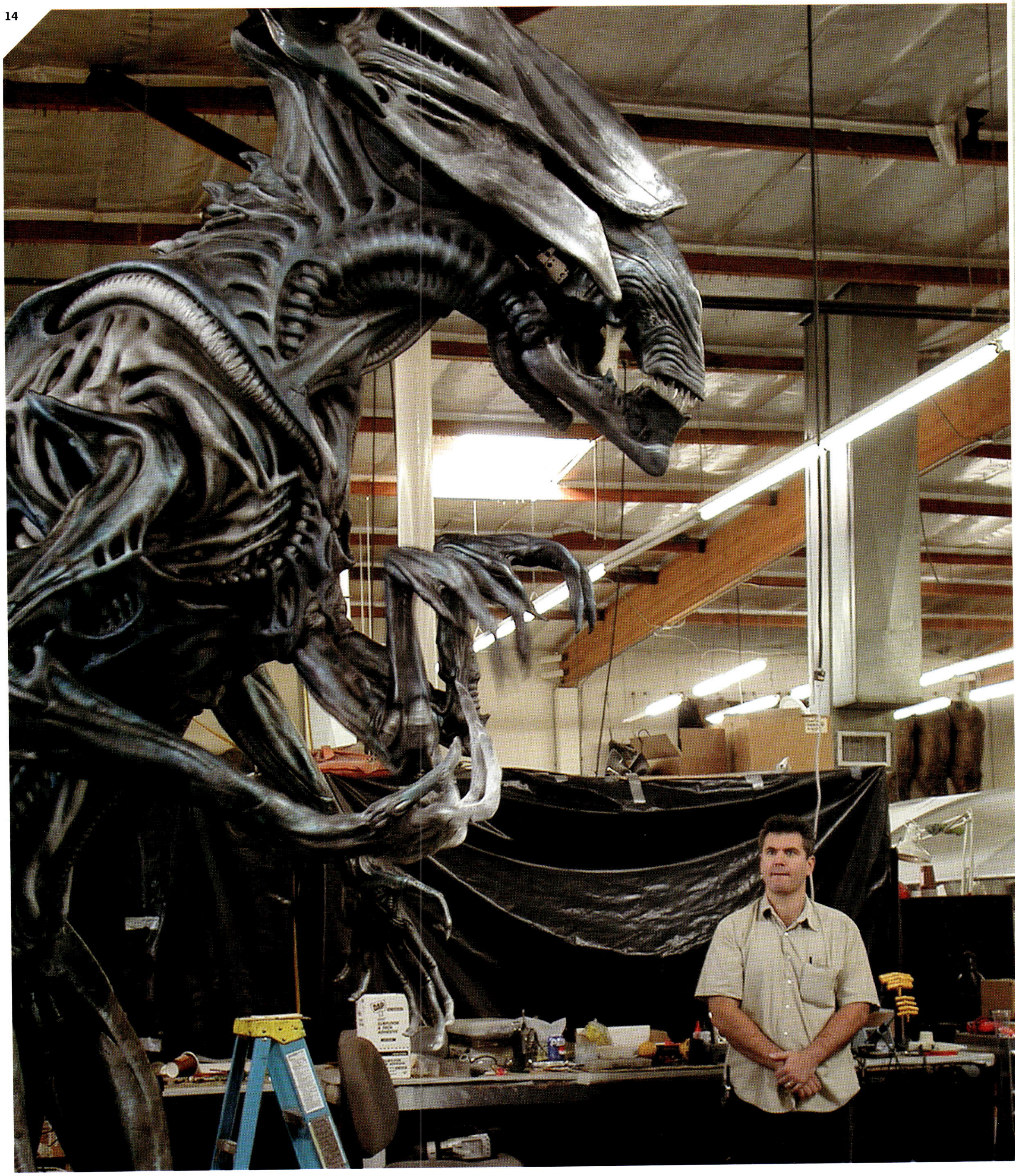

15

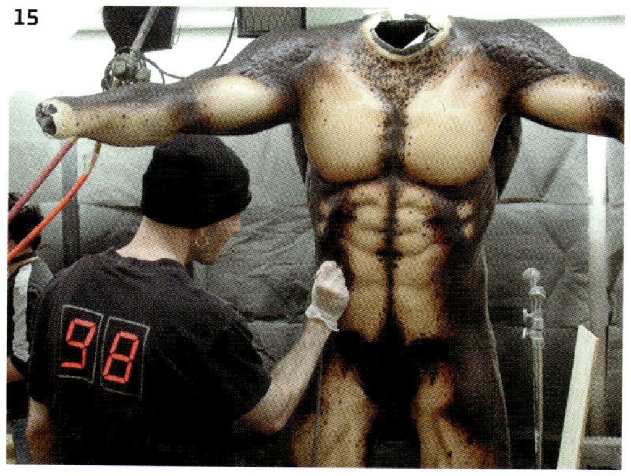

16

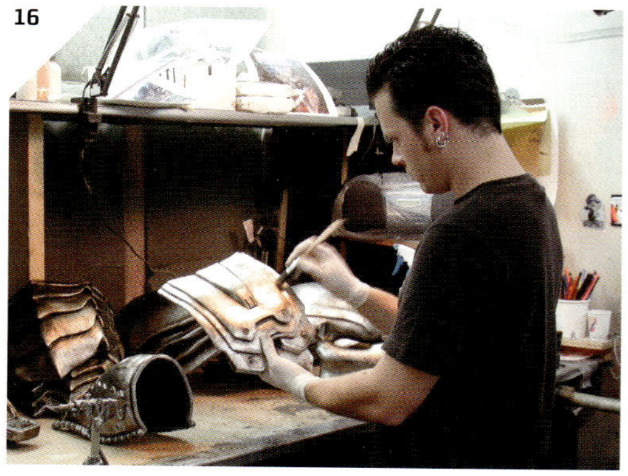

17

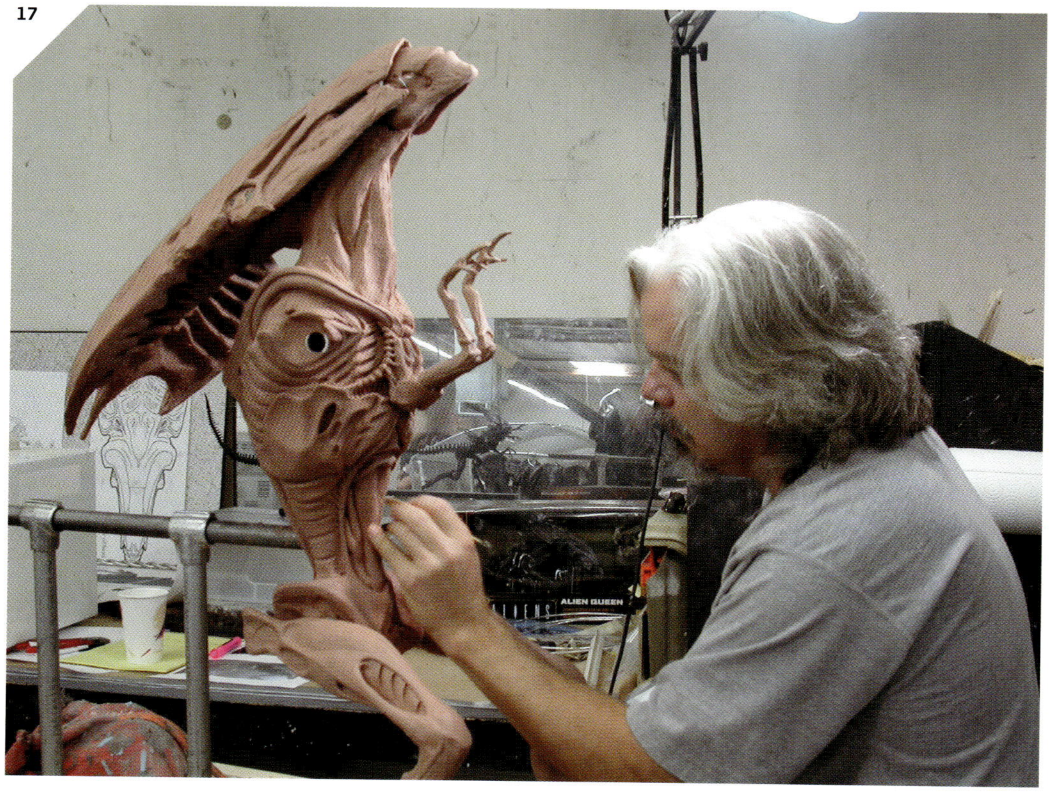

18

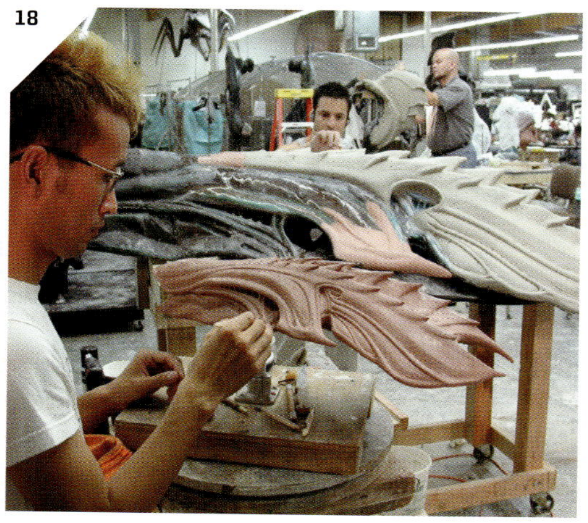

(15) Mike Larrabee airbrushes a finished Predator bodysuit for *AVP* **(16)** Justin Raleigh tests paint schemes on the urethane Predator armor pieces **(17)** Andy Schoneberg works on the detail of the quarter-scale Queen sculpture for *AVP* **(18)** Akihito Ikeda works on the quarter-scale Queen Alien head; Dave Selvadurai sculpts the full-scale version.

James Cameron's original concept art for *Aliens* had depicted the Queen as a very streamlined, insectile beast. However, the final design was much bulkier than originally planned, because its body had been enlarged to accommodate two internal performers. A quarter-scale puppet version had also required sufficient internal room for its cables and mechanisms.

For *AVP*: *Alien Vs. Predator,* ADI built a full-scale, 20ft-high (6m) fully animatronic Queen with an 8ft (2.4m) head. Modern technology allowed ADI's new Queen to retain the original insect-like thorax. "Because our Queen was mechanically actuated and didn't need internal performers we could really slim down the body," says Gillis. "Furthermore, the one-third-scale puppet versions that we built were controlled by cables and rods which can now be easily removed from a shot digitally. In the old days all these control mechanisms had to be concealed within the puppet."

However, time constraints again influenced the redesign of the Alien Queen. Although her body was a brand-new sculpt, her head was ultimately resculpted in clay on top of the original Alien Queen.

Redesigning such classic characters was a delicate process for Woodruff and Gillis, who consider themselves caretakers of the *Alien* creatures' legacy. They strove to produce characters that remained faithful to their original manifestations, but which had developed subtly to reflect the new drama in which they were cast. "On the one hand we didn't want to duplicate what had gone before, but change for change's sake is pointless. We realized we could never recapture the surprise and freshness of these characters [first appearance], but we tried to develop them and take them in new directions."

19

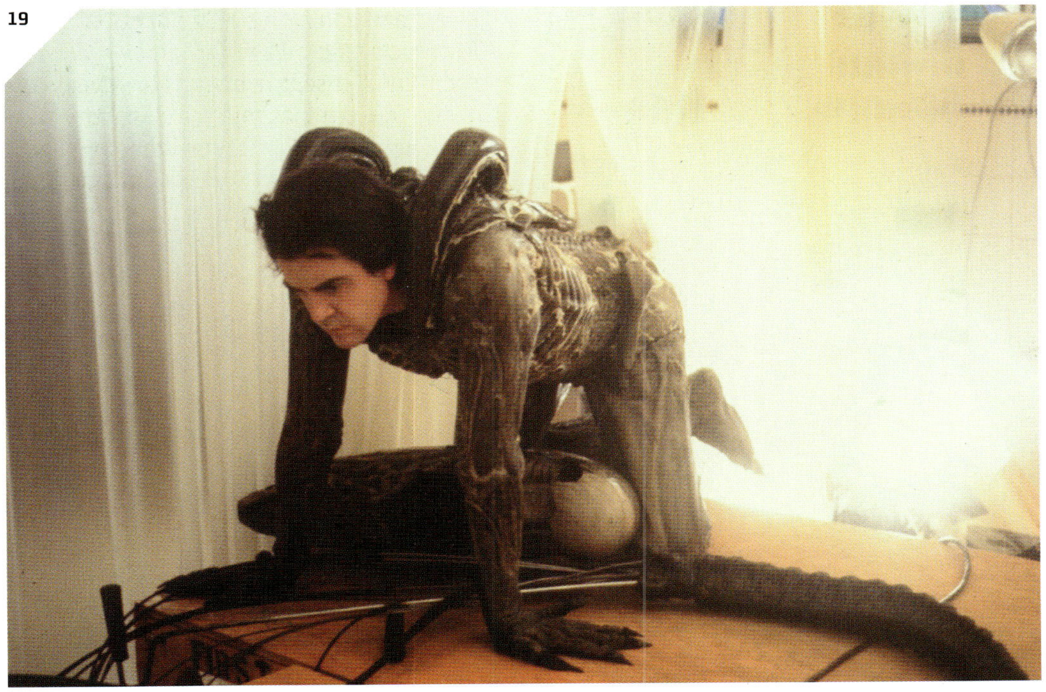

20

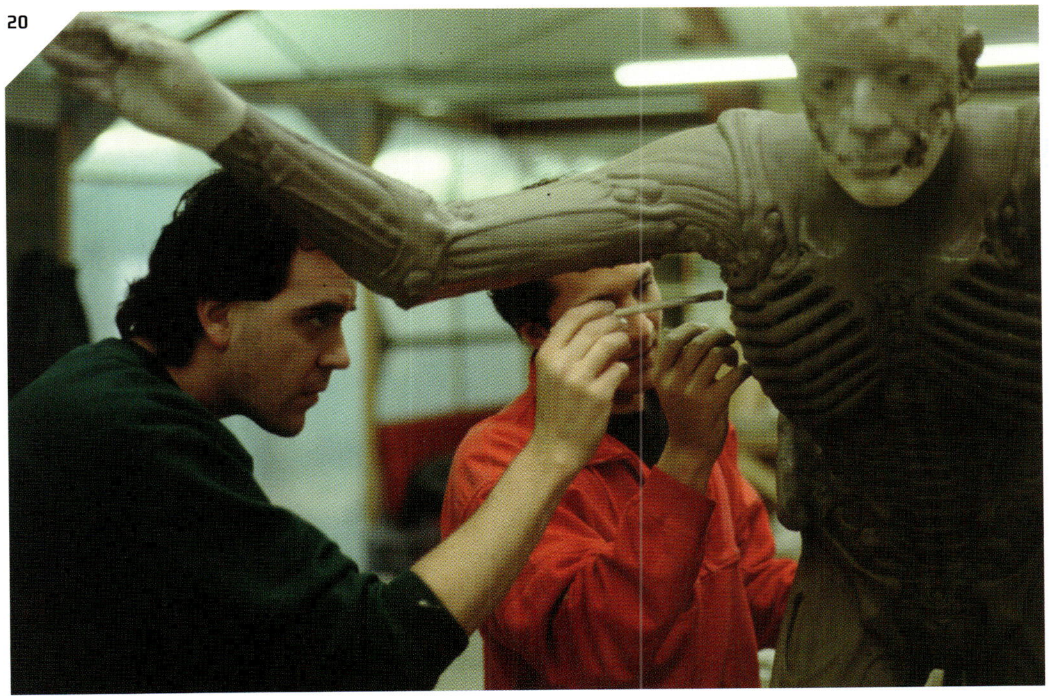

(19) Woodruff takes a break while dressed in the Alien body suit for *Alien*[3]
(20) Woodruff adds fine detail to the Alien body sculpt for *Alien*[3].

While ADI is recognized for its sinister science-fiction characters, some of its creations have been more family-oriented. ADI provided all of the prosthetic makeup and animatronics for *The Santa Clause* (1994) and its two sequels.

For the first film, ADI created a fat-suit to turn Tim Allen into a more rotund Santa. "We had never been terribly impressed by fat makeups in the past, and we searched for a material that would really look and behave like real fat," recalls Woodruff. "We always keep an eye on what materials other industries are producing, and one day a salesman asked if we had any use for an experimental glue that had gone wrong and produced a kind of blubbery vinyl which was wobbly like Jell-o, clear as water, and very stable. We realized it would be ideal for Santa's belly. People often assume that Tim Allen went on one of those potato-and-pasta diets that actors use to gain weight for their movie roles."

For the second film in the trilogy, ADI was asked to build lifelike performing reindeer. "For the first movie we had created reindeer which looked great but all they could do was just stand there," says Woodruff. "For the second movie, we managed to persuade the director that we could pull off a lot of walking and flying reindeer shots physically, saving the production time and money."

The look of the reindeer also needed to be subtly altered from the first film. "For *The Santa Clause* the production planned to use live reindeer in a number of shots, so we had no option but to build our animatronics to match the real thing," recalls Gillis. "For the second film, no real reindeer were going to be used, so we were able to ditch the totally accurate look. In addition, the reindeer had become more important characters, and needed to be quite expressive. We had a great time designing each of the reindeer faces; they had to combine the expressiveness of a cartoon character with the heart and soul of a real animal."

The build process began with clay reindeer sculptures that were used to create fiberglass cores into which the mechanics could fit. The central body framework was made of lightweight aluminum to keep the overall weight down. "Keeping it light was important, because otherwise you need bigger hydraulic rams, higher oil pressure, and so on," explains Gillis.

21

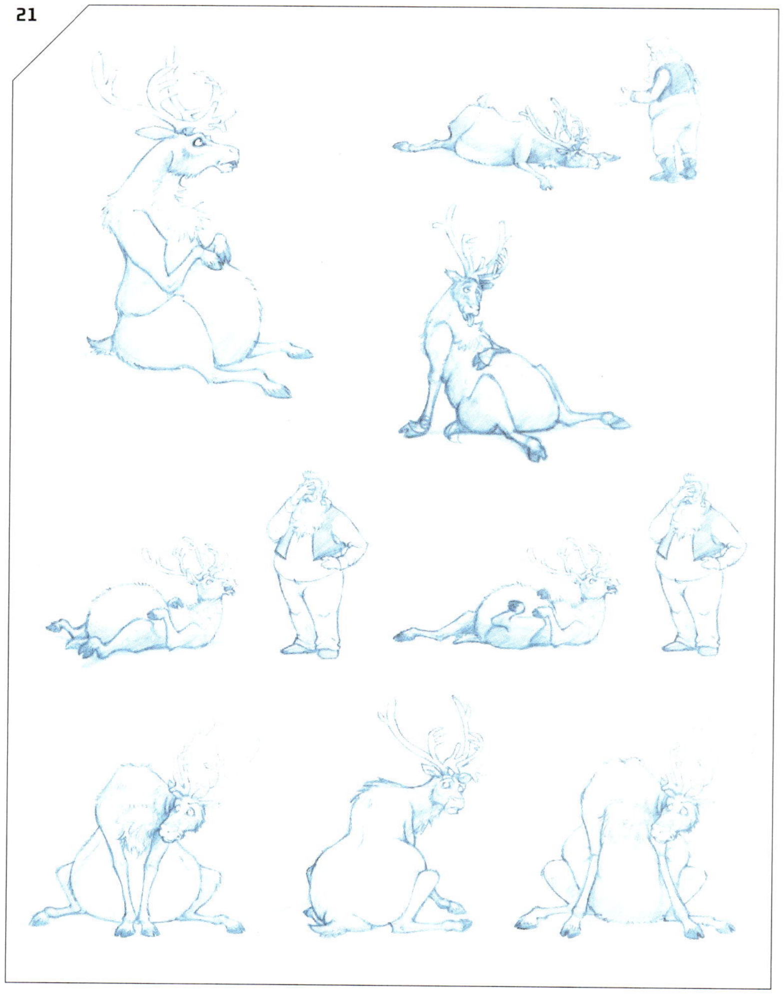

22

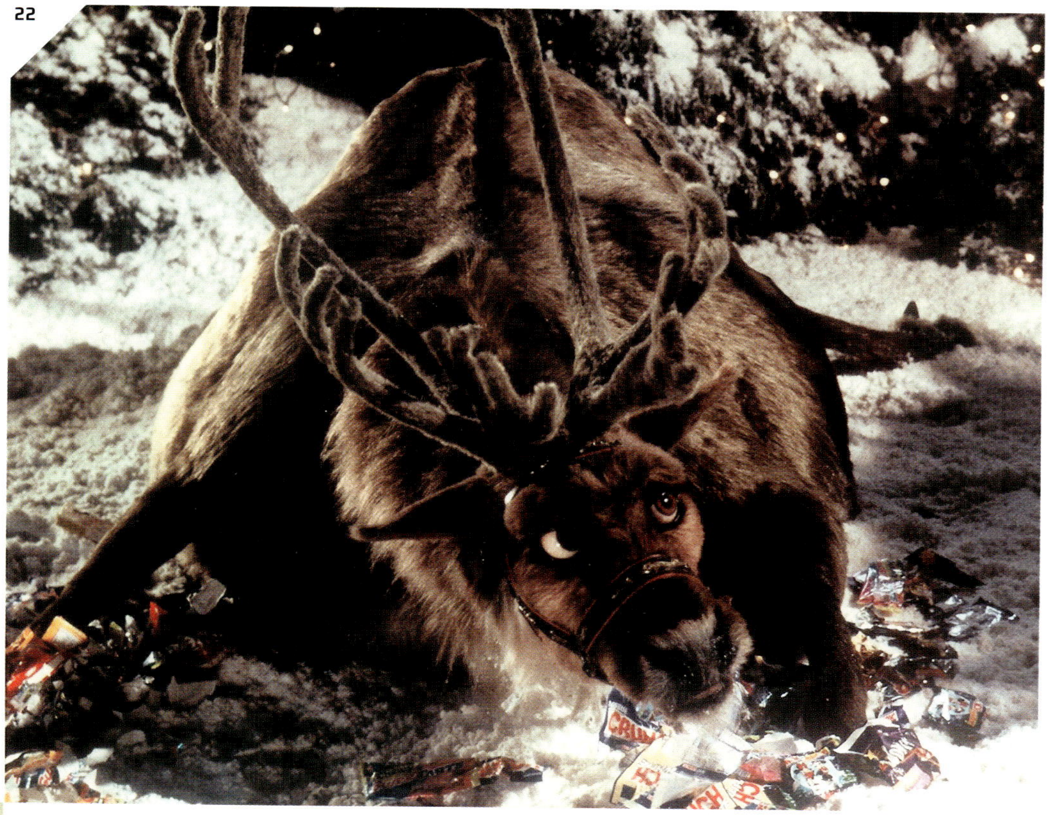

"The body mechanism was a staggeringly complex amalgamation of joints and pivots that could swivel and rotate exactly like the movements in a real creature, as well as stretching and compressing the torso to affect the overall proportions of the body during movement.

Mounted over the framework were pieces of fiberglass core—the result of the initial sculpt and molding process. On top of the core, the team fabicated a variety of shaped materials to recreate the muscle and flesh of a reindeer. A hair suit made of synthetic hair painted to reflect a reindeer's natural patterning was stretched over the body. The hair was on a superstretchy fabric backing to prevent the skin from tearing during the extreme motion of the underlying mechanics.

"The skin had to really stretch, especially in the area where the hip meets the belly, which is where the skin really moves around," says Gillis. "It took quite a bit of tweaking to get the skin looking right. First the skin was too tight, so we cut the fabric and inserted another panel. That worked fine when the leg was stretched out but when it pulled back in the fur would bunch up. To solve this we had to attach elastic bands to the inside of the fur and anchor it to various parts of the inside mechanism to keep it under control. It illustrates how amazing real skin is, with its ability to stretch and compress."

With the outer skin of the reindeer in place, some parts of the creature's interior needed to be modified. "Once the skin is on you see which parts of the mechanism aren't working well. You'll suddenly see a big lump that looks like some kind of tumor under the skin, and it'll be a bolt

(21) Concept sketches for the reindeer Comet (*The Santa Clause 2*, 2002)
(22) Still from *The Santa Clause 2*, 2002.
(23) Clay maquette produced after approved concept sketches
(24) Technical plans for reindeer mechanisms

23

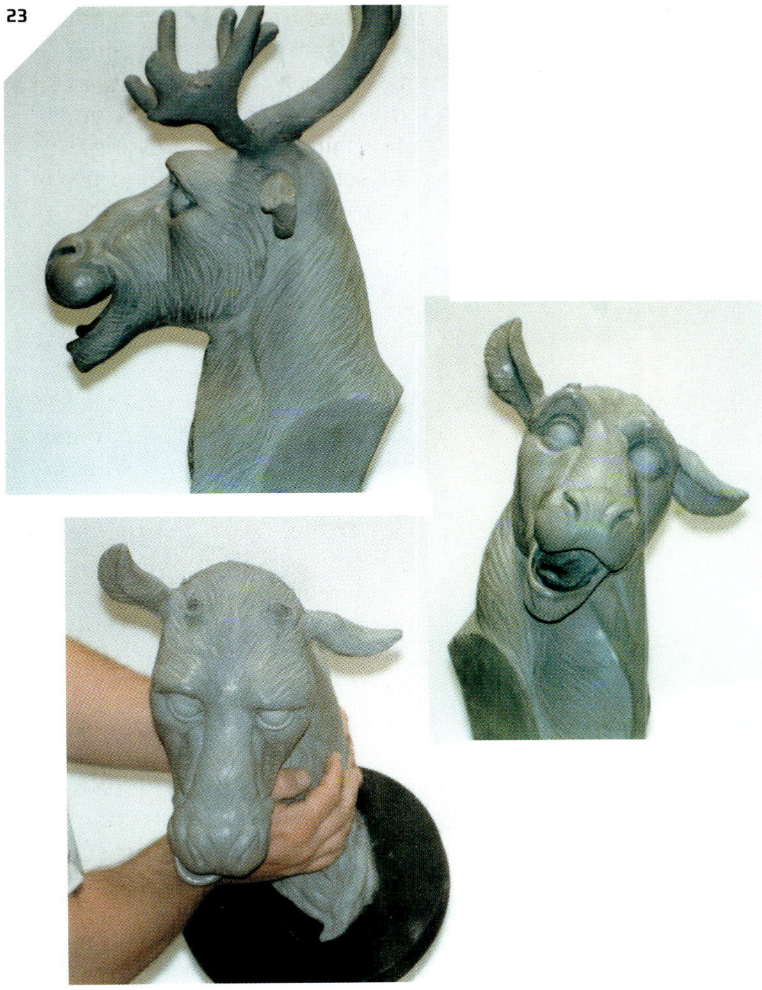

24

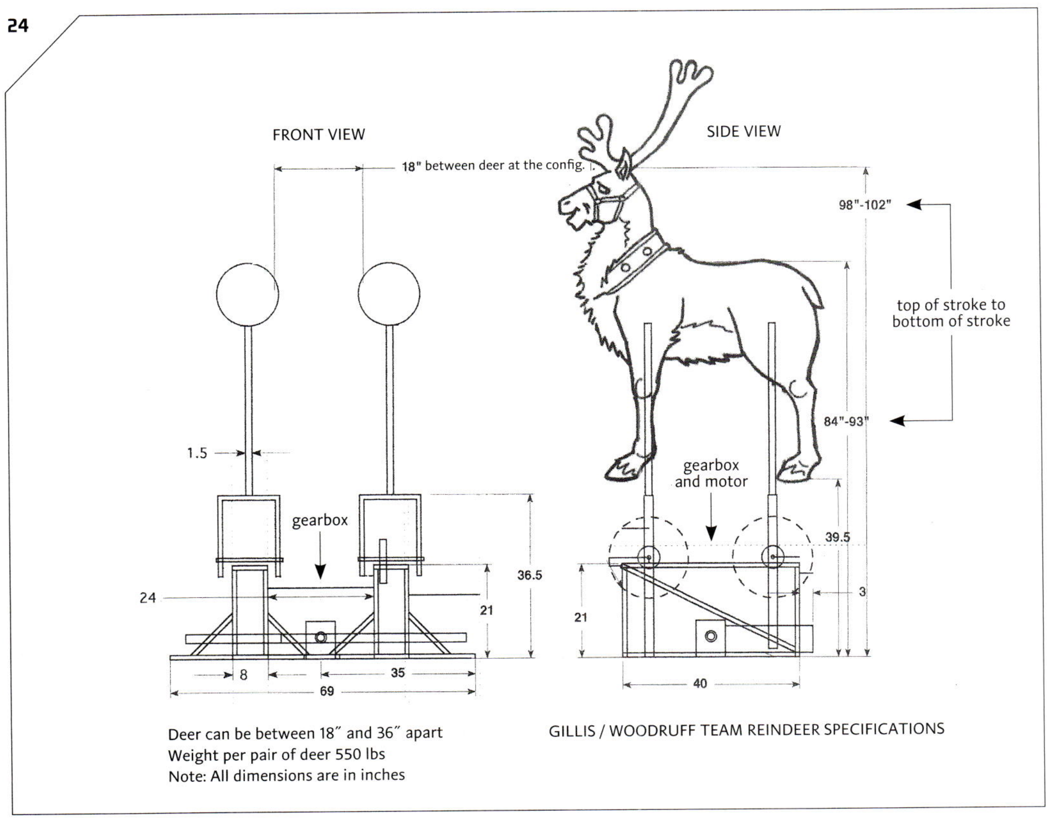

head or some other part of the mechanism that you have to go back and remove or conceal," says Gillis.

Only one animatronic flying reindeer was built, but its head could be removed and replaced, allowing the single body to portray both Comet and Chet, the lead reindeer characters of the film. The heads themselves contained dozens of servo motors to provide eye, lip, jaw, nostril, and muzzle movement.

The reindeer's movements were produced using hydraulic rams hooked to servo actuators, which in turn were linked to a computer. The computer itself was linked to a "waldo"—an aluminum control puppet that was a smaller version of the reindeer skeleton. As each of the small joints was hand-animated, the movement was translated to the full-scale creature.

"We spent weeks building up the performance of the reindeer, referring to footage of horses and creating seven or eight different run cycles," says Woodruff. "We would program the movement of a single leg, motor by motor, gradually smoothing out and enhancing its performance. Then we could cut and paste that performance and apply it to each other leg, off-setting the movement so that together they would move in a natural galloping pattern. We selected the appropriate run cycle, and it would work automatically while the three on-set puppeteers concentrated their efforts on the radio-controlled performance of the facial features, head, and neck."

The finished reindeer was mounted on an articulated boom arm that could be configured to allow filming from either the left- or right-hand side of the animal. The arm was used to control the pitch and rocking movement of the body and could also be mounted to the front of a fork-lift truck to lift the reindeer—and Tim Allen—25 feet (7.5 meters) into the air.

As well as a flying reindeer, ADI built a walking model with two fully functional front legs. The deer was mounted on a wheeled boom, allowing it to be walked into shots, or to rear up with a prancing movement as if about to take off.

25

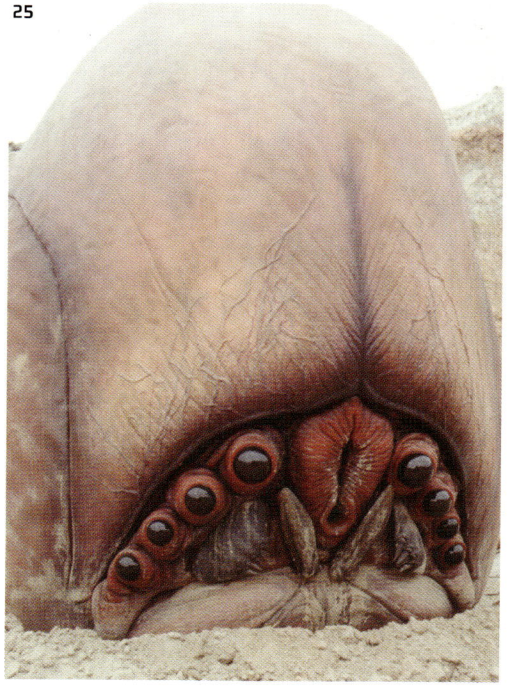

26

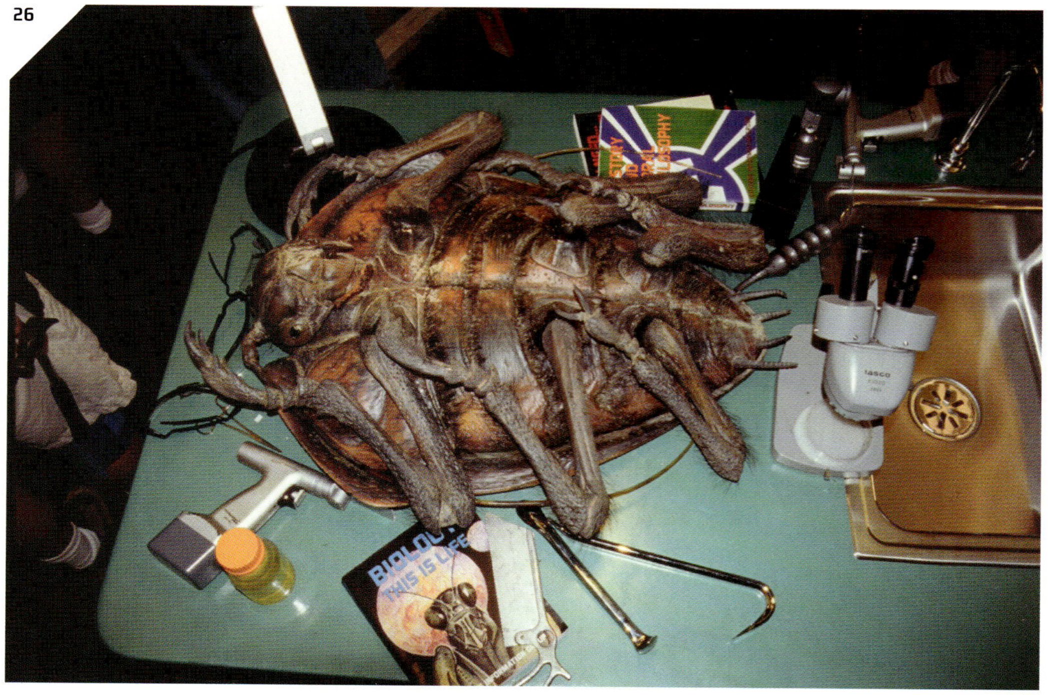

27

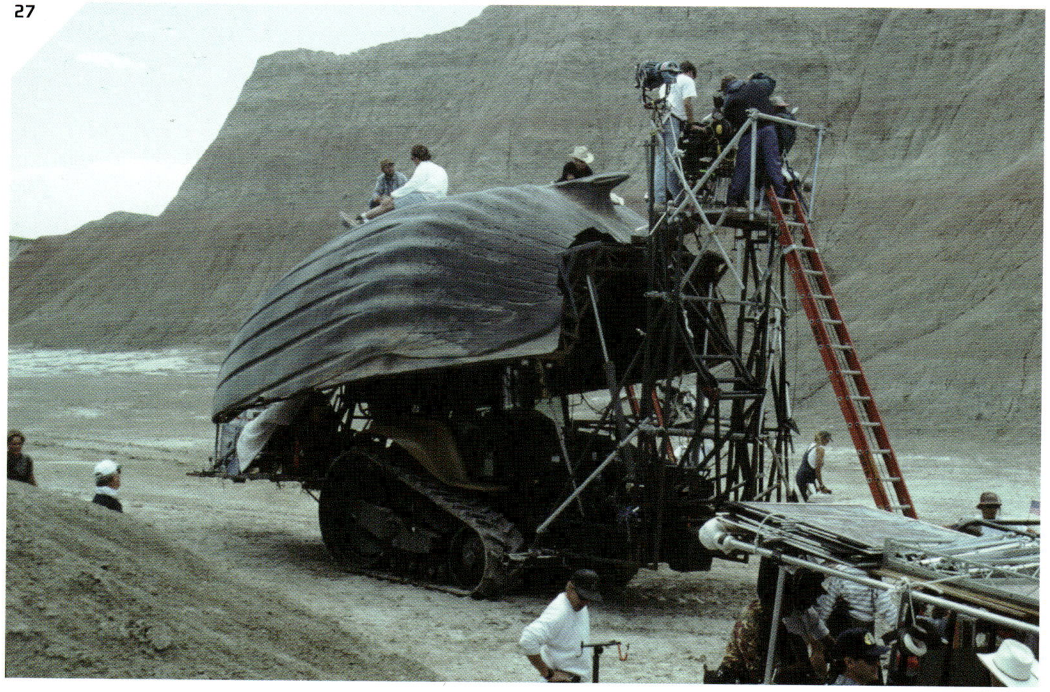

28

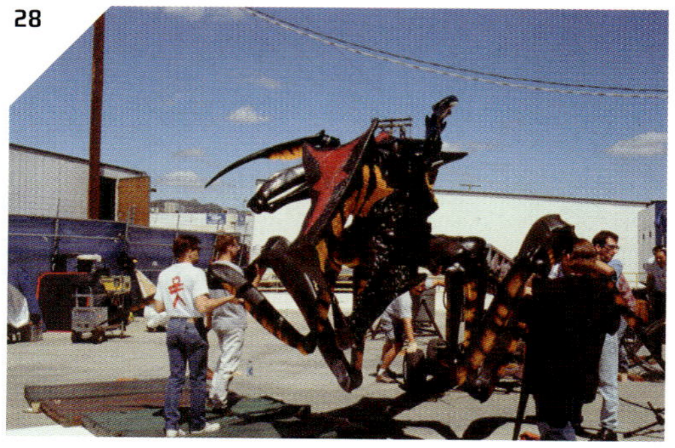

(25–28) ADI created the practical makeup for sci-fi monster movie *Starship Troopers* (1997). The alien bug creations ranged from small animatronic beetles to large-scale warrior bugs capable of grasping the stunt performers in their claws.

For Woodruff the reindeer for *The Santa Clause* has been one of the highlights of his career. "It certainly wasn't as high profile a creature as many of our others, but for us it was a real high-water mark in terms of creating a realistic-looking creature that gave a convincing, naturalistic performance," he says. "Seeing the finished mechanical reindeer moving was really an amazing illusion. It looked so real and moved so smoothly that your brain wanted to think it was a genuine animal. It was really only the big metal boom arm coming out of its side that shattered that illusion. And it didn't need a room full of animators and computer modelers to produce."

Gillis and Woodruff are the first to admit that practical (physical) effects have limitations, and that there are times when computer-generated creatures can outperform animatronics.

29

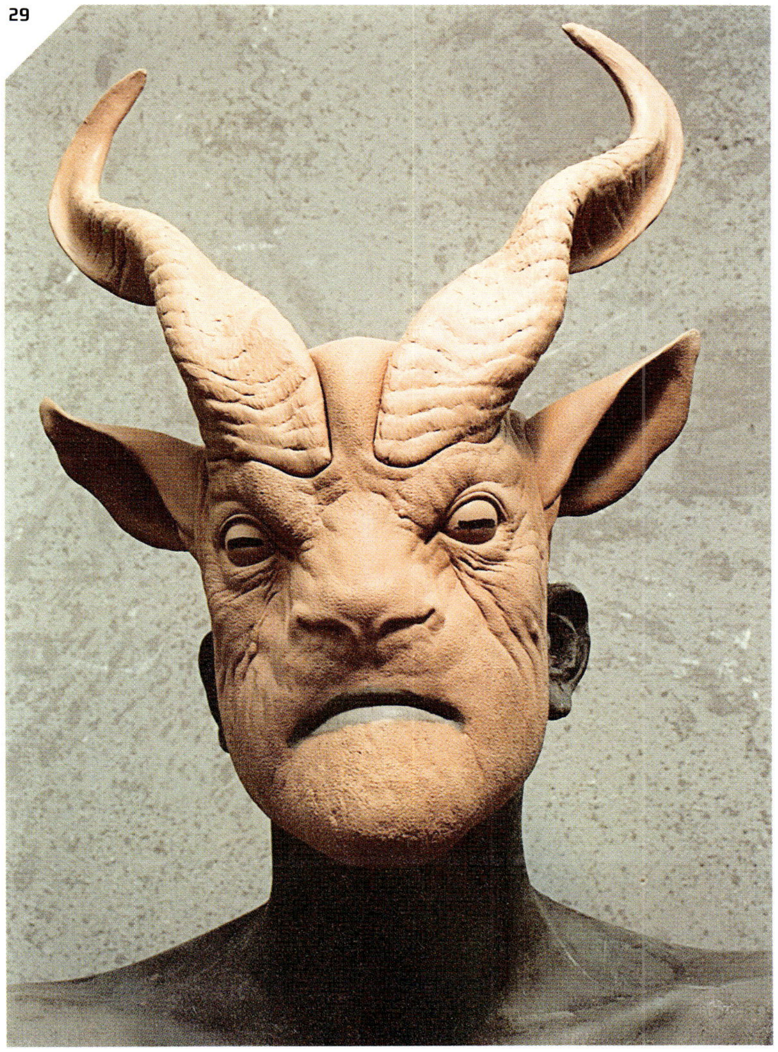

30

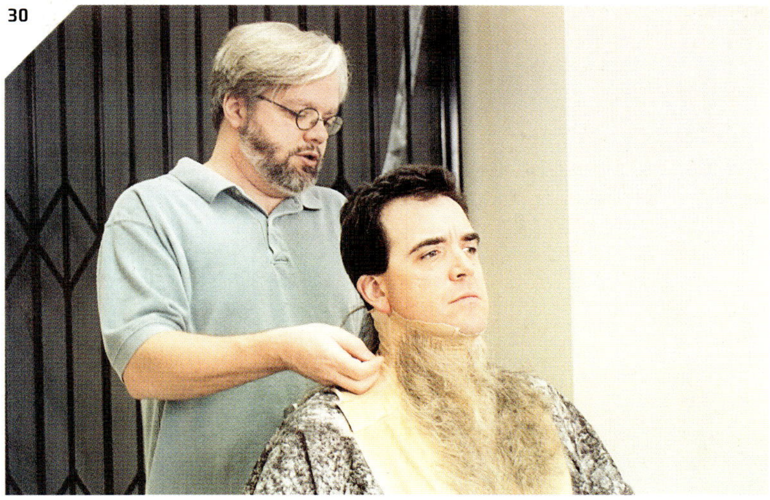

31

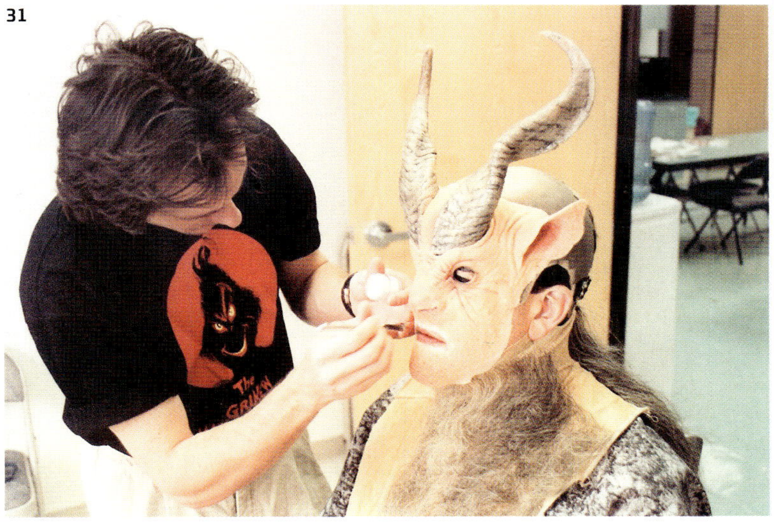

However, they find that the prevalence of CG visual effects has greatly affected the way their own industry is perceived and treated by film producers. "What's frustrating is the continually shrinking timescales available for creating character effects," explains Gillis. "Once a studio has committed to spending millions of dollars on a production, they want to get it in front of the cameras as soon as possible, leaving us very little time to create the work ready for filming. They also don't want to spend much money up front, preferring to spend as much as possible at the tail end of production so that they are not accruing interest on their investment.

"That's one of the big reasons studios prefer doing a lot of character stuff in CG—not because of the quality, but because it mostly happens in the later stages of production and they pay for it last. CG is also used when the movie looks like it isn't working very well and the studio is willing to pay out to fix the problems. The studios seem to have this mindset about spending vast amounts on CG effects when, in fact, we can often achieve much more—if only they were willing to commit more up front. At a time when box-office revenues are falling, we can produce great work for a fraction of the cost of CG."

(29) One of ADI's Satan designs, created for *Bedazzled* (2000), and sculpted over a lifecast of Tom Woodruff Jr. **(30–31)** Woodruff has the final "Satan" appliances attached to him.

AARON SIMS

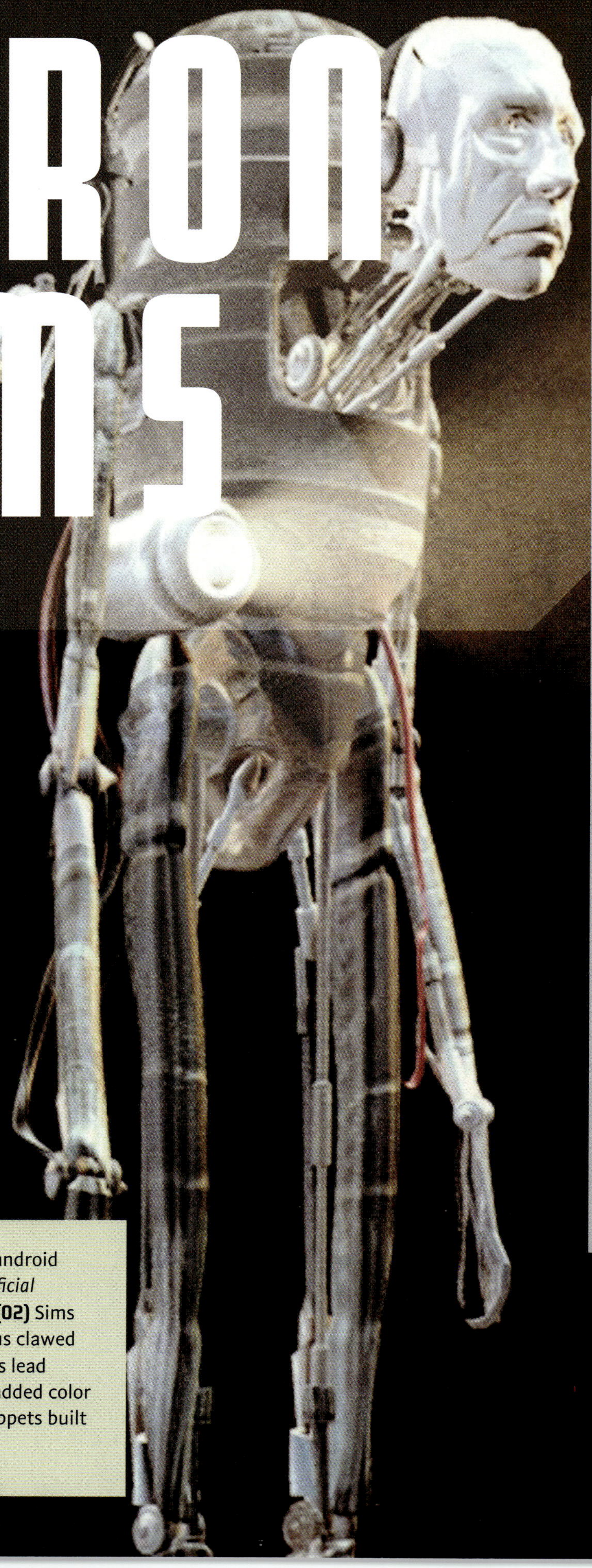

CV

Character designer, maker, and painter; b. Arlington, TX; father was an animator for classified military projects; originally pursued a career as an illustrator; moved to LA in 1985 to attend Art Center College of Design, Pasadena, but ended up working in Tower Records instead; invited by a friend to work on *From Beyond*, after which started designing and painting characters; hired by Rick Baker in 1988 as lead painter for *Gremlins 2*, afterward remaining with Baker as permanent employee; invited to set up a digital department at Stan Winston Studio, subsequently becoming art director of the physical department as well. Now runs his own design company.

SELECT FILMOGRAPHY

From Beyond (1986); *Gremlins 2: The New Batch* (1990); *Wolf* (1994); *Batman Forever* (1995); *The Nutty Professor* (1996); *Men in Black* (1997); *AI: Artificial Intelligence* (2001); *Terminator 3: Rise of the Machines* (2003); *Constantine* (2005)

KEY CHARACTERS

Worm Guys (*Men in Black*); robots (*Terminator 3*); Mammon (*Constantine*); Baron (*Doom*); aliens (*War of the Worlds*)

TECHNIQUES

ZBrush; Photoshop; Softimage XSI

(01) One of Sims' android designs for *AI: Artificial Intelligence* (2001) **(02)** Sims sculpts details of a monstrous clawed hand for *From Beyond* **(03)** As lead painter on *Gremlins 2*, Sims added color detail to many of the 150 puppets built at Rick Baker's studio.

02

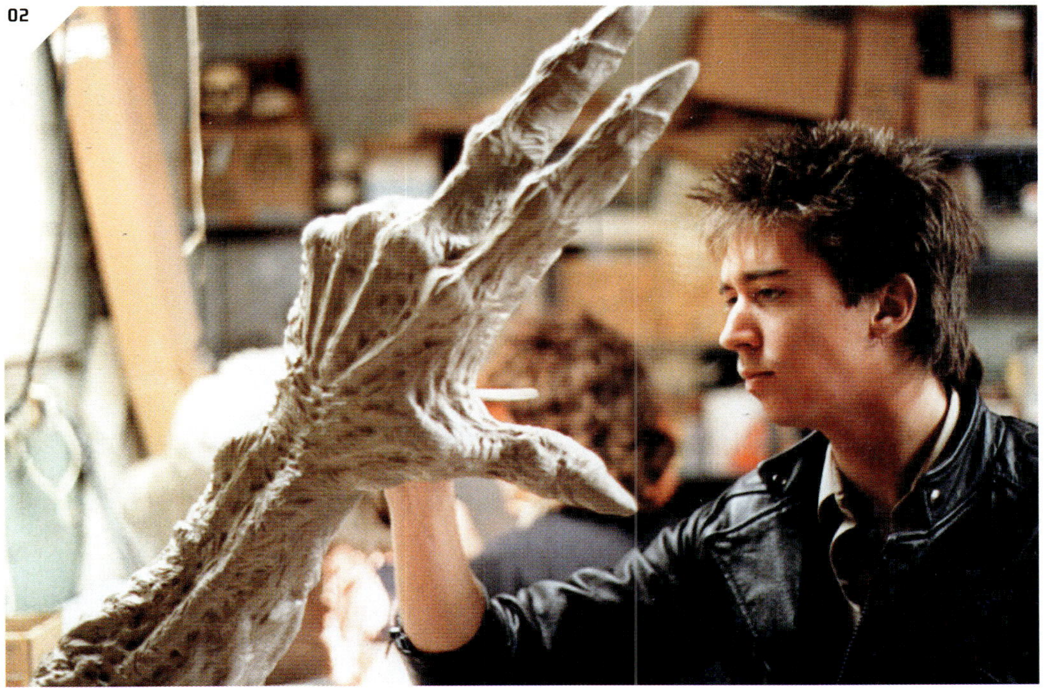

03

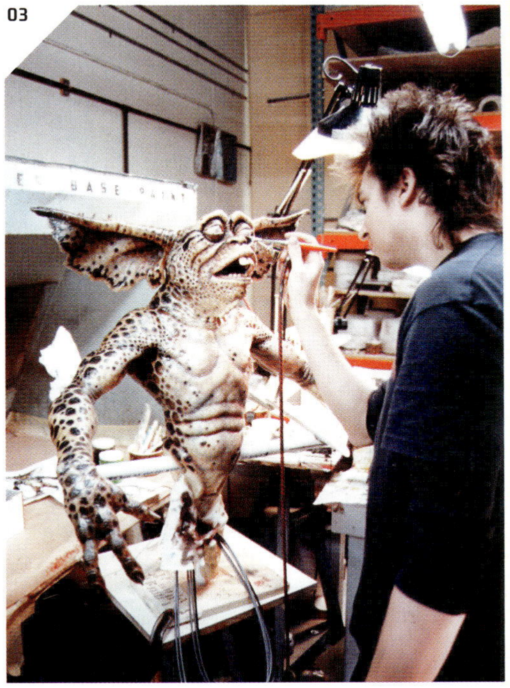

Aaron Sims was born in Arlington, Texas, where his father worked as an animator making movies for classified military projects. Sims would often try to copy his father's artwork, becoming a proficient draughtsman himself. "I was quite interested in what my dad did for a living, but early on I realized that I didn't have the patience to be an animator—drawing the same images over and over was hard work. I even tried doing clay-puppet stop-motion animation based on the Ray Harryhausen movies I'd seen on TV, but even that was just too laborious for me.

"I liked the idea of doing something artistic for a living, as I was always pretty good with a pencil and paintbrush. At high school I had a friend, Greg Punchatz, whose dad was an illustrator—he painted images for the covers of sci-fi books and *Time* magazine—and that seemed much more my kind of thing."

From an early age, Sims was a big movie fan, and often dreamed of working in the movie industry. "A lot of movies really influenced me as a kid," recalls Sims. "Even though I was too young, my mom took me to see *Jaws*—and I'm still afraid of the water! And *Star Wars* was a big deal for me. Everything about it was so exciting that it made me want to work in visual effects—I thought matte painting might be something that I could do. However, even at that young age I was pretty sensible, and I decided that a job in the movies wasn't a very realistic possibility—so instead I pursued a career as an illustrator."

In 1985 Sims moved to Los Angeles in the hope of attending the Art Center College of Design in Pasadena. But when college fees proved prohibitive he got a job creating window displays for Tower Records instead. One day Sims received a phone call from his friend Greg Punchatz, who was working with makeup supervisor Mark Shostrom on *Nightmare on Elm Street Part 2: Freddy's Revenge* (1985). Punchatz asked Sims if he'd be interested in helping to design a character for their next movie, *From Beyond* (1986).

"The door was suddenly opened and I was invited in," says Sims. "I was designing characters, sculpting them, and painting them. From then on I gave up the idea of illustration and dedicated myself to special-effects makeup."

Sims spent several years moving from workshop to workshop. "It was the mid 1980s, and special-effects makeup was really booming," he recalls. "Competition was really tough, as people were opening up workshops all over the place—from big studios like Kevin Yagher's to little places in people's home garage."

In 1988, Sims was hired by Rick Baker as lead painter on *Gremlins 2: The New Batch* (1990), a two-year assignment that involved creating over 150 puppets. When the project wrapped, Baker asked Sims to stay on. "I wound up staying for 12 years, an almost unheard-of period of time in this business," says Sims. "I worked on some exciting projects, including *Wolf* (1994), *Batman Forever* (1995), and *The Nutty Professor* (1996)."

04

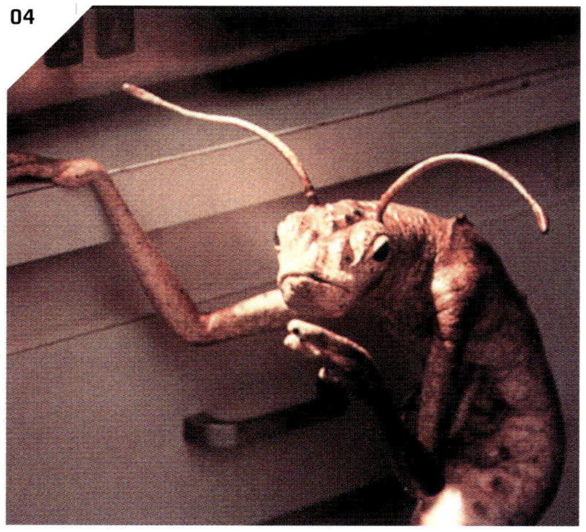

05

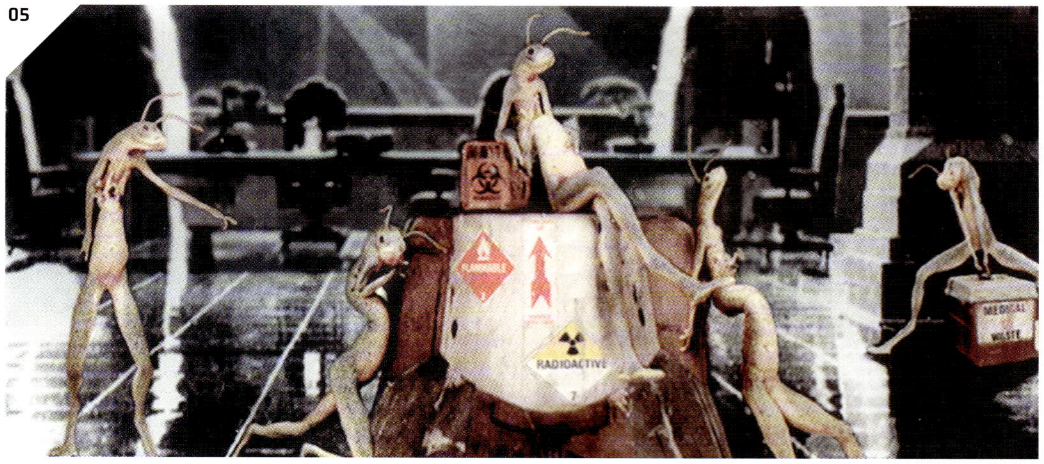

Among Sims's favorite creations from his time at Rick Baker's are the popular Worm Guys that he designed for *Men in Black* (1997). "There were lots of us churning out ideas, and I did a maquette of this worm-like creature," he recalls. "The director, Barry Sonnenfeld, really liked the character, and said he'd try to find a way to use it. I had originally intended the worm to be a one-off character who was about 6ft [1.8m] tall, but when he saw my 2ft [0.6m] maquette, Barry decided it was exactly the right size and he wanted a whole bunch of them!"

Sims's Worm Guys appeared in one of the movie's most memorable scenes, lounging in a kitchen and making themselves coffee. Sims helped to conceive the scene by generating concept art using the relatively new—at the time—image-manipulation software, Photoshop. "I took photographs of maquettes in various positions and used Photoshop to place them into a kitchen background. This helped us to visualize what puppets to build, how they would be set up, what mechanisms they needed, and how they would be puppeteered. The images I created in this way ended up being replicated almost exactly in the final film."

Using Photoshop for *Men in Black* opened Sims's eyes to the potential of digital technologies. "Rick loved Photoshop, and kept pushing me to use it and discover how it could help us design characters. I quickly discovered that it was a fast way of creating design options. I could sculpt a maquette in clay, photograph it, and then come up with a number of different paint schemes for a director to look at."

Sims threw himself into learning as much as he could about creating characters digitally, learning Softimage, the software used to create the dinosaurs in *Jurassic Park* (1993). At the time, Softimage was prohibitively expensive—almost $100,000 per license—and so Sims used demo versions to teach himself on his home PC.

During this period, Rick Baker decided to close his workshop, and so Sims set up an interview with the biggest makeup name in Hollywood, Stan Winston. "I told Stan how I wanted to use digital technology to design characters. He was very interested, and hired me to set up Stan Winston Digital, a branch of his company that would create digital character animation for shows where he was also providing the practical effects."

06

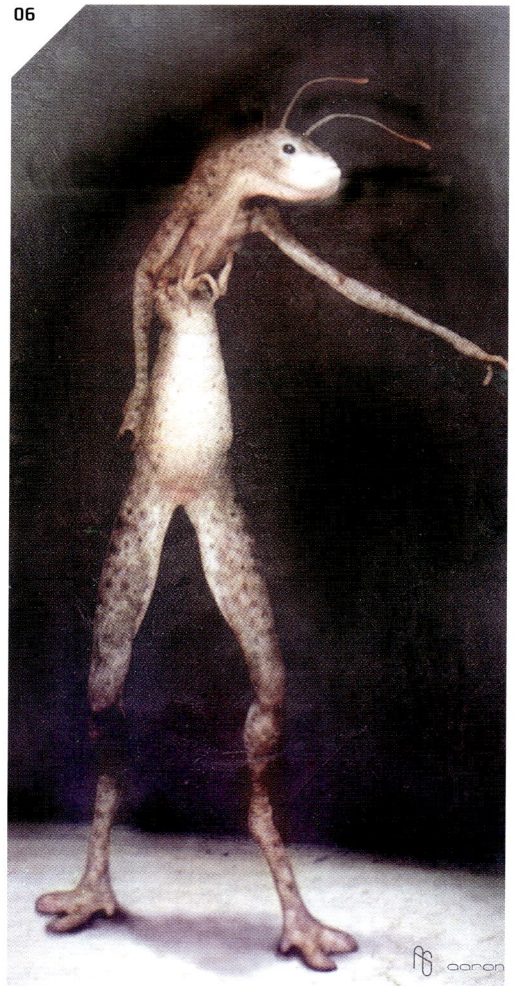

(04) A Worm Guy hangs out from *Men in Black* (1997) maquette. **(05)** Sim's made conceptual Worm Guy art by photographing his sculpted macquette and using Photoshop to create a montage. **(06)** Sims's Worm Guy.

07

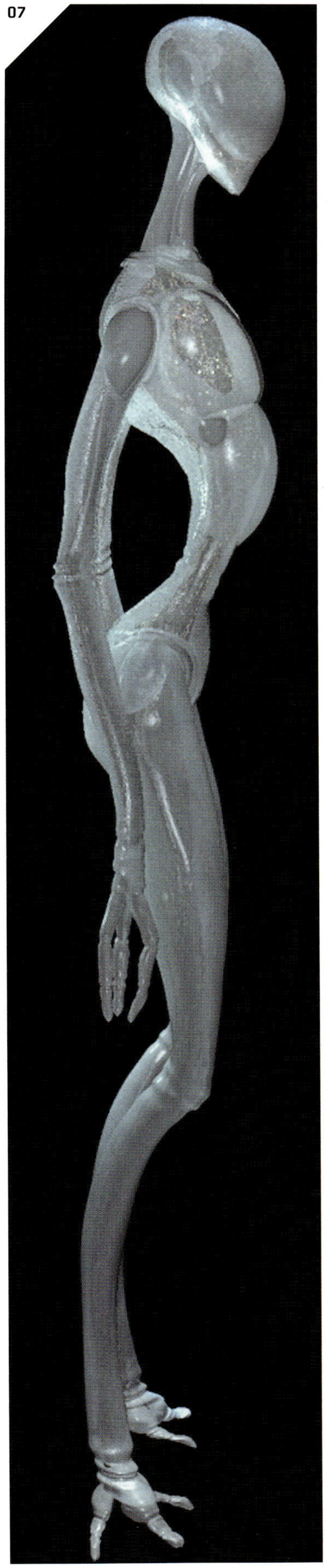

08

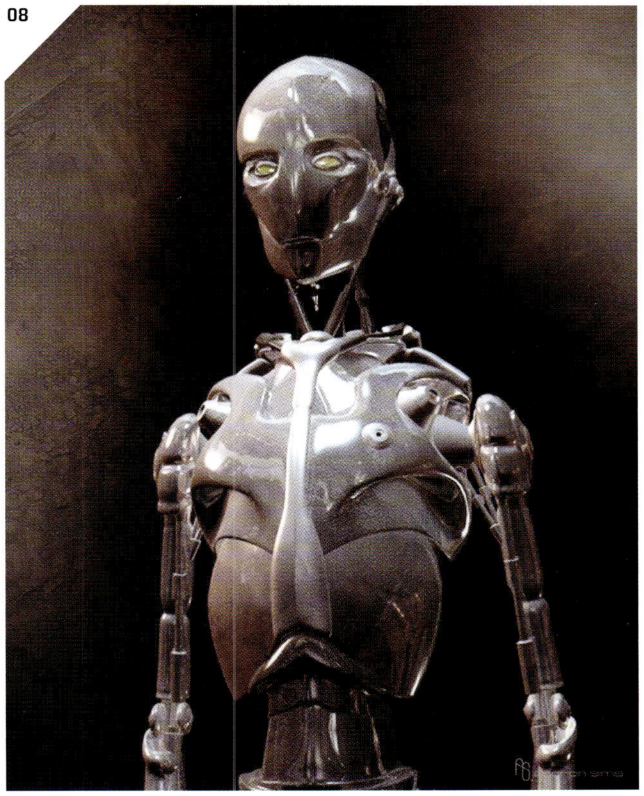

09

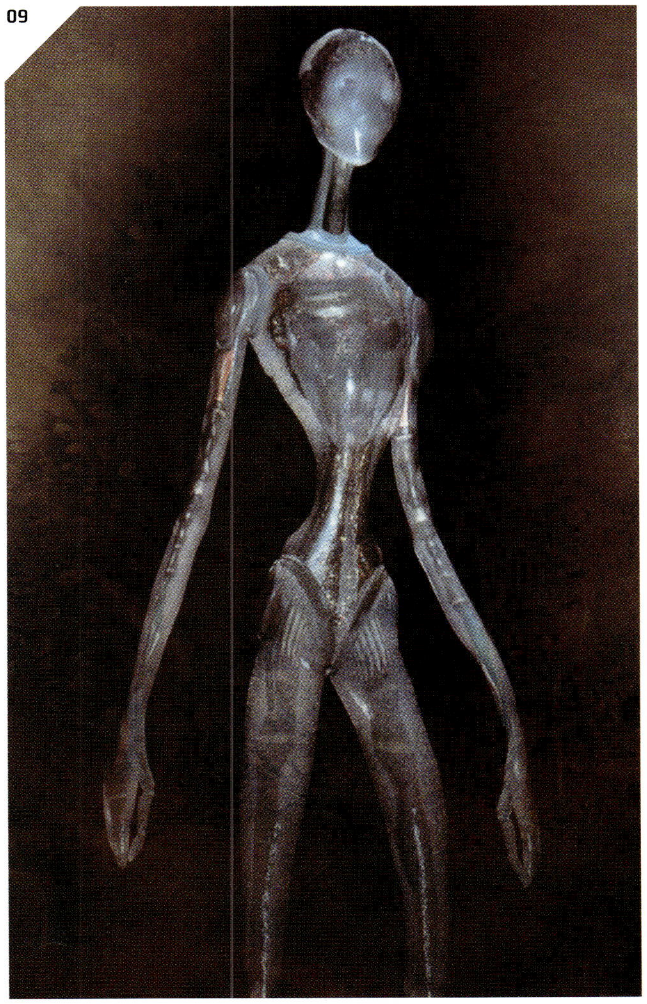

Sims ended up using 3-D modeling software to design many of the physical characters that would be built by Stan Winston Studio in the following years. One of the first projects he worked on was Steven Spielberg's *AI: Artificial Intelligence* (2001). "The shop was full of artists, including me, doing designs the traditional way. One day Stan said to me, 'Why don't you use the computer to see what you can do with your designs?' So I took a robot design that Steven had liked, and spent a day building it in the computer. Stan was ecstatic when he saw it—he loved being able to view a design from any angle so early on in its conception. I ended up doing a few hundred designs. It was amazing how quickly they could change and evolve once we had built them in 3-D." Shortly after *AI*, Sims was appointed art director of both the digital and physical departments of the studio.

In addition to designing the look of a character, Sims soon began to use the computer to aid the actual production of physical objects. "On *Terminator* 3, I designed all of the robots using 3-D models. Once the director had approved the concepts, I rebuilt the models using proper animation techniques so that they were rigged to move correctly when manipulated within the computer. That meant that we could check if a model would work from a mechanical point of view—could it walk, bend, stretch, or deploy its weapons once it had been built in the workshop?"

(07–09) Sims first used 3-D modeling techniques as a method of creating character concept art when working for Stan Winston Studio on Steven Spielberg's *AI: Artificial Intelligence* (2001). Here are three of his designs.

10

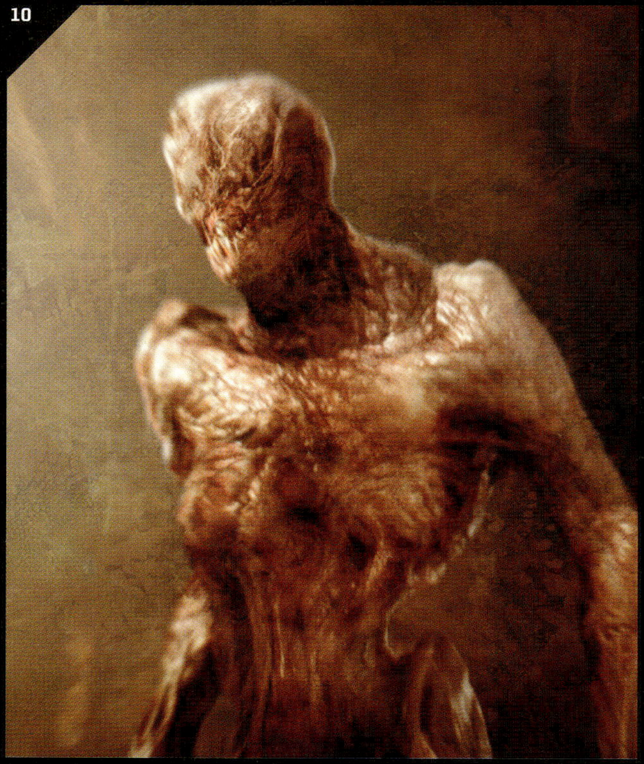

12

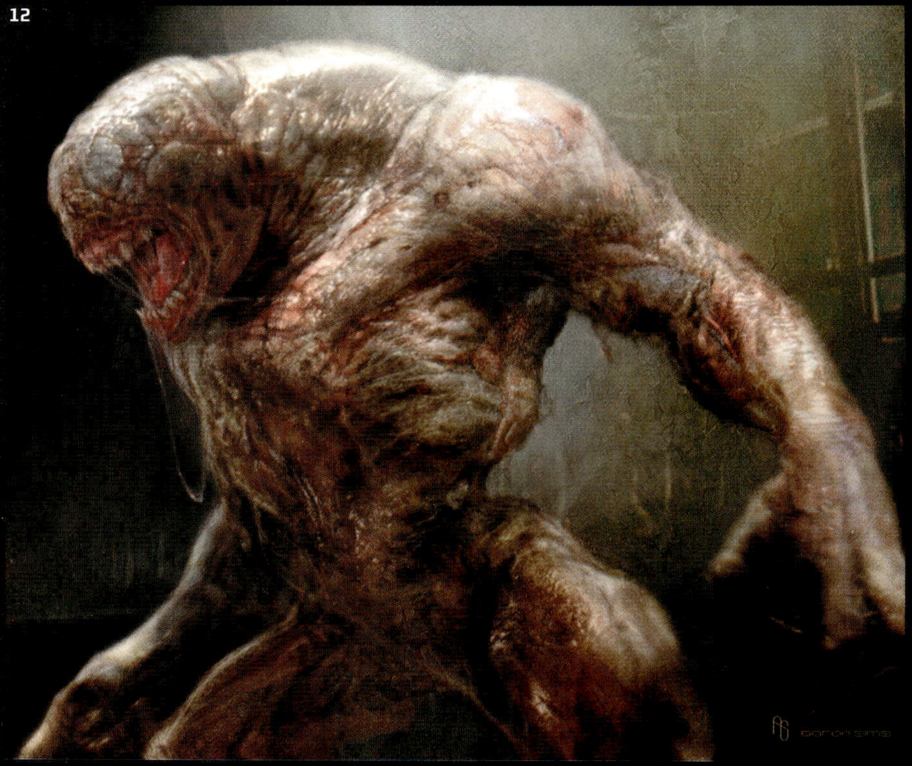

11

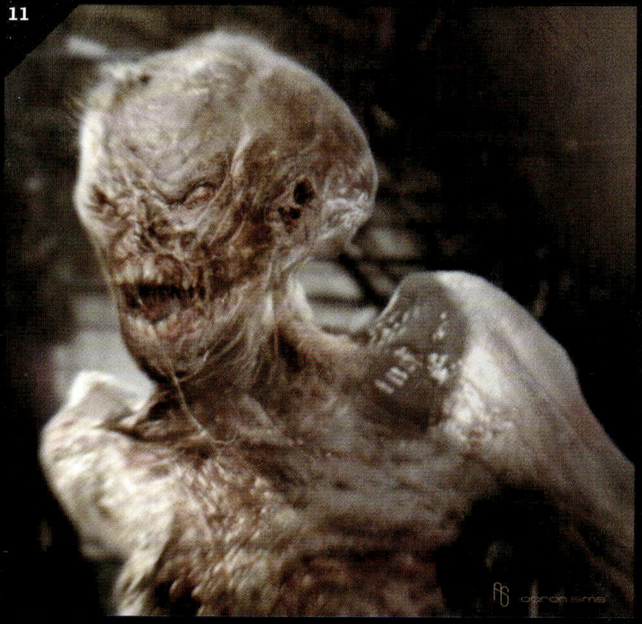

13

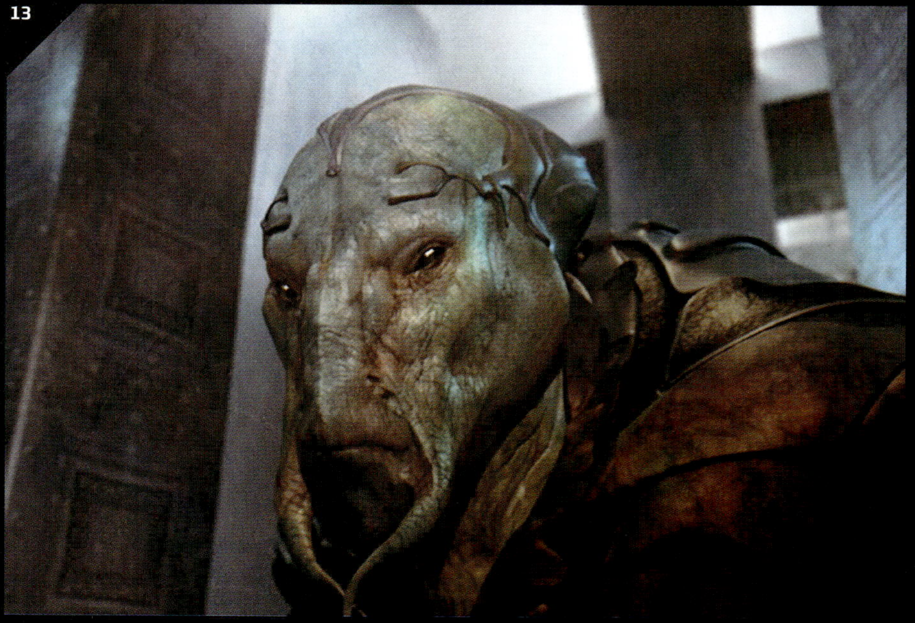

Designs for *Doom* (2005) produced by Sims at Stan Winston Studio: **(10–11)** Imp **(12)** Baron **(13)** Character from Sims' character project *Tethered Island*.
(14, 15) Concept designs for *Constantine* (2005): Mammon, and Half Breed.

14

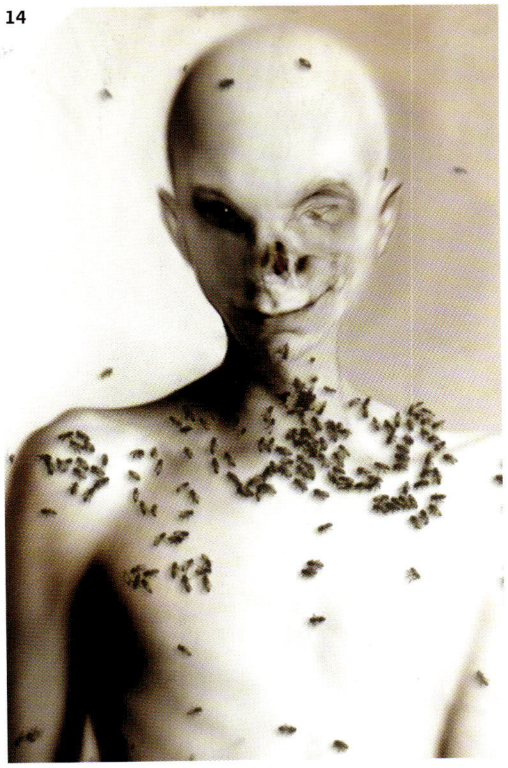

15

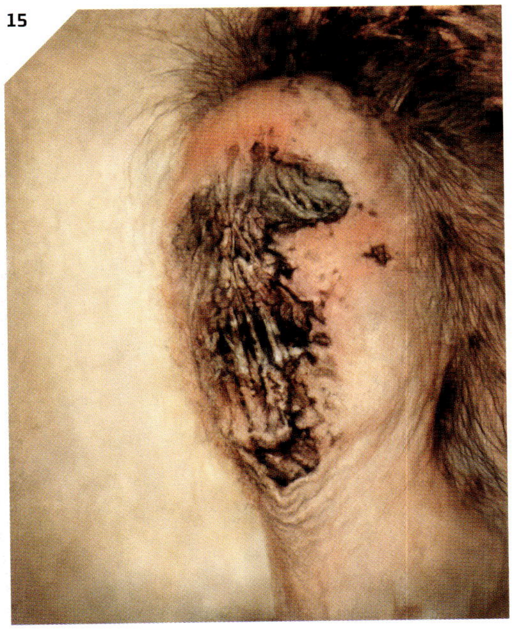

Sims's digital designs were also useful when it finally came to manufacturing the robots. The 3-D models were used by a computer-controlled milling machine to carve the necessary body parts in rigid foam or plaster. From these, molds were made so that parts could be cast in the appropriate materials before painting and polishing. Delicate mechanical details were made using stereo lithography to render small pieces in resin. Computer character designs were fed to the mechanical department, who used them in their CAD programs to plan the mechanisms, cables, and motors that would be needed to operate a puppet.

The angular, high-tech shapes of the *T3* robots lent themselves easily to the process of automated design and construction—not dissimilar to techniques now used to conceptualize and create real-world gadgets. However, Sims later proved that the process was equally capable of creating much more organic forms, such as the demonic characters built for *Constantine* (2005).

In 2005, Sims left Stan Winston Studio to establish his own character- and production-design studio and develop a number of ideas for movies. "I don't want a big workshop like some of those companies I've worked for in the past," explains Sims. "Creating practical makeup effects requires a great deal of investment in people and equipment. I'm really only interested in creating cool characters and production designs that other people will eventually execute."

Today Sims has an efficient character-design pipeline that combines old-fashioned design methods with the latest two- and three-dimensional software techniques. "When someone asks me to create a character, I still normally start by doing pencil sketches. I use these as my own shorthand way of blocking out shapes and ideas, but I rarely show them to clients. When I'm happy with the way things are going, I'll build the character as a 3D model in the computer. For this I normally use Softimage XSI."

Sims has developed a number of methods that make creating 3-D characters more efficient. "Every character I design in 3-D is made up of parts I have sculpted in the computer—limbs, heads, teeth, and so on. After each new project I add those parts to a library. So when it comes to creating a new character I can often assemble the basic form really quickly using ready-made pieces. The new design then builds on top of that. At this stage I'm trying to create quick concepts to show a client.

"The real time and effort goes into creating final designs. At the early stages I try not to build too much detail in 3-D. I get a rough shape together and, rather than sculpting textures, I'll project a texture image on to it. Then I'll pose the character, usually in a single, dynamic, three-quarters pose, which will best convey the essence of the design, before rendering out an image."

With a two-dimensional image of a character in a dramatic pose, Sims will then spend time artworking the design in Photoshop. "This is where I'll really work on the color, texture, and lighting details, getting the mood right. Photoshop's Liquefy tool is great for pushing parts of the image around in order to change shapes subtly that I haven't quite got right in 3-D. The Clone, Dodge, and Burn tools are also useful for adding detail."

16

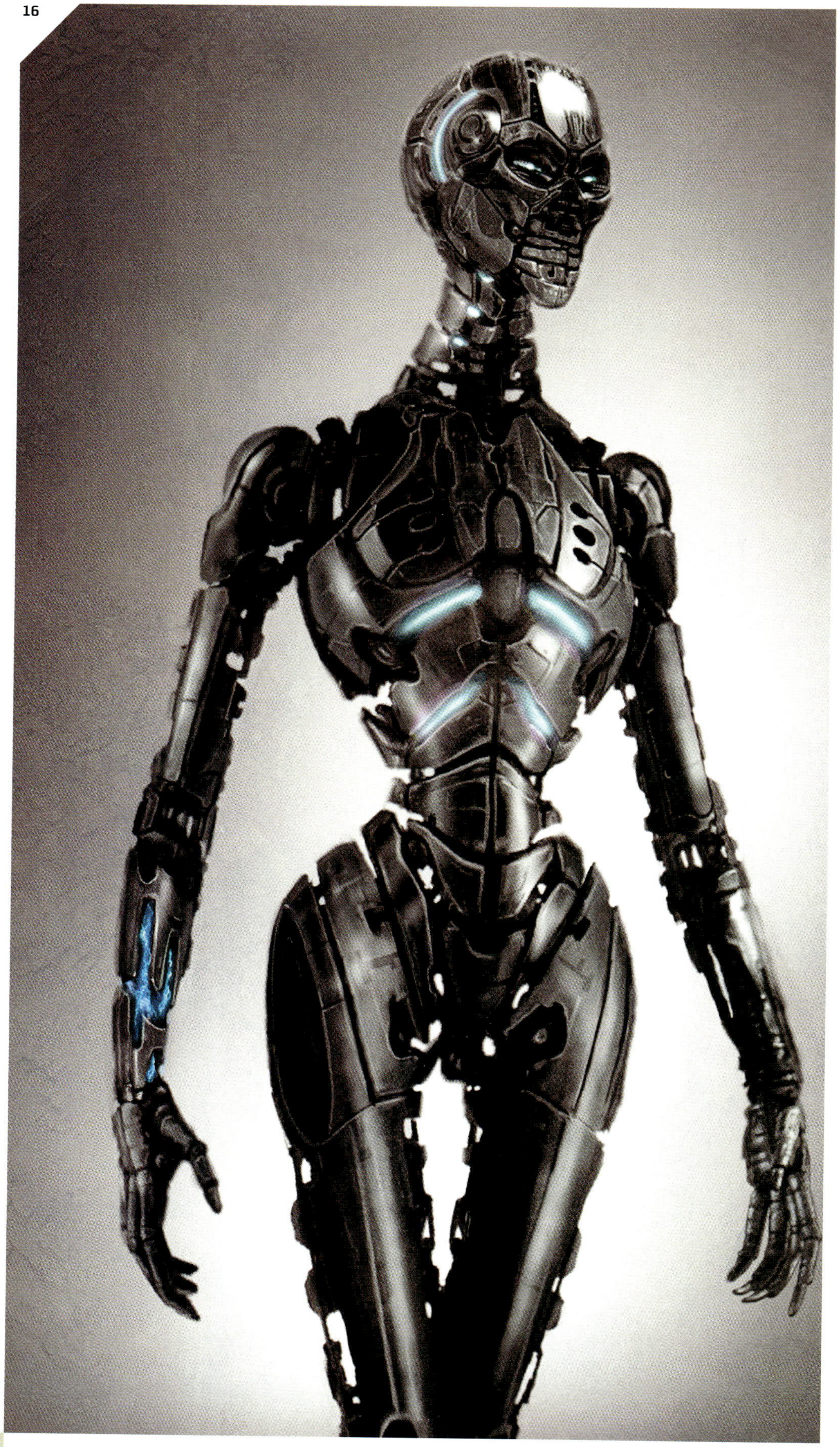

17

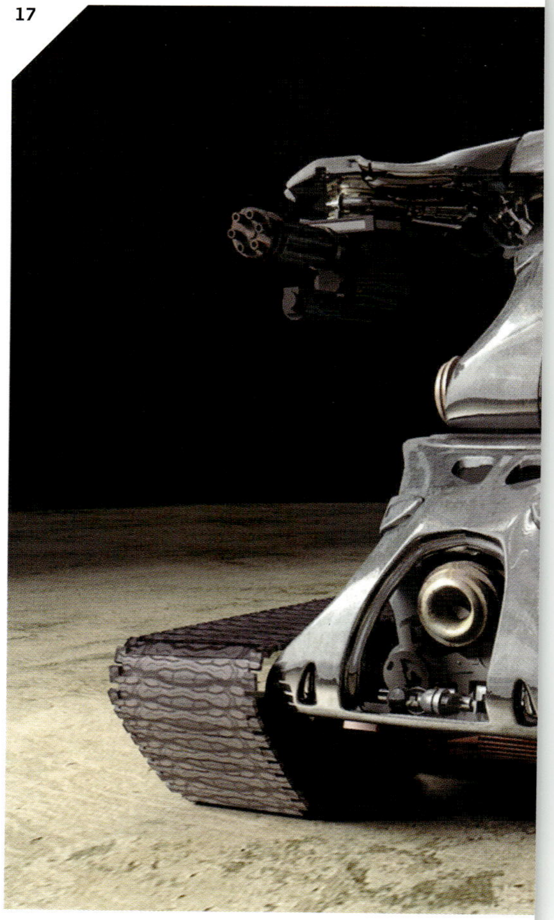

18

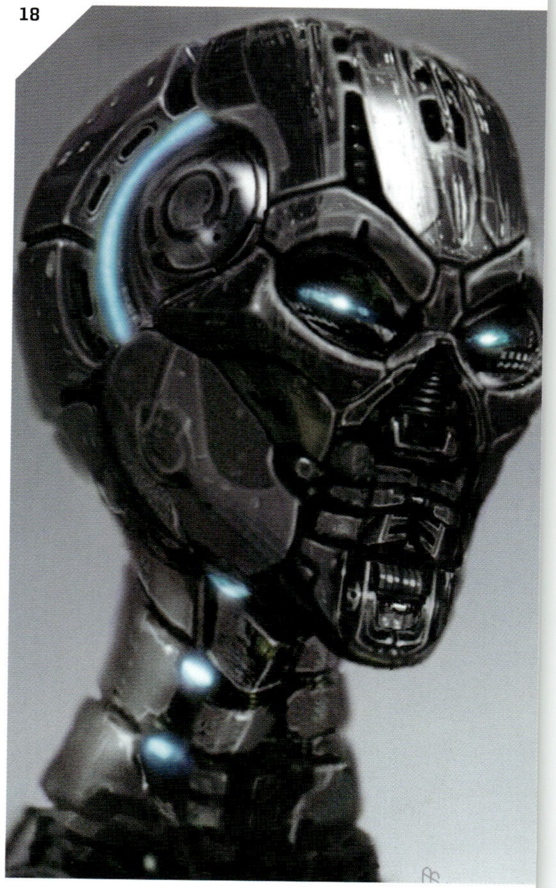

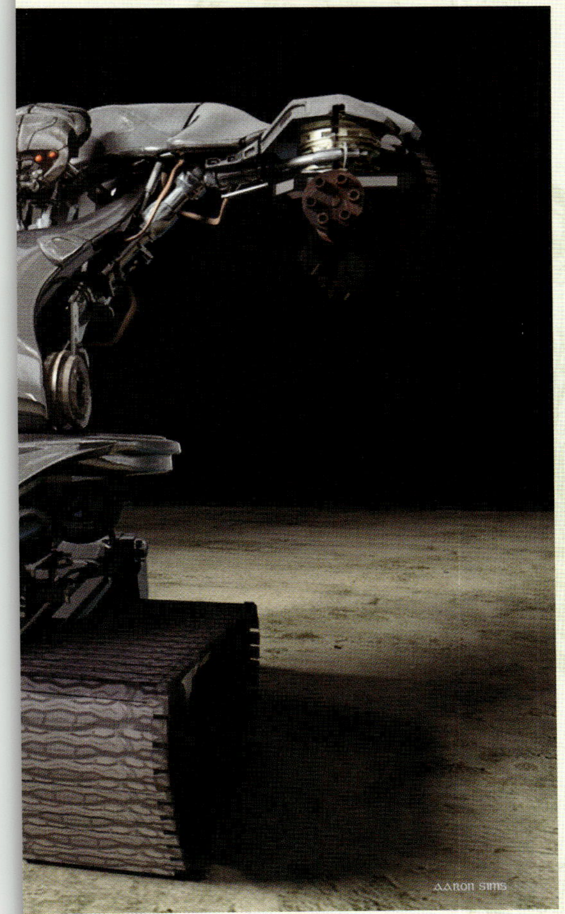

19

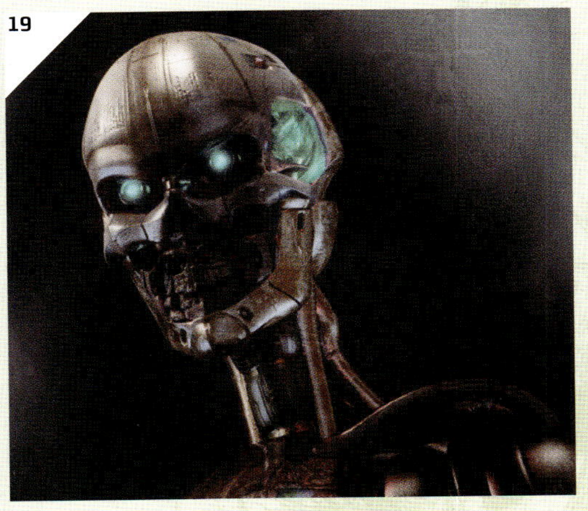

Once the client has signed off a design, Sims will often create final high-resolution models with modeling software ZBrush. “It’s the closest digital equivalent to actually sculpting in clay,” he says. “You can start off by assembling a bunch of digital spheres into the rough shape of your character. Then you gradually carve into the shapes using a variety of tools, just like you would with clay. Strangely enough, I found ZBrush quite hard to get used to because it’s so simple and intuitive. I’m used to complex modeling techniques that produce 3-D meshes, but ZBrush is almost like taking a step backward because it’s so ‘untechnical.’ But anyone coming from the traditional sculpting world will find this software really easy to learn.”

Sims finds ZBrush ideal for generating very high levels of refined surface detail, and so he tends only to use it in the later stages of the design process. “If a basic design is approved and needs to be created in more detail, I’ll export the basic model from Softimage into ZBrush and then begin to sculpt at a much higher level. Those models can then be used to create the practical makeup designs or handed on to a visual-effects studio for use in animation.”

Sims is one of a number of contemporary character-concept designers who are almost totally reliant on digital technology to manifest their ideas. Through his own writing and a series of instructional videos, Sims has tried to convey his enthusiasm for these processes to others in his industry. “I have found it frustrating trying to persuade traditional artists that digital techniques are what they should be learning. I guess that’s not surprising, because most artists get into doing this stuff because they are good with their hands. But in today’s fast-turnaround business these techniques are only going to become more vital. It’s important that artists know how to do this stuff and not just technicians.”

While some fear that using the computer to design will somehow impair their more traditional artistic abilities, Sims believes that technology has been nothing but an advantage to him. “Strangely, I’ve learned a lot from working in the computer that has only benefited my practical skills,” he claims. “I’ve recently started painting in oils again, and I’ve found that my ability has greatly improved. And my sculpting in clay is better now because modeling in the computer has helped me to develop new ways of looking at things, of seeing shapes and forms. I love creating work using all the traditional techniques—but I certainly miss having that ‘Undo’ button!”

(16,18) Final designs for the female TX robot from *Terminator 3: Rise of the Machines* (2003) **(17)** Final designs for the T1 battle robot from *T3* **(19)** An early design for the TX robot.

KNB

ROBERT KURTZMAN
GREG NICOTERO
HOWARD BERGER

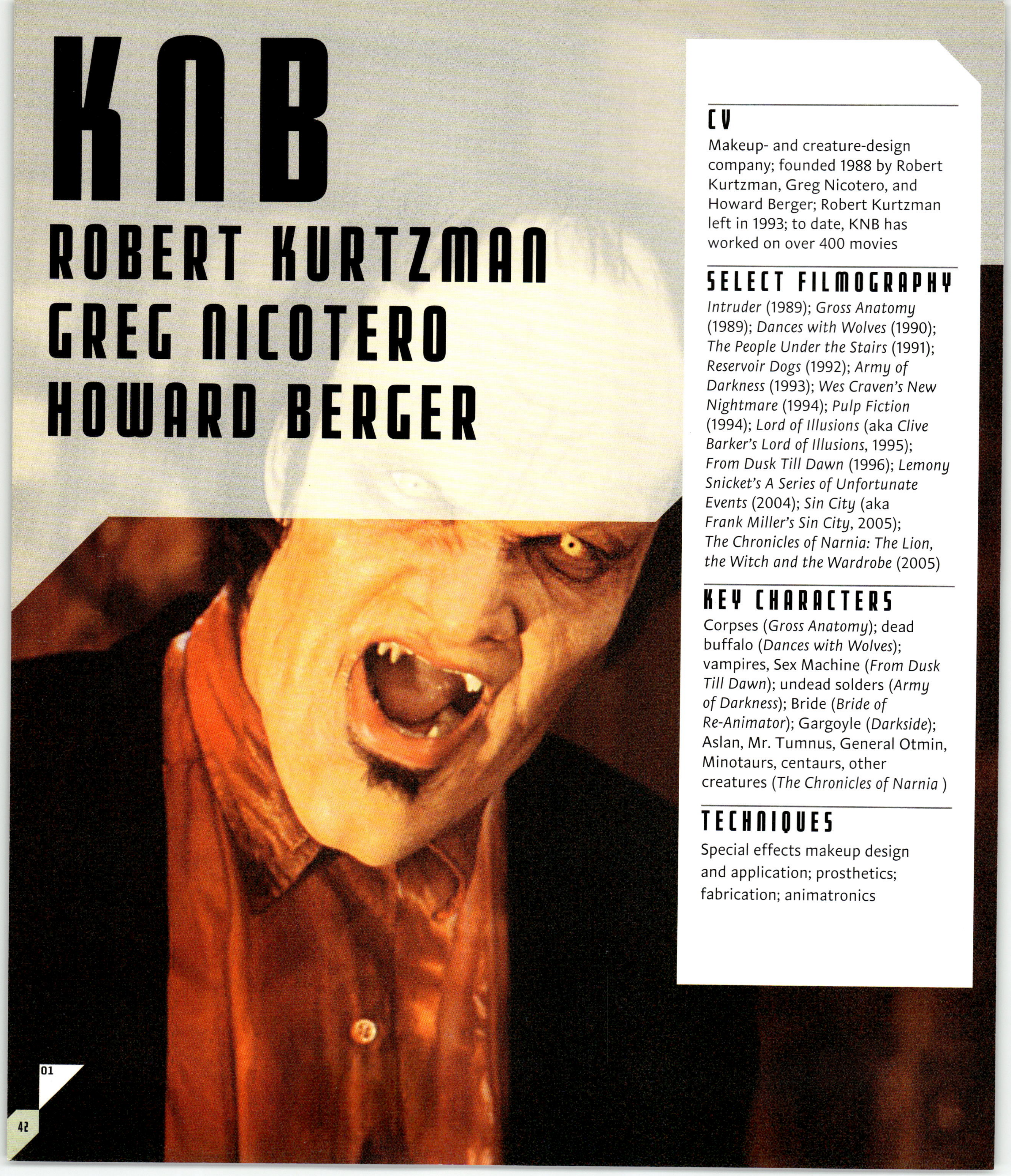

CV

Makeup- and creature-design company; founded 1988 by Robert Kurtzman, Greg Nicotero, and Howard Berger; Robert Kurtzman left in 1993; to date, KNB has worked on over 400 movies

SELECT FILMOGRAPHY

Intruder (1989); *Gross Anatomy* (1989); *Dances with Wolves* (1990); *The People Under the Stairs* (1991); *Reservoir Dogs* (1992); *Army of Darkness* (1993); *Wes Craven's New Nightmare* (1994); *Pulp Fiction* (1994); *Lord of Illusions* (aka *Clive Barker's Lord of Illusions*, 1995); *From Dusk Till Dawn* (1996); *Lemony Snicket's A Series of Unfortunate Events* (2004); *Sin City* (aka *Frank Miller's Sin City*, 2005); *The Chronicles of Narnia: The Lion, the Witch and the Wardrobe* (2005)

KEY CHARACTERS

Corpses (*Gross Anatomy*); dead buffalo (*Dances with Wolves*); vampires, Sex Machine (*From Dusk Till Dawn*); undead solders (*Army of Darkness*); Bride (*Bride of Re-Animator*); Gargoyle (*Darkside*); Aslan, Mr. Tumnus, General Otmin, Minotaurs, centaurs, other creatures (*The Chronicles of Narnia*)

TECHNIQUES

Special effects makeup design and application; prosthetics; fabrication; animatronics

02

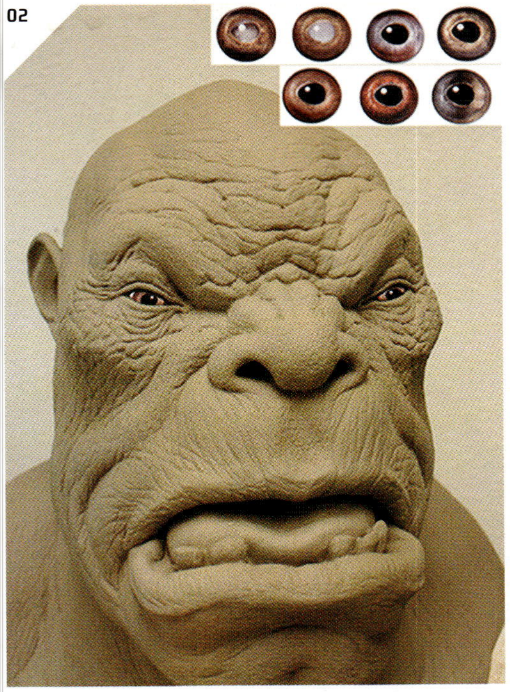

03

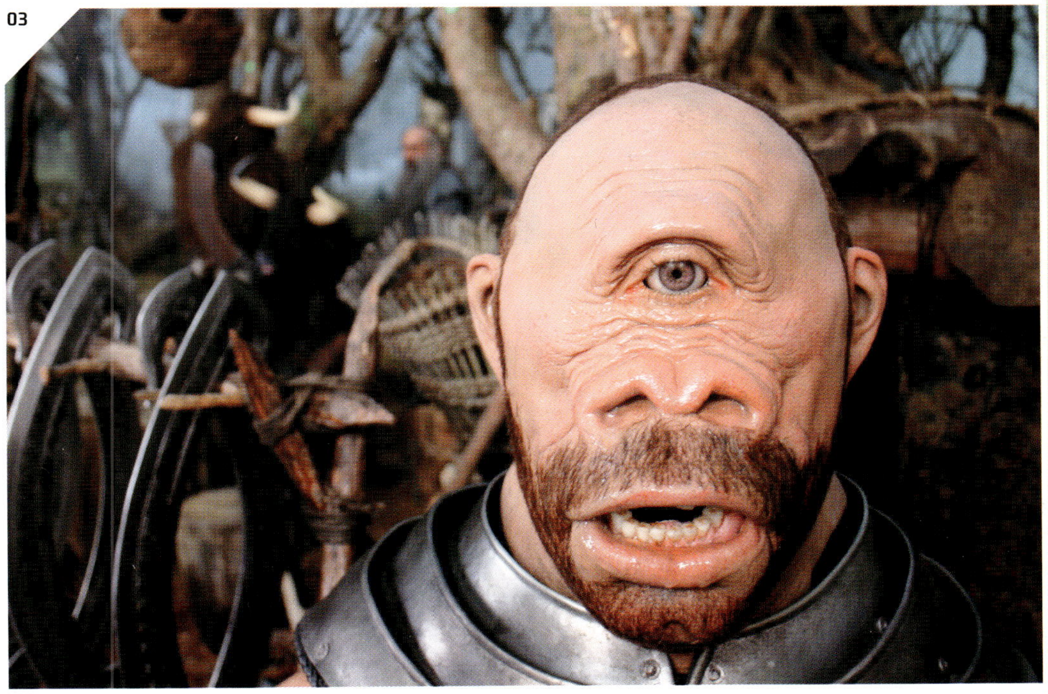

Robert Kurtzman, Greg Nicotero, and Howard Berger spent much of the 1980s toiling in the workshops of established makeup designers, such as Rick Baker, Tom Savini, Stan Winston, and Mark Shostrom. They met and became friends while working on *Evil Dead II* (1987). A year later, the three men, then still in their early twenties, decided that between them they had the talent, experience, and determination to strike out on their own.

KNB (Kurtzman, Nicotero, and Berger) was formed in 1988. The first assignment was for low-budget crime/horror movie, *Intruder* (1989). Working for only the cost of the necessary materials, the team was given its first screen credit in return, advertising the arrival of a new makeup effects company. KNB quickly gained a reputation for providing high-quality work on a fast turnaround, a reputation it retains to this day.

(01) *From Dusk Till Dawn* writer Quentin Tarantino in makeup as the vampire Richard Gecko **(02)** Ogre sculpt from *Narnia*, with range of potential eye designs **(03)** A finished Cyclops mask.

One of the team's first studio movies was Disney's *Gross Anatomy* (1989), for which KNB created anatomically accurate autopsy cadavers, complete with realistic internal organs. Having been noted for the quality of their dead humans, KNB was then contacted by Kevin Costner, who asked if they would make dead buffalo for *Dances with Wolves* (1990).

In the two decades since its formation, KNB has worked on a bewildering number of movies—over 400 to date—of all budgets and genres, from horror movies such as *The People Under the Stairs* (1991), to mainstream movies, including *Pulp Fiction* (1994), *Lemony Snicket's a Series of Unfortunate Events* (2004), *Sin City* (2006) and *The Chronicles of Narnia: The Lion, the Witch and the Wardrobe* (2005), for which the team won BAFTA (British Academy of Film and Television Arts) and Academy Awards for Best Makeup.

One of KNB's most fondly remembered makeup experiences was for the Robert Rodriguez movie *From Dusk Till Dawn* (1996), as it was based on an original treatment written by KNB co-founder Robert Kurtzman, as Howard Berger explains: "We all knew Quentin Tarantino when he still worked in a video store, and Robert [Kurtzman] paid him $1,500 to write a screenplay based on an idea he had for a vampire movie. The deal was that if Quentin managed to get the movie made, we would do the makeup effects for free. The movie didn't get made, but one day Quentin told us he was making *Reservoir Dogs*, and would we do the makeup? When that was a huge hit, it meant the studios started asking for anything else written by Quentin, and so out came *From Dusk Till Dawn*. The movie got green-lit with Robert Kurtzman as co-producer, Quentin Tarantino as executive producer, and Robert Rodriguez directing."

"With his movie finally getting made, Bob handed over all the storyboards he had made for the effects sequences," continues Berger. "Rodriguez just said, 'Great, let's do all of that.' So we started to gear up for what was our biggest makeup job up of that time. It was a lot of work, but it was meticulous because this was Bob's vision and he wanted everything done right." The scale of the work led KNB to move to new premises that could accommodate 60 artists.

Kurtzman's script called for a number of vampire characters, although his concept for them was very different from that of the traditional Hollywood vampire. "Bob wanted his vampires to look like heightened-reality versions of the actors selected to play them," says Berger. "Our artist Shannon Shea did some beautiful concept sketches of performers such as Cheech Marin and Danny Trejo, where their already interesting features were emphasized even more. It was a very subtle, but quite dramatic, design idea. Those were then beautifully sculpted onto the performer's lifecasts by Norman Cabrera. The makeups retained the essence of the performers, but added this creepy otherworldliness to them. It was a brilliant concept."

Another major task for KNB was the creation of a number of major transformation sequences, in which performers turned into vampiric creatures. "Our favorite is when the character called Sex Machine, played by [makeup artist] Tom Savini, turns into a rat-vampire," says Berger. "That sequence wasn't in the script, but I remember turning up to the set with this mechanical rat-vampire and Robert Rodriguez staring at it and saying, 'What the hell is that?' and us telling him it was something Bob had asked for. He just laughed and said, 'Go ahead, that sounds cool!'" KNB created a number of transformation makeups that showed the decapitated body of Savini gradually changing into a rat-like vampire, with clawed paws emerging from his sleeves and a furry body bursting from his clothes. "The makeup was great, but I like that scene because I got to chop Tom Savini's head off," recalls Berger. "We all had cameos in that film."

Berger remembers *From Dusk Till Dawn* as one of the most demanding but enjoyable times of his career. "We'd have a 7 a.m. call and know that meant Robert would be actually filming at seven—most directors on a 7 a.m. call won't film anything till ten. Robert would suddenly have some crazy idea that wasn't in the script, and we'd have an hour to find five bodies capable of being burned. On location we had 12 people working an average of 18- to 21-hour days. I used to go home, sleep for an hour, have a shower, and set out again, but it was such fun."

Deciding that he didn't want to raise his family in Los Angeles, Kurtzman left his partners at KNB soon afterward and moved back to his native Ohio, where he continues to pursue a directing career and runs a visual-effects company called Precinct 13 Entertainment.

04

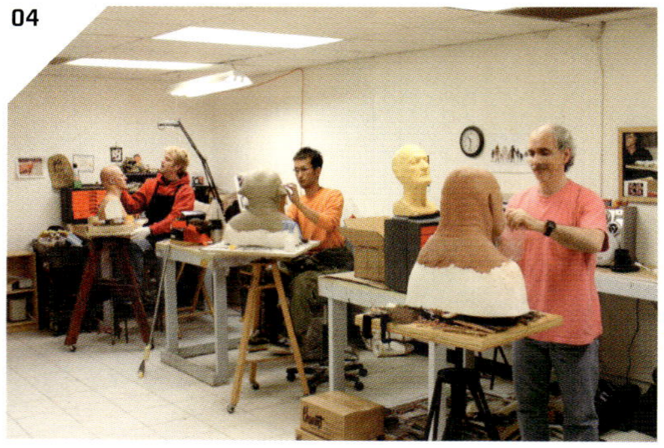

05

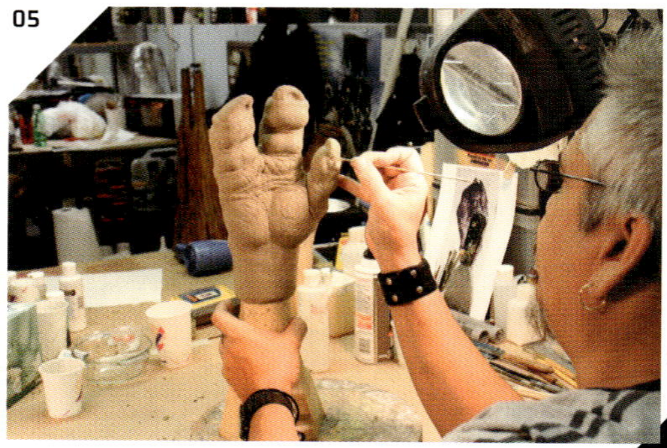

06

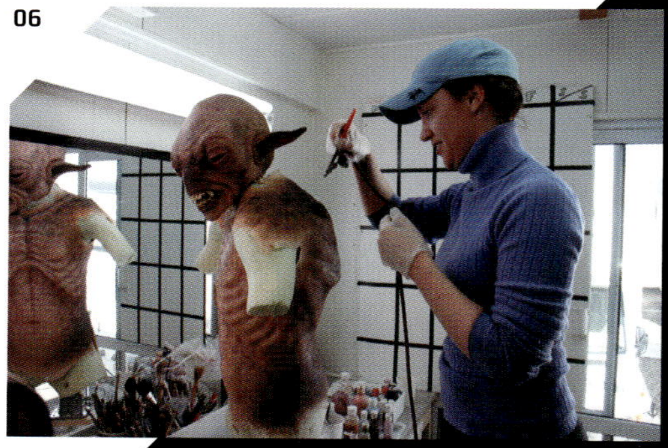

07

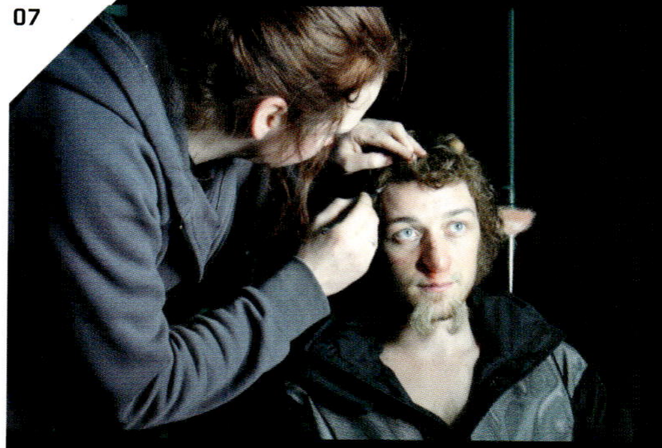

08

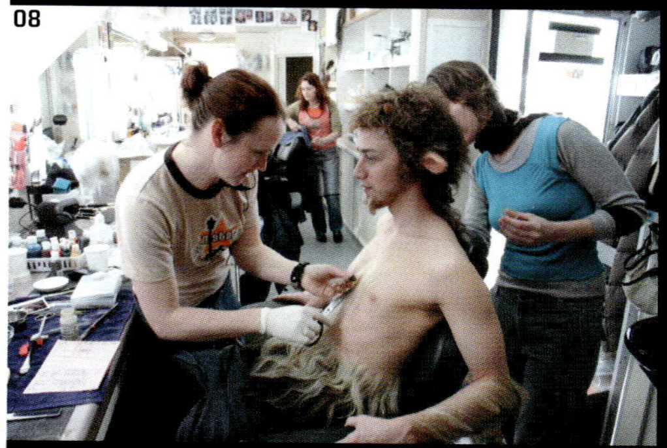

(04) Scott Patton (left) Akihito Ikeda (centre) and Mitch DeVane (right) work on facial sculptures for *Narnia* **(05)** Alex Daiz sculpts a Minotaur hand **(06)** Kathryn Brown airbrushes a goblin appliance **(07)** Tami Lane applies Mr Tumnus facial appliances to James McAvoy **(08)** Lane and Sarah Rubano apply chest hair to McAvoy.

09

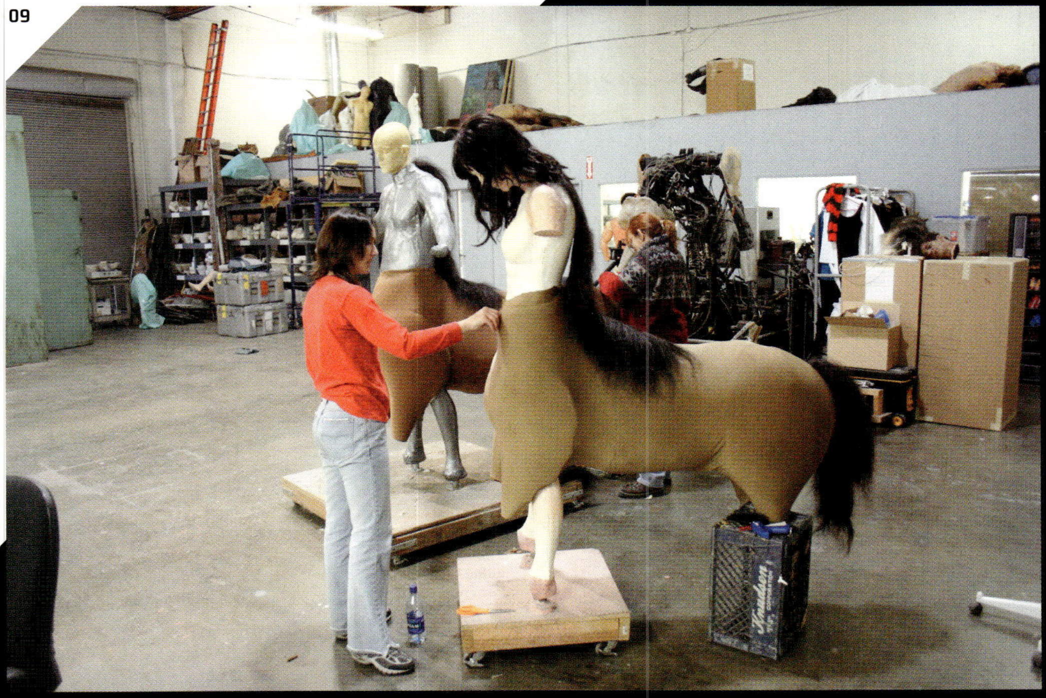

10

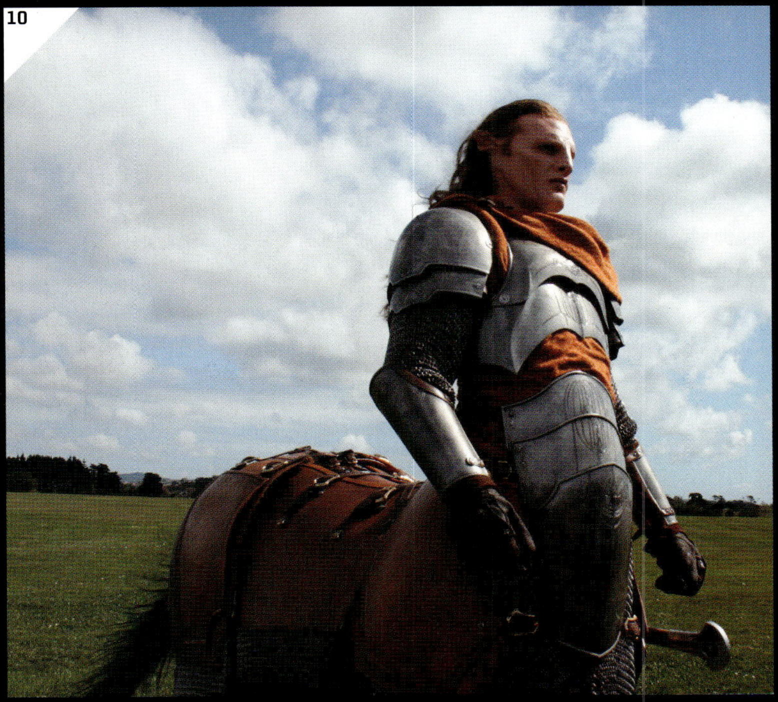

KNB's biggest makeup challenge came with the 2005 adaptation of C.S. Lewis's classic tale *The Chronicles of Narnia: The Lion, the Witch and the Wardrobe* (2005). Creature and makeup work for the movie was originally due to be produced by Weta Workshop in New Zealand. Under the supervision of Richard Taylor, Weta spent a year working with director Andrew Adamson to develop concepts for characters, weapons, and armor, but when *King Kong* (2005) went into production, Weta's alliance with director Peter Jackson meant that most of the company's energies were devoted to that movie instead. While Weta would still manufacture Narnia's weapons and armor, Taylor suggested that the work of bringing its character designs to life be awarded instead to KNB.

The production was a huge undertaking, requiring a staff of 120 artists to create over 170 creatures of more than 20 species, including centaurs, Cyclops, dwarfs, fauns, giants, goblins, Minotaurs, and unicorns.

"In January 2004 we inherited all of Weta's superb designs, which was really fantastic," says Howard Berger. "They had done all of the backbreaking early work of liaising with the director to develop the overall look and tone of the characters. In theory, that meant that we could just pick up those designs and run with them."

However, despite having much of the development work done for them, KNB's job was not as straightforward as it initially seemed. "Weta had been told that characters would largely be created and animated in the computer," says Berger, "but after seeing what we were capable of, Andrew Adamson decided that he wanted to achieve as many character shots as possible using practical [physical] methods."

(09) Dawn Dininger works on early Centaur prototypes **(10)** Early Centaur test combining human torso with prosthetic makeup, fabricated body, and armor produced by Weta Workshop.

Adamson's decision was brave, given his background as a director of entirely computer-generated movies, yet it was a sensible decision for several reasons, as Berger explains: "First, having character creations on set means you can get a finished shot there and then—with CG you often have to wait many months to see how—or if—a shot works. Second, the film starred a group of child performers, and it was easier for them to perform next to physical characters. And finally, even really sophisticated animatronics and prosthetics can be less expensive than CGI."

The decision for many effects to be achieved practically meant that most of Weta's designs had to be adapted to suit physical methods of construction and performance. "As soon as you need to put a human performer into a costume the dynamics have to change," says Berger. "You can't shrink a human's torso or remove their legs to fit a costume—the character design has to be created with the human performer in mind.

"Two good examples were the Cyclops and the centaurs. Weta's beautiful original Cyclops concept had a superflat facial design which we could never have fitted to a human performer's face. The Centaurs had a really elegant arched back, which had a crescent-moon curve from the hips up to the neck and shoulders—there was no way we could achieve that kind of form when the character was to be built around a human. So quite a bit had to change, but we worked hard to stay true to the original vision."

11

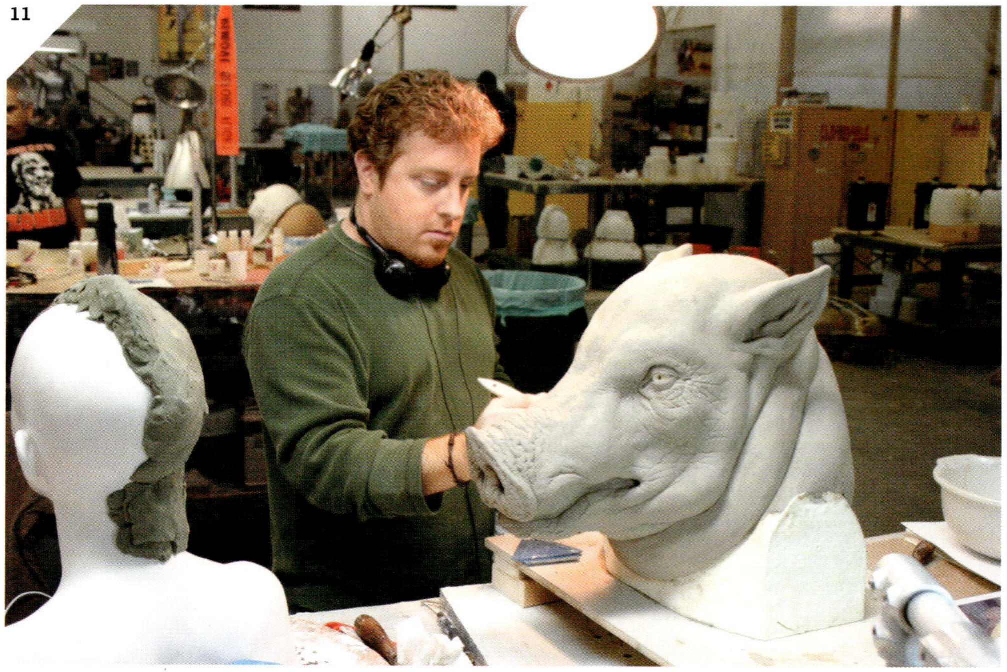

12

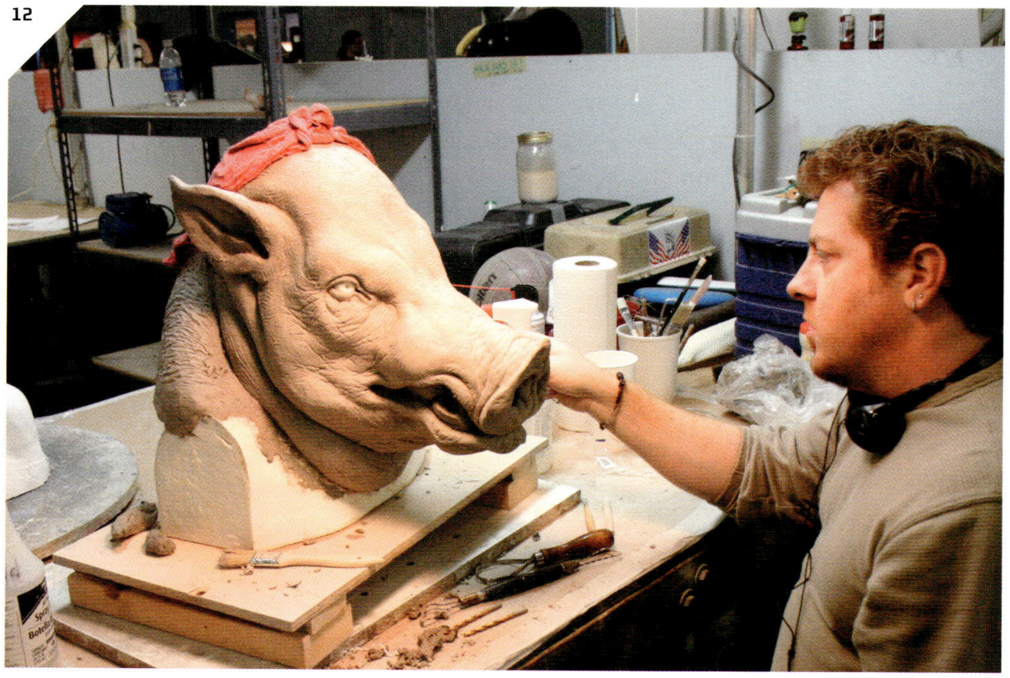

13

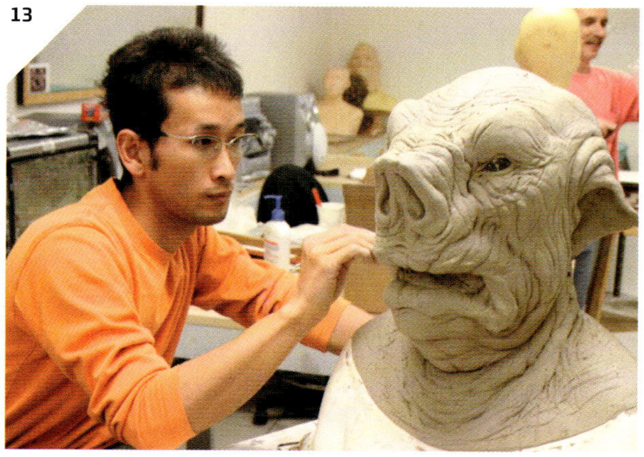

14

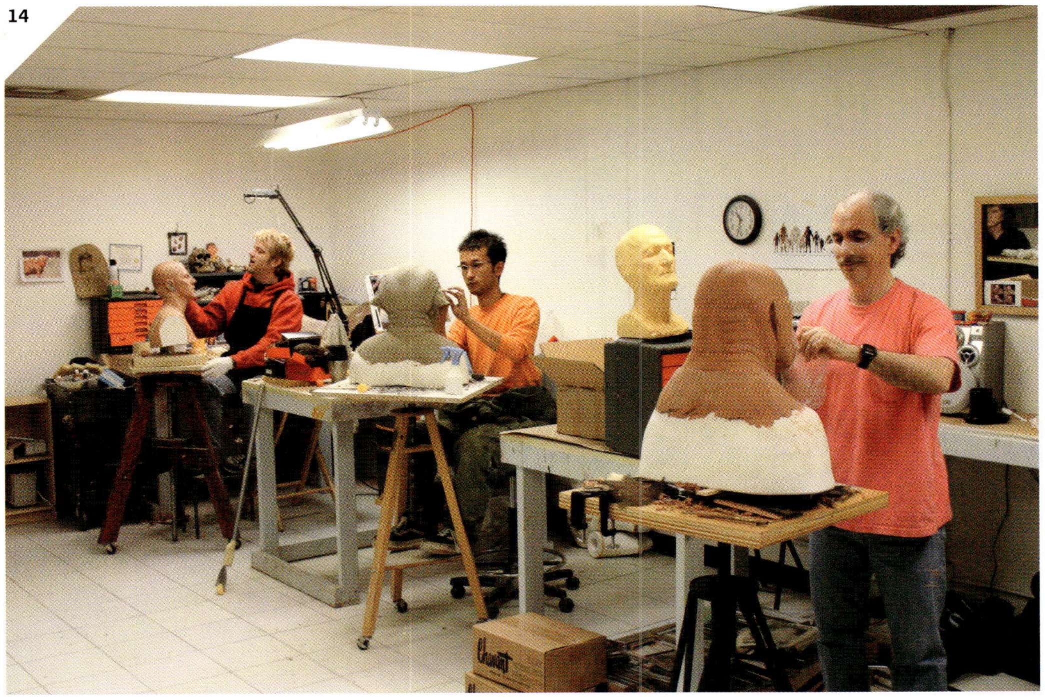

15

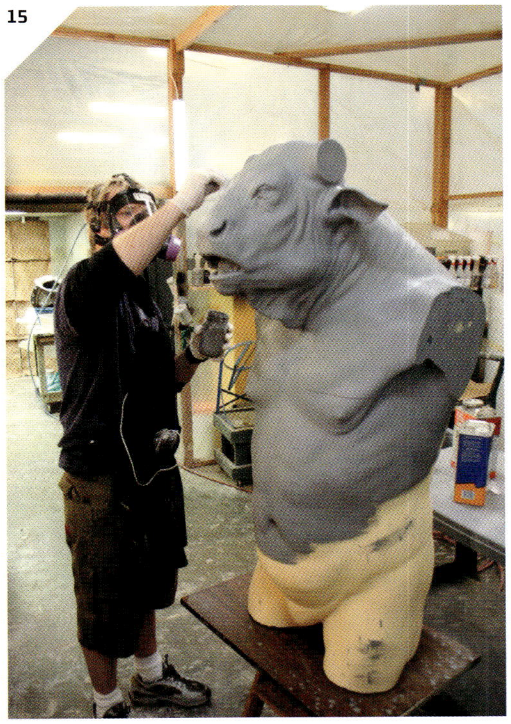

(11–12) Dave Grasso sculpts the head of a Minoboar **(13)** Akihito Ikeda works on a Boggle sculpture **(14)** Scott Patton (left), Akihito Ikeda (center), and Mitch DeVane (right) work on facial sculptures **(15)** Scott Patton works on a Minotaur sculpture.

The lion of the movie's title is Aslan, a noble cat of grand proportions. "Because Aslan wasn't going to have a human performer inside, we were able to keep largely to Weta's design," says Berger. "Weta sculpted a beautiful 3ft [1m] maquette, which we cyberscanned to produce a digital model. That information was used by a computer-controlled milling machine to carve a full-sized sculpture in rigid foam. We cut up that foam version and used it to make molds to create several versions of Aslan. One was a standing model that didn't have any performance mechanics and was used on set so everyone knew how big he was. The second was an animatronic head-and-back section, which was mounted on a mechanical rig. The children were filmed sitting on the back of this against a green screen for the scenes where they ride Aslan across Narnia. The final version was a fully animatronic lying-down model for when Aslan is shaved and then sacrificed on the stone table. This version was operated by radio control, and could breathe, create facial expressions, turn his head, and so on. We had to design the facial movement to match Aslan's anthropomorphic characteristics. For example, real lions don't blink—their brow and cheeks compress, but they do not have any eyelids. But to make Aslan more expressive we designed a blink mechanism and spent quite a bit of time designing the eye pattern and shape."

Ultimately, almost all of the shots of Aslan in the final movie were supplied by Rhythm and Hues Animation Studio, which recreated the lion in CG. However, shots of Aslan on the stone table largely used KNB's model. The version ridden by the children, although a stunning piece of makeup design, did not match the CG version that appeared in other scenes—its real mane did not undulate in the wind in the stylized manner developed for the CG shots in this sequence. Rhythm and Hues did, however, use the Weta/KNB designs to create their digital vision of him, scanning the models and photographing the finished version in order to replicate the color design and fur patterns.

One of the most unusual and demanding of KNB's Narnia creations was Mr. Tumnus the faun—a creature with the head and body of a man but the waist and legs of a goat. Berger and his team spent a considerable amount of time designing a makeup that could be applied to an actor without knowing who that performer would be. "Mr. Tumnus proved to be a really hard part to cast, and we were getting really close to production before Andrew Adamson finally decided on James McAvoy," recalls Berger.

The young Scottish actor was working on a television show in London. "James flew to LA, and from the moment he touched down we had just six hours until he had to be back on the plane," remembers Berger. "In that time we got him cyberscanned, took some lifecasts, and did makeup tests. The next time we saw him it would be for the filming in New Zealand."

16

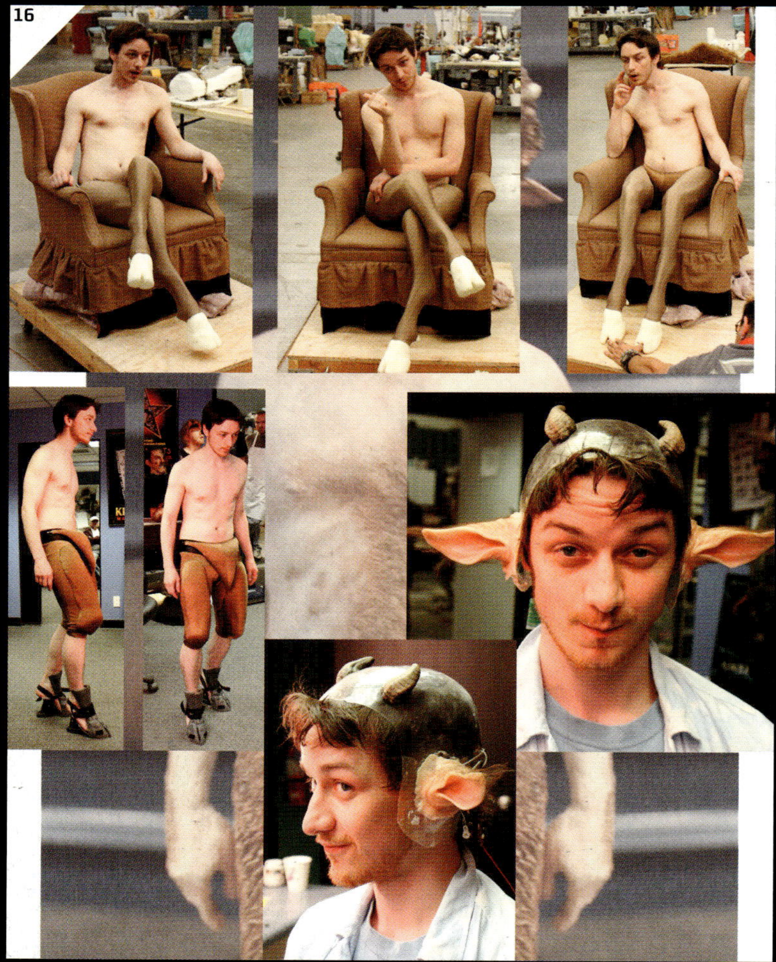

17

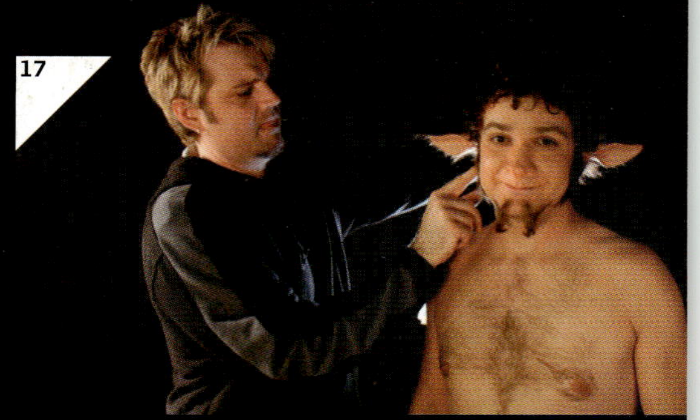

18

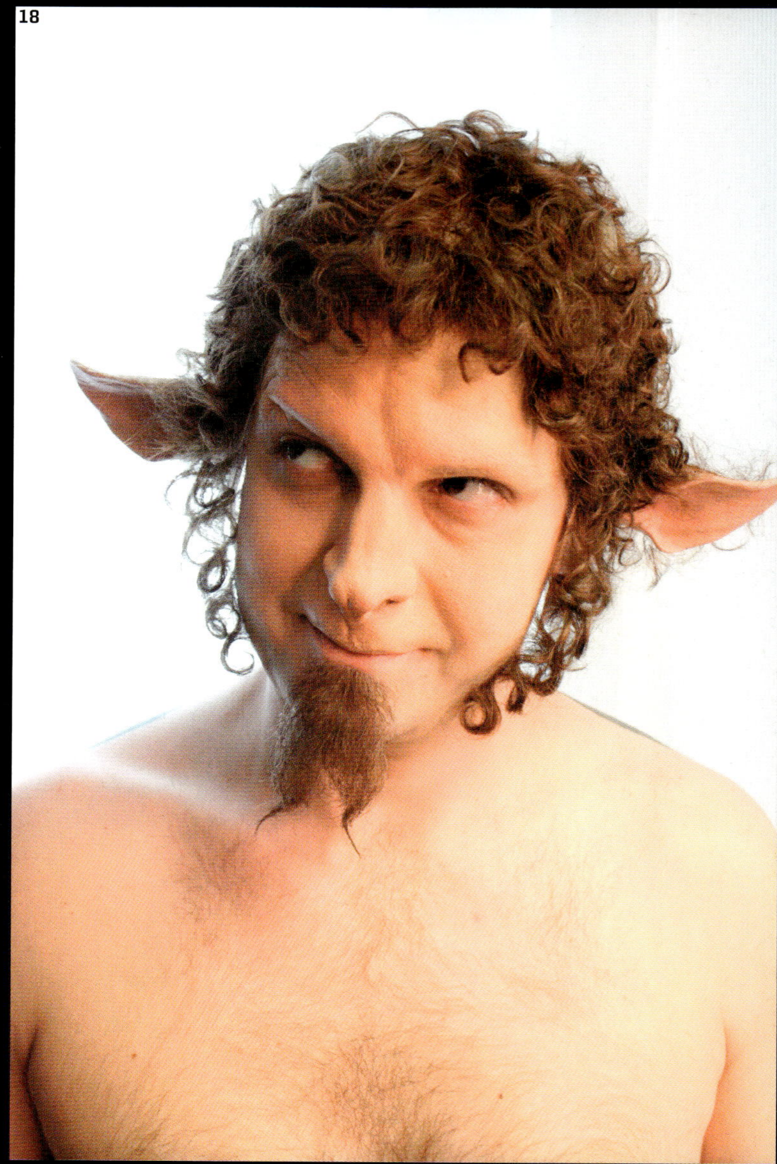

19

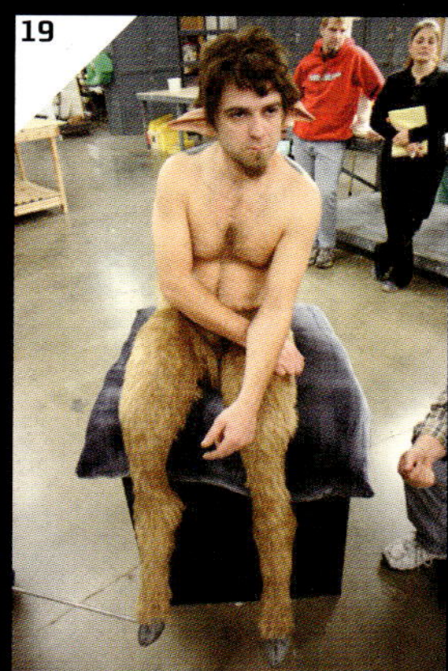

20

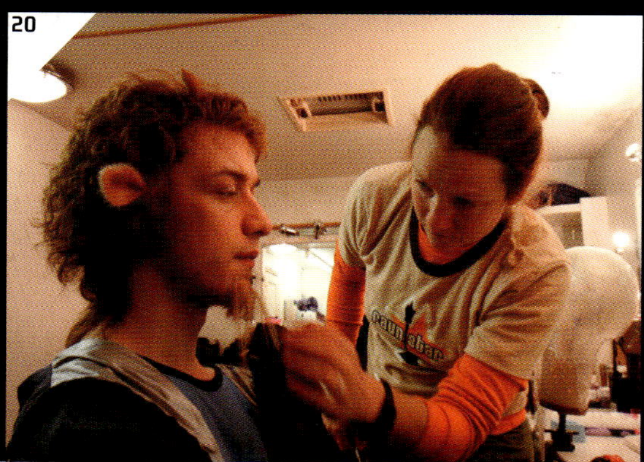

(16) The first, brief test session that KNB had with Mr. Tumnus actor, James McAvoy **(17)** Scott Patton applies the finishing touches to a test Tumnus makeup on KNB artist Ben Rittenhouse **(18–19)** Rittenhouse wearing the complete Mr Tumnus makeup
(20) Tami Lane applies final Mr Tumnus makeup design to McAvoy
(21–22) Display bust of McAvoy as Mr. Tumnus created for show at KNB
(23) McAvoy and producer Mark Johnson on location in Prague.

21

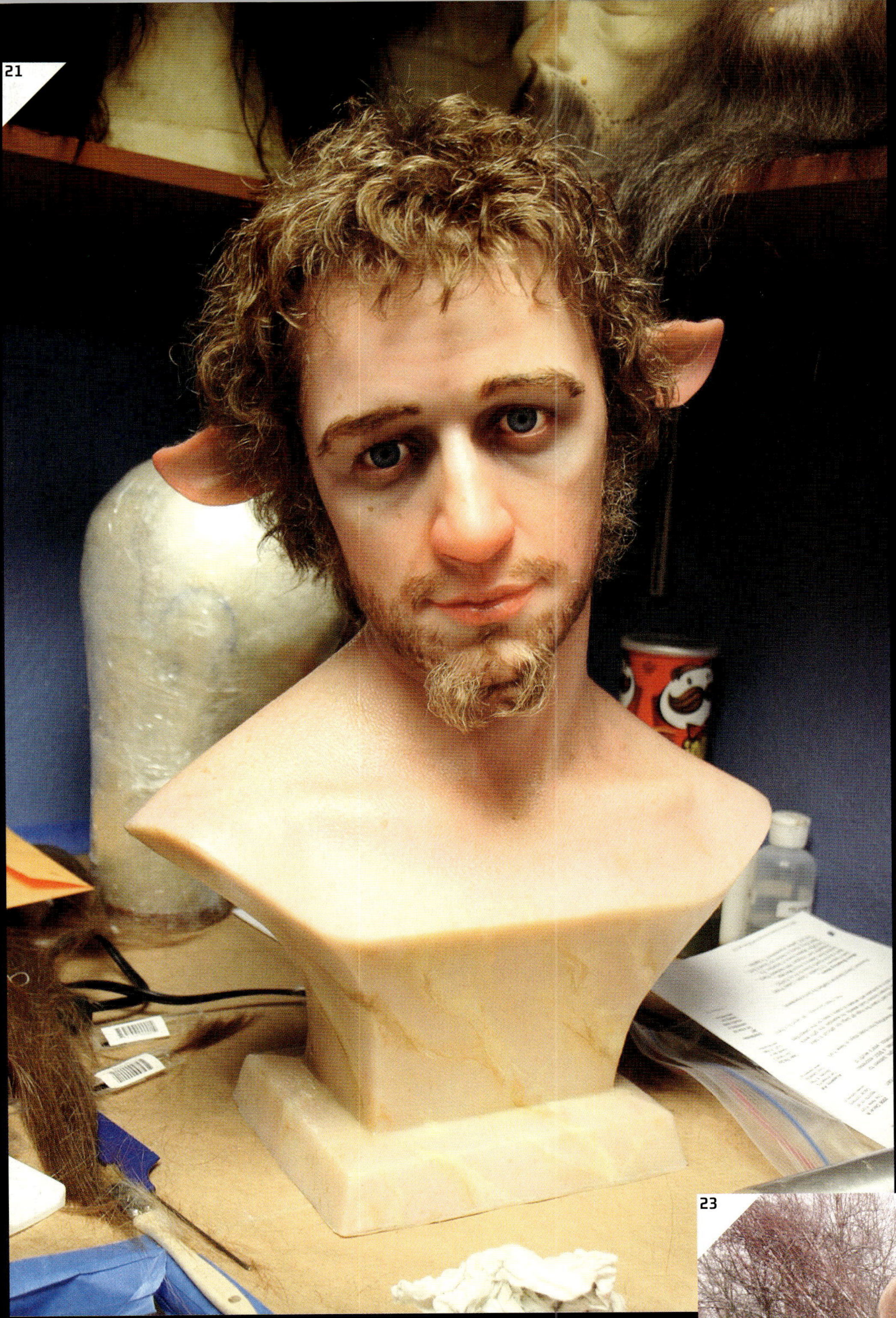

22

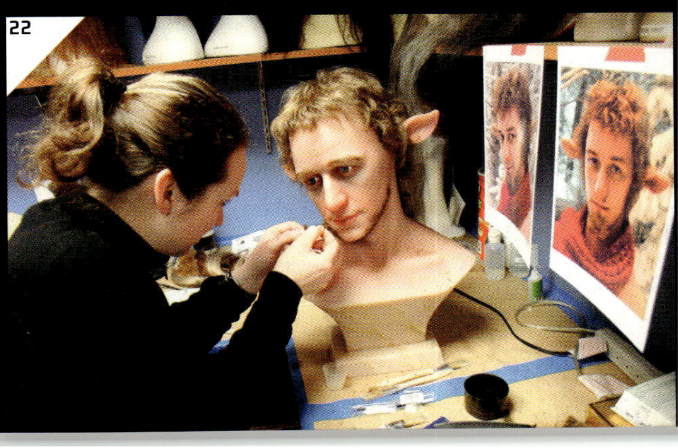

23

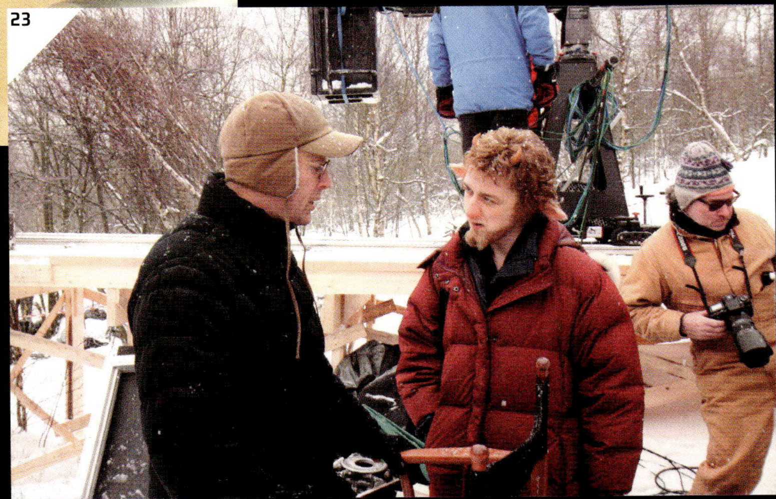

Each day of filming involved fitting McAvoy with a fiberglass skull cap containing small servos to twitch a pair of goat-like silicone ears—an effect that, in the end, was dropped during the editing process as the director found it too distracting. A wig went over the skull cap, and then small horns were screwed into the fiberglass headpiece. McAvoy's face needed little alteration to create the required look—only a subtle foam gelatin nose-tip was added for a more goaty profile. "We use foam gelatin a lot," explains Berger. "It's basically gelatin that is whipped up to create a foam, and therefore has the soft, slightly translucent qualities of gelatin, but is light and easy to apply like foam latex. It's much more durable than normal gelatin, the edges can be blended well into the performer's skin, and it paints nicely with a combination of alcohol and acrylic paint."

Next, attention turned to Mr. Tumnus's hair, which was painstakingly hand-laid onto his face and body—glue being applied to his skin and strands of hair being pressed onto it one layer at a time. Hair was added to McAvoy's face to create a beard and moustache, down the actor's bare back, on his chest and stomach, and along his forearms. Around his waist McAvoy wore Lycra biker shorts that had been thickly tied with hair which was then carefully blended with the hair on his stomach and back. Once all of the hair was attached, it was carefully styled and crimped using hot tongs.

"For Mr. Tumnus we exclusively used human hair," says Berger. "When you buy human hair you can get a huge variety—Chinese hair, African hair, Indian hair, and so on. Every race has a different quality of hair. For Mr. Tumnus we mostly used Russian hair, which is very fine but still has lots of body. We bought many kilos of it in a number of colors, which we blended to create the right shades for Tumnus." People don't give up their hair for nothing, and so dressing Mr. Tumnus cost an estimated $5,000 each day.

Berger, along with prosthetic supervisor Tami Lane, personally applied McAvoy's makeup each day of the *Narnia* shoot. "Unfortunately, when your passion becomes your career and then that career is then successful, you end up spending a lot of your time having to run a business," says Berger. "In the workshop we may have as many as 100 people or more working for us, so we don't get to do any hands-on stuff ourselves. We run the place and do the art direction and liaise with the clients. But when it comes to filming we're always on set, making sure things run smoothly and getting to be hands-on as much as possible. On *Narnia*, I worked on James McAvoy's makeup everyday. That's what I really get a thrill doing, and what I always wanted to do—creating makeup."

In the end, Sony Pictures Imageworks digitally erased McAvoy's legs below his fur-trimmed waist and blended in a pair of animated CG legs. During filming, therefore, the actor had to walk as if he had cloven hooves. "We tried all kinds of things, like building shoes with shock absorbers in them in order to get the top half of James's body to move as if the bottom half had these goat's legs," explains Berger. "In the end, though, James perfected a way of walking so that he put all his weight on his upper thighs and walked with bent knees. When they finally put the CG legs in there it really looked like he was walking on them."

24

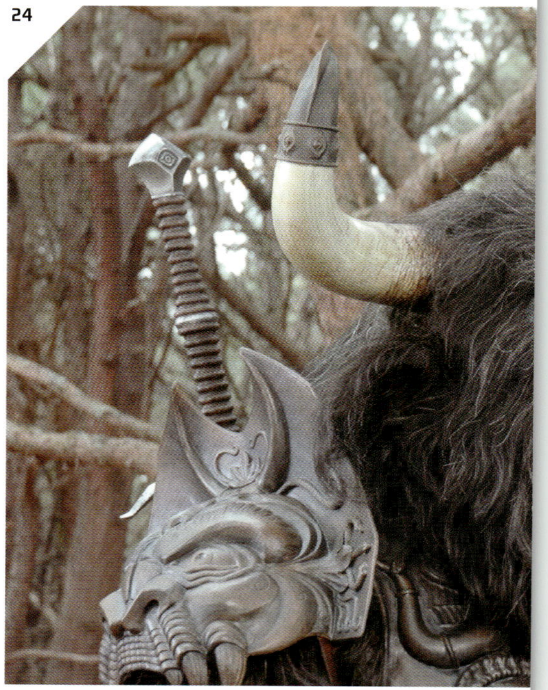

25

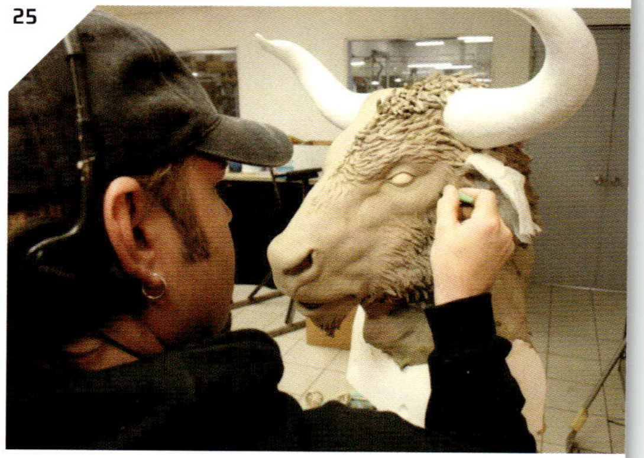

26

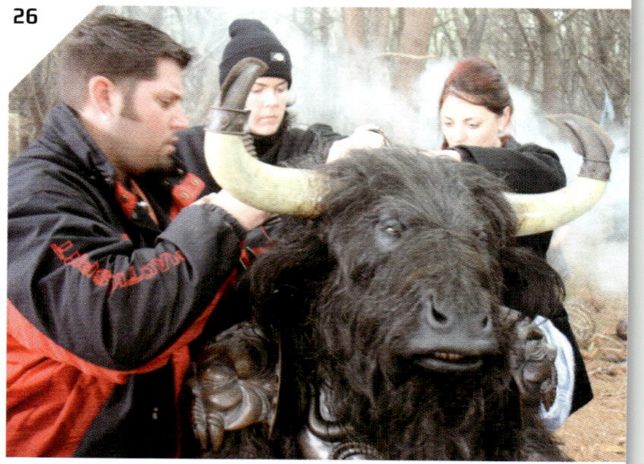

(24) The finished General Otmin on location in New Zealand **(25)** Scott Patton sculpts a Minotaur head onto a human lifecast **(26)** Rob Derry, Clare Mulroy, and Beth Hathaway prepare and dress General Otmin's animatronic head **(27)** An early test head to demonstrate Minotaur hair style and colouring **(28)** Finished ogre sculpt.

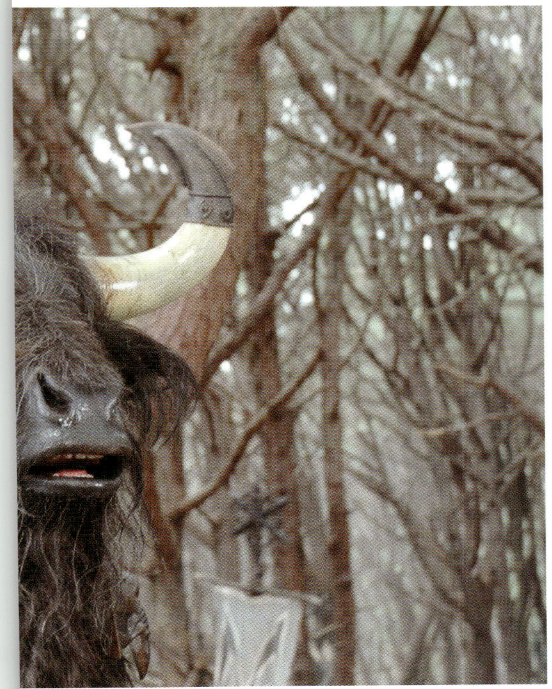

27

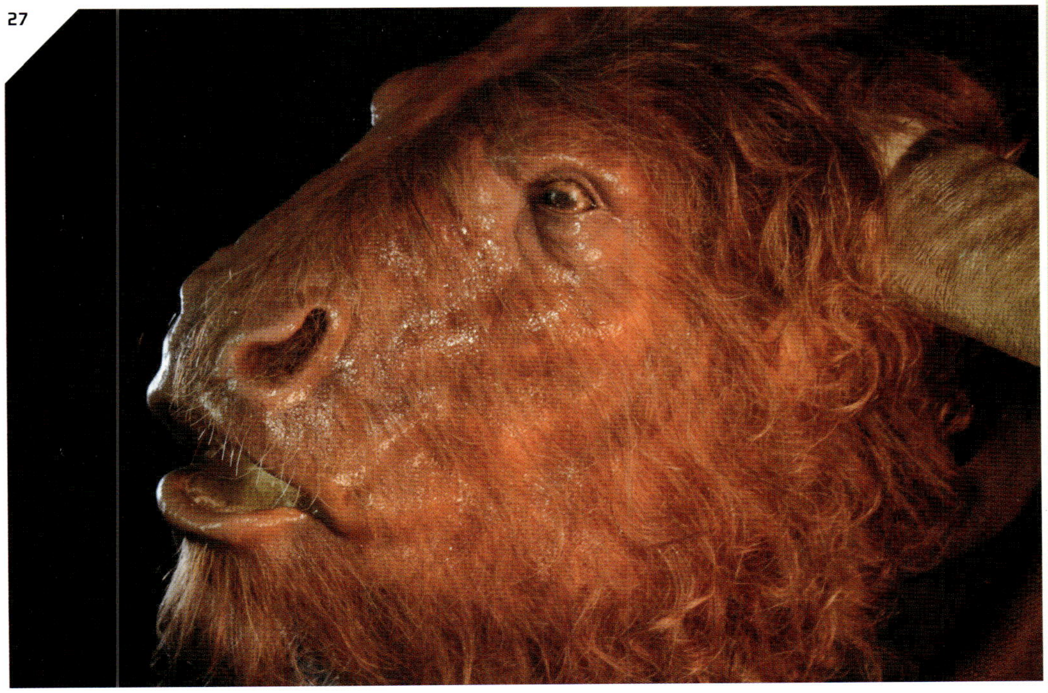

28

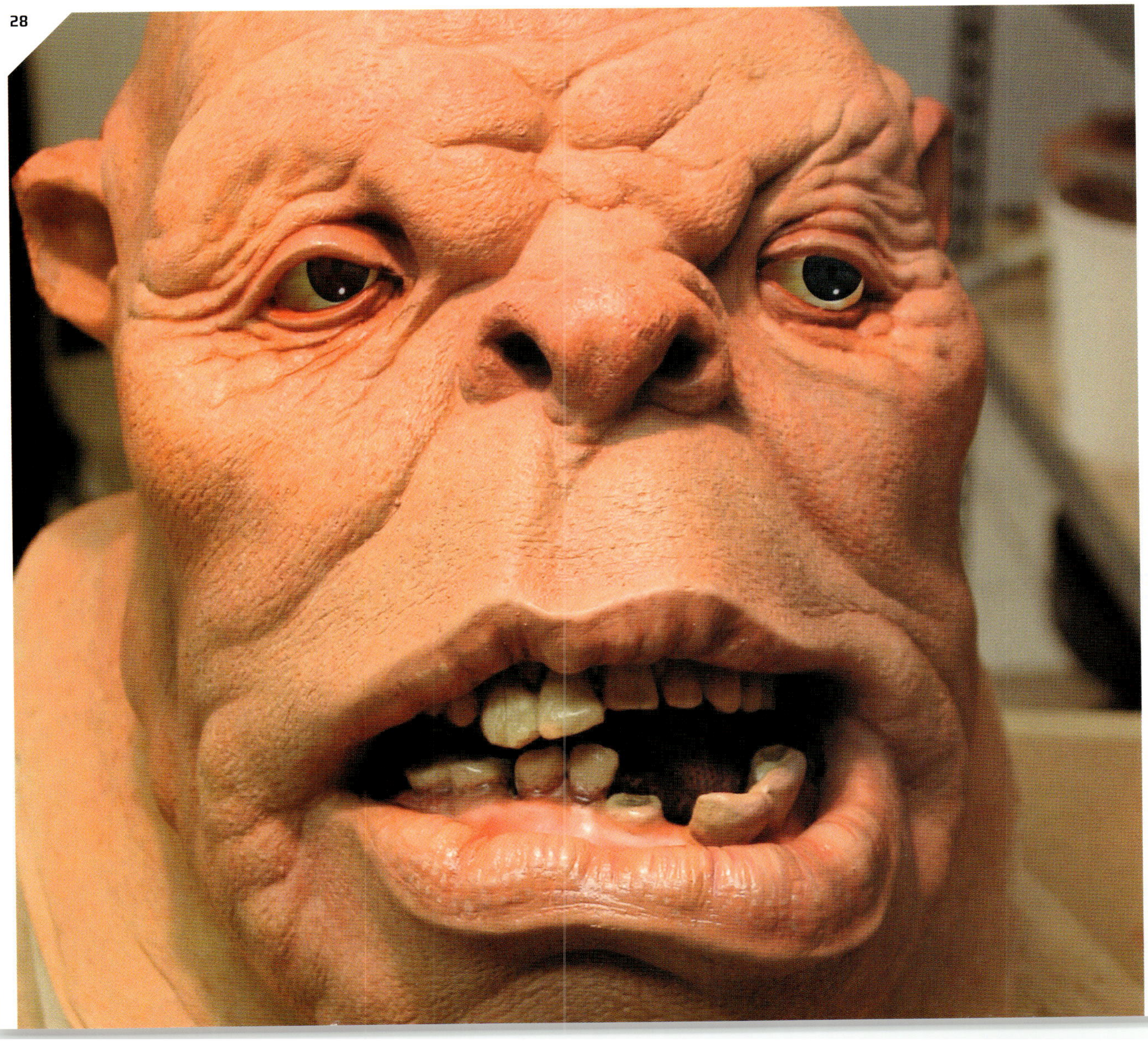

29

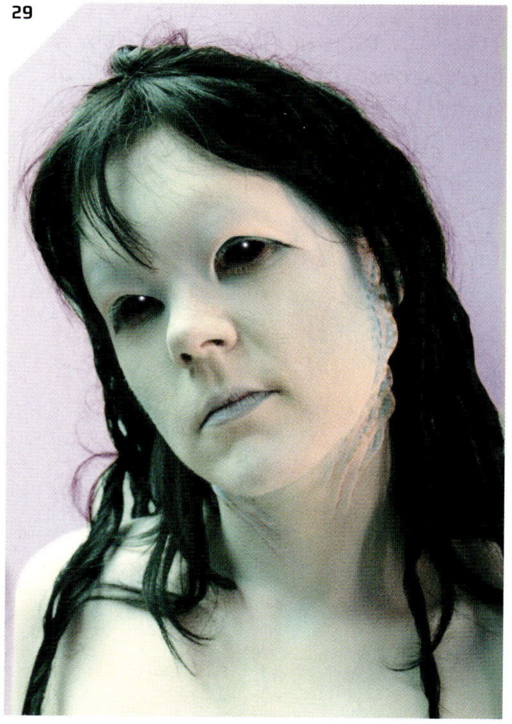

30

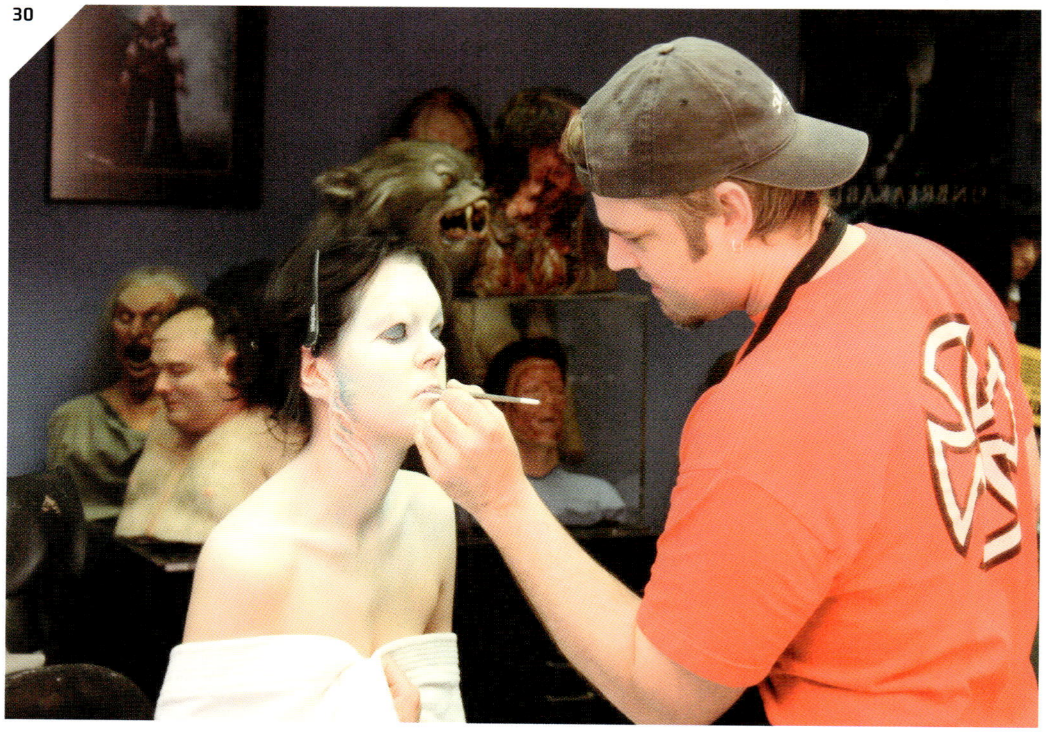

31

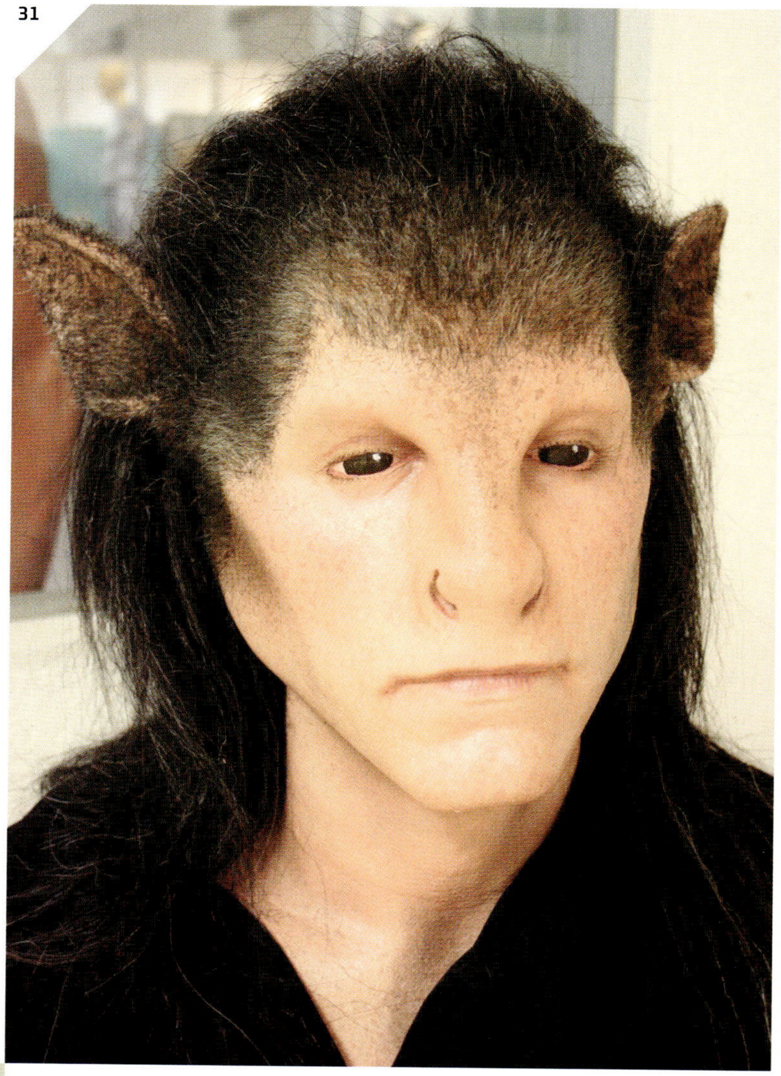

32

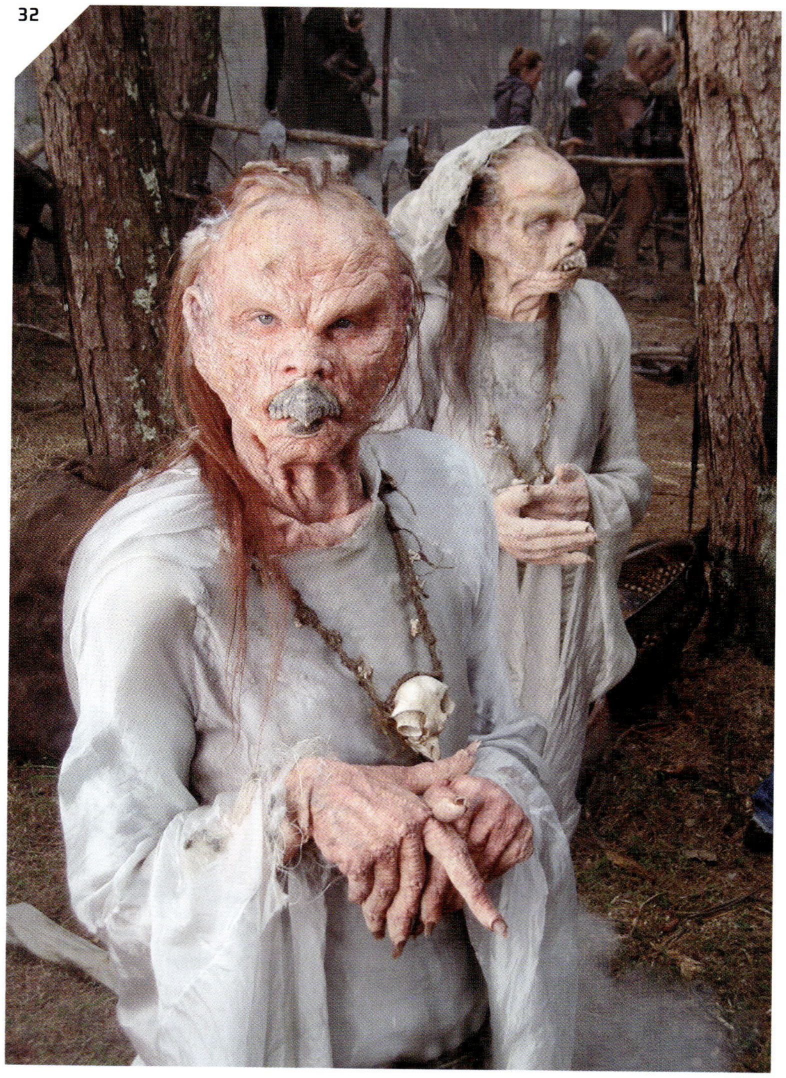

33

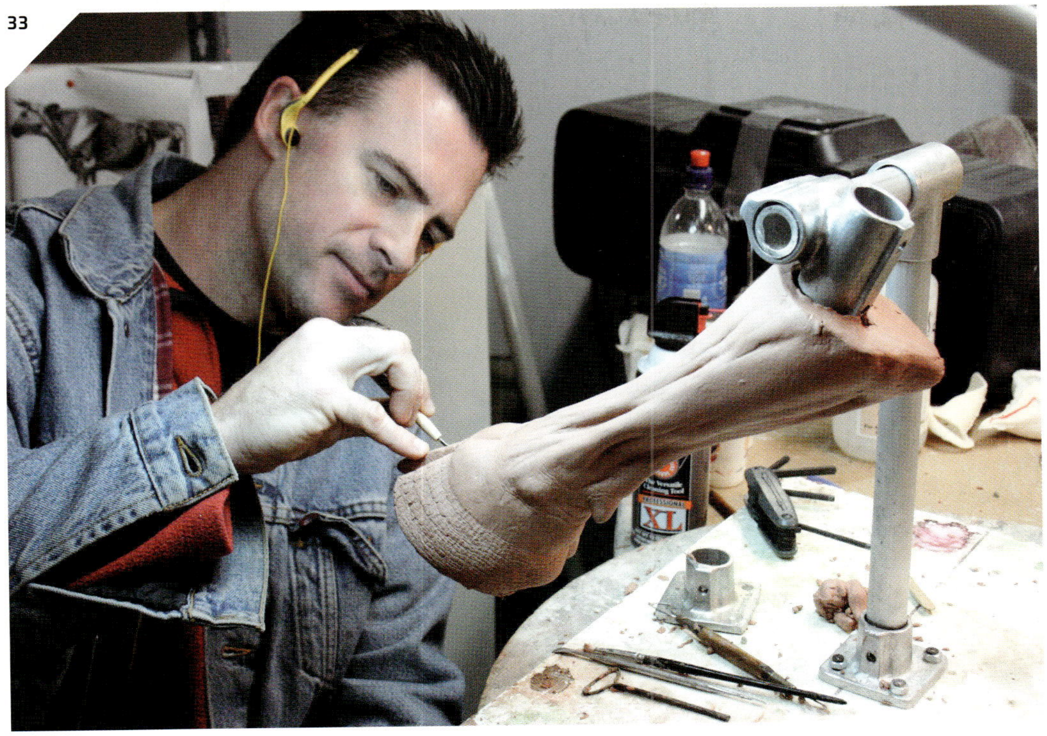

Among Berger's favorite characters in the movie were the Minotaurs, in particular their burly leader, General Otmin. "I was really looking forward to doing the Minotaurs. To me they are the perfect combination of buffalo, gorilla, and the characters from *Where the Wild Things Are*—one of my all-time favorite books."

KNB built 25 full-body Minotaur suits with unarticulated stunt masks that could be worn at a distance from the camera. Four fully articulated, servo-controlled heads with radio-controlled ears, eyes, brows, nostrils, jaws, and lips were also constructed for close-up work. "Normally underskulls are made from fiberglass, which really smells bad for the performer," states Berger. "But for this we vacuformed plastic skulls that were lightweight and didn't smell. We had to make 25 of them, so everything was done as a production line and put together like a model kit."

For Berger, it was crucial that the Minotaurs had a very real sense of power. "We wanted the Minotaurs to have weight, and jiggle as if they actually had layers of fat and muscle in their chest, arms, and thighs. We achieved this by creating an undersuit which represented the anatomy of the creature. This had various pieces sewn into it to simulate what was under the Minotaurs' skin. We used water-filled sacs to represent wobbly flesh and muscle, rigid foam to simulate bone areas such as the kneecaps, elbows, and ribcage. We created several layers of this muscle flesh and bone to simulate what should be going on inside the body. We later gave that information to the animation guys, who used it to build their CG Minotaurs.

"Once the performer was inside their undersuit, the character's outer skin was dressed over the top. This was made of spandex hand-tied with yak hair and had poppers to fasten it closed. Yak hair is used a lot in makeup because it's very thick and styles well to create the texture you are looking for."

Berger was happy with the final result. "I was really pleased with the way they looked on film—very powerful and majestic, but also very primal and clearly bent on destruction. To be honest, half of that was our work and half was down to the performer—it's really hard work in those suits, and getting a performance to come through the layers of fur and foam latex is quite an achievement."

Ultimately Berger believes that *Narnia* was a perfect example of the way that special-effects work has evolved in recent years. "What was really revolutionary about this film was that it was an incredible combination of all the available techniques. All of the effects vendors worked absolutely hand-in-hand to achieve this, and we had a great relationship with the CG people. Andrew Adamson wants us to do twice as much practical work for the second *Narnia* film—and we can't wait to get started."

Despite the inroads made by CG in the past few years, Berger remains buoyant about the future. "You know, a while ago everyone wanted to do stuff with computers, but we're starting to see a backlash now. I think audiences want to know that something was achieved for real. And directors who grew up thinking CG was the only way are starting to find out how much better things can look, or how much quicker or more economically they can be achieved, when done practically. I think we're entering a period when CG will not be seen as the be–all and end–all, and both old and new methods can sit more comfortably side by side."

(29) Makeup artist Clare Mulroy wears an early *Narnia* mermaid test makeup **(30)** Scott Patton applies the prosthetics to Mulroy. The mermaids were ultimately created as entirely digital characters **(31)** Bust of early Centaur design **(32)** Hags on the set of the White Witch's camp **(33)** Nick Marra sculpts a Mr. Tumnus hoof, later scanned to create the digital legs added to the live-action character.

CARLOS HUANTE

CV

Character designer-illustrator; b. East Los Angeles, CA; graduated from high school in 1983; studied life drawing at night classes at Art Center College of Design, Pasadena; worked as runner and junior artist at Filmation; clean-up artist at Ruby-Spears Productions; went on to work as an animation designer, but gave it up after becoming disillusioned; worked for Dinamation, which created animatronic dinosaurs for theme parks and museums; took on some work as a designer on a commercial, then went freelance as a character designer/illustrator

SELECT FILMOGRAPHY

Batman Forever (1995); *Mission Impossible* (1996); *Men in Black* (1997); *Deep Rising* (1998); *Mighty Joe Young* (1998); *Van Helsing* (2004); *Blade Trinity* (2004); *Hellboy* (2004); *War of the Worlds* (2005); *Eragon* (2006)

KEY CHARACTERS

Mikey (*Men in Black*); the worm and its victims (*Deep Rising*); Joe (*Mighty Joe Young*); aliens (*War of the Worlds*); Beast (*X-Men: The Last Stand*); Durza's Beast (*Eragon*)

TECHNIQUES

Traditional design and sculpture; Photoshop; ZBrush

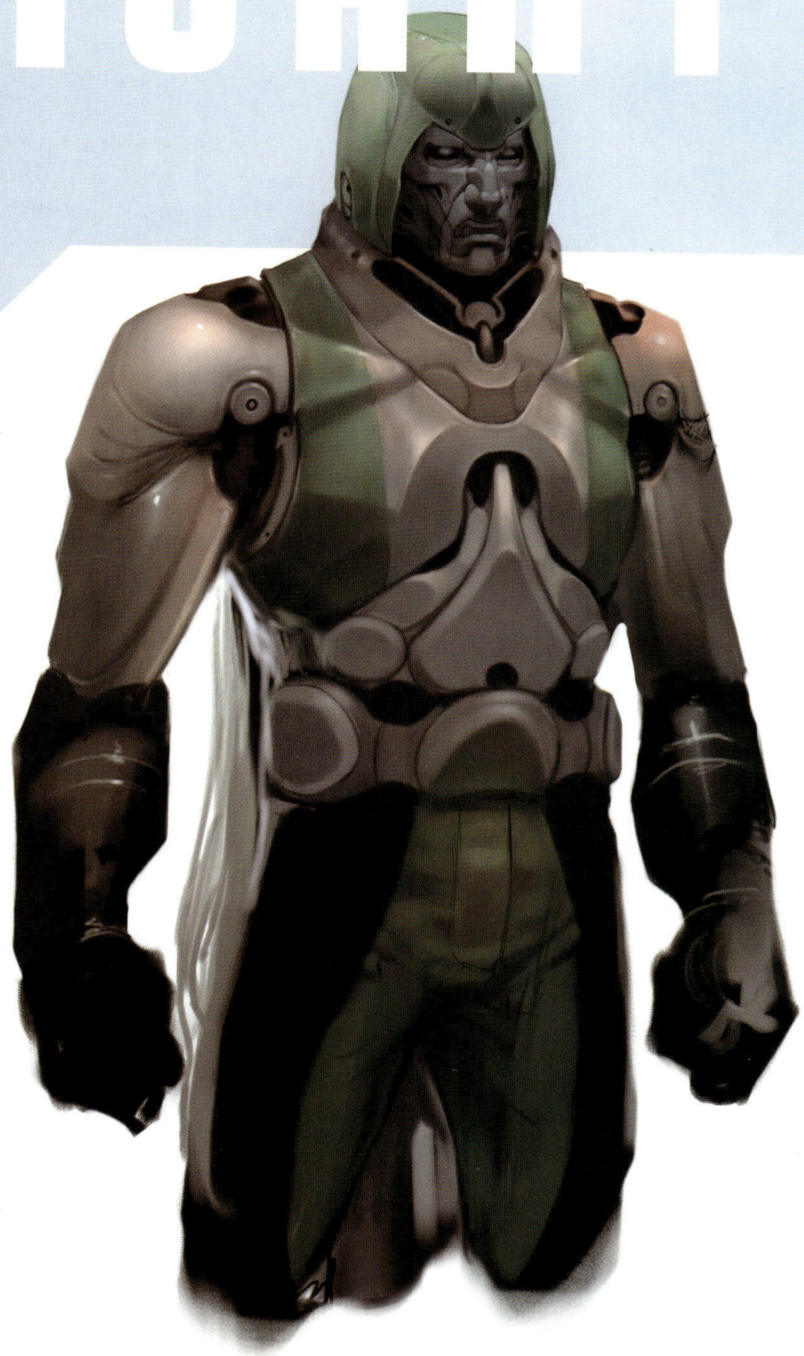

01

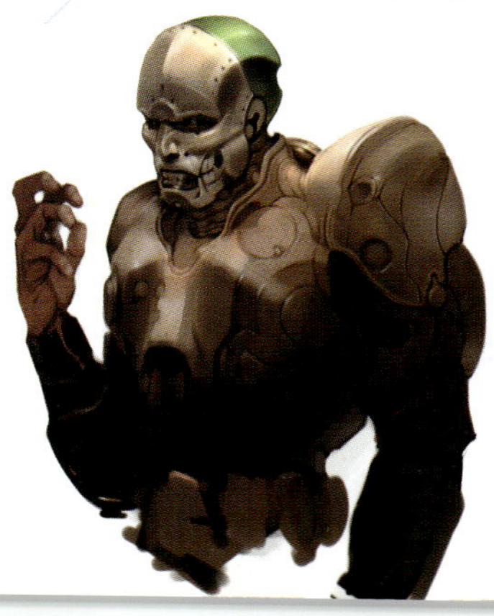

02

03

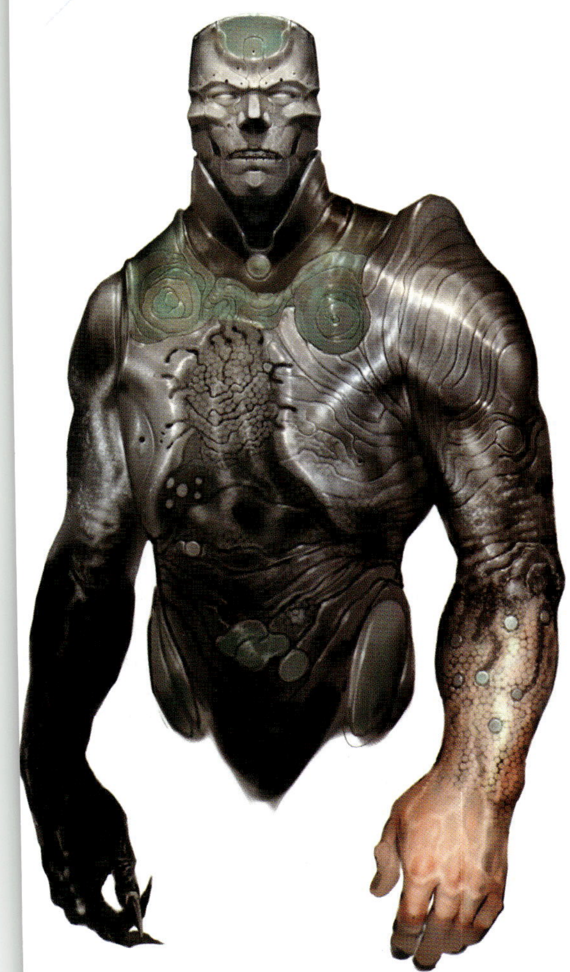

05

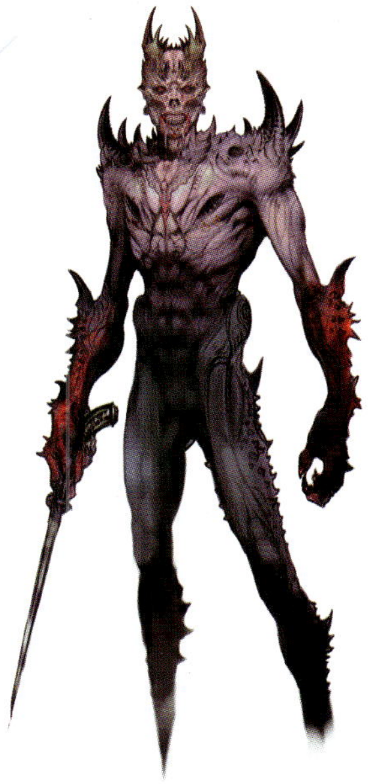

06

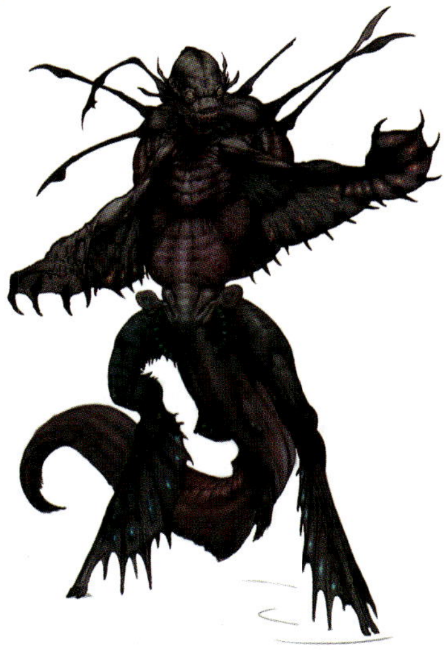

04

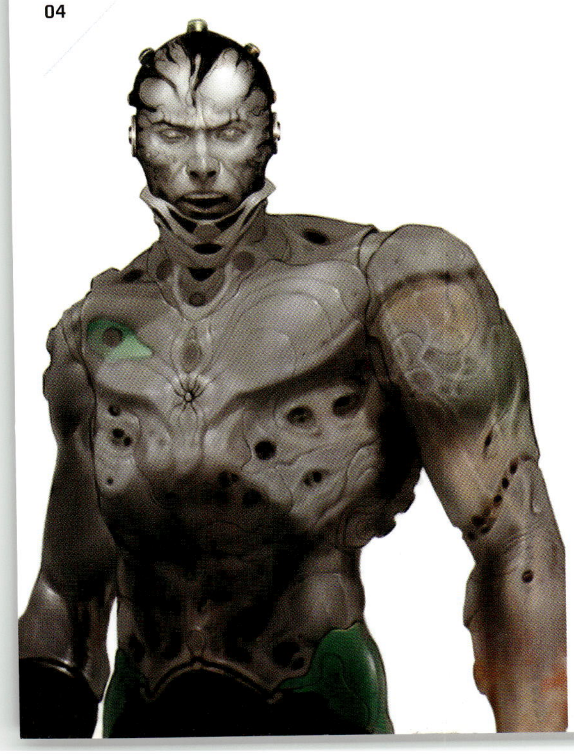

Carlos Huante is one of Hollywood's leading character designer-illustrators, respected for his vivid imagination and an ability to push form to its limits. He has created characters for movies including *Men in Black* (1997), *Mighty Joe Young* (1998), *Van Helsing* (2004), and *War of the Worlds* (2005). He is currently creature design supervisor at Industrial Light and Magic (ILM), where he is helping to develop their digital-creature shop.

Huante was born in East Los Angeles, CA, and grew up wanting to design monsters, a passion probably inherited from his mother, herself an avid fan of monster movies. "Even today my mom will call me up and tell me when *War of the Gargantuans* [1966] is on TV," laughs Huante. "She loves all that stuff!"

Huante's first artistic success came after a first-grade class in Mexican mask–making. The inspired youngster discovered how much he enjoyed designing and making masks, and was even photographed with some of his creations for the local newspaper.

After graduating from high school in 1983, Huante attended night classes in life drawing at Art Center College of Design in Pasadena, where he met Mike Spooner, an illustrator from Filmation, makers of the *He-Man* cartoon series. Huante worked as a runner and then as a junior artist in the layout department.

His next job was for another animation studio, Ruby-Spears Productions, where he worked on *Alvin and the Chipmunks*, redrawing and cleaning up the rough layouts created by senior artists. Despite the lowly position, Huante considers the job to have been a valuable experience. "Alvin is owned by the Bagdasarian family, and one of the family was the draftsman who set the style in which the characters had to be drawn. She was the quality control. This lady knew how to draw like classic Disney, and so my drawings had to match hers. Feathered lines got my mind thinking about the way that lines and motion hook up, how things flow. Drawing cartoons helps you to get that stuff inside your head and it still trickles over into my work today."

(01–04) Concept drawings for Dr. Doom (*Fantastic Four*, 2005) **(05)** Drake (*Blade Trinity*, 2004) **(06)** Huante's vision of the Creature from the Black Lagoon, dropped from the script of *Van Helsing* (2004).

07

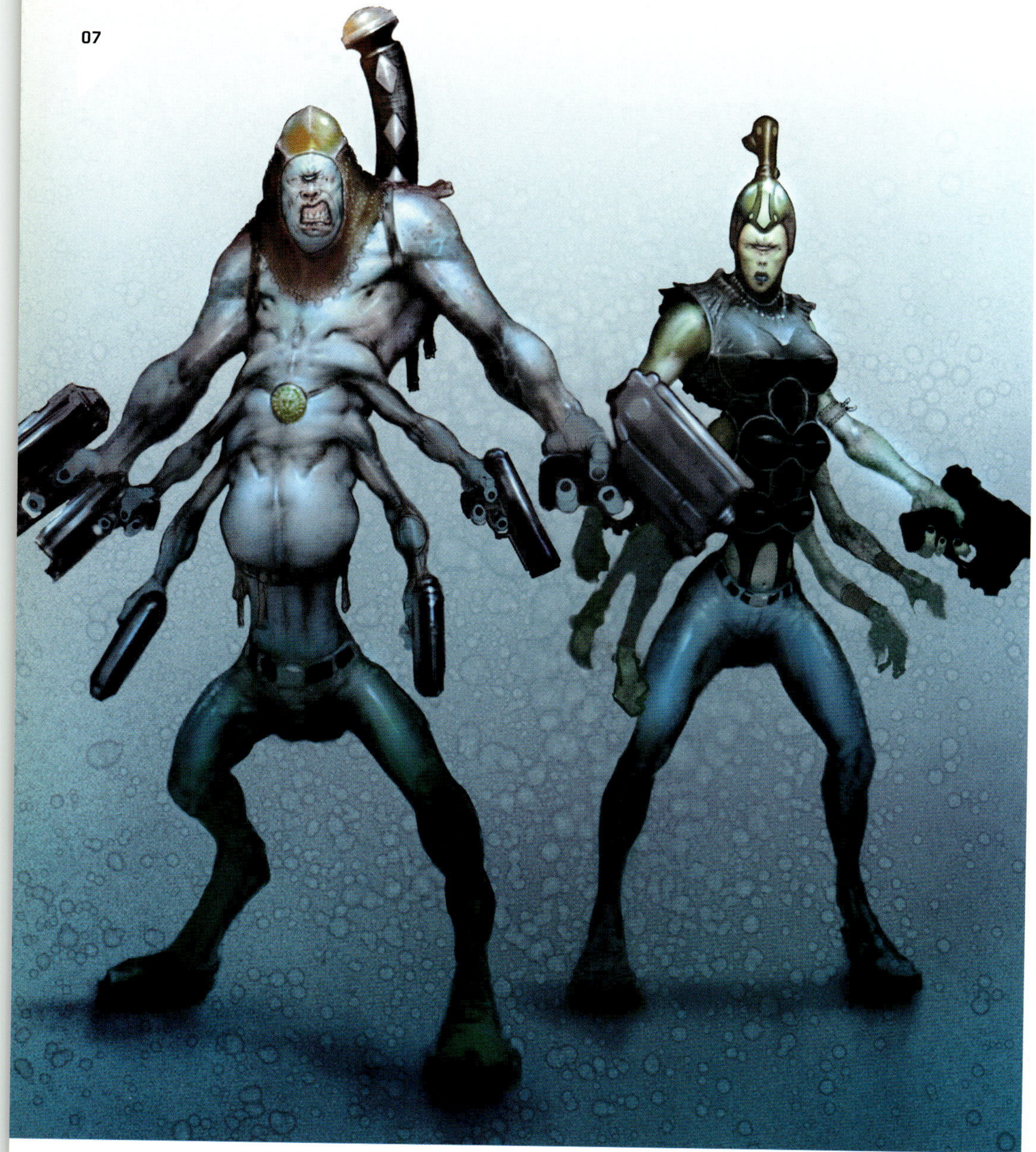

"Miles was the only person I knew who was freelancing as a creature designer at the time," says Huante. "Mostly, creatures were kind of thrown together by the guys who built them—they'd maybe do a few drawings, but since they were not necessarily draftsmen the drawings weren't great. They probably worked things out in clay, and for them that was the design process. Many great creatures were created that way, so who am I to say it didn't work? But Miles was working as a freelance artist and getting to create these great character designs. When Miles couldn't finish some work on a commercial because he got offered a movie job, he handed the excess work to me. From then on I was designing characters for feature films. That was the late 1980s."

(07–08) Alien warrior concepts (*Men in Black*, 1997)
(09) Pencil sketch of Serleena, from the same movie.

08

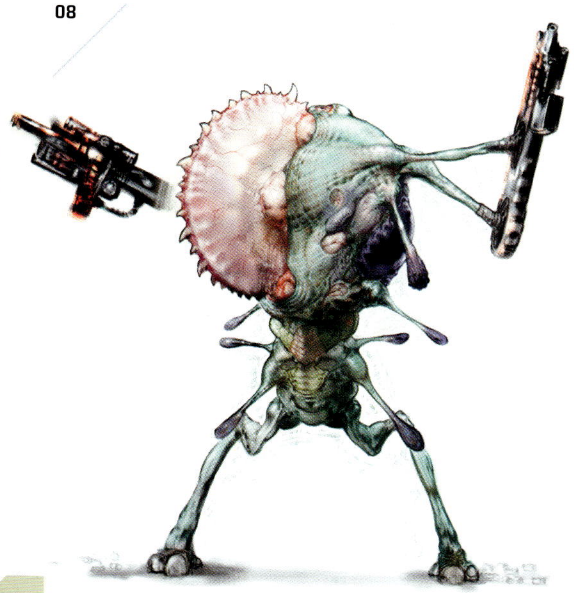

Huante pursued a career as an animation designer, landing a job creating characters for the *Ghostbusters* cartoon series. However, the artist became disillusioned with working in a business that seemed ruled by egos and internal politics and eventually gave up his job. He then spent three years unsure of what he wanted to do, even working in a kitchen under his younger brother—but he never stopped drawing.

After working for two years at Dinamation, a company that built animatronic dinosaurs for theme parks and museums, Huante was introduced to Miles Teves by a mutual friend.

09

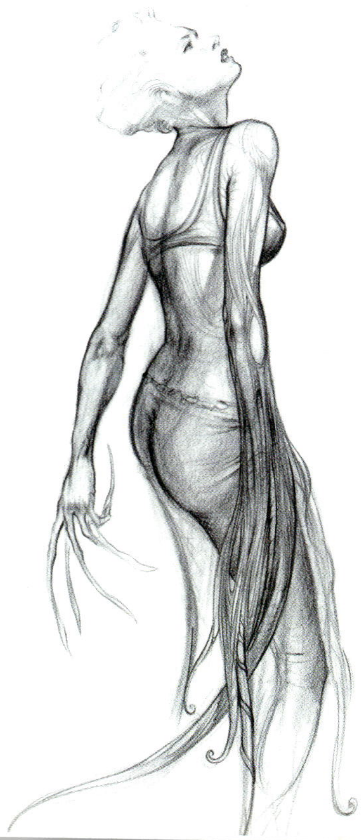

10

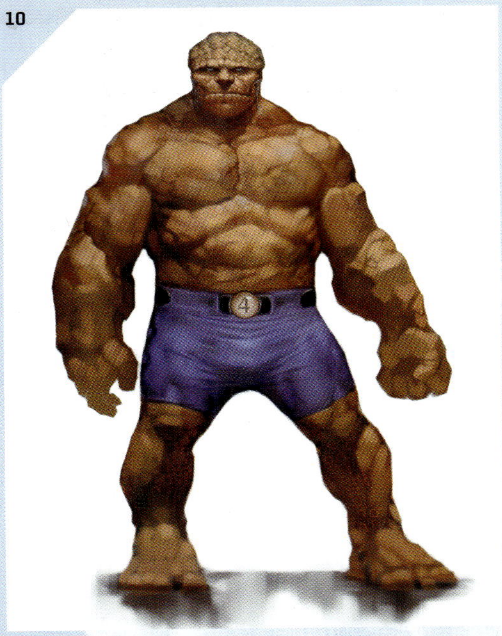

After working on a number movies, including *Batman Forever* (1995), Huante got what he considers his first major character-design job on *Men in Black* (1997). "I worked on that while it was still in the very early development stages at Amblin Entertainment [in 1995]," recalls Huante. "It was hard because there wasn't really a script to look at, so I didn't have much of an idea for the feel of the film. I designed all these crazy aliens, they were realistic, but had a kind of hip-hop, cartoony edge, which amused me but the guys at Amblin just didn't get it. After a while, I was starting to doubt my abilities, I left the job and went off to work with Rob Bottin on *Mission Impossible* [1996]. When *Men in Black* went into production, they hired Rick Baker to do the makeup, and he rehired me as one of the designers. I did a bunch of designs similar in style to those I had done before. After Rick had his first production meeting with Amblin, he came out and said that a lot of the stuff they had liked was mine! That was really redeeming."

Huante's favorite creation for *Men in Black* was Mikey. "Mikey was a really fun character, although there are aspects to his design that aren't fully developed because of the changes that got made. My original idea was to have the character continually farting from the top of his head. So I gave him these paddle-like hands which he would use to fan the smell away. In the end he didn't do the farting thing and his paddles remained a bit undeveloped. But I think he worked great all the same."

Huante is known for his free-flowing creativity and remarkable imagination. However, he considers one of his most interesting conceptual designs to be the imposing giant gorilla for *Mighty Joe Young* (1998), later built by Rick Baker's team and also computer-animated. "A lot of people might wonder what there is to design in a gorilla," says Huante. "After all, it's a beast that exists in nature. But there are a huge number of things to consider: Is he a mountain gorilla or a lowland gorilla? Is he a youth or a mature silverback? All of those options have different characteristics to their personality. If he's a silverback, maybe he looks wise and regal, but old silverbacks also have pot bellies, which make them look dumpy. Is he going to look square and Hulk-like, or is he going to be round and soft, or a combination of soft edges in some areas and hard edges in others, so he can look both menacing and kindly? That's the way we went in the end.

"It was also important to design a personality and not just an animal. One of the things I did was to give him a kind of Fu Manchu goatee beard to make him that combination of both sinister and wise. Matt Rose sculpted Joe, and he did an absolutely fantastic job. I thought he looked great in the movie—even the computer-generated version. That was the first time I saw CG fur work."

Huante loves designing characters for the movies, but sometimes finds it hard coming to terms with the fact that he is hired to generate ideas that other people will use in whatever way they wish. Huante counts one of his recent design experiences as just such a disappointment. "I thought *War of the Worlds* (2005) was a great film, and I really like the attitude

11

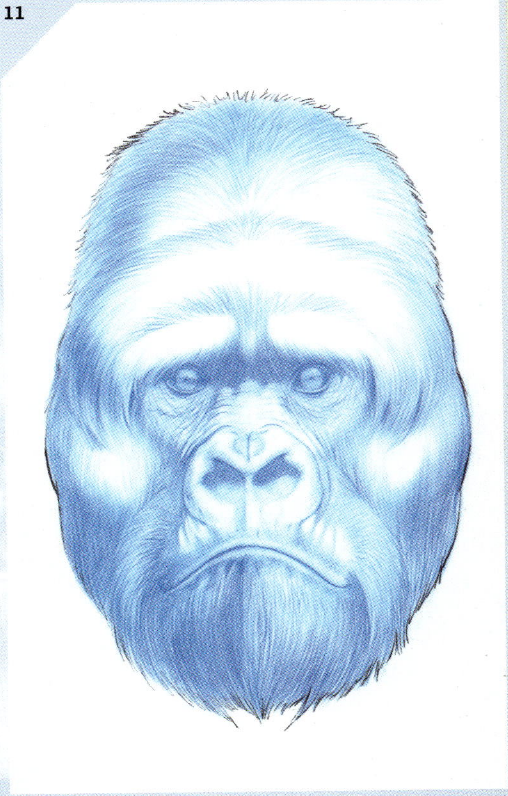

12

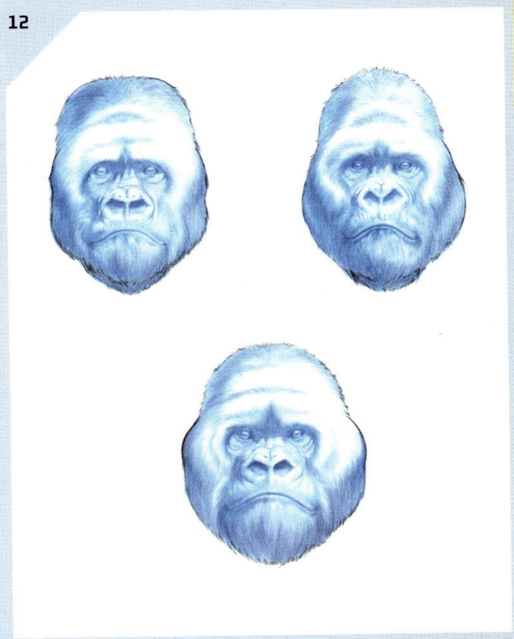

(10) *The Fantastic Four*'s The Thing **(11)** Huante's final rendering of the gorilla's head for *Mighty Joe Young* (1998) **(12)** Head variables created during the design of Joe.

and the feeling of the alien war machines. However, I worked on the designs for the actual alien creatures. A group of artists, including myself, came up with several designs, but they ended up cherry-picking the bits they liked from two separate designs—one by me, the other by Chris Alzmann. They took the head from here, the mouth from there, the legs from this, the arms from that, and so on. That's no way to produce a character for a film. Creating characters is not like a pick-and-mix. I had originally envisaged a body similar to the final version—though full of tentacles and with a different head that had no eyes, which I thought would look really nightmarish. But they wanted eyes. I thought to myself, 'Alien had no eyes, and that's about the scariest movie monster ever.' For such a great movie I thought the aliens were really anticlimactic. It's hard when you can see how great it ought to be in your mind's eye, but the reality turns out different."

Even when Huante is pleased with a finished design, there is no telling how it might evolve once turned into a puppet, makeup, or computer-generated model. "When you love a final design, you start worrying about what other people are going to do to your work," he says. "One thing you can do is make sure you create a design that can be physically made. The best design is a perfect marriage of experimentation with crazy proportions and an understanding of the practical application. That's to say, it's good if you know the restrictions of the medium you are designing for, be it for CG, puppet, or makeup. If you don't apply this understanding, the people fabricating your design will have to rein it in so that they can make it work, meaning your design will be massively revised. The result is a character that looks nothing like the original concept.

13

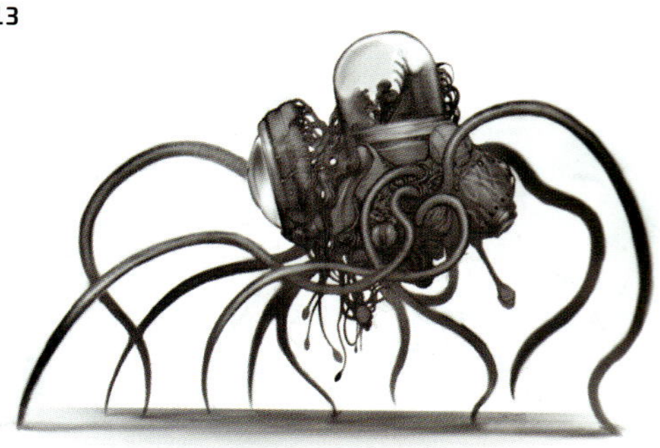

"That's why there is a problem in hiring illustrators from outside of film. They might be great draftsmen, but they often don't know the restrictions of film and practical makeup—what you can and cannot do with arm and leg extensions, for example. So, if it's a character that will be performed by a human, I will always make sure the design will fit a human. It's all about shifting the weight of the character design around within the three-dimensional silhouette of the human form. And that's a test of a good designer, to find the design you like and then to make that design work on a person."

One of the ways that Huante now ensures that it is his design that makes it through to the screen is by using the latest in computer technology. "We used to create a design as a 2-D image on paper; latterly we would design it in the computer before handing it over to be made into a practical creature or CG model. But now I can have a hand in the actual creation of a character by modeling it in the computer. I'll block out my character in ZBrush, which is like having digital modeling clay. This is great because having a 3-D model means you can have orthographic views—be able to see it from any angle. Then I'll hand that basic digital model to a skilled computer modeler who can create the final model directly from what

14

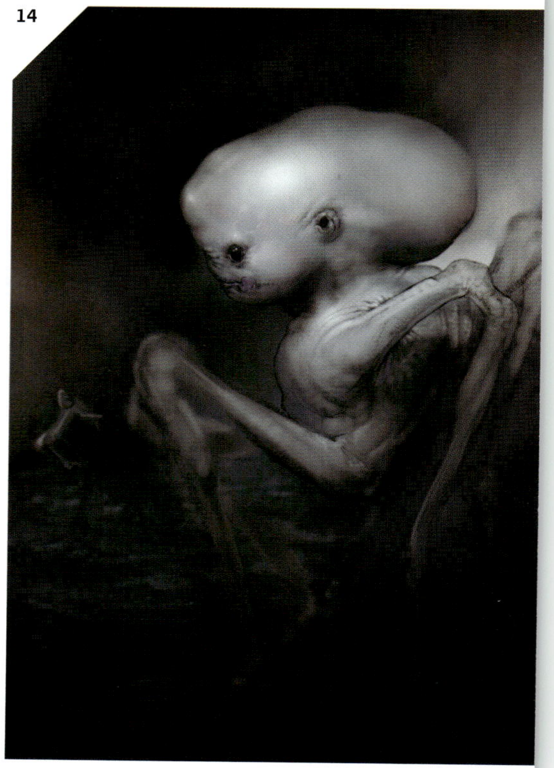

15

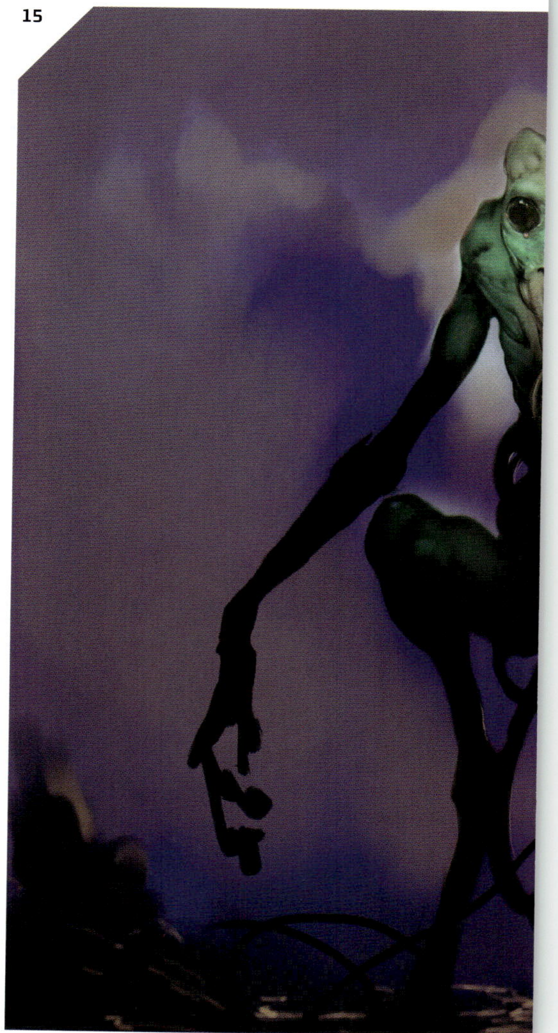

16

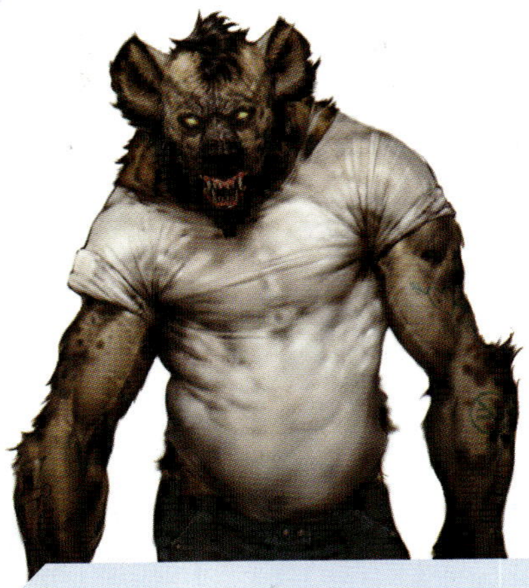

17

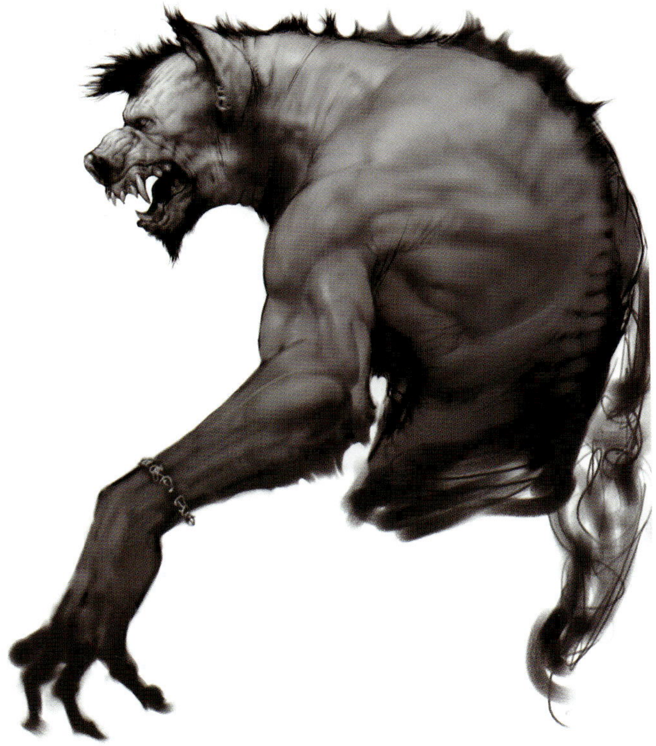

(13) Alien capsule for *War of the Worlds* (2005) **(14)** An original alien concept for the same movie **(15)** 1950s-inspired work for *War of the Worlds* **(16-17)** Werewolf concepts for *Van Helsing* (2004)

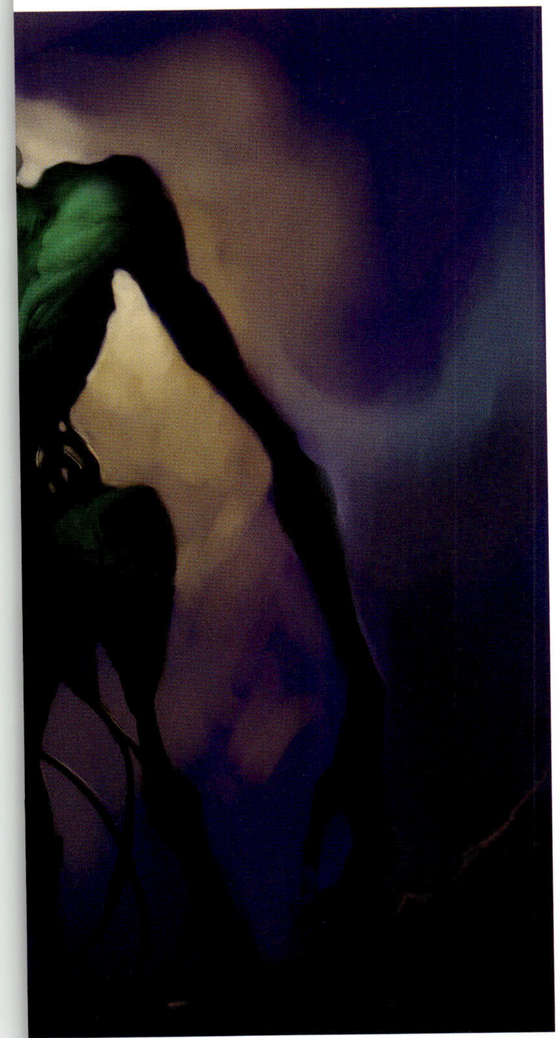

I originated—not from a piece of 2-D art, but from an actual three-dimensional object. And what's really cool is that they can pass their version back to me, and I can sculpt back on top of it or paint on it as a 2-D image and send it back again. I recently used this back-and-forth process for the first time to block out designs for Durza's Beast for *Eragon* [2006]."

Huante believes that the quality of his design depends greatly on his relationship with the people with whom he works. He cites makeup designer Rob Bottin as one of his greatest influences: "I worked for Rob designing the worm and its victims for *Deep Rising* [1998], and I can tell you he is an absolute genius when it comes to design. I would show him designs thinking that I had nailed it and he would always spot the one bad angle or flaw. That really pushes you to create your best stuff. I used to study the full-size version of Robocop that he had there in the shop, and I can tell you it is a design masterpiece. You can look at it from every angle and it works perfectly. I can't imagine the work that went into it." Huante has also loved working with Mike Elizalde and Guillermo del Toro on *Blade: Trinity* (2004) and *Hellboy* (2004). "Working with those guys is always guaranteed to be a good experience. And you know that whatever you design for Guillermo is going to end up in the movie, and I love that. Normally so much of what we do is just never seen."

Although Huante is reserved about the success of computers in creating characters for film, he believes that the technology will ultimately give artists more influence over how their creations make it to the screen. "Animation and modeling software is getting cheaper and easier to use all the time, and so are all other aspects of modern filmmaking. In a few years I hope it will be so affordable that production will again be in the hands of people with great ideas—not the guys in suits who run studios and have no idea about creativity."

STEVE WANG

CV

Makeup artist and painter; b. Taiwan; moved to USA when he was nine; became fascinated by Halloween masks as a child, and established a mask-making business while a teenager; moved to LA in 1985, finding work at Stan Winston Studio; then he moved on to Rick Baker's Boris, Inc., subsequently going freelance

SELECT FILMOGRAPHY

Invaders from Mars (1986); *Harry and the Hendersons* (1987); *The Monster Squad* (1987); *Predator* (1987); *Gremlins 2: The New Batch* (1990); *Guyver* (1991); *Godzilla* (1998); *Hellboy* (2004); *The Cave* (2005); *Underworld: Evolution* (2006)

KEY CHARACTERS

Gill Man (*The Monster Squad*); Predator (*Predator*); Abe Sapien (*Hellboy*); Marcus (*Underworld: Evolution*)

TECHNIQUES

Special effects makeup and prosthetic design; art direction; traditional design and sculpture; painting; Photoshop

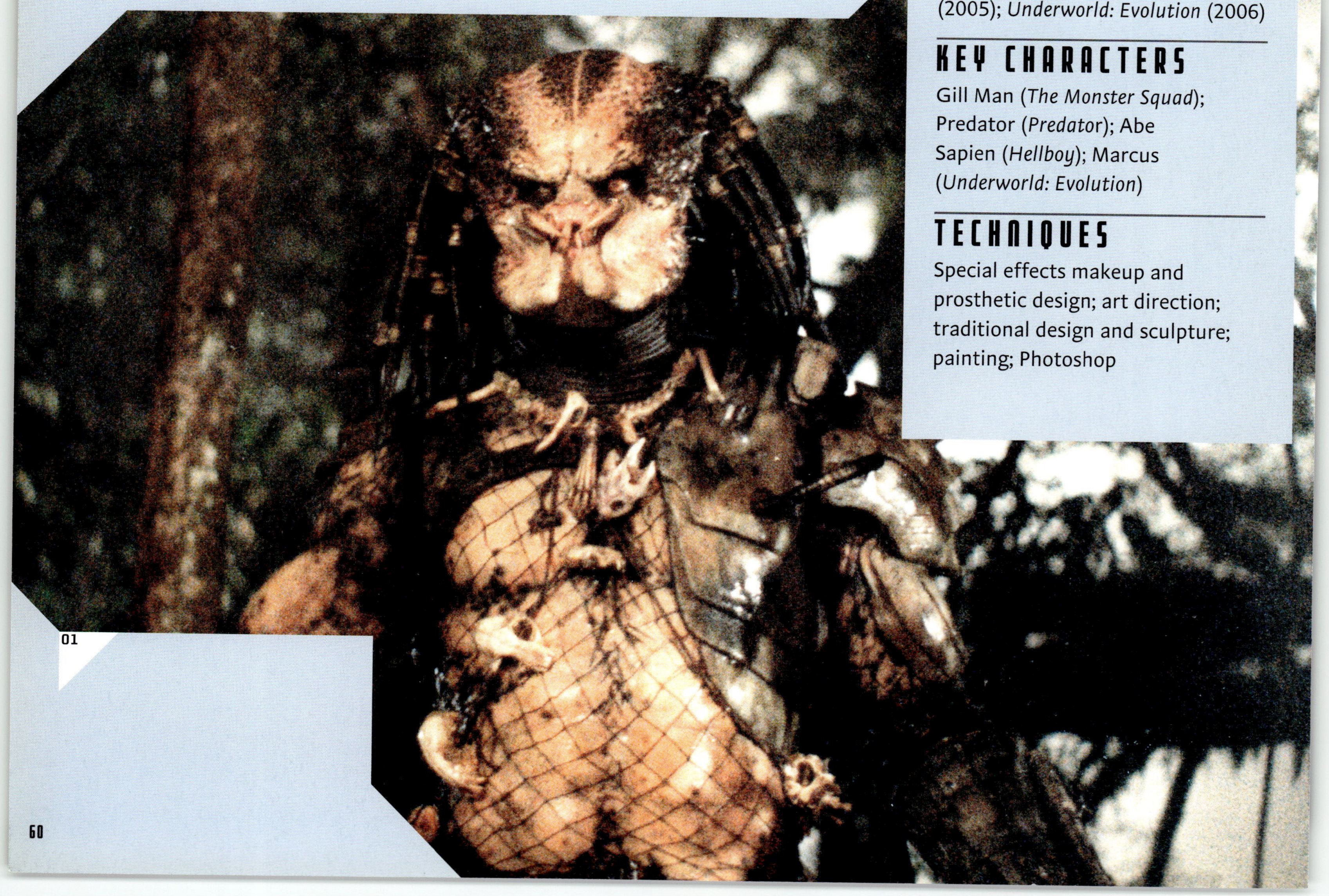

01

02

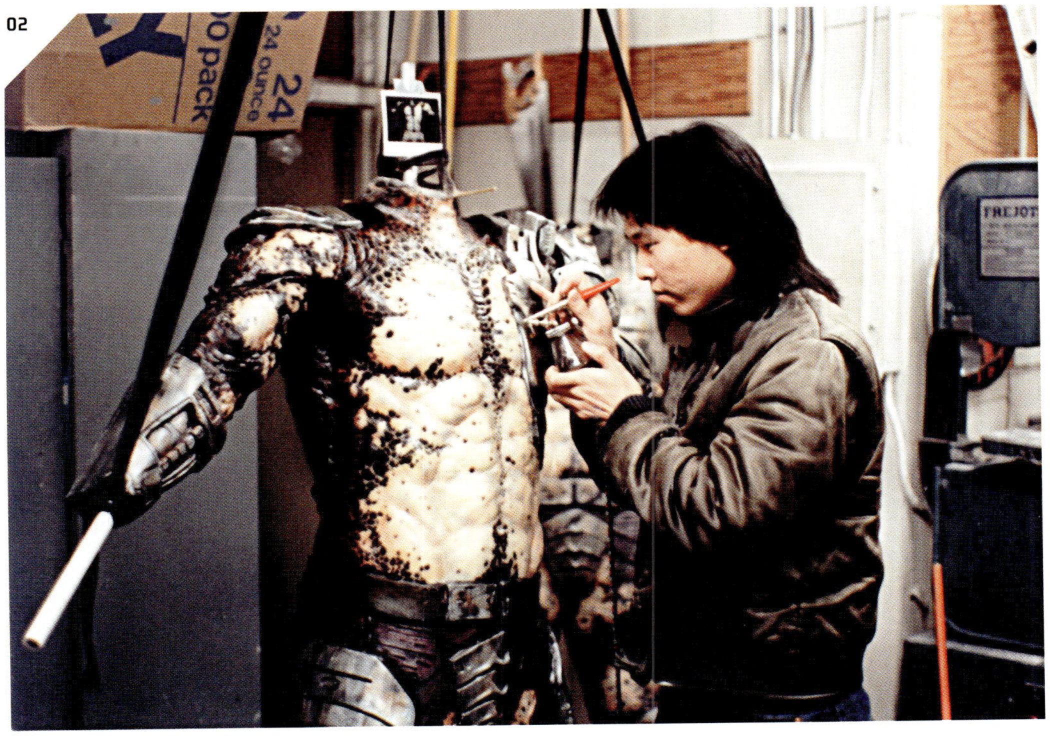

03

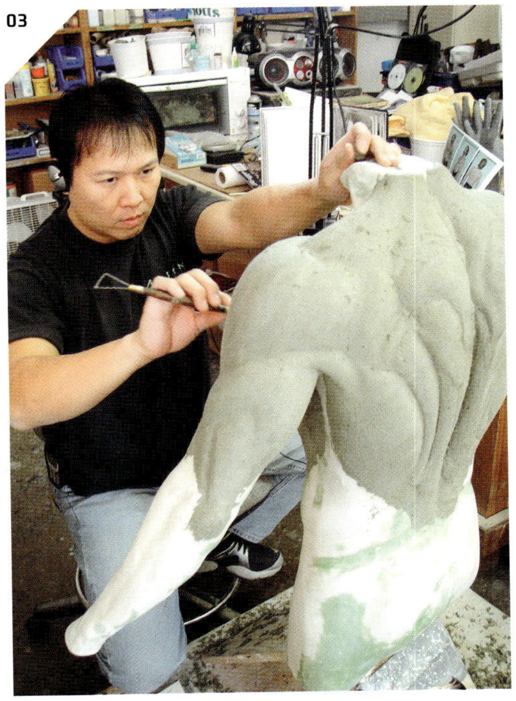

Steve Wang is one of Hollywood's most respected makeup artists. His talents as a designer, supervisor, sculptor, and painter are constantly in demand. He is particularly known for his striking naturalistic color designs and paintwork for characters in movies such as *Predator* (1987), *Gremlins 2: The New Batch* (1990), *Godzilla* (1998), and *Hellboy* (2004).

Wang was born in Taiwan, but moved to the USA with his family when he was nine. Much about life in America was new to him, but one of his discoveries triggered a passion that would lead him to become one of the most in-demand makeup talents in Hollywood. "A little while after we arrived in the US I noticed that the shops in the local mall were suddenly filled with these amazing rubber masks," explains Wang. "I'd always had a fascination with masks as a kid, but back in Taiwan the masks we had were pretty simple—just cardboard cutouts with an elastic band on the back. But these new masks were very elaborate and covered your whole head. Of course, I soon discovered that the masks were for Halloween, something we didn't have in Taiwan."

Wang began collecting rubber masks, and within four years had accumulated over 40. "Pretty soon, simply owning masks was not enough for me, and I wanted to know how to make them," he explains. "I got hold of a bunch of books about theatrical makeup, but they weren't very useful. However, I studied the photos in *Famous Monsters* magazine carefully, and worked out that it all started with sculpting. Then I got hold of some really cheap modeling clay, and started shaping it with my hands and digging away at it with forks and spoons." Wang's skills as a sculptor quickly improved, perhaps because he was already very accomplished at drawing and painting. By the age of 18 he had established his own mask-making business with fellow enthusiast Matt Rose.

Wang and Rose decided that they wanted careers in the movie business, and so in 1985 they moved to Los Angeles. "We went around the different makeup studios and were pretty lucky. Within a week we were hired by Alec Gillis at Stan Winston Studio to work on *Invaders from Mars* (1986). We weren't doing anything creative, but we learned how to run foam, clean molds, and all that kind of thing." Toward the end of the project, Wang had proved himself enough to be assigned a major painting job on one of the movie's creatures. "I got to paint the brain part for the drone characters, which was a pretty big job. I think my work on that made a good impression at the studio."

(01) The Predator is perhaps Steve Wang's best known paintwork achievement **(02)** Wang paints an original Predator suit at Stan Winston Studio **(03)** Wang sculpts the torso of the vampire, Marcus, for *Underworld: Evolution* (2006).

04

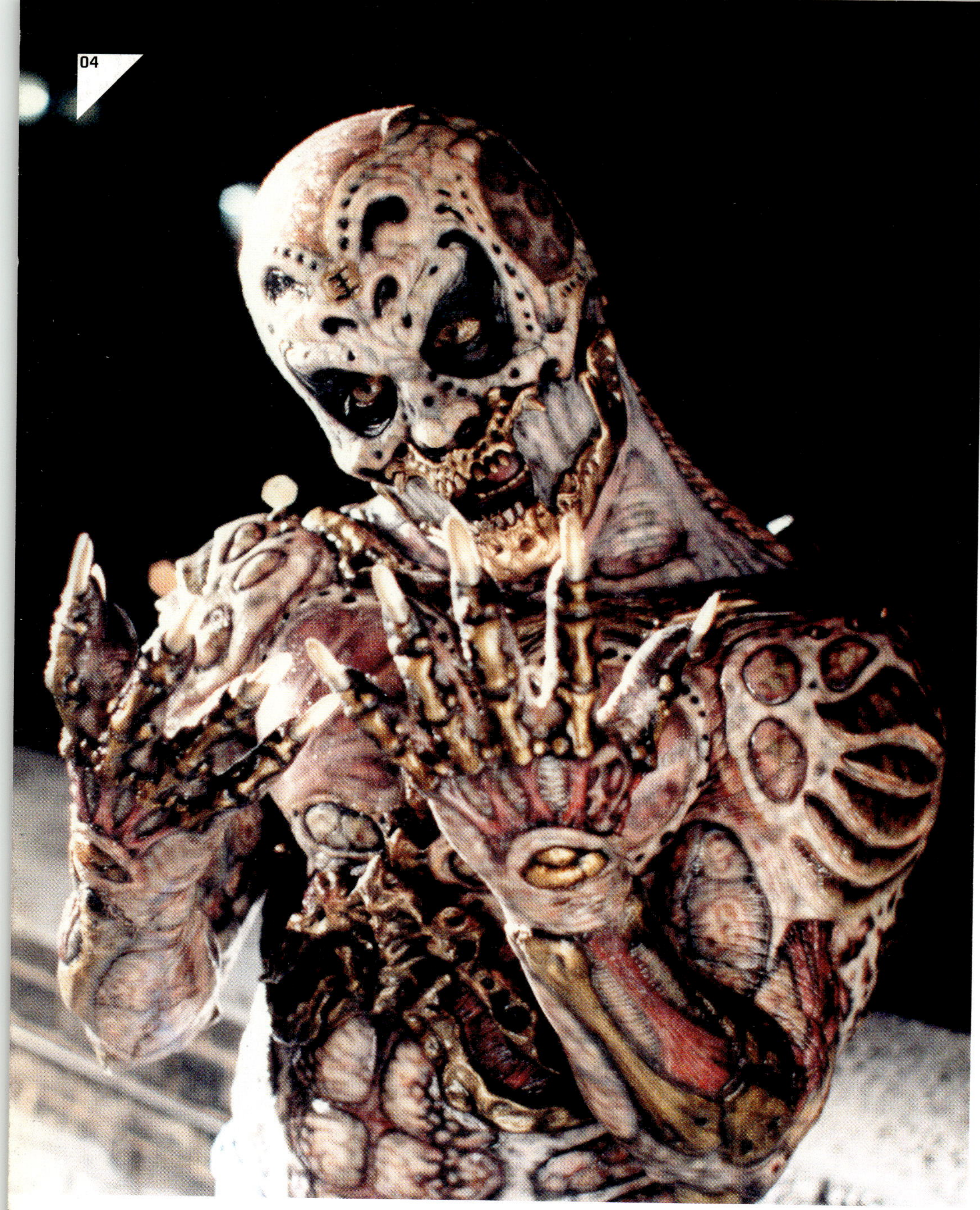

Working freelance, like most artists in the makeup business, Wang moved from one job to another, learning different skills and techniques at a number of studios, including Boss Films and Kevin Yeager Productions. Eventually he found himself back at Stan Winston Studio, where he worked with Matt Rose to create a seamless monster suit for the Gill Man character in *The Monster Squad* (1987).

Wang is particularly proud of the paint job that he did on Gill Man, considering it to be one of his early achievements. "I had been influenced by the alien paintwork done by Chris Walas for *Enemy Mine* [1985]," says Wang. "Those designs used a kind of aquatic camouflage pattern, which I thought was good, but a bit crude and flat-looking. For Gill Man I designed a color scheme that was very influenced by aquatic creatures; I thought that if this character lived under the water his patterns and coloration should really resemble a fish. When I showed my paper designs to Stan he just shrugged them off dismissively. However, at about the same time I made a hermit crab monster suit with a similar camouflage-like pattern, which I entered into the first annual Screaming Mad George Halloween contest—a contest for makeup professionals. It was being judged by Rick Baker, Dick Smith, Tom Burman, and Stan Winston. The suit won first prize and got lots of praise for its paintwork and color design. After that Stan came up to me and said, 'So that's want you want to do on Gill Man, huh?' And so that is what we did!"

05

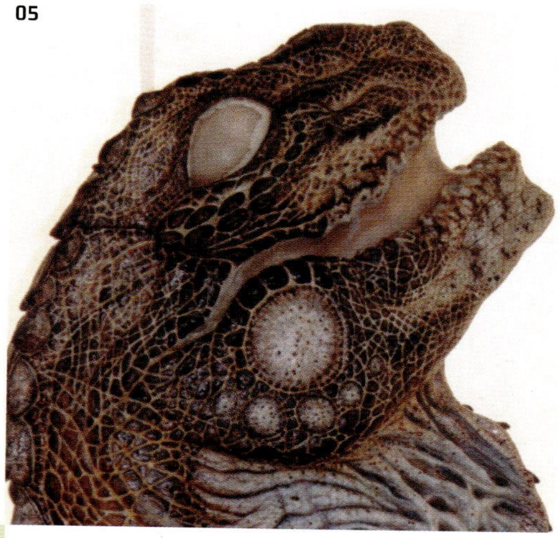

Wang and Rose next worked as sculptors at Rick Baker's studio—then known as Boris, Inc.—on various projects, including *Harry and the Hendersons* (1987). "It was very nerve-racking; Rick really threw us in at the deep end," remembers Wang. "The first thing I sculpted was a set of hands, something I'd never done before. But I learned really fast because I was in a creative environment and surrounded by great artists. I probably learned more in my first year in Hollywood than in the previous six years put together."

06

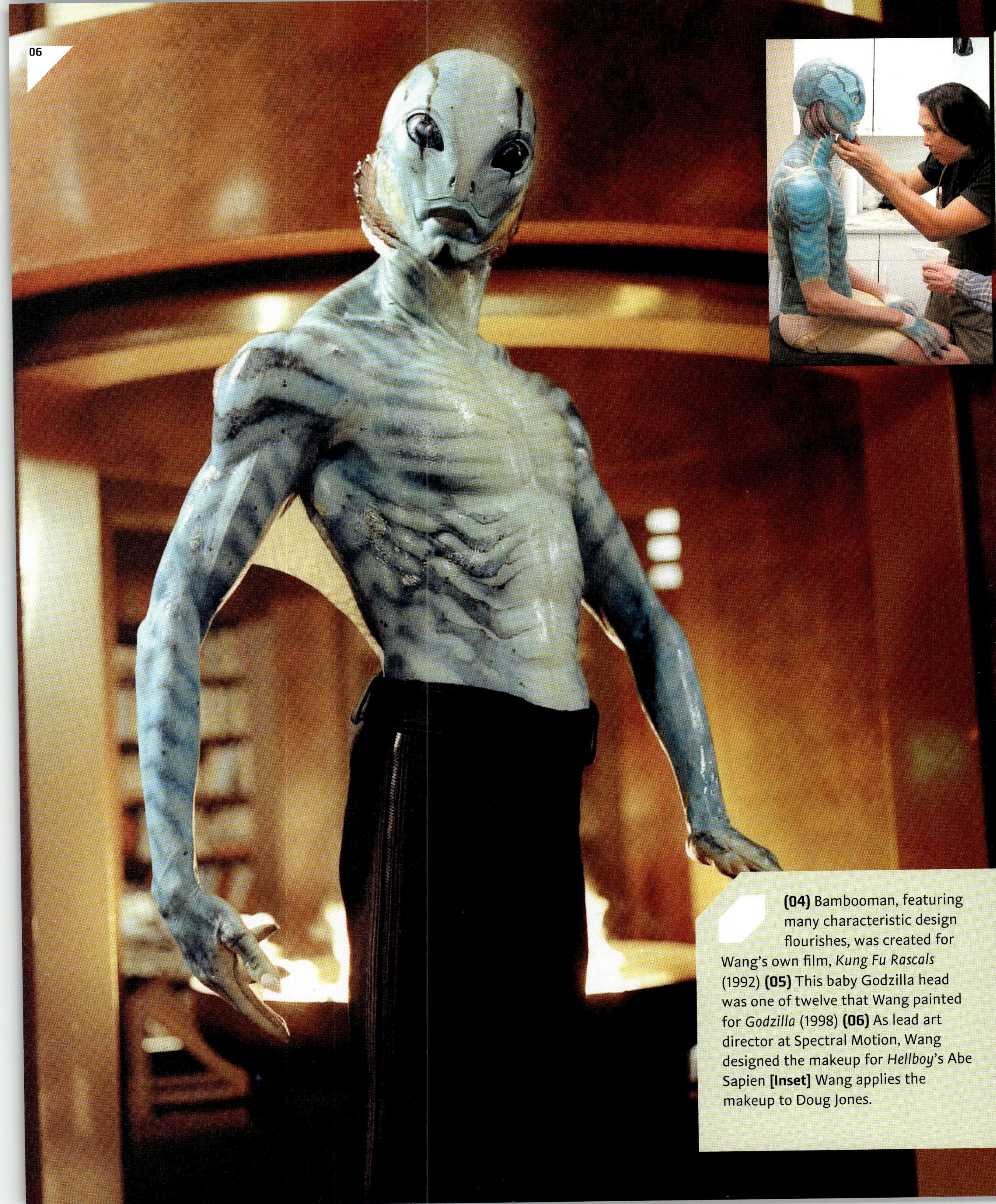

(04) Bambooman, featuring many characteristic design flourishes, was created for Wang's own film, *Kung Fu Rascals* (1992) **(05)** This baby Godzilla head was one of twelve that Wang painted for *Godzilla* (1998) **(06)** As lead art director at Spectral Motion, Wang designed the makeup for *Hellboy*'s Abe Sapien **[Inset]** Wang applies the makeup to Doug Jones.

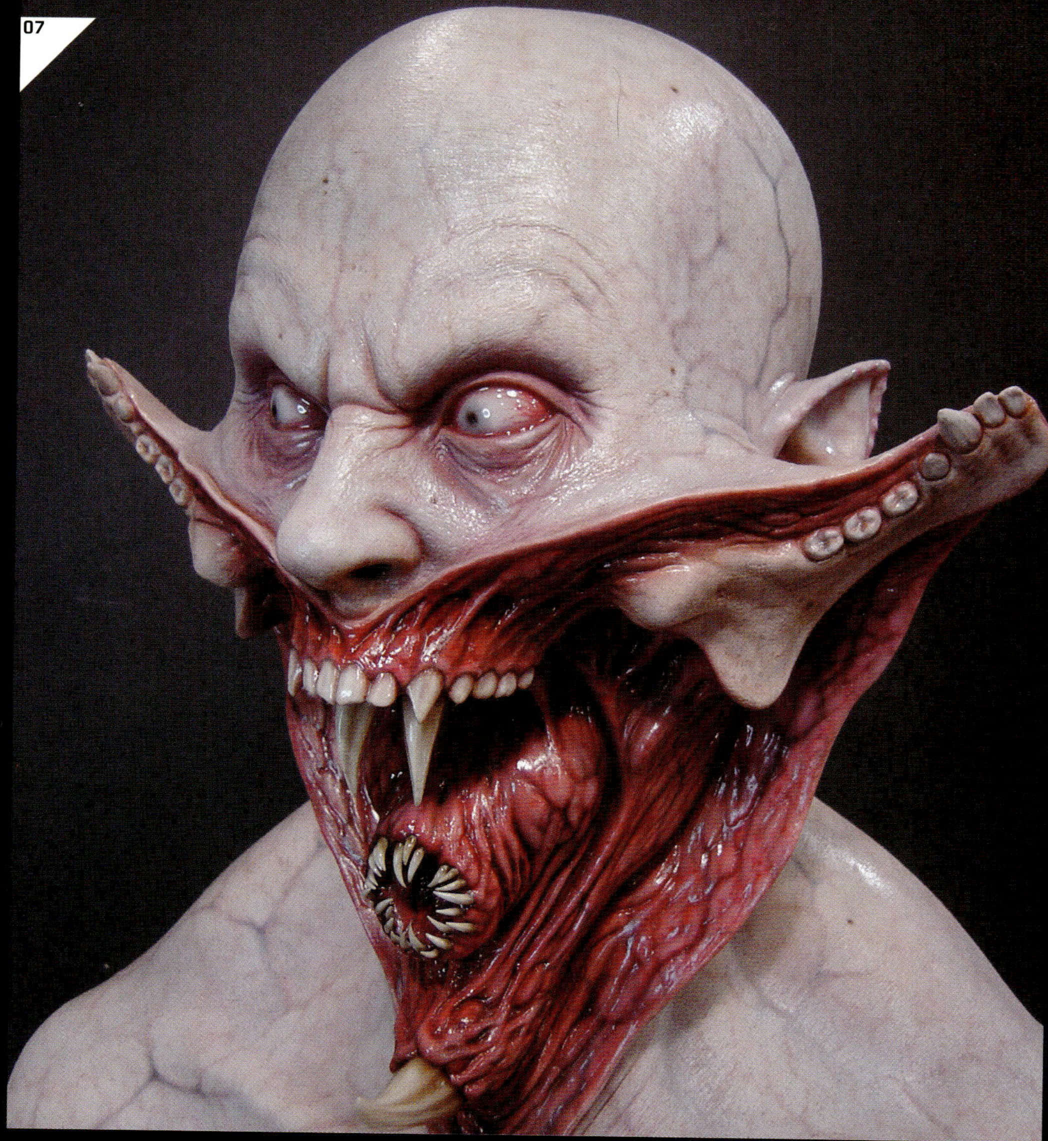

07

Stan Winston next hired Wang to work on the makeup for *Predator* (1987). "I really wanted to do something great with *Predator*, and to build on what I had done with my paintwork for Gill Man," says Wang. "I spent a lot of time studying fish like koi carp and insects such as locusts to get a sense of how the colors should work, which areas should be more or less translucent, how the areas of pigment broke up around the face, and so on." Wang's paintwork on *Predator* produced a startling creature that remains a favorite among many fans to this day. The style was so distinctive that it was emulated in a number of other characters, becoming known as the "Steve Wang paint job."

Wang describes the process he typically uses to design one of his color schemes: "I usually begin on paper first, starting with basic pattern designs, often in pencil, before developing the colors in watercolors or, more often today, painting in the computer. I use a paint program called Painter. Unlike Photoshop, which most people use, Painter does not allow you to paint your image in editable layers. You paint colors on top of other colors and if you make a mistake you have to paint over it, just as if you were using real paint. It's a trickier way to work, but because it's closer to traditional forms of painting I feel it helps me to remain practiced at the art and remain sharp.

"Once I've designed the colors and patterns on paper I do a written color breakdown, in which I note which colors to use, which order to use them, and how the different colors will react with one another. A lot of people find being this meticulous a bit unnecessary and tedious. I remember when I was planning the Gill Man color scheme, and Stan Winston asked what I was writing, when I told him what I was doing, he said, 'That's not how you design paint jobs. The way you design paint jobs is you put paint in an airbrush and start painting.' I was a bit young and cocky, and I told him that was not how you make a paint job—it's how you make a mess! Of course, a lot of good people do just go straight into painting, but I like to do all the planning up front. That way, when I am painting all I have to concentrate on is getting the detail and look of the colors absolu tely perfect."

Like all artists Wang uses a range of materials and techniques to produce the final result. "For foam-rubber and latex costumes I use a rubber-cement paint which is mixed with universal tints to get the color I need. That mix is then thinned down with either naphtha or Bestine thinner until it's the right consistency to be sprayed through an airbrush. This color is instantly absorbed when it is sprayed on, to give a really good finish.

"I always use a technique called underpainting," explains Wang. "Some people just paint a base coat and then paint the highlights and the shadows on top of that. This can work OK, but I don't feel it gives enough complexity or depth. I always start with a base coat—the basic flesh tone—then I'll go in with various shades, like reds and browns, to make really subtle mottling all over the skin, which always makes it look a bit of a mess. Then you go in and add the veins and arteries. I then overpaint all of that with another coat of paint which is similar to the original base coat. Depending on how dark or heavy that coat is, I can really affect the levels of opacity or translucency in the skin—if you look at your own skin you'll see that some areas look more translucent than others and that's what I try to achieve."

Using these techniques to apply a coat of paint just a few microns thick, Wang is able to give solid foam rubber an amazing sense of depth and translucency, transforming an inert material into something that appears to be alive. However, the process does not stop there. "Once I have applied that second layer of overpaint, I have then created my first-stage base coat. This is my basic skin, on which I will build the majority of the patterning and color that gives a character its true appearance. Using my written plan, I then add all of the highlights and shadows, patterns, blemishes, age-spots, and so on, using just one color at a time over the entire creature.

"Many of the characters I do with camouflage patterns contain a lot of blacks and dark colors, and with those it's only with the very final couple of colors that the creature will come to life and look any good. Until then it'll be a messy mixture of tones that don't really work. The final addition will be several different types of gloss that add the appearance of additional translucency, or perhaps slime or mucus. In order to tell how the character is likely to look under the lights during filming, I'll normally take a few Polaroid or digital photos as I go along.

08

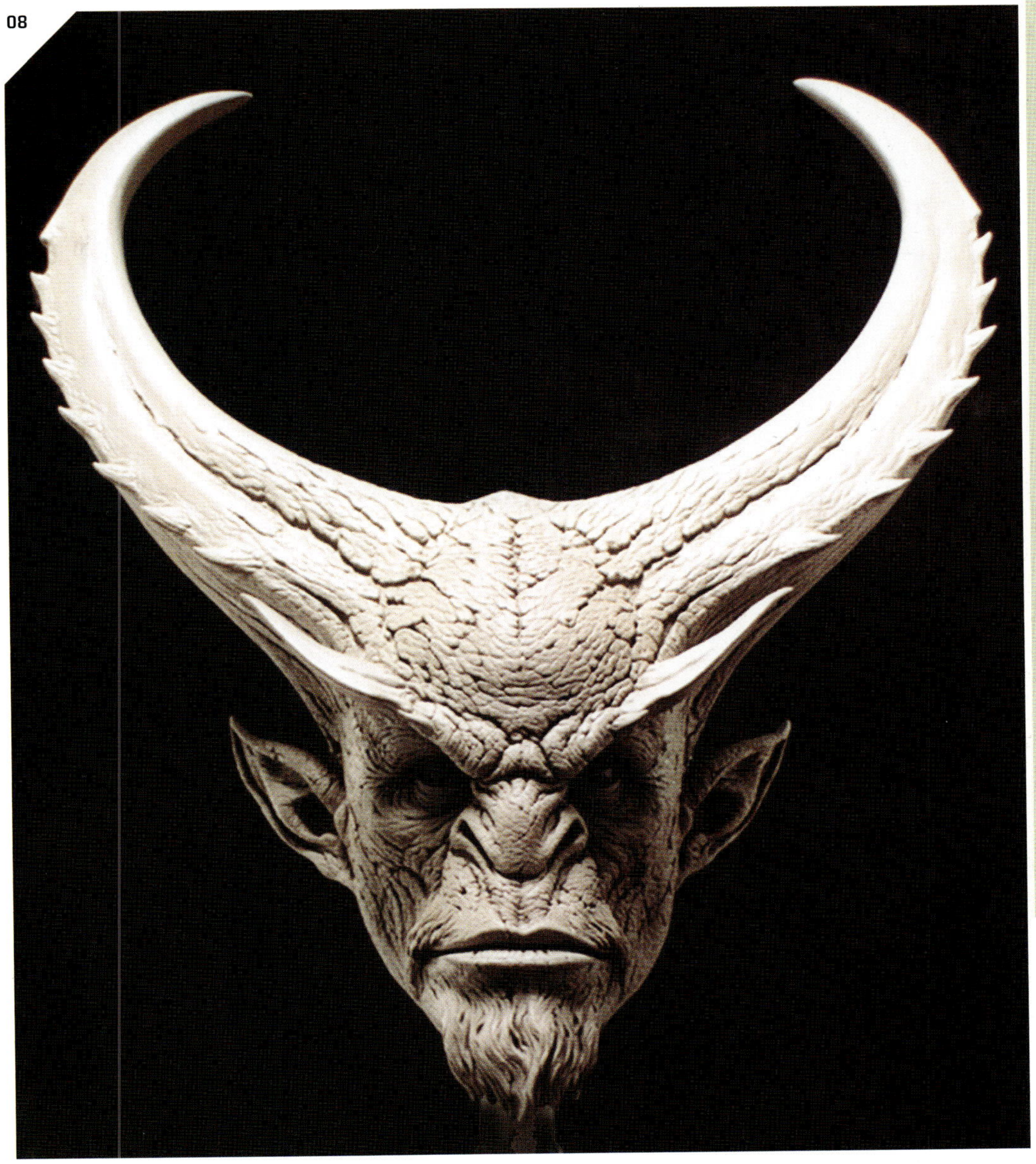

09

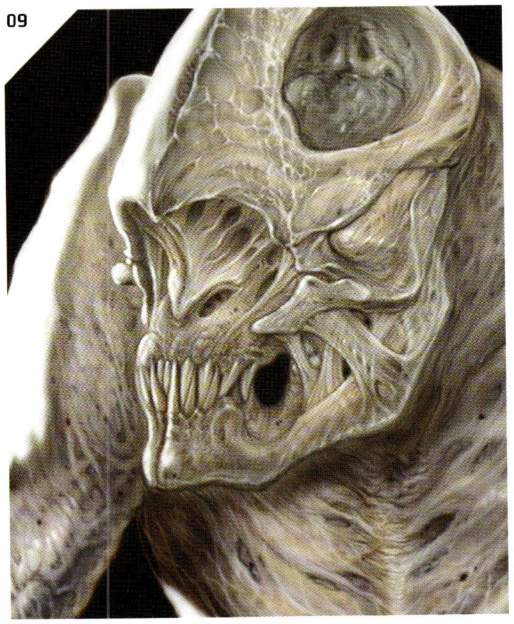

(07) Wang made this tribute to the Reaper vampire makeup in *Blade II* (2002), with which he was not involved, for a private collector **(08)** Wang sculpted this Demon character while working on *Bedazzled* at ADI **(09)** One of many paint designs created by Wang for *The Cave* (2005).

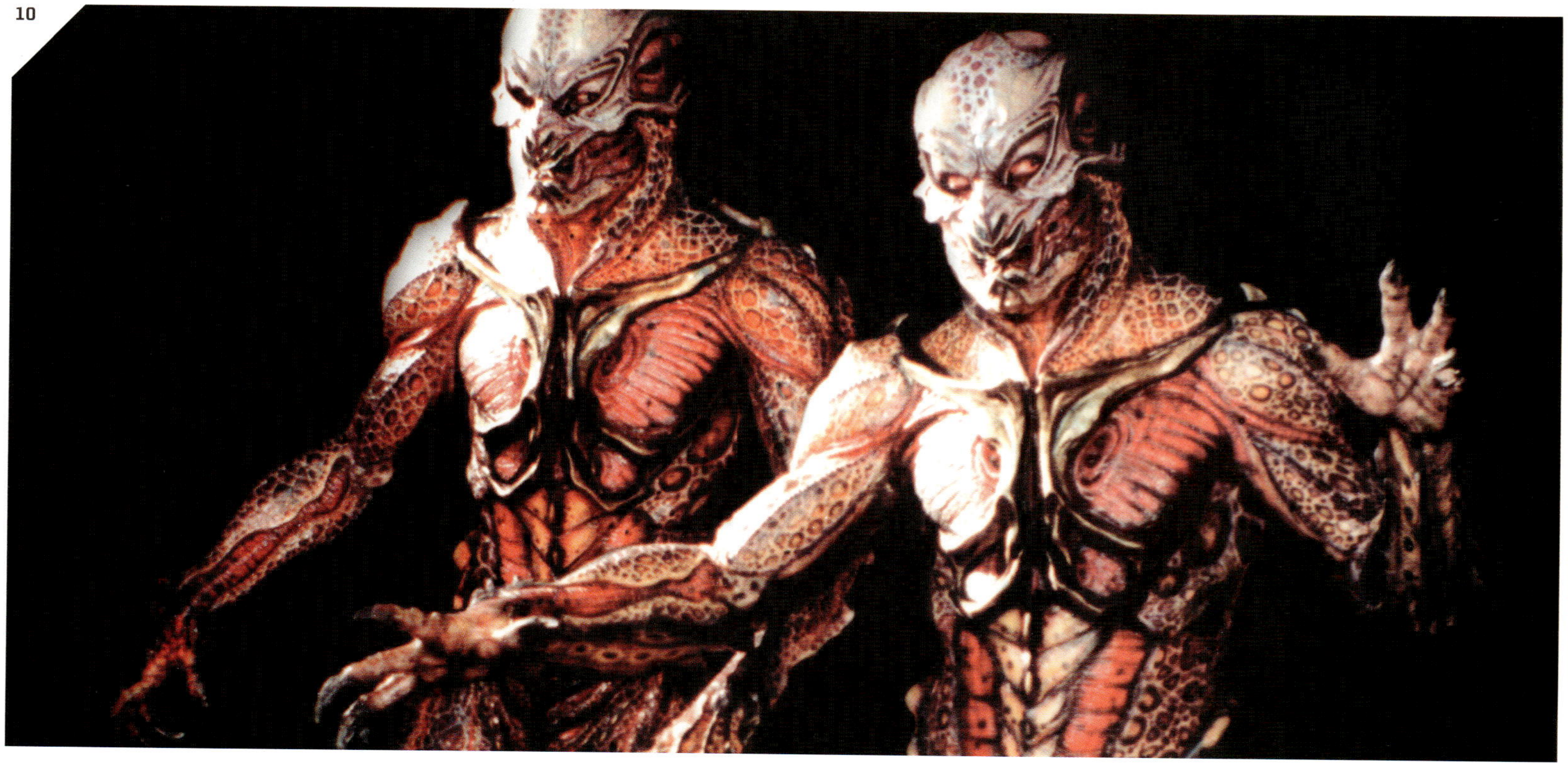

"This really allows me to step back and see how the character looks when photographed and provides a sense of distance, an objectivity, that is useful when evaluating the work. I often spot things in a photo that weren't obvious to the naked eye."

When painting, Wang is always conscious that his work must complement the original sculpture. "When you sculpt a character you tend to make detail more exaggerated than in real life because you want those details to show up on film," he explains. "If you were sculpting scales or folds in skin, for example, you might make them around 20 percent deeper than they would be in reality. However, it's very easy to obliterate that work with a flat paint job. Your job as a painter is to accentuate the design, adding highlight, shadow, and color to emphasize what the sculptor has done and to draw the eye to the important details, like the mouth, the eyes, and the muscle tone. Although we are very often inspired by nature, our aim is not always to reproduce nature—our work is very theatrical, and is there to serve the movie. Equally, sometimes nature does things we wouldn't dare to copy—there are some crazy bright-red-and-blue tree-frogs out there, but if we apply those color schemes to our artificial characters they're just instantly implausible, however hard we try to make them look good."

Ultimately, though, it is nature in all its forms that inspires Wang. "Animals are inspirational, but so are natural phenomena. I can spend a long time looking at an oil slick on the pavement—how the colors pattern, swirl, clump, and break up. I remember one time years ago when I was on a flight and I looked out of the window, there were ice crystals forming on the glass. I looked at all the incredible patterns in the ice, and then I noticed the mountains on the ground below—where rivers had carved out canyons and the stone had fractured, and so on. It struck me that the patterns I was seeing in the ice and on the ground were really similar. It is all part of the grand design: that the forces of nature govern everything on the planet. I try to reflect that in the flow of my sculptures and the look of my paint jobs, and I think that brings a strong sense of reality to what I create."

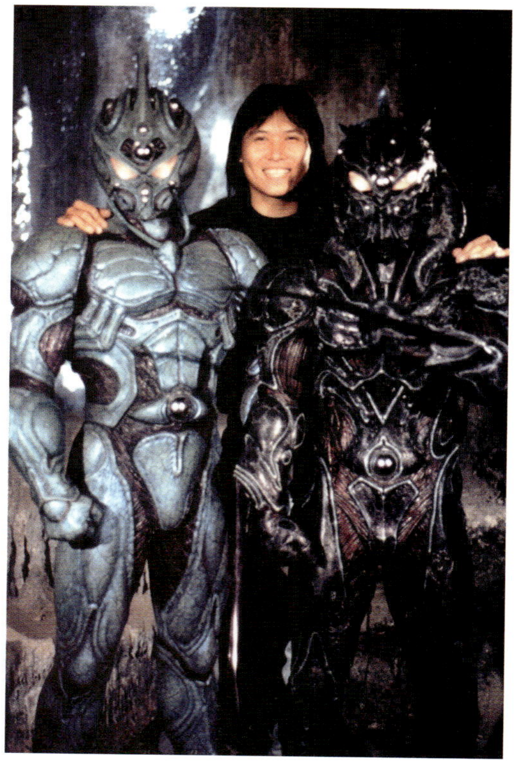

12

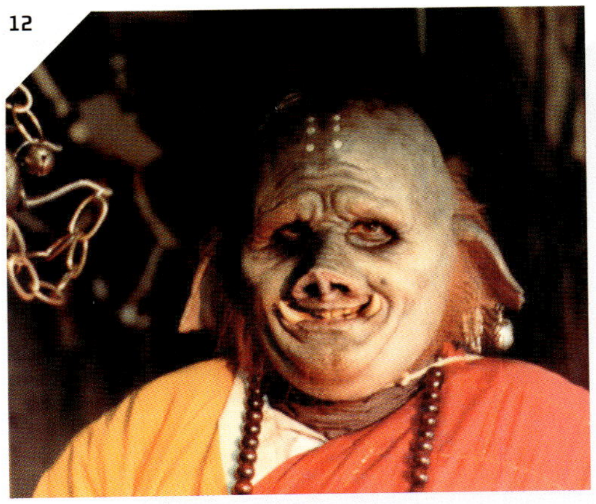

13

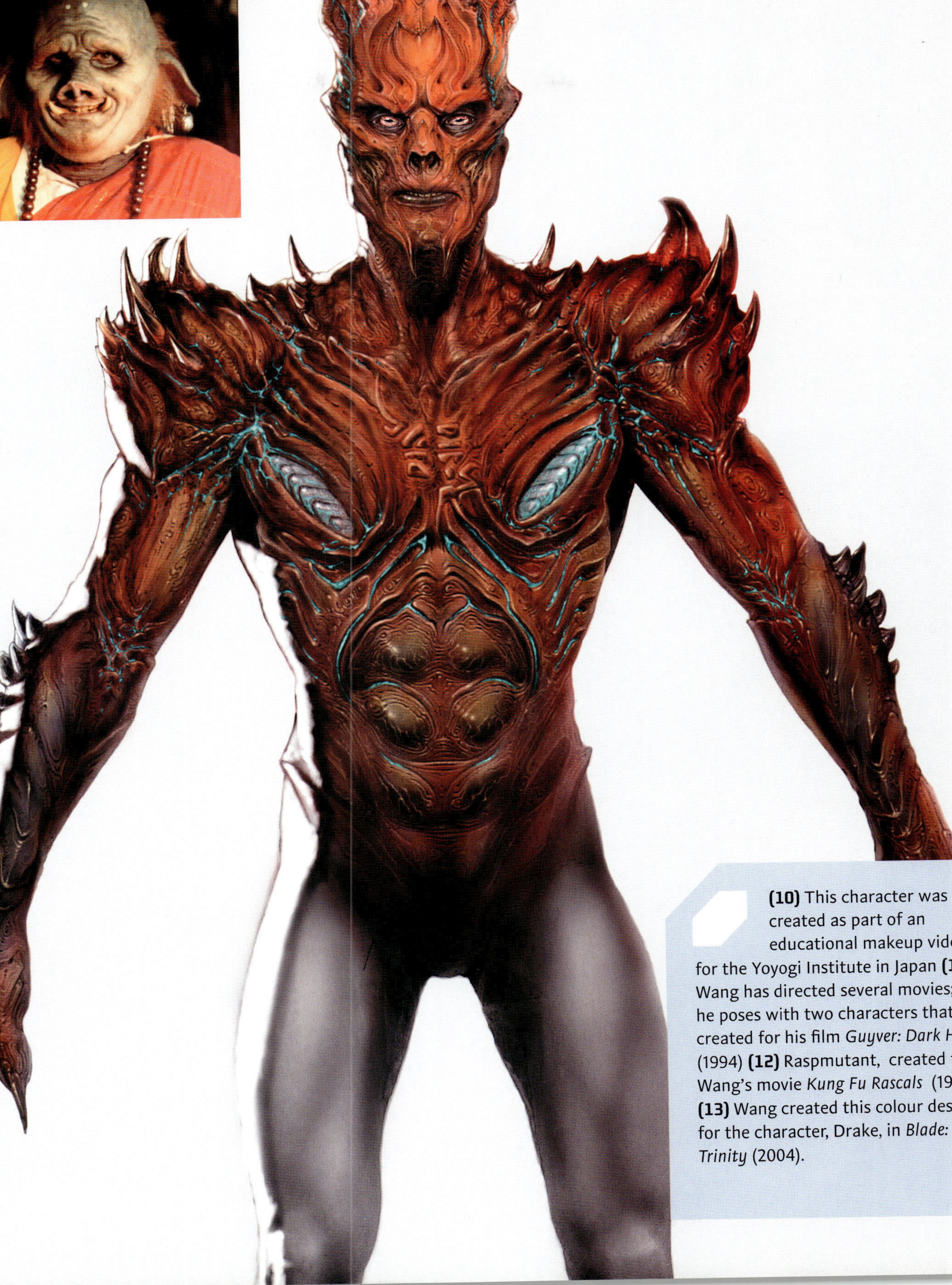

(10) This character was created as part of an educational makeup video for the Yoyogi Institute in Japan **(11)** Wang has directed several movies; here he poses with two characters that he created for his film *Guyver: Dark Hero* (1994) **(12)** Raspmutant, created for Wang's movie *Kung Fu Rascals* (1992) **(13)** Wang created this colour design for the character, Drake, in *Blade: Trinity* (2004).

PATRICK TATOPOULOS

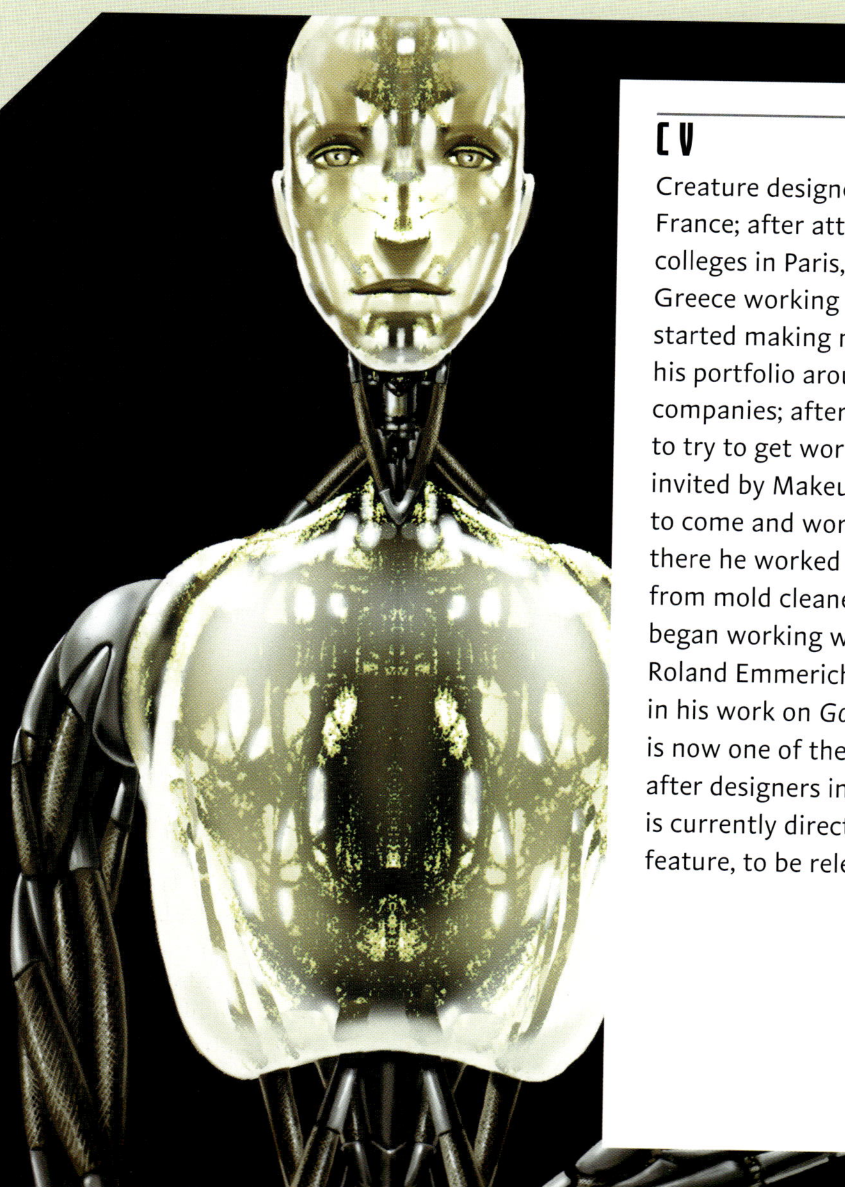

CV

Creature designer; b. Paris, France; after attending art colleges in Paris, spent time in Greece working as an illustrator; started making models and sent his portfolio around US makeup companies; after a visit to the US to try to get work, was eventually invited by Makeup Effects Group to come and work for them; there he worked his way up from mold cleaner to designer; began working with director Roland Emmerich, culminating in his work on *Godzilla* (1998); is now one of the most sought-after designers in Hollywood; is currently directing his first feature, to be released in 2007.

SELECT FILMOGRAPHY

Beastmaster 2: Through the Portal of Time (1991); *Super Mario Bros.* (1993); *Bram Stoker's Dracula* (1992); *Stargate* (1994); *Independence Day* (1996); *Dark City* (1998); *Godzilla* (1998); *Stuart Little* (1999); *They* (2002); *Underworld* (2003); *I, Robot* (2004); *Underworld: Evolution* (2006)

KEY CHARACTERS

Ra, Horus, Anubis, Mastadge (*Stargate*); aliens (*Independence Day*); Godzilla (*Godzilla*); Stuart Little (*Stuart Little*); werewolves (*Underworld*); NS-5 robot (*I, Robot*); Marcus (*Underworld: Evolution*)

TECHNIQUES

Character and production design; sculpting; special effects makeup and prosthetics; animatronics, CAD software

02

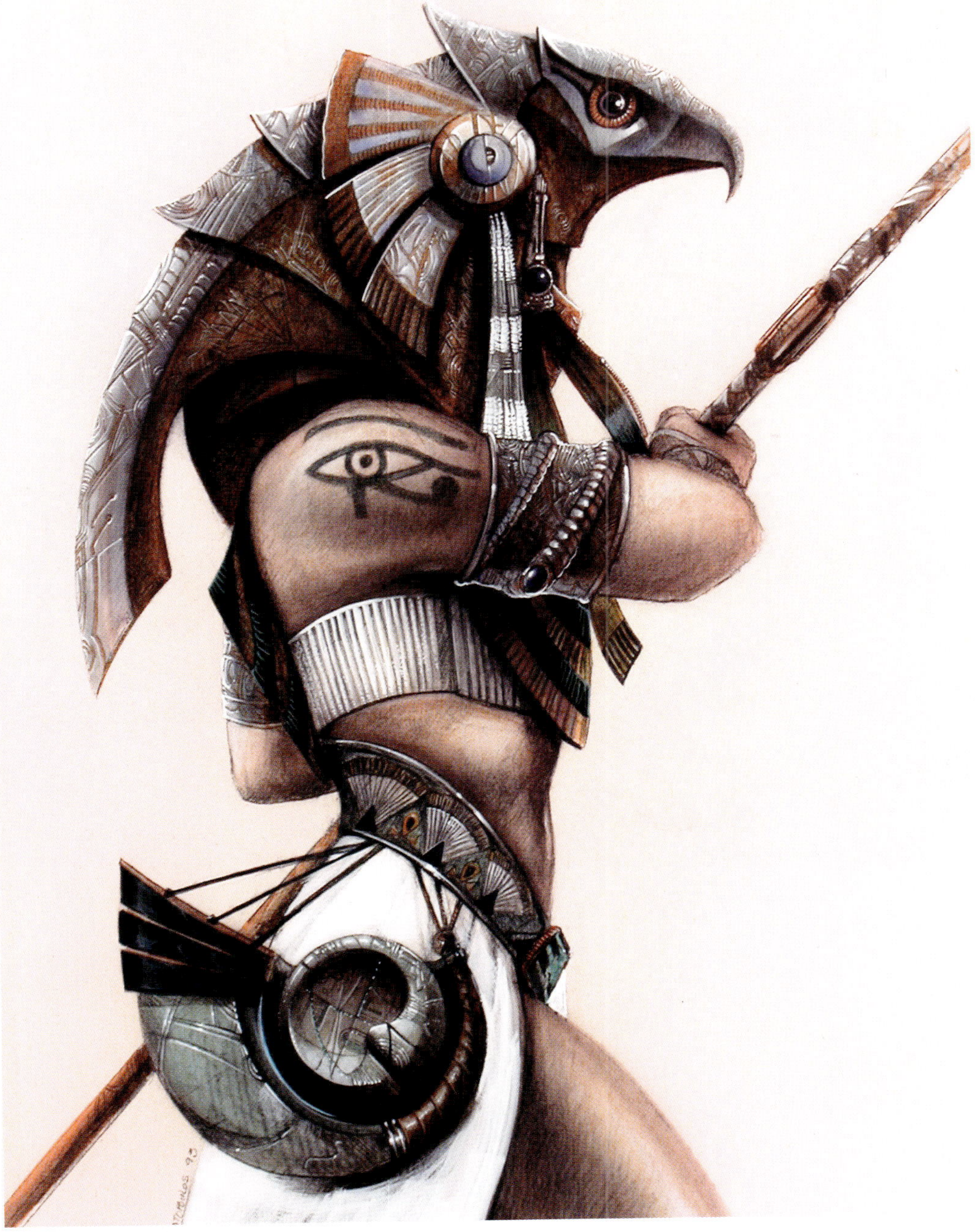

(01) Patrick Tatopoulos was production designer on *I, Robot* (2004), where his work included the design of the movie's central robot characters **(02)** This magnificent Horus was one of the initial *Stargate* designs by Tatopoulos.

Patrick Tatopoulos was born in Paris to a French mother and Greek father. As a child he would spend the weekends watching his grandfather, a keen amateur artist, painting and drawing. Tatopoulos studied art at the Ecole d'Art Décoratif de Paris, the Ecole d'Art Appliqués de Paris, and the city's famous Ecole des Beaux-Arts. "Then one day in 1983, a friend showed me a copy of *Cinefex* magazine," he says. It showed the makeup and effects for *Something Wicked This Way Comes* [1983]. I thought it was so cool. At about the same time I saw John Carpenter's *The Thing* [1982] and the creature effects were just amazing. I thought to myself, 'Somebody out there is actually creating all this stuff!' Then I knew that was what I wanted to do."

Tatopoulos threw himself into creature design. "I went straight out and bought some clay. Not sculpting clay, but ordinary clay—I didn't even know there was a difference," laughs Tatopoulos. "I sculpted about five characters, which I painted and then photographed to produce a portfolio. Then I called all the big makeup companies in America."

Arriving in the USA, Tatopoulos discovered that his portfolio had been lost in transit. He spent a frustrated few days visiting luminaries such as Stan Winston and Rick Baker with nothing to show them. With one day left, the missing luggage arrived, but only Makeup Effects Group (MEG) could see him at short notice. A month later they called and said they could give him some work and help him get his Green Card.

Working at MEG for two years, Tatopoulos learned about every aspect of creating makeup, prosthetics, and animatronics, working his way up from making molds to designing characters for the *Star Trek: The Next Generation* TV series and the movie *Beastmaster 2* (1991). His first job as production designer came with *Super Mario Bros* (1993), but then his dark, sumptuous makeup designs for Francis Ford Coppola's *Bram Stoker's Dracula* (1992) brought Tatopoulos to the attention of director Roland

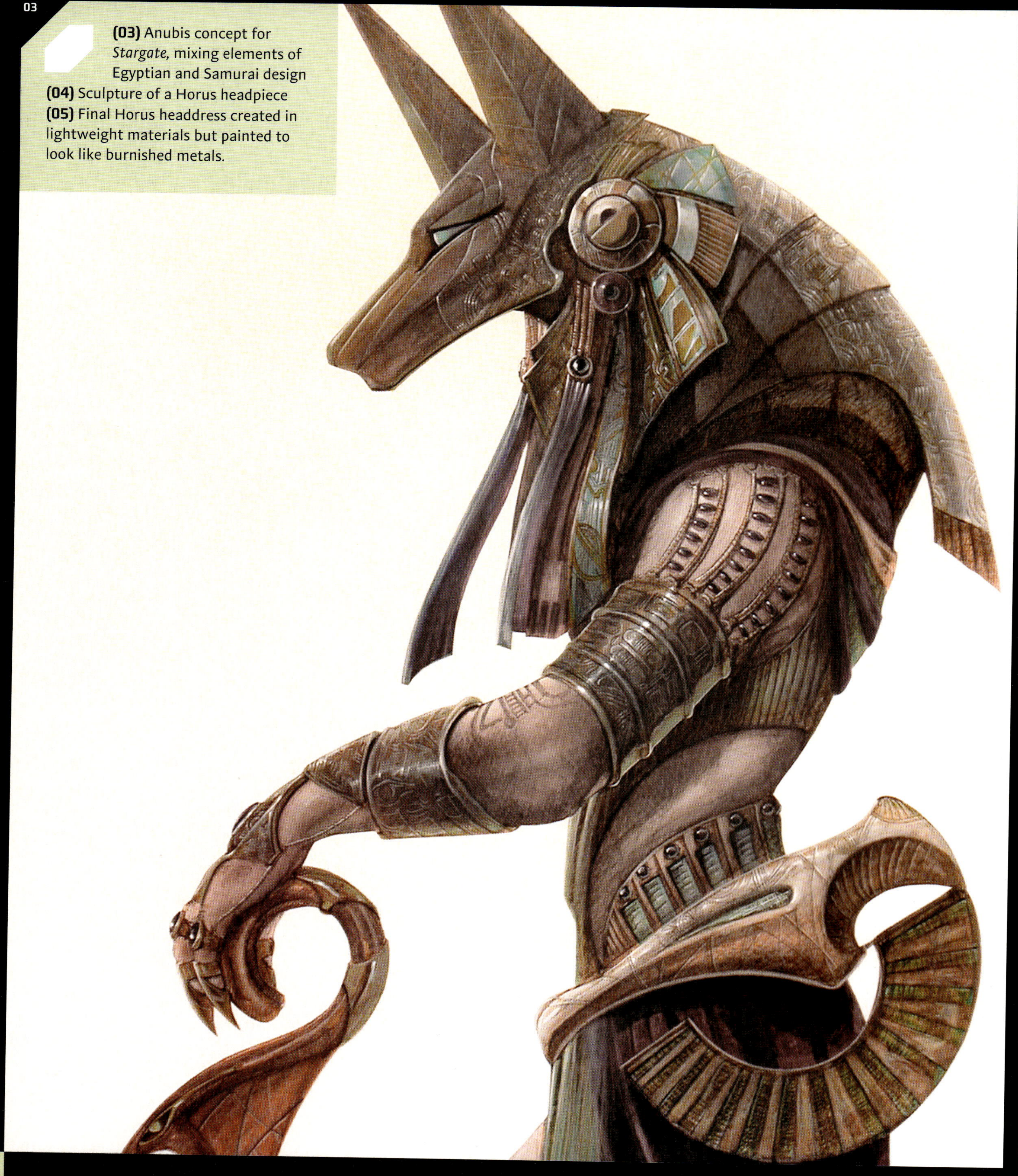

(03) Anubis concept for *Stargate*, mixing elements of Egyptian and Samurai design
(04) Sculpture of a Horus headpiece
(05) Final Horus headdress created in lightweight materials but painted to look like burnished metals.

04

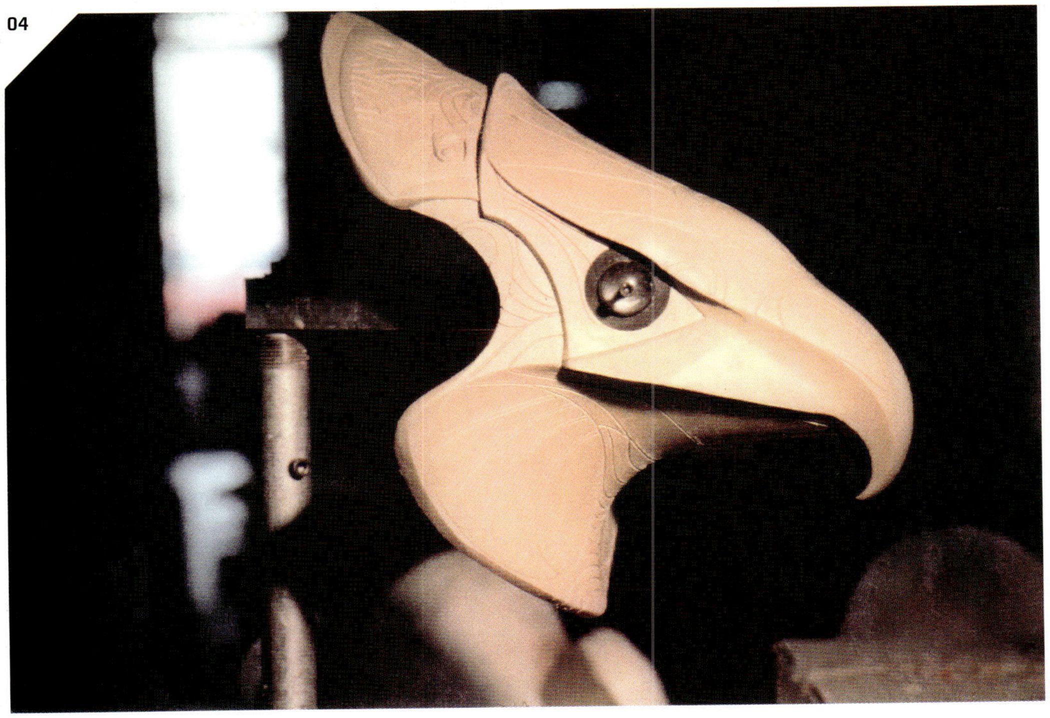

05

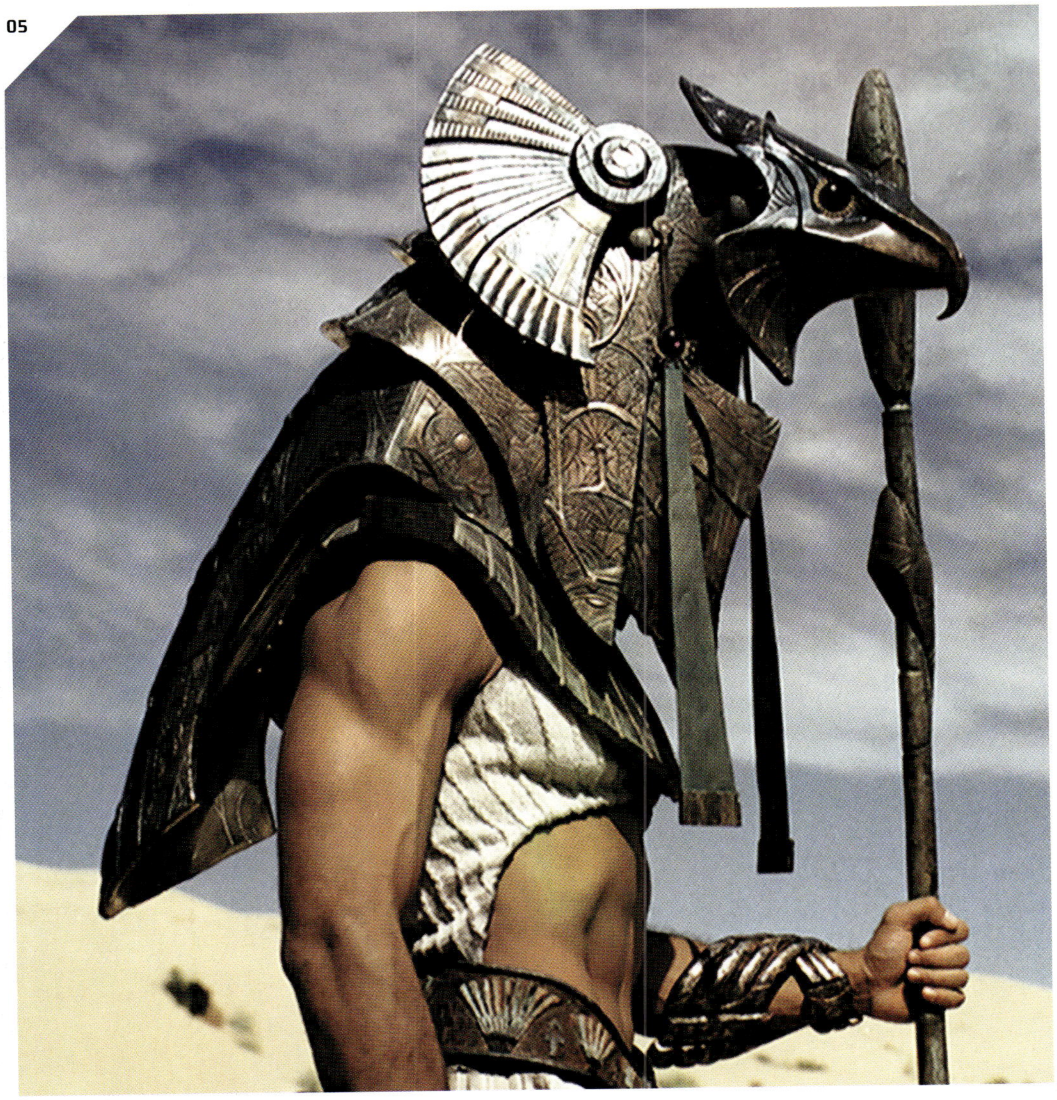

Emmerich. The German director hired him to design characters for his first Hollywood movie, *Stargate* (1994).

"The three main characters to create were Ra, Horus, and Anubis," says Tatopoulos. "When I'm asked to design a character, all I need to do is read the script. Then I sit and I draw. To be a good designer I think you need to have a wealth of knowledge about artistic and cultural styles, about biology, anatomy and different types of animals. You are constantly observing these things. Then, when you draw, you don't need to think about these things, they will inform your work almost instinctively." Emmerich asked him if he would also build the designs himself. "I took a deep breath and said yes. Within a few weeks I had found a building, hired many of the best people I had worked with over the last few years, and set up my own company. It was a scary thing to do."

In addition to the humanoid characters, the *Stargate* script called for a large animal called a Mastadge that could be ridden across the desert like a camel. "There was no money for CG or complex animatronics, yet we had to find a way to make walking creatures," says Tatopoulos. "The obvious answer was to use a real animal and dress it up."

Tatopoulos decided on a massive Clydesdale horse. "The horse wore a normal saddle, and attached to that was the lightweight metal framework on which the Mastdadge body was hung. The body, complete with a huge camel-like hump, was covered in long yak hair that trailed down over the sides of the horse. The horse's legs were dressed with slip-on Lycra leggings that were also covered in yak hair."

The head of the Mastadge took six redesigns until the final look—a leathery combination of a camel and a cow, with a few traces of lizard—was cast in foam latex and mounted on a steel bar that was attached to the horse's neck. Facial movement was controlled by motors and servos that were built into the head

06

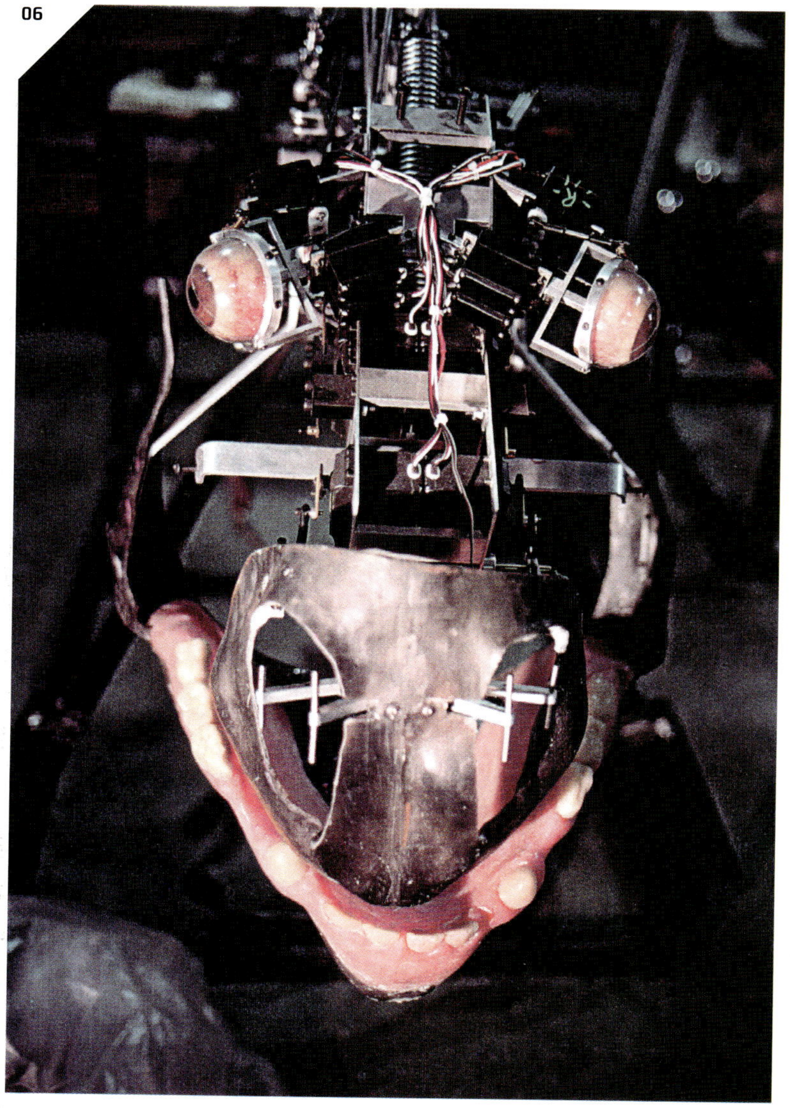

07

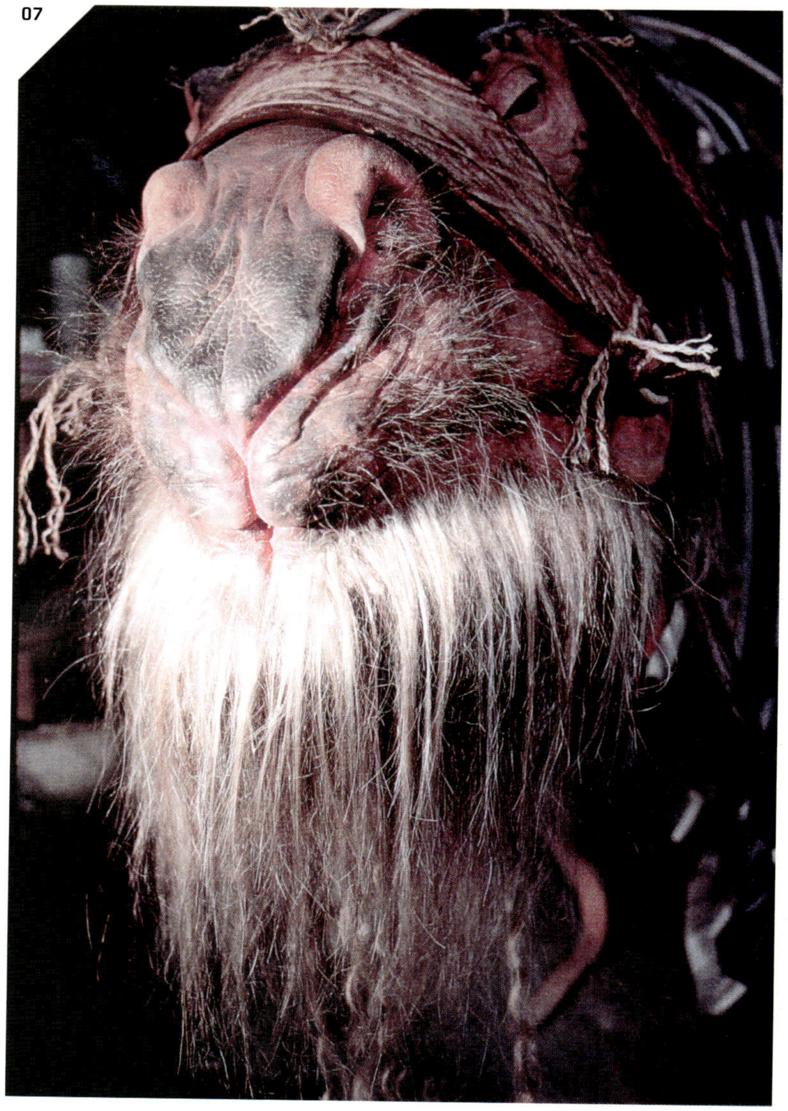

08

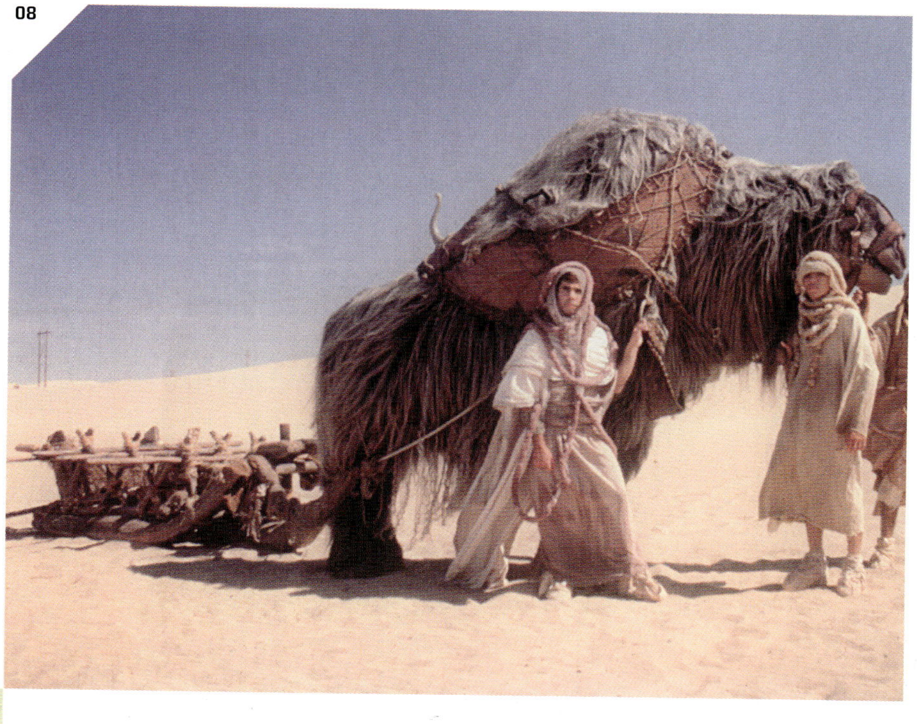

09

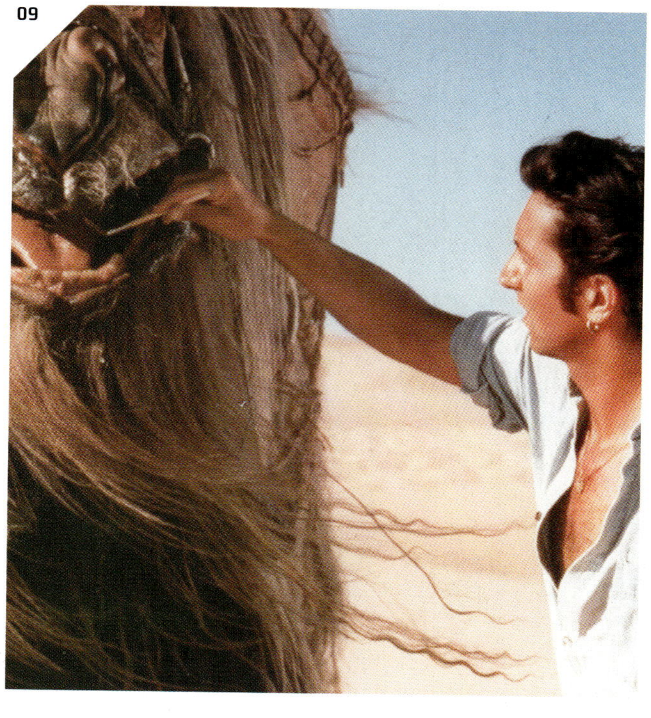

and radio-controlled by a team of four puppeteers. The beast was controlled by a small rider, who sat in a cage over the animal's haunches. The costume was gradually introduced to the animal over a long period so the horse would not be terrified by the experience.

"The problem was we needed a few shots of the Mastadge galloping across the sand dunes, and that would have been dangerous for horse and rider," adds Tatopoulos. "So we thought, 'Why not put a costume on another animal?' We built a small version of the costume that fitted an Australian shepherd dog. We then made a doll of the actor James Spader and filmed the dog running across the dunes dragging the puppet behind him. It was filmed at high-speed so the final footage made the dog look heavier and slower."

After he had finished all scheduled work on *Stargate*, Tatopoulos was asked to create a character for a last-minute change to the ending of the movie. "Roland decided that he wanted to see the alien that inhabited the Ra character, but the finished shot was needed in just a couple of weeks," explains Tatopoulos. "I quickly designed a very classic-looking alien. Within a week it was sculpted and we had produced a foam-rubber puppet that was operated with rods and had radio-controlled eyes and lips.

"Roland wanted to see this alien burning and turning to ash. For this we used the same mold, but filled it with papier mâché to produce a head made of thin paper. After it was painted the head was prescored so that it was covered with invisible cuts. Then we placed small explosive squibs on the inside of the head and filled it with shredded gray and black paper. During filming we blasted the head with high-pressure air at the same time as detonating the squibs. The head exploded into dust. This was all mixed together with footage of flames."

10

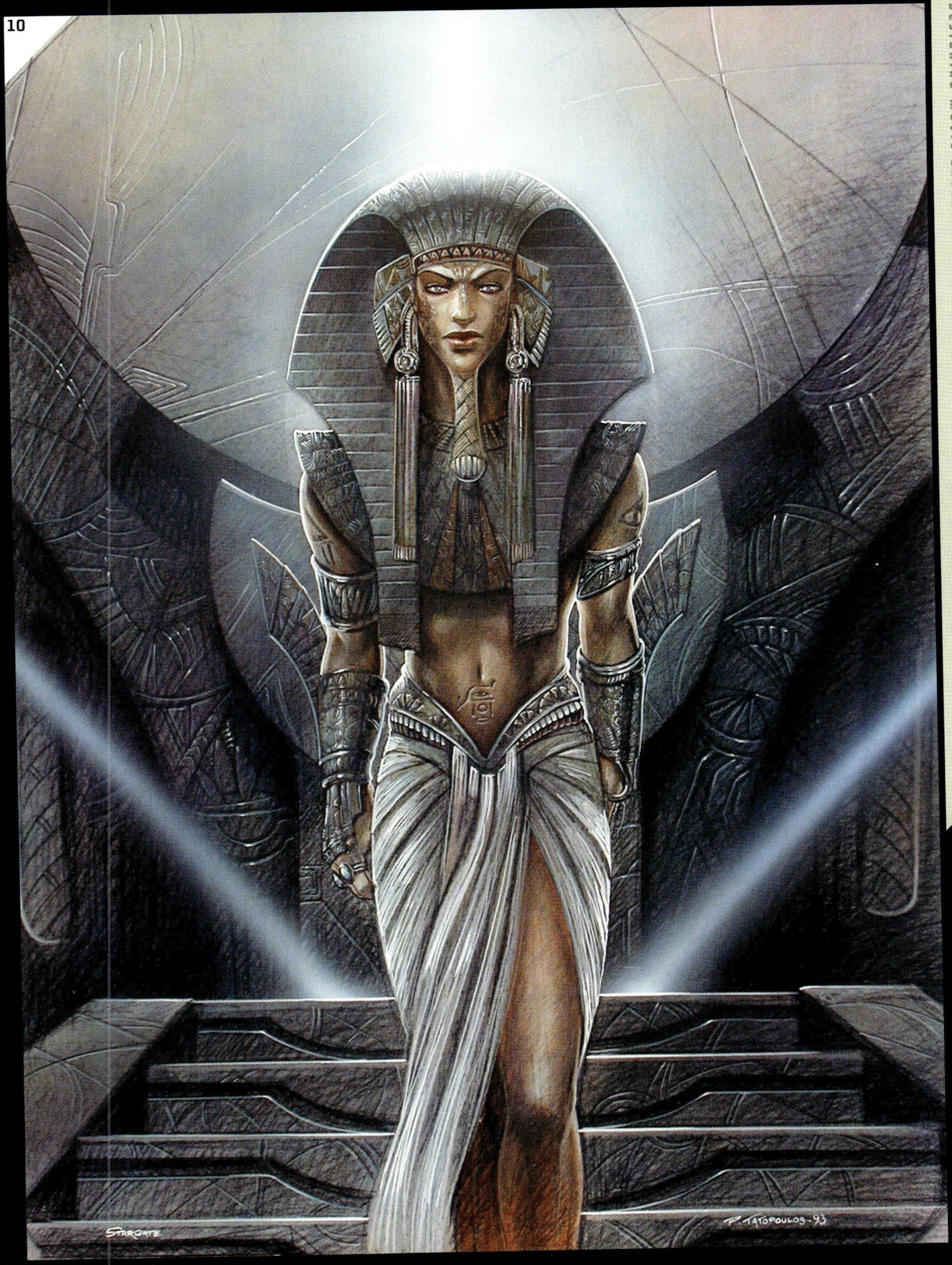

(06) Understructure of the animatronic mastadge head for Stargate **(07)** Mastadge muzzle complete with yak-hair beard **(08)** Walking shots were created by mounting the costume on a horse **(09)** Tatopoulos retouches the mastadge head on set **(10)** Concept design for the *Stargate* character, Ra.

Following his successful stint on *Stargate* Emmerich asked Tatopoulos to be both production designer and creature designer for his next movie, *Independence Day* (1996). The alien character he designed became the first movie creature to appear on the cover of *Time* magazine.

In 1998 Emmerich contacted Tatopoulos again. "Roland asked if I wanted to work on *Godzilla* [1998]," recalls Tatopoulos. "Of course I did! I asked Roland what he wanted his Godzilla to look like and he said, 'Do whatever you like. Completely redesign him. The only thing to remember is that our Godzilla is fast. I want him to run at 200 miles per hour [320kmph] through New York.'"

"So I started thinking about how to redesign Godzilla. What did I really like about him? How would I make that classic lumpy creature capable of moving so fast? I realized that I loved the original design so much that it would be a terrible thing to try and adapt him. It would really be disrespectful to the original creators to say, 'We're going to use your design, but make it better.' I decided that if we were going to have a new Godzilla it would have to be different in every way."

Tatopoulos flew to Paris, where Emmerich was promoting *Independence Day*. "I took him the two drawings I had done. One I didn't like—it was just something to show Roland—and the other I liked very much. Luckily he picked the good one. At that time Roland was not sure if he really wanted to do Godzilla, but I think the drawings helped him make up his mind."

The next task was to get the design approved by Toho Studios, the original creators of Gojira (Godzilla). "Back in the States we made a maquette of our Godzilla. Then we flew to Japan and met with the board at Toho," recalls Tatopoulos. "Sadly, the original creator of Godzilla, Tomoyuki Tanaka, was ill so he wasn't there. After talking for a while about our ideas we unveiled our model Godzilla. First there was silence. Then they started discussing the model in great detail, pointing at different parts. At that time the interpreter stopped translating and we couldn't tell what they were saying. We were very nervous. Then they asked if they could let us know the next day. We hardly slept that night, but in the morning we got a very definite 'Yes.'"

11

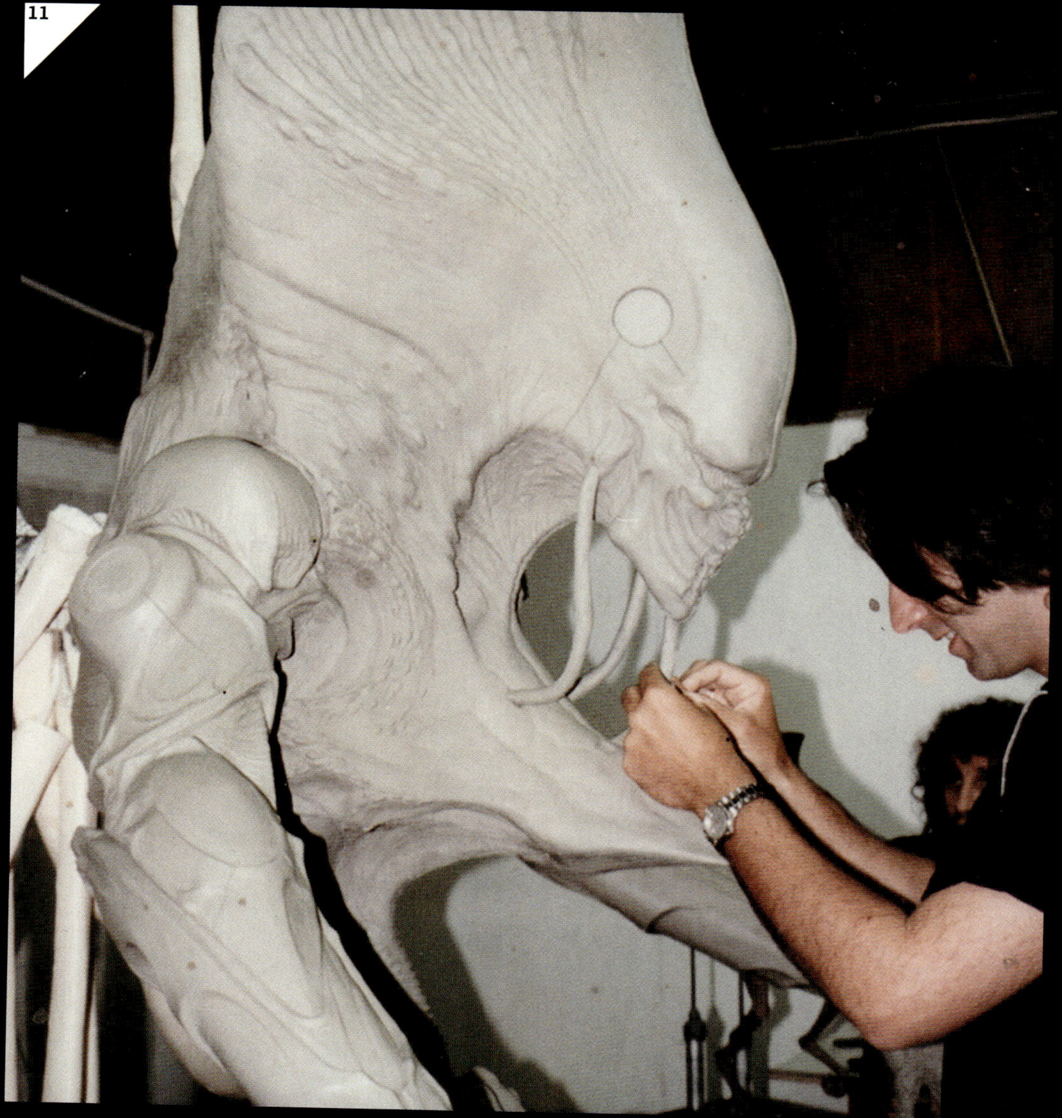

Tatopoulos's design was for a huge, sleek beast that combined the appearance of a number of animals. "It was supposed to be a reptile that has been affected by radiation, so it had elements of crocodile and iguana in it." There were other, more unexpected, influences too. One of Tatopoulos's favorite animated characters is Shere Khan, the tiger from Disney's *The Jungle Book* (1967). "I always thought Shere Khan was such a noble creature, but also scary and evil. One day I tried to analyze why. I decided it was because of

12

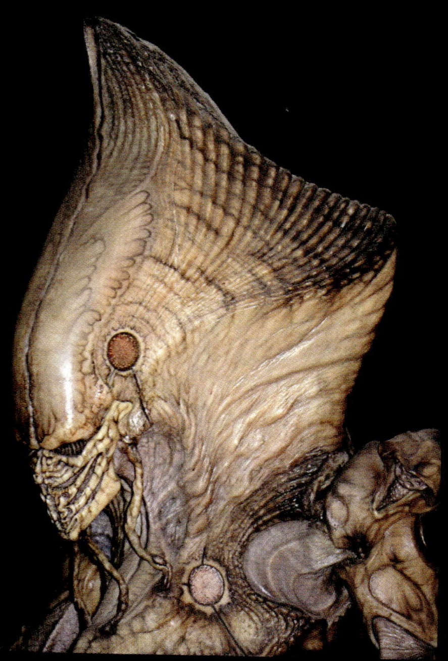

13

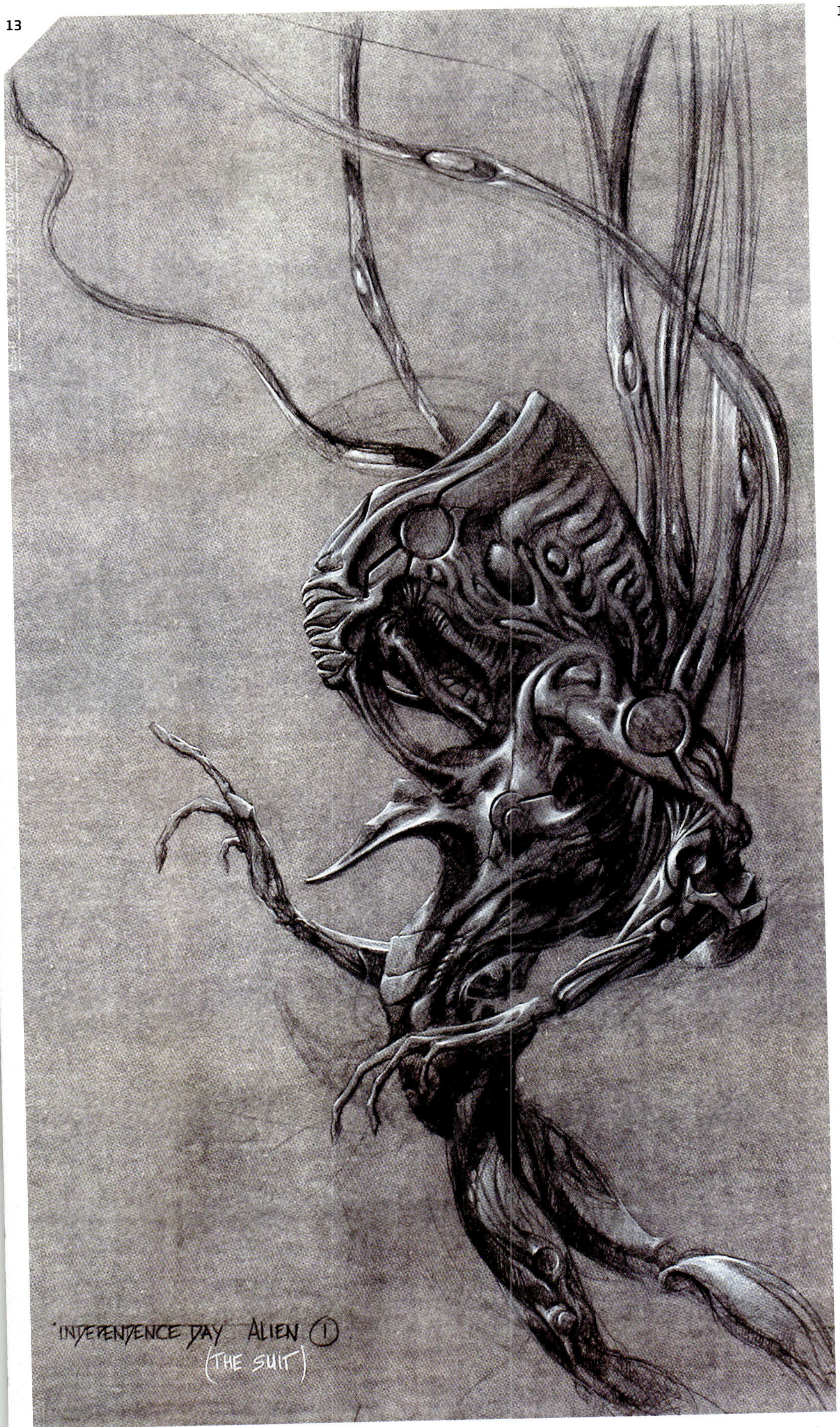

14

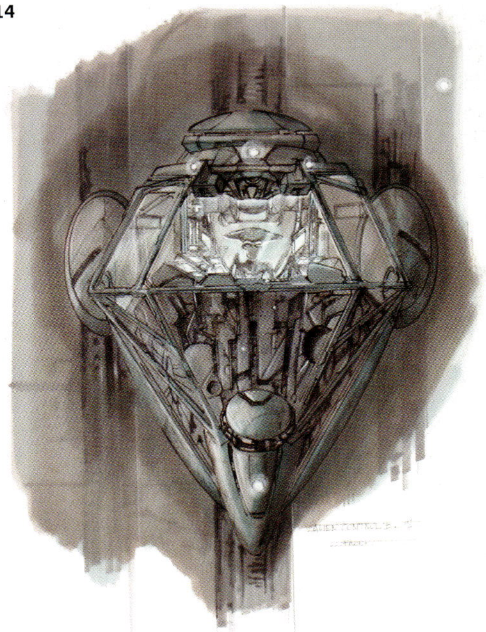

the large, forward–jutting chin and the big squared-off nose. I ended up giving Godzilla a similar jaw line—though I only realized afterward that this is what I had done. In fact, much of Godzilla's look was feline. I often think that if we covered him in fur he would resemble a giant panther. The original Godzilla, on the other hand, is more like a dog."

With the beast needing to move at incredible speed, Tatopoulos looked for inspiration to one of the few real-life two legged sprinters—the legs, and in particular the feet, have more than a touch of ostrich about them. The patterning of Godzilla's scales and leathery skin also came as a result of studying nature. "I don't draw every tiny detail when I'm designing a creature like this—my job is to get the essence of the character

(11) Tatopoulos works on the alien biosuit sculpture for *Independence Day* (1996) **(12)** Finished costume **(13, 14)** As production designer for *Independence Day*, Tatopoulos integrated the appearance of alien characters with their technology, as in these concept designs for the biosuit (left) and alien control booth (right).

on paper: its overall physiognomy, its proportions and lines. Refined details like skin texture are something I will discuss with the sculptor when the time comes. In this case we looked at lizards and crocodiles as well as the scaly, leathery legs and feet of ostriches."

Tatopoulos spent some time considering the color design of his creation. "I knew for sure I didn't want him to be green and lizard-like," says Tatopoulos. "At first Roland considered having him change color like a chameleon, blending in with his background. This would have been difficult to achieve in a puppet. Instead, I looked at the colors of New York: browns and ochres from the brownstone buildings, and blues from the chrome and glass. By using these colors carefully we hoped to achieve a character that blended in and looked at home in that environment." Another cue for the coloring came from a pet owned by Tatopoulos at the time. "I had a lizard—a sailfin dragon—and it had these random pearlescent scales that would catch the light. I would never have thought of including anything like that for fear it would look fake, but it was there in nature, so we applied that pearlescence to the larger scales on his back, arms, and shoulders, and it gave him a weird, glowing appearance."

Tatopoulos assembled his crew of over 200 to construct the necessary Godzilla puppets and animatronics. The mighty creature was built at a number of sizes and brought to life using different techniques according to the needs of the production. "We created versions that could be worn as suits by performers," states Tatopoulos. "These were 24th-scale, and had very complex animatronic heads. We spent a lot of time engineering the tails so that as the performer moved the tail would sway naturally in response. Then there was a large waterproof head that was mounted on rails so that it could rise up from the water near some miniature boats and a pier. We also made other head and neck pieces that were used to interact with miniature bridges and buildings. But the biggest task was to create a sixth-scale head and torso."

15

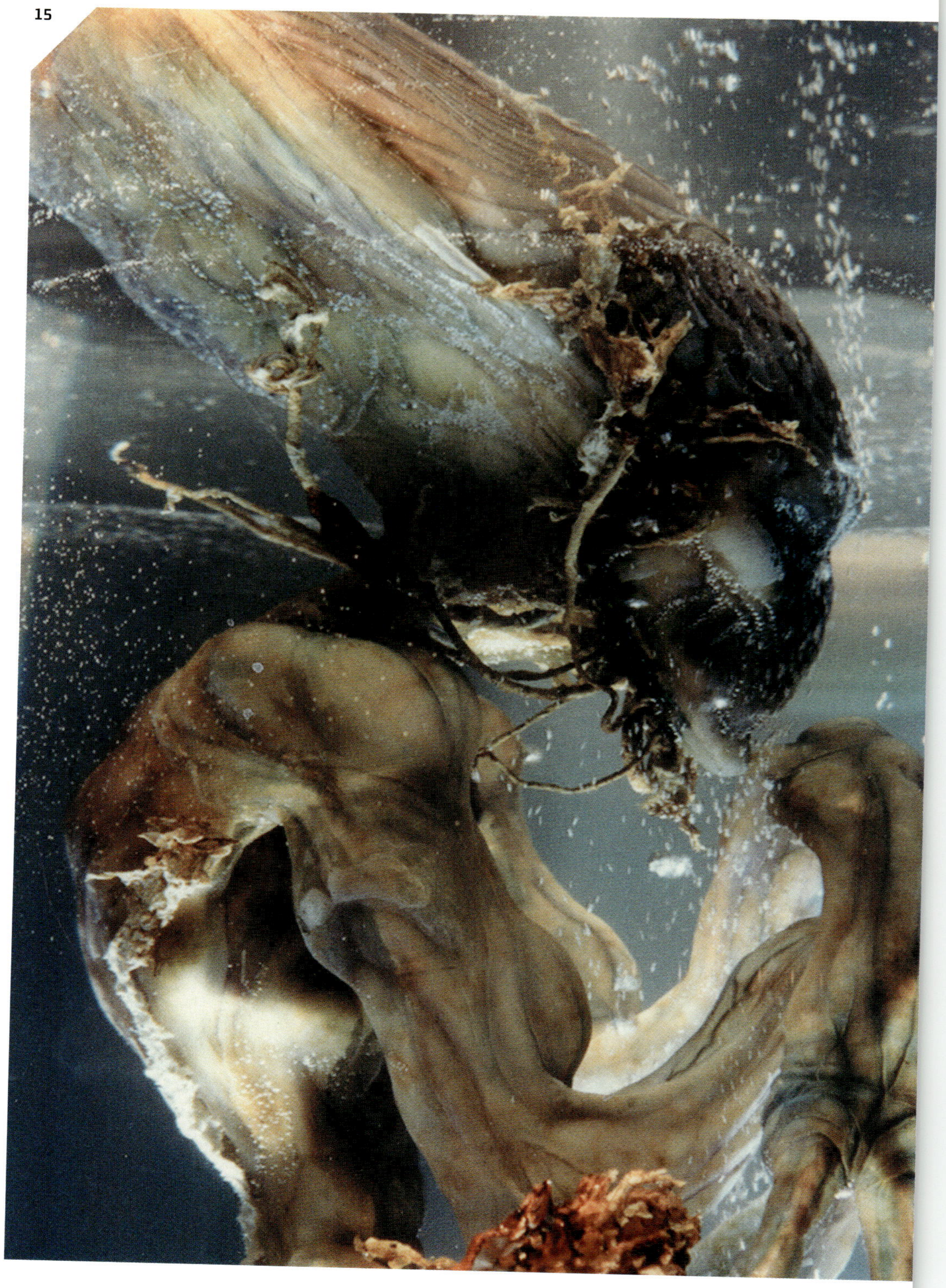

(15–17) Alien puppets built by Tatopoulos and suspended in tanks of water on the *Independence Day* set.

16

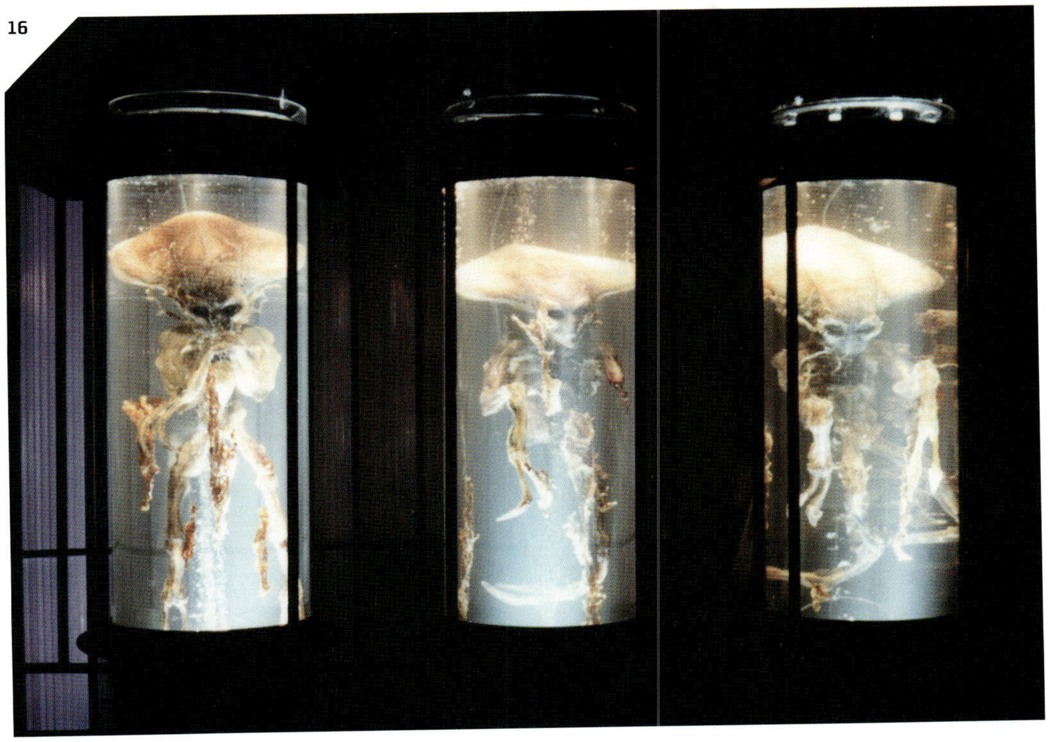

17

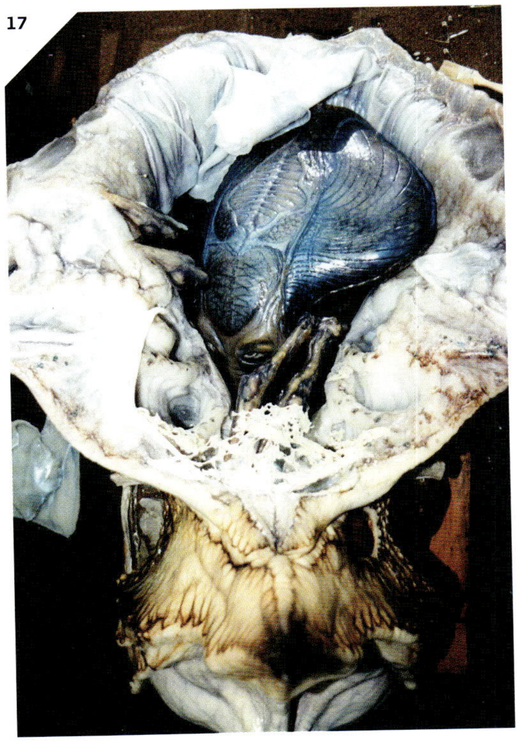

The sixth-scale animatronic "miniature" was truly a monstrous undertaking. This incarnation was used when Godzilla was seen colliding with scaled-down model architecture and when it was required to attack and bite model vehicles. It would have been an enormous task to sculpt such a huge model in clay. Instead, the Tatopoulos team created a framework on which they sprayed a two-part urethane foam, like the yellow foam that is sprayed into cavities to insulate homes. When this foam had set the sculptors hacked away at it until they had created the rough shape. Using precision tools they then carefully carved, shaved, scraped, and etched until they had created every scale, ridge, and skin pore in perfect detail. The resulting 30ft-high (9m) sculpture was then used to create fiberglass molds, which in their turn were used to cast foam-latex skins that were baked in industrial-size ovens. The resulting skins were then mounted on a fabricated Godzilla shell and painted.

The task of bringing the creature to life mechanically proved equally challenging. "The bust was filled with servos that operated the eyes, mouth, lips, nostrils, and the facial muscles. We even had a very subtle form of lighting to make his eyes glow," says Tatopoulos. "The whole thing was mounted on a computer-controlled hydraulic motion base that could rise, tilt, surge, and twist in all directions—the same motion base had previously been used to move the jet planes in James Cameron's *True Lies* [1994]. This thing had so much power that we had to build in lots of safety features. If our Godzilla had malfunctioned he could easily have killed someone for real." The motion of the behemoth was controlled by manipulating a puppet miniature, the movements of which were recorded by a computer and edited to produce a performance that was relayed to the full-sized model.

Despite the superb craftsmanship and technical brilliance, the beasts were not always up to the job of representing Godzilla on the screen. "Of course, many shots were created using a computer-generated creature," says Tatopoulos. "It would have been impossible to get an animatronic character to run around and jump in the way that Godzilla needed to. But at least our designs were used to create the computer-generated Godzilla—it was exactly the same as our physical versions."

The CG Godzilla was created and animated by Centropolis, a visual-effects company established by director Roland Emmerich and producer Dean Devlin to create the effects for *Independence Day*. Tatopoulos supplied a 6ft-high (1.8m), 24th-scale sculpture that was digitized to produce a three-dimensional computer model. Hundreds of photographs of the finished Tatopoulos sculptures and puppets were then used to reproduce the exact skin texture and coloring on the digital Godzilla.

As well as determining the appearance of the beast, Tatopoulos also helped influence the way that it moved. "The way a creature moves is almost as important as the way it looks when it comes to establishing its character. Thinking about that movement should be part of the design process. The feline element of the design seemed to suggest that he should move like a big cat—sleek,

18

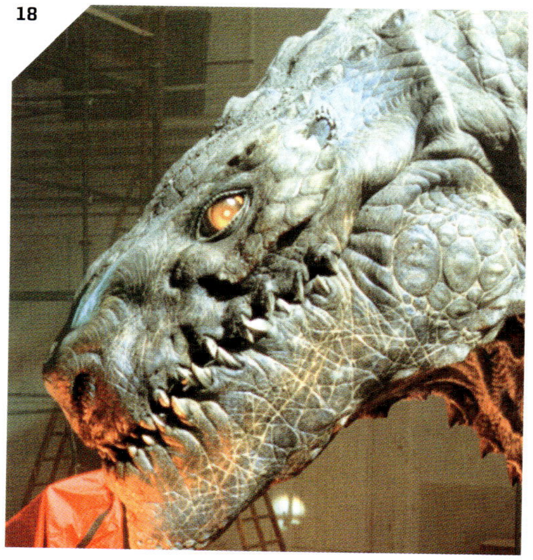

19

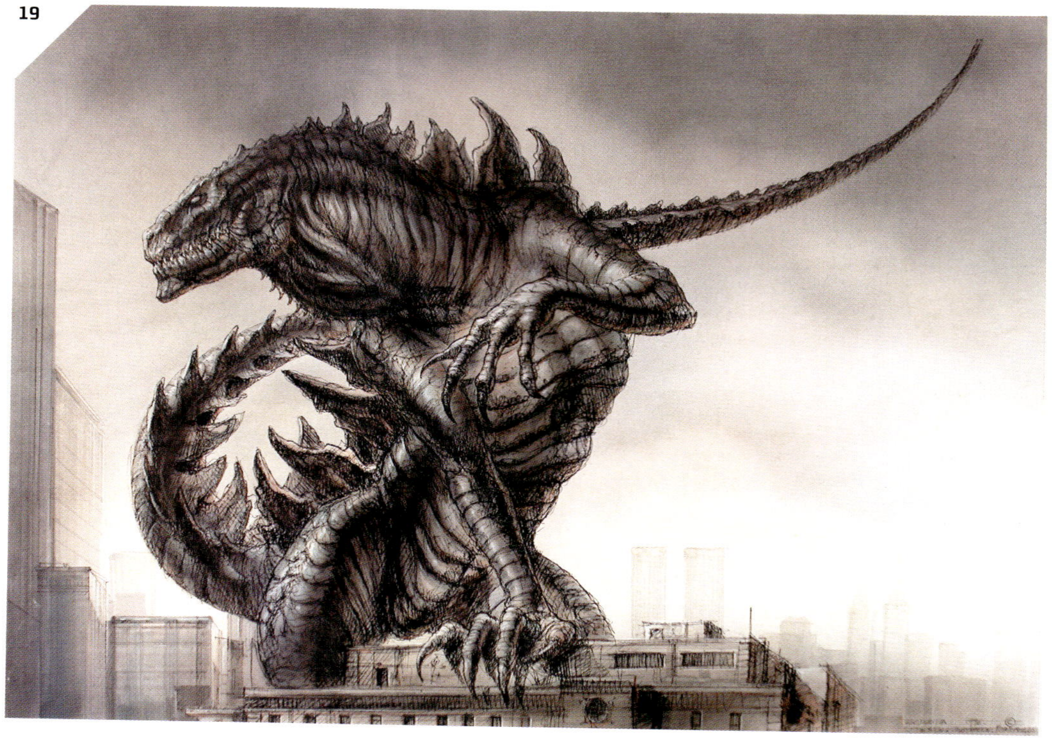

sinuous, and very controlled. I also like the way that crocodiles move—if they become aware of your presence they don't simply turn to look at you; first they just freeze and observe, thinking carefully about what to do, and then they move swiftly and decisively. That initial stillness is very compelling, you get a real sense of a thinking, calculating mind, and it's very hard to take your eyes away. It was this combination of feline and reptilian motion that we asked the costume performers and the computer animators to give to our Godzilla."

A decade after the completion of Godzilla, Tatopoulos looks back on the movie as a highlight in his career. "Unfortunately we don't get to make creatures like that anymore," he says. "It is we, the creators of practical creatures and makeups, who are now becoming the dinosaurs."

Tatopoulos went on to work on a variety of other movies—his creations varying widely from the loveable rodent star of *Stuart Little* (1999) to the hideous forms that appear in *They* (2002)—before he was offered work as production designer for a movie adaptation of Isaac Asimov's novel *I, Robot* (2004). Working with director Alex Proyas, for whom he had previously designed *Dark City* (1998), Tatopoulos quickly realized that the design of the movie's central robot character was the key to unlocking the look of the whole movie. The NS-5 robot was a signature piece of technology from which all

20

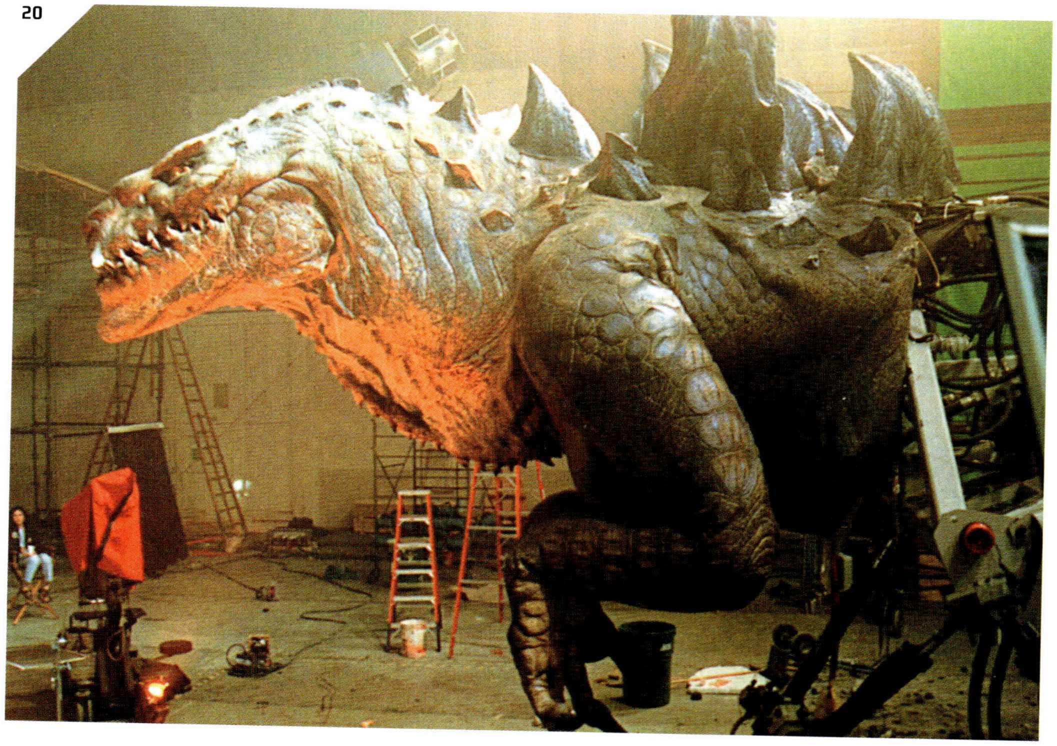

(18) Close-up of animatronic Godzilla, showing intricate skin detailing **(19)** Tatopoulos' powerful concept for an updated Godzilla **(20)** The finished sixth-scale Godzilla, one of the biggest mechanical monsters ever made for a movie.

21

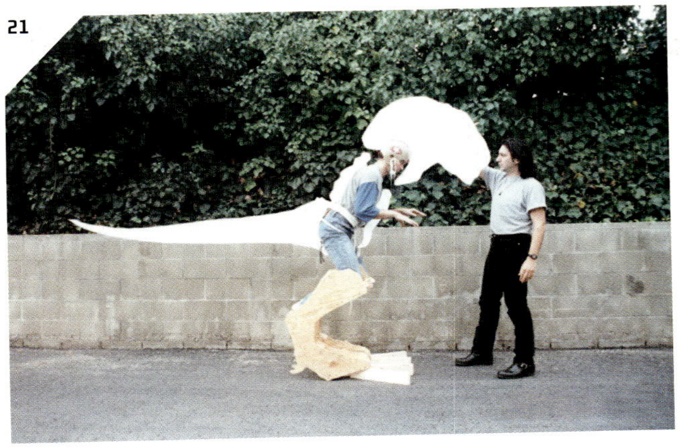

22

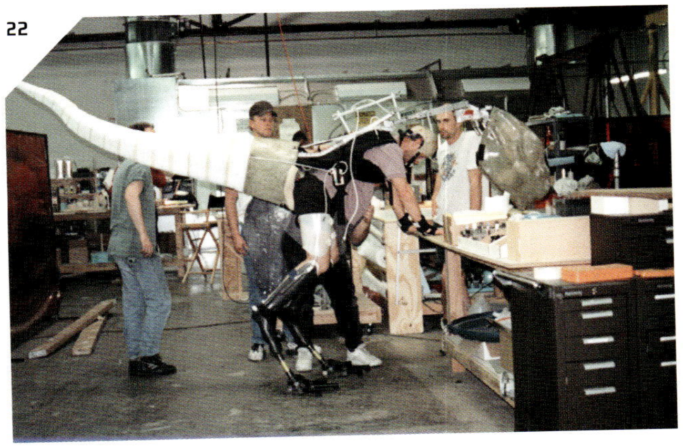

24

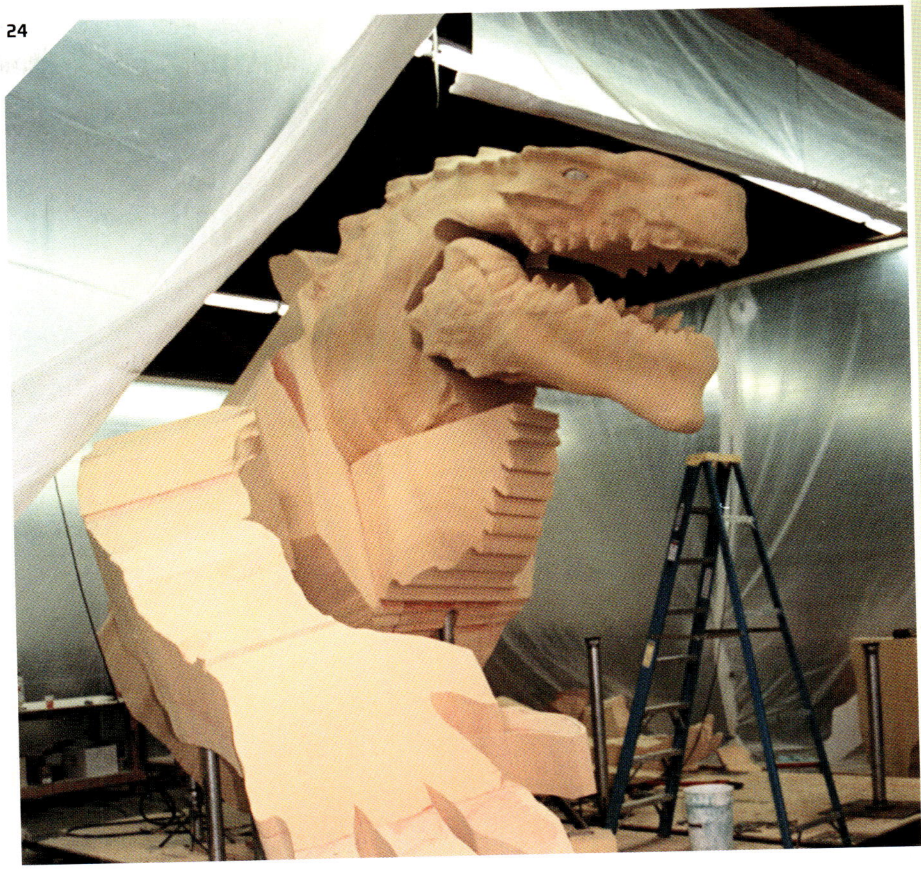

23

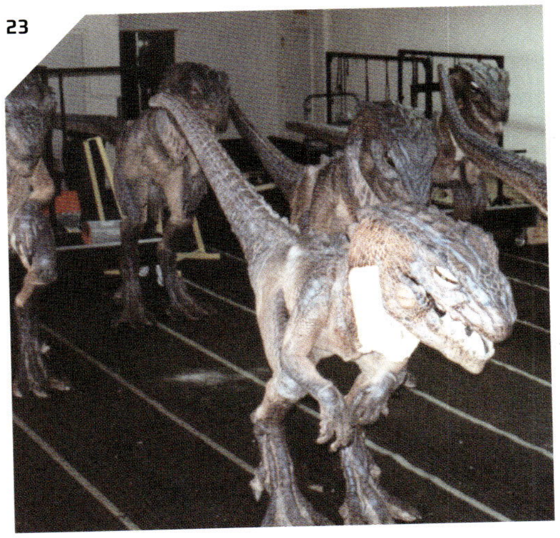

(21) Early tests for the baby Godzilla costumes, using cardboard cutouts for scale **(22)** A performer tests a baby Godzilla suit during the build **(23)** Twelve baby Godzilla costumes were built for the movie **(24)** The 30ft Godzilla was first assembled from blocks of rigid foam before being carved to produce the final sculpture.

other aspects of the movie's world—architecture, vehicles, clothing, and color schemes—would be extrapolated.

Tatopoulos spent six months experimenting with different robot designs, eventually creating over 50 concepts, drawing on research into existing robot designs from science-fiction art, movies, and genuine robotic projects such as Honda's ASIMO. "Alex and I decided that the movie robot we most liked was Maria from *Metropolis* (1927), which is very elegant and in some ways very human," he comments. "We didn't like more recent attempts like the endoskeleton in *The Terminator* (1984), which we found far too menacing and mechanical for this film.

"Our movie was to be set 30 years in the future, so I compared modern technology with the way similar technology had looked 20 or 30 years ago," says Tatopoulos. "Computers made 20 years ago were just gray, functional boxes. While they might have been designed to make your life easier, they weren't designed to be esthetically pleasing or to feel like a part of your life. But when I looked at my assistant's iMac computer, I realized that it had been turned into a fashion item. The [first-generation] iMacs didn't hide their technology—their translucency makes the internal mechanisms visible. The fact that you can see the technology means it is not mysterious, frightening, even if you don't understand it.

"At the same time I was beginning to think about the environments that I was going to design for the film. I looked at the work of architects like Santiago Calatrava and Zaha Hadid. Many of their buildings feature a lot of glass, making the interior visible from the outside. This makes them much more welcoming; they have nothing to hide. All these ideas appealed to me, and I decided to make a feature of them in both the architecture and the robots."

Tatopoulos then imagined how real robots, such as the Honda ASIMO, might look in 30 years time when their technology has advanced. To these ideas he added transparency, which became even more

25

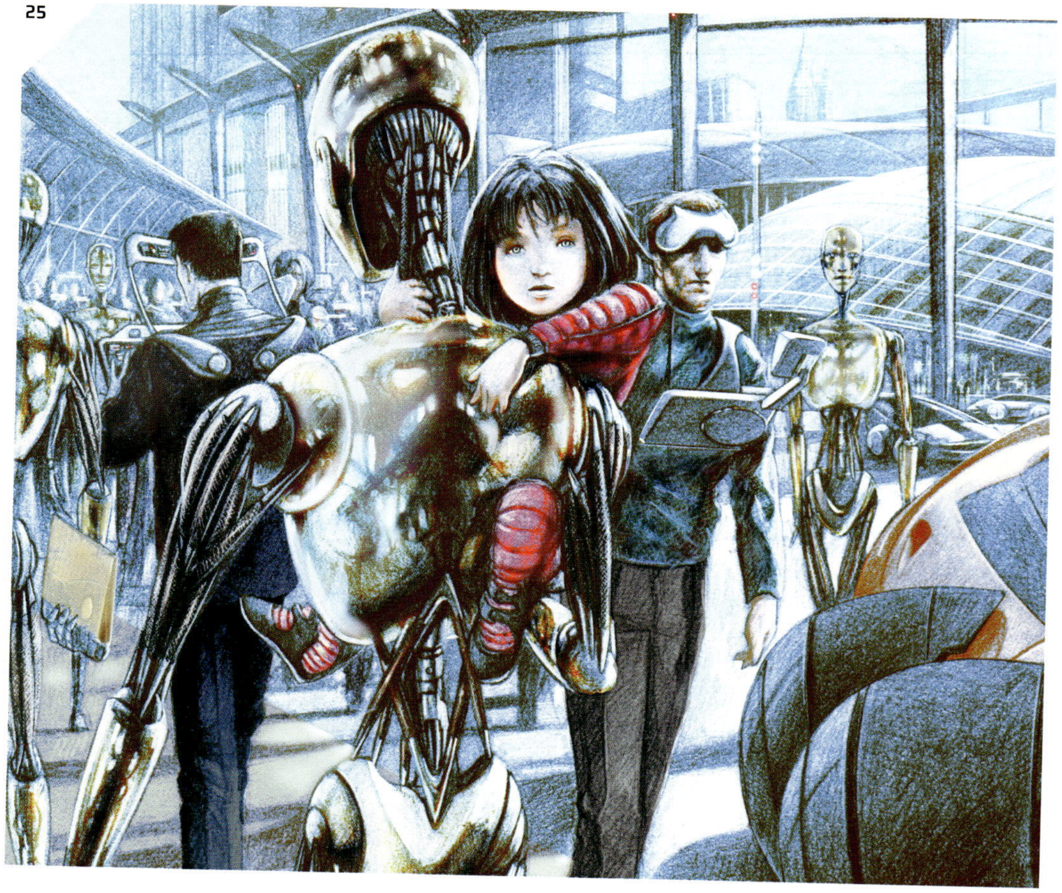

26

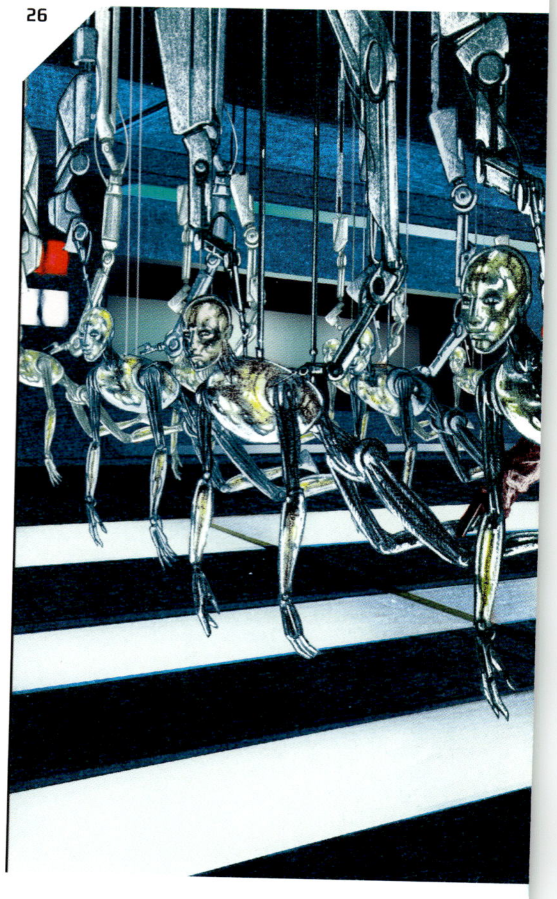

relevant when it was decided that all of the film's robots would be computer-generated. "Once I knew that, then I could really push the sleek, translucent look," he says. "I knew that there wouldn't have to be any physically accurate mechanics to clutter my design or need to be concealed."

The most difficult challenge was finding the right look for the NS-5's face. First, the robot needed to be fully expressive, speaking and conveying emotions. This would mean deciding how movement on the surface of the face should appear to be mechanically created. The second question was what—or who—the features of the robot should resemble.

"We spent a long time discussing whether the robot should be male or female. Alex suggested thinking about the face of an angel—he wanted it to evoke a sense of innocence. I sketched many designs, and eventually came up with a generic face that seemed neither strongly male nor female, and was not distinctively of any particular race," says Tatopoulos.

"The next question was how the face should move. In the past, movie robots have had relatively unemotive faces. They tend to have a fixed overall expression that can only change by mechanically raising the eyebrows or opening and closing the mouth in a very limited way. I wanted to find something that could give us a much more refined performance."

As part of his research for the movie, Tatopoulos had looked at technology being used for prosthetic limb replacement in humans. One of the materials he discovered was a form of artificial muscle that could inflate or deflate pneumatically to drive the movement of a limb. "I thought it would be cool to have muscle like this driving certain parts of our robot," says Tatopoulos, "but instead of working pneumatically our robot muscle would work electrically. The idea was that thousands of electrical pulses flowing into the surface of the muscle would cause it to expand and contract, producing movement. I designed the robot to have this type of muscle on the forearms, lower legs, chest, and face. It was like a silicone sleeve that fitted over these parts and which would change shape either to make a limb move or, in the case of the face, articulate expressions and emotion."

After paper designs were approved, a final version of the NS-5 was built as a computer-generated model, with every detail produced in minute detail. "The final computer design was used to drive a computer-controlled router to create each of the components of our robot physically," explains Tatopoulos.

(25–26) Tatopoulos' production design for *I, Robot* was influenced by architects such as Santiago Calatrava and Zaha Hadid **(27)** Design for the movie's featured robot, the NS-5 **(28)** Early Robot and environment concepts.

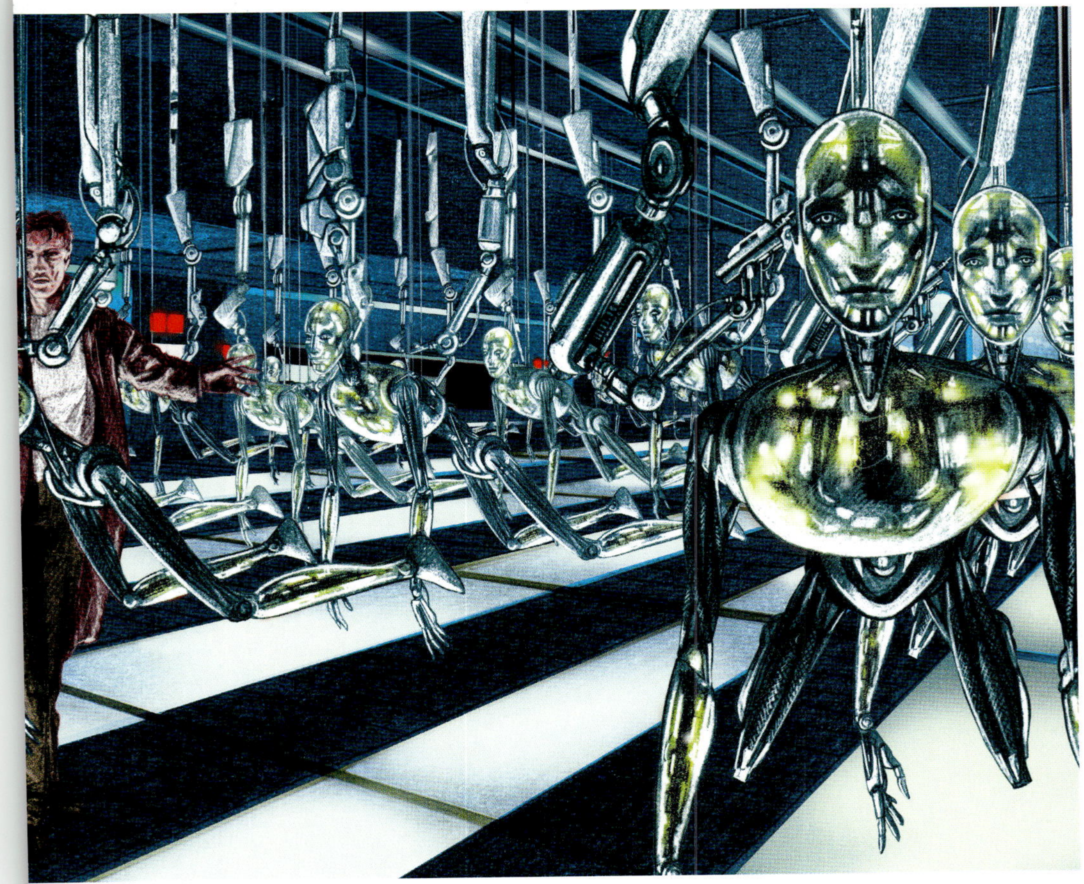

27

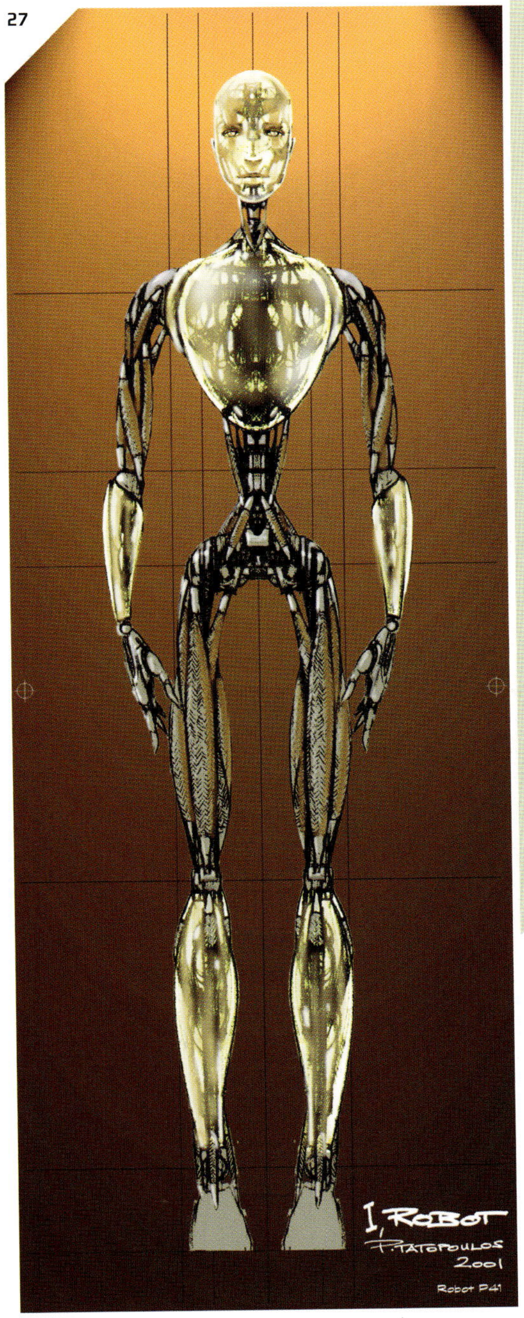

28

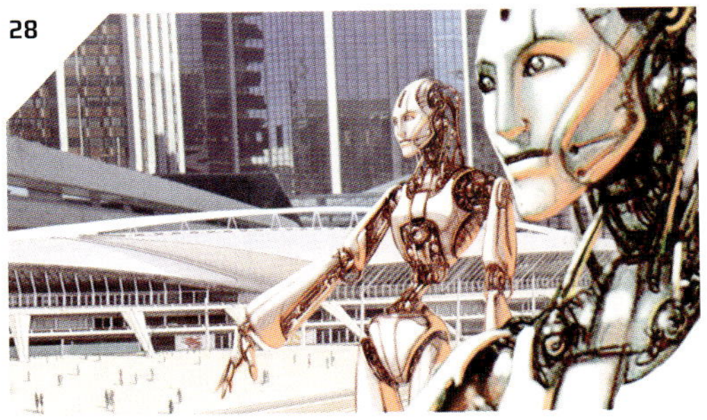

"We used these to create molds in a platinum-based silicone, so that we could cast really smooth, detailed pieces of the robot in various plastics and resins. These parts were then painted or metalized to produce the final finish, and then assembled to create two full-scale versions of the robot. The areas of muscle were produced in a material called braided fiber, which behaves much like real muscle and is cast into the shape you require. When stretched this material changed shape but maintained its volume, and when unstretched it always returned to its original shape. The finished robots were absolutely perfect and resembled precisely how the CG versions should eventually look. They were totally articulated and could be posed into any required stance."

Although creating physical versions of the robot was not strictly necessary, it did help Tatopoulos to see how his designs would translate to the screen "We spent quite a bit of time sand-blasting the transparent pieces in order to find the right levels of translucency. For example, we made the front of the head fairly opaque so you can't see too much of what is underneath, but that drops off as we move around to the side of the head so you can start to see more of the interior. We also discovered that you could light the robot in different ways according to the dramatic needs of a scene. If the robot was lit from the front you could see through the shell and it looked quite pleasing, but when lit from behind you couldn't see through it so well and the robot took on a more menacing appearance. This technique was used more in the later scenes when the robots are more threatening. We also placed a red light inside which would glow when there was any danger."

Tatopoulos's designs were used by visual-effects company Digital Domain to create computer-generated versions that could be animated according to the requirements of the movie. "The only change we made to the design for the CG version was that their shoulders

29

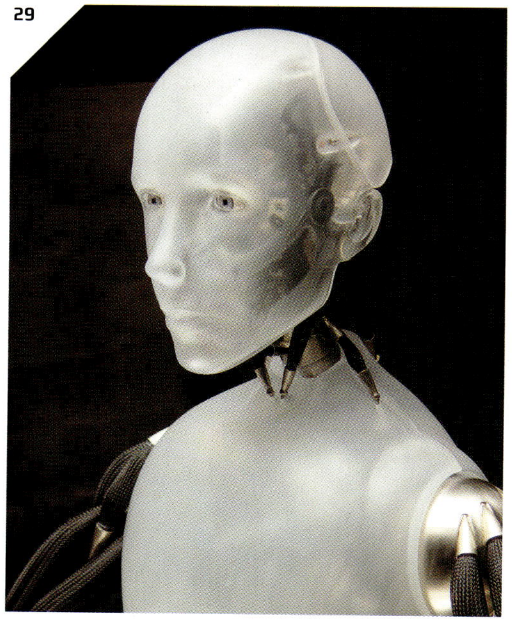

30

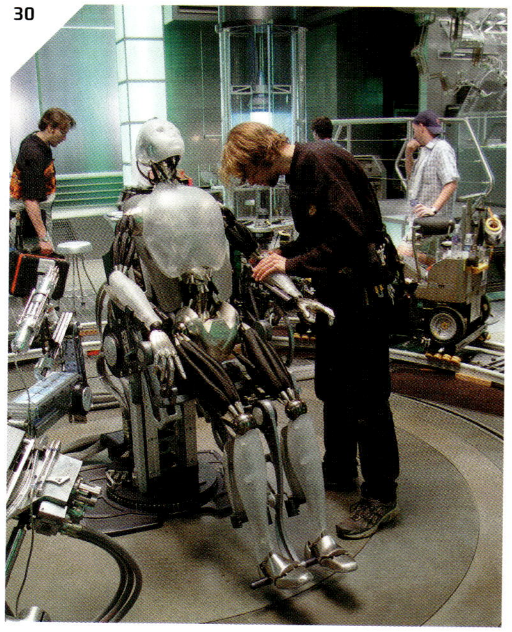

were more flexible. The original arms were fixed to the shoulders in a ball-and-socket fashion, which meant they could only swivel around that point. By making the shoulders more flexible—able to collapse forward like those of a human—the robot had much more movement in the upper body."

The practical versions of the robot created by Tatopoulos were used on set, being placed into every shot so that the actors had something with which to interact as well as to produce a lighting reference for Digital Domain. "Alex Proyas wouldn't sign off on any digital-robot shots until he had seen the same shot with the practical robot in it," says Tatopoulos. "Our practical robots were always removed from each shot and replaced with the digital versions for consistency. There are, however, just a few shots in the film in which they appear—but I'm sure no one will ever work out where they are!"

In 2003, Tatopoulos was asked to design the characters for the modestly budgeted horror movie *Underworld*, directed by Len Wiseman, whom Tatopoulos had befriended when the director was a mere prop assistant on *Independence Day* and *Godzilla*. "Len wanted me to design something very different for the werewolves for *Underworld*," says Tatopoulos.

Werewolves are one of the more frequently created creatures for the movies, so Tatopoulos found plenty of previous examples for inspiration. "Of all the movie werewolves my favorites are Rick Baker's from *An American Werewolf in London* [1981] and, above all, Rob Bottin's wolf from *The Howling* [1981]. When I looked at those movies again I thought the wolves looked the coolest when they were still turning from people into wolves. Somewhere in the middle is where I thought they looked the best, especially with *American Werewolf*. So that's how I drew my wolves, with a shorter muzzle which was almost cat-like. Len was really unsure about this approach. He liked it but was a bit uneasy about the cat-like appearance. I tried really hard to persuade him and eventually he decided to go that way." The final designs were built as a series of transitional puppets and the full werewolves were created as costumes with animatronic heads worn by performers.

Following the success of the first movie, a sequel, *Underworld: Evolution* (2006), was made with a higher budget. For the second outing Tatopoulos was asked to act as overall production designer as well as working to extend the range of devilish characters. "We brought back the same werewolf designs, but made some major improvements," he says.

"The original werewolf had this really thick neck, but we found that it limited the performer's ability to turn his head left and right. This wasn't unnatural—gorillas, for example, have very thick necks that prevent them from turning their heads much. But for the new film we wanted to keep the design but find a way to allow head movement. In the end we replaced the sculpted foam-latex neck with a fabricated neck which was covered in spandex. But spandex cannot be painted to look as good as foam latex, so to cover the new neck we decided to make the wolves in the second film much more hairy."

New characters for the movie included Marcus, a vampire. "Len wanted Marcus to be really hideous, so I designed him as this really ugly bat-like creature. But the most interesting thing was his wings. I've never really liked winged characters before, the way their wings fold up on the back and look kind of stuck-on. I thought it would be really cool to have a character whose wings fold up and completely disappear into their body. I wondered how to achieve this, and thought about how the wings of a butterfly unfold when they emerge from a chrysalis—they fill with blood and unfurl. Also, Len wanted the wings to act as weapons that could attack and grab people."

(29) The finished NS-5 was influenced by the sleek design of Apple's original iMac computers **(30)** A single physical NS-5 was built by Tatopoulos and used as a reference for adding CG robots during post-production.

31

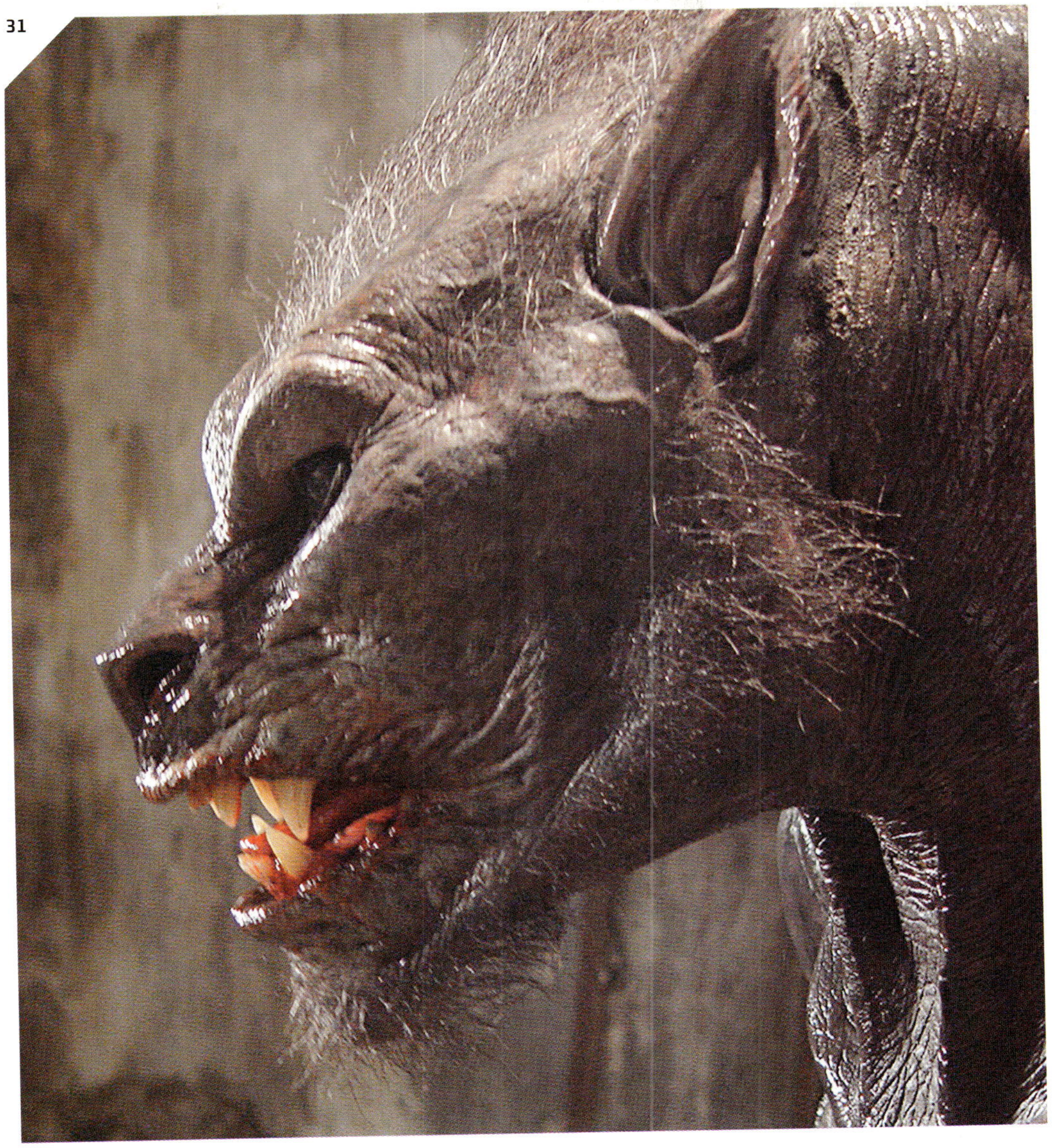

32

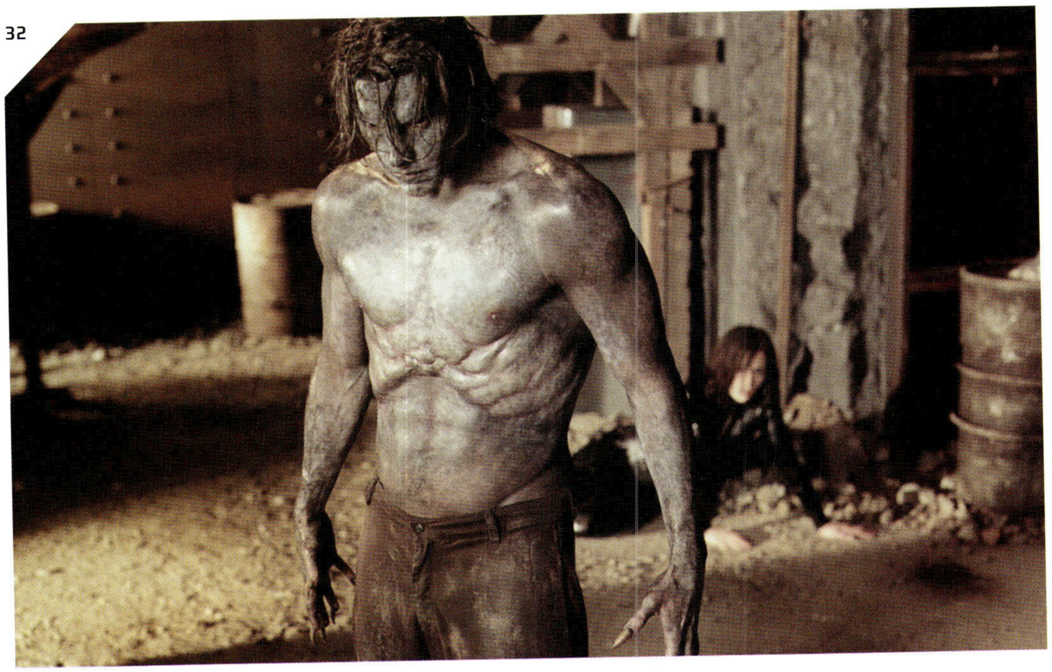

(31–32) Some of the original creations from *Underworld* (2003).

Tatopoulos designed a unique wing system that allowed the arm-like appendages to fold out from the body. When required, the wings could then unfurl from the under edges of the arms like a membrane. While most of the shots with the arms were achieved practically, whenever the fully extended wings needed to flap, CG wings were added to the practical costume. "Whenever you see him flying it isn't a CG character," notes Tatopoulos, "it's a performer in our makeup flying on wires. Just the wings were added in CG."

Tatopoulos acknowledges the increased use of CG creature effects, but he does not think the technology is about to replace practical work altogether. "CG will replace a lot of the big stuff, for sure. But I think directors are starting to enjoy working more with practical makeup effects again. The initial enthusiasm to do everything in CG has died down and people are realizing that great work can be achieved with practical makeup effects. Some of the CG in *Underworld: Evolution* was great, but a few shots that were done quickly because of script changes really weren't so good. It's now all about finding the right mix of CG and practical, knowing what can be done best, fastest, and most economically with either medium."

MITCH DEVANE

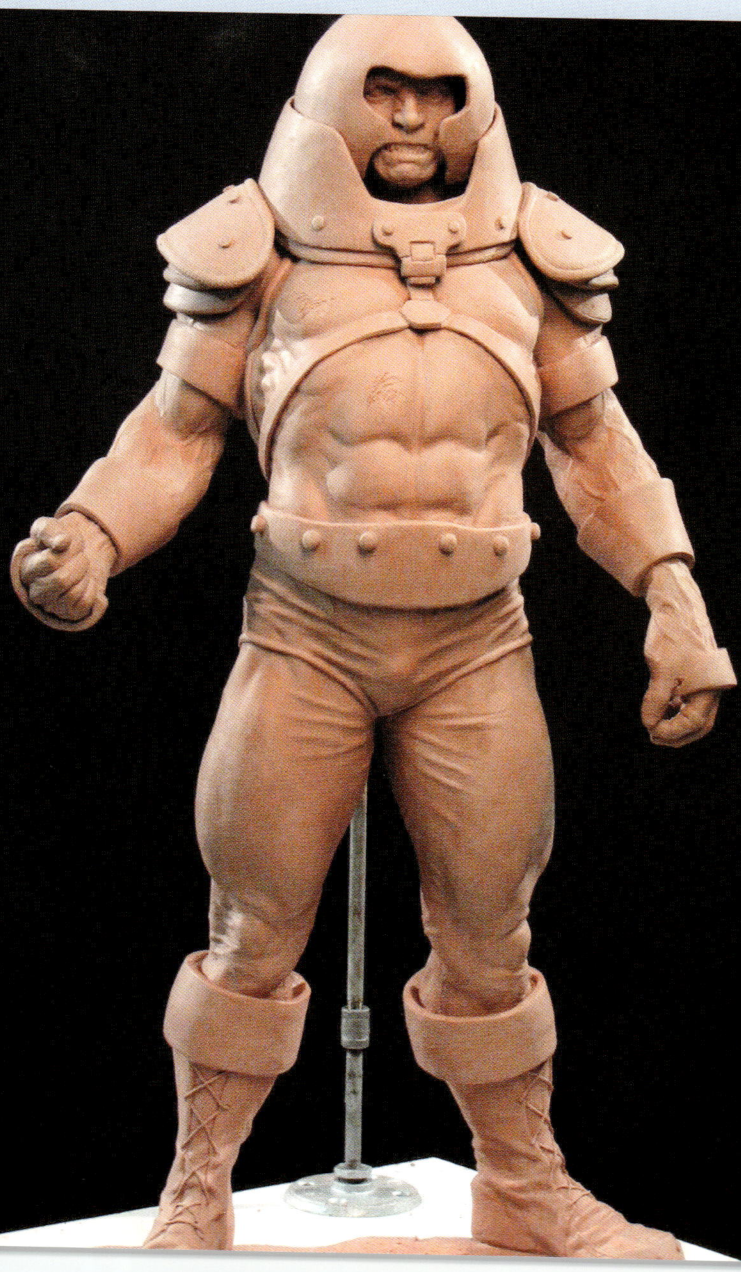

CV

Sculptural makeup creator; b. Columbus, GA; built on a childhood interest in modeling by taking art classes at a local college; spent five years as a touring musician before working in a hospital; then discovered movie makeup, moving to Hollywood, where he enrolled at Joe Blasco Makeup School; got started in the business working at John Buechler's workshop; has subsequently worked with many studios, latterly mostly for Rick Baker, but also for Spectral Motion, Patrick Tatopoulos, and KNB.

SELECT FILMOGRAPHY

Hook (1991); *Bram Stoker's Dracula* (1992); *Mrs. Doubtfire* (1993); *The Nutty Professor* (1996); *Men in Black* (1997); *Planet of the Apes* (2001); *The Ring* (2002); *The Chronicles of Narnia: The Lion, the Witch and the Wardrobe* (2005); *X-Men: The Last Stand* (2006)

KEY CHARACTERS

Granny Wendy (*Hook*); Edgar (*Men in Black*); Sherman Klump (*The Nutty Professor*); Cyclops (*The Lion, the Witch and the Wardrobe*); Juggernaut (*X-Men: The Last Stand*)

TECHNIQUES

Traditional character design and sculpture

01

02

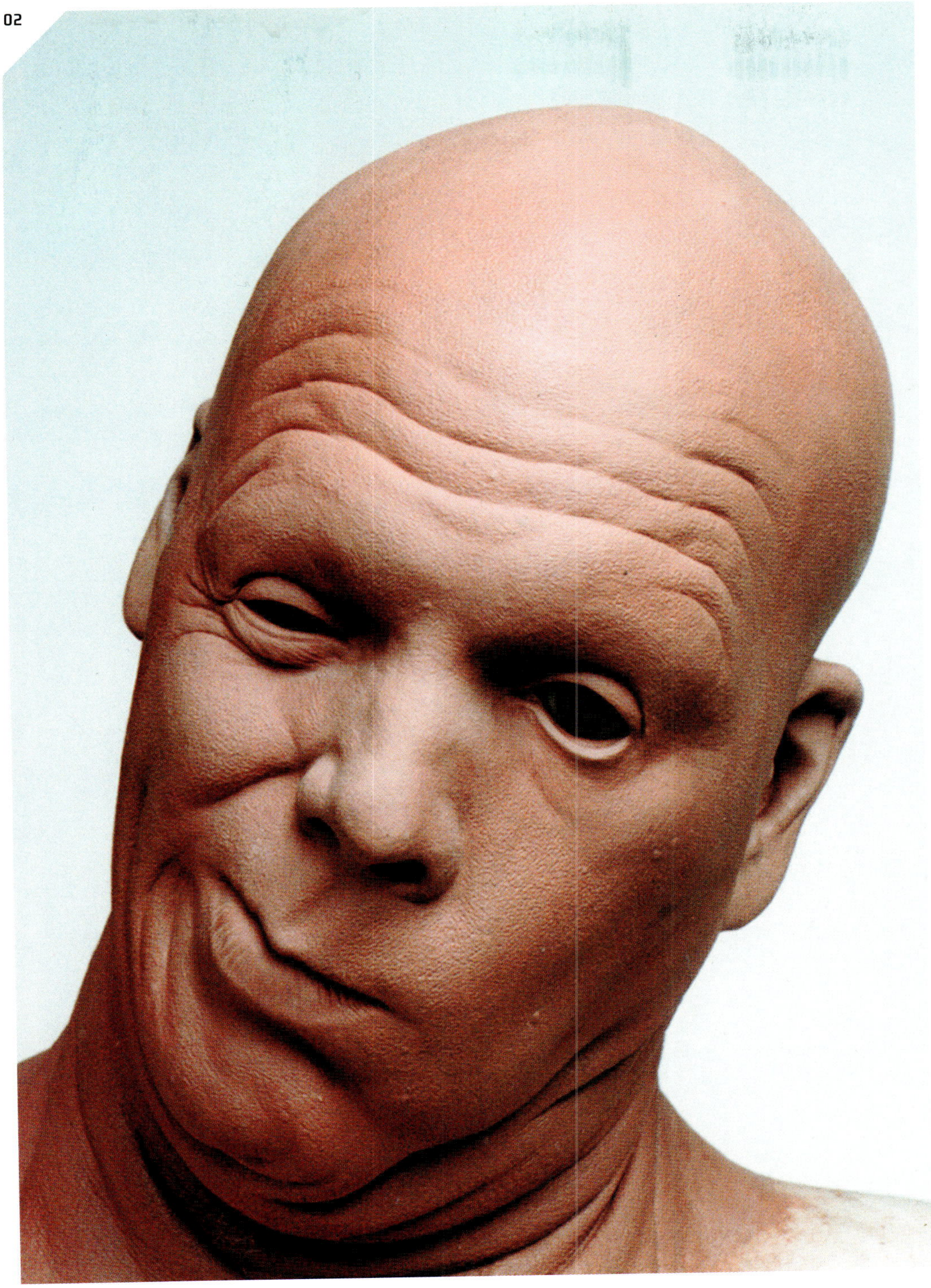

Raised in Columbus, Georgia, Mitch DeVane grew up loving comic books, teaching himself to sculpt at an early age by recreating some of his favorite fictional characters in multicolored modeling clay. Unusually for someone now working in character design, DeVane wasn't obsessed with monster movies. "I did see *The Exorcist* [1973] about 20 times, though I think that was because I enjoyed all the bad language, but I was never really into movies in a big way."

Instead, DeVane spent five years as a touring musician before working in a hospital, sterilizing medical equipment. At this time he saw a copy of movie magazine *Fangoria* in his local comic store. "Inside the magazine I saw this image of a sculpture that was done for *Howard the Duck* [1986], and that made me realize that there might actually be some practical application for my sculpting skills."

After moving to Hollywood, DeVane enrolled at the Joe Blasco Makeup School, which led to a job at John Buechler's makeup workshop. "I met a lot of great guys there, including Howard Berger, Greg Kurtzman, and John Vulich." DeVane has since worked as a sculptor for many leading artists and studios, such as Greg Cannom, Dick Smith, and Mike Elizalde. However, since the early 1990s most of his work has been for Rick Baker.

Although DeVane will turn his hand to any form of sculpture, he is known best for his human-character work. "If I'm creating a new face or prosthetic makeup, I'll start with a lifecast of that performer. Then I'll start sculpting clay on top of that."

(01) Mitch DeVane sculpted this maquette of Juggernaut as part of Spectral Motion's work on *X-Men: The Last Stand* (2006)
(02) Bust of actor Vince D'Onofrio as Edgar in *Men in Black* (1997).

03

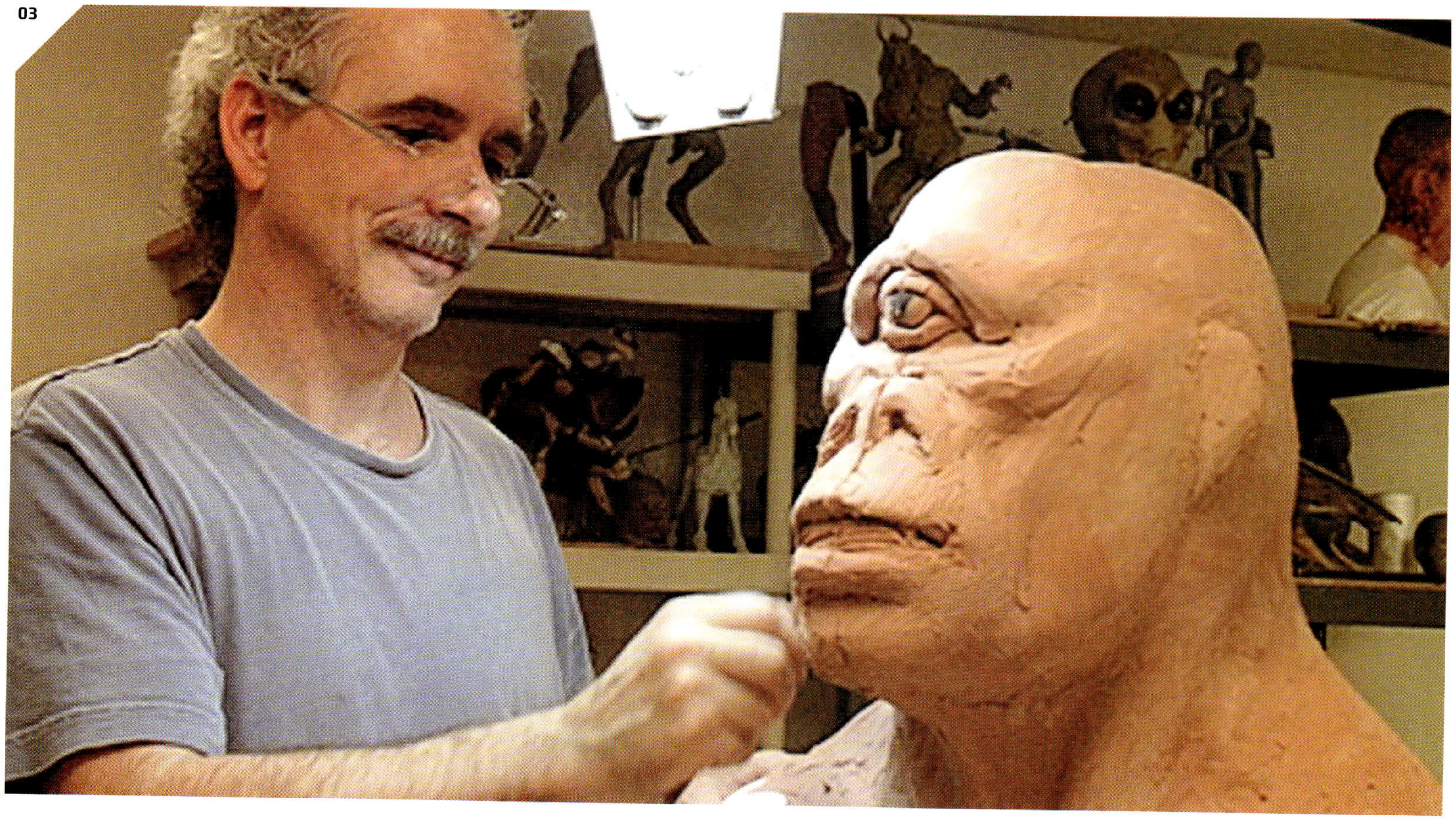

"I mainly use Chavant NSP [non-sulphurated plastelene], an oil-based clay that does not dry out and can be worked for a long time without cracking," says DeVane. "It's important to use sulphur-free clays when the later molding process will use silicones, because sulphur and silicone are not compatible. The clay comes in different grades of softness and can be heated in an oven to make it more malleable. It can even be melted and poured. I mainly use a medium grade, as the harder stuff can be tough to work. The harder clay is good if you want to do sculptures with very fine, hard-edged details, like mechanical forms or jewelry."

Although the common perception of a sculptor is that of an artist vigorously shaping and scraping with their bare hands, DeVane does this only during the earliest stages. "The clay comes out of the oven really soft. I quickly press it onto the lifecast, blocking out shapes in broad strokes. That clay then cools and hardens in just a few minutes, becoming too hard to move about with your hands.

"I start with getting the basic features in the right place. A sculpture can look fairly featureless for a long time, so I often like to add in a few temporary things to remind me what I'm working on. I'll often add very roughly finished-looking eyes with a little ball of clay on them to represent a glint, or eyelashes if it's a woman, and maybe an earring. These are just little things to make a very rough work-in-progress look a bit more human."

DeVane is frequently required to sculpt masks of movie stars that can be worn by doubles or stunt performers. "For some shots that don't show a star in close-up, or when they're involved in dangerous action scenes, someone else will be filmed instead of the star. That person will have to wear a mask that makes them look like the performer," says DeVane. "This is a strange aspect of sculpting. We have to take a lifecast of the double and then sculpt the face of the star on top of it. This can be a bit like trying to sculpt a mouse on top of an elephant. People's faces are such different shapes and sizes that you can't just go putting one on top of another. There are some things you just can't change on a face, like the size of the nose and the distance between the eyes. One way of doing it is to press clay into the negative mold of the star's face to form a kind of clay mask that is then pressed on to the positive cast of the double. But that tends to distort the features. I prefer to do it from scratch, sculpting the nearest thing I can get to the star's face over the double's cast."

04

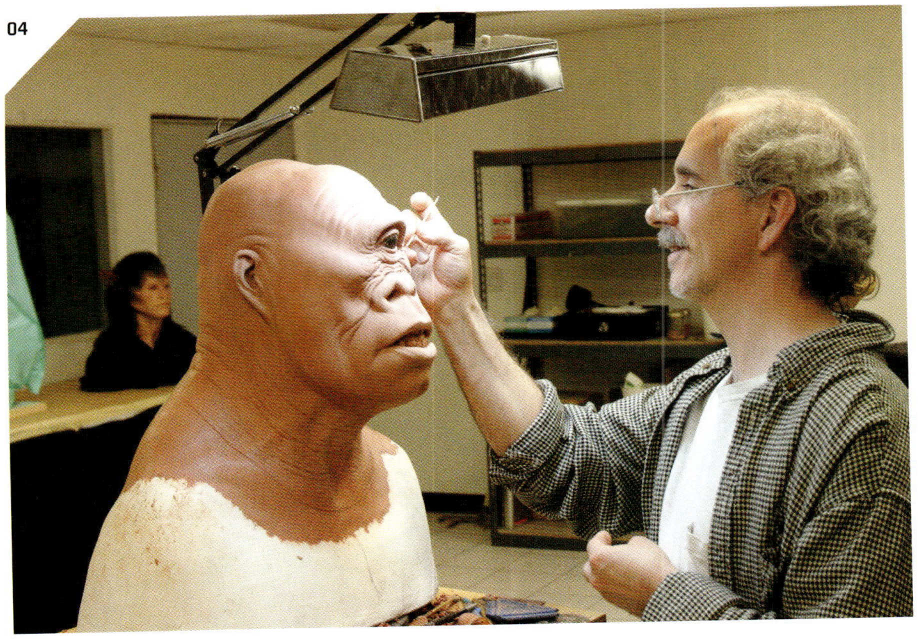

05

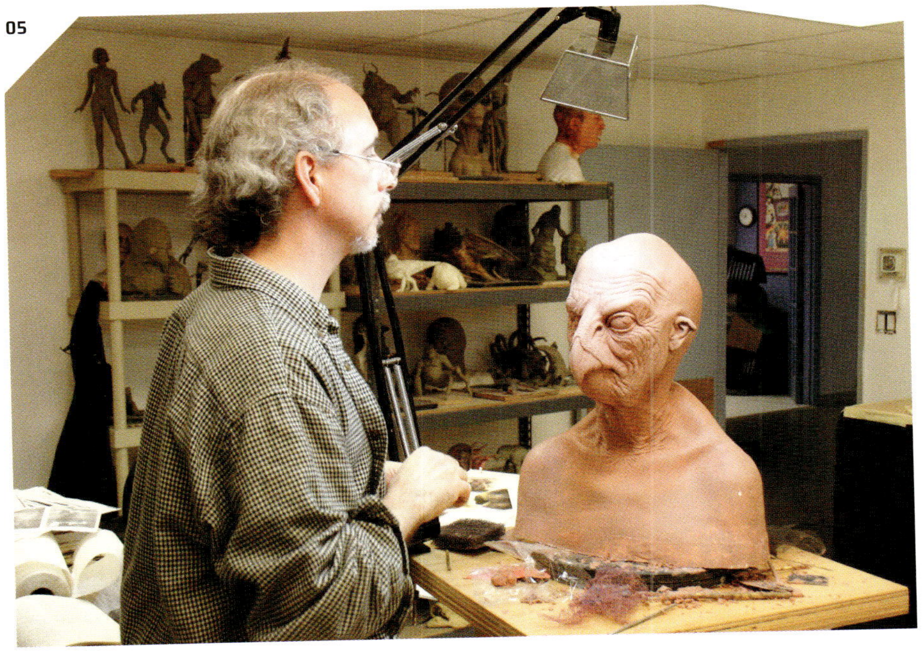

06

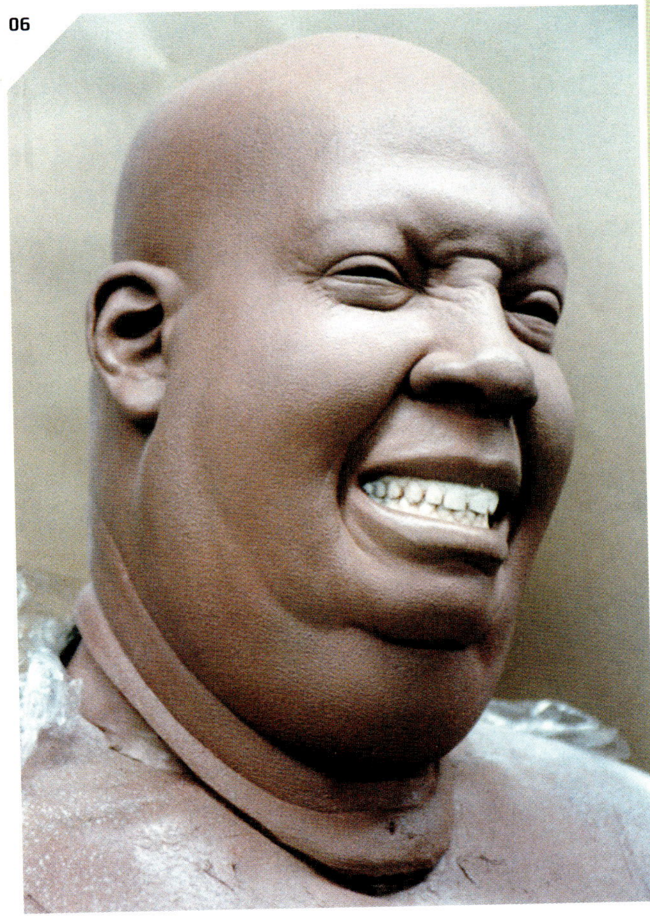

07

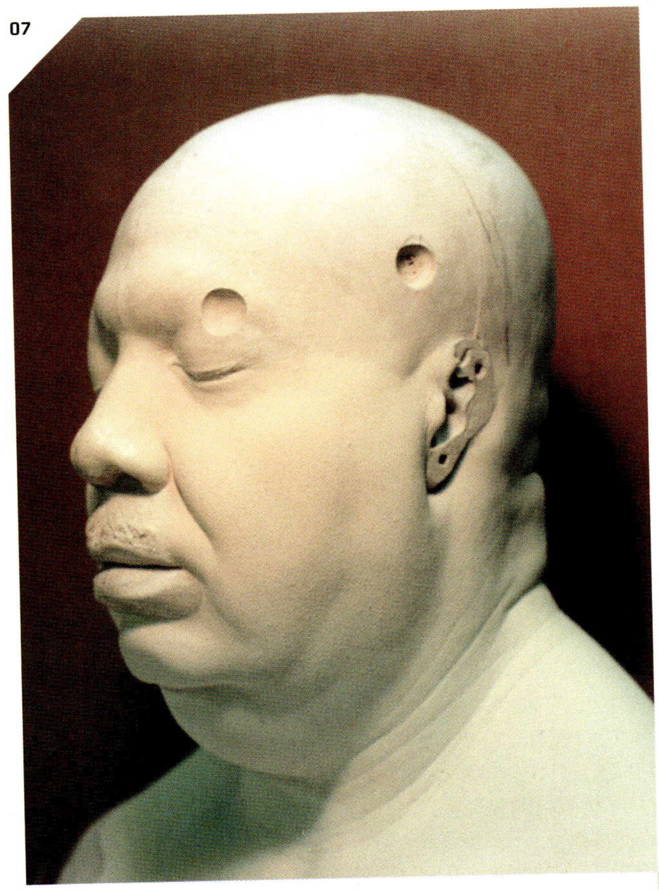

(03–04) DeVane works on early and later stages of a Cyclops for *The Lion, the Witch, and the Wardrobe* (2005) at KNB **(05)** DeVane sculpts a Hag for KNB **(06–07)** Sherman Klump sculpts for *The Nutty Professor* (1996). After makeup tests the design was changed to make the face fatter. Once approved, DeVane sculpted two more identical versions so that enough foam appliances could be created for the lengthy production process.

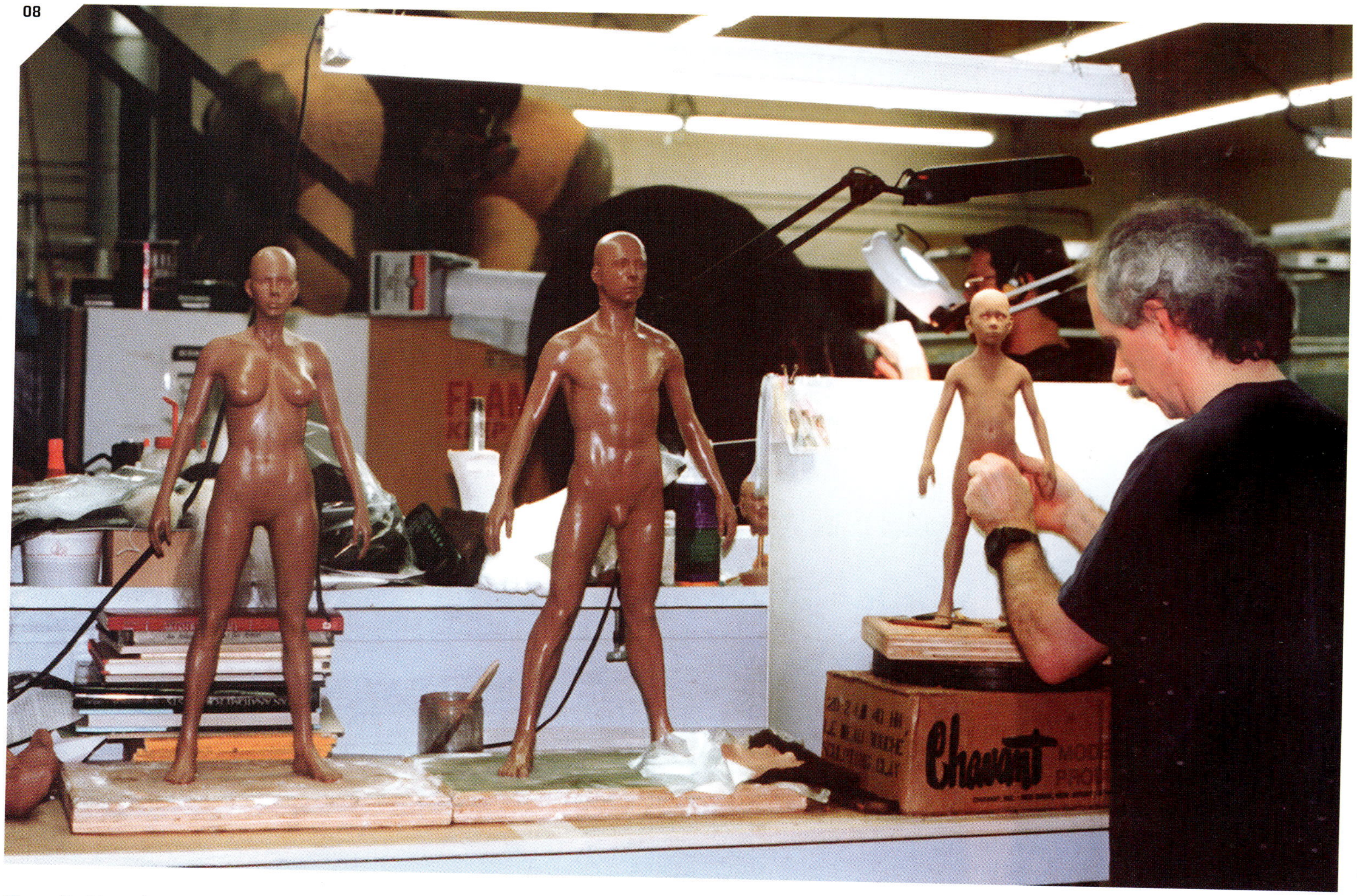

Once DeVane has shaped a clay face with his hands he will start using various tools to whittle away at the material and produce the final sculpture. "Like most sculptors I tend to make most of my own tools," says DeVane. "My most important ones are made from different grades of piano wire bent into a loop which is the size and shape that I want and then threaded into a piece of brass tubing which is crimped shut to make a handle.

"The first tool I'll normally use when I start shaping a sculpture will be a length of piano wire that I've doubled into a loop and then twisted into a spiral. That twisted wire is really good for scraping away broad strokes of clay. Coping-saw blades are also good. You can heat them up with a blowtorch and then bend them into a shape you like. I scrape those across a surface and remove clay to the depth of the teeth on the blade."

Every sculptor likes to work in a different way, emphasizing different parts of a form before others, or perfecting one area before moving on to next. For DeVane it is important to be sure the whole face is fully formed before any type of refinement is made. "You need to get the broad detail right before doing any refinement, because if you make a change to one thing you're actually changing the whole face. If you make a nose a bit wider you're not just widening the nose, you're also making the whole face look thinner, and so on.

"I often see [other sculptors] getting interested in one part of a sculpture and putting a lot of work into it and doing some finishing work when they should probably still be working on the broad shape. Having said that, I do spend a very long time getting the overall form right before doing any refinement."

While DeVane sculpts he often likes to be reminded of whose face he is working on by viewing videos of their previous movies. "Watching a performer on screen really helps me to get a strong sense of their form, the space that they occupy."

More often than not DeVane is trying not to create a likeness of a performer, but is attempting to reshape their existing features to produce someone—or something—new. For this he will refer to designs already created by a concept artist, be they two-dimensional artworks or three-dimensional maquettes. However, DeVane is not as complimentary about all of the design work he receives. "What's really frustrating is when I get given artwork that just isn't proportionately or anatomically correct. The artist might have sold a great-looking concept to the production, but that design may not actually fit the human form over which I have to sculpt—maybe the hips are too narrow or the nose too thin. In such cases, it feels like the designer has made a promise that I can't keep. That can be frustrating and embarrassing because when the sculpt doesn't look like the designer's artwork, people think it's me who can't do my job properly."

To convey a character's personality many artists draw their designs with dramatic facial expressions. This is something that DeVane has to interpret broadly in his sculpture. "Expression in a drawing gets across a sense of character, but we don't have those expressions permanently etched onto our faces. When it comes to a sculpture you need to create the same face when it's relaxed. The performer will use their own face to work the makeup. A lot of people can't resist putting at least a bit of expression into a sculpt, but a face with too much expression will look as dead as one with none."

The ability of a performer to create facial expressions when wearing prosthetics is something else the sculptor must consider. If a face needs to be highly supple it is important that appliances are as responsive as possible. While the final quality of the foam latex or silicone affects the performance of an appliance, its thickness also has an influence. "When you're creating forms on top of a lifecast it's easy to keep piling on the clay to get the shape you want," says DeVane. "In fact, you need to think about how thick the clay is on each area. The more supple the area, the thinner the clay should be."

When DeVane is happy with the overall form, he will start to finish it off, refining small areas and adding intricate surface detail. "A lot of time is spent removing all evidence of the artist. For makeup you have to conceal any suggestion of human involvement to create something that's completely natural-looking."

DeVane uses a number of materials to smooth down the clay surface of a sculpture, subtly influencing the surface forms. "I rub down the surface using different grades of canvas or plastic window screen, which is a fine plastic mesh that can be rubbed over the surface to smooth it down and polish it. Next I'll start on the fine detail of the skin, like pores and wrinkles. The first thing I do is go over the surface with a piece of ScotFoam, that can start to give a light texture to the skin."

Much time is spent creating the tiny pores and wrinkles that cover even the smoothest skin. "There are many ways to create them. You can use a little star-shaped arrangement of needles which you press into the clay through different grades of plastic sheeting. Plastic has the effect of softening the edges of your holes. If it's a tool with a number of points on it you have to be careful to avoid building up too much repetition in the pattern of the pores. You need to think carefully about the size, placement, angle, and depth of each pore, otherwise it will start to look repetitious and manmade.

"As well as adding indentations you need to add bumps. For example, men often have little bumps on their skin from razor burn. To reproduce this effect you can lie a needle so that it's almost flat to the surface, then you poke it in and use it to kind of lever up a bit of clay from underneath."

09

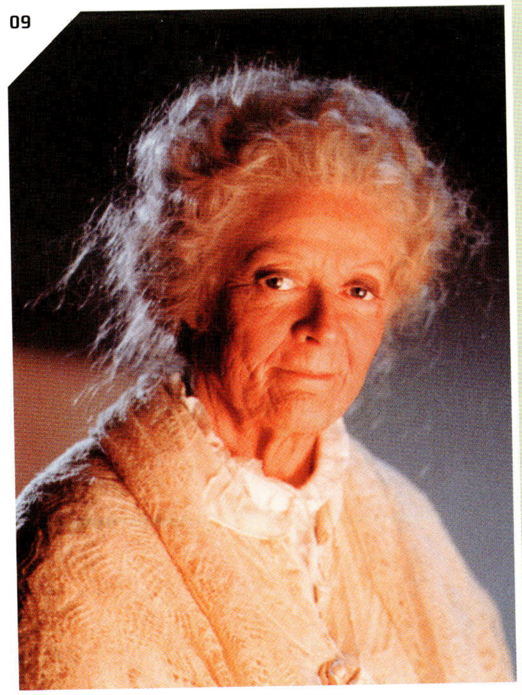

(08) DeVane sculpted these perfect human figures purely as scale comparisons for performer John Alexander when he wore a gorilla suit for *Mighty Joe Young* (1998) **(09)** Old-age makeup for Maggie Smith in *Hook* (1991).

Finally, DeVane creates the very fine texture of the skin surface. "One of my favorite tools for finishing is a dog-grooming brush. I drag that along over plastic, especially on areas like necks, cheeks, and foreheads, and it really unifies the surface and helps to tie all the other textures together. A final polish with a soft brush and powder, and you're done!"

THE ART OF MAKING MOLDS

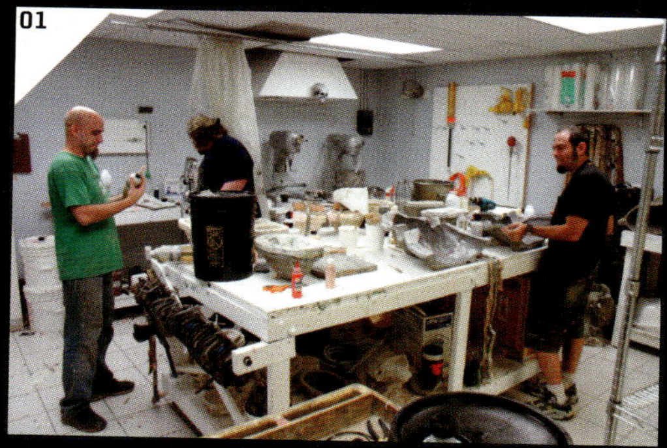

When a creature design has been sculpted, the next step is to produce the molds from which a final foam-latex or silicone character suit, animatronic skin, or prosthetic appliance will be cast.

The starting point for any human-based makeup is usually a lifecast of an actor's head or body. This is created by covering the performer in a fast-setting alginate mixture that solidifies to form a kind of dense rubber. This is ladled over the performer, making sure that it works its way into every bodily feature, with only the nostrils kept clear so the actor can breathe. To protect the flexible alginate, bandages dipped in plaster are layered over the top of it.

When the alginate and plaster has set, the mold is carefully cut in half and removed. The two resulting halves are then fitted back together to form a hollow shell.

A hard-setting plaster or artificial stone is then poured into the mold, which, when set, is removed. The result is a lifecast, a perfect copy of the performer complete with every wrinkle, pore, and blemish.

A modern alternative to the lifecasting process is cyberscanning. This uses a laser to record the performer's body or face as a three-dimensional digital model. The data can then be used by a computerized milling machine to carve an exact replica, at any scale, in rigid foam.

A finished cast is only the start of the molding process. Next, the physical character changes that are to be made to the performer—whether giving them a larger nose or transforming their entire body into that of a monster—are sculpted in clay over the top of the lifecast. The result is an entirely new body form built on top of the performer's natural shape.

The parts that have been added to the lifecast in clay then need to be reproduced in a material such as foam latex or silicone. This is done by making another mold, either in a stone material or, on larger sculptures, by painting on a resin and reinforcing it with fiberglass. The resulting mold is a perfect negative of the clay sculpture; if this were then filled with foam latex, the result would be an identical copy. However, what is usually needed is a copy of only the additional face and body elements that have been sculpted onto the lifecast in clay. To achieve this, the original lifecast of the performer is placed inside the mold. The gaps between the lifecast and the new mold are injected with foam latex or silicone, forming a prosthetic appliance that will be the shape of the performer on the inside and the shape of the new clay sculpture on the outside.

Instead of an actor, animatronic characters will be filled with the various mechanics and motors necessary to produce a performance. The starting point is a clay sculpture of the character. A mold is made of the sculpture to produce a negative version of the creature's exterior.

In order to create the skin to cover the internal mechanisms, another mold, or core, needs to be created. This core is placed inside the main mold, producing a gap into which foam latex will be injected. To create the core the inside of the mold is carefully lined with clay to the desired thickness. The depth of the clay will eventually be reflected in the thickness of the skin. Areas that, in the performance, need to produce subtle movements will be kept thin while less responsive areas will be made thicker. When this clay skin has been sculpted over the inside of the mold, it is coated in a material such as fiberglass. The result is a mold of the inside of the skin, which is the core. The clay is then removed from the original mold, the core placed inside that mold, and foam latex added to the void between the two pieces.

As the core is exactly the size and shape of the creature's body beneath the skin it can be used to create the main framework for the animatronic body. The core is cut up into pieces, enabling various parts of the body to move, and mounted over the top of the creature's internal mechanisms, which will have been made separately. When the animatronic body of the character has been completed, the painted foam skin is placed back over the core, fitting it perfectly.

As we've seen, creating molds is essentially a matter of producing negative and positive versions of a sculpture and using the difference between each to create a prosthetic appliance, creature suit, or skin for an animatronic character. However, the mold maker needs to know which materials will be used to make the creature's skin, as this will influence the material that the mold is made from. Some mold-making materials adversely affect the foam or silicone that will be used inside it, and vice versa. The mold maker also needs to know how many copies of an appliance will be made; this again determines the mold material.

Complex characters will need to have molds made in perhaps as many as 20 interlocking pieces. This means that the mold maker must decide exactly where the seams of each section will run before making each piece separately. The walls between each section need to have keys built into them so that each section of the final mold will line up and slot together.

Working with a foam technician, mold makers will also decide how and where it will be best to inject foam into the mold, allowing the foam to run freely through the cavities and expelling any air bubbles. The mold will then have stand pipes built into it ready for the foam to be injected.

Mold making is simple in principle, but in reality a complicated process requiring consummate skill. Each mold-maker has their own methods and secrets, and each a favored range of materials. The process can be hot, dusty, smelly, and often toxic. It is, however, an essential part of creating movie creatures and characters.

02

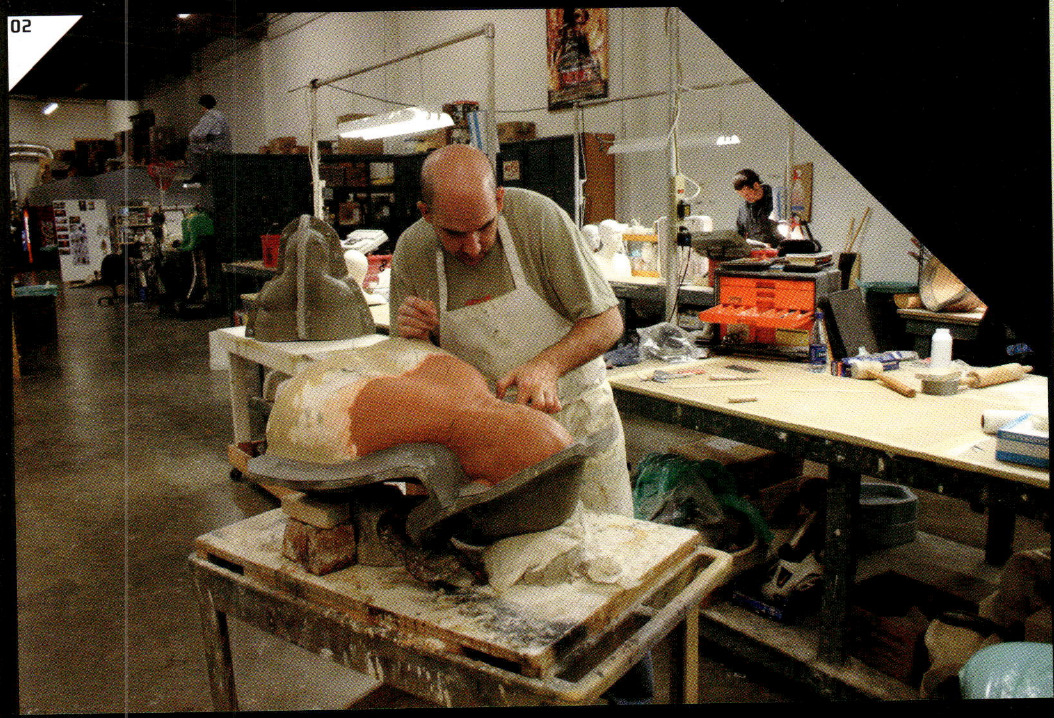

03

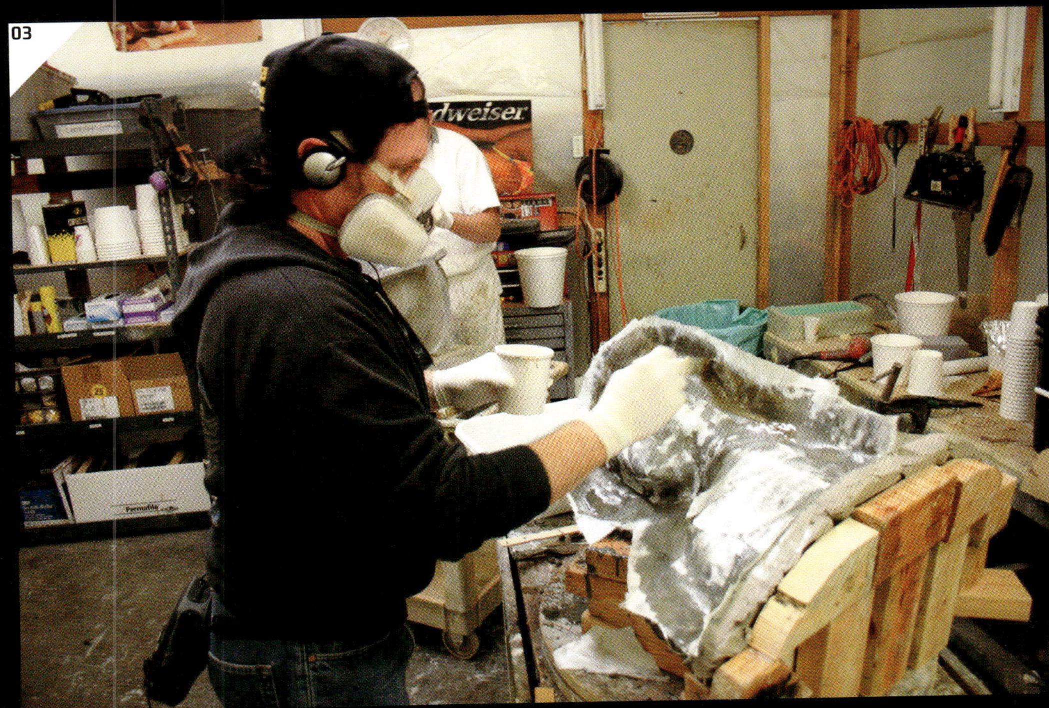

04

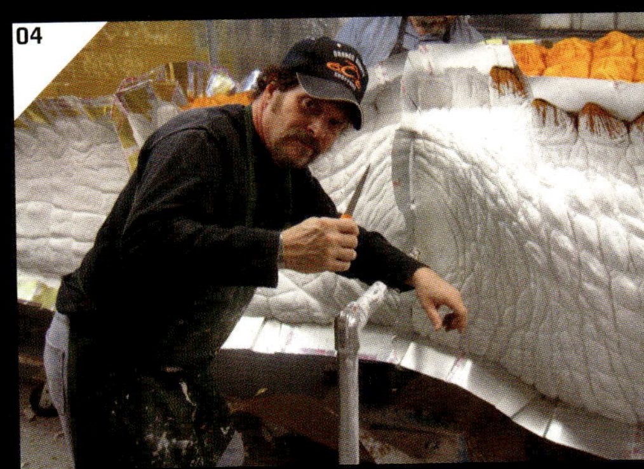

(01) Mold-makers at work
(02) A three-piece mold is removed from a clay sculpt
(03) The casing of a mold is built-up with additional layers of resin.
(04) Preparing a sculpture for a multipart mold by inserting metal dividers.

MONSTER MATERIALS

Foam latex is by far the most commonly used material for creating prosthetic appliances and creature costumes. Every project requires a different quality of foam latex, depending on the character's size and shape, the way it will be used, and how it will perform. The production of foam latex, known as foam running, is both an art and a science.

The basic ingredient of foam latex is liquid latex, a sticky white syrup, to which various components are added, including a foaming agent, which helps to create bubbles, a curing agent that will cause it to set, and a number of other additives that will affect qualities such as the foam's density, the speed at which it sets, its color, and so on.

When all the ingredients have been measured and mixed, the resulting liquid is tipped into a large bowl and whipped up into a froth. The degree to which the mixture is whipped will greatly affect the consistency of the resulting foam. Small bubbles will produce a dense, heavy foam, while larger bubbles will create a lighter, more flexible, material.

A heavier foam might be used for a large animatronic creature whose skin is thick and leathery, such as a dinosaur; a light foam would be used to create flexible prosthetic facial appliances, or wrinkly, soft skin. Often several densities of foam will be used in one mold. For example, a strong, dense foam might be used to create the hard-wearing feet of a costume character, while a medium-density foam would be used for the rest of the skin.

Before the foam is added to a mold, any areas that might experience excessive wear and tear—such as elbows and knees—will be lined with pieces of nylon or Lycra to help reinforce the finished piece. These areas might also be brushed with a layer of denser foam. In the case of creature suits, a spandex unitard is stretched over the mold's entire inner core before the foam latex is introduced. The result is a stretchy bodysuit with a sculpted foam-latex outer skin.

Small molds have the foam mixture carefully spooned into them, while larger or more complicated molds will have the foam injected using a giant syringe. This forces the foam into every cavity and out through small vent holes that are there to prevent air bubbles from forming inside the mold.

Once filled, the mold is left for a while to allow the gelling agent to set the foam. The entire mold is then placed in an oven and baked—or cured—for between one and 12 hours, depending on the size of the mold and the desired quality of the foam. Like baking a cake, longer cooking at cooler temperatures will produce something that is softer and more consistent. Baking slowly also helps prevent the foam-latex object shrinking inside the mold.

When the oven is opened the smell of ammonia—released from the foam during the curing process—wafts out. The mold is then opened and the foam-rubber piece allowed to cool before being removed and thoroughly washed to minimize its unpleasant aroma. The resulting foam-latex item will be a perfect positive copy of the mold in which it was cast, with every minute wrinkle and skin pore of the original sculpture appearing on its surface. When the small flanges of foam that result from the seams and air vents of the mold have been trimmed from the cast, it is ready to be painted.

(01) Several gallons of liquid foam latex is pumped into a large fiberglass mold. The mold has several plugs through which the foam can be injected to ensure it reaches every corner.

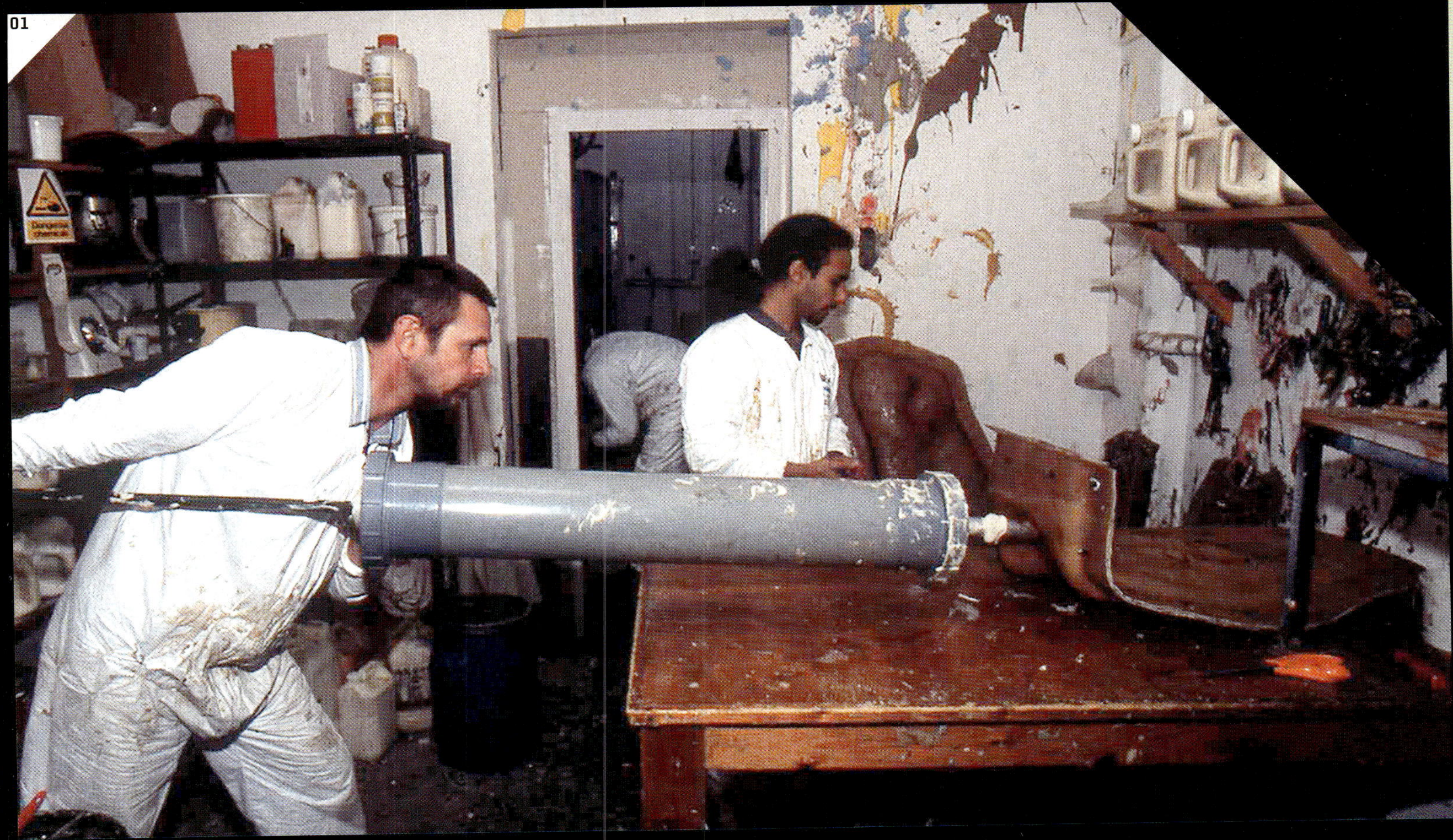

Foam latex has been the mainstay of special-effects makeup appliances since the late 1930s and is still used for the vast majority of work. It is good at producing tough, leathery-looking skin, but many types of skin, particularly that of humans, are actually translucent. Some skillful artists are able to paint the opaque surface of foam latex to make it look translucent, but it rarely looks exactly like human skin. To produce completely naturalistic, translucent skin, silicone is now used as an alternative.

Silicone is a greasy cream similar to soft petroleum jelly, and is supplied in large tubs. In order to turn the liquid into a rubber it is mixed with a catalyst that solidifies it over a period of several hours. Other ingredients added to the mix include plasticizers, which will determine how rubbery the finished material will be, and dyes.

Because silicone can be difficult to glue and paint, another material is often painted onto the surface of a mold to produce what will be the outer skin of the appliance. This material could be a rubber, vinyl, or a less oily silicone. Once this skin has dried, the mold will be closed and the catalyzed silicone is injected.

Although silicone looks good, it does have disadvantages: it is very heavy, and so can be impractical for large creature skins or character suits. Some varieties of silicone can react badly to other materials used during the manufacturing, and so the combination of materials and processes used at each stage must be carefully planned in advance.

A third material, less frequently used than either foam or silicone, is gelatin. This is an animal extract normally used to set foods such as Jell-o, and it comes in a powder called gelatin sorbitol. This is mixed with glycerine and water and heated up before being poured into molds. After a few hours the gelatin sets to form a jelly-like solid.

Gelatin is usually only used for small appliances such as scars. Because it can be melted by heat it is easy to blend the edges of an appliance into a performer's skin, but this also means that the heat of studio lights can cause a gelatin appliance to melt and slide away from the skin.

THE SCIENCE OF APPLIANCE

Once a makeup or character suit has been designed and manufactured, it will, of course, be worn by a performer. In the case of a full creature suit, the performer steps into the costume while assistants zip and popper it shut around the body.

Many makeups, however, are applied directly to the performer, with pieces of latex or silicone being glued onto their skin and painted to look as if they were always there. This is a crucial stage of the makeup process—the culmination of months of work by designers, sculptors, mold-makers, foam runners, and painters. This is when a few pieces of lifeless material are used to transform an ordinary human being into an extraordinary character.

The final application of a makeup is sometimes done by the people who designed, sculpted, and created it, but often the process is handled by specialist makeup artists who only become involved in at a project's later stages.

Before filming begins, makeup artists apply a test makeup to the performer who will be wearing it on-screen. This is normally done alongside the makeup designer to ensure everything remains true to their intentions. At this stage, any small changes to the paints, glues or other materials to be used will be made, and the exact methodology with which each appliance is fitted will be decided.

When shooting starts, makeup artists are normally among the first people on set in the morning. Before performers arrive, artists will prepare the appliances, tools, and paints ready for use. Depending on the nature of the makeup, the actual application process typically takes between one and four hours, so if a performer is required to appear in the first shots of the day a makeup artist might have to arrive on set in the early hours of the morning.

The first stage of applying a makeup is to attach prosthetic appliances to the performer's face and body. The goal is to hide the blend lines. Well-made appliances have extremely thin edges that are easy to hide along natural skin creases.

Appliances are always pre-painted to get them as close to the color of a performer's skin as possible, but once attached they will need a little more painting to blend them completely. In the case of aliens or monsters, the performer's skin will need to be painted to match the appliance. It is vital that paintwork looks exactly the same each time a makeup is applied, and so makeup artists will refer to original designs and Polaroids of previous applications as they work.

However, there are some clever methods of making this easier. For *Hellboy* (2004), the character of Abe Sapien was created by gluing intricately patterned appliances to the body of performer Doug Jones.

(01) Makeup artist Bart Mixon nears the end of a lengthy appliance session during which he has transformed Kelsey Grammer into Beast for *X-Men: The Last Stand* (2006).

01

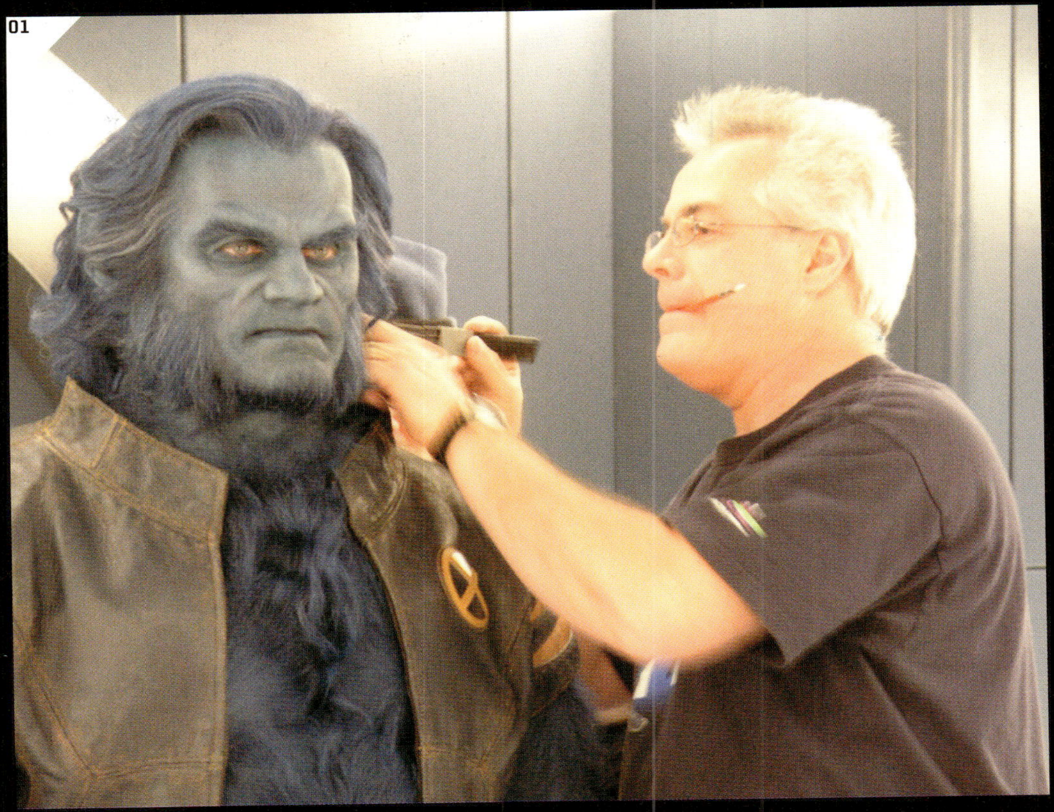

The durability of a makeup can greatly depend on the care shown to it by the performer who wears it. The more considerate actors will take good care of their makeup—resisting the urge to scratch any itch that's lurking underneath.

Once filming is over and the rest of the crew leave for the night, the makeup artist often has plenty of work ahead of them—complex makeups can take almost as long to remove as they do to apply. Makeup artists are undoubtedly among the longest working members of a film crew, putting in long hours and often staying away from home. However, the final part of a character's creation is often in their expert hands.

The remaining areas of his bare skin were then painted to match. To make sure that the swirling, fish-like patterns were identical for each application, and to ensure the patterns linked each foam latex appliance, a special template was created. Thin plastic was vacuformed around Jones' lifecast and the pattern of the design was then cut out of the plastic to make a kind of three-dimensional stencil. Once the latex appliances were stuck down and a base-coat of color had been painted on the skin, the plastic stencil was placed over the performer's body and black skin-ink sprayed through the holes.

Applying complex makeups can be something of an endurance test for both makeup artist and performer. A complicated design may require two or even three artists to work on the performer simultaneously, with each concentrating on a different part of the body. In such cases, makeup artists hope that the performer is both patient and understanding, allowing them to work in a pleasant and relaxed atmosphere—although that is not always the case!

Once makeup is applied and painted, additional features such as false teeth, contact lenses, and hair appliances are added to complete the effect. The performer may even need to visit the hairdresser so that any artificial hair can be appropriately coiffured.

Once a performer is ready for the cameras, the makeup artist's job is by no means over. Almost as soon as it is completed a makeup will start to decay. From behind the camera makeup artists will watch the action, carefully keeping an eye on the makeup and its performance. The artist will know the limits of each design, and if the performer should move in an unexpected way they will be sure to check appliances for any stretching or tearing.

To avoid removing and re-applying any damaged appliances, running repairs can be made on set. Makeup artists often make "blenders"—the equivalent of sticking plasters. A range of sizes and shapes will be made that have the same surface texture and color as the rest of the appliances. If anything rips, one of these will be patched in as a quick fix.

KAZUHIRO TSUJI

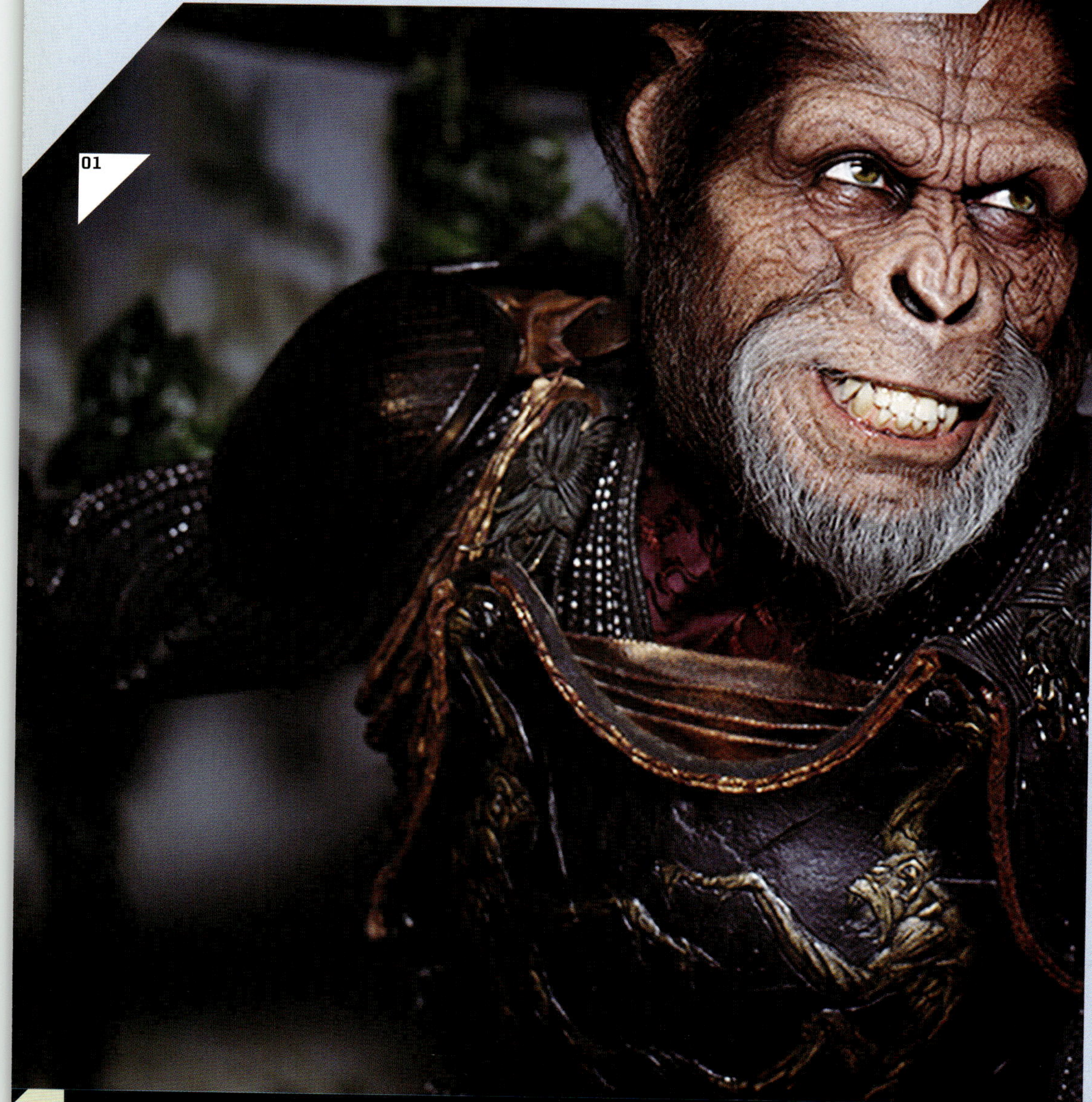
01

CV

Makeup artist and sculptor; b. Kyoto, Japan; became interested in a career in movie makeup while still at school, and corresponded with Dick Smith; when Smith was filming *Sweet Home* (1989) in Japan, he invited Tsuji to work on the film; after more film work in Japan and teaching, was invited by Rick Baker to work on *Men in Black* (1997), and moved to the USA; since then has worked on numerous films as a designer and makeup creator.

SELECT FILMOGRAPHY

Batman and Robin (1997); *Men in Black* (1997); Mighty Joe Young (1998); *How the Grinch Stole Christmas* (aka *Dr. Seuss' How the Grinch Stole Christmas*, (2000); *Planet of the Apes* (2001); *The Ring* (2002); *The Haunted Mansion* (2003); *Hellboy* (2004); *The Cave* (2005)

KEY CHARACTERS

Joe (Mighty Joe Young); Thade (Planet of the Apes); Dick Smith (tribute portrait); Samara (The Ring); The Grinch

TECHNIQUES

Traditional design and sculpture; Photoshop; ZBrush; makeup

02

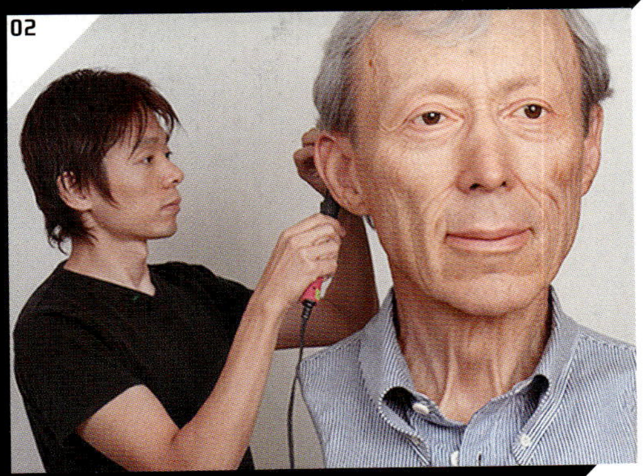

03

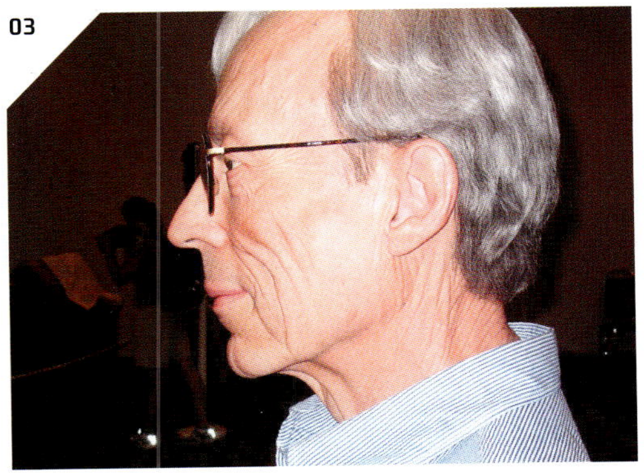

04

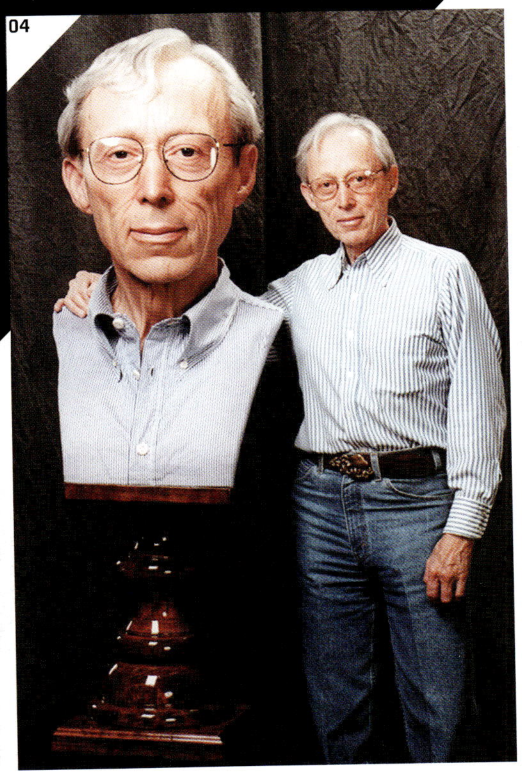

Kazuhiro Tsuji grew up in Kyoto, Japan. When he was eight, Tsuji saw *Star Wars* (1977) and became fascinated with production design and special effects. While still at junior high school he began to make home-movies and experiment with all kinds of special-effects techniques, including miniatures, stop-motion animation, and matte paintings. At this stage he avoided the makeup pages of the movie books and magazines he collected, as he was squeamish. However, after seeing Dick Smith's old-age makeup for *The Exorcist* (1973) and Rick Baker's transformation sequences in *An American Werewolf in London* (1981), Tsuji realized that special-effects makeup could be powerful without involving too much blood and gore.

When Tsuji was 17 he saw an article in movie magazine *Fangoria* about Dick Smith's makeup for *North and South* (1985), in which he turned actor Hal Holbrook into President Lincoln. From then on Tsuji decided that he wanted to be a makeup artist, spending all his spare time and money making sculptures and makeup appliances—and even turning himself into Lincoln.

Like many other young hopefuls, Tsuji wrote to makeup master Dick Smith and, as is usual, received a courteous and helpful reply. Tsuji then wrote regularly to Smith, sending photographs of his work and receiving advice in return. When Smith was hired to create the makeup for *Sweet Home* (or *Suito Homu*, 1989), which was being filmed in Japan, he invited Tsuji to work with him as an assistant. After working on a number of movies and teaching for several years at the Yoyogi Animation Institute, Tsuji was hired by Rick Baker to work on *Men in Black* (1997). Baker had been impressed by some photographs of Tsuji's old-age makeups and decided to sponsor his immigration to the USA. Since then, Tsuji has designed and created creature and character makeups for many movies, often in association with Baker, including *How the Grinch Stole Christmas* (2000), *Planet of the Apes* (2001), *The Ring* (2002), and *The Cave* (2005).

Of the many aspects of makeup at which Tsuji excels, he has become known for creating incredibly realistic human facial sculptures. The sculptural portraits that he produces are so startlingly realistic that a photograph of one of his creations could easily be mistaken for that of a living person. "I love human faces, they fascinate me," says Tsuji. "Of course, I love the imagination involved in creating weird and wonderful characters for the movies, but reproducing nature is the ultimate challenge."

When creating a human portrait, Tsuji does not start with a lifecast, preferring instead to sculpt from scratch. "A lifecast can only capture the shape and basic detail of a face, but not the life in it," he says. "Every face presents a different challenge; there are so many tiny subtleties on each person's face that you won't find on anybody else's. Faces change and evolve according to the life that someone has had, and capturing that sense of history and experience is the greatest artistic endeavor." Tsuji can sculpt a realistic bust just by looking at photographs of the front and side view of a person's face, but he prefers to meet his subject in person. "That's how you get a real sense of who someone is, their personality and life," he says.

At the sculptural stage, Tsuji considers that the tiny details of a face are every bit as important as the major features. "It's important to make sure that the surface of the skin is right," he says. "Everyone has different skin with different textures and pores. I have to get that right if the portrait is going to look alive."

(01) Kazuhiro Tsuji created stunning ape makeup for Planet of the Apes (2001). This is a display version of Thade, which Tsuji created for show at Rick Baker's studio **(02)** Tsuji styles the hair on his incredibly realistic bust of Dick Smith **(03)** Detail of Dick Smith bust. **(04)** Smith poses with the larger-than-life portrait created in tribute to him by Tsuji

05

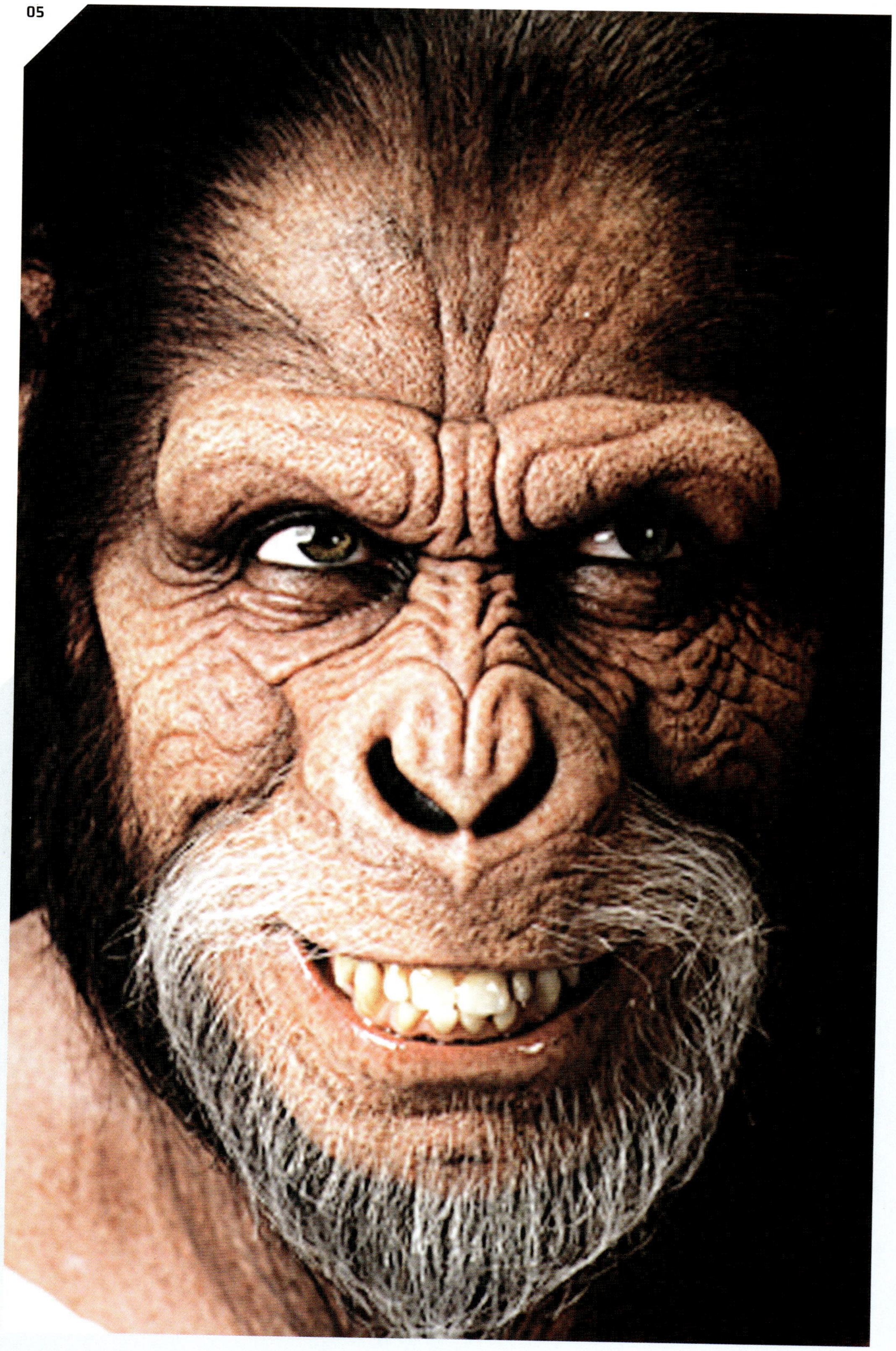

06

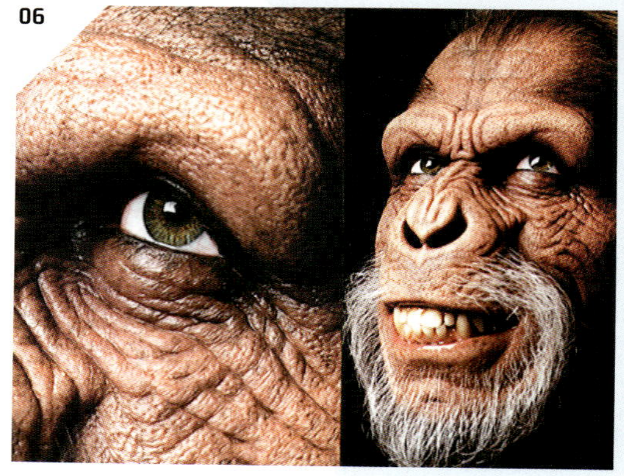

To give the skin on a human face its microscopic pores, Tsuji uses tools that have several needle tips poking out of them to push thousands of tiny indentations into the surface of the clay. Nevertheless he must still press these into the clay of each face many hundreds of times. He often lays a thin plastic sheet over the clay and presses the tool into the plastic in order to give the pores below a smoother edge.

Tsuji casts his human faces in silicone, and strives to ensure that the result is as close as possible in color and opacity to the required final appearance. "I mix the silicone with flocking, which is thousands of tiny, very fine, colored hairs," he explains. "That makes the silicone more opaque, more like the appearance of skin. Silicone alone is too translucent. I will also dye the silicone the right color. It's important to get the color right. If it's too light or dark then I will have to change it during painting."

To paint his silicone Tsuji uses oil paints or acrylics that have been mixed with silicone and thinned down with a solvent, such as naphtha. Each layer of paint is thinly airbrushed on to the silicone, one color at a time to build up the final appearance. "I will normally use a blue, two different reds, a yellow, two different browns, a green and a black. I'll layer those one color at a time in different combinations until I get the look that I want. The browns usually go last to give the effect of the melanin in the skin." Tsuji also uses a very fine brush to add detail, such the appearance of blood vessels under the skin.

(05–06) Display bust of Tsuji's design for Thade, played by Tim Roth in *Planet of the Apes* **(07–09)** This looks like a photograph of a living person, but it is actually a bust sculpted, painted, and finished by Kazuhiro Tsuji.

07

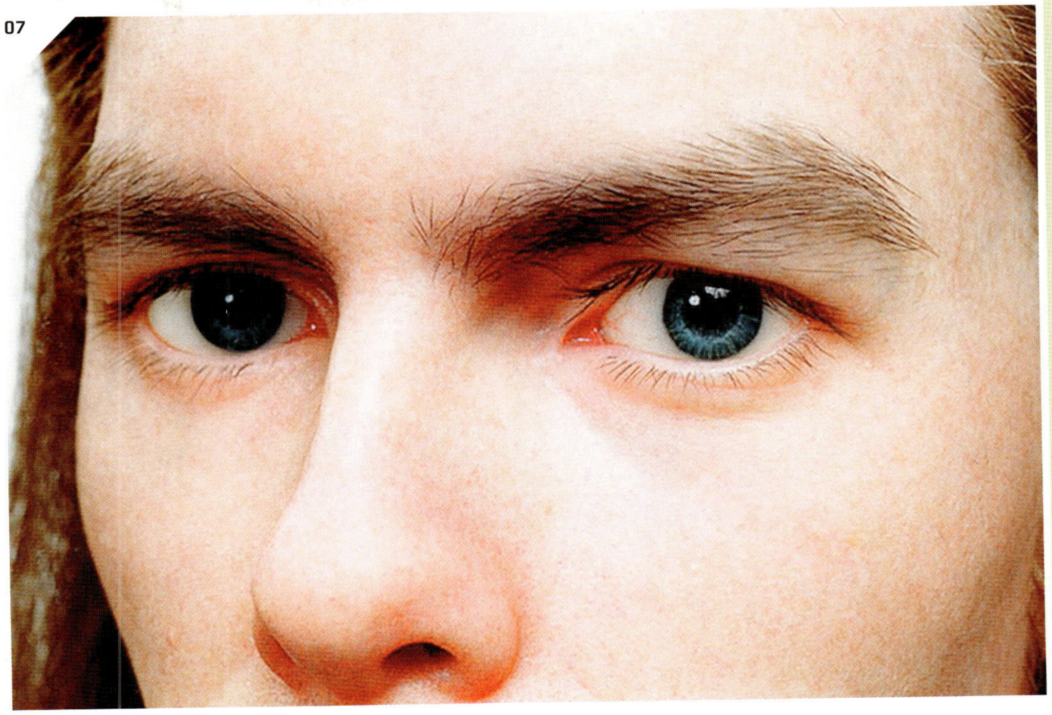

08

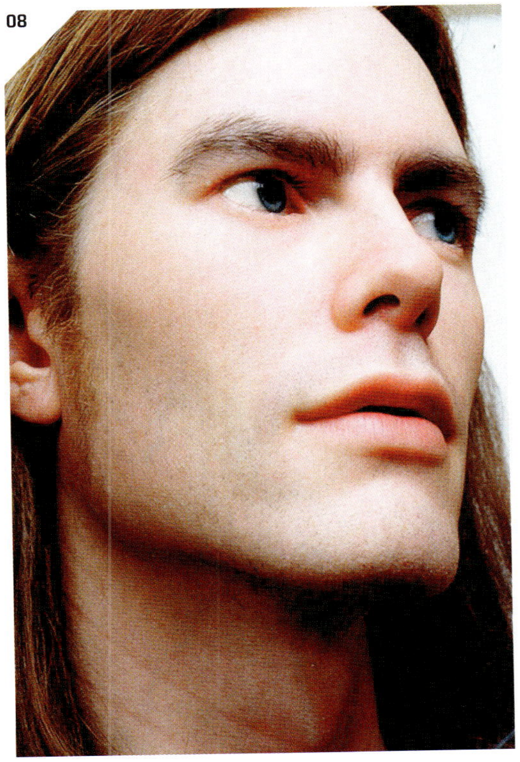

09

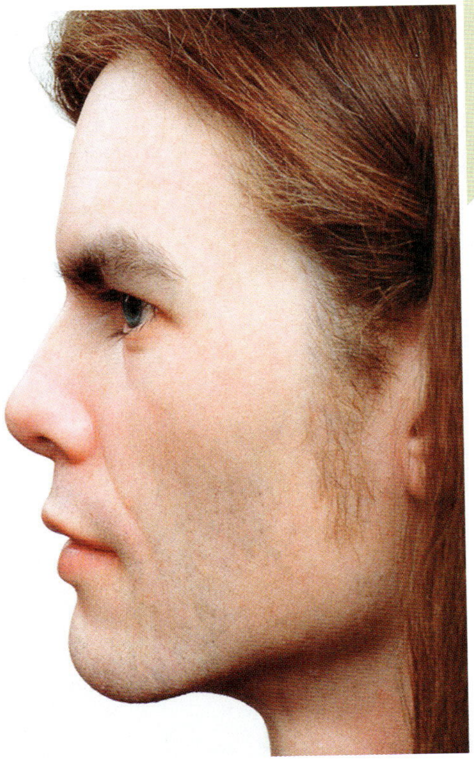

Hair is added by hand-punching each strand into the silicone. Perhaps unsurprisingly, Tsuji uses human hair for the head, but he prefers to use rabbit hair for the eyebrows and eyelashes. Rick Baker was so impressed by the eyebrows created by Tsuji for some fake bodies he made for *Batman and Robin* (1997) that he awarded him the nickname "King of the Eyebrows." For men's stubble Tsuji uses yak hair, punching long strands into the silicone and then giving the character a shave to achieve the right look. He sometimes shaves the hair right back to the skin so that while no stubble protrudes from the actual surface of the skin, it remains visible below the surface as if actually growing there. For the finishing touches Tsuji makes the eyes from polyester resin and creates teeth from dental acrylic.

Although Tsuji is one of the most admired people in the makeup industry for his incredible makeup work, his sculptural portraits have become famous because of one particular subject. In 2002 he made a twice-life-size bust of Dick Smith to commemorate the legendary makeup artist's 80th birthday. Although those seeing Tsuji's sculpture of Dick Smith are startled by its extraordinary likeness, Tsuji remains less sure of its accuracy. "It isn't meant to be an exact replica of him," he says, "it's a portrait. That means that I have tried to capture the essence of him as I see him, as I think of his personality and the things he has achieved. When Dick saw his portrait he was absolutely amazed and he cried," recalls Tsuji. "I think he realized that I was only able to make it because of all of his help, and what he had taught me. That was the greatest tribute I can imagine."

MARK SETRAKIAN

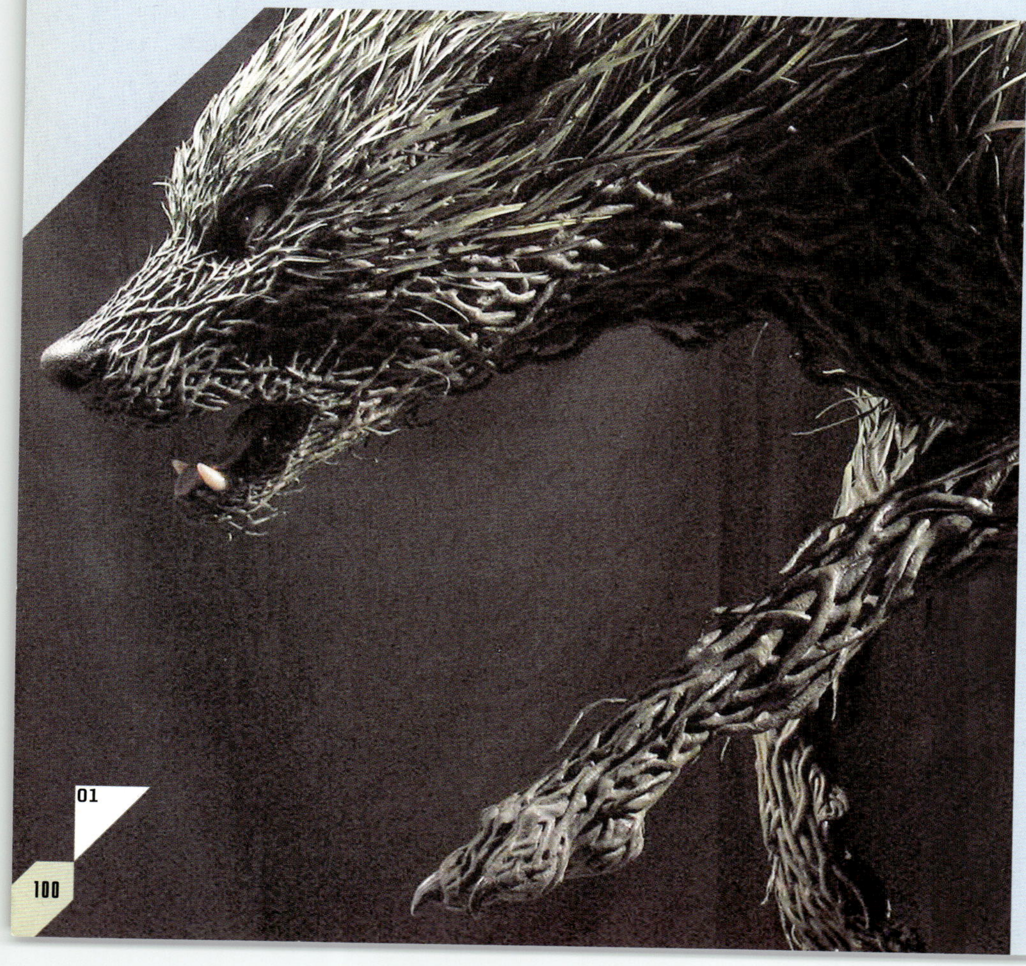

01

CV

Animatronics designer and puppeteer; grew up in Marin County, CA; at 19 started work in the local creature lab—George Lucas's Industrial Light and Magic (ILM); moved to LA in 1988; now one of the world's most sought-after designers; has also created robots for *Battlebots* and *Robot Wars* TV series.

SELECT FILMOGRAPHY

Howard the Duck (1986); *The Golden Child* (1986); **batteries not included* (1987); *Innerspace* (1987); *Spaceballs* (1987), *The Blob* (1988); *Robot Jox* (1990); *Gremlins 2: The New Batch* (1990); *Batman Forever* (1995); *Men in Black* (1997); *Mighty Joe Young* (1998); *How the Grinch Stole Christmas* (2000); *Hellboy* (2004) *Lady in the Water* (2006)

KEY CHARACTERS

Howard (*Howard the Duck*); Brain Gremlin (*Gremlins 2: The New Batch*); alien controlling a human robotic body (*Men in Black*); Abe Sapien, Sammael (*Hellboy*); the Scrunt (*Lady in the Water*)

TECHNOLOGIES

Animatronics; Gilderfluke machine; CAD software; Max programming

02

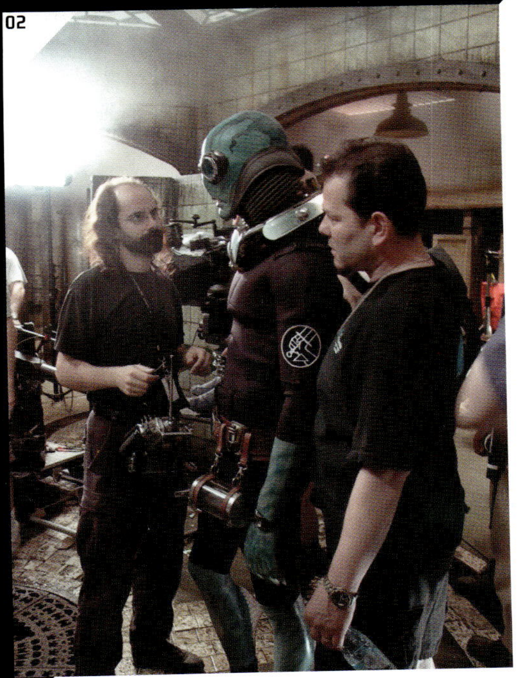

Mark Setrakian grew up in Marin County, California. His childhood heroes were Leonardo da Vinci and marine explorer Jacques Cousteau, and his favorite toys were anything that he could take apart, from the kitchen toaster to an old camera. If asked what he wanted to do when he grew up, Setrakian would always reply: "I want to be an inventor."

Setrakian fell in love with movie monsters. "Growing up in Marin County, my local special-effects company was George Lucas's Industrial Light and Magic," recalls Setrakian. "Having ILM just down the road from where I lived made me realize that it wasn't an impossible dream, but I was pretty realistic about how hard it would be to get in. I was getting a lot of very bad advice, such as, 'Write a letter to George Lucas.' I knew perfectly well that wasn't going to work! I had to find a way to meet someone who worked at ILM."

When he discovered that some of ILM's employees also taught art at the local junior college, Setrakian signed up for sculpture classes. Before long he met Lorne Peterson, then head of ILM's model shop. "I had this tiny mechanical puppet with me that I had made," he recalls. "Lorne thought it was great, and told me I should meet with Charlie Bailey in ILM's creature shop."

So, at the age of 19, and with no formal mechanical or engineering training, Setrakian started work in the creature shop at ILM, designing and building animatronics—first of all for *Howard the Duck* (1986). Setrakian helped to construct fully animatronic puppet versions of the giant-size duck, as well as suit versions worn by a performer. He also got to be a puppeteer for the character during location filming.

"Looking back, I realize that my three years at ILM were my college education," he says. "Twenty years later, the skills I learned are the foundation for everything I have learned since. Every project is an opportunity to learn. ILM was a great place for me because, to be honest, they didn't know a lot about this stuff themselves at that time. Many of the techniques that are now standard were still being developed. We were all making things up as we went along."

Setrakian worked with ILM on a number of movies that required increasingly sophisticated animatronics and performance systems, including *The Golden Child* (1986), **batteries not included* (1987), *Innerspace* (1987), and *Spaceballs* (1987). However, with ILM being the only effects facility in the area, Setrakian found work opportunities were sporadic. Setrakian got a call from Lyle Conway inviting him to work in Hollywood on *The Blob* (1988), and he decided to move south permanently. The move paid dividends when he was hired by Rick Baker to work as an animatronic designer on *Gremlins 2: The New Batch* (1990). It was the start of a 15-year collaboration.

Setrakian remembers *Gremlins 2* as an opportunity to learn new techniques —in particular, methods of coaxing synchronized speech from the puppets. "The Brain Gremlin was voiced by Tony Randall," recalls Setrakian. "Production would send me these reel-to-reel tapes with Tony's dialogue on them. I would synchronize the playback to a huge motion-control computer called a Gilderfluke machine. To program the puppet, I would run the tape at half-speed and place my hand into a glove-like puppet controller to perform the movements of the Gremlin's mouth in sync with the voice track. I would do a few passes: first, I would focus on the broad jaw movements, then the vowels and consonants, and then a final pass would control the tongue for things like Ts and Ds. These passes could then be combined and played back from the Gilderfluke, which sent signals to the servos in the Gremlin's head. Now, I can do everything from my PowerBook!"

Working for Baker, Setrakian created mechanical characters for *Batman Forever* (1995), *Mighty Joe Young* (1998), and *How the Grinch Stole Christmas* (2000).

(01) The Scrunt by Setrakian and Spectral Motion for *Lady in the Water* (2006)
(02) Setrakian (left) and Mike Elizalde make adjustments to Abe Sapien on the Prague set of *Hellboy* (2004).

03

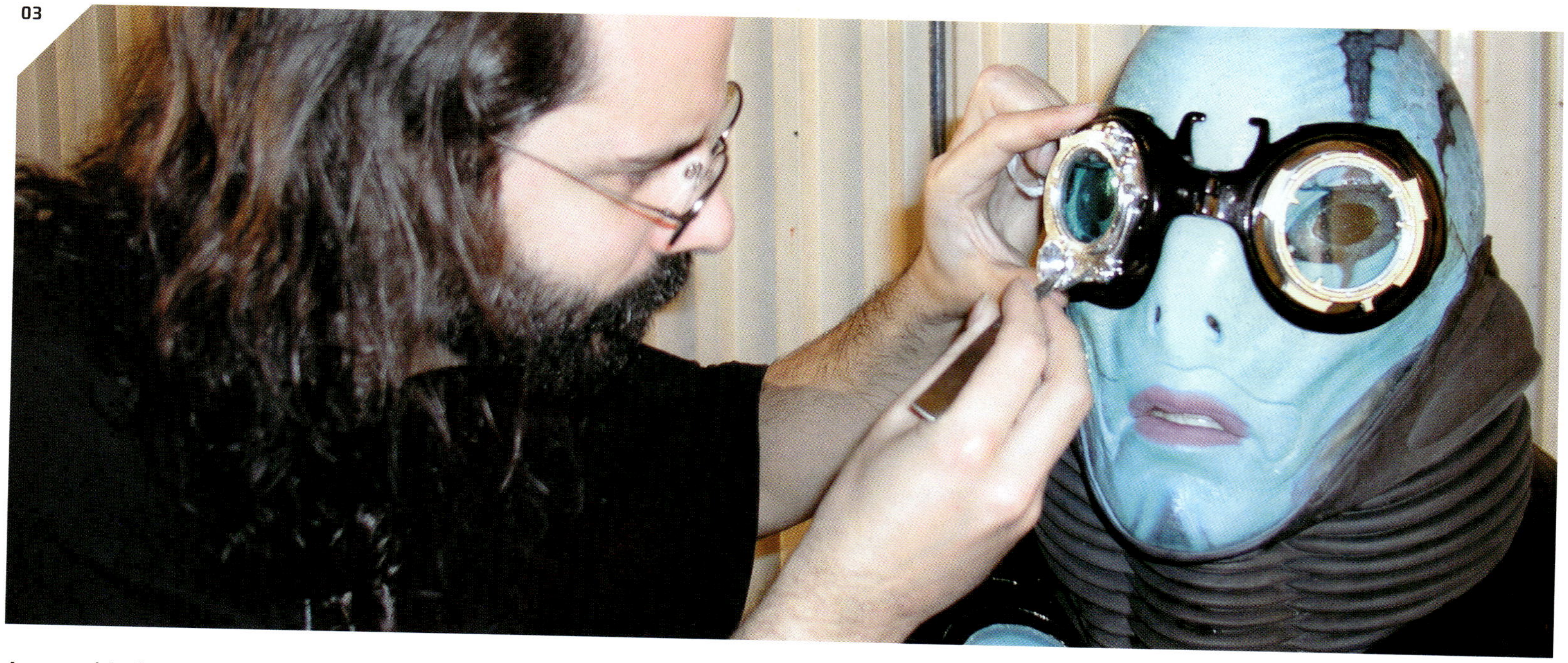

Among his favorite work from the period is the small green alien who sits in a control-room housed within a human character's head in *Men in Black* (1997). "One of the reasons I like that little alien is that I actually created that character," recalls Setrakian. "In an early draft of the script, there was a short scene where a guy lifts some skin up around his neck and we see light come out, showing that he's an alien. I thought it would be better to do something more specific, so I did a little sketch of the whole face opening up to reveal a tiny alien in a cockpit controlling a robotic human body. The director liked this idea so much that he threw out the original scene and wrote a whole new sequence with a page of dialogue."

Setrakian built two versions of the alien-in-the-head puppet. One was actual size, with a tiny mechanical puppet that could move when the actors were filmed next to it. While filming with actors Will Smith and Linda Fiorentino, Setrakian operated the tiny alien and also spoke his dialogue. For close-up shots, a version six-times actual size was constructed, allowing a better mechanical performance from the alien. Close-ups were filmed using the dialogue spoken by Setrakian to control the alien's lips in a way similar to that used for *Gremlins 2*. Much to his surprise, his voice performance made the final cut.

Since *Men in Black*, animatronic technology has vastly improved. One of his more recent constructions was the horrific Scrunt, made by Spectral Motion for M. Night Shyamalan's *Lady in the Water* (2006). Setrakian describes what the project involved: "The Scrunt is like a big wolf made of roots and dirt with grass for fur," he explains. "Night wanted as many shots as possible to be achieved practically during filming, which meant constructing a creature capable of a wide range of expression and movement—including walking and running."

Constructing a walking puppet was a bold move that bucked the convention of using animatronic creatures for close-ups and static shots, and CGI whenever a character needs to walk or run. "Like an increasing number of directors, Night sees the benefit of going to set with a physical puppet, and having CGI pick up where the puppet leaves off," says Setrakian. "It means that he can direct it, the camera crew can shoot it, and the actors can interact with the creature. It benefits the CG guys too, since they have the best possible reference for their animation." Creating a character as sophisticated as the Scrunt means that Setrakian needs to get involved as early as possible. "The usual process is to produce concept drawings, which are then sculpted to create maquettes, then a full-sized sculpture, a mold, and then a fiberglass core. Based on the core, we build a mechanism that fits inside and makes the final character look alive. However, if I can see the designs during the planning stages, I can often find interesting ways to get the creature to move. This may mean suggesting subtle changes to the design."

However, as an engineer Setrakian is careful not to step too far into the territories of character designer or sculptor. "Part of my job is to give the sculptors as much design freedom as possible. I don't ask for a change unless there is a valid technical reason to do so. Anything that is well sculpted in an anatomically realistic way can be made to work mechanically—one way or another. If the creature is a weird shape with limbs so impossibly thin that it's hard to get a mechanism in there, then chances are that creature could never exist."

Setrakian does, however, make design suggestions that he feels might help to improve the dramatic impact of a character. "When I saw the early drawings of the Scrunt, I saw that it had a really long tail. That's when it occurred to me that I could give this thing some really frightening qualities—like a tail that lashes in a serpentine kind of way. The director liked that idea, so I requested

04

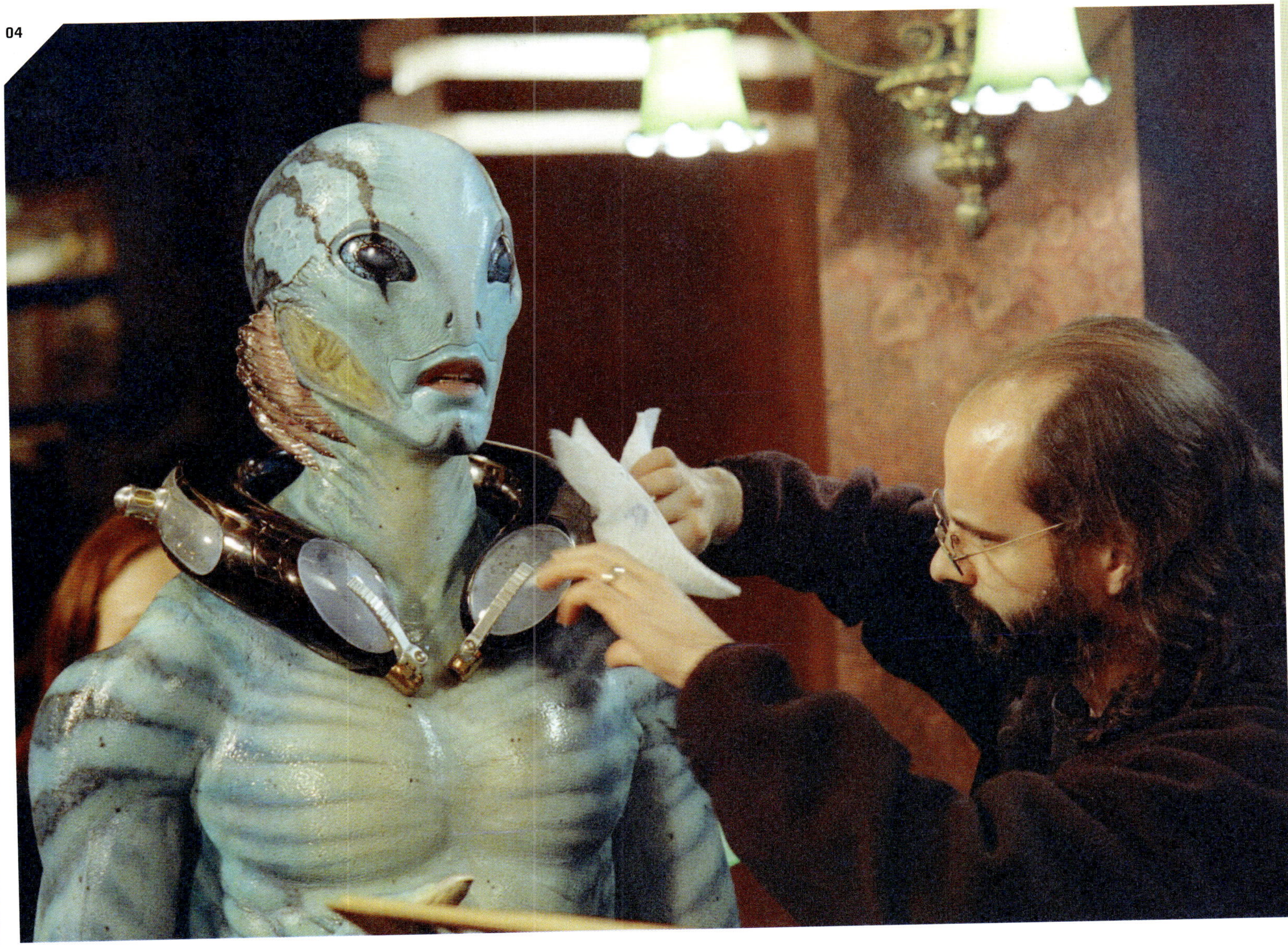

a change to the way the tail was sculpted so it would accommodate the mechanism. "The other thing about getting involved early on is that it just gives you more time to think about the job—how you're going to make stuff work and what equipment you need. That's particularly important today, because production schedules are so tight. On *Men in Black* we had eight months to build everything. Today, that would be a luxury! Now we might typically have only three months on a project—which is sometimes barely enough to draw up designs and order the parts. The servos for the Scrunt took eight weeks to arrive after ordering."

Luckily, modern technology can speed up the design process. Setrakian now uses his computer to start design work as soon as he is able to obtain dimensions from the design team. "With *Lady in the Water* I started taking digital photographs of the character's profile as soon as the full-sized sculpture was under way. Using CAD [computer-aided design] software, I then started planning the mechanisms to fit inside the outline of that profile. This gave me a real head start in preparing for the job ahead.

"Once the sculpture was molded, I had the fiberglass core scanned so I had an accurate 3-D model of it in my computer. With that I was able to start precisely designing the internal structures and work out how the joints were going to work, where the servos needed to go, and so on. This also allowed me to see where parts might interfere with each other."

(03) Setrakian works on Abe Sapien's glasses (*Hellboy*, 2004), which allow the aquatic creature to see when out of water **(03)** Abe Sapien was created as a makeup worn by performer Doug Jones.

05

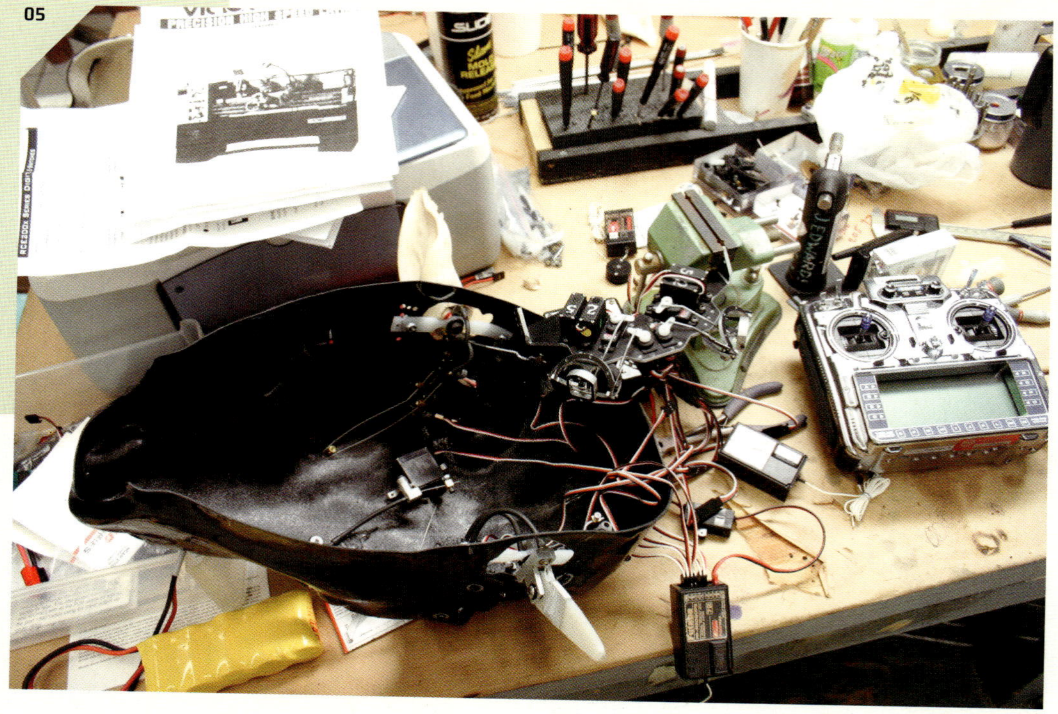

It is not only the design process that has been affected by digital technology. "We used to have to make everything by hand using shop-tools like milling machines and band saws, working from hand-drawn designs," says Setrakian. "Now there are almost no limits to what I can design and build. For example, I designed the tail vertebrae of the Scrunt in my CAD program. Then I e-mailed the files to a company that quickly cut out the parts using a water-jet machine—a computer-controlled tool that cuts through inch-thick [2.5cm] metal with a high-pressure mixture of water and garnet dust.

"Another part was made by a rapid prototyping machine, called an FDM machine [Fused Deposition Modeling]. This thing uses a heated nozzle to extrude liquefied polycarbonate, building up any three-dimensional shape one layer at a time. When the part is finished I can take it and bolt it straight into my mechanism. Things like this are what makes it possible to even consider producing what we do in the incredibly short schedules we now have to work with."

Setrakian also relies on computers to help control his finished creatures. "One of my hobbies is creating electronic music using [interactive music authoring and control language] Max. It has turned out to be a really versatile programming language that I have started to use to write motion-control software. For *Lady in the Water* I wrote a motion-control package to control the running and walking action of the Scrunt. I ran this software on my laptop and used a wireless transmitter to send the performance data to the creature. With a joystick and the keys on my laptop I could control the huge number of servos within the puppet using algorithms similar to those I might write to control a musical performance."

Setrakian built two versions of the Scrunt. One was entirely self-contained. This version could not actually walk but could crouch, lunge, move subtly, or thrash about. Another version was built with a support arm that protruded from the belly of the beast or from the side that was away from camera. This arm supported the creature and moved it forward while it was running.

"The legs could brush the ground as it was moving and it really looked as if it was running flat out," states Setrakian. "In reality there was no friction between the feet and the ground and it was the arm moving along on a track which provided the forward motion."

(05) Animatronic engineers fill the empty shell of a Minotaur head with mechanisms that will produce lifelike movement **(06)** Testing a mechanism **(07)** Creating the performance of Blawp (*Lost in Space*, 1998).

06

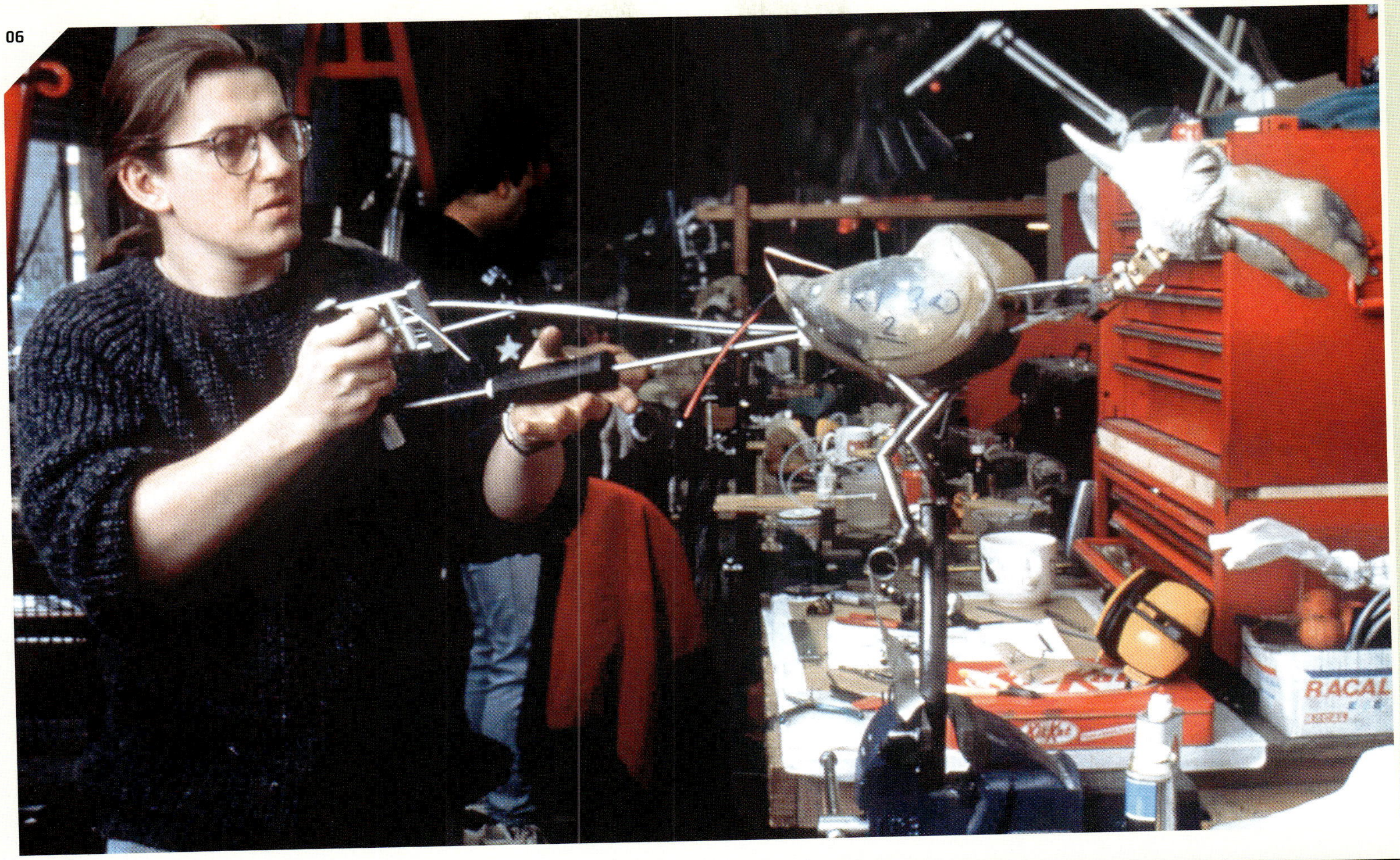

07

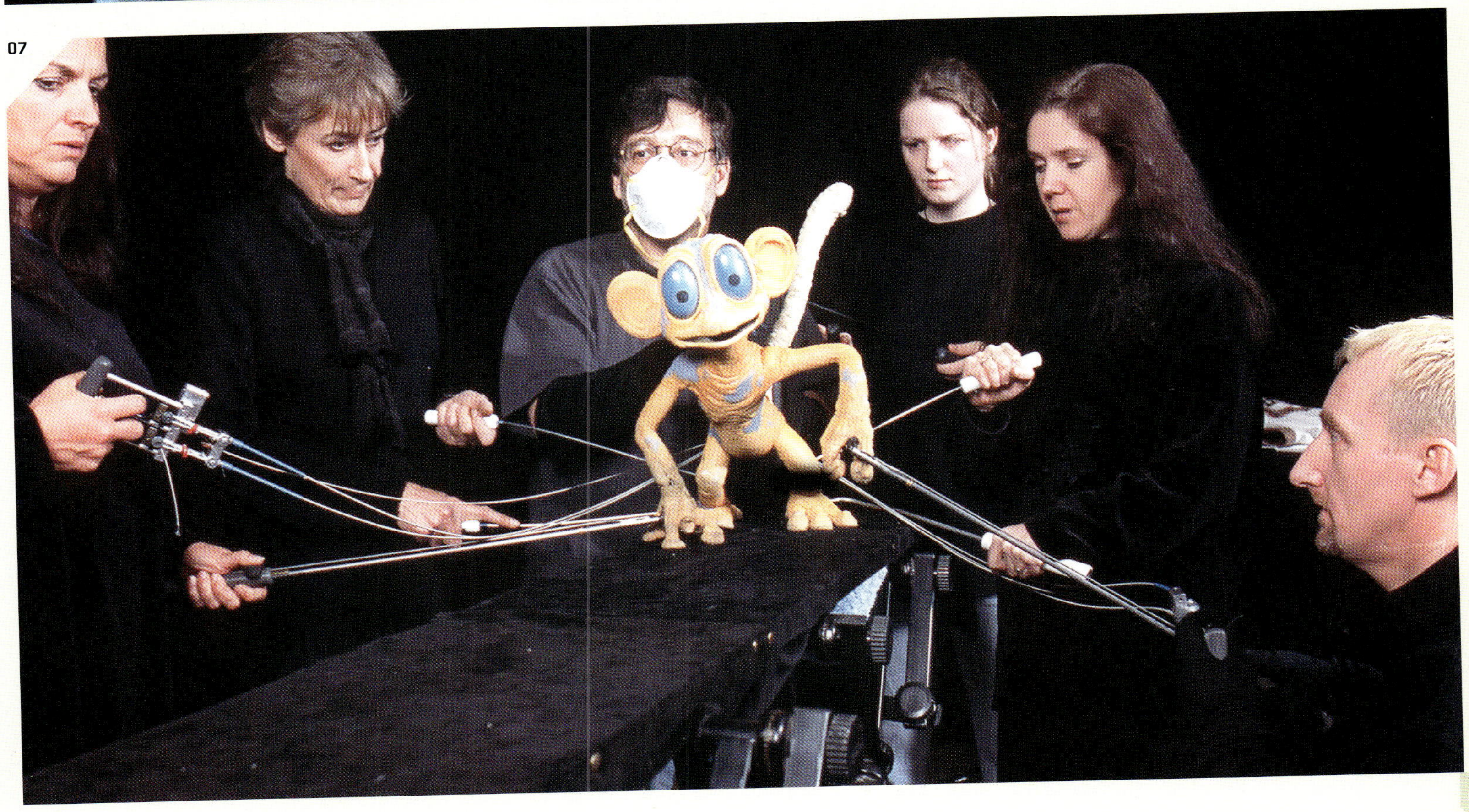

For shots in which the Scrunt was walking at a slower pace, the robotic creature could support its own weight and walk forward without any exterior propulsion. In such cases the support arm was used only to provide balance. The arm and track were digitally removed during post production.

Setrakian admits that there are some things that computer-animated characters can currently do far better than puppets. "I would say that CGI is definitely capable of creating powerful performances—look at the recent *King Kong* [2005], for example. But I believe animatronics also have the potential to provide incredibly expressive facial expressions and movements.

"One of the biggest problems is that animatronics have to be designed and built from scratch every time. While I can make incremental improvements to my performance software from one project to the next, every new character essentially needs to be fabricated from the ground up. I may already know how to build a brilliant eye mechanism, but it's still going to take three months to machine all the parts.

"CG characters, on the other hand, can use animation tools and systems that are built upon and improved with each new movie. In the case of *King Kong* (2005), Weta Digital was building on what it achieved with Gollum in *The Lord of the Rings*. I believe we are capable of creating astonishing animatronic performances, it's just a matter of dedicating enough time and money to allow that to happen. Most of the time producers and directors would rather assign those resources to computer animation."

When he has finished building them, Setrakian frequently operates the puppets he has created—a subtle art that is seemingly at odds with his engineering skills. "I don't think about the fact that my job is technical," he says. "Mostly my job is not about designing equipment, but about designing movement. I am there to

08

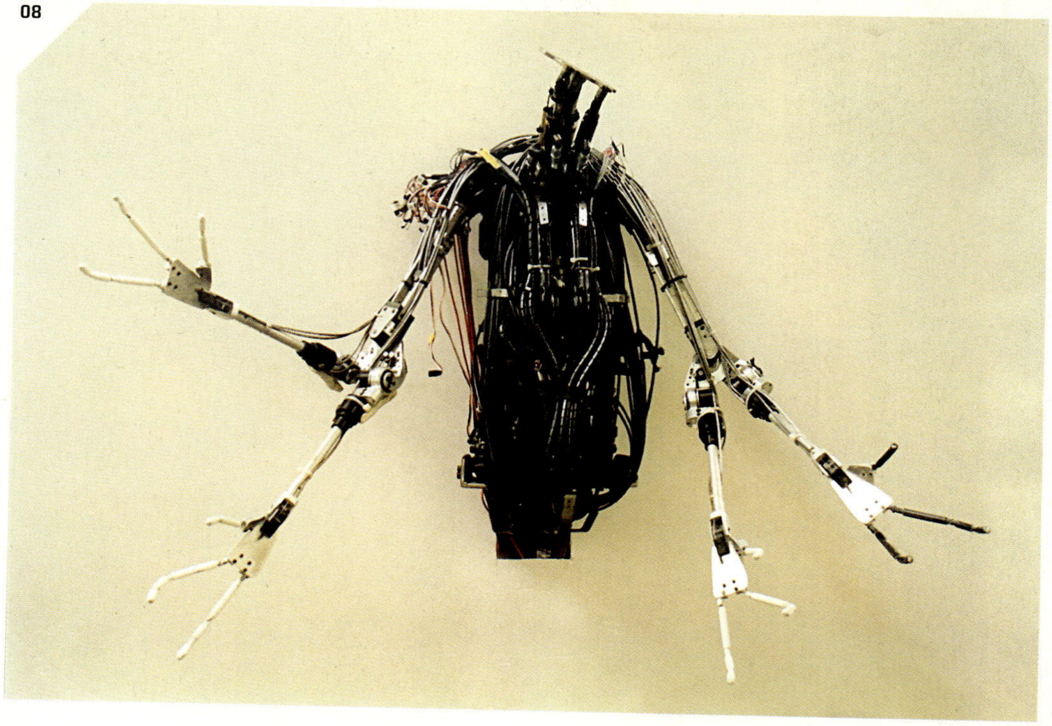

make a performance not just possible, but believable. I think of myself as a puppeteer who is also able to design the machinery that makes it possible. Many of the characters I create are highly engineered, very complex pieces of technology. But the thing I am most passionate about is getting a great performance out of them."

A wide range of techniques is used to create facial and body performances in animatronic characters: "Our job is to choose which techniques are most appropriate—depending on the size and type of creature, how and where it will be filmed, and the budget and schedule.

"My favorite tool for making creatures move is the servo. A servo is a motor that exactly follows the commands of a control signal. So, as the puppeteer moves a joystick back and forth, the motor will respond by moving whatever object it is attached to it in the same direction and speed. In this way, we can make fingers and eyes move, and mouths open and close." First becoming widely available in the 1960s, servos have developed into fast, strong, and often very small motors. They are available in a wide range of sizes, either off the shelf or custom built.

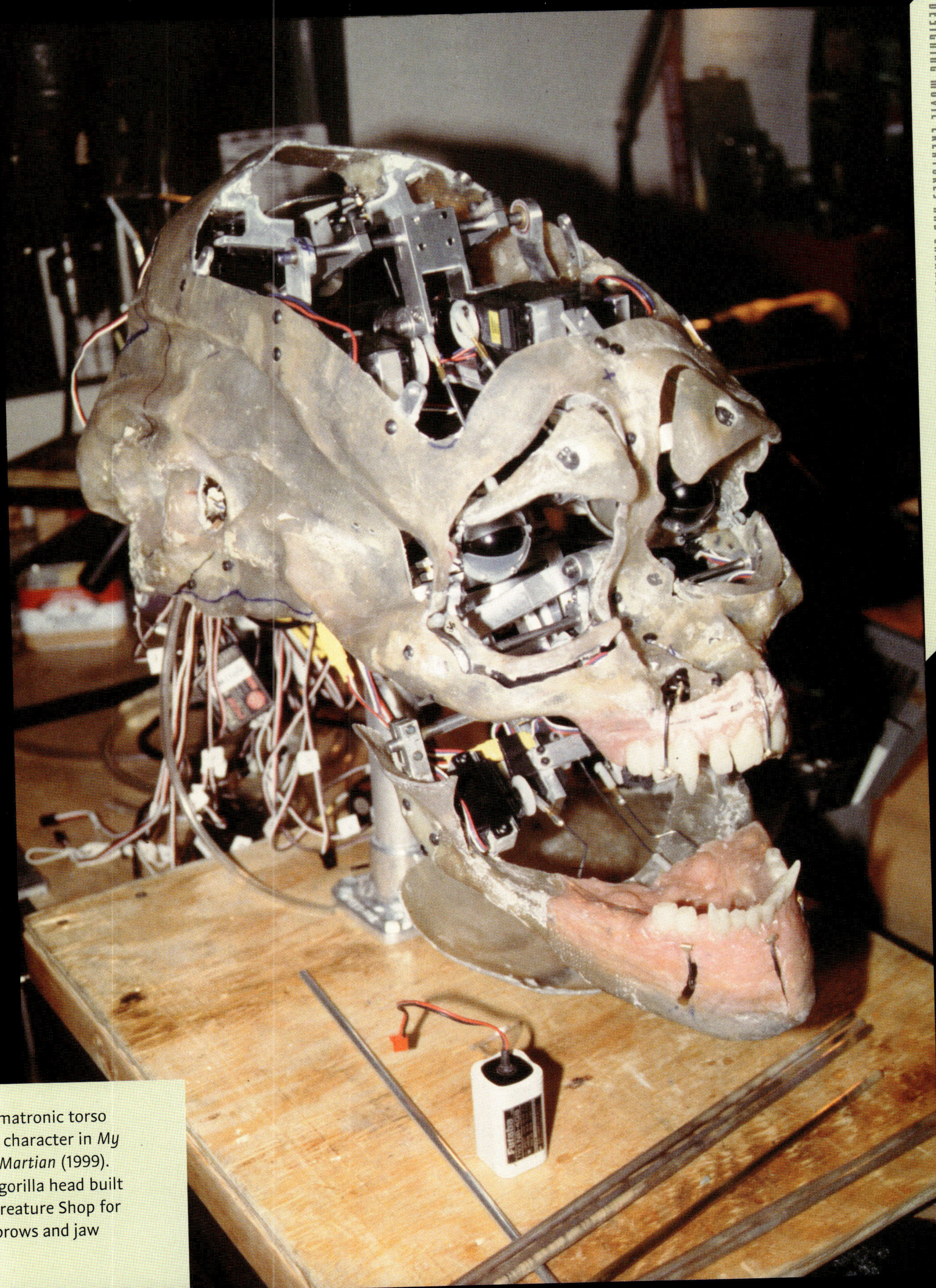

(08) Animatronic torso for alien character in *My Favorite Martian* (1999).
(09) Animatronic gorilla head built by Jim Henson's Creature Shop for *Buddy* (1997). Eyebrows and jaw are articulated.

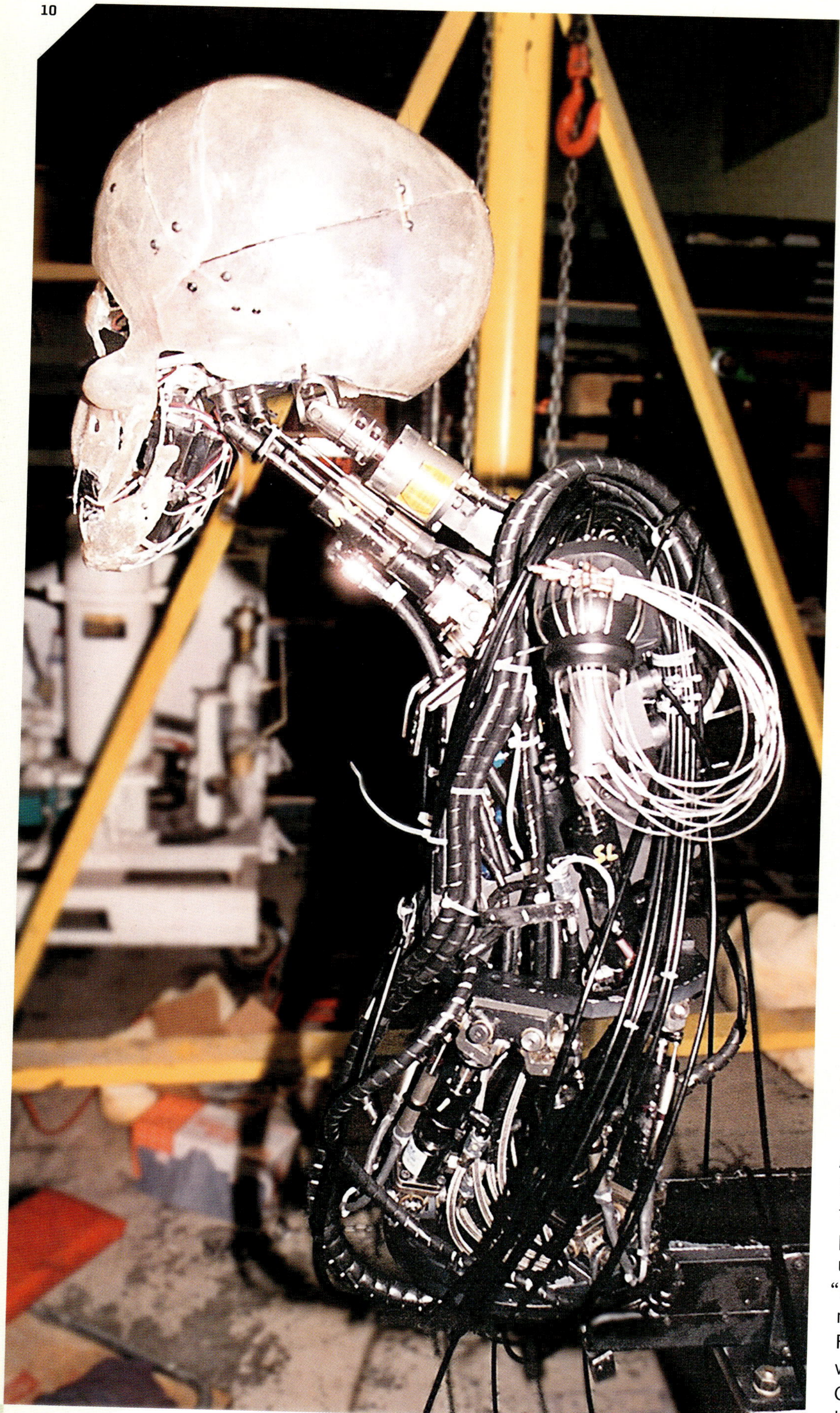

The main, less expensive alternative to servos is cable control, using Teflon-lined housings through which cables are run—much like the cables used for bicycle brakes. When the cable is pulled by a puppeteer working a lever, it physically moves part of the creature. E.T., for example, was completely cable controlled. Setrakian finds cable control most useful when a character is too small to contain servos. However, he tries to avoid the technique. "The longer a cable, is the more friction there is, making it harder to get a responsive performance. When I was in Prague working on *Hellboy* [2004] with Mike Elizalde, we had this big cable-controlled creature called Sammael. The creature had, say, 40 cables coming out of it connected to big, heavy controllers. Mike and I had a tough time trying to set this thing up on a freezing-cold location. After a while I said, 'I never want to build another cable-controlled creature again.'"

That said, Setrakian sometimes favors a hybrid technique. "For Sammael's hand in *Hellboy*, I ran cables from his fingers out a short distance to a bank of servos. We radio-controlled the servos, the servos pulled the cables, and the cables moved the fingers."

When it comes to much larger creatures or heavy limbs requiring a lot of power to control their movements, hydraulic rams are another option. These use a large external pump to squeeze high-pressure fluid through cylinders that can push or pull a mechanism. These complex and expensive systems tend only to be used for the biggest creations, such as the larger dinosaurs in the *Jurassic Park* movies.

At the other end of the scale, Setrakian is also responsible for designing systems that control subtle and emotive facial performances. "Faces are still controlled using cables and servos," he explains. "However, they need to be controlled in a much more precise and delicate fashion. For example, there are several common ways to articulate a character's mouth. One method is the so-called eight-cable lip mechanism. The mouth is divided into

11

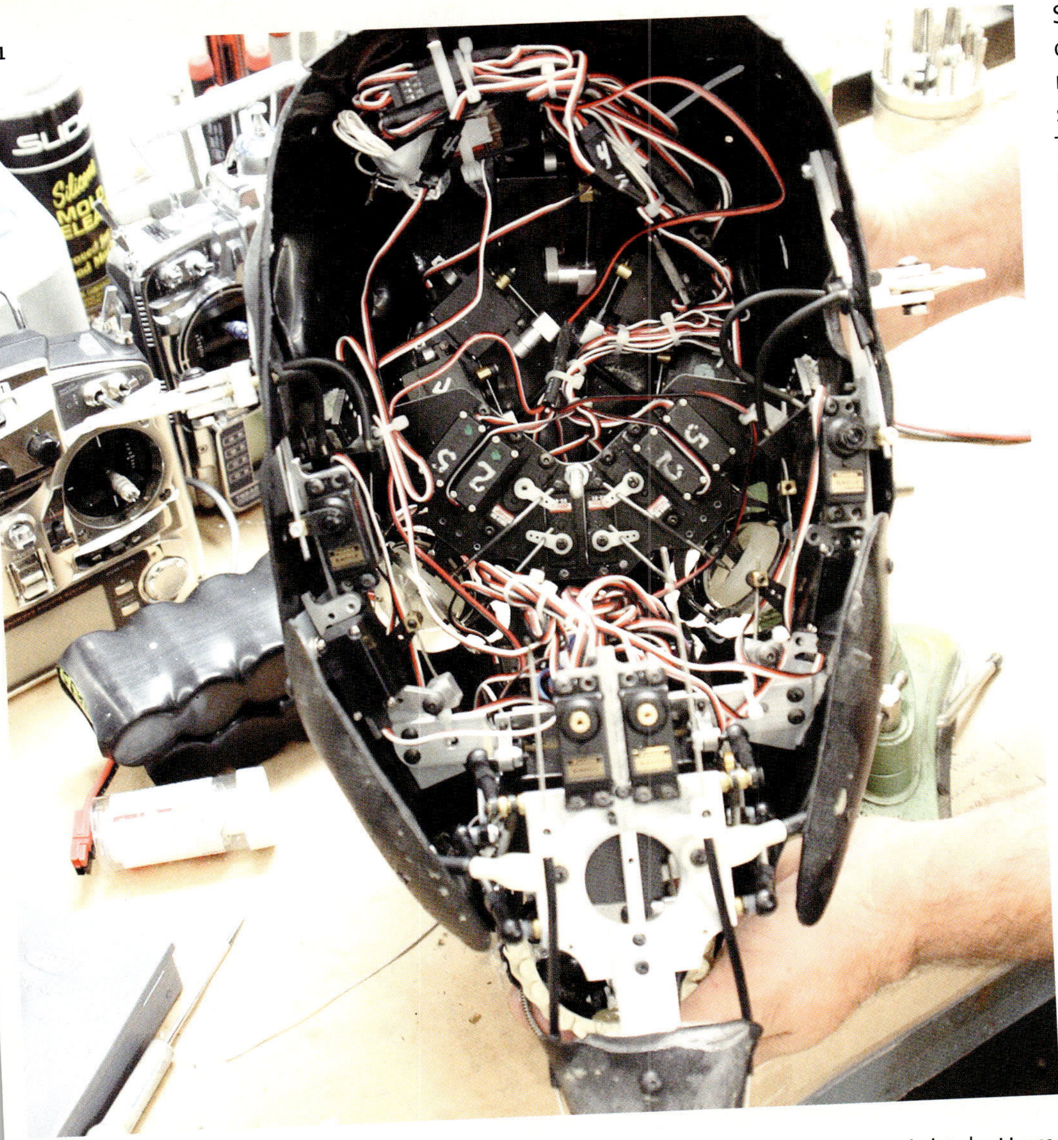

four quadrants, top left, top right, bottom left, and bottom right. Each quadrant is controlled by two cables, one horizontal and one vertical. Using a joystick controller called a quad-box, servos push and pull the cables to make the lips form any of a number of shapes."

Another method, known as the paddle technique, uses servo-controlled hard paddles, or patches, which are attached to the underside of the skin material. "By embedding paddles in and around the lips of a character you can move and stretch them to articulate all the different shapes—the 'oohs,' 'eees,' and 'aahs'—required to emulate speech," Setrakian explains. "Paddles can move very fast and are excellent for speaking characters, but they aren't always that natural looking."

Setrakian often prefers to use a hybrid of the two, which he calls the drawstring method. "I use long, very small-diameter springs lined with little segments of Teflon tubing. I run a cable through the spring, and by pulling on that cable, usually via a servo, I can make the spring contract or expand, like a muscle. I'll take these drawstrings and embed them within a creature's foam skin wherever I need movement. Check out *Mighty Joe Young* [1998] for a good example."

Setrakian believes that when it comes to speech, chin movement is also vital. "You can make a character that has limited lip and jaw movement look much more expressive by adding some movement to the chin. A good example is the mummified-corpse from *Hellboy*." Other aspects of a face, such as cheeks, noses, and eyebrows, can be manipulated using a combination of all these operating techniques.

For Setrakian, the outer skin of a character is much more than simply a wrapping for his mechanical marvels. "I think of the skin as part of the mechanism," he says. "It isn't just something that goes over the top of the mechanics. Many artists have switched completely to using silicone skin. I still really like working with foam latex; it's much lighter, and works well with mechanisms that I frequently embed deeply into the skin itself. Making sure the skin is the right thickness and density makes a big difference to the way a character reacts in relation to the underlying mechanisms."

(10) Animatronic torso and head for *My Favorite Martian*, showing the technical skill involved, from hand-machining limbs and joints to designing control mechanisms **(11)** Nearly complete head. When an animatronic mask is worn by a performer, these motors and mechanisms must be fitted into the spaces surrounding their head.

JON DAWE

CV

Animatronic designer, specializing in eyes; after leaving school, moved to North Hollywood and worked in an art store; started working in an effects workshop and moved into animatronic design and mechanics; hired by Stan Winston Studio in 1991 to work on *Batman Returns*; worked on building eye mechanisms for *Jurassic Park*; in this and subsequent work has developed increasingly challenging but realistic eye mechanisms for characters.

SELECT FILMOGRAPHY

Batman Returns (1992); *Jurassic Park* (1993); Mousehunt (1997); *I, Robot* (2004); *Blade: Trinity* (2004); *Hellboy* (2004); *Fantastic Four* (2005); *Underworld: Evolution* (2006); *Silent Hill* (2006)

KEY CHARACTERS

Penguins (*Batman Returns*); dinosaurs (*Jurassic Park*); mouse (*Mousehunt*); Sammael (*Hellboy*); werewolves (*Underworld: Evolution*)

TECHNIQUES

CAD; animatronics

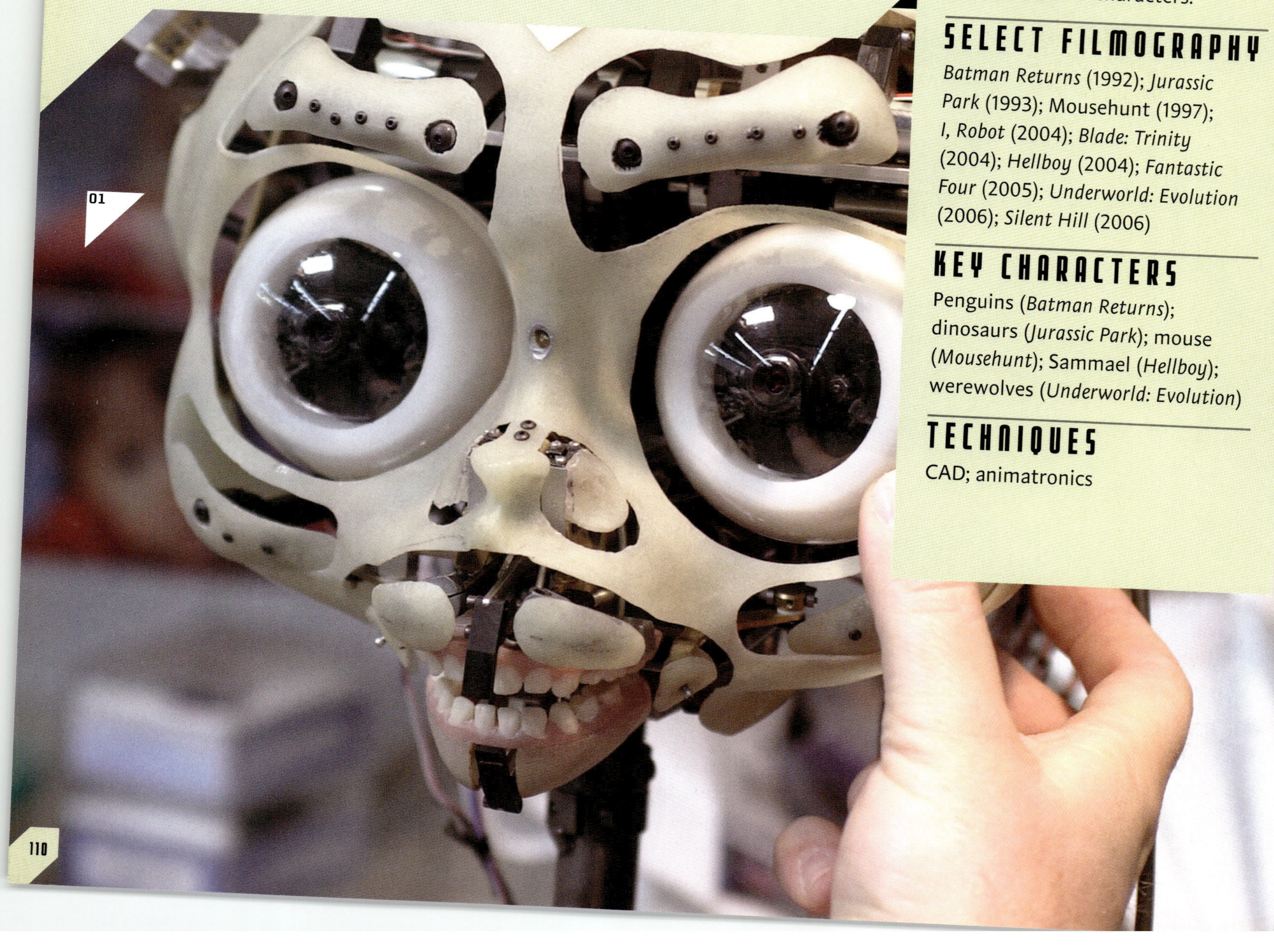

01

02

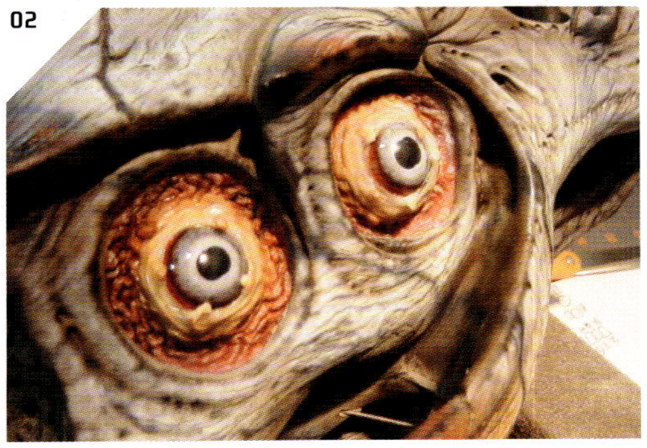

03

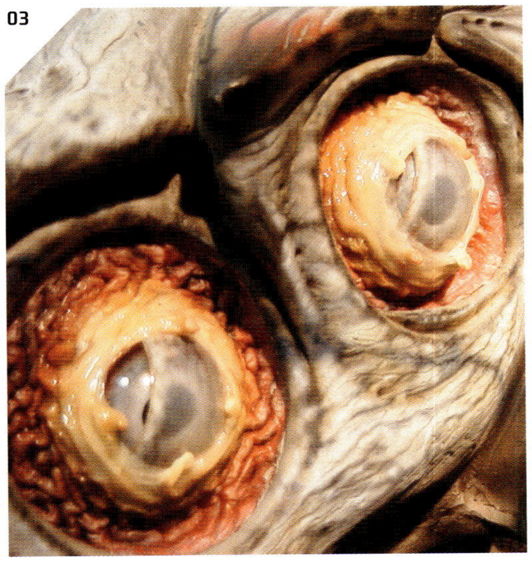

04

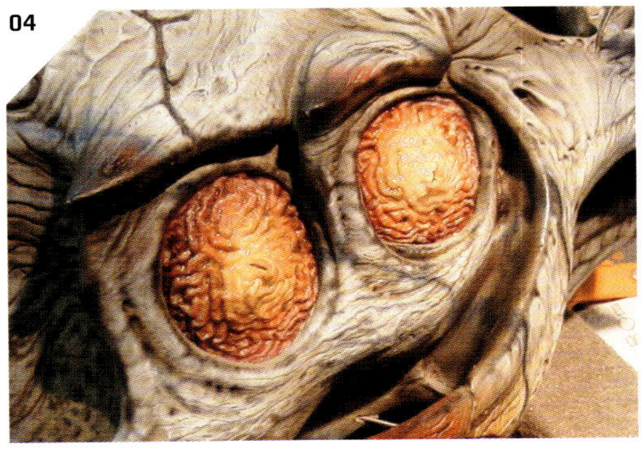

(01) As well as his movie creature eyes, Jon Dawe created this research character for the Massachusetts Institute of Technology. These eyes are cameras and can actually "see." **(02–04)** Dawe engineered these eyes for the devilish character, Sammael, in *Hellboy* (2004). The eyeballs could look around, protrude from their sockets, close with a meaty iris, blink with a mucus membrane, and the pupils dilate.

Character artists must strive to produce convincing eyes for the creatures that they build to help create the illusion of life where none exists. Animatronic creatures' eyes also need to move naturally.

Jon Dawe is an engineer who specializes in building complex eye mechanisms for animatronic characters—a job he fell into by accident when he had to make a delivery from the art supplies shop he worked in to a special effects makeup studio. With his art and machining skills he was offered part-time work, which soon turned into a full-time position. "Animatronics was pretty sophisticated by that time in the late 1980s," he recalls, "but the one thing that bugged me was the mechanical eyes—they seemed really crude and bulky. Many heads had to be sculpted bigger so the mechanisms to swivel the eyes and make the eyelids blink could be fitted into them. So I decided to try redesigning the eye mechanisms."

In 1991, Stan Winston hired Dawe to help with the animatronic penguins for *Batman Returns* (1992). This was followed by designing and building eye mechanisms for one of the biggest monster movies of all time, *Jurassic Park* (1993). One challenge was the scale of the eyes, ranging from the tiny eyes of small creatures to the grapefruit-sized eyes of the iconic T-rex.

In one thrilling scene, the T-rex peers through a jeep window at two terrified children. "Stan asked me to create a pupil that would dilate when the girl shone her torch in its face," says Dawe. After months of experimentation, Dawe eventually hit upon a technique of using a very stretchy, yellow piece of rubber with a small hole at its center, through which a black pupil could be seen. This was mechanized, and driven by radio-controlled servo motors that would stretch or shrink the size of the hole and create the desired effect.

Dawe's other major mechanical challenge for *Jurassic Park* was to create "nictitating" eyelids for the velociraptors. "Some wild creatures, such as crocodiles and lizards, have a milky-colored membrane that they flick quickly across their eyeball from the side in order to keep it clean and moist," explains Dawe. "Stan originally wanted to use this nictitating effect, as it is known, for the T-rex, but it was used for the velociraptors instead.

"The challenge in creating the nictitating membrane was to find space for another moving part within the eye mechanism, and then find a way to make the blink happen so quickly that it didn't look mechanical. I tracked down a tiny electromagnetic drive motor of a type commonly used in vending and pinball machines. When a current was applied a small piston would shoot in or out, quickly driving a small, semi-translucent plastic membrane over the eyeball, and back." The effect gave the velociraptors a malevolent, reptilian presence.

As well as creating the mechanisms to control a character's eyes, Dawe also creates the eyeballs themselves. Artist-supplied designs are usually pasted or painted onto the flat surface of a small resin hemisphere. That is then suspended in a larger semi-spherical mold into which a clear resin is poured, encapsulating the iris and pupil. Most finished eyeballs are not complete spheres, but are normally a little over half a sphere, leaving room behind the eye for the mechanism.

Real eyeballs are not completely spherical, usually having a noticeable lump on the front—the corneal bulge—which makes eyeballs more elliptical than spherical. This can present problems: the working of mechanical eyelids (often swivelling hard shells that have the creature's foam skin attached to them) ideally depends on the eyeballs being perfect spheres. One solution is a flexible eyelid that actually touches the eyeball and changes shape in a very natural-looking way as it is dragged over the corneal bulge.

05

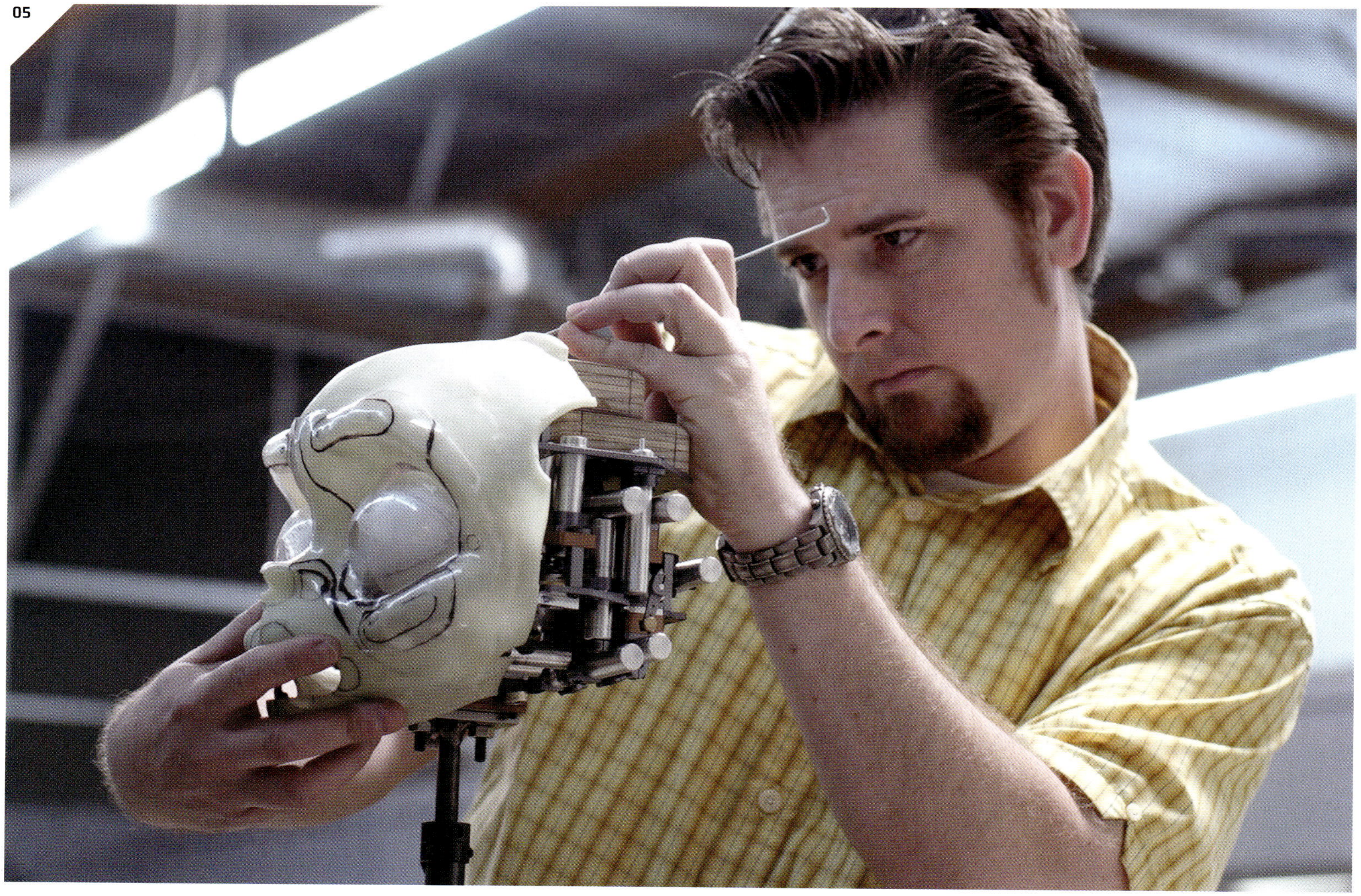

06

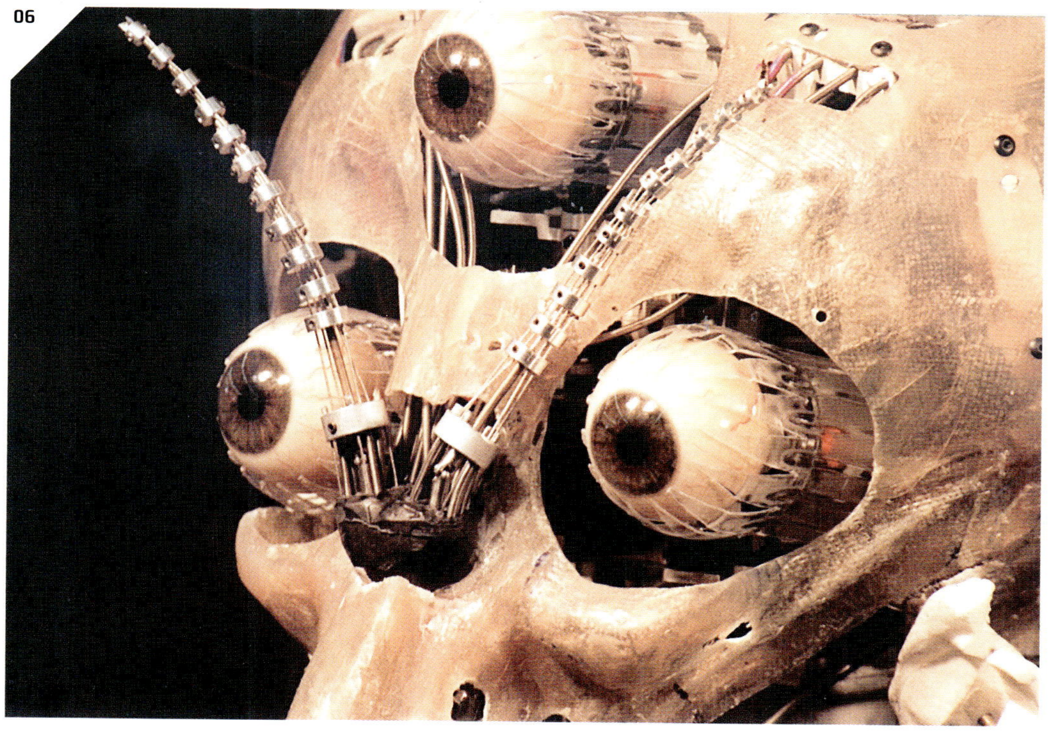

07

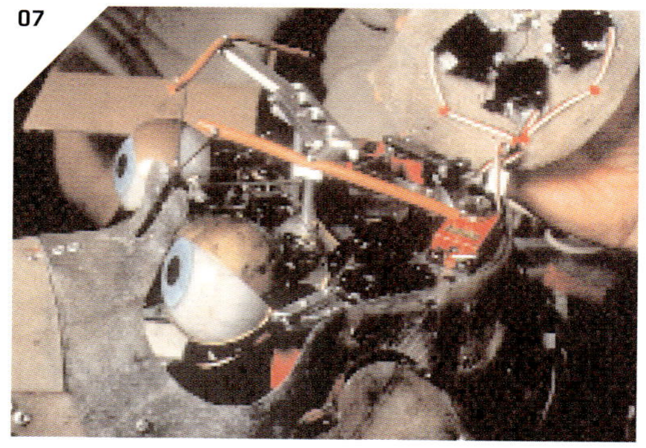

08

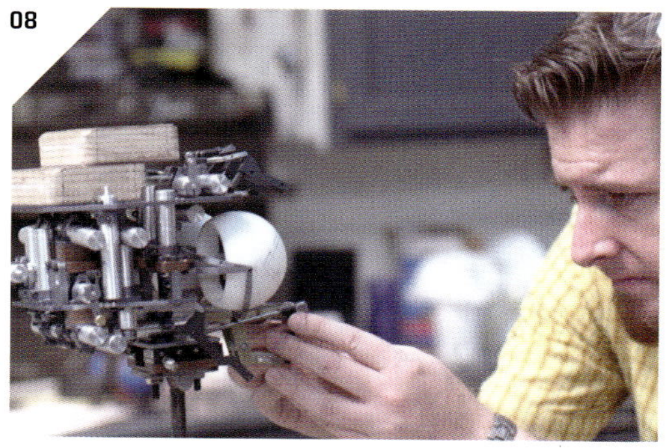

09

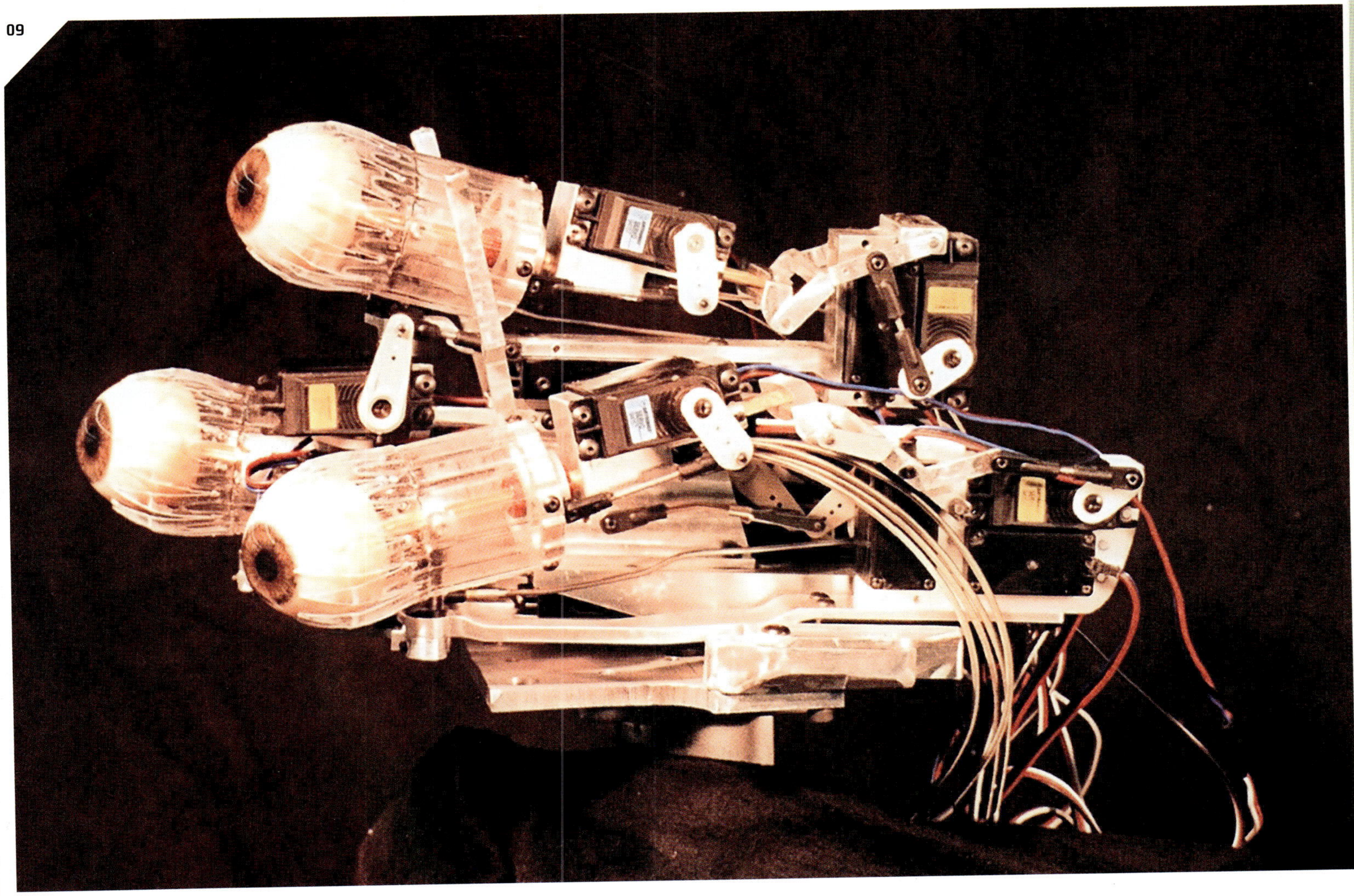

"To make the eyelids move at the same time as the eyeballs we used to separately puppeteer the eyelids and eyeballs in an attempt to make them look as if they were working in tandem," says Dawe. "What I do now is make such movements automatic by mixing the signals used to control the mechanisms. For example, if you want to make the eyes look upward, you would just use the eye control to produce the movement, but some of the signal will be automatically mixed through to the eyelid channels, making them move a little bit in response as well —it's all about making the puppeteering process as easy and intuitive as possible, so the character looks real."

Dawe has created animatronic head and eye mechanisms for a number of recent movies, including *Blade: Trinity* (2004) and *Underworld: Evolution* (2006). However, perhaps his most challenging task was to create the eyes for Sammael in *Hellboy* (2004). "Sammael had three differently sized eyes, each of which had five functions. As well as the usual up-down, right-left movement, the figure-eight shaped pupils had to dilate, there were nictitating eyelids, it blinked with this horrible, sphincter-like eyelid, and the eyes themselves could bulge in and out of their eye sockets. All those movements required seven servos for each eye. This was all done with small human-size eyes, so it was really an engineering challenge."

For Dawe, creating a character's eyes is akin to creating its soul—a task made all the more challenging by the technical nature of the work. "When you see something built on a workbench and it's just a bunch of screws, fiberglass, and motors, it's hard to imagine that it could ever represent life, so it's always a thrill to see it come to life."

However, Dawe admits that it isn't only mechanics that bring eyes to life. "Good eyes rely on good puppeteering," he says. "A well-observed reaction, such as an almost imperceptible squint when a character walks from shade into light, can make all the difference between a machine and a living creature."

(05, 08) Dawe at work on his creations—note the space that eye mechanisms take up in a skull **(06)** Unusual mechanism built by ADI for *My Favorite Martian* **(07)** Old-style brass eyelids by Jim Henson **(09)** Servo motors are visible here as small black boxes with white "arms."

BETH HATHAWAY

01

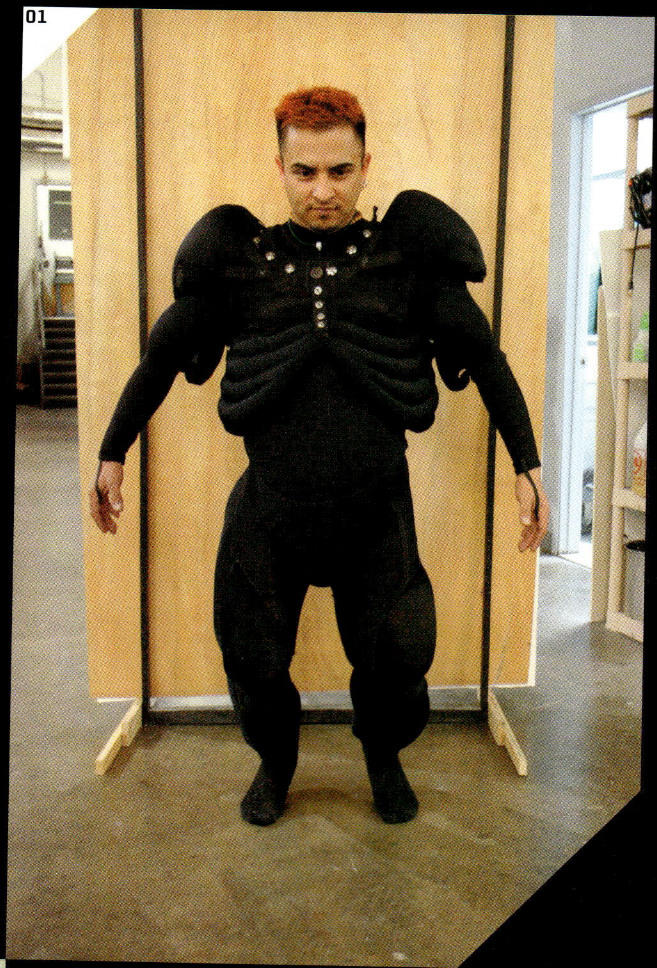

CV

Fabricator; first worked as a teenager for her stepfather, Steve Neill, who had his own makeup company; joined Stan Winston Studio in the early 1980s, staying for ten years; now runs the fabrication department at KNB.

SELECT FILMOGRAPHY

Edward Scissorhands (1990); *Terminator 2: Judgment Day* (1991); *Batman Returns* (1992); *Jurassic Park* (1993); *Gordy* (1995); *The Relic* (1997); *Instinct* (1999); *The Time Machine* (2002); *The Chronicles of Narnia: The Lion, the Witch and the Wardrobe* (2005); *The Reaping* (2006)

KEY CHARACTERS

Inspector Gadget (as puppeteer); Gorillas (*Instinct*); Minotaurs, Minobaurs, Cyclops, General Otmin (*Narnia*)

TECHNIQUES

Hairworking and fabrication; puppeteering

02

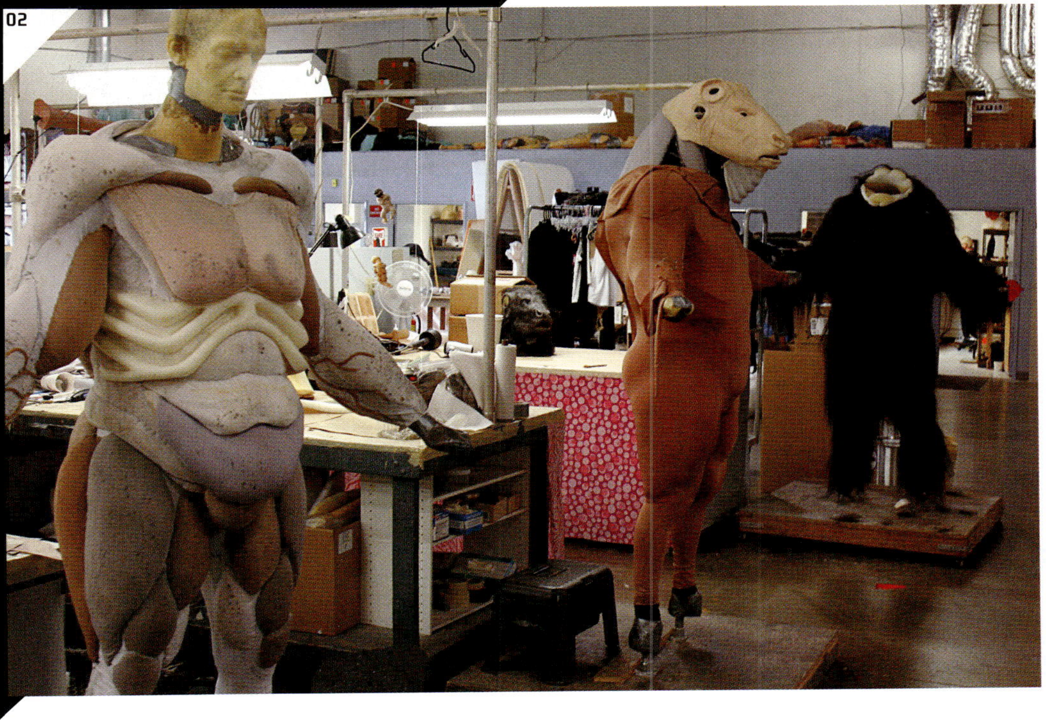

03

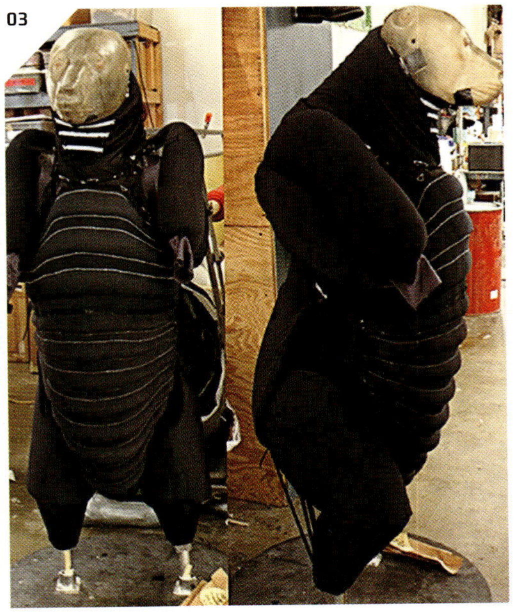

(01) KNB makeup artist Harrison Lorenzana wears the fabricated foam body of a Minotoar from *The Chronicles of Narnia: The Lion, the Witch and the Wardrobe* (2005) **(02)** A selection of fabricated suits in the workshop of KNB. **(03)** A fabricated bear suit created by KNB for *Narnia*.

While many movie monsters are created using the classic "rubber-suit" techniques that produce an all-in-one foam latex skin, many creatures require a more complex, modular understructure of bones and muscles, covered in a looser layer of skin, fur, or clothing. Assembling a body from multiple pieces in this way combines the art of the sculptor with the skills of the seamstress in a process called fabrication.

Beth Hathaway is one of Hollywood's leading fabricators. Getting her start in the business when she was 18, Hathaway first worked for her stepfather, Steve Neill, who ran his own workshop and created makeup for movies including *Ghostbusters* (1984) and *Fright Night* (1985). It was during her subsequent ten years at Stan Winston Studio that Hathaway began to specialize in fabrication techniques, creating the understructure and suits for *Batman Returns* (1992) and *Jurassic Park* (1993), among others. Hathaway now runs the fabrication department at KNB, creating suits for movies including *The Time Machine* (2002), *The Chronicles of Narnia: The Lion, the Witch and the Wardrobe* (2005), and *The Reaping* (2006).

Hathaway explains the key differences between casting a character's skin in foam latex and fabricating a suit: "If a creature is humanoid and its appearance is essentially a shaped extension of the performer's own skin, then that will typically be created as a rubber suit. This is then worn by the performer like a tightly fitting wetsuit." Classic examples include the Gill Man suit made for *The Creature from the Black Lagoon* (1954), and the suits for the *Alien* movies.

"However, many creatures have a body which is very different in size or shape to the performer who will wear it," says Hathaway. "In such cases, the body of a character is fabricated—built up from scratch using various materials to form the individual pieces of bone, muscle, and flesh. These fabricated pieces will respond to the actions of the performer, creating anatomically accurate movement beneath the character's skin, fur, or clothing." An example of this type of suit might be a realistic bear or gorilla costume.

Like sculpting a character in clay, often fabricators start with a bodycast of the performer who will wear the suit. Since a fabricated suit does not always have to fit its performer as precisely as a rubber suit, the body used might actually be from anyone who is of roughly the right build. The body form—usually made of rigid foam so that fabricators are able to stick pins into it—is then dressed in a spandex suit. This is what will ultimately be worn against the body of the performer. The spandex suit is then gradually built up by sculpting and attaching individual pieces of "muscle" or "bone."

"This is where the real art of fabricating comes in," says Hathaway. "When a character is sculpted in clay before being cast as a rubber suit, the artist has to sculpt a surface that suggests what forms of bone, muscle, and flesh lie below the skin, even though they are not present. We do things the other way around. We normally look at a sculpted maquette that shows the exterior of a body and then have to figure out what's going on beneath the surface. When we've made and assembled all the bits and pieces and placed a skin over the top, it should end up looking like the original sculpture."

04

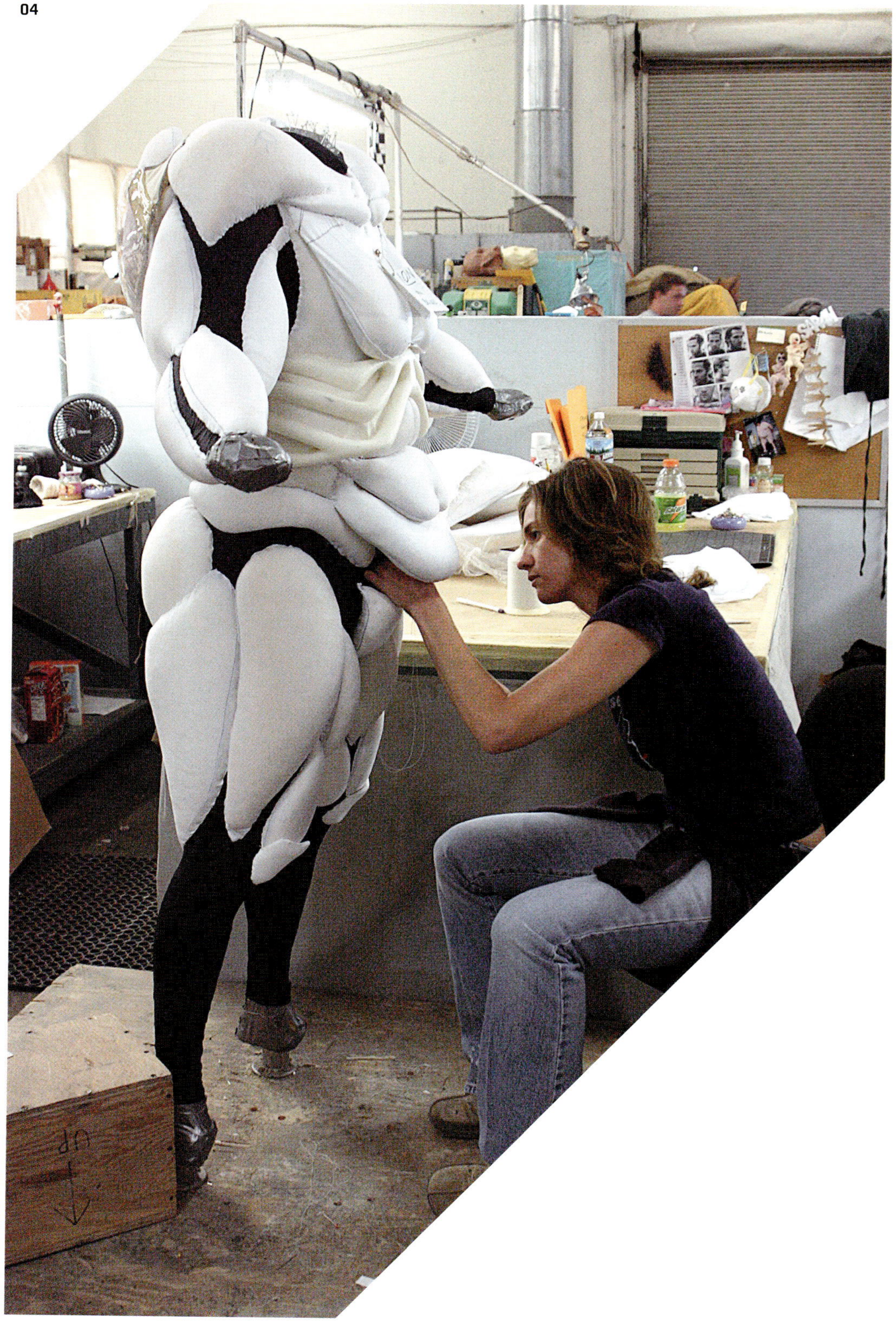

05

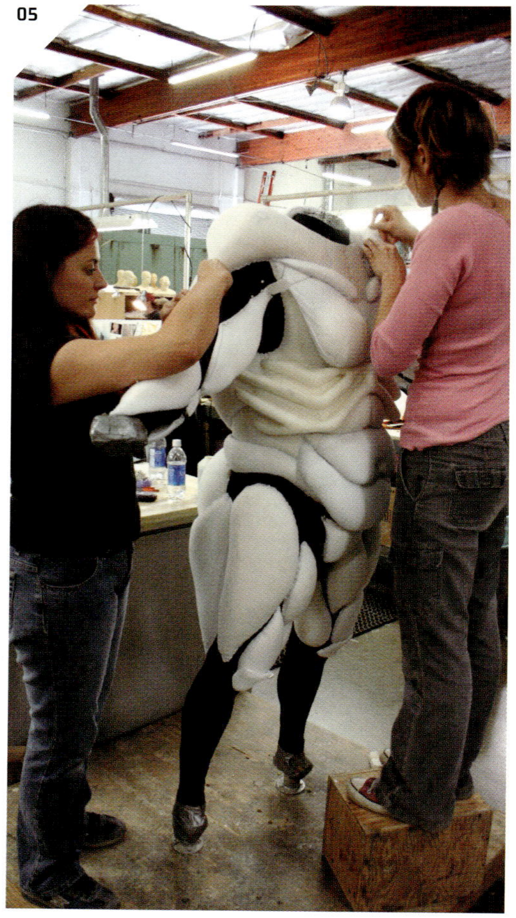

The basic materials for creating fabricated suits are a range of foams of varying weights and densities. "Sometimes I use foam latex, which is whipped up in the mixer and then formed into a rough shape with a spatula. Then when the foam has solidified I can sculpt it to produce the shape I want before baking it," says Hathaway. "Most commonly used is a medium-density sheet foam similar to that used to make cushions for chairs; then there is ScotFoam, which has a very open structure, allowing the air to travel through it to help keep actors cool. L200 is a very dense foam that we use to sculpt bones and ribcages—that sort of thing. Once sculpted, it can be coated with plastic, which hardens to make it tough and smooth.

"When we shape these materials we're essentially still sculpting, but we use foam instead of clay. We start with a chunk of foam and then use scissors, blades, and even electric breadknives to cut it and clip it until it's the right size and shape.

06

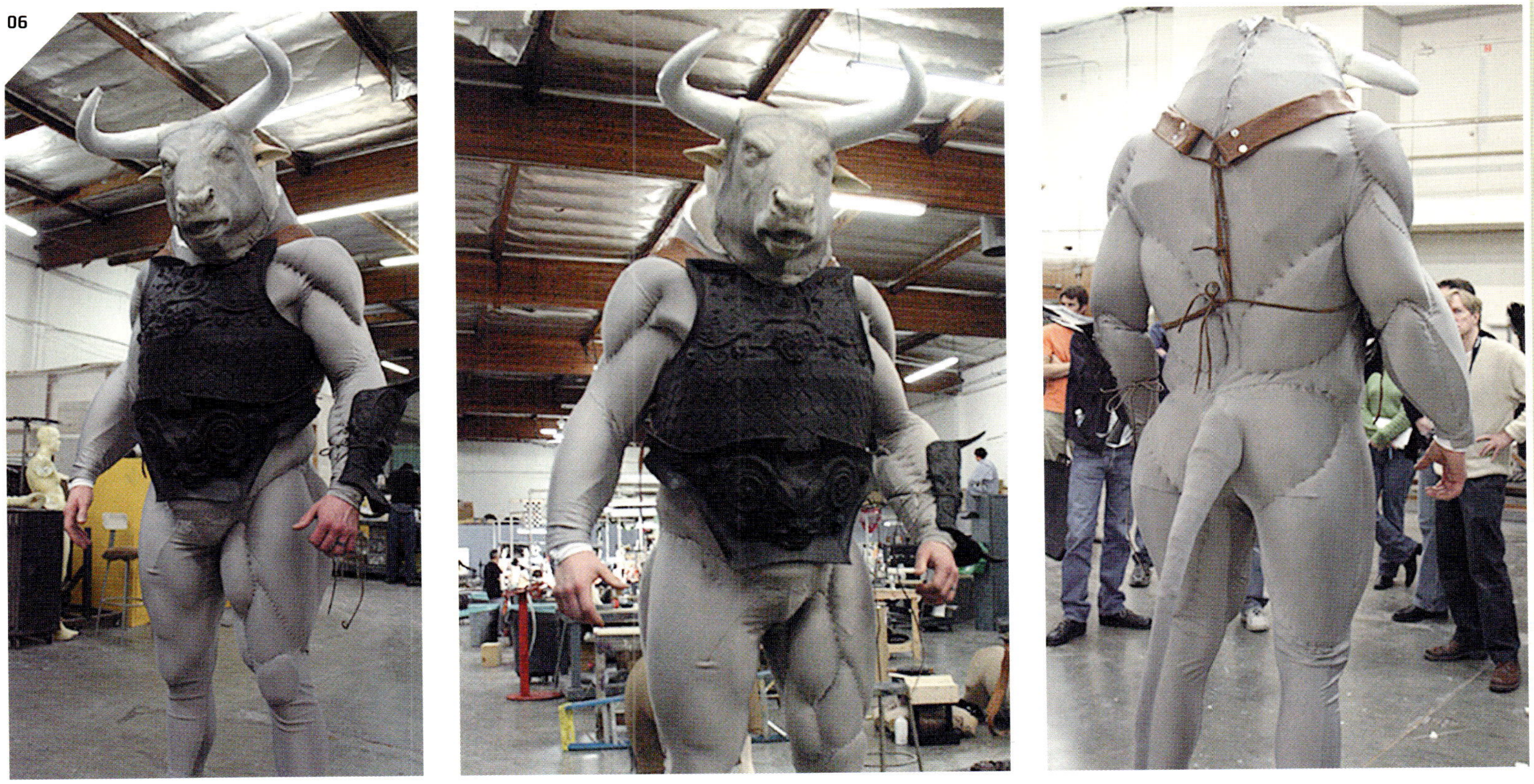

"At [Jim] Henson's [Creature Shop], where they make a lot of fabricated puppets, like the Muppets, they have people who sit and do this all day. They call them 'clippers.' When we've clipped a piece of foam to the right shape, we refine it by checking it against the body to make sure it fits, and then trim or even sand it down until it's exactly the right shape and is really smooth."

In addition to foam, other materials will be used to achieve different effects. Rippling muscles or bulging fat might be created by casting pieces in silicone. If areas such as the chest or biceps need to jiggle, they may be created using water sacs, or by filling bags with nylon beads.

For Hathaway, a comprehensive understanding of anatomy is vital in order to ensure that her work is as authentic as possible. "I've learned all about the way bodies work, where the bones are and what all the different muscle groupings do," she says. "That's the only way to ensure that fabricated suits look realistic and not like a big, bulging bag of lumps."

When the pieces of a fabricated suit have been made, they need to be assembled and attached to the spandex body suit. The finished parts are often individually covered in spandex or silk in order to allow them to slide freely against each other as well as the artificial skin that will be laid over the top of them. "One of the most important tasks is ensuring that everything will move together organically," says Hathaway. "You can have the most beautifully put-together sculpture, but if the parts don't move correctly it will still look fake."

The various pieces of understructure are attached to the spandex suit and to each other with varying degrees of elasticity, making sure that they react to each other in the proper way. To replicate the look of tendons, individual pieces of spandex, elastic, or hot melt will be stretched between and over the muscles and bones, especially in the neck area.

With the understructure complete, a latex skin or hair suit will finally be fitted over the top. This outer layer also needs to move in the right way, with areas being attached to the understructure with

07

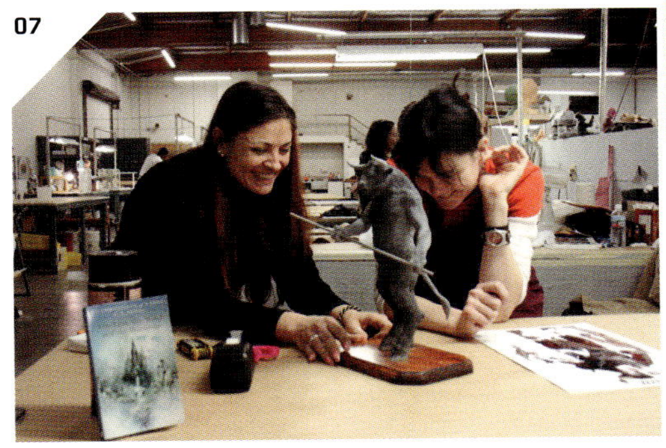

(04) Sarah Rubano sews fabricated foam muscles to a *Narnia* Minotaur suit **(05)** Beth Hathaway (left) and Sarah Rubano work on the Minotaur, which used foam muscles and rigid-cast ribcage, knees, and elbows **(06)** Once the fabrication is complete the muscle and bone is covered with spandex to simulate skin **(07)** Beth Hathaway (left) and Clare Mulroy study the Minotaur macquette created by Weta Workshop.

different degrees of tightness. In this way, the outside of the suit will slide freely over some parts of the understructure while clinging tightly to others, like real skin over bones, tendons, and muscles.

Unlike creating a rubber suit, fabrication is a highly flexible process, allowing alterations throughout the build. "Whenever we have a fitting or a viewing by the director or supervisor, I'll be standing by with my scissors ready to chop bits off my carefully sculpted pieces," she says. "We'll hack stuff about and move it around until everyone is happy. Then we'll have to remake those muscles properly afterward."

Hathaway usually travels to the film set, standing by to make any alterations that may be necessary to her creations during filming. "Whenever a suit is on camera, I'm always standing by with my scissors, needles, and thread in order to make small changes so that things look their best; cutting open a shoulder blade or an arm pit to insert more materials or make running repairs."

Hathaway cites her work on the dozens of creatures in *The Chronicles of Narnia: The Lion, the Witch and the Wardrobe* (2005) as some of her most challenging to date. "The sheer quantity of really detailed costumes was immense," she says. "In particular, creating the Minotaurs was a huge task."

Twenty-five Minotaurs were built, each requiring fabricated pieces, including ribcages, biceps made from bags of nylon pellets, and an understructure of bladders to make them jiggle when they moved. "Jeff Himmel and Clare Mulroy created one prototype Minotaur suit, and when that was approved we set up a production line to produce multiples of each muscle and bone, as well as the hair suits and all the animatronic facial mechanisms. It's rare to create multiples of a fabricated suit, as they are normally carefully crafted one-offs. Multiple-costume production is really more suited to the foam-rubber molding and casting process."

The artist is also very proud of the gorilla suits that she helped create for *Instinct* while she was at the Stan Winston Studio. "The quality of those suits was absolutely superb. Every ape had its own dedicated designer who worked hand-in-hand with the fabricators for over a year. We had at least 20 fittings with each performer to ensure that everything worked perfectly —though they weren't particularly comfortable to wear.

"To create the costumes we used a standard spandex suit to which we attached ScotFoam-sculpted muscles with an L200 ribcage. Over the top of those went another spandex suit on which we had molded a silicone chest and belly. Over the top of that went the hand-tied hair suit. The hair was then quilted down into the fabricated suit—sewing areas of the hair suit down between the individual muscles so that the muscle definition could be seen through the hair. There were also a number of other innovations, including a new type of arm extension that helped to make the performances more naturalistic. I think those suits were the closest we have ever come to creating absolutely convincing gorilla suits for the movies."

For Hathaway, fabrication is the most enjoyable part of the creature-making process. "It allows you a great deal of freedom to experiment and find out what works best for each character," she says. "Plus there are none of the nasty chemicals that you have to deal with when working with foam latex or silicone. It also allows you to get out of the workshop and go on set with your costumes, which is always great fun."

(08) Beth Hathaway worked as part of the team that created gorillas for *Instinct* (1999) at Stan Winston Studio. The suits were quilted to produce refined muscle definition and used a new type of arm extension **(09)** Kathy Sully works on a *Narnia* wolf stand-in to represent on set creatures that would be created digitally **(10)** The fabrication department at KNB resembles a clothing factory **(11)** Beth Hathaway (left) and Clare Mulroy prepare their fabricated Otmin suit, worn by Shane Rangi, for *Narnia*.

08
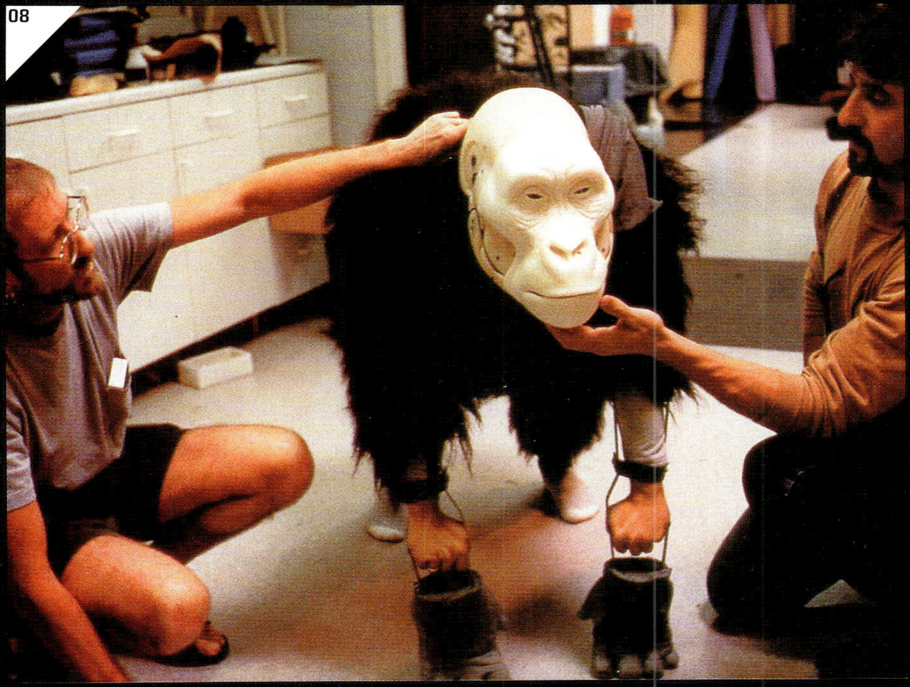
09
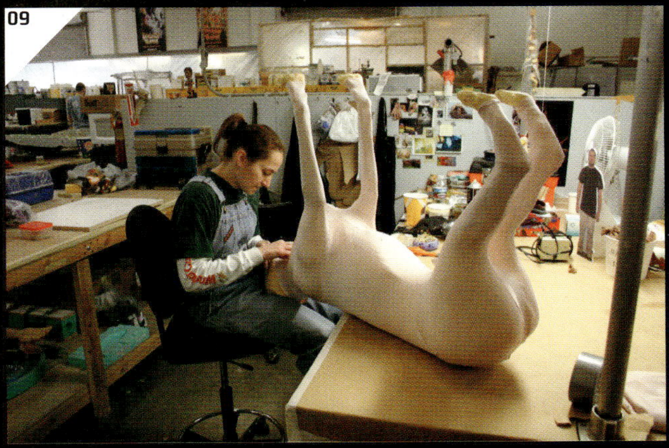
10
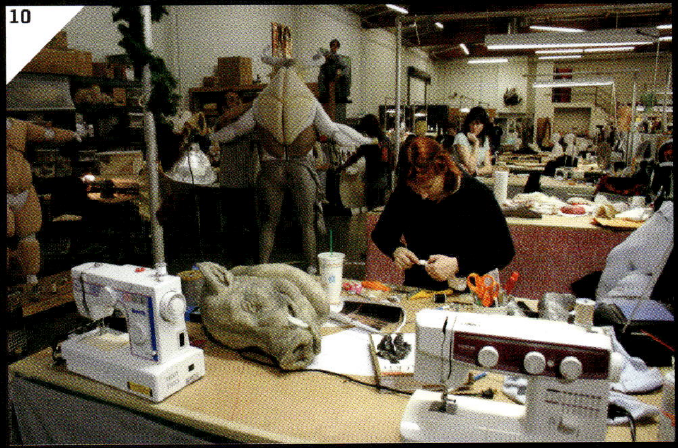
11
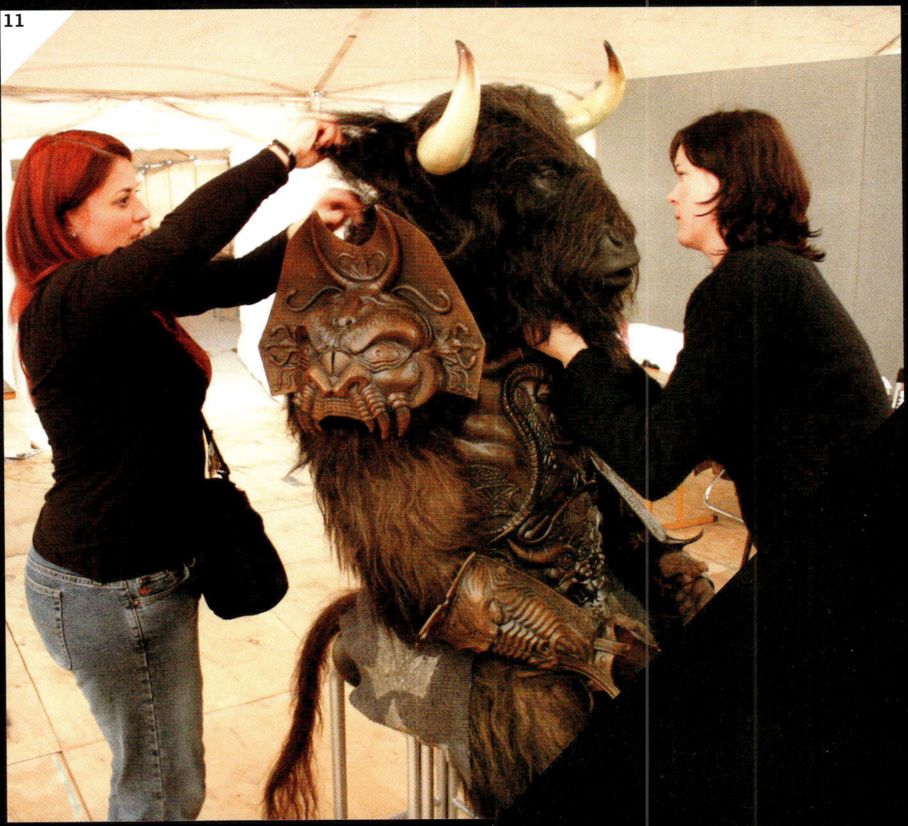

JEFF HIMMEL

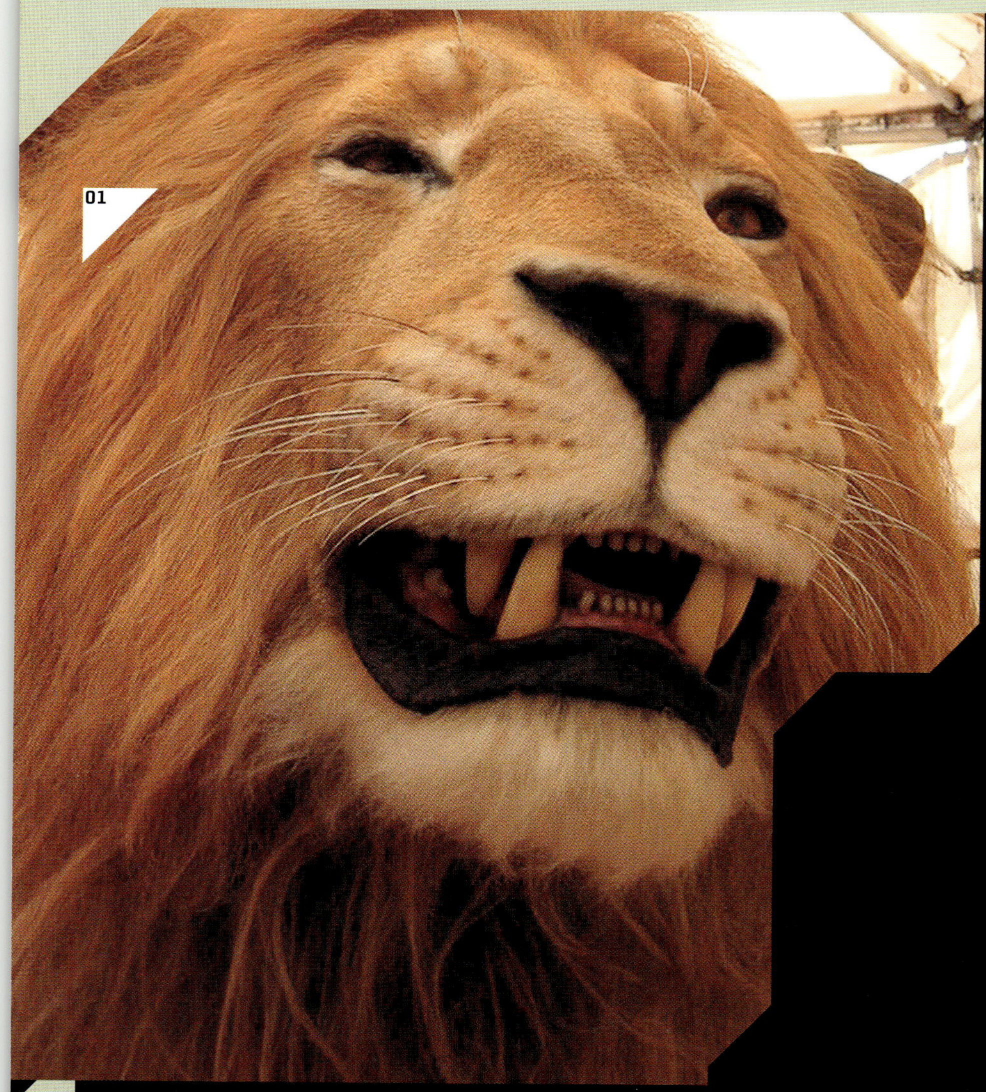

CV

Specialist in hair, fur, and feather coverings; grew up in Los Angeles, CA; internship in small makeup shop enabled him to learn about practical makeup, fabrication, and animatronics; later specialized in fur and hair for makeup and animatronic characters.

SELECT FILMOGRAPHY

George of the Jungle (1997); *Bicentennial Man* (1999); *Hollow Man* (2000); *Cats & Dogs* (2001); *Blade II* (2002); *The League of Extraordinary Gentlemen* (2003); *The Village* (2004); *The Chronicles of Narnia: The Lion, the Witch and the Wardrobe* (2005); *Unearthed* (2006); *The Reaping* (2006); *10,000 B.C.* (2007)

KEY CHARACTERS

Cats and dogs (*Cats & Dogs*); jungle creatures (*George of the Jungle*); Aslan (*The Chronicles of Narnia: The Lion, The Witch and the Wardrobe*)

TECHNIQUES

Fabrication and hairwork

(01) KNB's Aslan, given its lustrous coat and flowing mane by Jeff Himmel
(02) Himmel created the hair on this cow built for *The Reaping* (2006)
(03) Himmel also gave this cow its covering for *Say It Isn't So* (2001)
(04) This range of synthetic hair samples made by National Fiber Technologies, was considered for use on KNB's Centaurs for *The Chronicles of Narnia: The Lion, the Witch and the Wardrobe* (2005).

02

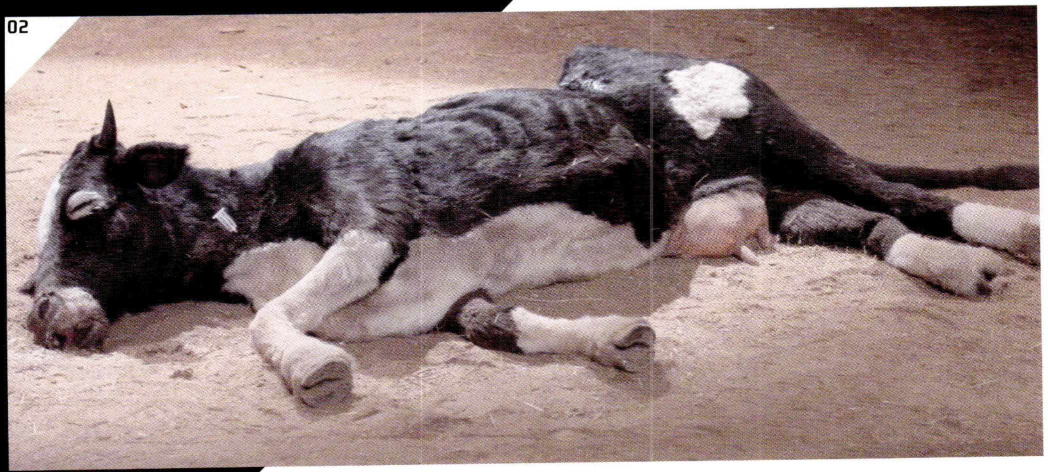

03

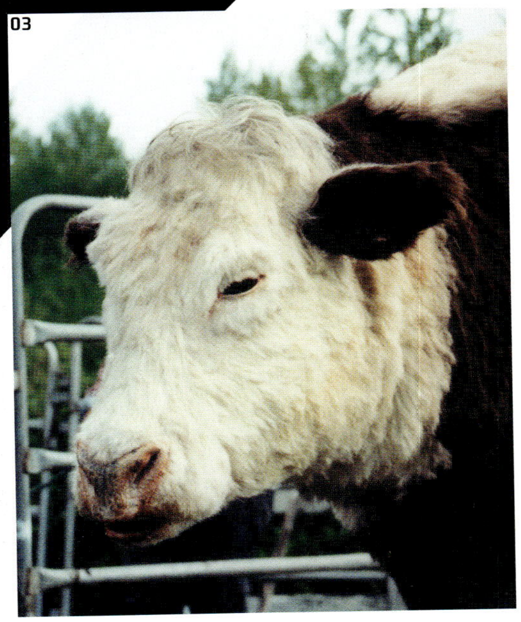

04

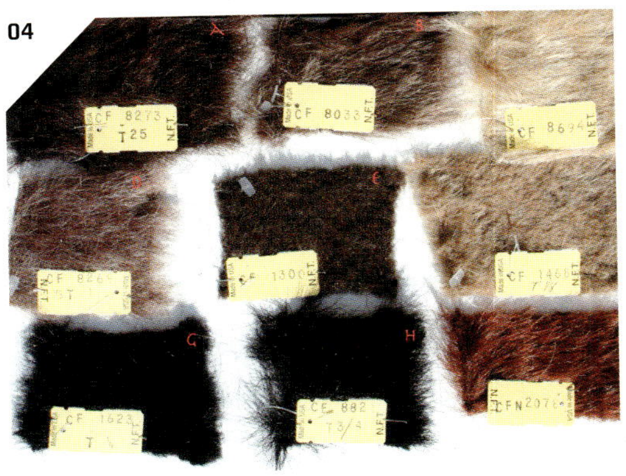

While foam latex and silicone are ideal materials for creating leathery outer skins, many characters need to be partially, or even completely, covered in hair. There are a number of methods for giving animatronic creatures or costumes a head of hair, layer of fur, or coat of feathers—some so intricate and time-consuming that this can be by far the most lengthy part of the production process.

Jeff Himmel grew up in Los Angeles, CA, where watching Elvira ("Mistress of the Dark") present horror movies on television encouraged a childhood fascination with special effects makeup. In the early 1980s, classics such as *An American Werewolf in London* (1981) and *The Dark Crystal* (1982) also caught his eye, fueling a desire to work in the movie makeup business. Practicing facial designs on himself, his younger brother, and friends eventually led to an internship at a small makeup shop where he learned about sculpting, molding, animatronics, and fabrication.

While Himmel is a skilled artist who practices other aspects of makeup production, he has become best-known for his expertise with hair, fur, and feathers, having contributed to movies including *George of the Jungle* (1997), *Cats & Dogs* (2001), *The Chronicles of Narnia: The Lion, The Witch and the Wardrobe* (2005), *The Reaping* (2006), and *10,000 BC* (2007).

"The easiest way to give a creature fur is to buy it ready-made," says Himmel. "Fur can be manufactured according to exact specifications by a company called National Fiber Technologies (NFT), located in Boston, Massachusetts. We can specify exact hair thickness, density, length, color, and so on. It is then produced on a range of backings, such as stretch fabric, ready to be glued or stitched to a character's body. However, there are many occasions when premanufactured fur is unsuitable, in which case several alternative methods can be employed."

One technique used to create a covering of fur is flocking, a process with industrial applications that range from making artificial velvet to adding the hair to Action Man's head. "Flocking is mostly used to apply an even coat of short hair over a fairly wide area," explains Himmel. "The first thing we do is prepare the hair. We use a variety of synthetic hairs as well as human and yak hair. I generally prefer using natural fibers, which tend to react better in the flocking process.

"When I've selected the hair I want to use, I bundle it up with elastic bands to produce a long, tight bunch. I'll feed that hair into a metal tube until just the right amount is poking out of one end. Then I'll trim that length off with clippers and let it fall into a bucket. I'll carry on doing that until I have a bucketful of clippings. I'll usually do the same for several types and colors of hair, clipping each into its own bucket. Then I'll mix up the different types of hair a few handfuls at a time as if they were paint until I reach exactly the color and mix that I want to use."

The next task is to prepare the area that needs to be covered in fur. "The character to be flocked has its skin sealed with a layer of Pros-Aide glue," says Himmel. "Then I'll apply a few additional layers of the same glue to the area of body that I want to cover in hair. It's important to plan which areas are to be covered, because it's difficult to add more hair at a later time without leaving an obvious join. If two areas of a skin need to be flocked at different times, or perhaps using different types of hair, I will look for places to hide the joins, such as natural creases in the skin or around the creature's joints.

"One of the hardest flocking jobs I've done was Aslan from *The Lion, the Witch and the Wardrobe*. He was about 8ft [2.5m] long and really smooth with nowhere to really hide any joins, so I practically had to flock the whole body in one go. I used five or six colors of human hair."

With the area to be flocked prepared, the hair can now be applied. Flocking works by using electrostatic energy to make each hair stand on end when it falls on to the glued surface. This is achieved by giving the hairs a positive charge before spraying them on to a surface that has a negative charge.

The cut hair is loaded into a basket that is attached to one end of a flocking wand. A custom-cut and formed screen is placed over the basket to hold in the fibers and to regulate the quantity that will exit during each passing of the wand. A wire from the opposite end of the flocking machine is attached with a crocodile clip to the area of skin to be flocked to create a negative charge. The wand is then passed over it, dispersing a shower of positively charged hairs that will land, standing up on their ends, in the glue.

"Once I've passed the wand over the surface a couple of times it will have a coating of hairs sticking upright in the glue," explains Himmel. "Next, I'll shake the surface of the skin so any hairs that haven't stuck properly will fall off. Then I'll gently brush the remaining hairs in the direction I want them to lie. I may repeat the process a few more times, passing the wand over to build up the density of the fur and then brushing it down in the right direction. Guiding the direction of the hairs like this is important to the realism of the fur coat. Animal hair doesn't all stick out at the same angle from the surface of the skin, and there are places on a body where the fur subtly flows in different directions or even changes direction abruptly, causing furry ridges."

Flocking is only suitable for covering a surface with relatively short, straight hairs. Anything longer than about an inch (2.5cm) will need to be produced using other methods. "Quite often we'll find a suitable type of fur that is attached to an unsuitable backing—something that is not flexible enough for us to wrap around and glue to intricate areas or which won't be supple enough if the character's furry skin needs to flex and move," says Himmel. "In these situations we put the fur on a new, more flexible backing using a fur-transfer system."

05

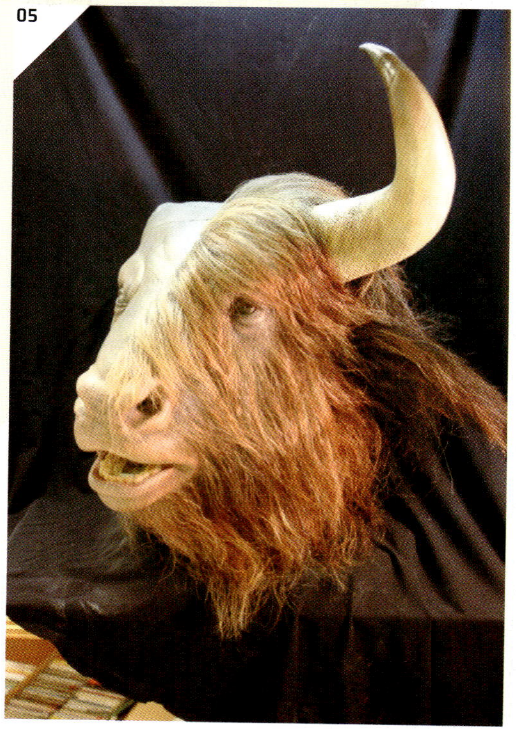

There are a number of methods of transferring fur from one backing to another but all follow the basic principle of the technique used by Himmel. The fur is glued or pinned to a flat surface. The hair is then steamed and combed until it lies as flat as possible. Heavy-duty, low-tack tape or sticky-backed paper is then laid over the top of the fur and pressed down to make sure all hairs are firmly attached. Using electric clippers, the hair is then carefully shaved away from its original backing, which is removed to expose the base of the fur. Several layers of Pros-Aide glue are then sprayed or brushed over the base of the fur, which forms a new backing when set. The tape is then carefully removed from the front of the hair and the result is a piece of fur that looks identical to the original but now has a very thin flexible backing. The new fur can be cut according to a pattern and glued to the foam-latex skin or surface of the character. A complex shape, such as a head, might be covered with a patchwork of ten or more individually tailored pieces.

(05) Minotaur head hand-punched with Yak hair to test length, color and styling during development work on *Narnia*. **(06–07)** Here, individual hairs are being pushed into foam rubber to create the gorilla from *Buddy* (1997).

06

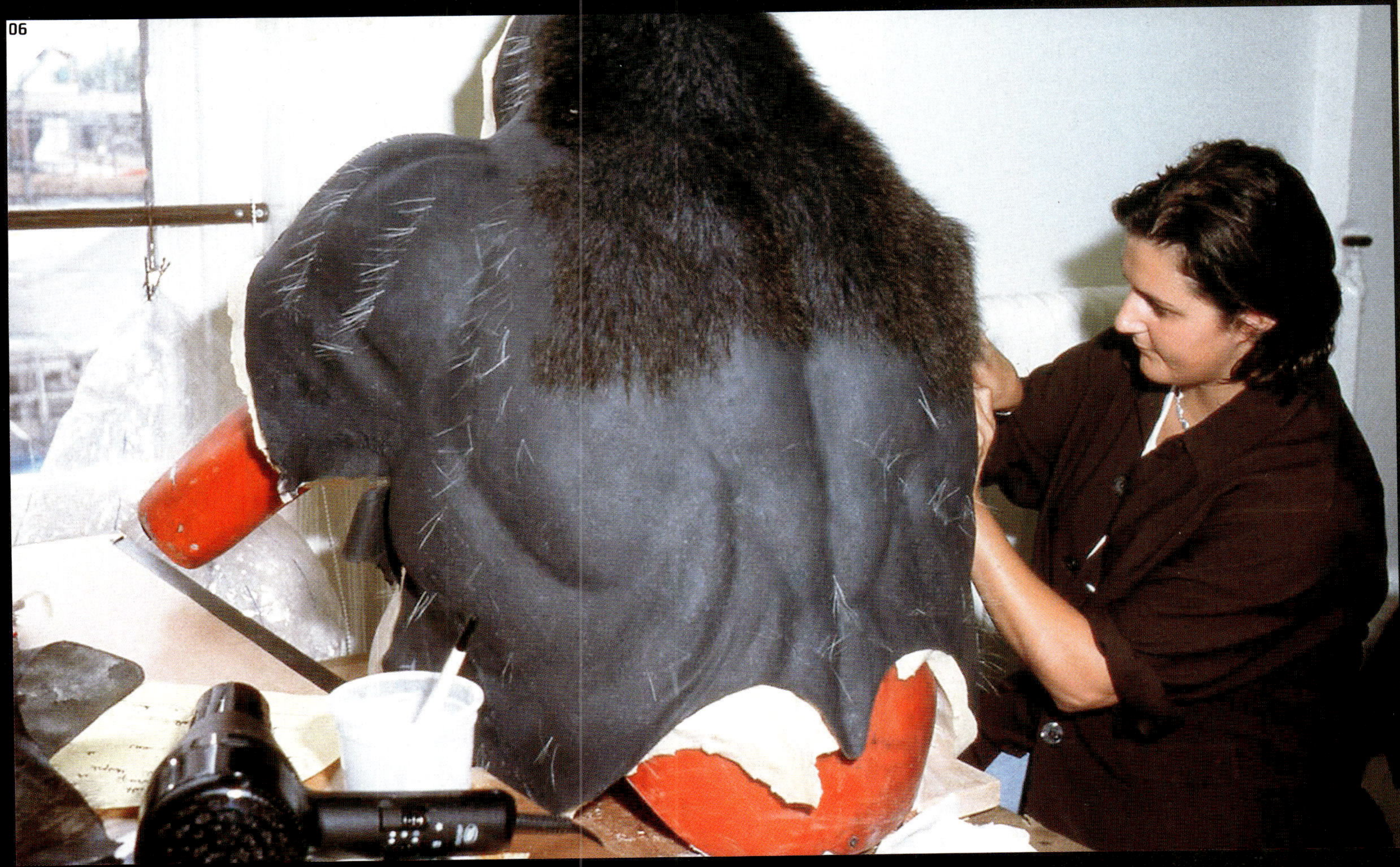

07

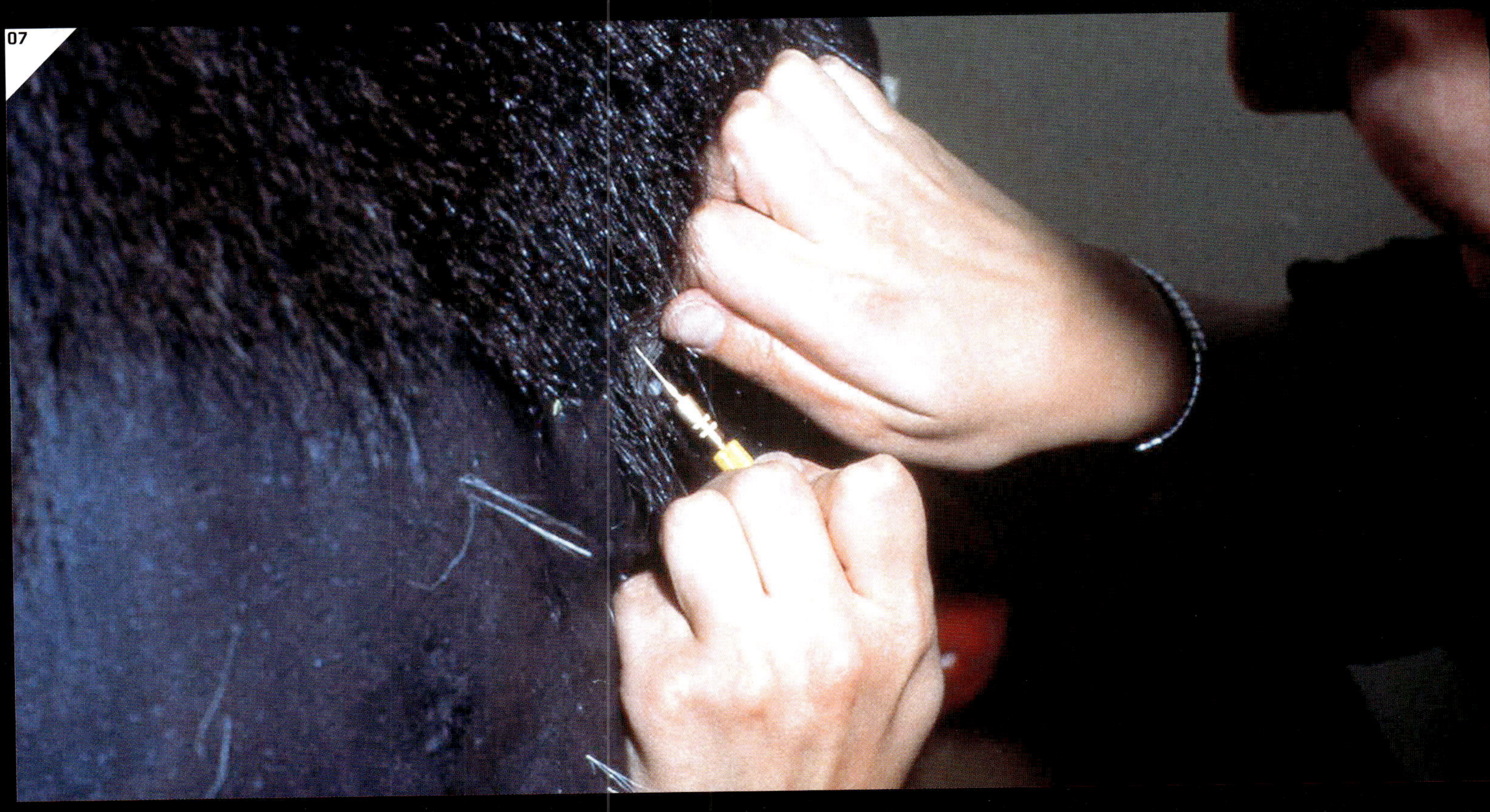

A similar technique can also be used to transfer fur from its original backing directly onto the surface of a character's skin. Once the original backing has been removed, the fur—with its temporary covering of sticky tape—is pressed directly onto the glued surface of the creature. When the tape is removed, the fur will remain attached to the exterior of the creature as if growing from its skin.

A far more painstaking method of giving a character a coat of hair is to individually punch each hair directly into the skin. Hair punching is extremely labor intensive, but offers the most freedom to produce exactly the required finish. The technique is often used to create the fur on complex-shaped creatures to which it would be hard to glue any ready-backed fur.

"To punch hairs into a character's skin we first make our own tool," says Himmel. "We use very thin beading needles and then cut off the top of the eye to make a tiny forked instrument. Using fine sand paper, we work the ends of the fork into a J-like shape. We then lay our hair against the skin one strand at a time and use our punching tool to push that hair down into the foam latex or silicone skin of the animal. The hair will then stick up out of the skin as if it is actually growing there.

"The angle at which each hair is punched must correspond to the angle of its neighbors so that all of the hair appears to be growing in the same direction; however, the direction of most creature's hair changes across its body. We have to very gradually change the angle we punch the hair at as we work our way across the body toward certain features. For example, the hair on the back of an ape might grow horizontally away from its spine, but then start to curve around and downward on the outer edges of its back and then change direction again as it goes up over the shoulders."

Hair punching is often used as a method of blending different areas of hair. For example, an area of long, fabric-backed fur that meets an area of short, flocked hair may have hairs of an intermediate length and color punched into the flocking to make the two types merge.

Another technique for creating hair is to hand-tie every strand to a fabric backing. This technique is usually used for creating wigs as well as facial hair that will be glued to a performer's skin. To tie hair—a process also known as ventilating—each hair is bent into a loop and the loop is pushed through the tiny hole on a piece of fine silk or lace. A very small hooked instrument is used to pull the loop of hair through the hole and then push the loose ends of the hair through the loop to tie a knot. Hairs in the center of a wig can be tied several at a time, while the more noticeable hairs around the edges will be done singly. The hair for a human head would require between 30,000 and 40,000 individual hairs, taking over a week to tie.

It is rare that a character's hair needs are met using only one method, and so a combination of techniques is normally used to get the best effect. "We usually have to mix a number of different fur techniques for each creature in order to create the range of textures and looks that most animals naturally have," says Himmel. "A good example, again, is Aslan. His body was mostly flocked. His mane fur was custom made by National Fiber Technologies from a combination of natural and synthetic fibers on a stretch fabric backing. To blend the mane into the flocked head we used hand-punched human hair. Punching was also used to create the longer fur along his belly, paws, tail, and the whiskers on his face, which were actually ostrich feathers stripped down to their quill."

Once hair of all varieties has been applied, it is trimmed and styled—perhaps painted to create more subtle colors. Additional hair is sometimes punched back into areas that have been trimmed and painted to create a less "manicured" look. Finally, the hair will be dressed using a range of chemicals, hair products, or hot tongs to achieve the perfect look before the cameras roll.

(08) Jeff Himmel flocks Aslan's face with a flocking wand. The white area on the lion's face has been painted with glue, ready to receive the hair **(09–10)** Himmel created the fur coat for this dead Beagle made by KNB **(11–12)** Aslan's face fur was flocked, the mane was ready-made synthetic fur on a backing material, and a hand-punched mixture of human and synthetic hair was used to blend the two areas together.

08
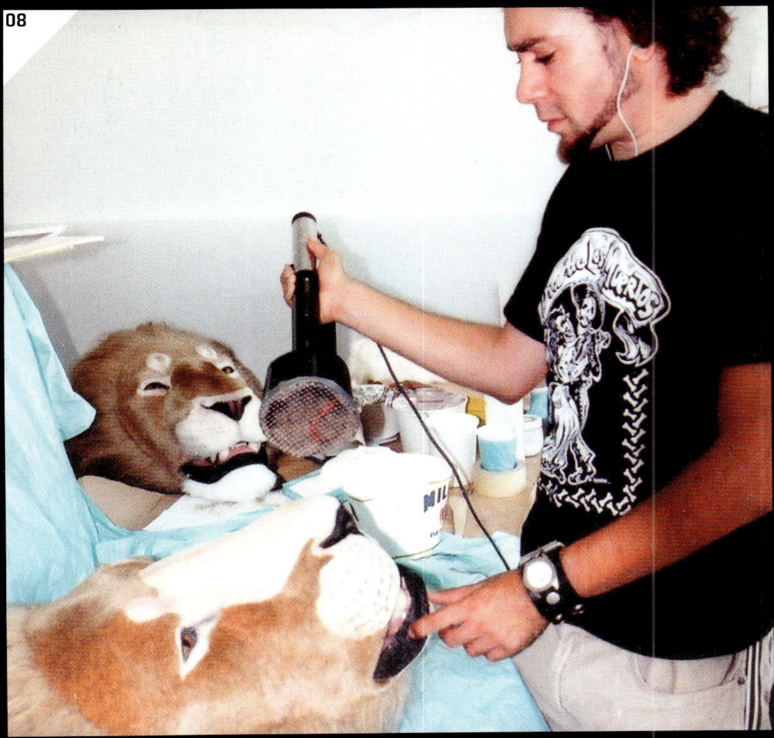

09
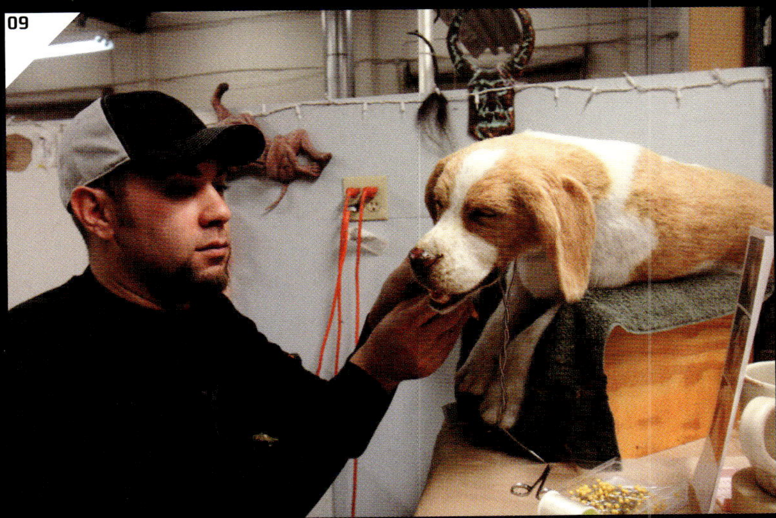

10
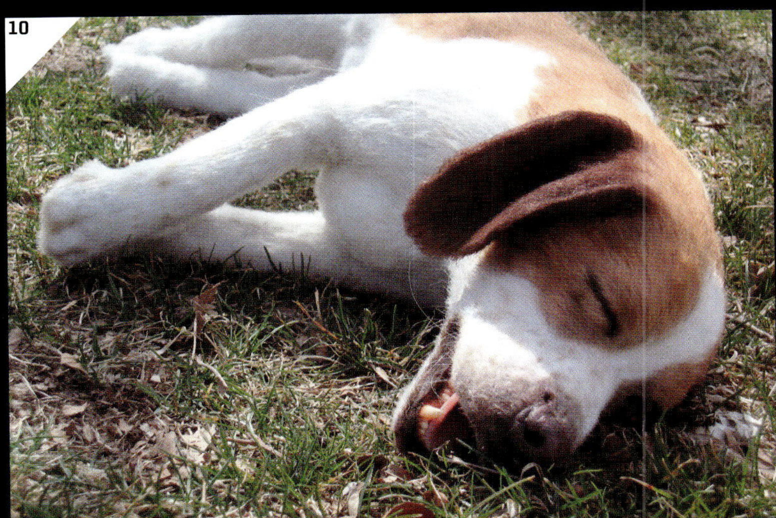

11
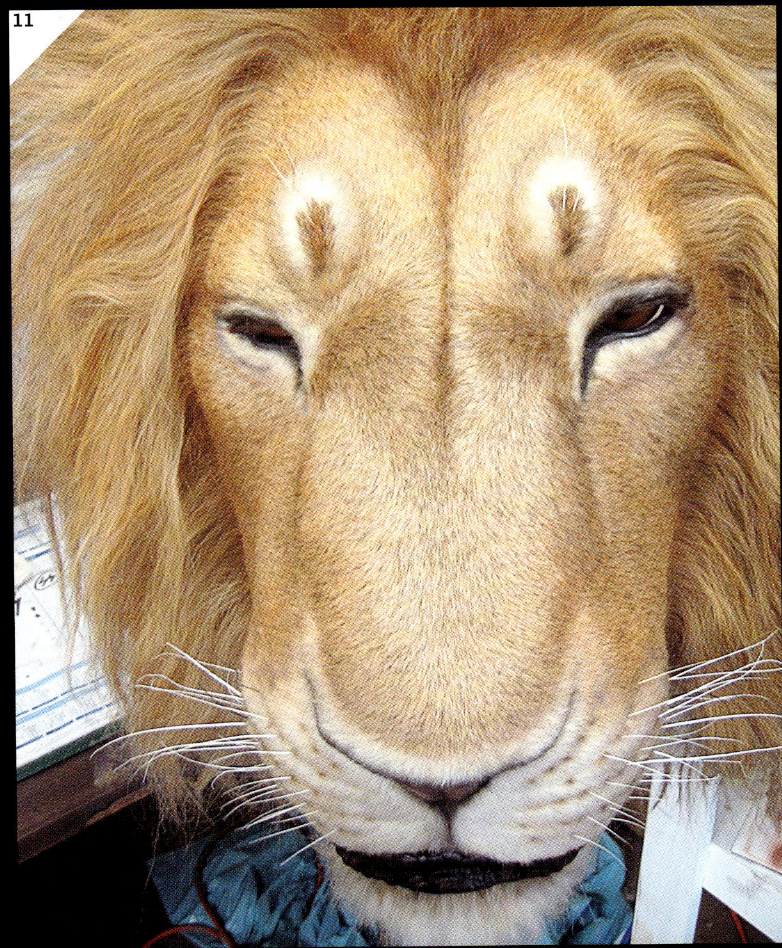

12
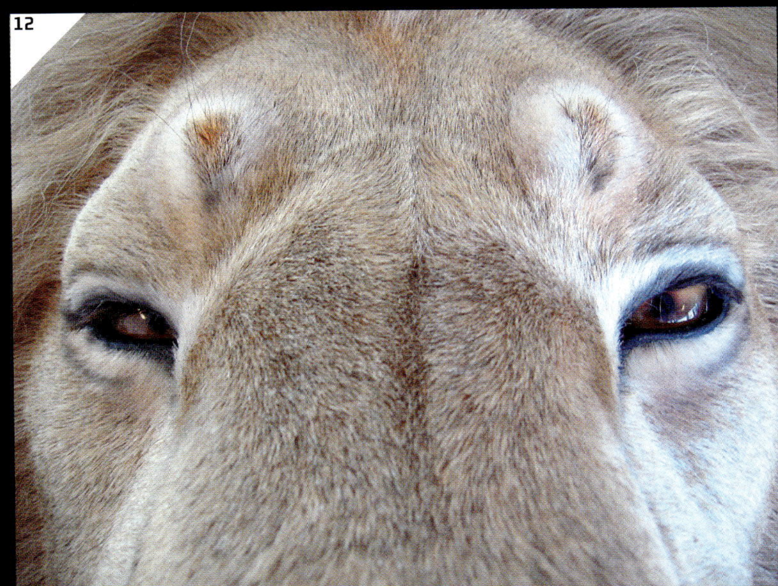

SPECTRAL MOTION

MIKE ELIZALDE

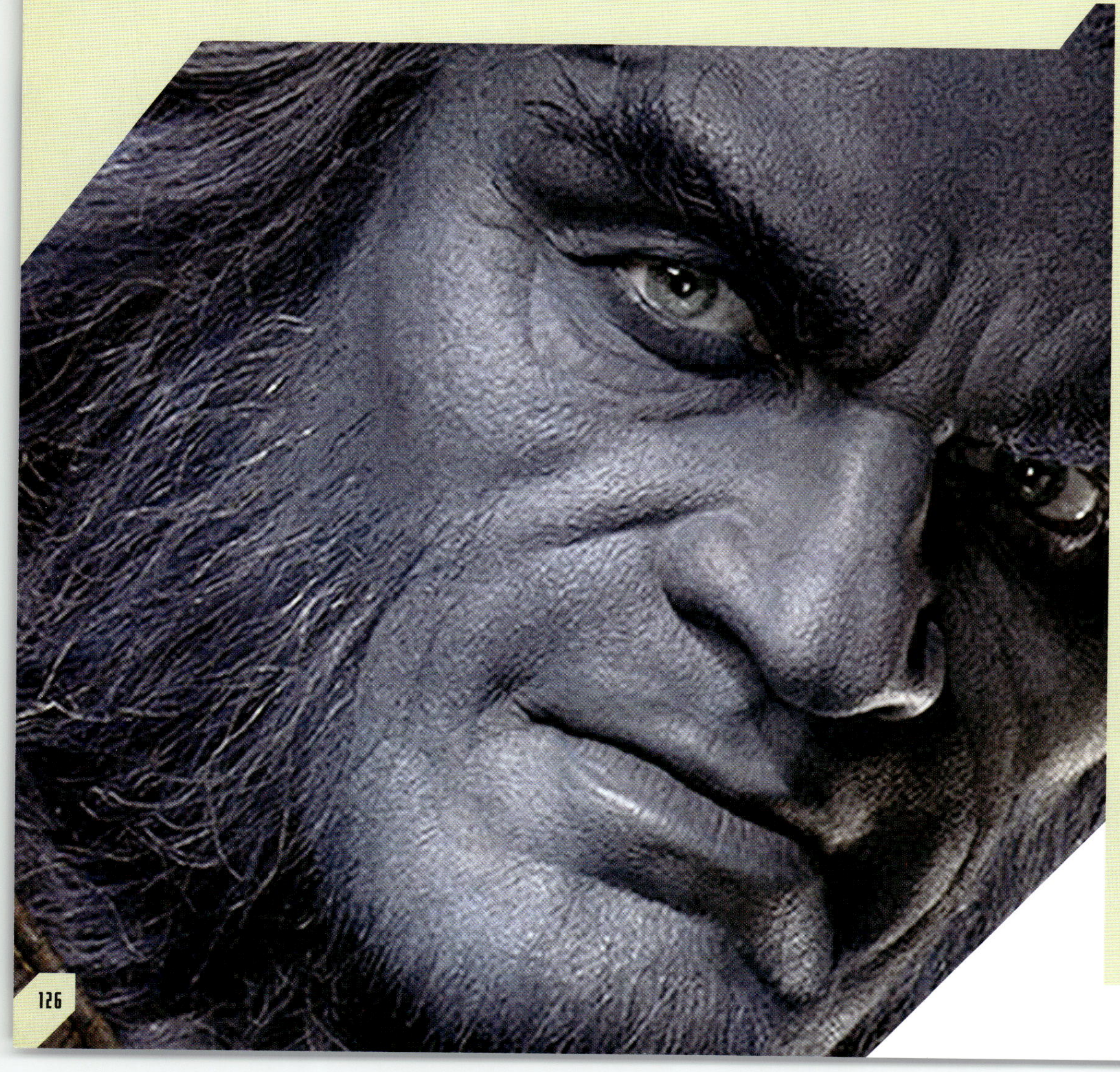

CV

Makeup producer, animatronic designer/manufacturer, and puppeteer; after high school, joined the Navy; on leaving, took up painting and sculpting; landed a job with John Beuchler's Magical Media Industries, after which he worked for the Dave Miller Studio, where he learned to apply makeup; worked as a freelance, during which time he became increasingly drawn to animatronics and puppeteering; formed Spectral Motion with his wife Mary in 1994.

SELECT FILMOGRAPHY

Arena (1989); *A Nightmare on Elm Street* (1989); *Nothing But Trouble* (1991); *Coneheads* (1993); *Blade II* (2002); *Blade Trinity* (2004); *Hellboy* (2004); *Fantastic Four* (2005); *X-Men: The Last Stand* (2006); *Lady in the Water* (2006)

KEY CHARACTERS

Abe Sapien, Sammael (*Hellboy*); Drake (Blade Trinity); Angel, Beast, Juggernaut (*X-Men: The Last Stand*); The Scrunt, the Tartutic (*Lady in the Water*)

TECHNIQUES

Design, makeup, and animatronics; Photoshop; Softimage XSI

02

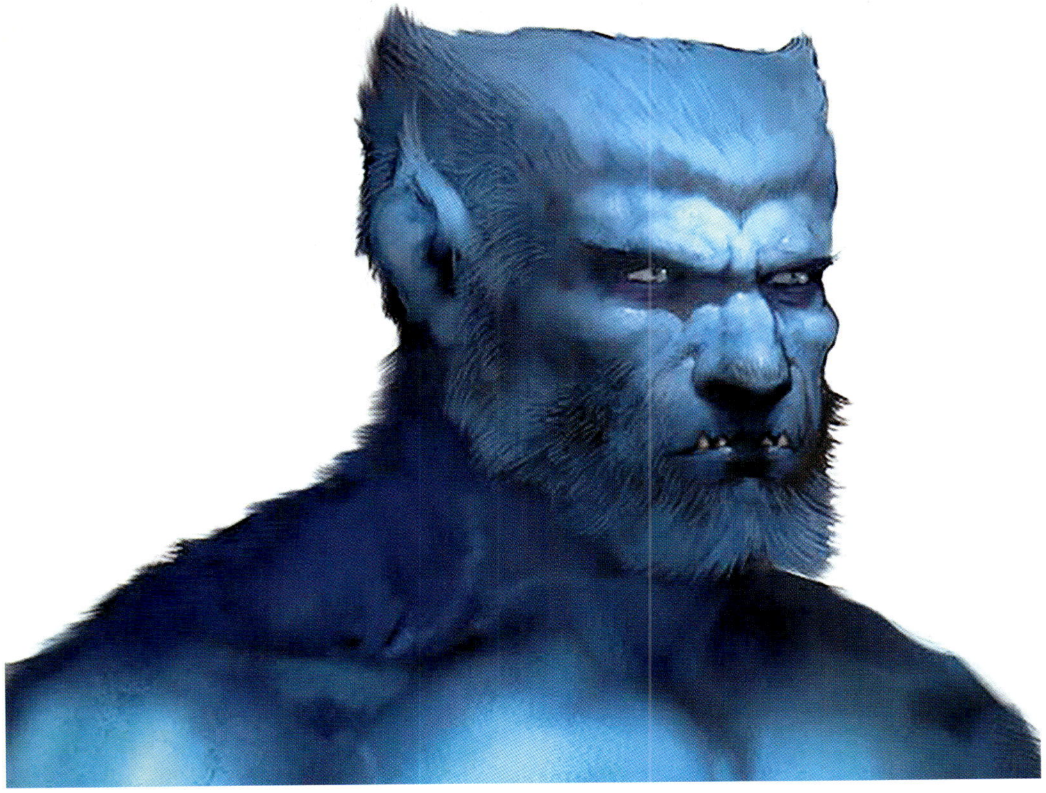

03

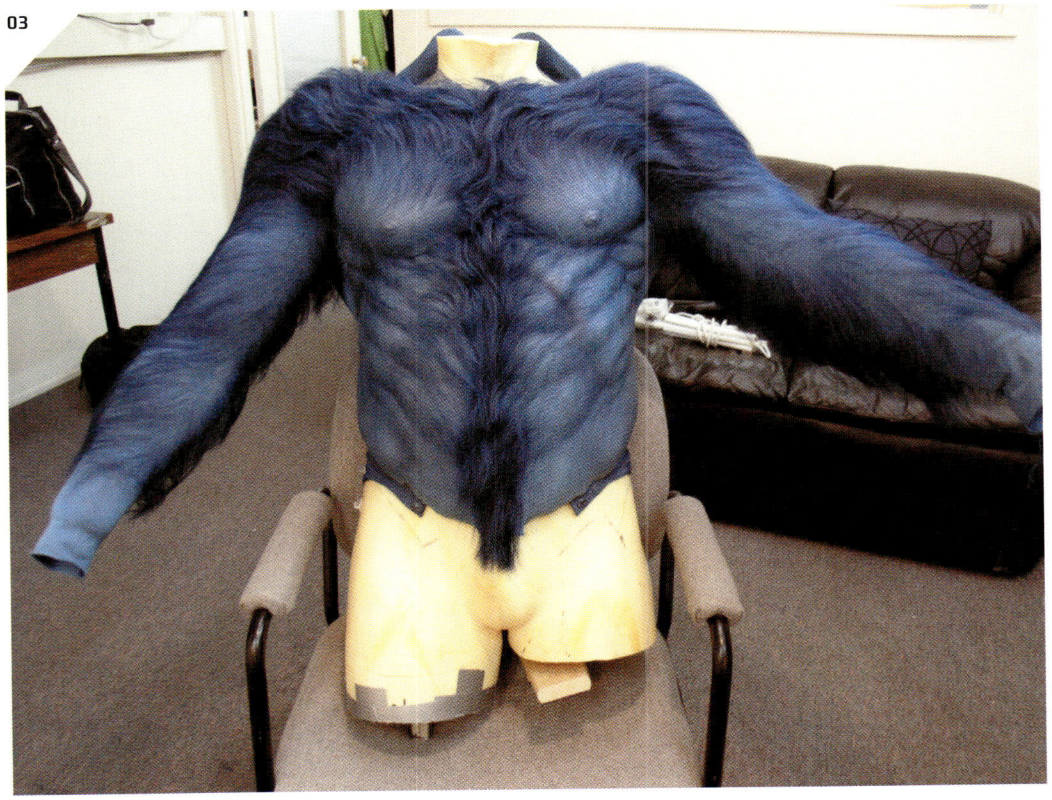

(01) Spectral Motion transformed Kelsey Grammer into Beast for *X-Men: The Last Stand* (2006) **(02)** Early Beast concept art by Carlos Huante **(03)** Final Beast body suit, prepainted and punched with hair, ready to be applied to Grammer.

Mike Elizalde's interest in the movies was kindled by his father. "We spent many hours together watching Vincent Price, Hammer Horrors, the original *Frankenstein*," remembers Elizalde. "That got me interested in movie monsters from a pretty early age."

After high school Elizalde served in the US Navy, before realizing that movie makeup was his real calling. "During my second enlistment I saw *An American Werewolf in London* (1981), and started reading about Rick Baker and Dick Smith—that made me painfully aware that I was in the wrong business. Then I found a book by Lee Baygan called *Techniques of Three-Dimensional Makeup*, and it really caught my imagination and made me start to work on my skills."

Elizalde left the Navy and began sculpting and painting, sending examples of his work to Hollywood makeup shops. He found a job with John Beuchler's Magical Media Industries (MMI), working on a science-fiction movie called *Arena* (1989). "It was a big show for MMI, so instead of starting off at the bottom and working my way up, I was sculpting and painting right from the start," he says. "One of the other people was Steve Wang, and I got to learn a lot from him. I later worked for the Dave Miller Studio, where one person had to do everything—sculpting, molding, casting, cleaning-up, painting. We worked on movies like *Nightmare on Elm Street* [5 and 6; 1989, 1991]. That's when I learned the art of applying makeup."

04

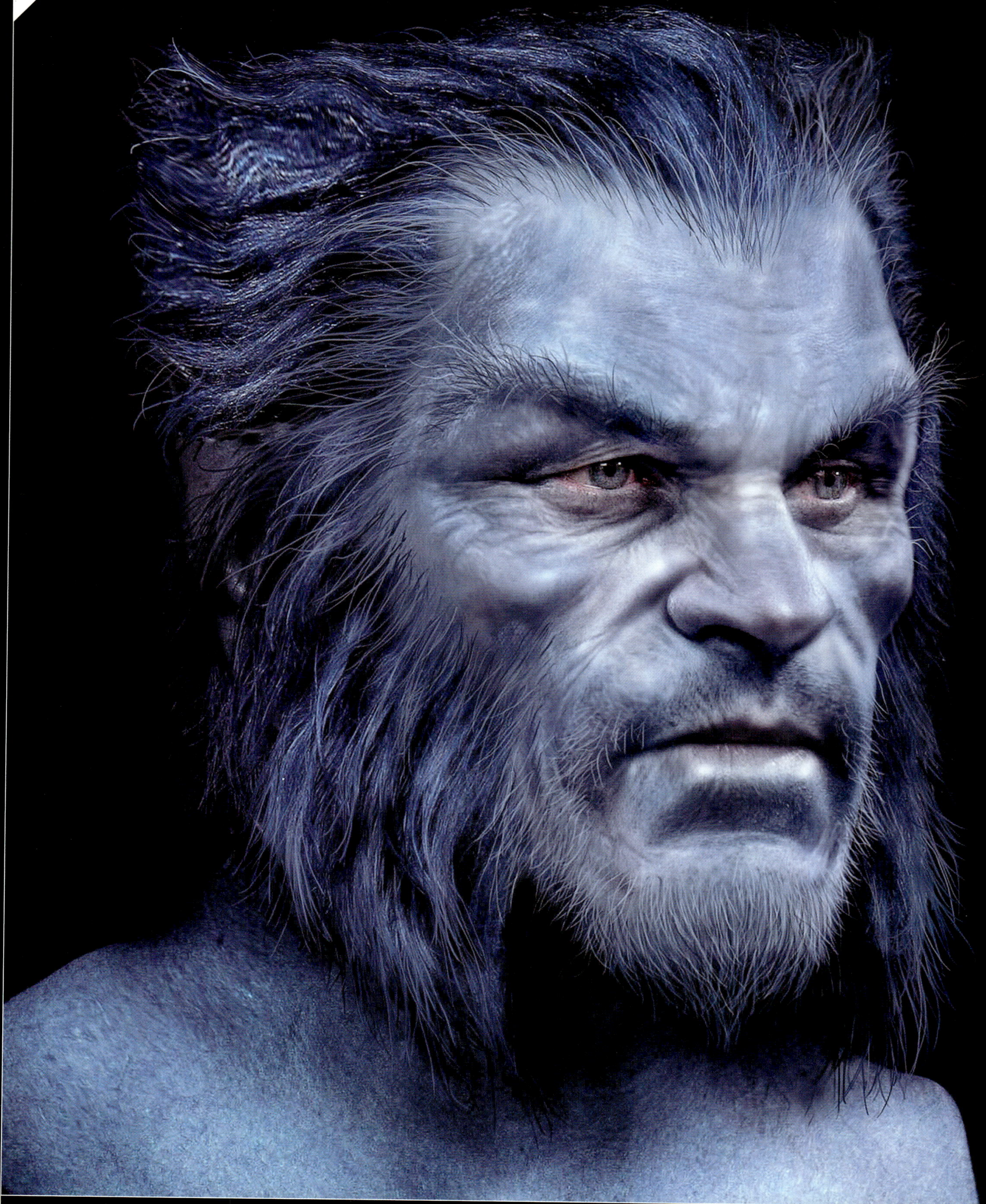

05

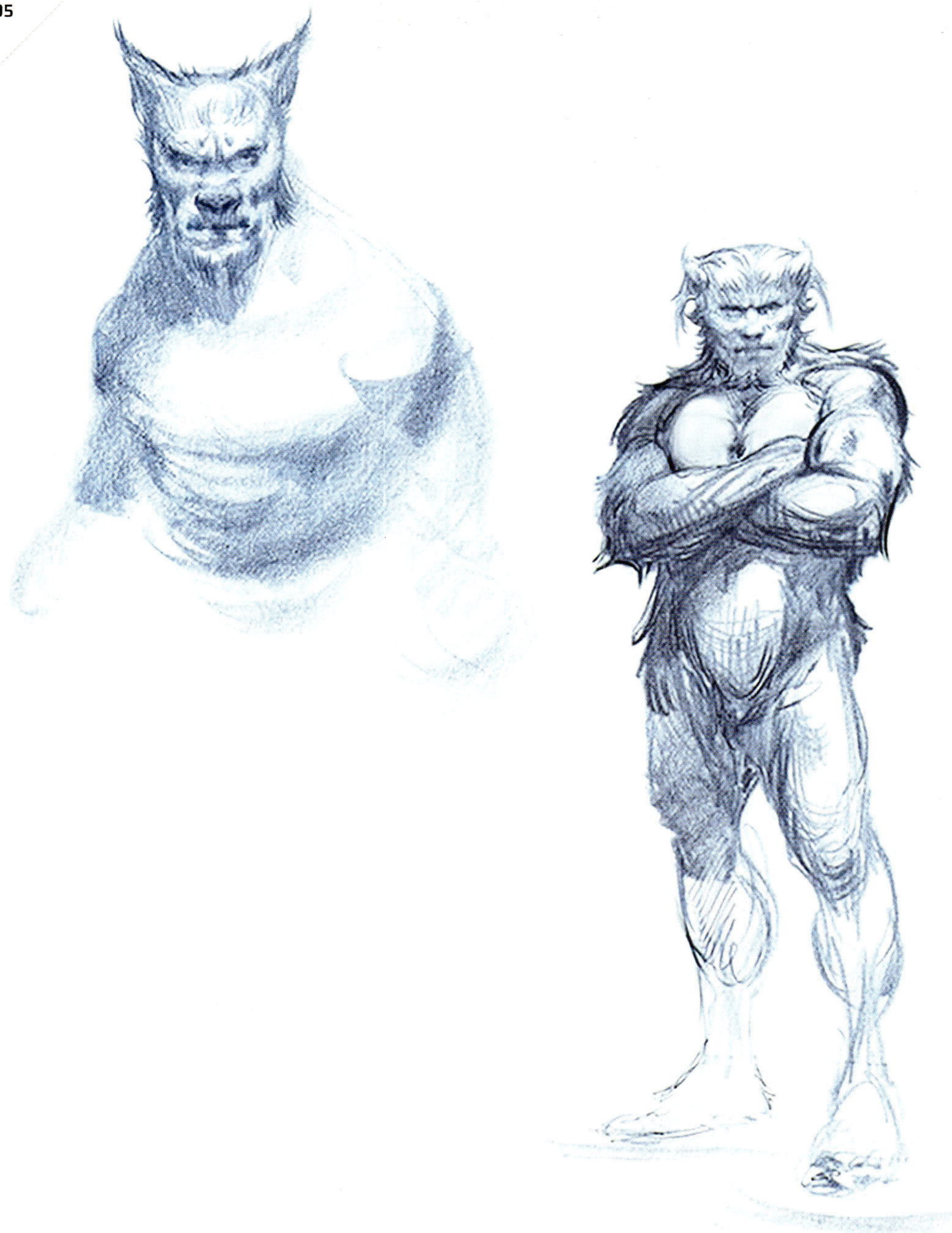

Elizalde found himself increasingly drawn toward animatronics and puppeteering. "If you're designing or sculpting characters, everyone has some input and you're essentially piecing together someone else's ideas. But with animatronics you get a brief in terms of how the character has to perform, but after that it's down to you to figure out how to make it work."

For a while Elizalde lived the typically nomadic life of a Hollywood makeup artist, then in 1994 he and his wife Mary established their own company, Spectral Motion, initially to sell original-character modeling kits, but also hiring out Mike's talents to other studios.

While working for Steve Johnson on *Blade II* (2002), Elizalde befriended the movie's director, Guillermo del Toro, himself a former makeup artist. One of the projects del Toro was then trying to get off the ground was an adaptation of Mike Mignola's 1994 graphic novel, *Seed of Destruction*, which had been renamed *Hellboy*.

Hellboy (2004) had a six-year evolution from comic book to movie. Long before the movie went into production, Matt Rose and Chad Waters at Rick Baker's Cinnovation Studios sculpted their interpretation of the Hellboy character by grafting a version of the comic-book character onto a facial lifecast of actor Ron Perlman. Del Toro was so pleased with that first attempt that it remained largely unchanged until production began almost five years later.

With Rick Baker's studio working on Hellboy himself, del Toro offered the remainder of the character work to Elizalde. "We didn't have our own workshop at that time. I found a property, purchased equipment, and started hiring the best people we could find. Suddenly Spectral Motion turned into a fully fledged makeup studio."

06

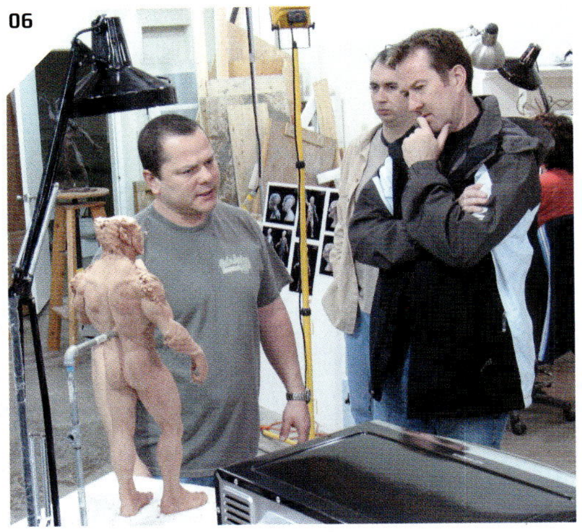

(04) Beautiful Constantine Sekeris' artwork for an optional Beast hairstyle **(05)** Early concept sketches by Carlos Huante **(06)** Mike Elizalde (left) discusses an early Beast maquette with Spectral Motion production supervisor Brian Walsh and *X-Men* producer Ralph Winter

07

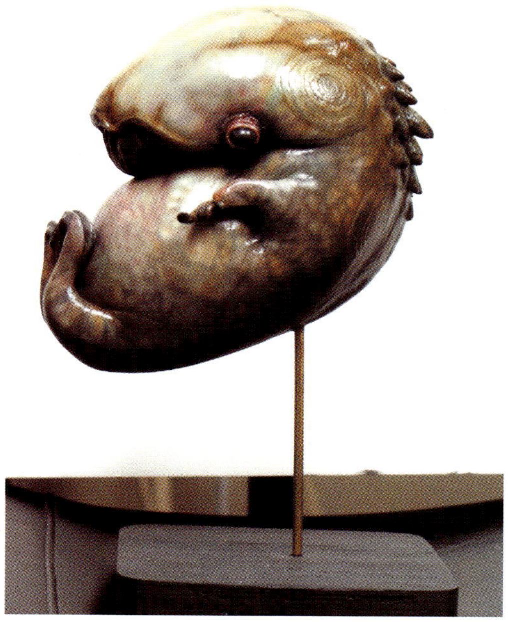

08

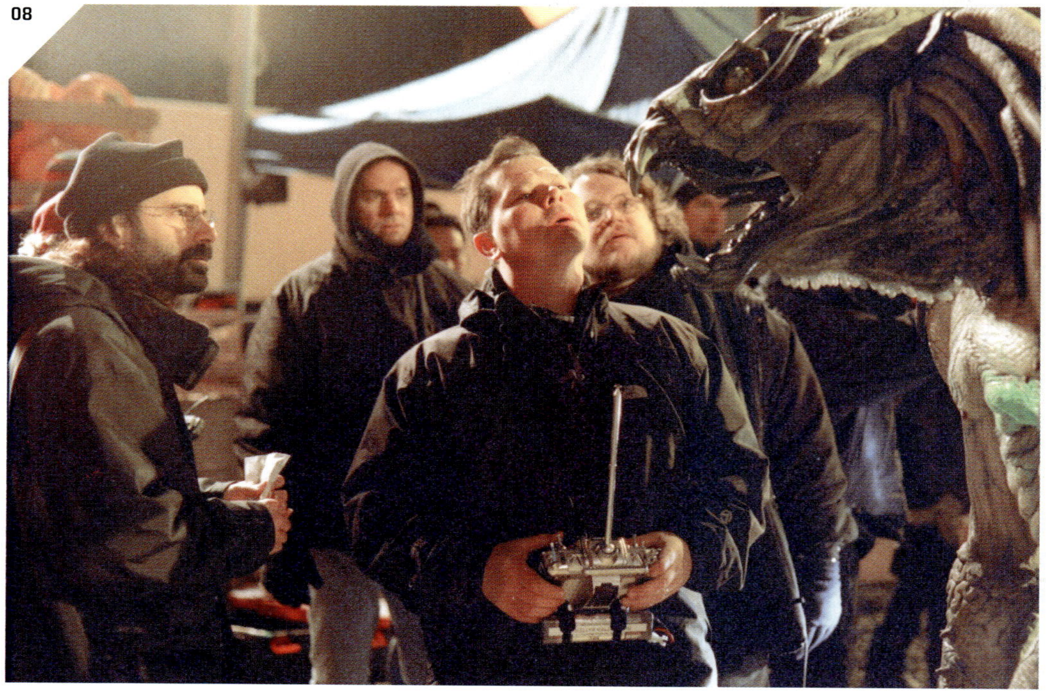

Among other characters, Spectral Motion was asked to create the amphibian, Abe Sapien, and the demonic Sammael. Elizalde recalls that Abe Sapien really caught his imagination with his human physiognomy, plus fins, gills, and webbing.

Abe evolved through a series of designs by artists including Wayne Barlowe, Mike Mignola, and Steve Wang. With the final paper design approved, a 2ft-tall (0.6m) maquette was sculpted by Jose Fernandez and approved by del Toro. Wang was then charged with turning the concept into a practical makeup design. "Steve did a wonderful job of figuring out how the maquette could be turned into a series of pieces that would then be applied to performer Doug Jones," says Elizalde. "Steve also created the color design—who else but Steve Wang would you go to for aquatic camouflage?"

(07) Maquette of baby Sammael (for *Hellboy*, 2004) **(08)** Mark Setrakian (left) watches Mike Elizalde test Sammael's radio-controlled eye mechanisms **(09)** Elizalde makes adjustments to Sammael on-set **(10)** The finished Sammael.

Using a bodycast of Doug Jones, Wang sculpted each piece of Abe's body in clay to create a system of modular appliances. Elizalde recalls what it took to turn Jones into Sapien: "On the body there was a shirt-like torso section, upper arm, and leg pieces, and front and back neck appliances. There were transparent membranes that stretched between his body and arms to produce a webbed effect, and transparent fins that ran down his legs and back. Doug wore gloves with extended webbed fingers and rubber boots that created Abe's feet. The face was made from a series of overlapping foam-latex appliances. Around the mouth the mask was blended off on the inside of Doug's lips. When the prepainted appliances had been glued onto his body, makeup artist Thom Floutz blended them together with more paint and also painted any remaining areas of Doug's bare skin."

"One of the things Guillermo requested was that Abe's face didn't look like it had been built right on top of a human face," continues Elizalde. "In particular, he didn't want to see human eyes looking out from the makeup, which can often happen with facial appliances. We designed these big, oval, resin eyes that were very angular and spaced widely apart. From inside the makeup Doug could just about peer out

09

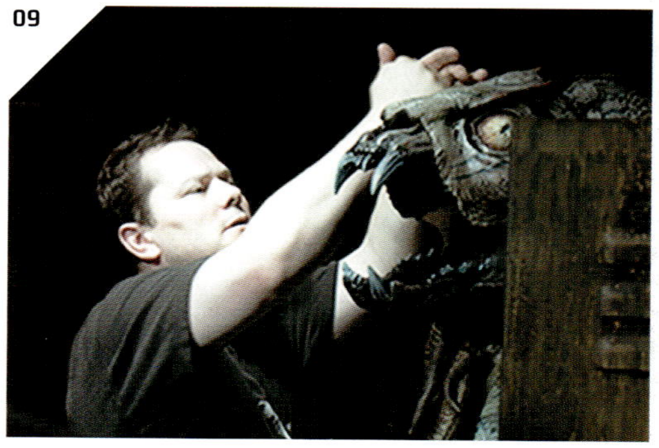

of the bottom inside corners of the eyes. In addition, the front of the mask was very flat, so Doug's nose had to be squashed under the makeup. We also created a set of three gills on each side of the face, which Mark Setrakian engineered to flick open and closed in an amazingly delicate way."

A number of materials were used to create the appliances. "Silicone is very heavy, and in the quantities used for Abe, it would have weighed the performer down," he says. "Instead we went for foam latex, which is much lighter, and easier to apply and blend into the actor's skin. The translucent look was achieved by building up the paint in layers."

10

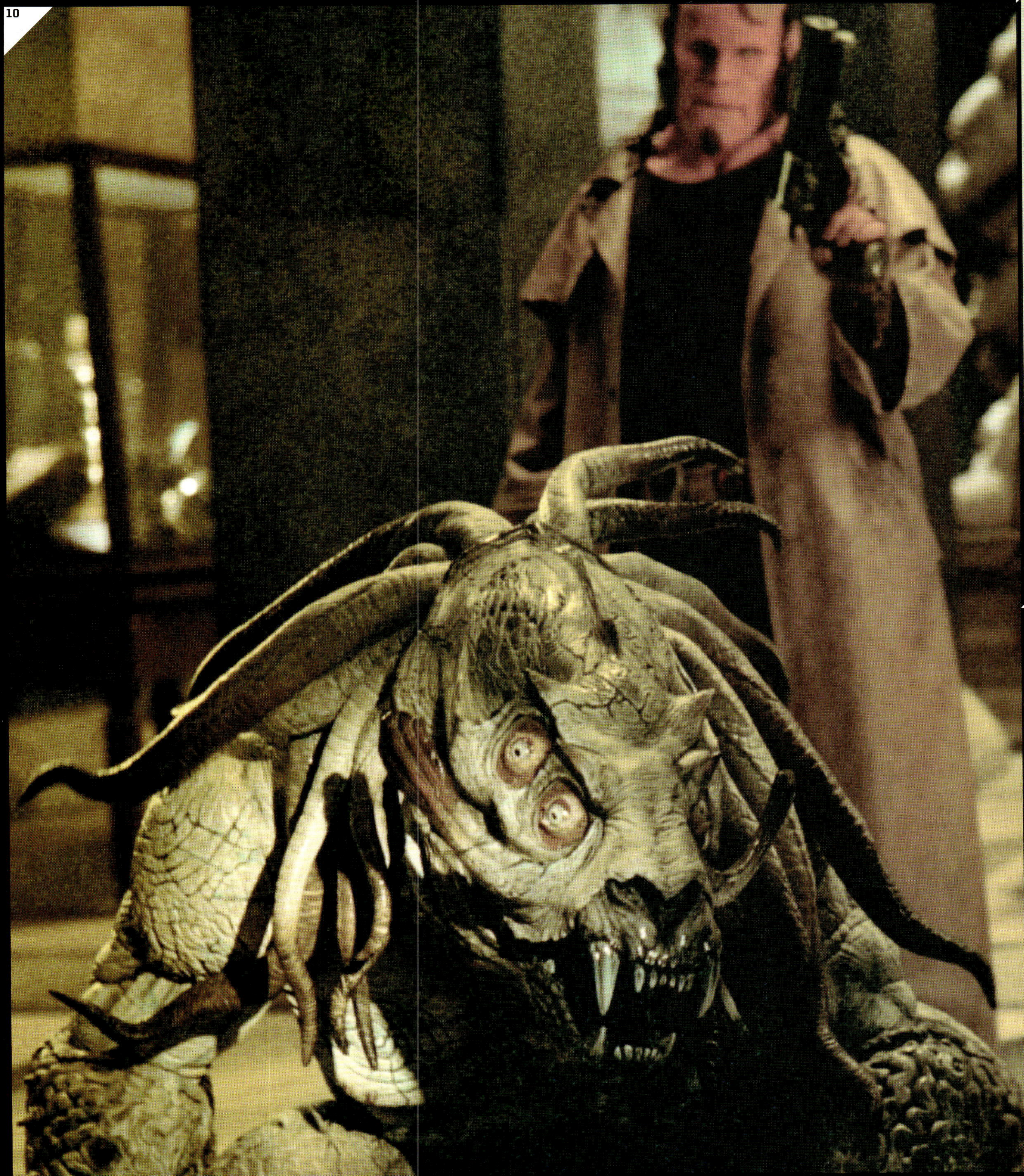

11

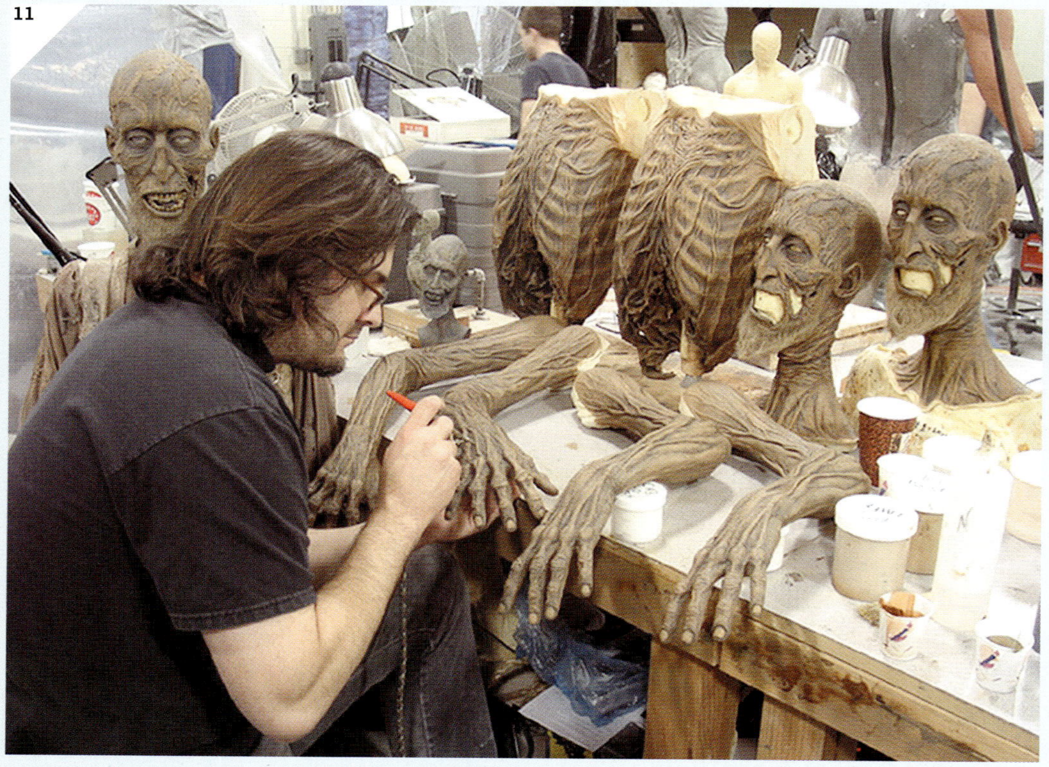

13

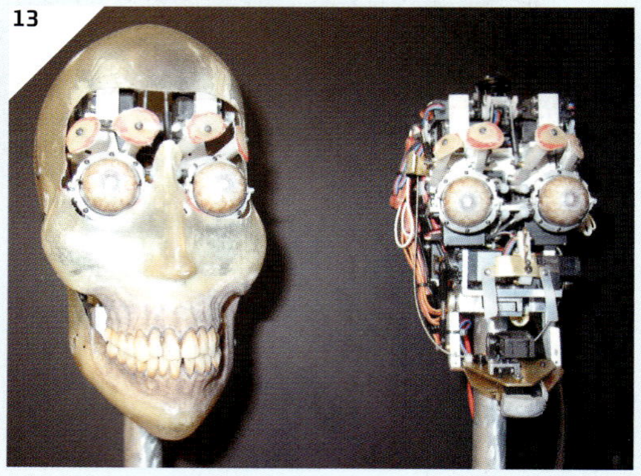

12

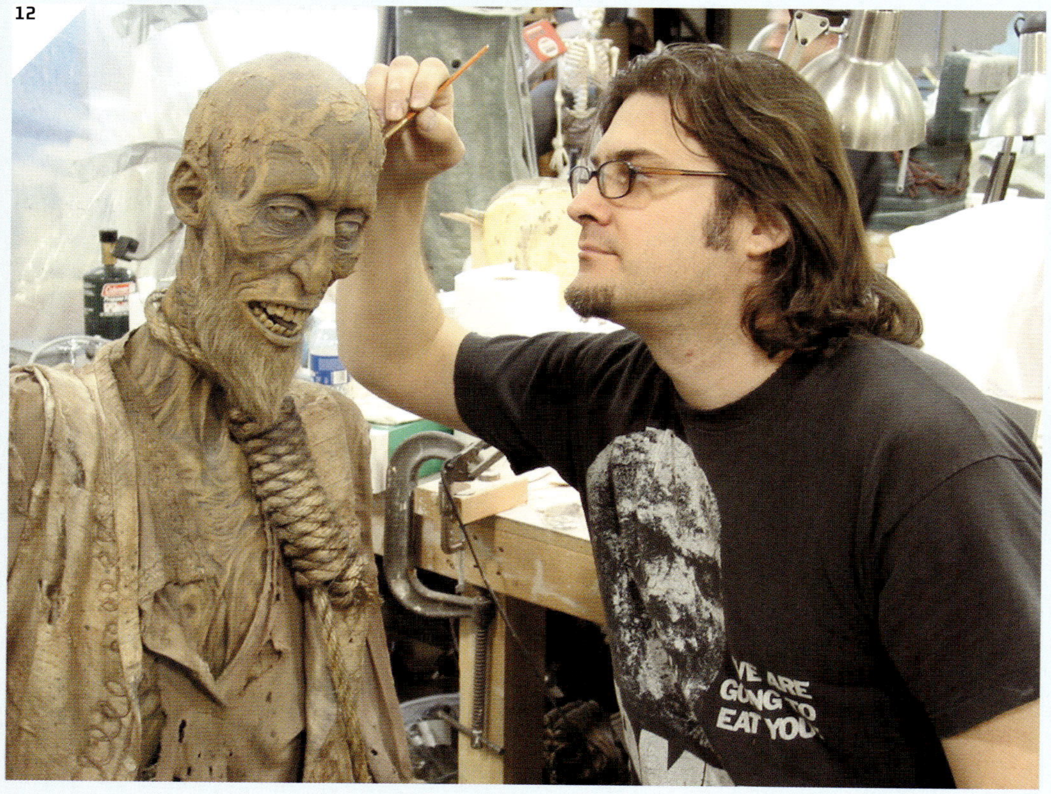

Abe's aquatic look was aided by a slathering of gel to give his skin a glistening, wet appearance, but for underwater scenes the effect had to be played down. "We filmed a number of scenes on a smoked-up stage with Abe hanging from wires to look like he was swimming," says Elizalde. "Even shiny objects look matte and dull underwater, so for these shots we had to make sure there was no sliminess on his skin."

More unusual materials were employed for some of Abe's non-standard body parts. "For the fins down his spine and on the backs of his legs, we used a semi-flexible urethane. The webbing under his arms was made from a thermal-gel material which is melted at high temperature before casting. It sets to form a piece with a very good memory—you can stretch and distort it but it always comes back to its original size and shape." Applying the Abe makeup took between four and six hours each morning. To save time—and allow the makeup artists some sleep—Jones even wore the makeup home at night on a few occasions!

(11) Norman Cabrera paints a mummified corpse for *Hellboy* **(12)** Cabrera applies fine detailing **(13)** Corpse internal facial mechanisms **(14)** Spectral Motion created the Tartutic (designed by Crash McCreery with makeup supervised by Steve Wang) for *Lady in the Water* (2006).

14

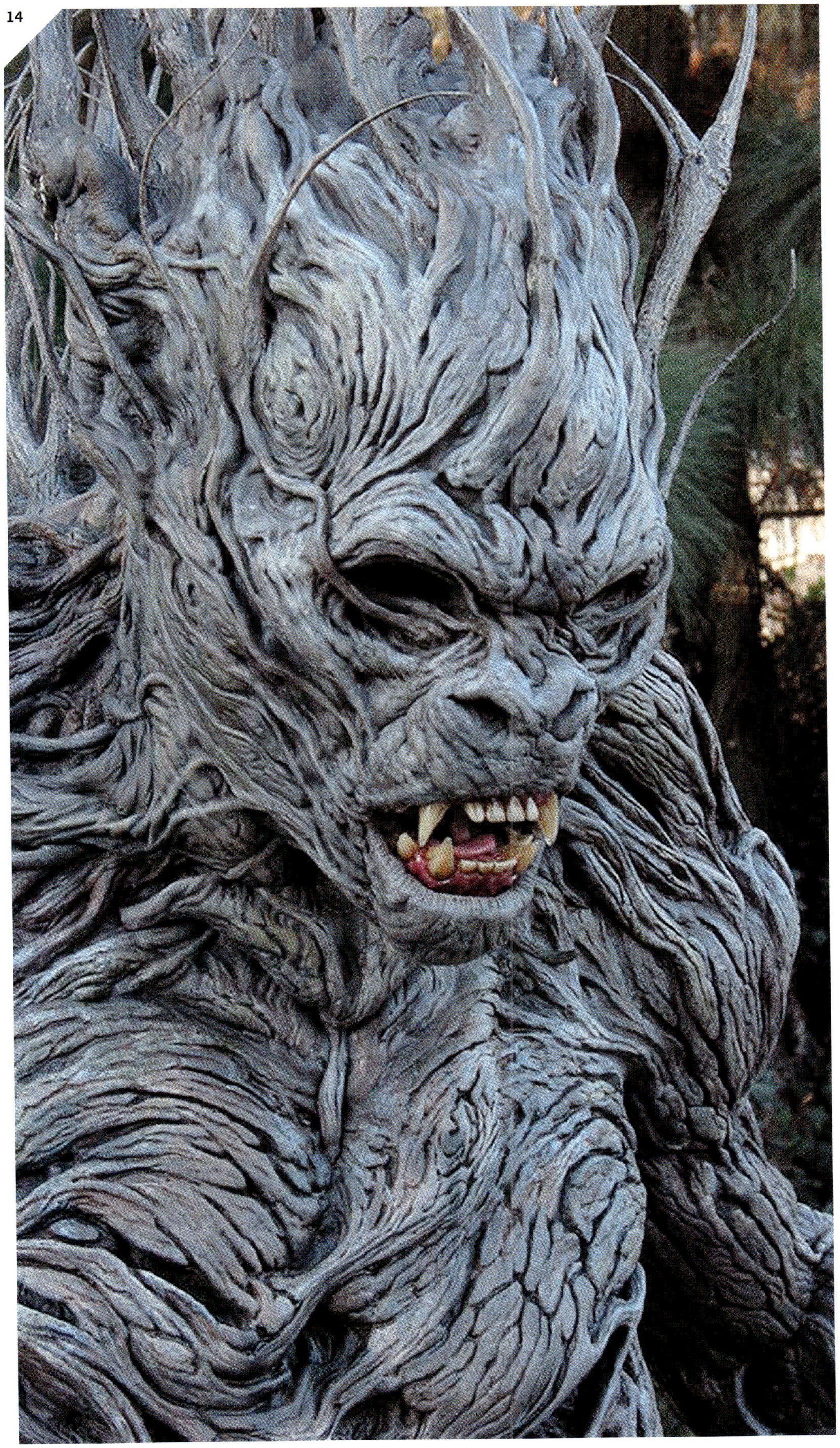

The practical (physical) Abe makeup was subtly aided by some minor digital additions during post-production. Because Abe's mask was designed to sit so closely against Jones's face, there was no room for mechanisms to make his eyes blink. Visual-effects house Eden FX therefore created digital blinks, and added a few facial expressions in scenes where the director wanted a little more emotion. "They were very subtle effects—a great example of the two disciplines working well together," says Elizalde.

Spectral Motion's other major character for the movie was Sammael, the devilish beast that looks part ape, part dog, and part dragon. "Sammael was a fascinating character to work on," recalls Elizalde. "Almost everything about him was unusual or a challenge. From the design point of view, Guillermo kept using the word 'Lovecraftian' [after the American fantasy author H.P. Lovecraft], which I took to mean dark, mythical, and demonic. The final design was largely the result of collaboration between Guillermo and concept artist Wayne Barlowe."

One of the key design features was an unconventional lopsidedness. "Guillermo wanted Sammael to be unsettling to the eye," Elizalde explains. "He wanted part of that to come from a lack of symmetry. He had one arm larger than the other and even had one eye on one side of his face and two on the other."

Sammael was designed by Steve Wang as a creature suit to be worn by performer Brian Steele, consisting of a torso piece with separate head, arms, legs, hands, and feet. "We knew early on that Brian would be inside the suit, so we did a cyberscan of his body, and that was used to mill out a 2ft-high (0.6m) version of him. Our Sammael design maquettes were sculpted by Motoyoshi Hata on top of that, so we knew that the full-scale version would work on Brian's physique," says Elizalde. "Often a maquette is sculpted purely to sell a design to the director, but when you come to make the creature you have to make compromises because it won't fit the physique of your performer."

15

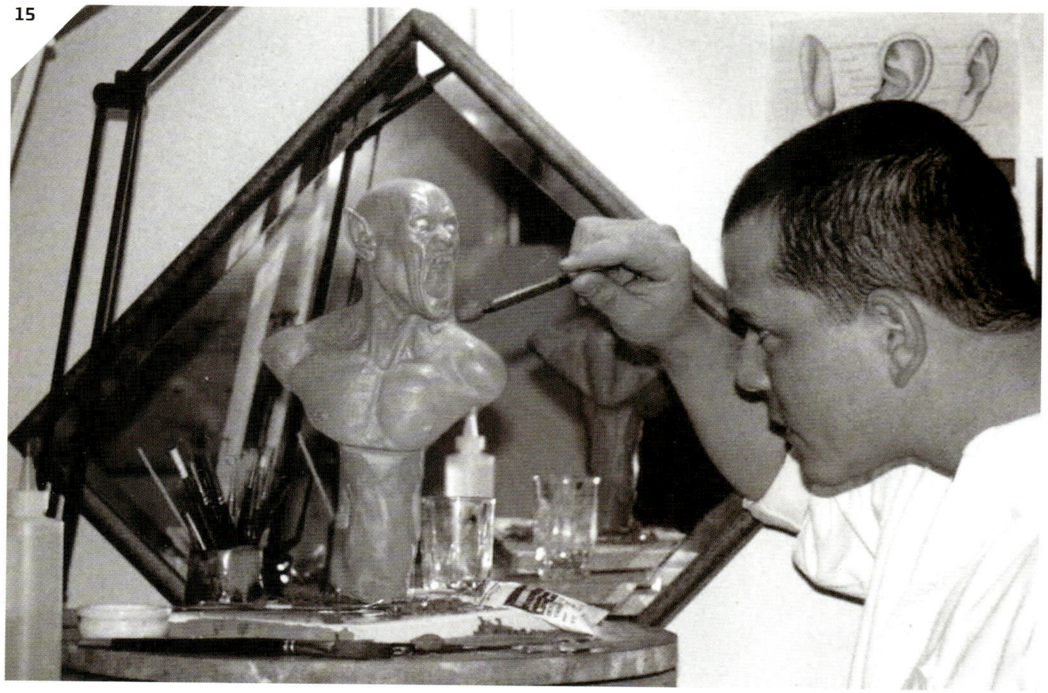

16

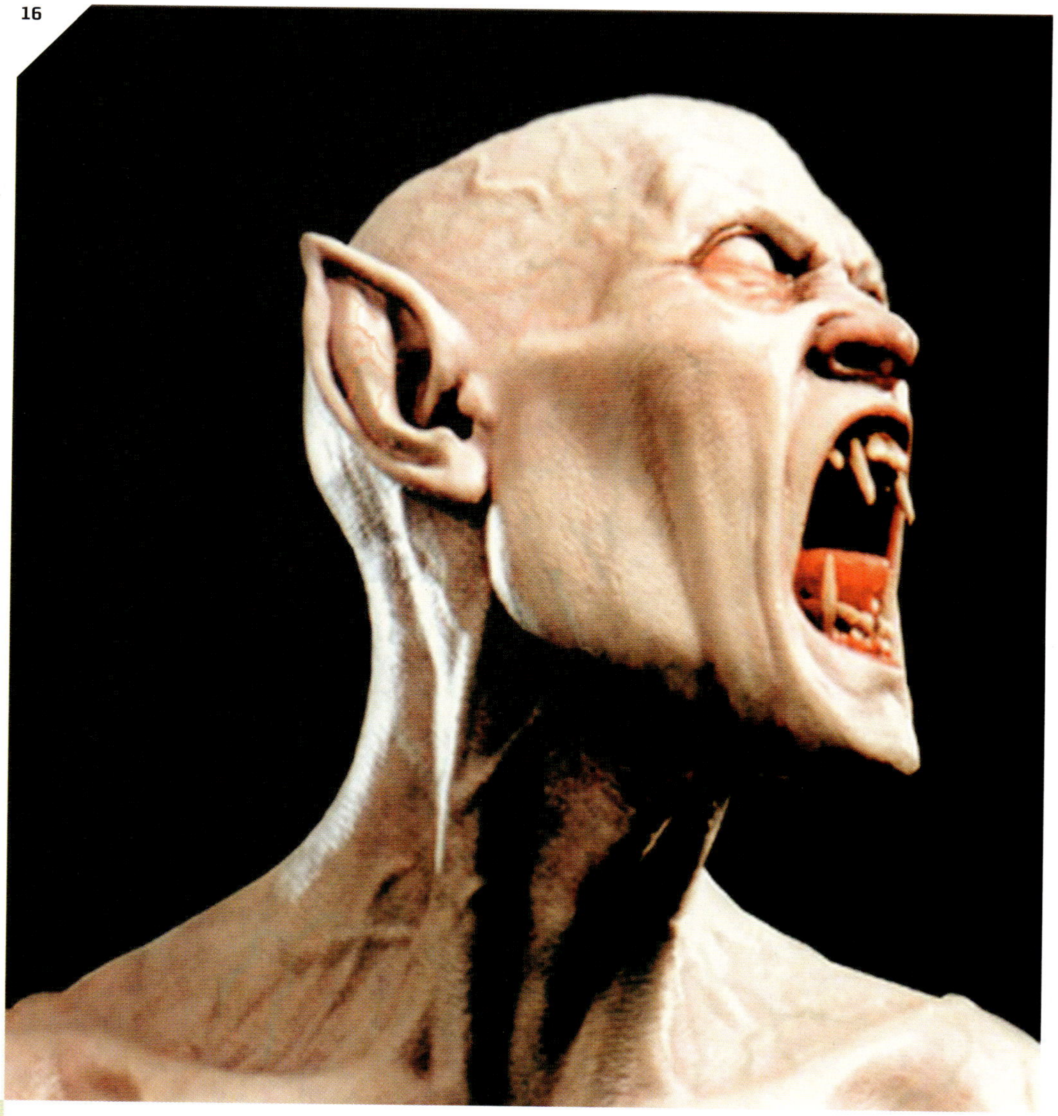

With the maquette design approved by del Toro, production of the full-scale character got under way. "First we used Brian's cyberscan to mill out a full-size, rigid-foam version of his body in several pieces, using a computer-controlled milling machine," says Elizalde. "The pieces were then reassembled to form an exact copy of the performer's body. In this case, though, we found slight discrepancies between the pieces, and we couldn't guarantee an exact replica of Brian's body, so we elected to do a lifecast instead."

Before sculpting, the plaster lifecast of Steele's body was slightly reduced in key places, delicately shaving small amounts away from the surface so that the suit would be a very tight fit. "Because the suit was such a snug fit in the stomach, rib, and chest areas, there was really lifelike movement on the outside of the suit whenever Brian breathed," says Elizalde.

Some of Sammael's features were designed to distort his physiognomy, shifting it away from the humanoid shape of the performer. "Guillermo really didn't want Sammael to look like a guy in a rubber suit. One of the ways to do that is to play around with proportions. On Sammael, one of the things we did was to give him enormous forearms that had extending bones that he could use as a weapon. For stunts and running shots, the hands were unarticulated and Brian could put all his weight on them to run like a gorilla. For shots where he needed to flex his fingers and grip objects, we had articulated versions. The torque required to move the huge fingers was too great for internal cable controls that Brian could operate, so we had cables that ran up inside the arm and out of the suit where they could be actuated by servos operated by puppeteers via radio control."

One of Sammael's most unusual features presented Spectral Motion with a unique technical challenge. "Guillermo wanted Sammael to have a crop of writhing tentacles for hair," says Elizalde. "He wanted them to have a truly fluid, serpentine look to them. At one time there was a plan to create the hair

17

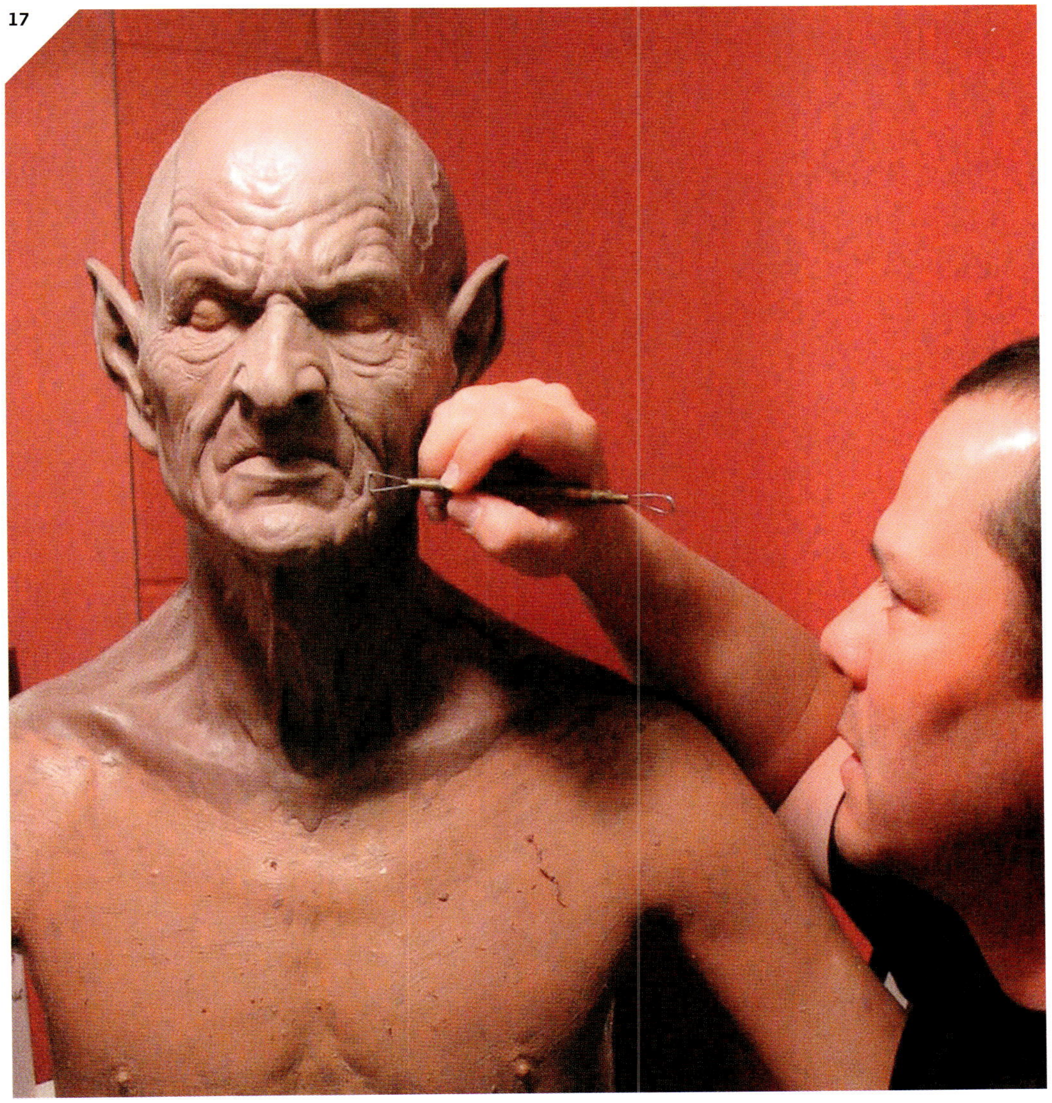

18

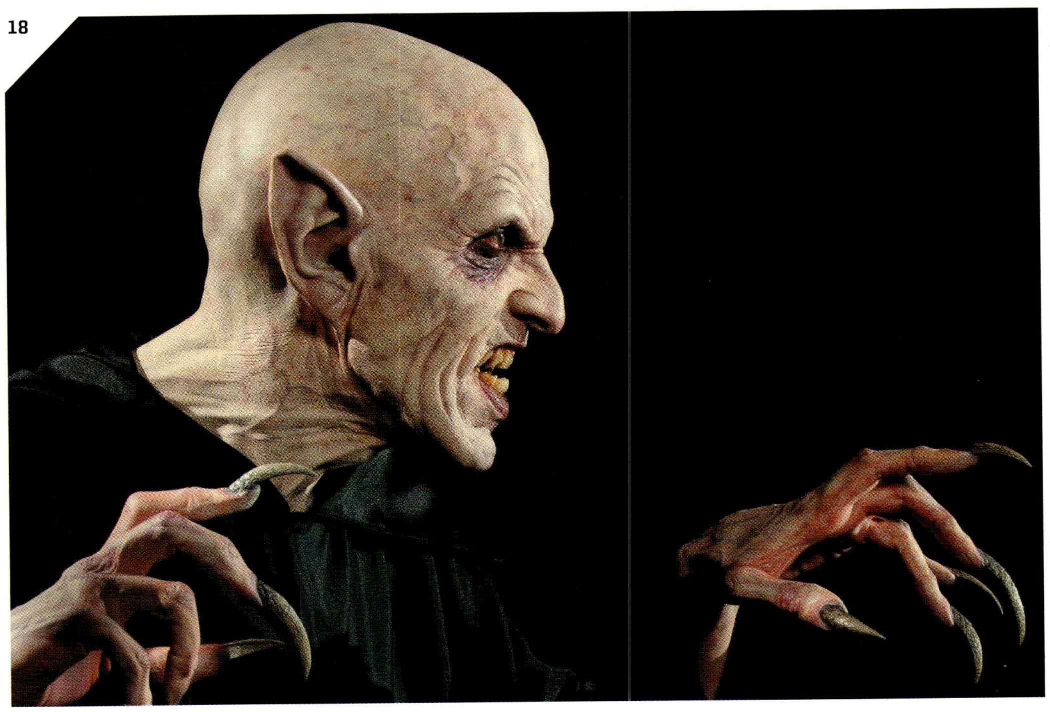

(15) Elizalde sculpts a Spectral Motion collectable figure, Alex the Vampire **(16)** The finished model **(17)** Elizalde sculpts a vampire makeup design **(18)** Doug Jones wears the finished makeup.

digitally, adding it onto the practical character in post-production. That seemed slow and expensive, so we decided to create it as a practical effect."

Spectral Motion's mechanical designers set to work on the problem. "Traditionally, the way to make something like a tentacle move is to have a number of joints and then a cable linking them. When the cable is pulled the tentacle curls," explains Elizalde. "But in this case there wasn't the room to have masses of cables inside Sammael's head. Instead, Mark Setrakian built the system by which an array of about ten servo motors was placed one after the other inside each of the 14 tentacles. Each set of servos had a controller board which instructed them to move sequentially." The radio-controlled tentacles, each covered in a skin of foam latex, writhed and twisted like eels to create a repulsive sight. "But after all our efforts people thought it was a CG effect!" says Elizalde.

Along with Jon Dawe's eye designs and complex mechanisms, Sammael's revolting appearance was also aided by tubes that squirted saliva when he opened his mouth and a mechanical tongue that could move out and splay into three separate pieces.

Like Abe Sapien, Sammael was digitally finessed when practical makeup effects reached their limits. His tongue was replaced with a digital tongue to allow it more complex writhing motions, and the beast was replaced by an entirely digital character—animated by Tippett Studio—for nine shots in which he is seen leaping and moving in ways that would be impossible for any puppet or performer.

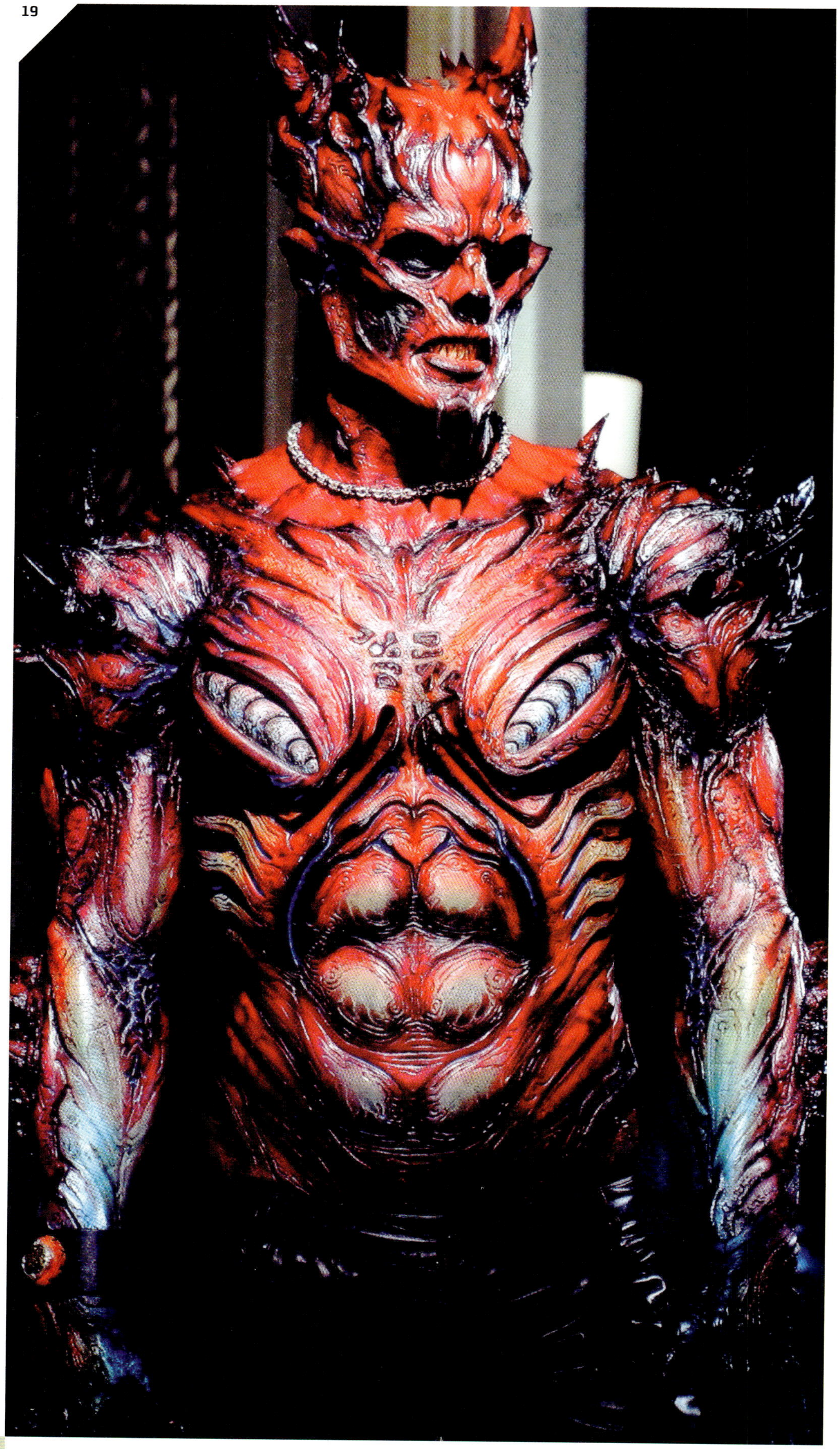

"I'm really happy that the vast majority of creature shots in *Hellboy* were created practically," says Elizalde. "Digital was used sparingly to create things that couldn't be done on set."

Following the success with *Hellboy*, Spectral Motion was approached to work on more high-profile features, including *Fantastic Four* (2005), *X-Men: The Last Stand* (2006), and *Lady in the Water* (2006).

For *X-Men: The Last Stand*, Elizalde oversaw the creation of a number of new superhero makeup designs, developing the characters of Angel, Beast, and Juggernaut, as well as inheriting designs from the previous two movies. "The most straightforward of the new characters was Angel," says Elizalde. "We went through several wing designs, eventually settling on a version that looked a bit like white sparrow wings when they were folded up. We created the wings as very lightweight appliances, covered with a combination of real feathers on the arm and shoulder areas and large fabricated foam feathers for the main parts of the wing. We made a form-fitting frame derived from a lifecast of [actor] Ben Foster's back, which was glued to him before having the individual wings attached during filming." As is often the case today, Spectral Motion's practical wings were replaced by digital wings for action scenes where they were required to move and perform in ways impossible or impractical to achieve during filming.

Kelsey Grammer's Beast took more work. "We had to find a design that encompassed the central dichotomy of the character—he's a feral creature on the outside, but a brilliant, educated man on the inside," Elizalde says. "In the comic, Beast tends to change between a very animalistic, lion-like appearance and a more human look. We tended toward the human look by combining primal and intellectual elements with Kelsey's own features. It can be tricky to build a design onto the face of a name actor like Kelsey [known for the US series *Frasier*], because you want to retain their features. If you can cover the whole face it's often easier."

Like most designs, Beast evolved, with a number of artists contributing. "It's rare to be able to say that a single person designed a character," says Elizalde. "Sometimes you get a design right first time—like Abe Sapien from *Hellboy*. But normally one person will do some initial sketches—that might be someone here or working for the art department of the movie. Then, when we've discussed those early ideas with the director, one of our own artists will do some more designs. Then the director will normally provide more feedback, and the artist will either have another crack at it or we'll give it to another designer who will bring a fresh perspective.

"Sometimes several designers will do drawings of the same character and the director will select elements from each design that they want to combine. When the paper design is done, we'll sculpt a maquette. This adds another hand to the design process. Finally, the full-sized sculpture will be created by one or more artists, bringing yet more subtle design elements to the mix."

In the case of Beast, concept designs were done by Carlos Huante, Chris Ayres, and Chet Zar; the maquette by Ryan Peterson; the body sculpture by Mario Torres, and the facial sculpture by Motoyoshi Hata.

One of the challenges of Beast was his color scheme, as Elizalde explains: "Beast was covered in blue fur and skin—which is not the most natural-looking color. If we weren't very careful he could easily have ended up looking like some furry cartoon character or a teddy bear." Elizalde and his team did exhaustive tests, using a range of furs. "In the end, hair specialists

20

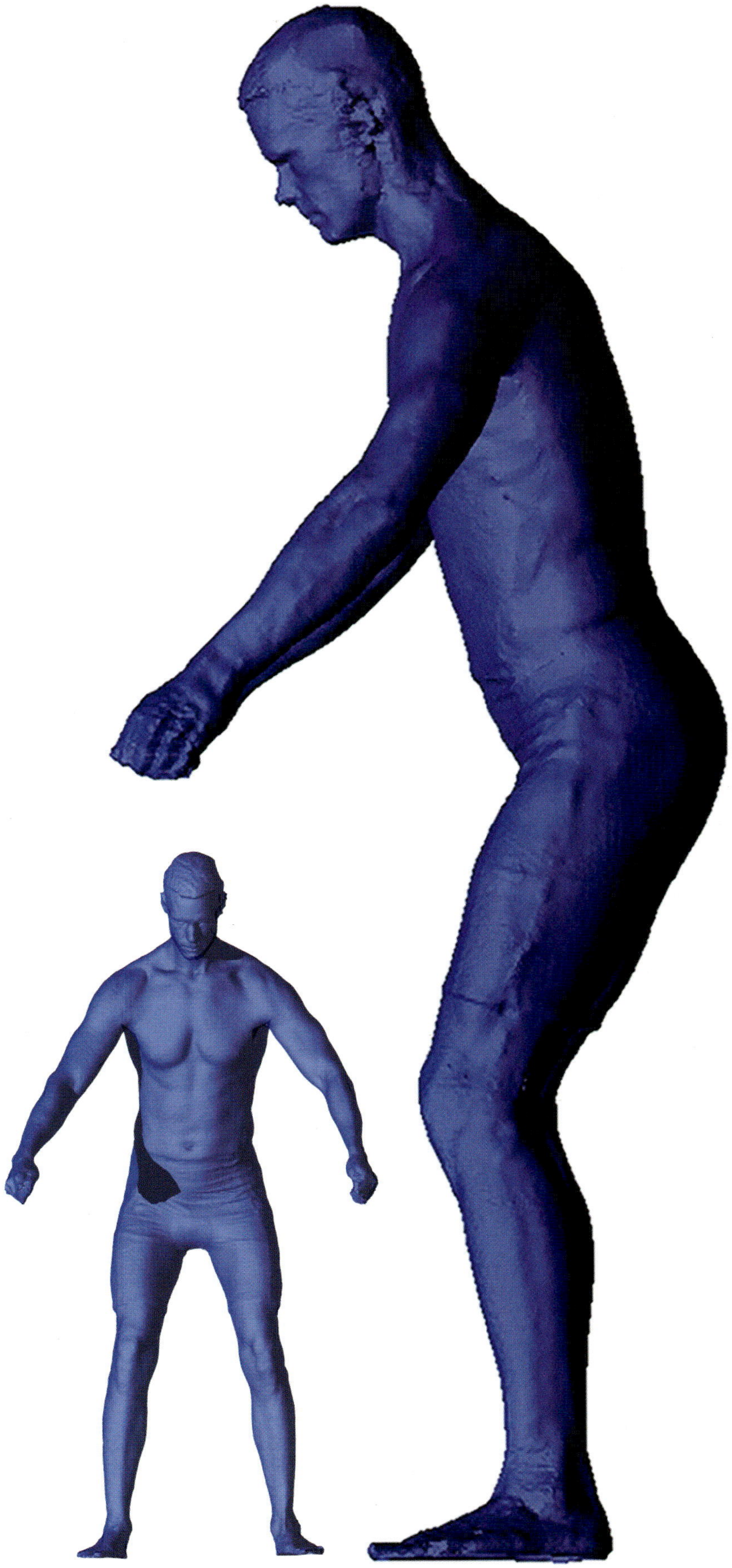

(19) Elizalde oversaw the creation of the Drake bodysuit for *Blade Trinity* (2004), with paint design by Steve Wang **(20)** Drake performer Brian Steele was cyberscanned to obtain his exact physical dimensions.

21

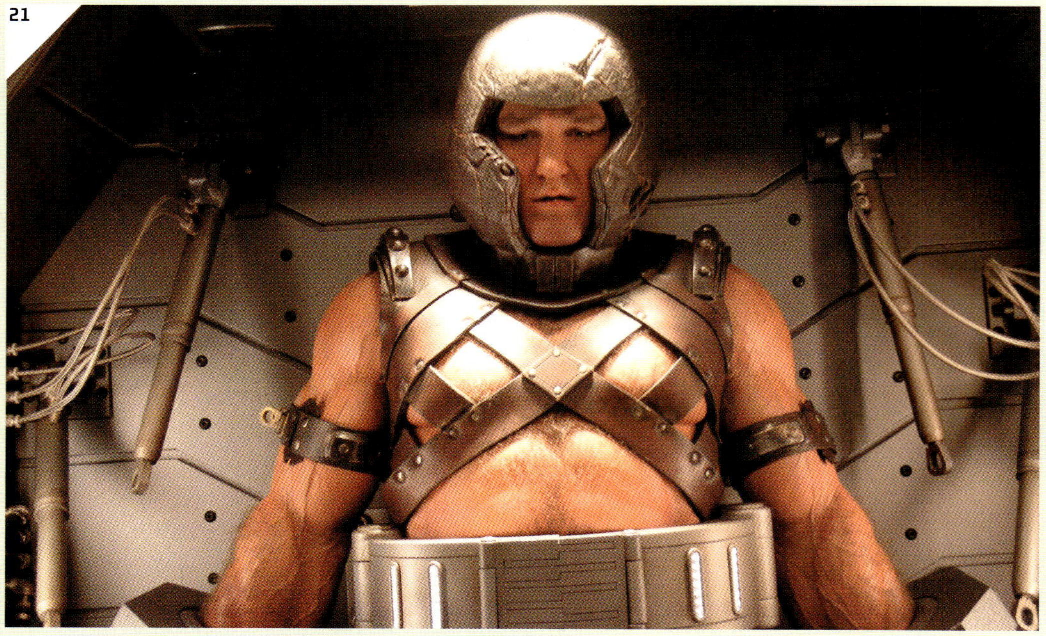

22

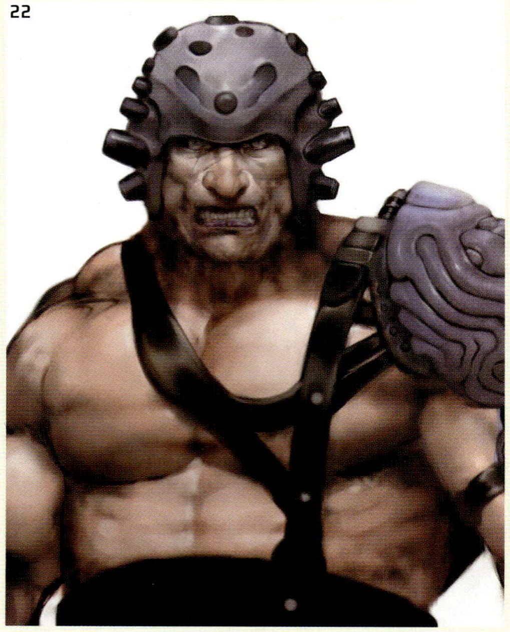

Diana Yun Soo Yoo and Silvia Nava used a combination of yak and human hair, which was mixed in varying quantities, thicknesses, and lengths to achieve the right look on different parts of the body. The hair was dyed a variety of colors, from a range of blues to more organic browns and auburns, which added a more subtle, natural look. The other trick to keeping him on the naturalistic side was to illuminate him with tungsten light, which is more orange, so his blues didn't look too vivid and glossy."

Spectral Motion's other major new creation was Juggernaut, played by former UK soccer player, Vinnie Jones. "Vinnie has a fearsome reputation, so we were slightly nervous about working with him! But he turned out to be a real gentleman with a great sense of humor," says Elizalde. "Taking our cue from the comic book, we initially designed Juggernaut with massive shoulders and a bullet-shaped helmet which is capable of smashing down buildings. Unfortunately, the costume department decided that the original design didn't work for them and would be impractical to work with. There was also the possibility that the very dramatic costume might have somewhat dwarfed the talent. So, in the end, we ended up with a watered-down version which had a much smaller helmet and virtually no shoulder pads.

"I think it was a shame to lose the comic-book aspect of the character. I believe our original design was much more imposing and dramatic. Unfortunately, we don't always get to do stuff the way we like.

"To create Vinnie's Juggernaut makeup, we first did a lifecast of Vinnie. We could have done a cyberscan, but those we've done in the past have been less than perfect. They required quite a bit of work before the milled-out piece was ready to use for sculpting, so they didn't really save much time. However, recent advances in the process have ironed out some of the problems. Scans are great if you have a performer who's terrified of having a lifecast done, or if you can't get access to them for very long. They're also great if you want to create a miniature version of someone—you can just scale down their size when milling out the cast."

Norman Cabrera then sculpted a muscled body suit and facial appliances on top of Jones's cast. The resulting foam-latex appliances were carefully punched with hairs to give them a natural appearance. The pieces were prepainted to look like real skin by Margaret Prentice, and then applied and painted on set by Thom Floutz. When applied to Jones, the result was an extremely convincing super-muscular body of which Elizalde is very proud. "I remember driving up to wardrobe one time, and Vinnie was standing outside, and my driver gasped and said, 'Look at the size of that guy!' It's nice to get that kind of reaction when a character has been skillfully lit and photographed, but when someone is sold on your work when they see it in broad daylight it's just great."

In 2005, Mike Elizalde was hired to create the creature makeup effects for *Lady in the Water* (2006), directed by M. Night Shyamalan. The creations built by Spectral Motion and based on designs by Mark "Crash" McCreery included the Scrunt, three tree-like beasts called the Tartutic, and an unusual prosthetic muscle suit worn on just one half of actor Freddie Rodriguez.

"The Tartutic were one of the oddest creations we've worked on," says Elizalde. "They were these kind of walking trees with a very simian, elemental feel to them. Crash McCreery did a great job designing them, and their sculpture was supervised here by Steve Wang. Their sculpture was really intricate. They were made using normal foam-rubber techniques, but really looked like they were made of gnarled old wood once they were painted. Steve Wang introduced a technique of heating and stretching polyethylene to create wispy, twisted twigs that protrude from the character's head."

23

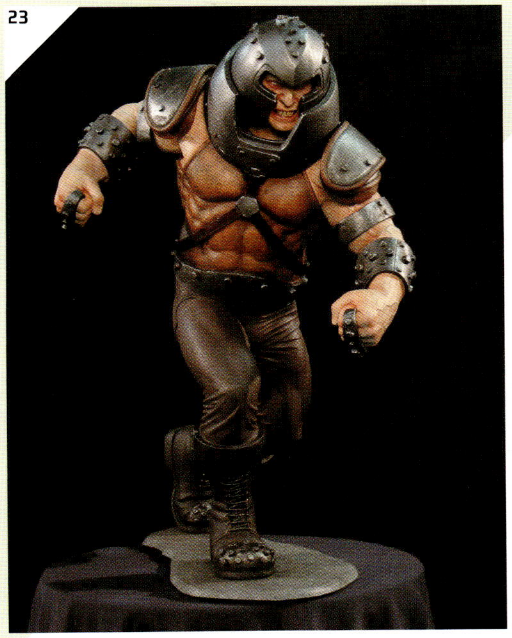

24

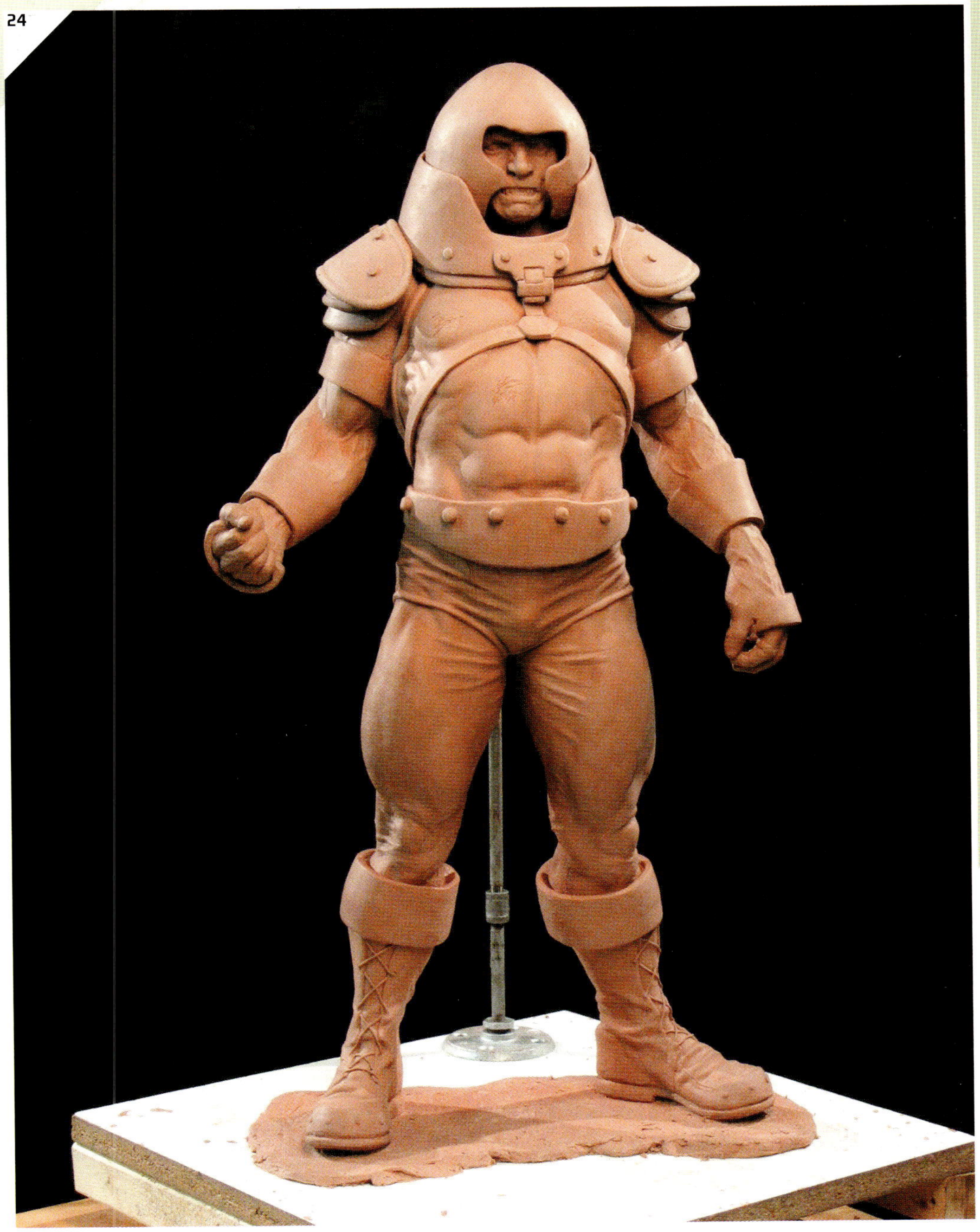

Elizalde admits that he was initially unsure how successful the Tartutic would be because of their unconventional design. "Something that's interesting about the Tartutic is that they were fairly unrealistic-looking characters. It was hard to imagine that anyone would believe in them as characters because they looked so outrageous. But there is an important lesson for makeup artists and moviemakers here, because in the final film they worked beautifully. That goes to show that however brilliant—or bad—a makeup design is, its success depends greatly on the story it is being used to tell, the director, and the way it is filmed. So far at Spectral Motion I've been honored to work with some of the most inspiring and creative people in the business. I hope that continues for a long time."

(21) Vinnie Jones as Juggernaut in *X-Men: The Last Stand* (2006) **(22)** Juggernaut concept art by Carlos Huante **(23)** Juggernaut maquette created by Moto Hata **(24)** Juggernaut maquette by Mitch DeVane.

BRIAN STEELE

CV

Costume performer; trained as an actor, but didn't like the personal attention; from 1987–90 became one of the costume characters at Universal Studios (Frankenstein's Monster, Harry from *Harry and the Hendersons*); played Harry in *Harry and the Hendersons* TV series, after which started to get movie work as a performer; since then has played creatures in numerous movies.

SELECT FILMOGRAPHY

Harry and the Hendersons TV series (1991-1993); *The Relic* (1997); *Men in Black 2* (2002); *Hellboy* (2004); *Doom* (2005); *The Cave* (2005); *Underworld: Evolution* (2006); *Lady in the Water* (2006); *Creature from the Black Lagoon* (2006)

KEY CHARACTERS

Harry (*Harry and the Hendersons TV series*); Kothoga (*The Relic*); Sharkmouth (*Men in Black 2*); Curtis Stahl/Hell Knight (*Doom*); Drake (*Blade Trinity*); Sammael (*Hellboy*)

01

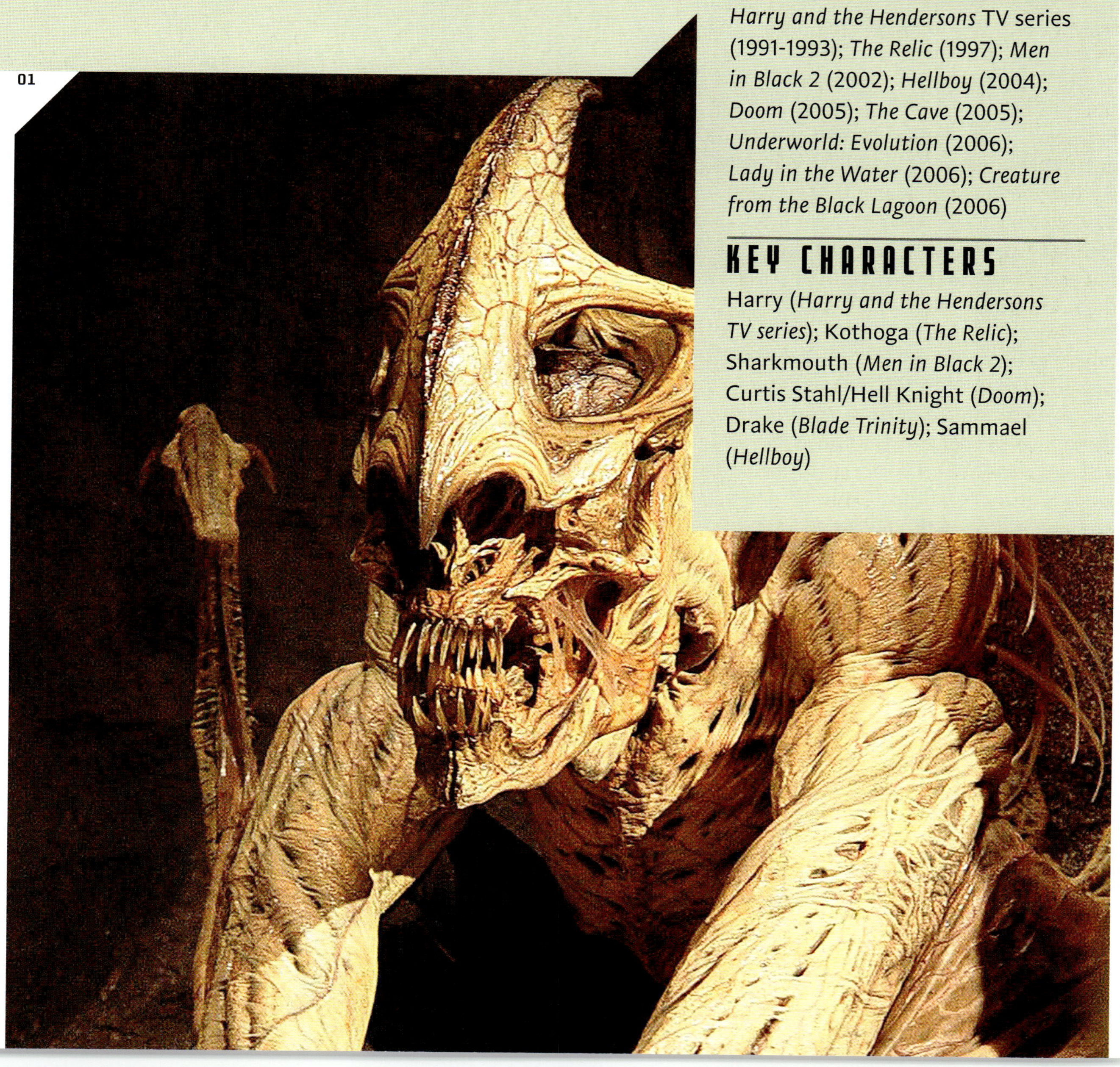

Brian Steele trained as a theatrical actor, but found that he didn't like the attention of being in the public eye. For any actor who doesn't enjoy being stared at, one option is to go under cover, concealing himself or herself behind makeup or a costume. In 1987 Steele found a job that suited him perfectly: dressing as Frankenstein's monster and walking around the Universal Studios theme park entertaining guests. "If you had your photo taken with the monster between 1987 and 1990, there's a good chance it was me," laughs the actor. "It was a thrill, because I've always been a fan of Boris Karloff and the characters he created."

Steele was happy performing behind makeup, and was soon asked to play the bigfoot star, Harry (from *Harry and the Hendersons*, 1987), another costumed character that roamed the Universal theme park. "At that time they were shooting the *Harry and the Hendersons* television series at Universal, but the performer playing Harry, Kevin Peter Hall, passed away. After auditioning numerous times during the show's enforced hiatus, I landed the role. After initially being the understudy for 24 episodes, I took over as the main performer for the following 24."

With experience as a costume performer, Steele was next asked to play Kothoga, beastly star of *The Relic* (1997), as created by Stan Winston Studio. "Working on that was a real eye-opener," recalls Steele. "The biggest difference was that I was working as a quadruped. The ape impersonator and performance coach John Alexander came in and taught me and the other costume performer, Vincent Hammond, how to walk on all fours."

02

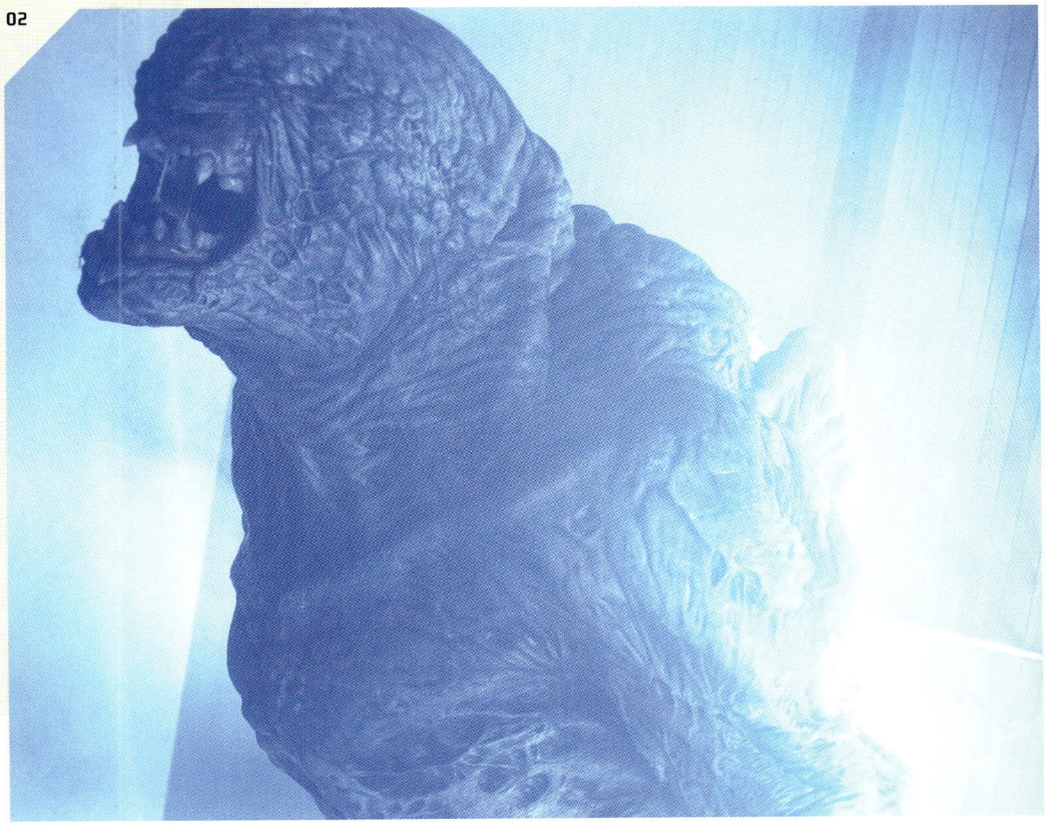

Steele has since played costume characters in a number of major movies, becoming one of the most respected artists in the field. When creating any new character, his first job is to attend the makeup studio for a full bodycast. "It's not much fun having a cast made of your body or face, with all that alginate being poured over you. Luckily most makeup studios now have my bodycast, headcast, and handcast, so, unless I gain a lot of weight, I shouldn't have to do too much more of that!" The casting process has been greatly improved by laser scanning technology. "We often do cyberscans. Instead of hours of discomfort, I stand on a platform for 30 seconds, the laser spins around me, and it's done. The great thing is that if the scan is no good or they want to try a new pose, we just do another."

Once the workshop has a cast or scan of Steele's body, they begin sculpting the character's outer skin on top of it, typically taking at least a month before the performer's input is needed again. However, this is by no means a pause in production as far as Steele is concerned. "Once I know that a part is coming up, I start to prepare myself for it. I always work out and keep fit for my job, but I will start to do additional training to develop the muscle groups that will be important to perform that particular creature. I do a lot of swimming, boxing, weight training, yoga, and Pilates to ensure I am both physically and mentally prepared."

Steele tries not to think too much about the performance of a character until he wears a suit during a first fitting at the

(01) Costume performer Brian Steele is here hidden behind the makeup as this creature from *The Cave* (2005)
(02) The Hell Knight from *Doom* (2005), a makeup designed by Stan Winston.

03

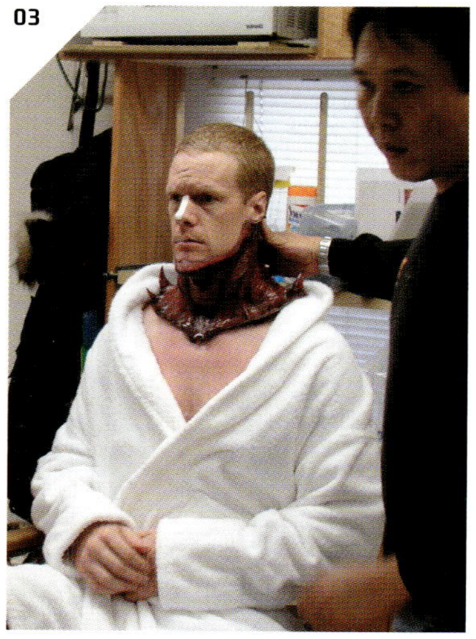

04

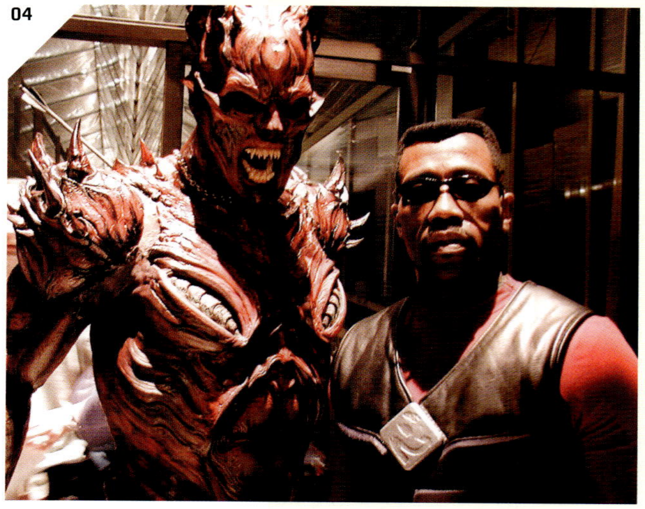

Although his face is usually not visible, Steele likes to give a complex facial performance beneath the mask. "It's really important to use your face as a means of creating emotion," he says. "You can't actually see me growling and roaring or baring my teeth, but it's all going on under there and it definitely helps bring the character to life." In fact, all of Steele's interior movements are more exaggerated than they appear from the outside. Creature suits absorb much of the motion of a performance, so every move has to be larger than life. "Each small movement or gesture as seen from the outside is typically a fairly large movement for me inside. With each new costume I have to learn how much is coming through the foam latex and regulate my performance accordingly."

makeup workshop. "The key is to let the form of the creature guide the movement, so it isn't until I wear a suit that I can see how a character might need to perform. I always video myself in costume, because what's really important is how something looks, not how it feels. When you're in a costume you can't just move in a way that feels comfortable or appropriate, because more often than not that just won't look right on the outside. You have to establish the outside appearance and then figure out how you're going to create that from the inside. Getting the balance right is particularly important. I will naturally walk in a way that is balanced for the shape and mass of my own body, but when you're inside a creature you need to move in a way that creates the correct balance and sense of mass for that body."

To bring his characters to life, Steele often refers to real wildlife, watching videos of animals in motion to help establish the movement style for each new creature. "If I'm walking on four legs, I often start off with a gorilla movement combined with the look of some big cats.

"Depending on how fast they are moving and what they are doing, every quadruped has different styles of movement—with their legs off the ground at different times. That's hard to coordinate because we walk with two feet, lifting one leg up as we put the other foot down. But on all fours, the motion is completely different, and there should normally be three legs in different stages of motion while only the fourth is on the floor. You have to train your brain to produce what for humans is a very unnatural rhythm."

Steele tries to imbue his performances with a sense of character and personality. "Without dialogue to perform it can be hard to convey what a character is thinking or feeling. However, I always try to be aware of what the creature's emotions are, what its story arc is, so that I can hopefully portray a thinking creature rather than just a crazy beast who just wants to attack people."

(03) Steele prepares to be transformed into Drake for *Blade: Trinity* (2004) by Steve Wang **(04)** As Drake, Steele towers over Wesley Snipes **(05)** As Curtis Stahle in *Doom* **(06)** In test transformation makeup as part of Patrick Tatopoulos' work on *Underworld* (2003) **(07)** Testing Tatopoulos-designed leg extensions for a werewolf in Underworld: Evolution **(08)** Transformed into the werewolf.

Working in a suit can be a tiring process. "It's mentally exhausting because you are continually thinking about how to make your character move, plus you have to remember all your directions, timings, and marks. It's also physically exhausting because you're carrying a heavy suit, you're forcing your body to move in ways that are unnatural for a human, and the temperature inside can range from hot to *very* hot! It can also be a really long day. On *Hellboy* I was doing 14-hour days, six days a week, for five months."

Enduring such extremes can take its toll, and Steele has lost over 14 pounds (6.5kg) in weight during a month-long shoot. "I now get up twice each night of filming to load my body with carbs and protein to give me the energy to perform at a consistently high level without losing too much weight."

05

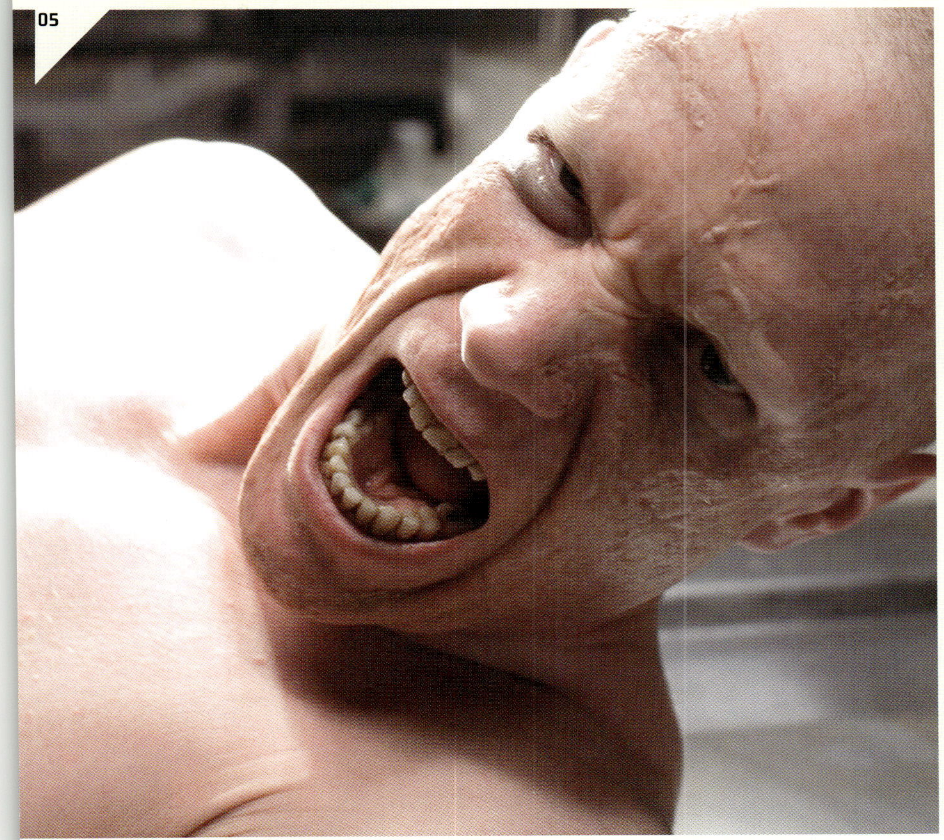

06

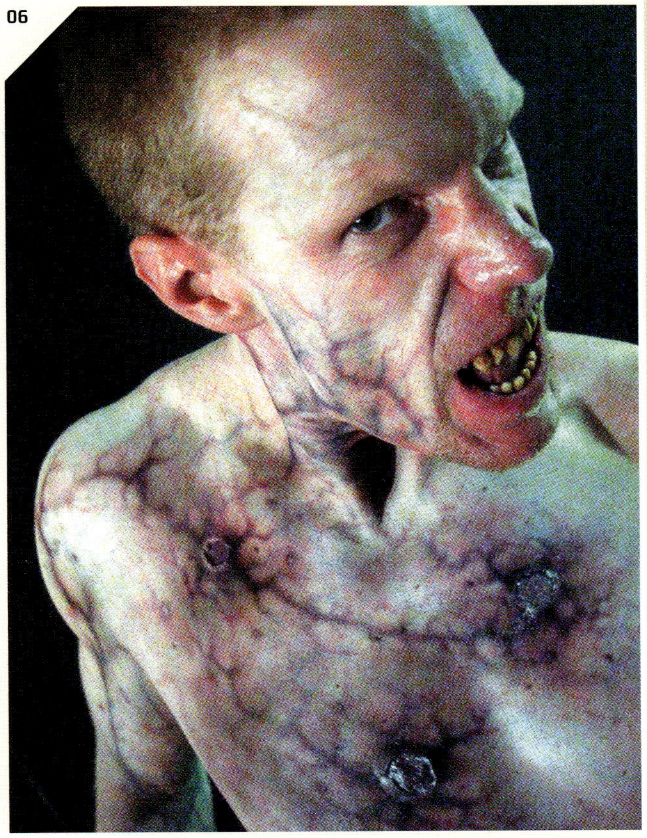

07

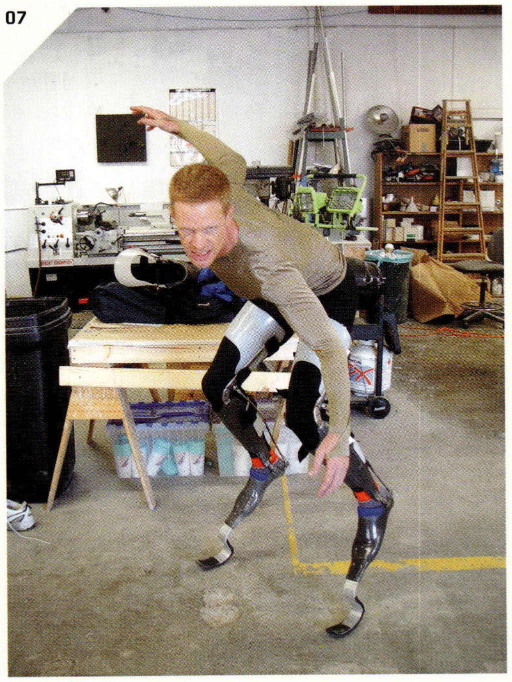

08

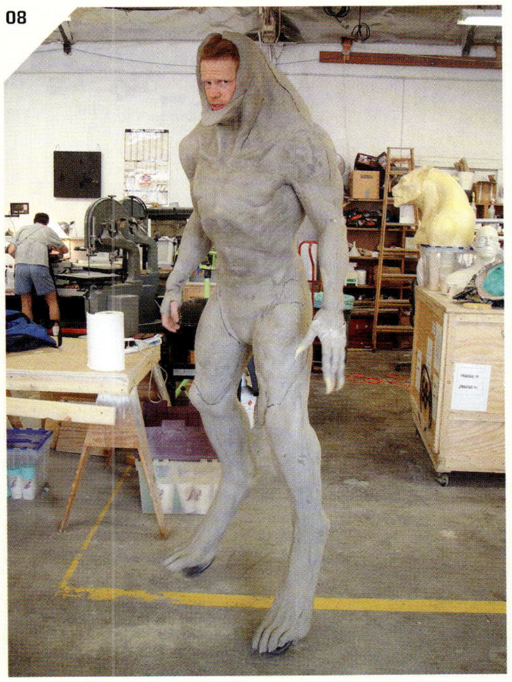

One of the toughest aspects of performing in a character costume can be wearing the arm and leg extensions that are frequently used to alter the proportions of a creature's limbs. Arm extensions typically take the form of a type of grip or glove into which the performer fits their own hands. Sometimes the performer's hands will operate cable controls that move the character's mechanical hands in a similar way; other times the character's hands—or front legs—might stay unarticulated, designed only to take the performer's weight while walking on them.

The more uncomfortable leg extensions are those that require the performer's foot to be angled downward with the toes slotted into the extension without any rear heel support. In this way a foot,

09

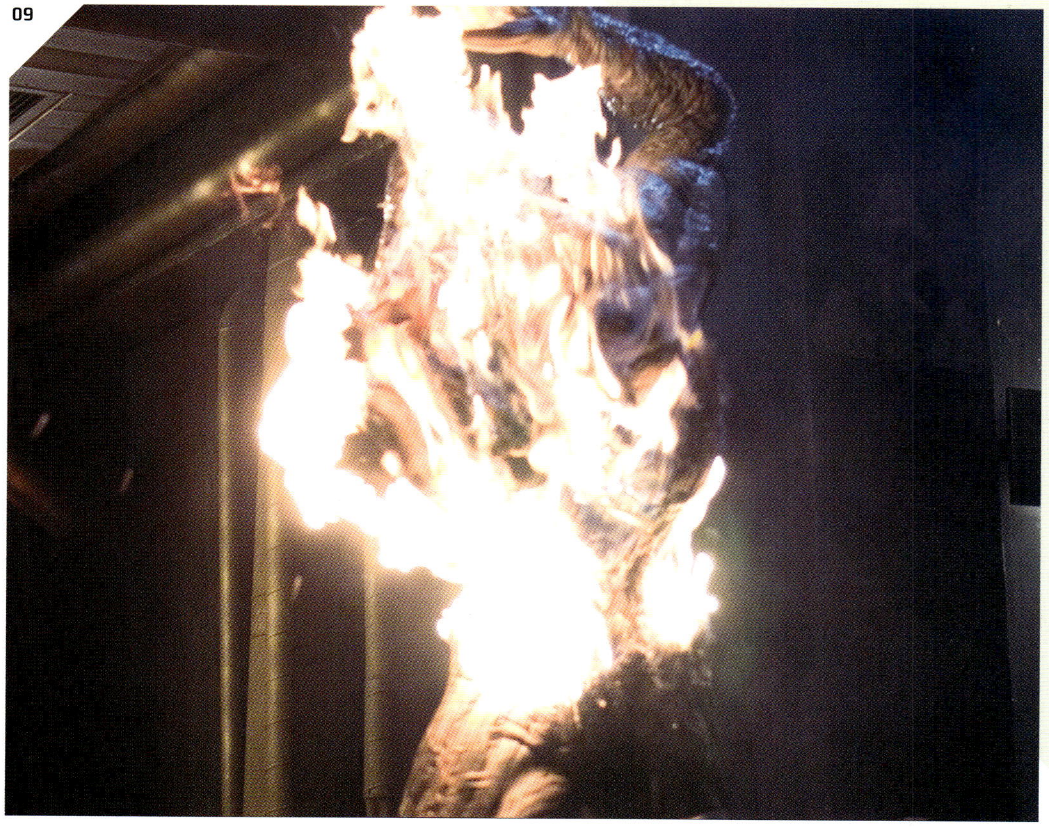

(09) The Hell Knight costume was set on fire with Steele still in it, for *Doom* **(10)** As Sammael, in *Hellboy* (2004) **(11)** Steele takes a break during the filming of Underworld: Evolution, as makeup artist Bruce Spalding Fuller pumps cool air into the suit **(12)** Steele's friendlier beginnings as Harry from *Harry and the Hendersons* TV series.

10

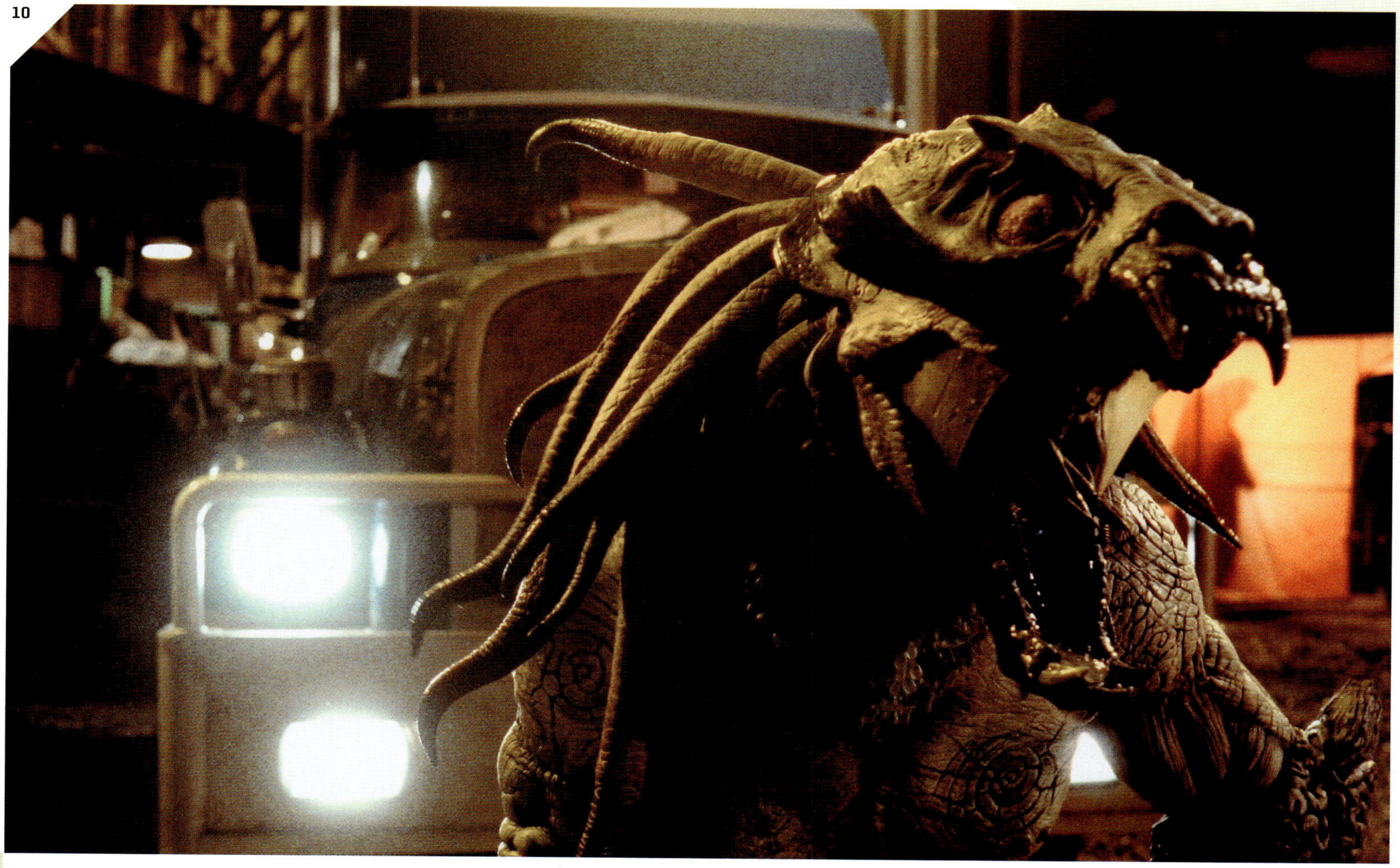

11

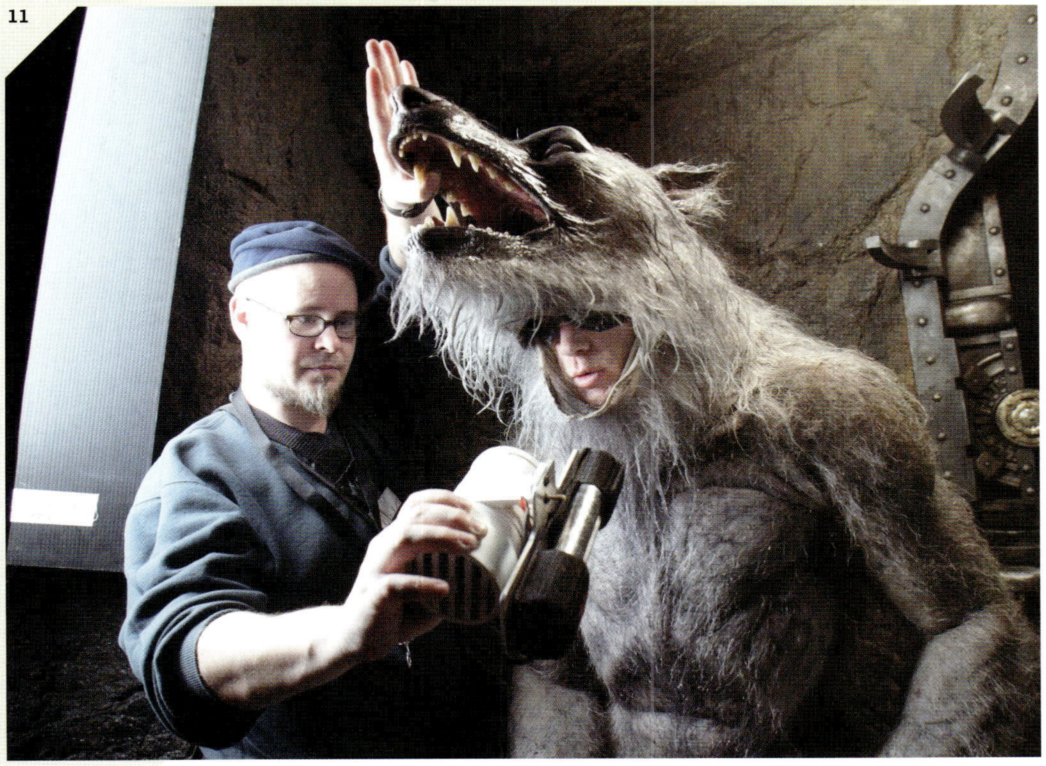

12

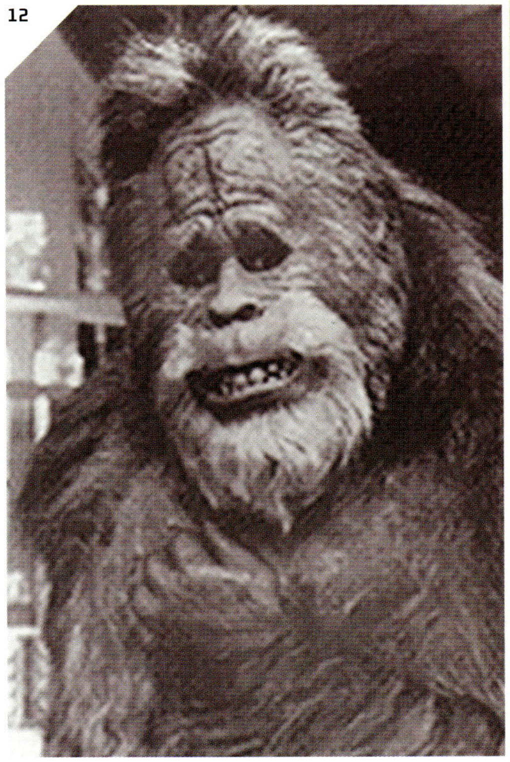

which should be at right angles to a leg, is bent so that it fits within the lower half of a creature's leg. The creature's foot may be another eight or ten inches further down than the performer's. When a performer walks in leg extensions it can be like walking on tiptoes while on stilts —meaning lengthy practice to produce a convincing walk or run.

Steele explains what it takes to create a performance during the shooting of a movie: "I'll show up in the morning and start having conversations with the director, other performers, puppeteers, stunt coordinators, and anyone else who needs to be involved. We talk about the shots that need to be filmed and how we plan to achieve them. We all have to know how every shot is going to work—when I'll move, when I'll roar, what objects I have to interact with.

"A creature performance is the result of a lot of different people working together. I provide the overall body movements, but puppeteers need to know when I will raise my head so that they can make the mouth roar, the eyes open up, and the ears swivel backward, for example. We reduce each shot down into a series of beats—who's doing what and when. We just have to remember that the beats are not a series of discreet actions, but part of a flowing, organic performance.

"When we know what we're doing, we'll normally go on set and act out a shot with me in my regular clothes and everyone practicing whatever they have to do. This is an important time for me, because it is where I am most aware of the environment in which I am performing and what will be happening around me. When we know the drill, I will get suited up. A foam-latex suit normally takes about an hour to get glued into. Before the head goes on we'll have another run-through on set. This time I can still see what I'm doing, but it will feel very different because I'm in costume. It's also an important stage for the puppeteers, because they'll be watching my face for cues as to when they need to operate the various facial functions of the mask.

"Once I'm fully costumed we'll do one rehearsal, checking it all works and that I can hear instructions through an earpiece. With the head on, my visibility is normally reduced to almost nothing, so all the rehearsals will have been very important!"

Although Steele had a brief unmasked appearance in *Doom* (2005), he prefers to remain a performer who remains largely unrecognized by those outside the industry. "I enjoy the anonymity of performing inside a costume. As far as I'm concerned, people I respect in the industry or fans who really love this stuff know who I am, and that means a lot to me. But what I really enjoy is the terrific challenge of breathing life into an inanimate object. Taking a creature assembled from foam latex, animatronics, and fiberglass, and creating a character that lives and breathes, is an awesome experience.

"Another thing is that when I see the movie I'm not seeing myself on screen. Some actors can't enjoy a film because they find themselves watching their own performance. But if I do my job right, when I watch the film, all I will see is the creature, not myself."

WETA WORKSHOP

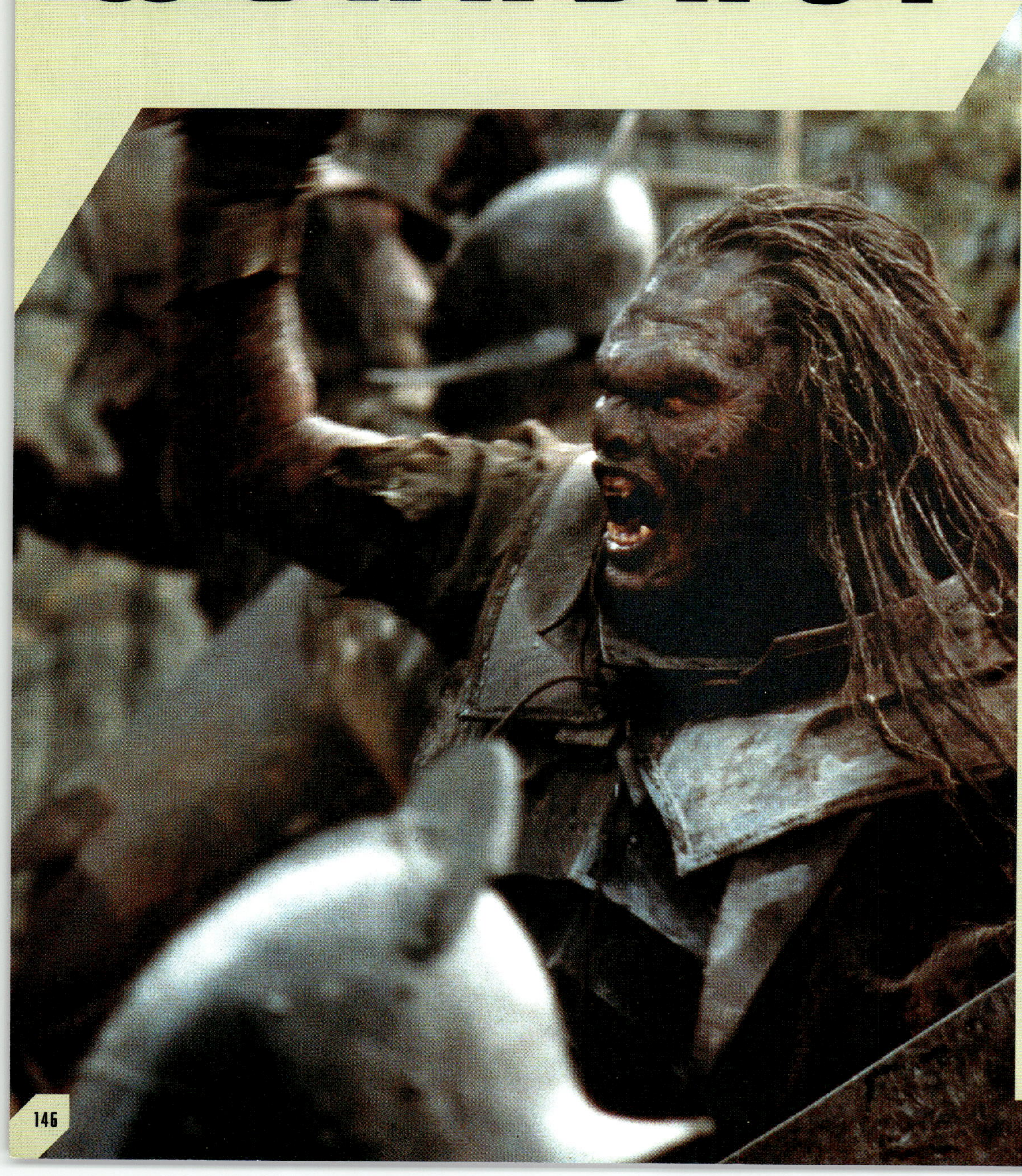

CV

RT Effects set up by high school friends, and later husband and wife, Richard Taylor and Tania Rodger, in a bedroom in Wellington, New Zealand; found work making table sculptures out of margarine for a local restaurant; made puppets for satirical TV show; joined forces with Peter Jackson, an ambitious local movie-maker; formed Weta Workshop with Jackson, Peter Selkirk, and James Booth in 1994 to handle practical effects for Jackson's movies (with Weta Digital handling CG effects); success followed with *Heavenly Creatures* and *The Frighteners* before the global phenomena of *Lord of the Rings* and *King Kong*.

SELECT FILMOGRAPHY

Meet the Feebles (1992); *Braindead* (1992); *Lord of the Rings* trilogy (2001, 2002, 2003); *Peter Pan* (2003); *The Chronicles of Narnia: The Lion, the Witch and the Wardrobe* (2005); *King Kong* (2005); *Black Sheep* (2007); *The Waterhorse* (2007)

KEY CHARACTERS

Mermaid (*Peter Pan*); Watcher, Gollum, Cave Troll, Shellob, Uruk-Hai, Orcs, Mumaks, Hobbits, and Elves (*Lord of the Rings* trilogy); Dinosaurs, Kong (*King Kong*), Minotaurs, Minoboars, hags, Centaurs, Mr. Tumnus (*The Lion, the Witch and the Wardrobe*)

TECHNIQUES

Design and sculpture; special-effects makeup and prosthetics; fabrication and animatronics

02

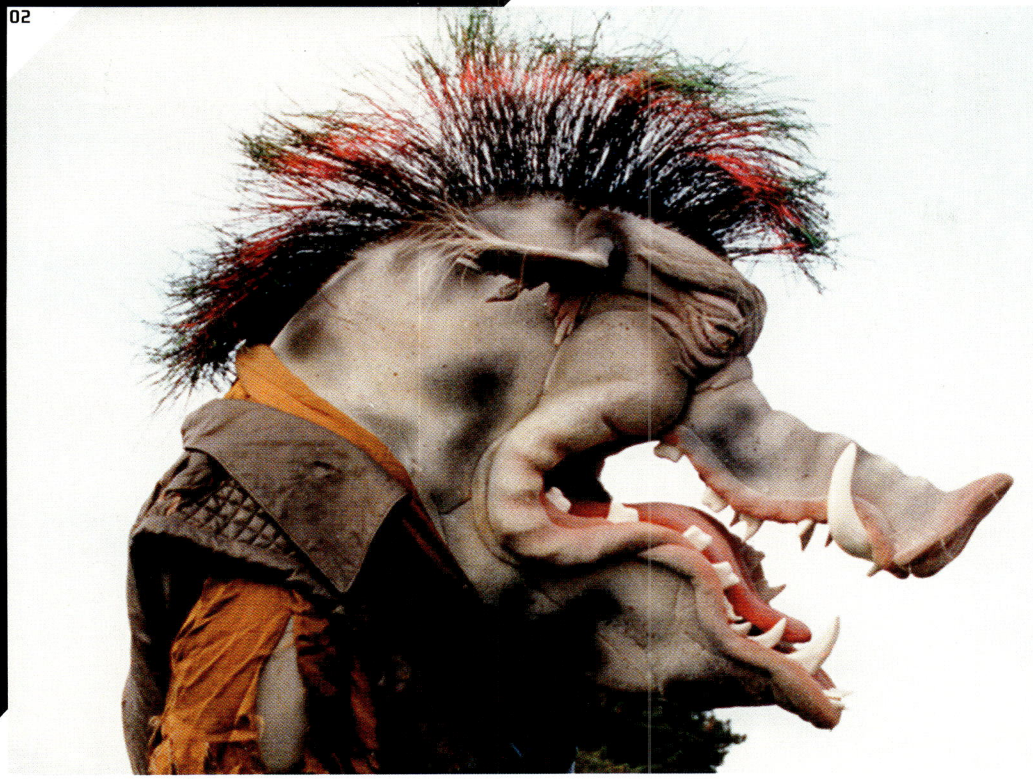

03

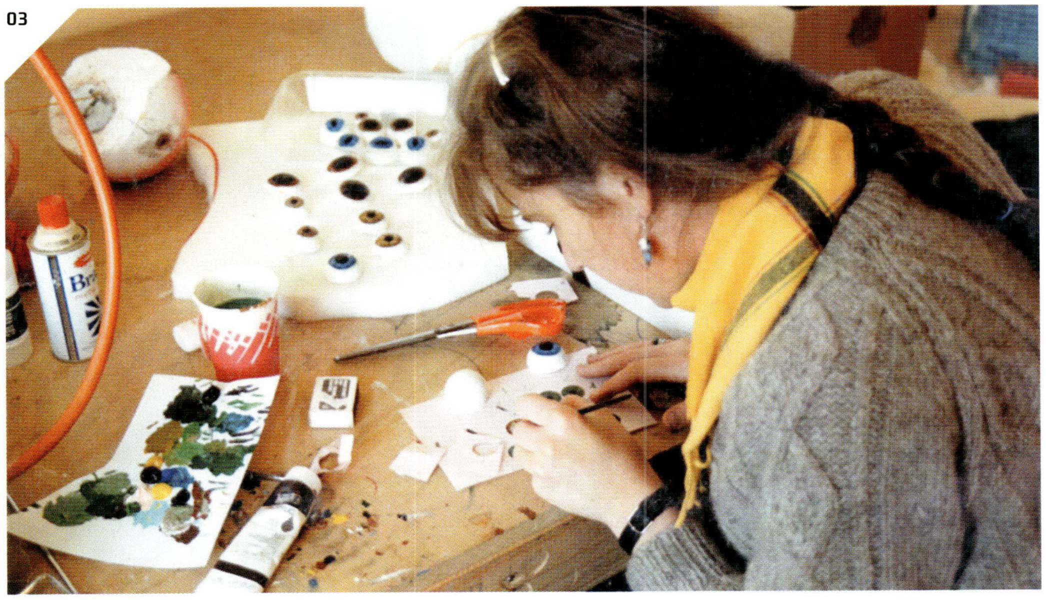

(01) The Uruk-hai, one of Weta Workshops' creations for *Lord of the Rings* **(02)** Cedric the Boar from Peter Jackson's *Meet the Feebles* **(03)** Tania Rodger paints ping-pong ball eyes for *Meet the Feebles.*

Richard Taylor grew up in a tiny, rural community on New Zealand's North Island. "Most people in this business will tell you how they watched monster movies as a kid and did makeup in their garage," says Taylor, "but I don't think it even occurred to me that people did that kind of thing for a living. I got into making things because, growing up in New Zealand, if you wanted something you usually had to improvise and build it yourself."

Taylor met his future wife and business partner, Tania Rodger, when they both started high school. From an early age the pair determined they wanted careers in the arts. In 1987 the pair set up RT Effects in the capital, Wellington, based in their back bedroom. "We hoped people would commission us to make things for their theater productions, shop displays, or museum exhibits. Any kind of creative work that was offered to us. We became friends with the chef in a hotel restaurant and persuaded him to let me create table sculptures for their Saturday night buffet—for free food!"

A big break came in 1988 when a local TV production company was commissioned to make a current affairs puppet show called *Public Eye*. "I got hold of some photos of the boss and created a rubber caricature of him. He called me up and said, 'You've got the job if you want it—but you needn't have bothered with the stunt because no-one else has applied!'"

Taylor, Rodger, and sole employee Clive Memmott made 72 puppets. Taylor sculpted the caricatures in margarine —a technique he had developed for the restaurant—and the puppets were molded in rubber and painted by Rodger, with Memmott building the internal mechanisms. "We just improvised, using materials that came to hand," says Taylor. "We used the balls from roll-on deodorant bottles to make the characters' eyes."

It was a chance meeting while working on a TV commercial that would decide the course of Taylor and Rodger's careers. "A local chap had been invited to come and see how things were done on a big shoot. We knew of him because there were these rumors about a local person making a feature movie in his parents' basement. We immediately struck up a good relationship." Taylor and Rodger's new friend was Peter Jackson.

Then an unknown amateur moviemaker, Jackson had recently finished making his first no-budget feature, *Bad Taste* (1987). He, Taylor, and Rodger agreed to help each other achieve their ambitions.

04

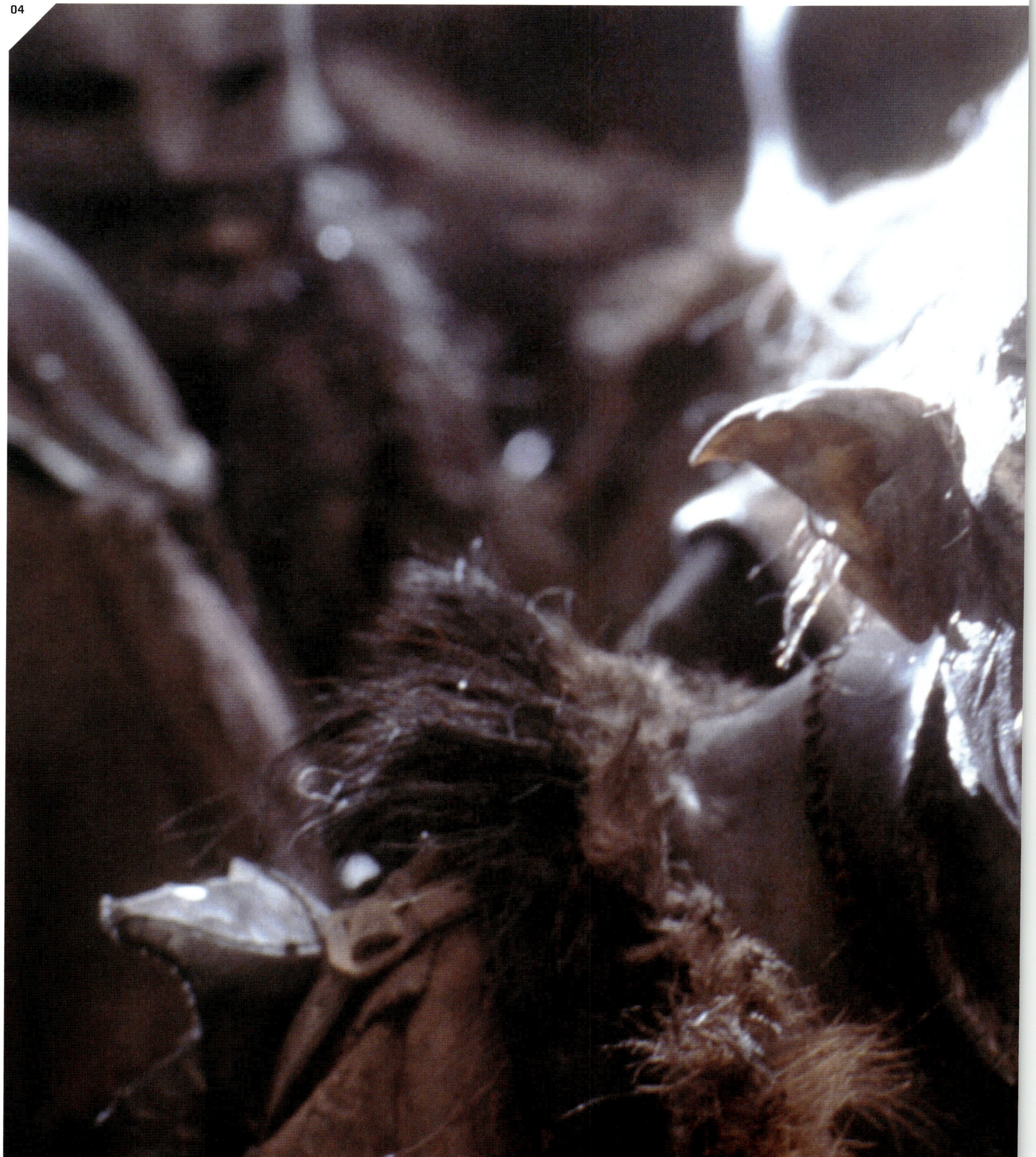

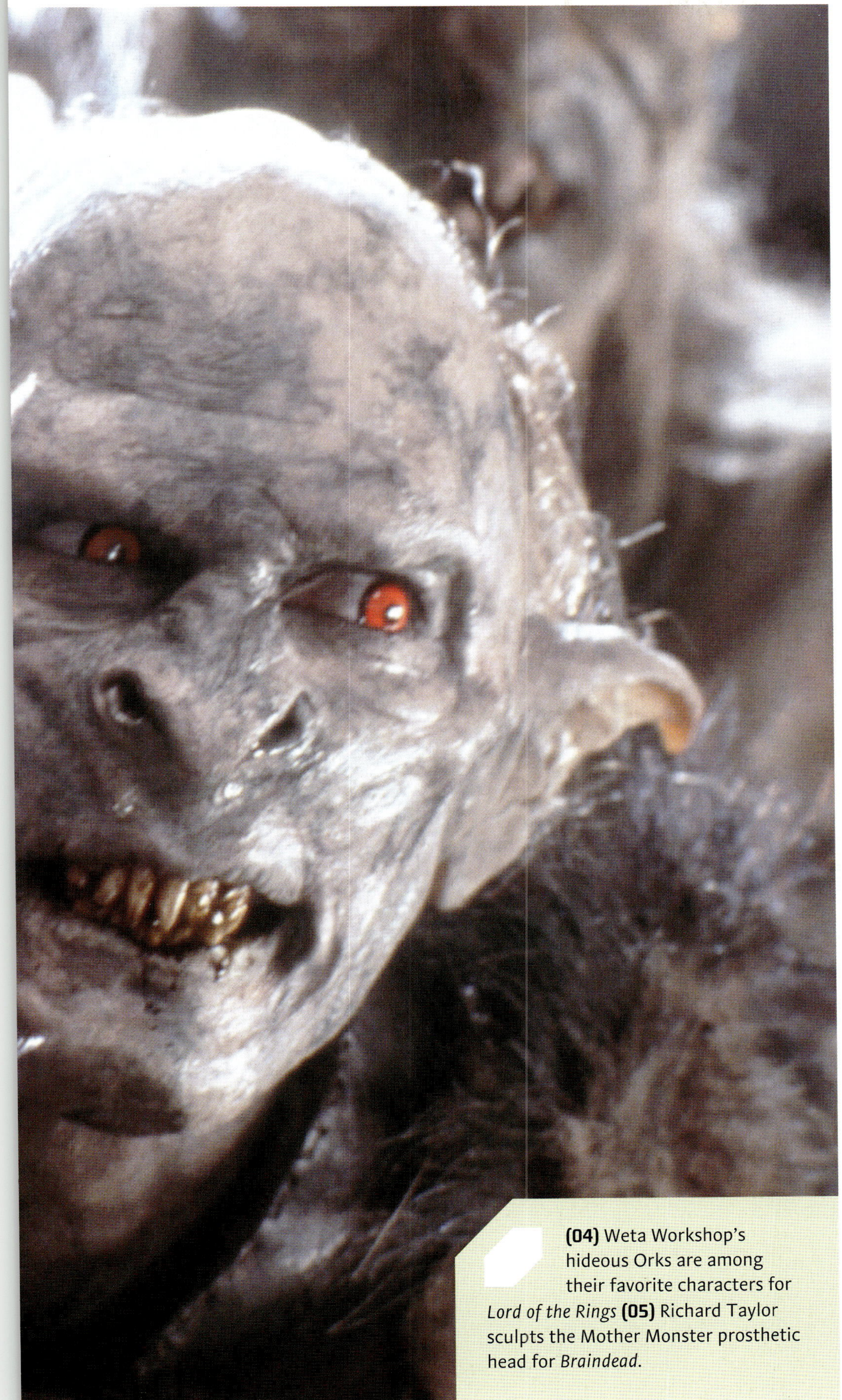

(04) Weta Workshop's hideous Orks are among their favorite characters for *Lord of the Rings* **(05)** Richard Taylor sculpts the Mother Monster prosthetic head for *Braindead*.

05

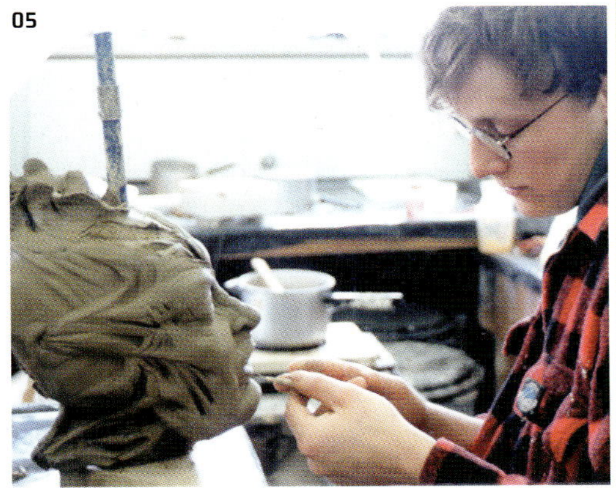

Progress was slow. The first project, *Braindead*, collapsed. However, Jackson's next movie, *Meet the Feebles* (1989), did get made. Taylor and Rodger worked with puppet designer Cameron Chittock to create dozens of Muppet-like characters at a workshop in a dilapidated railway shed. A year later, Jackson resurrected *Braindead*, inviting Taylor and Rodger to oversee the creatures and copious gore effects. *Braindead* (1992, a.k.a *Dead Alive*) was a cult success. Gradually, Taylor and Rodger's skill and experience grew with the scope of Jackson's movies. *Heavenly Creatures* (1994) called for more than just practical (physical) effects, and so the Southern Hemisphere's first Silicon Graphics workstation computer was leased and transported from America. "At the end of the movie we realized this computer was the future of visual effects and that if we let it go, we would have lost a tremendous opportunity," says Taylor. "So a small group of us pooled our resources and formed a company."

Weta was formed in 1994 by Taylor, Rodger, Peter Jackson, his movie editor Peter Selkirk, and inspirational producer James Booth, who tragically passed away soon afterward. With its sole computer, Weta became a fully fledged effects facility, but by the time Jackson directed his first Hollywood-backed movie, *The Frighteners* (1996), Weta had 14 workstations to generate a then-astonishing 420 digital effects shots.

Taylor and Rodger ran the practical side of the business, Weta Workshop, while the digital effects department was run as a sister company, Weta Digital.

06

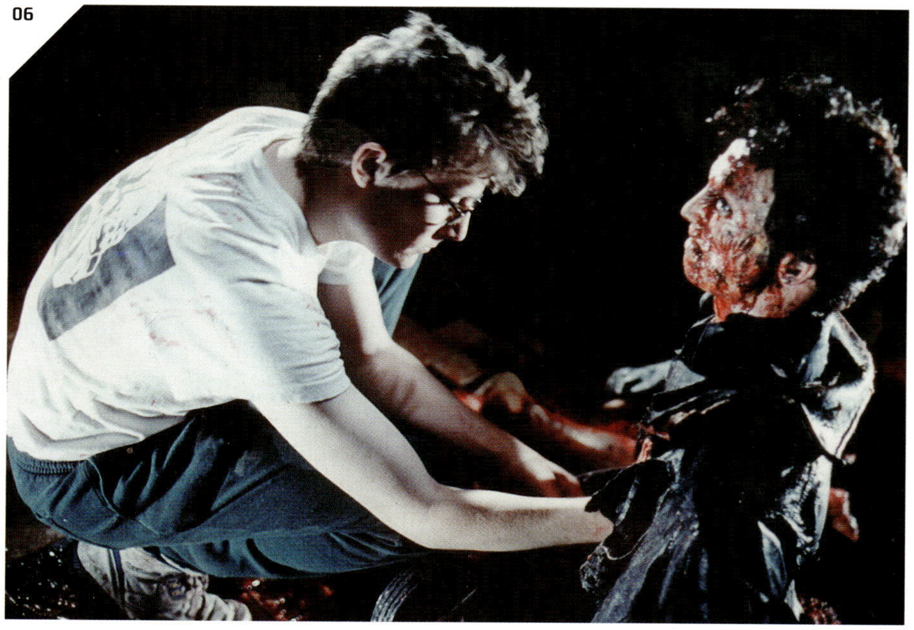

07

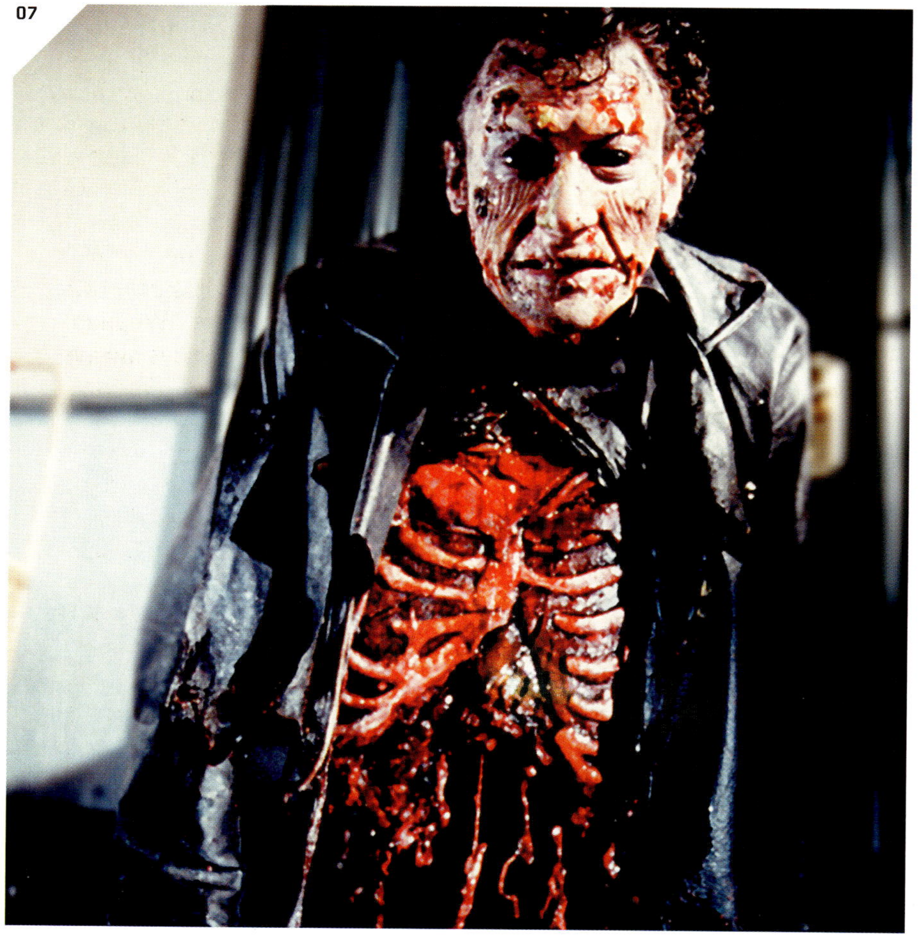

"As we were finishing on *Heavenly Creatures* we were contracted to start providing props and makeup for two TV series, *Hercules* and *Xena: Warrior Princess*," says Taylor. "Those two shows provided us with so much work and enabled so many people in New Zealand to gain experience that, without them, I think we would have struggled to pull off *Lord of the Rings*.'

Jackson's *Lord of the Rings* trilogy (2001-2003) required seven-and-a-half years' work, and visual and special effects of a scale that would daunt any of the world's biggest studios. Weta Digital worked on several thousand shots, while Weta Workshop produced a staggering quantity of creature designs, prosthetic makeups, animatronics, models, weapons, armor, and miniatures.

With the inspiration of designers Alan Lee and John Howe, Weta Workshop designed and created an incredible array of characters, including Orcs, Elves, Hobbits, elephant-like Mumaks, soaring Fellbeasts, and the trilogy's signature character, Gollum.

"We've found that we can't effectively create the characters that populate a movie without first doing what we call 'world design,'" says Taylor "If we know what a world looks like, what its culture and history are, we can better design the characters that live in it. The first thing we do is to talk about an environment in great detail. We decide on all of its attributes—whether they will be seen in the final movie or not. You'd wonder how this could ever be cost-effective, but a few hours chatting between the team can throw up the broadest array of concepts, some of which will lead to designs, and others that will help inspire the team to create a greater wealth of detail and authenticity."

Taylor cites the Uruk-hai warrior, Lurtz, as among his favorite character designs. "As you grow up you realize that monsters don't live under your bed. The only things to be scared of in the world are other human beings. I think it's the mixture of human and base animal elements that makes the Uruk-hai, and in particular Lurtz, so effective," he says. "Another character I'm proud of is the Balrog. One thing we always try to do with even our most fantasy-inspired designs is to make sure they are believable on a physical level. The Balrog was described in Tolkein's books as being of smoke and shadow, which are intangible qualities. So to try and ground the character in a reality we gave him the combined physical attributes of, say, a bull and a sumo wrestler, which helped make such an extraordinary character all the more believable."

08

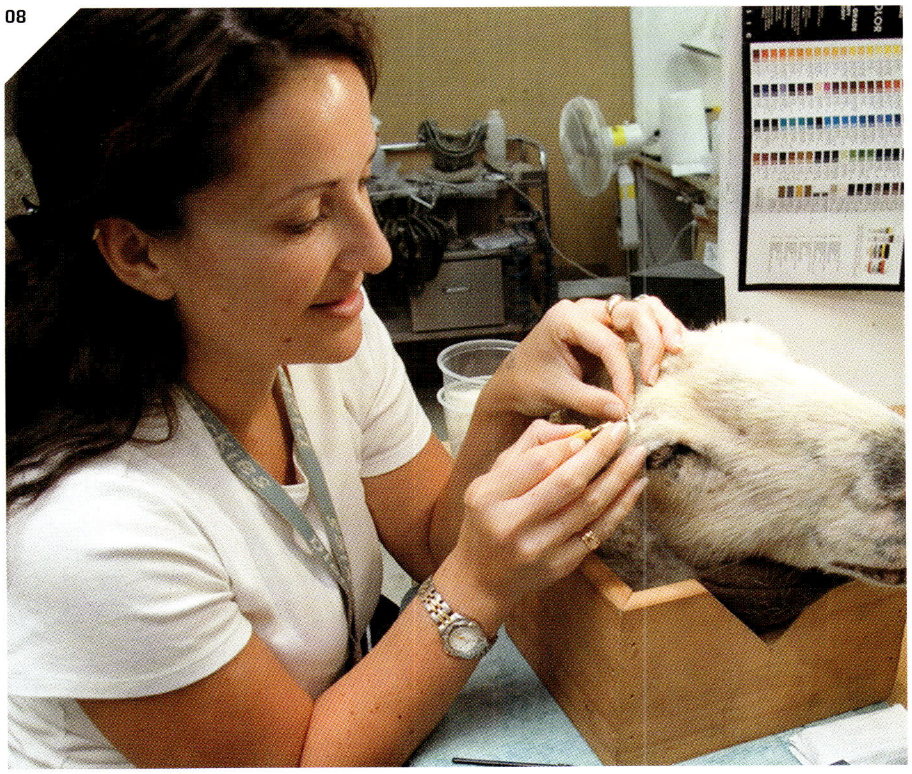

09

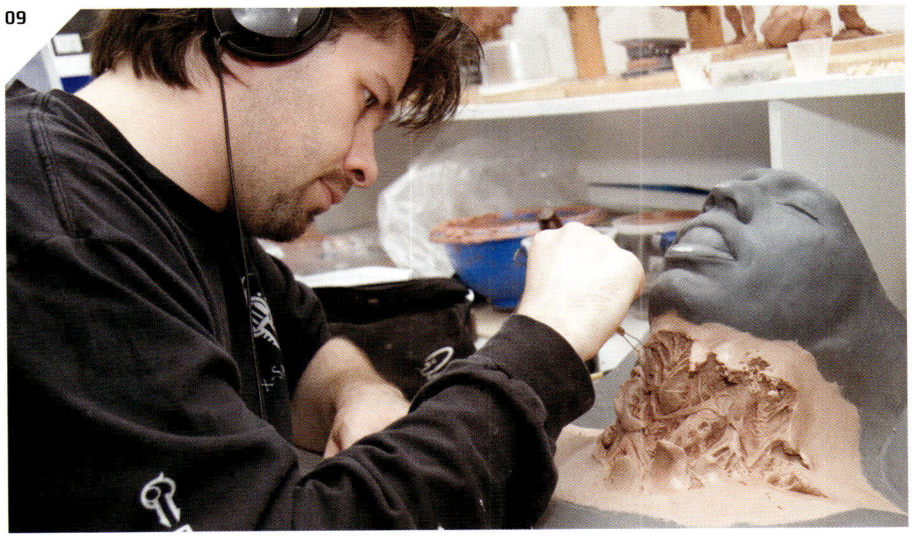

(06) Richard Taylor prepares the dummy of Void for a scene in *Braindead* **(07)** Jed Brophy wearing a prosthetic chest rig as Void in *Braindead* **(08–09)** Weta artists create animatronic sheep and prosthetic wounds for *Black Sheep* (2006).

After completing *Lord of the Rings*, Weta Workshop worked on a number of projects at the same time. Among these was the design of creatures, cultures, armor, and weapons for *The Chronicles of Narnia: The Lion, the Witch and the Wardrobe* (2005). Weta created maquettes of the movie's many characters and manufactured large amounts of weapons and armor, but had to give up the work to create the fantastic flora and fauna of Peter Jackson's *King Kong* (2005). "Designing Skull Island was a fantastic challenge because we needed to create a prehistoric environment that had apparently survived into the modern age," says Taylor. "We weren't supposed to be designing ancient creatures, but ones that had continued evolving for another 65 million years after every other dinosaur had become extinct."

The design team produced thousands of conceptual drawings and hundreds of sculptures to illustrate their world design. They conceived creatures of the air, land, and sea, engineered complex food chains involving exotic plants and beasts, and imagined how the island's geology, geography, and climate affected its life forms. Only a proportion of the work created ever made it on to the screen, although it helped to inform everything that was seen in the final movie.

To Taylor it was important that the creatures of Skull Island were designed and rendered as "real" animals, and not simply fantasy beasts. "When it comes to living creatures, the real world is always our inspiration. That means including authentic physiological and anatomical detail. One of our senior designers, Ben Wootten, has a degree in zoology as well as a degree in fine art. That combination of knowledge and skills helped to keep our designs very true. Jamie Beswarick, one of our long-time sculptors, also happens to be an amateur paleontologist—he knows as much about prehistoric creatures as some professionals."

One of the vilest creatures was the writhing, slug-like Carnictis. "The idea was that all kinds of revolting creatures had evolved to live in this pit, devouring anything unfortunate enough to fall into it," says Taylor. "Peter had described that part of the movie as a horror show and wanted everything that lived in the pit to be revolting to humans. As a team we discussed what would be the most unpleasant and disgusting ways to be killed and we decided that being slowly eaten alive by a slug-like creature would be pretty gruesome. I happened to be wearing a floppy jersey and, improvising, I pulled my hand back into the arm of the jersey, pulling the jersey in with it, and then performed the motion of my fingers rolling vast amount of detail we included, right down to the skin pores and scales. The one-meter-tall sculpture represented a creature that was 35ft (10.5 meters) tall, so it was imperative that every small surface detail was perfect."

Taylor believes that geographical isolation has been a mixed blessing for Weta. "We work with a group of people raised among Southern Pacific art and culture, and that has helped impart a certain look of the exotic and the mystical to our work. The disadvantage is that we don't have great libraries and museums. But in many cases ignorance has been our ally. We've explored many opportunities that we probably would have shied away from if we had been a little better educated!"

10

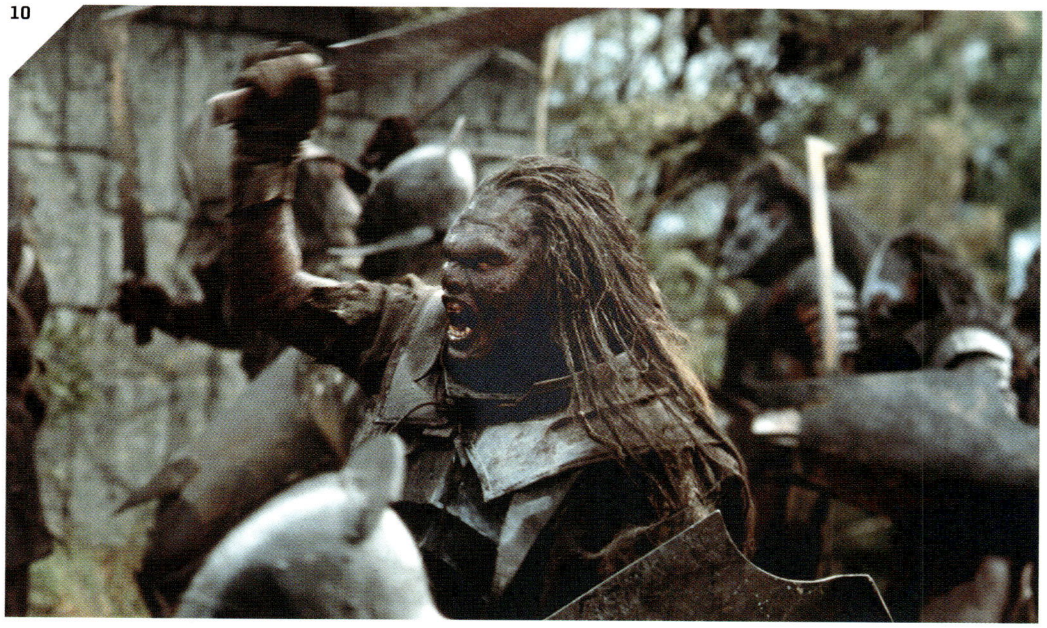

11

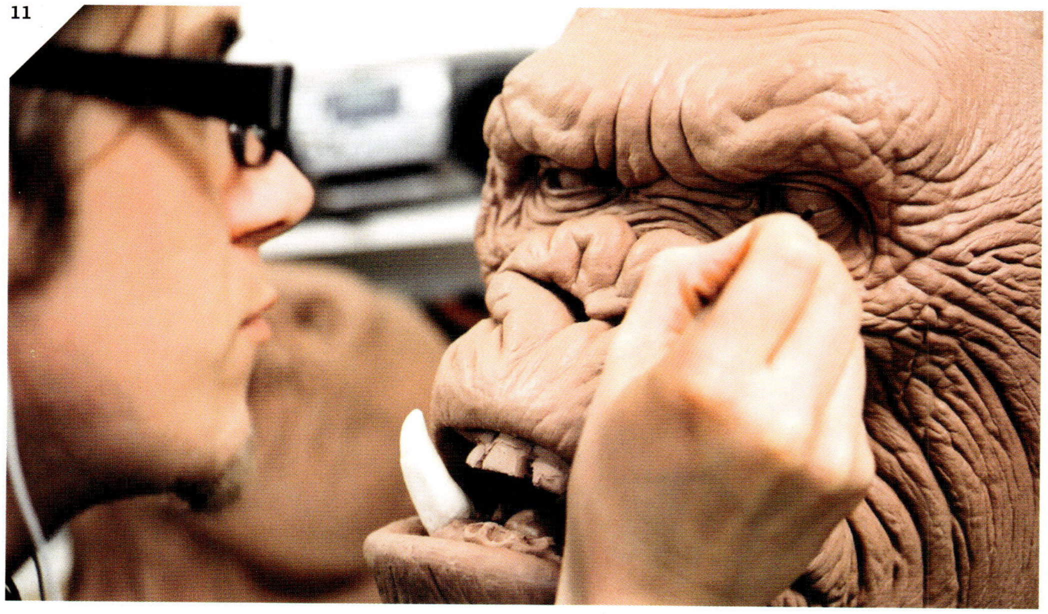

out of the end like teeth. If you watch the scene of Lumpy the cook being eaten alive you'll see it is exactly like the motion of a hand being pulled back inside a jersey. I find it really exciting how conversations with your colleagues can lead directly to this kind of on-screen action."

Weta designed many dinosaurs that were evolved versions of genuine fossil finds, such as the T-rex and Brontosaur, but they also created a number of fictional beasts. "A favorite creature of mine was what we called the 'Wetasaur,'" says Taylor. "Peter came to us and said he'd written a scene between a dinosaur and Anne Darrow and he wanted to use a totally new type of dinosaur, something that wasn't based on any known creature. We did about 40 conceptual sculptures, combining all our favorite dinosaur features, and whittled it down to something we all liked before creating a sculpture that could be scanned and then animated by Weta Digital."

The sculpture of the Wetasaur took an incredible nine months to create, though this was by no-means the greatest time spent on a single sculpture. "The T-rex took over a year to sculpt, with up to five sculptors working on it at a time," says Taylor. "It took so long because of the

(10) Weta Workshop created thousands of pieces of weaponry for Lord of the Rings **(11)** Sculptor Jamie Beswarick works on the face of King Kong **(12)** Kong protects Anne Darrow (Naomi Watts) from the T-rex. The creatures were computer generated by Weta Digital from designs and sculptures by Weta Workshop **(13)** The "Wetasaur" from *King Kong* (2005).

12

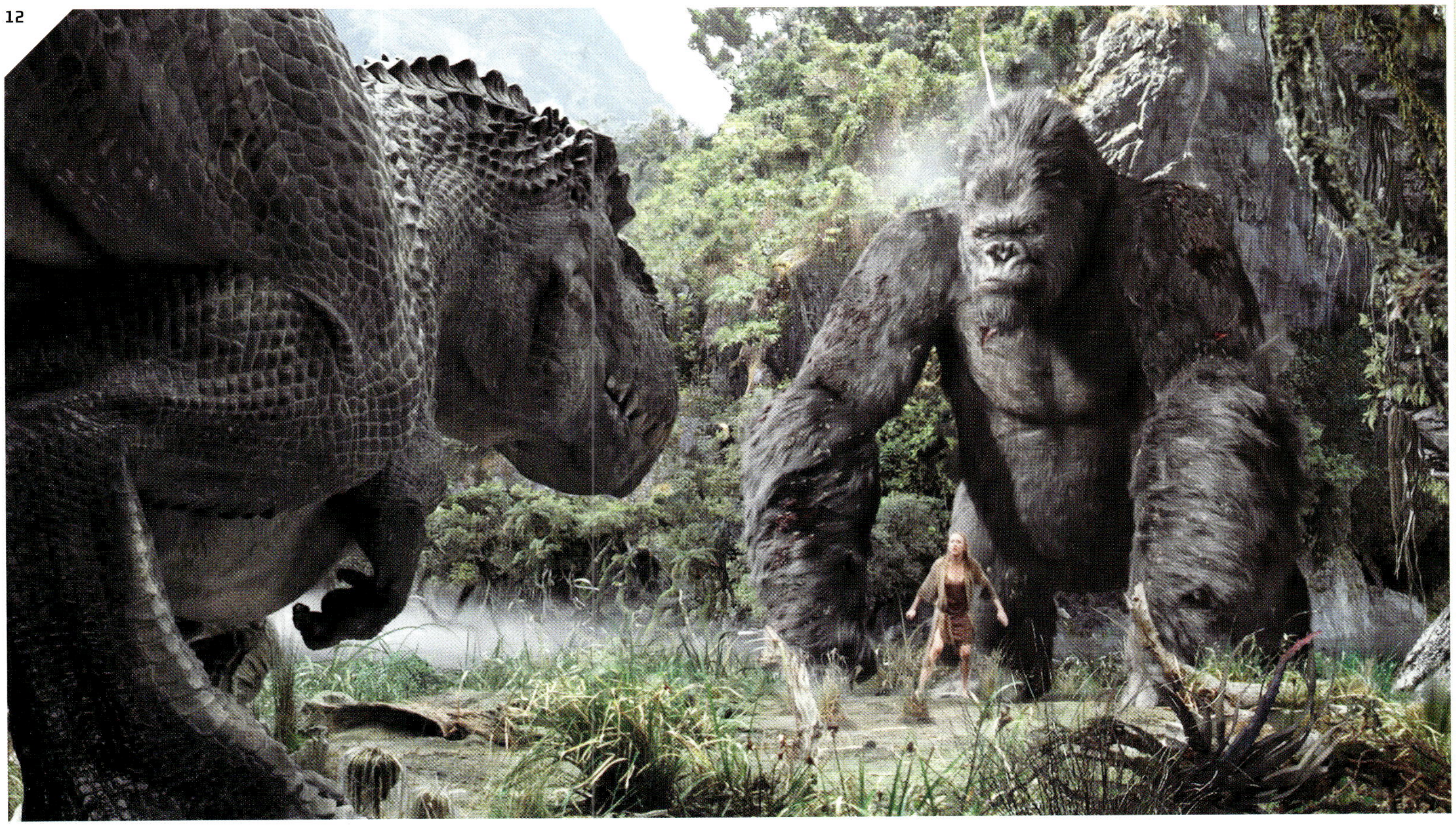

13

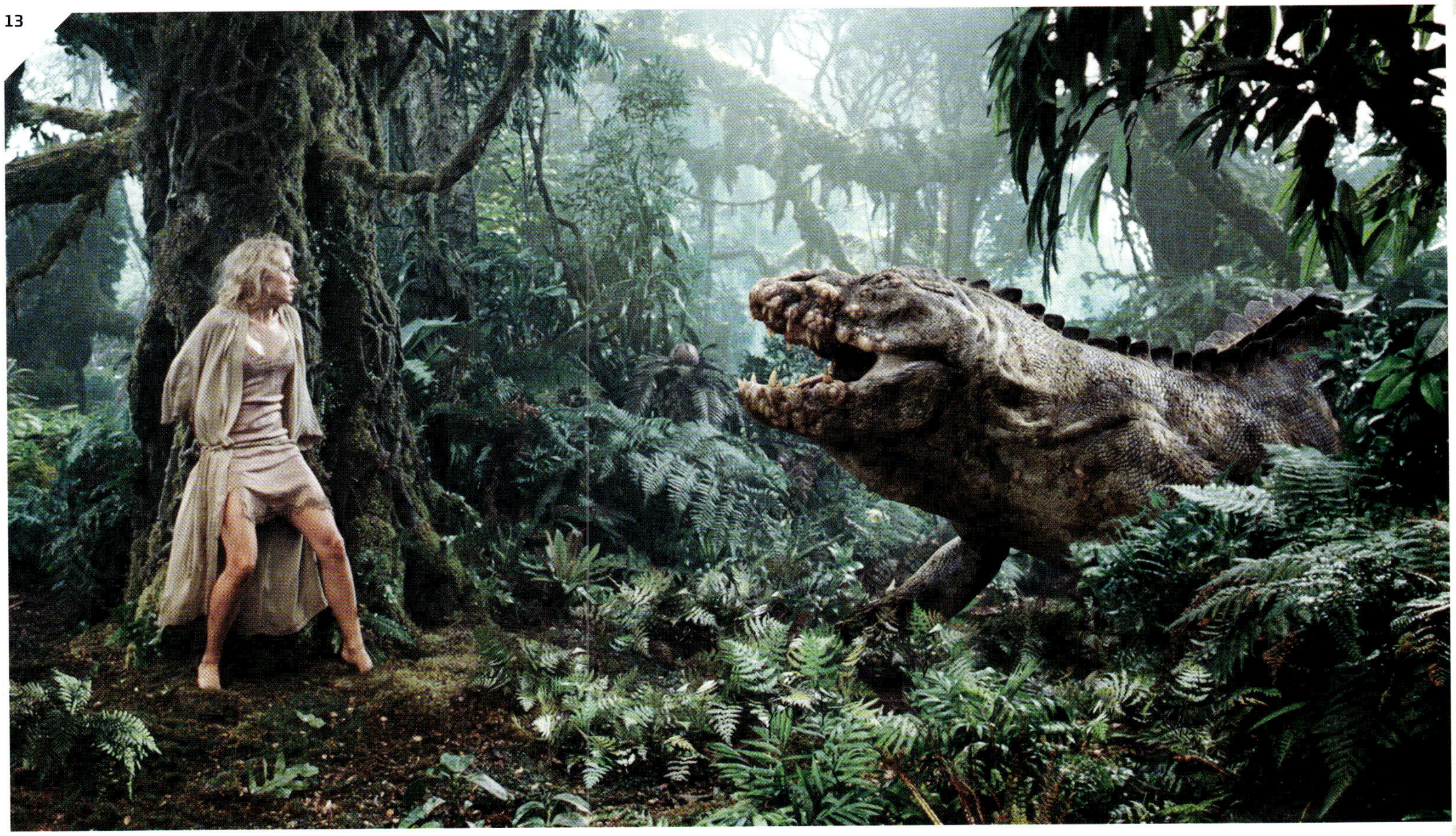

CRISTINA PATTERSON CERET

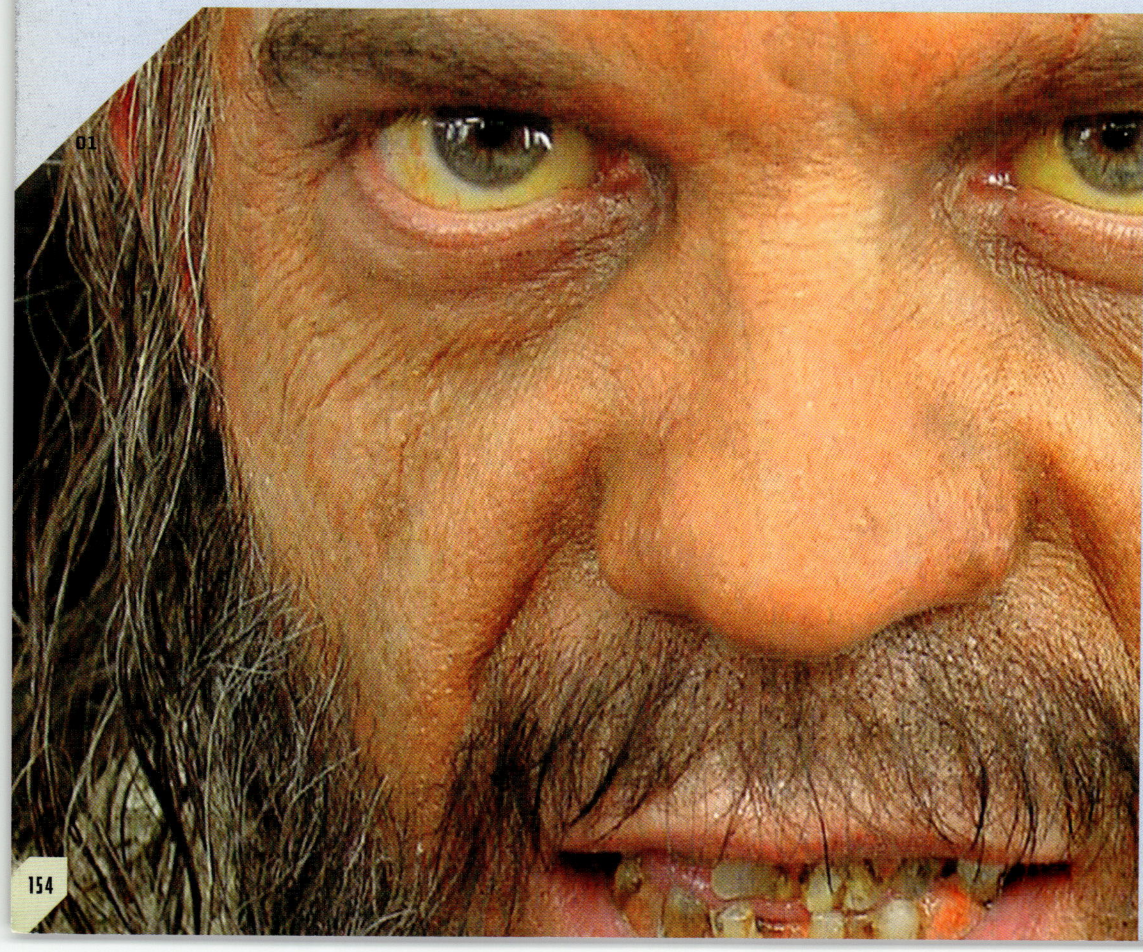

01

CV

Contact-lens artist; born Madrid, Spain; moved to Los Angeles, CA, at the age of one; became movie makeup artist in 1980s; joined Professional VisionCare as contact-lens technician in 1995, becoming special effects coordinator in 2002.

SELECT FILMOGRAPHY

Batman and Robin (1997); *Galaxy Quest* (1999); *Planet of the Apes* (2001); *Hulk* (2003); *Underworld* (2003); *The Lord of the Rings: Return of the King* (2003); *Pirates of the Caribbean* series (2003, 2006); *Van Helsing* (2004); *Sin City* (2005); *King Kong* (2005); *Superman Returns* (2006); *Spider-Man 3* (2006); *Pirates of the Caribbean: Dead Man's Chest* (2006)

KEY CHARACTERS

Dracula (*Bram Stoker's Dracula*); Skull Islanders (*King Kong*); Orcs, Uruk-hai (*LOTR*); Hulk (*Hulk*); Selene (*Underworld*); Pintel, Ragetti (*Pirates of the Caribbean*)

TECHNIQUES

Contact lens design and painting

02
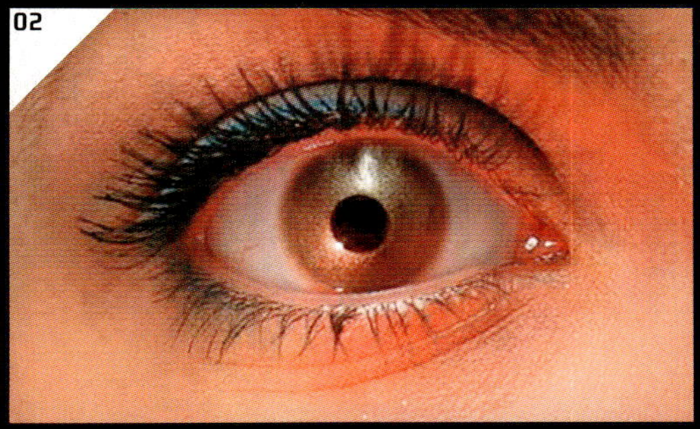

03
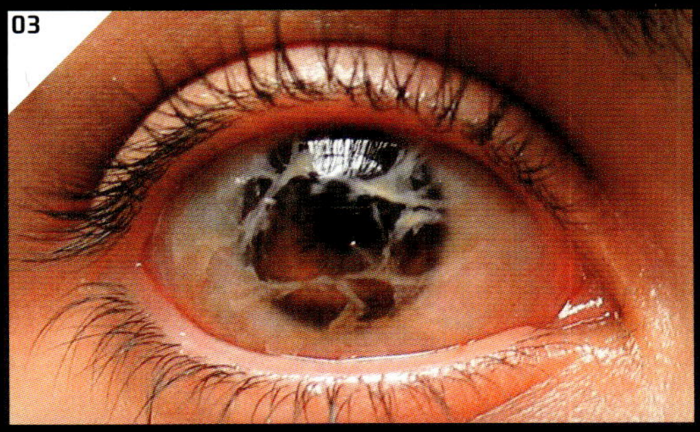

04
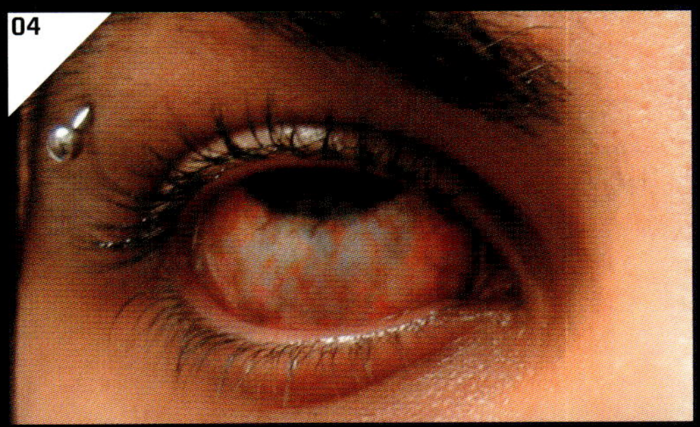

05
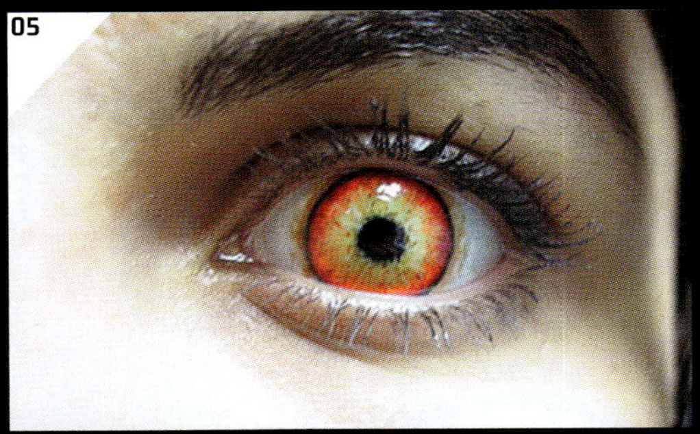

06
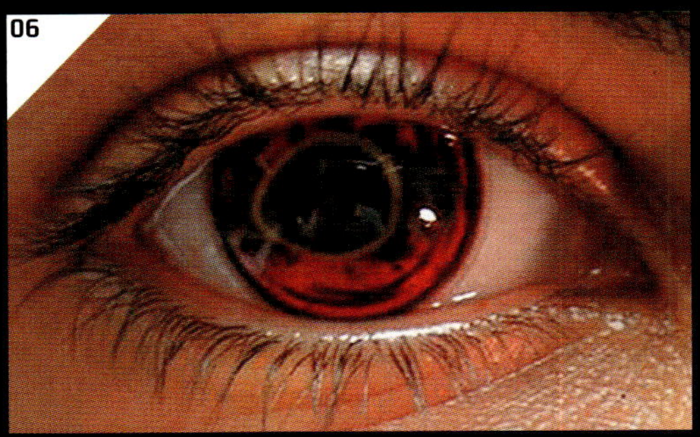

07
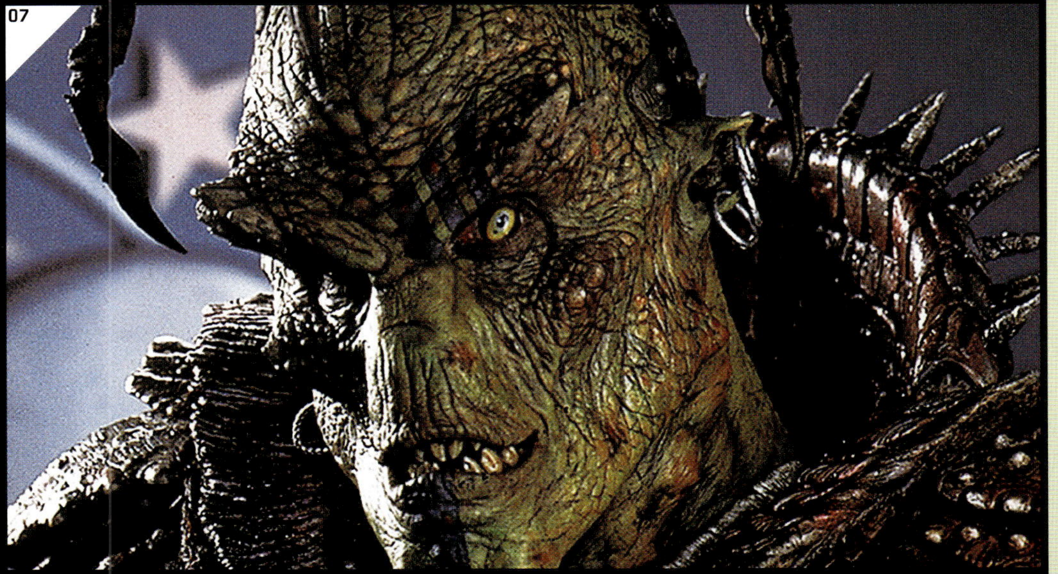

Cristina Patterson Ceret is one of the world's leading contact-lens artists, having created the eye designs for characters played by human performers in hundreds of films, including *Pirates of the Caribbean: The Curse of the Black Pearl* (2003); *The Lord of the Rings: The Return of the King* (2003); *Van Helsing* (2004); and *Superman Returns* (2006).

Born in Madrid, Spain, Ceret moved to Los Angeles at the age of one. Her mother, Raffaelle Butler, was a makeup artist on films including *To Kill a Mockingbird* (1962) and Doctor Zhivago (1965). Often accompanying her mother during filming, Cristina became intrigued with makeup application, becoming a makeup artist herself during the 1980s. In 1995 she became a contact-lens technician at Professional VisionCare Associates, the leading supplier of specialized contact lenses for the movie and television industries since 1939. In 2002, Ceret was promoted to Special Effects Coordinator, designing and painting contact lenses, overseeing fittings and exams, and training and supervising all on-set technicians.

Creating a set of unique contact lenses begins when a movie's makeup artist or designer sends an eye design to Ceret —or requests she design one for them. "When I see a design, the first thing I decide is what type of lens we'll have to use," says Ceret. "There are two basic types: a corneal lens and a scleral lens. Corneal lenses are like the lenses used by most contact-lens wearers to improve their vision. They fit on the front surface of the eye, the cornea, covering only the iris and pupil to change its color or pattern. Scleral lenses are much larger, and they cover the whole surface of the eye including the white of the eye—the sclera."

Before lenses can be created, the performer who will wear them attends a fitting and exam at Professional VisionCare's office. "I usually attend the exam with the performer and discuss the process of using contact lenses while they have a full eye examination with one of our doctors," says Ceret.

(01) Lee Arenberg as Pintel in *Pirates of the Caribbean: The Curse of the Black Pearl* (2003), wearing lenses painted by Cristina Patterson Ceret **(02–06)** A range of her painted lenses **(02)** *Blade 2* **(03, 04)** *King Kong* **(05)** *Lord of the Rings* **(06)** *The Chronicles of Narnia: Lion, the Witch and the Wardrobe* **(07)** Eye design is an integral part of a character costume, as with this alien character created by Stan Winston studio for *Galaxy Quest* (1999).

08

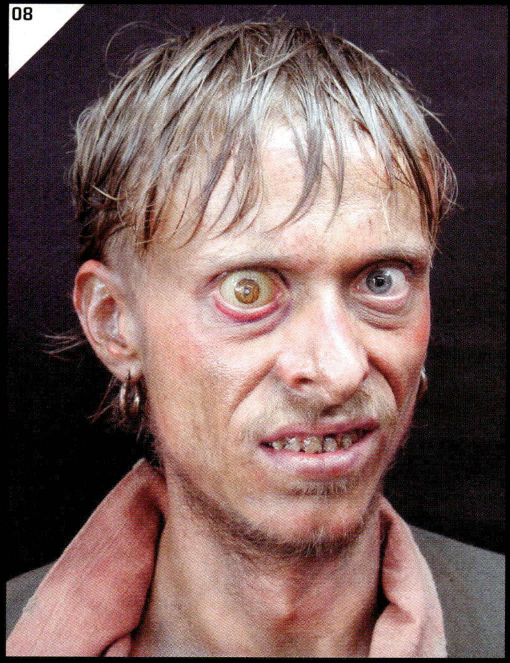

09

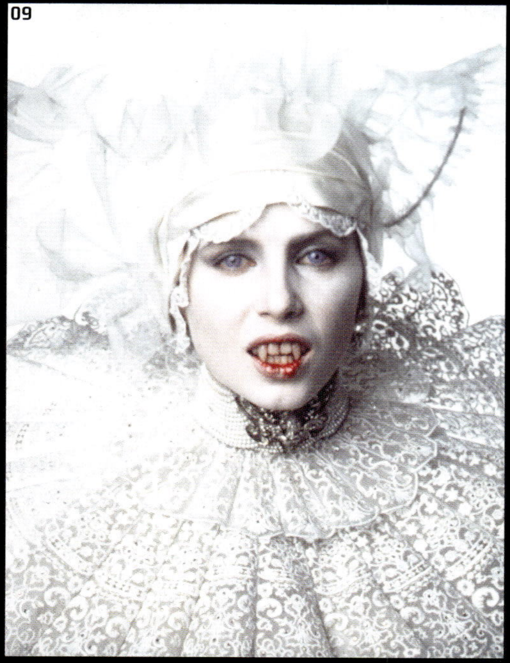

"For scleral lenses there's no method of measuring the whole eyeball, so the doctors have to try a few variations," she explains. "It's very important that lenses are properly fitted by an optometrist, otherwise the eyes could be injured. During the exam we also get the performer to try a lens that is similar in design to the one they will eventually be wearing so they know what to expect. Some people can be very claustrophobic, hyperventilating and passing out once lenses are applied."

The vision of the performer will be affected by the type of design used on the lens. "If we're just changing the color or design of the iris, then the performer will be able to see as normal, though their peripheral vision may be impaired," she explains. "If we paint over the pupil area, they will have blurred or milky vision. If the design involves covering the whole eye with a strong pattern then the performer may not be able to see anything. For example, the wandering eye Brad Pitt wore in *Twelve Monkeys* [1995] was totally opaque, as was the wooden-looking eye worn by Mackenzie Crook in *Pirates of the Caribbean*."

Once a contact lens is fitted it will follow the movement of the eye. However, because they are circular, lenses can also rotate. This does not matter in most cases, but where the design of the eye depends on the lens remaining at a certain angle—when the pupil is a vertical slit, for example—a special lens called a prism-ballast lens is required. These are thicker on the area of the lens that needs to be at the base of the eye. The extra weight at the bottom ensures that it does not rotate and spoil the appearance of the design.

Once the requirements of the lens have been determined and designs are approved, Ceret can begin to create the pattern and color. "Referring to the design artwork, I will individually hand paint each lens using extremely fine brushes," she explains. "Sometimes I will paint on the front surface of the lens and at other times it will be painted on the underside so that the thickness of the lens will make the eye look deeper."

Ceret uses a variety of paints and pigments to create her designs. The special-effects lens business is so competitive, however, that the exact materials remain a trade secret. "All our materials are FDA approved for use in and around eyes, but other than that we don't tell anyone what we use," she says. "I have come up with many of my own tricks and techniques, which will remain with me until I find someone to pass them on to."

Colored fashion lenses sold to consumers to change the appearance of their eyes are machine printed, but there are no mechanical means of producing unusual designs of the type required by special-effects artists. "I can enhance commercially printed lenses," says Ceret. "For example, I can take a blue-printed lens and paint additional details like a limbus ring—the dark edge that encircles an iris—or an arcus ring, which is a sort of gray deposit that older people develop around the edge of the iris that makes the eye look gray and soft."

The finished lenses are shipped to the production ready for filming. However, that is rarely the end of Professional VisionCare's involvement. "Performers typically have to build up their tolerance to lenses," explains Ceret. "If they are not normally lens wearers, they will need to wear the lens first for an hour at once, then two hours, and so on. Often performers don't want to do this—and scleral lenses are impossible to fit without assistance—so we have to have a technician on set with them to take the lenses on and off between takes, care for the performer's eyes, and also look after the lenses."

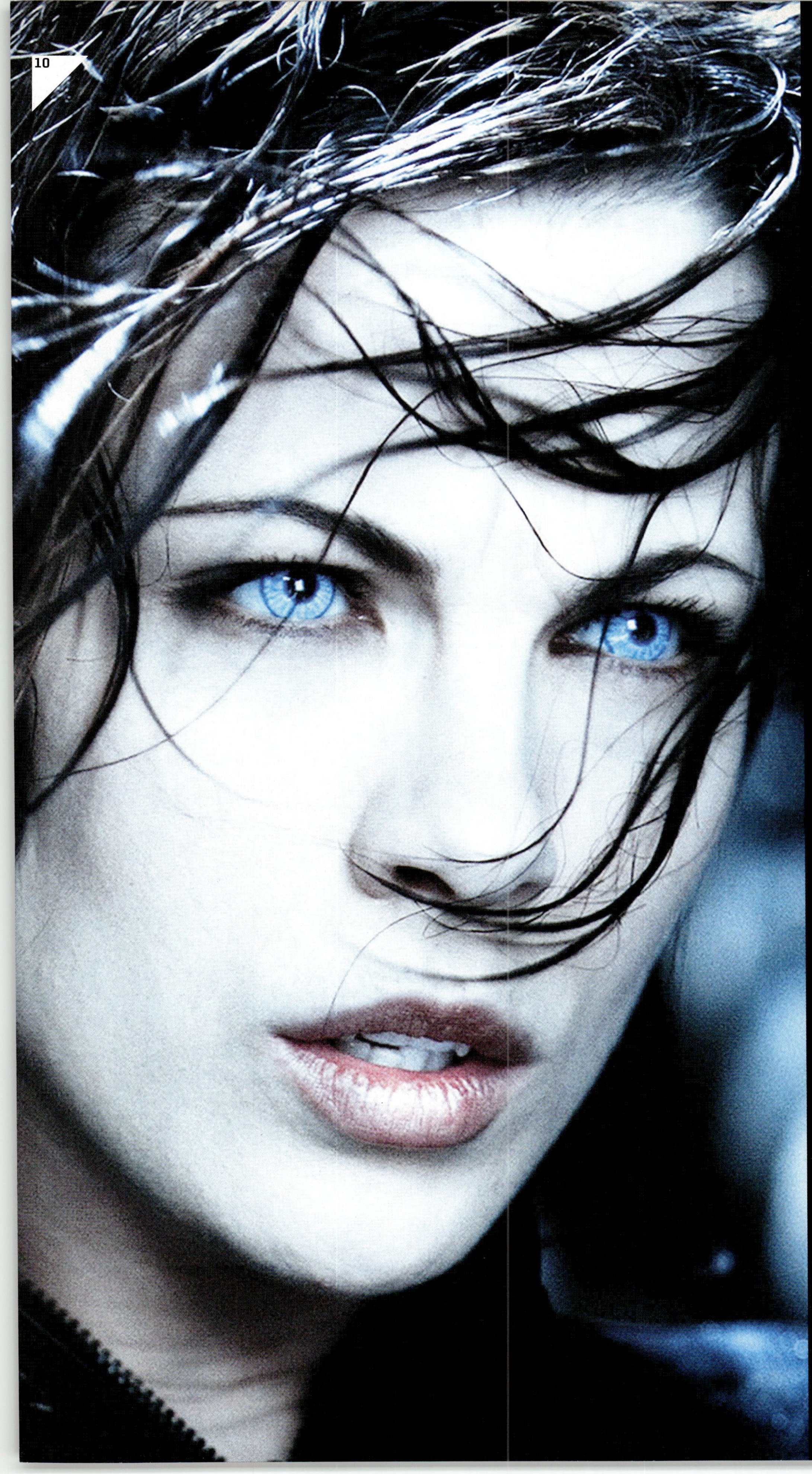

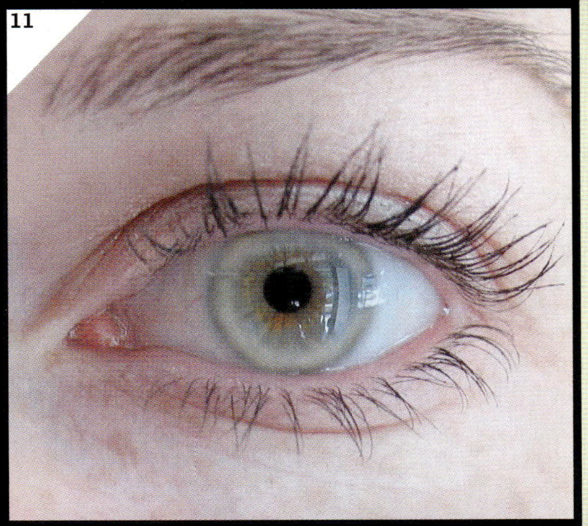

Ceret's favorite and most challenging pieces have been for the recent *King Kong* (2005). "Gino Acevedo from Weta Workshop sent me over a design, and I had never seen anything like it. I had to develop a whole new technique to achieve the multilayered cobweb effect, but the final look was unique and I'm really proud of those lenses.

"When it comes to eyes, the two greatest designers are Gino Acevedo and Dave Elsey. They always send designs that really push the limit for a contact lens. I always try my best to get as close as possible to their design. I hate saying no, and I usually don't. Although there was a time when someone wanted to glue tiny suction cups to a lens, we had to put our foot down that time!

(08) This bulging corneal lens was fitted to actor Mackenzie Crook for his role as Ragetti in the *Pirates of the Caribbean* series. The lens was painted to resemble carved wood **(09)** Sadie Frost sports icy blue eyes as a vampire in *Bram Stoker's Dracula* (1992) **(10)** The shocking blue eyes of Kate Beckinsale in *Underworld: Evolution* (2006) were integral to the movie's stylized look **(11)** Old-age makeups often use lenses that mimic the natural condition arcus senilis.

WALT CONTI

CV

Animatronics designer; b. Palo Alto, CA; worked in the early 1980s with a company that created educational robotic toys; studied Robotic Engineering at Stanford University; 1986 started work for George Lucas's Industrial Light and Magic on *Star Trek IV*; formed his own animatronics company, Edge Innovations.

SELECT FILMOGRAPHY

Star Trek IV: The Voyage Home (1986); *The Abyss* (1989); The *Free Willy* series (1993, 1995, 1997); *Flipper* (1996); *White Squall* (1996); *SeaQuest DSV* TV series (1993–96); *Anaconda* (1997); *Deep Blue Sea* (1999)

KEY CHARACTERS

Humpback whales (*Star Trek IV*); submersible vehicles (*The Abyss*); killer whales (*Free Willy* series); dolphins (*Flipper*); snakes (*Anaconda*); sharks (*Deep Blue Sea*)

TECHNIQUES

Design and contruction of animatronic systems capable of underwater performance

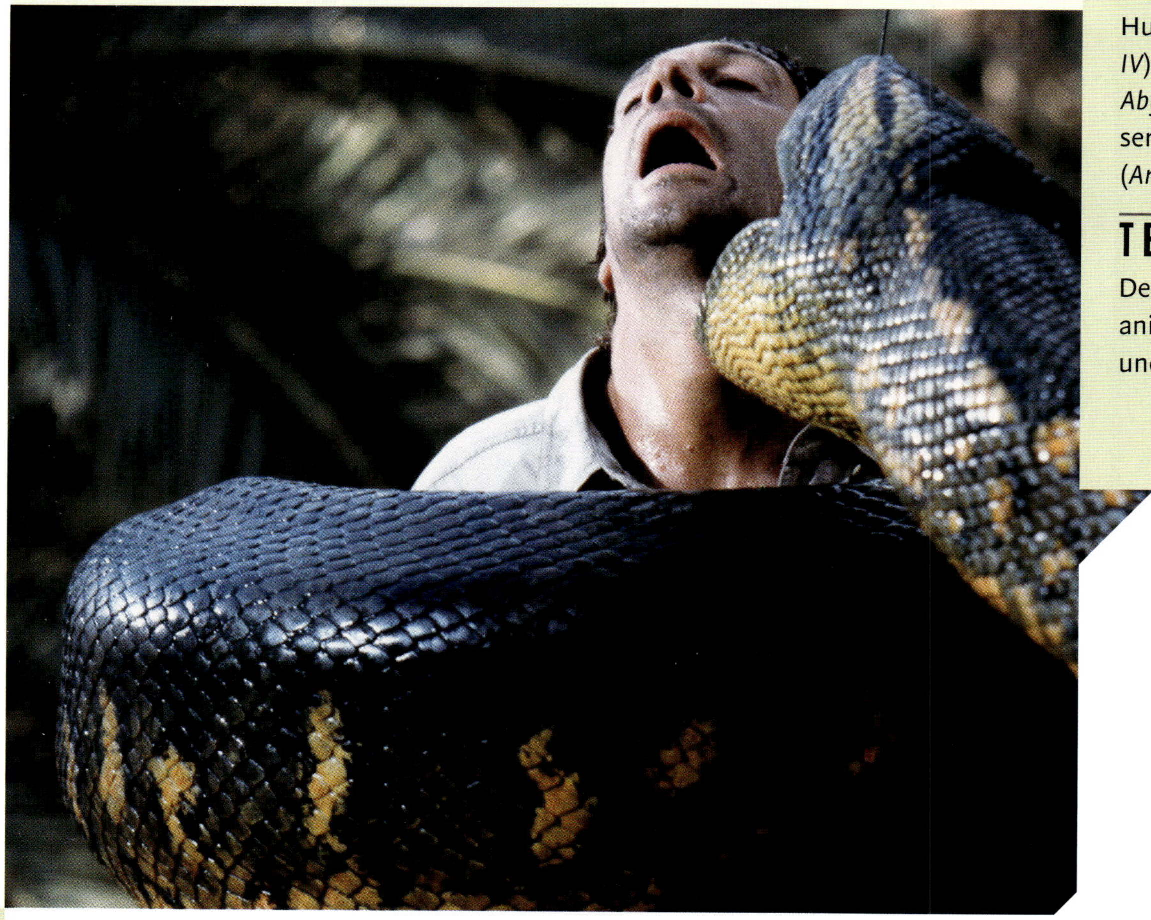

02

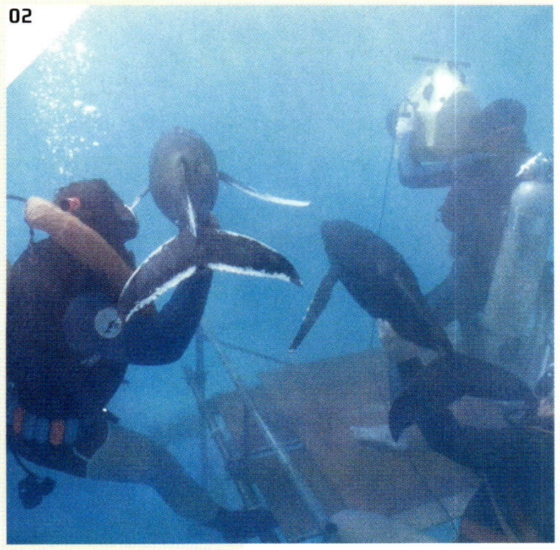

03

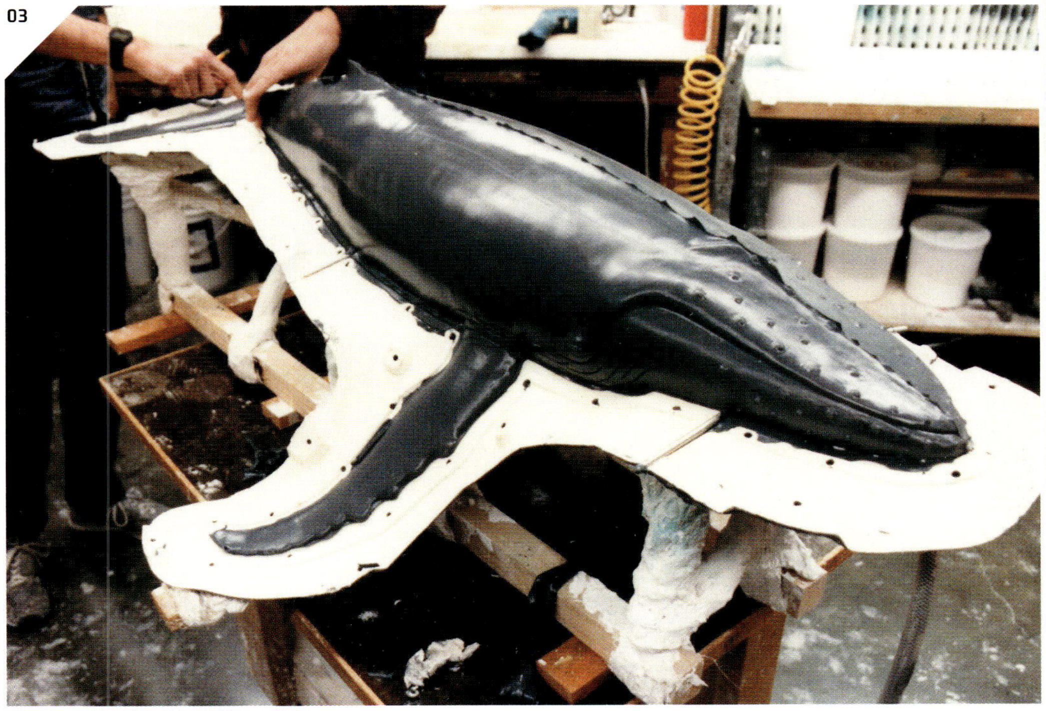

While most animatronic characters have to combine delicate design features with a fabrication robust enough to withstand the rigors of filming, few have to be built to the demanding specifications of those made by Walt Conti and his company, Edge Innovations. Conti's creations have had to operate almost exclusively underwater, delivering naturalistic performances despite the difficulties presented by waves, currents, sunlight, and salt water.

Walt Conti was born and raised in Palo Alto, California. From a young age he was building contraptions out of Lego and experimenting with all things mechanical. He studied robotic engineering at Stanford University, where one day he picked up a copy of special-effects magazine, *Cinefex*. "It was 1981, and the magazine had an article about how the animatronic puppet was being created for *E.T.* [1982]," recalls Conti. "I was just blown away by what went into making that guy walk and talk. Of course, I'd seen and loved films like *Jaws* and *Star Wars*, but I'd never really considered that making movies was something to which I could apply my engineering and robotics skills. I tried really hard to get a job at ILM."

Having no success with ILM, Conti found work with a company creating educational robotic toys. There he befriended the project art director, Nilo Rodis-Jamero. "Nilo had been an art director on *Star Wars*, and still did a lot of work at ILM," says Conti. "One day he asked me if I would be able to apply my knowledge in robotics to a special-effects project they were having trouble with."

At the time, ILM was working on *Star Trek IV: The Voyage Home* (1986). The movie required extensive footage of humpback whales that would be impossible to achieve by filming the real creatures. "They'd tried just about every method of artificially creating whales, including animating models filmed in a smoked-up studio, but nothing was working very well. They had even reached the point where they were considering rewriting the script to leave the whales out," says Conti. "I had no experience of underwater engineering, I wasn't a diver, and I didn't know much about whales. But Nilo thought I might be able to come up with something interesting."

Conti was hired to create model animatronic whales that could be filmed actually swimming underwater. He started by studying hours of video footage of whales to become familiar with how they moved. He then set about building a number of rapid prototypes in order to establish the mechanics. It quickly became obvious that the weight of the models would be a major obstacle. "It became an exercise in using only lightweight materials and using as little of them as possible."

Conti also discovered that it would probably be impossible to keep the inside of the whale dry. "We decided it was easier to accept the inevitability of water inside the creature and just work with it," says Conti. "The inside of the whale was fully open to the water and all of the mechanisms were designed to operate safely and effectively while submersed.

(01) A scene from *Anaconda* (1997), with Conti's creation **(02)** Conti's first underwater animatronic challenge was the humpback whales for *Star Trek IV: The Voyage Home* (1986) **(03)** The inner mechanisms of the whales were placed into molds and the outer skin of urethane was cast around them.

04

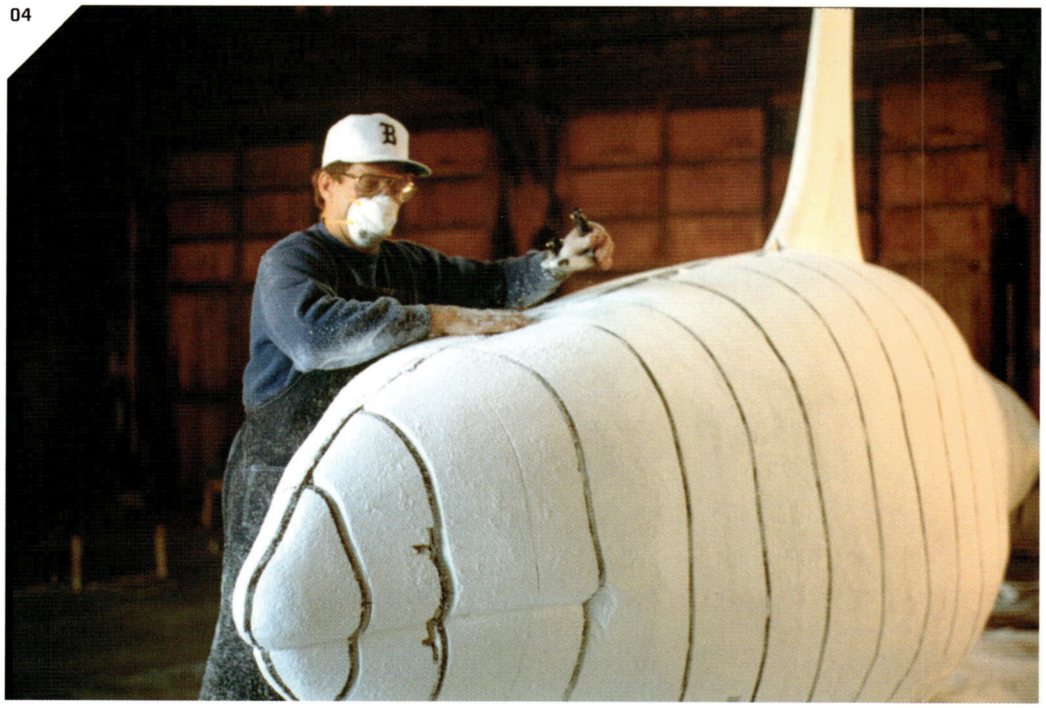

05

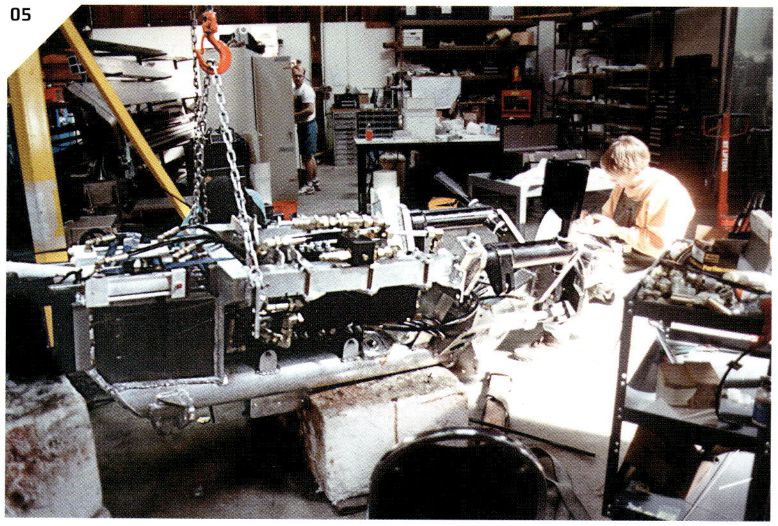

06

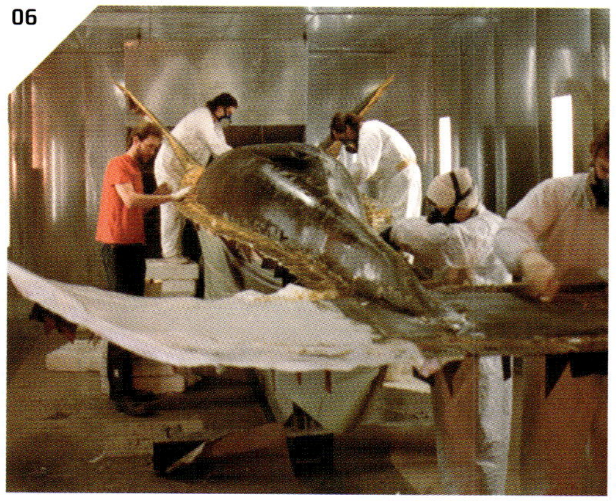

(04) The orca of *Free Willy* (1993) was carved out of sheets of polystyrene **(05)** The 250-horsepower hydraulics needed to drive the whale robot are prepared at Edge Innovations **(06)** The whale sculpture is encased in fiberglass to create the mold **(07)** The finished whale, with the mechanisms inside, is painted ready for use **(08)** One of the full-sized robots is lifted from the water by a support ship **(09)** Walt Conti's orcas could swim, dive, and spray water, as in this scene.

With the body filled with water and not air, the models were also more stable. All of our aquatic characters since then have been open to the water." The demanding conditions in which the animatronic creatures would be working called for some unusual engineering solutions. "We couldn't use standard servos because they simply weren't strong enough to push a fin or a tail through the weight of the water. Instead, I managed to locate some servos that had been designed for use in Korean missiles. They were very powerful and worked well underwater."

The whales' main propulsion was provided by their tail, which flapped up and down just like the tail of a real whale. Long pectoral fins on the sides of their bodies could move up and down and produce a circular motion both to propel the creature and to steer it through the water. Under the skin the fins themselves were made of flexible steel, allowing them to bend subtly as they moved through the water.

The way in which the motors and other internal mechanisms were fitted into each model was important to the whales' ability to operate. Everything had to be evenly distributed and carefully balanced, so that the model would lie absolutely level in the water without rolling over or nose-diving.

Another challenge was finding a suitable material for the skin of the models. "At that time, all animatronic creatures were made with foam latex. But that's basically just sponge, which will soak up water and make the creature even heavier. Instead, we experimented with various materials and ended up using urethane, which is very soft but doesn't absorb water. Urethane is also very strong, which is vital when you're working with underwater characters that are likely to crash into things. We've used it for almost all of our movie characters ever since."

At 4ft (1.2m) in length, the finished whales were a tenth of the size of a real adult whale. To make the models look much larger, they swam at an

07

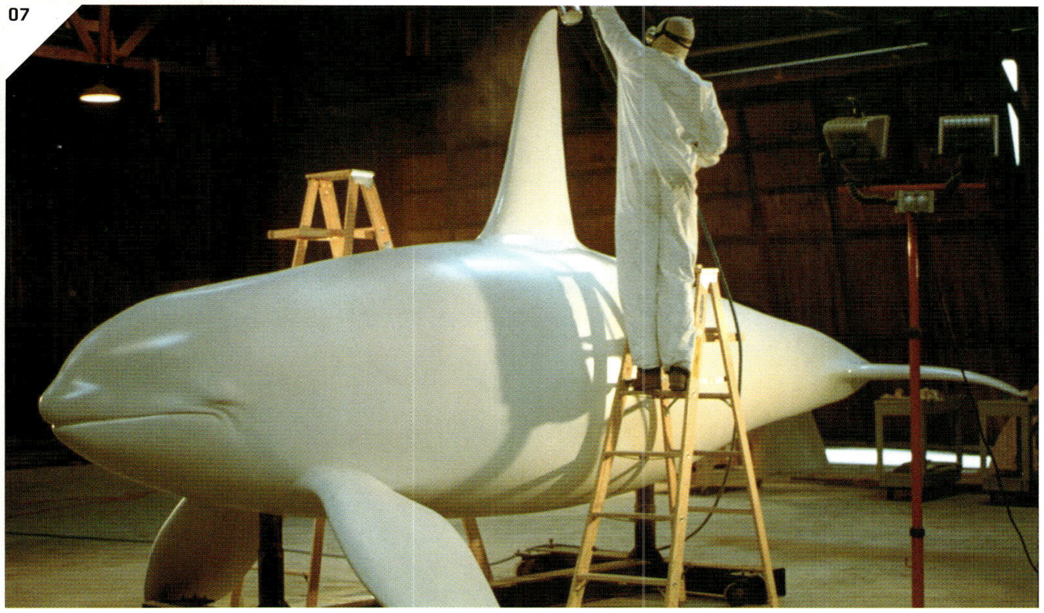

08

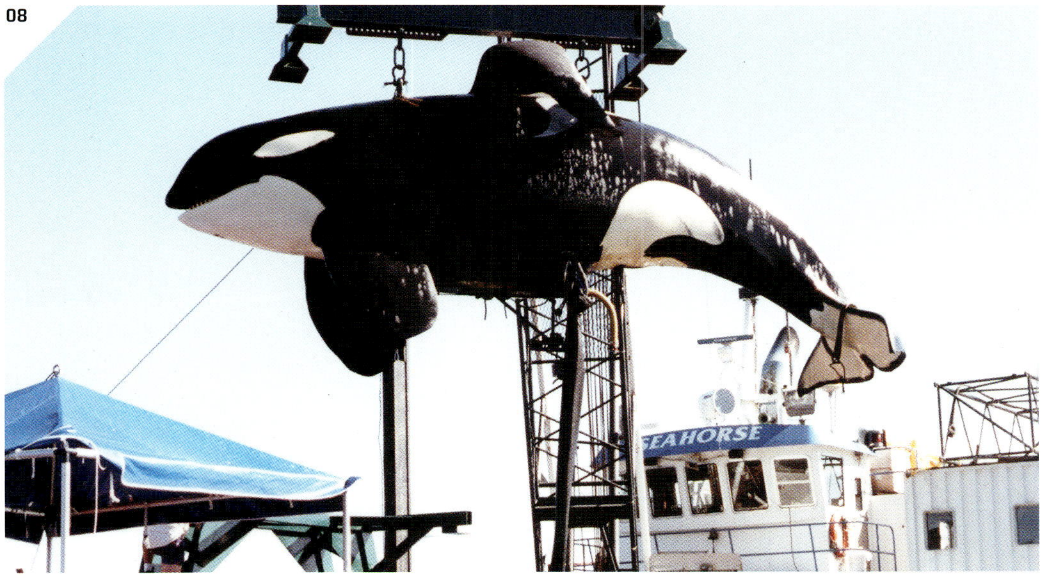

09

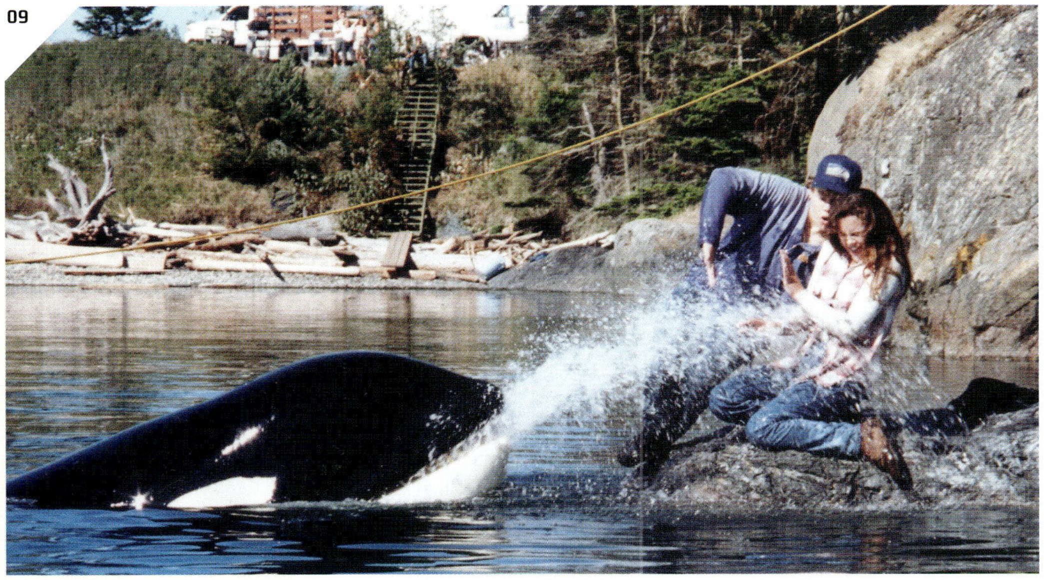

accelerated pace and were filmed at high speed. The resulting slow-motion footage made the creatures look enormous and graceful. "The whales were filmed in a large swimming pool by underwater cinematographer Pete Romano," says Conti. "The pool had an underwater viewing window, allowing the puppeteers to watch the whales while controlling them using standard radio-control handsets. Radio waves don't travel through water very well, so we had to boost the signal with some underwater amplifiers."

Despite his thorough research and testing, Conti was nervous about whether his whales would actually be able to propel themselves under the water. "I was pretty sure they would be able to move their head, tail, and flippers convincingly, but had no idea whether they would actually be able to 'swim' like the real thing. Just in case they didn't, we built in a water pump that could suck water in through the mouth and expel it from the end of the tail—just like a jet boat. In the end we didn't need to use the jet-propulsion at all, since they swam naturally using only their fins and tail to power them."

Conti's experience at building remotely operated underwater models next won him the job of building animatronic killer whales, also known as orcas, for *Free Willy* (1993). The success of the film led to two sequels, requiring more whales with better performance capabilities.

"In the first film, our artificial whale was the double for a live whale named Keiko," says Conti. "Our whale was used for maybe 50 percent of the shots, while Keiko performed in the rest. In the second film, our whales were used for most shots except for some wildlife footage of real orcas. For the third film, our robotic whales were pretty much the only ones you see throughout the whole film."

10

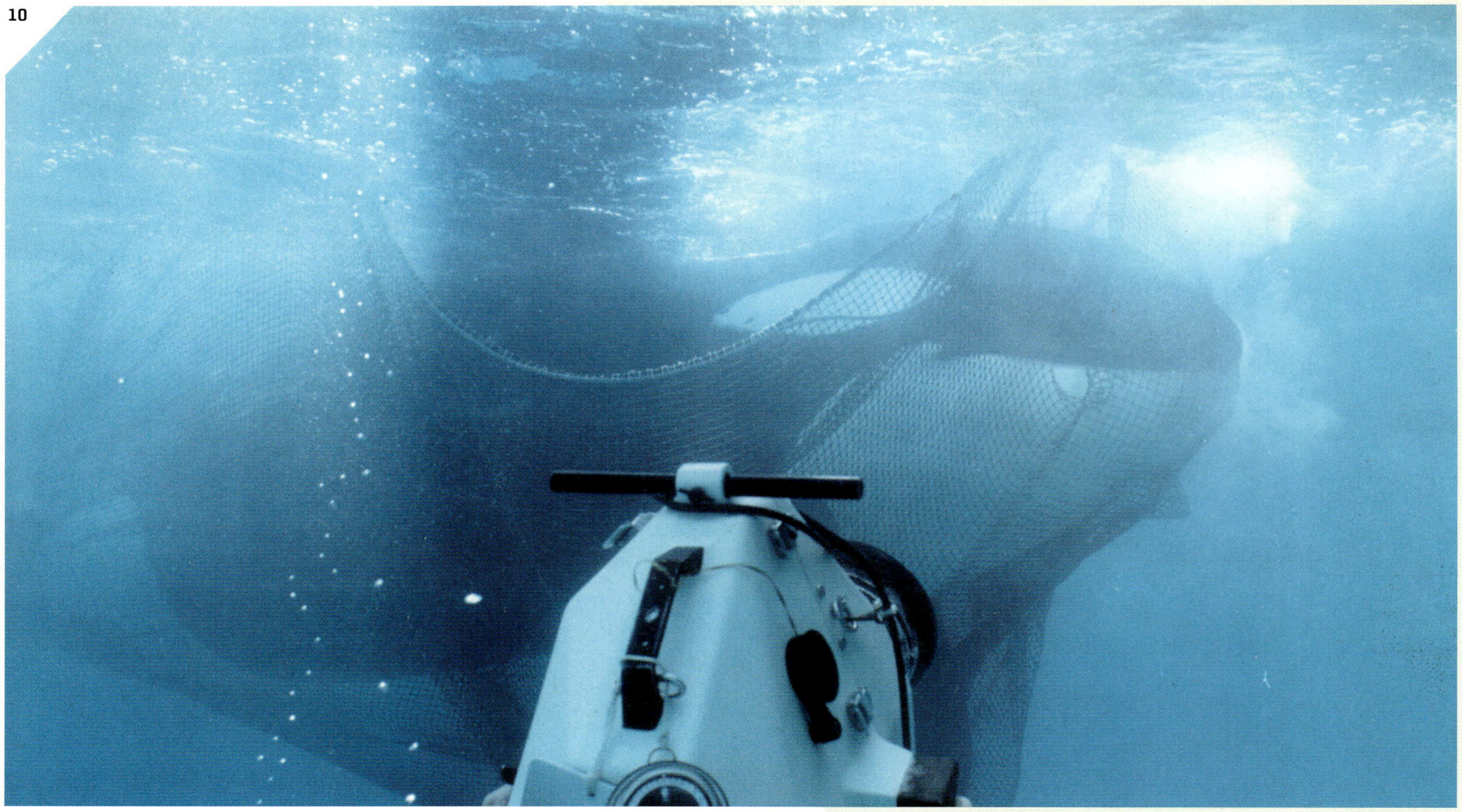

11

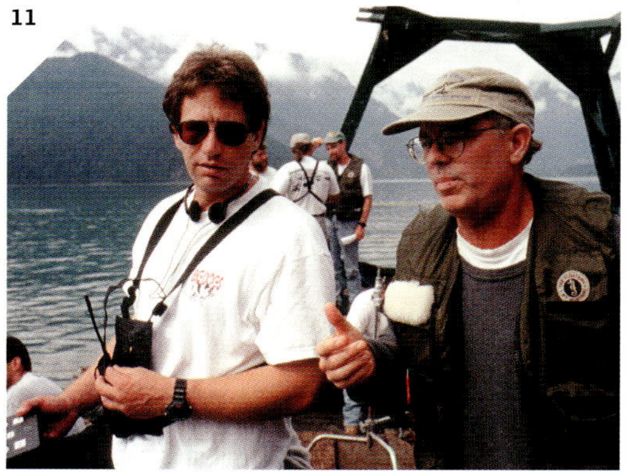

12

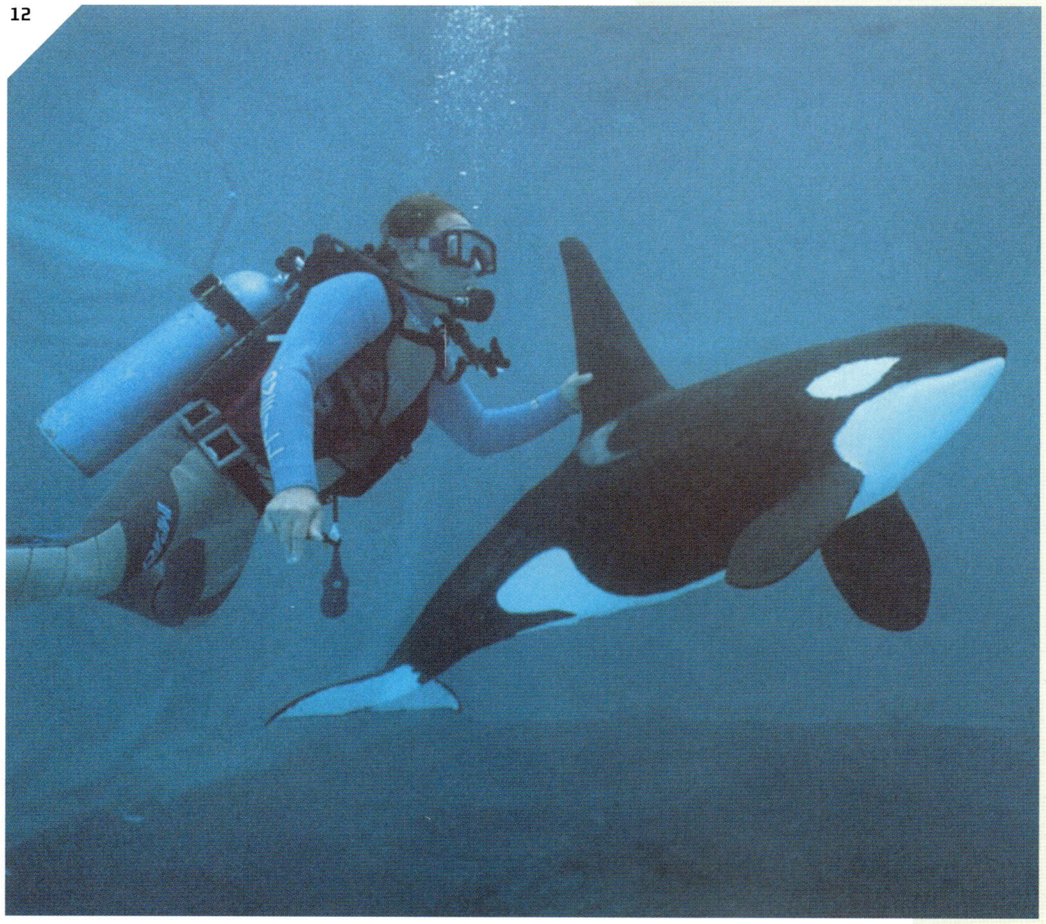

(10) One of Conti's hydraulically controlled whales is filmed from below the waves as it struggles in a fishing net **(11)** Walt Conti (left) holds one of the consoles used to control the performance of his whales during the filming of *Free Willy* **(09)** Many shots of the free-swimming Willy were achieved using this miniature, quarter-scale model, filmed in a swimming pool.

13

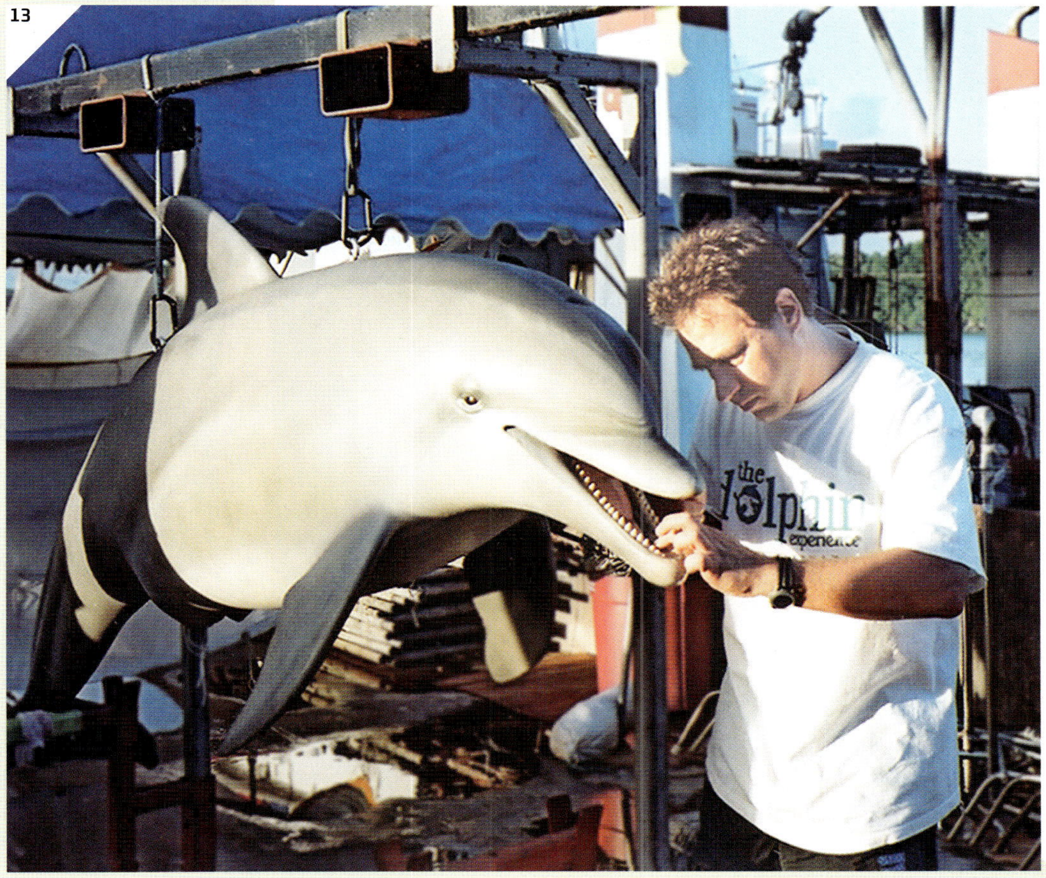

14

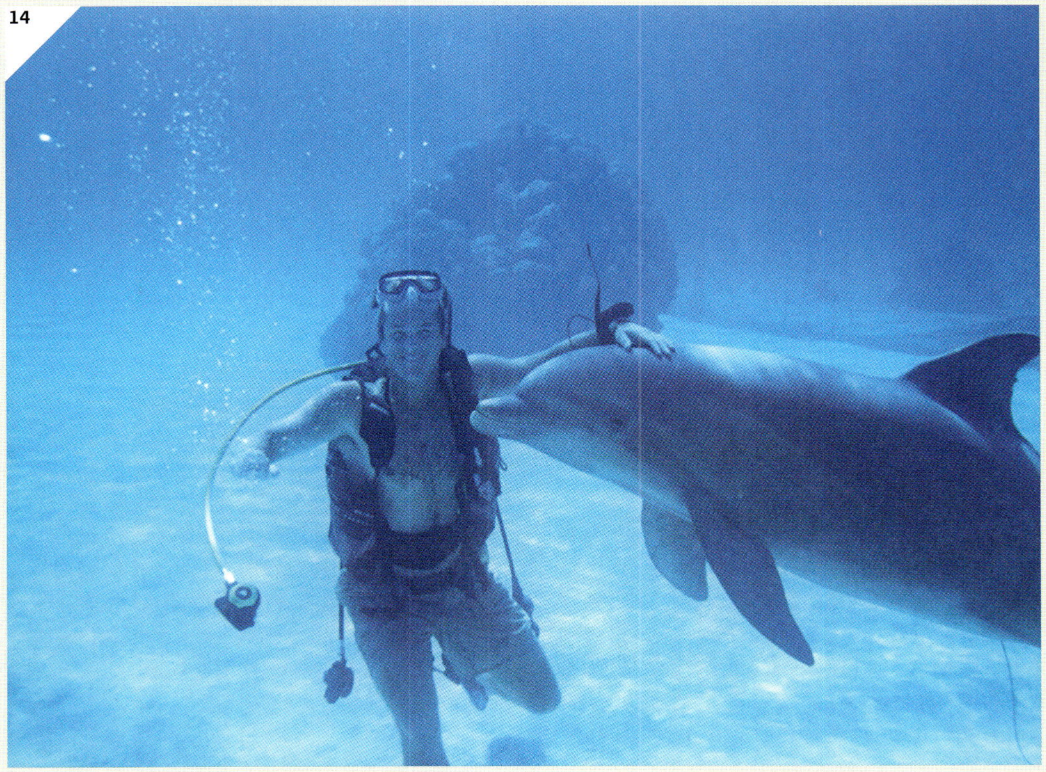

15

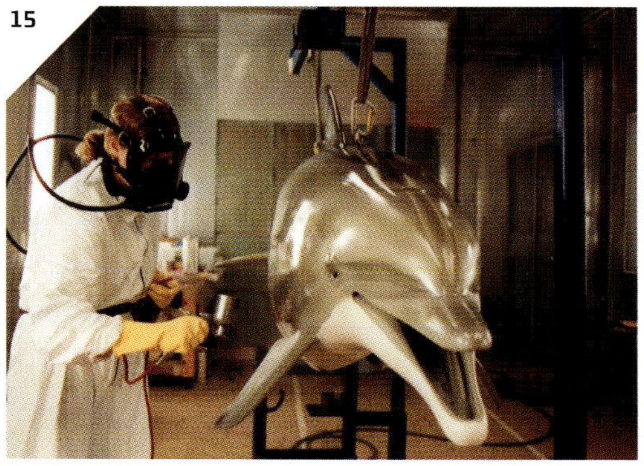

16

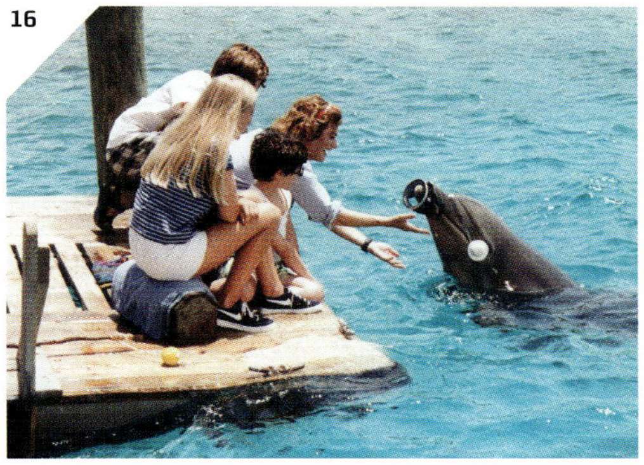

17

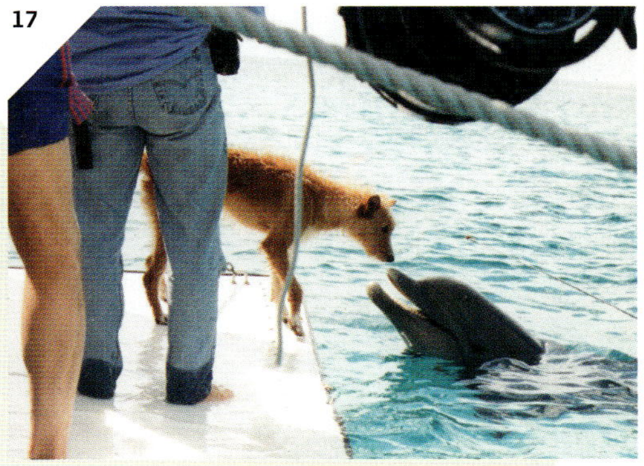

(13) Conti makes final adjustments to one of his animatronic dolphins before filming **(14)** Conti's dolphins are capable of swimming completely freely, just like the real thing. In this image the umbilical control cable is just visible trailing from the creature's belly **(15)** Spray-painting an animatronic dolphin. **(16-17)** Conti's dolphins are so controllable they can accurately interact with actors—and even dogs, as in these shots from *Flipper* (1996).

18

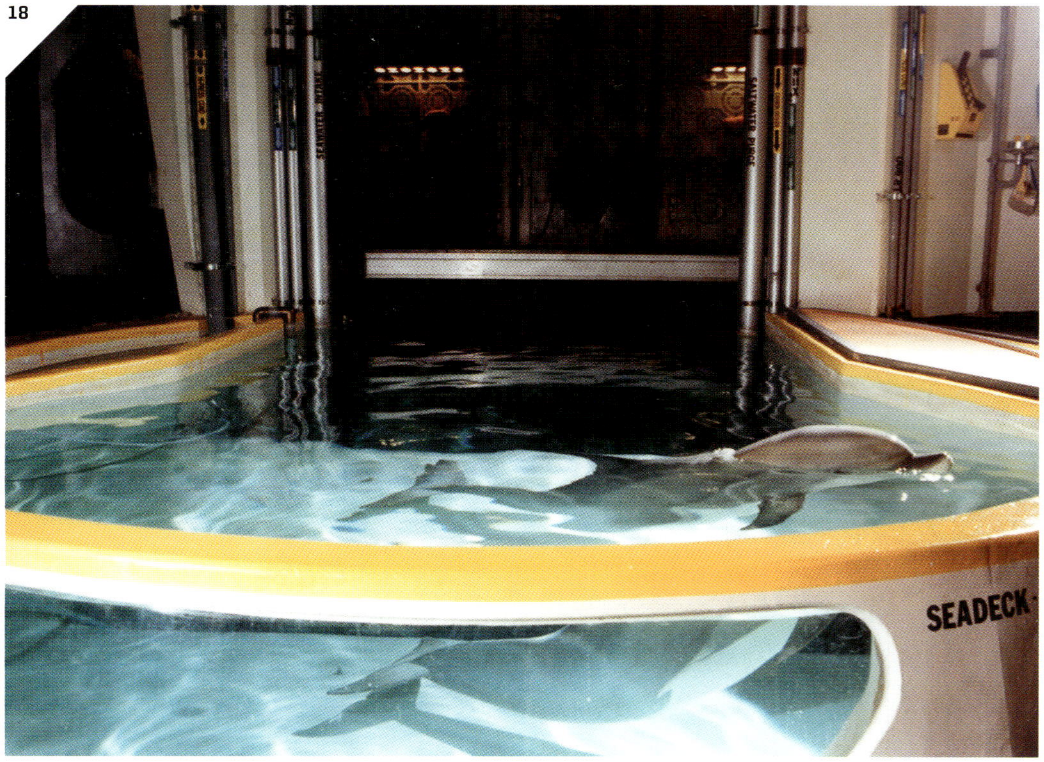

The *Free Willy* orcas presented Conti with the biggest challenge of his career. "Even though I had experience of making whales for *Star Trek*, building full-sized whales was a huge leap in terms of technology. The sheer size was also a complicating factor, with the final orcas weighing around 10,000 pounds [4,536kg] each."

"From an engineering point of view, the body has to endure incredible amounts of stress, especially at the peduncle, which is a narrow point at the base of the tail where the body meets the tail fin. That required very strong materials and some complex engineering. In many ways, it was much like building an aircraft. We used the strongest, most lightweight materials we could find: aluminums, titanium, and the kind of high-tech composite materials normally used to make things like helicopter rotor blades."

The orcas were controlled by hydraulics, the only power source capable of providing the huge forces needed to propel a full-size whale through water. Each whale required over 250 horsepower to produce its lifelike swimming movements. "When you start trying to get a robotic character to thrash its tail around and shift huge quantities of water, you really come to appreciate the power of the real creatures," Conti says. The whales' internal hydraulic rams required a pump to pressurize the oil and produce the movement, as Conti explains: "We kept the hydraulic power units out of the water on a support vessel and they pumped high-pressure oil to the whales through an umbilical cord. The cord also returned low-pressure oil back to the pump, supplied the power to drive the other internal mechanisms, and delivered control signals from the puppeteers."

The 300ft-long (91m) umbilicals were an engineering and logistical task in themselves. "So that they wouldn't be seen by the camera, the cords could be made to exit from either the side or from underneath the whale, depending on the angle they were filmed from," Conti explains. "The cords were also really heavy and could have dragged the whales down into the water, so we had to attach floats to them to make them neutrally buoyant. When we had three whales swimming together the cords would get all tangled up, so we had one person whose job it was to watch the whales and copy their movements using three pieces of string. That way when we'd finished filming a shot we could work backward and untangle the whales." The problem of unsightly umbilical cords became less of a problem in the later films when the technology to remove them digitally from shots improved and became much less expensive to use.

The whales' outer skin was again made of urethane. "We did lots of tests to find the right recipe, using plasticizers and other ingredients to make the material strong and very flexible. In addition, we had to make sure that the outer skin would stay wet when it came out of the water. If you look at a real orca when it puts its head out of the water, it is very shiny and wet. But plastic materials like urethane cause water to run right off them, making them look dry except for small beads of water sticking to the surface. We had to use a special wetting agent on the skin of the whales so that water would cling to them and make them look alive, not plastic."

The sheer size of the orcas also presented a challenge when it came to creating the skin. "We sculpted our whale in foam that was then covered in smooth fiberglass in much the same way that surf boards are made. From that we produced an articulated fiberglass core into which all our control mechanisms, motors, and electronics fitted. The only way to get the skin of the whale over this core was to cast the skin as one single piece around it. The core, complete with finished and tested mechanisms, was placed inside the steel-reinforced glass-fiber whale mold. We then mixed three tons of liquid urethane with black dye before finally adding the catalyst that would cause it to solidify. From then on we had half an hour to inject the urethane into the mold before it set. We had to rehearse the procedure precisely so we all knew who was doing what and when."

19

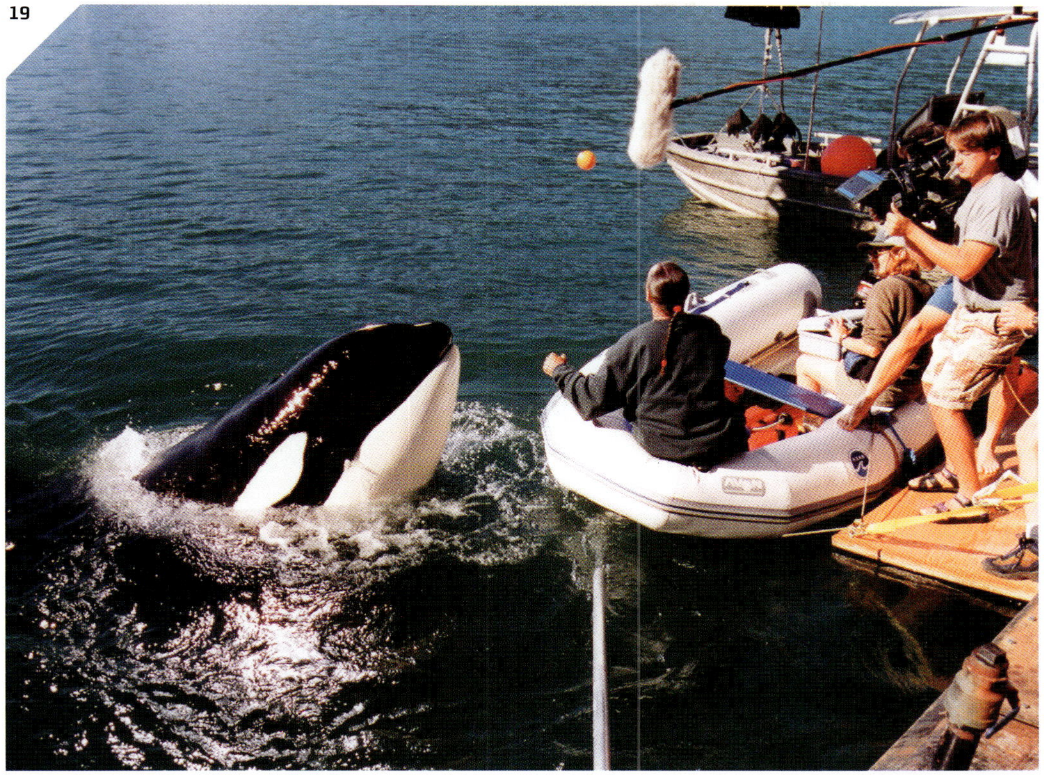

20

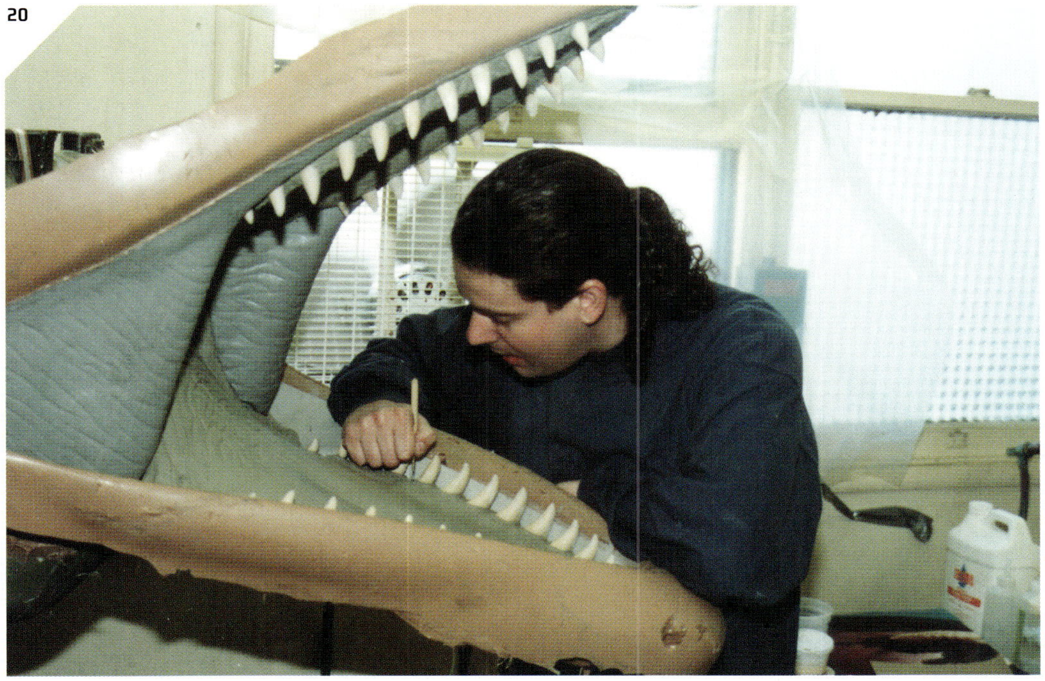

(18) Conti's dolphins made regular appearances in the TV series, *SeaQuest DSV*. Viewers assumed the dolphins were trained animals **(19)** On location for *Free Willy* **(20)** A bit of robot dentistry for the animatronic whale.

It was pretty hair-raising. When the whale was removed from the mold it was essentially complete, other than for exterior modifications such as painting. All of the mechanisms were permanently sealed inside. If we wanted to access anything we had to crawl in through the whale's mouth, but we could never get to a lot of the parts."

Despite the incredibly high-tech solutions employed by Conti, his goal remained the creation of entirely convincing orcas capable of giving a naturalistic performance. "One of the problems with the whales was making them appear alive," says Conti. "For such huge creatures, orcas have relatively few movements. That may make it sound simpler for the puppeteers to produce a performance, but with so little to move it starts becoming hard to create the impression of a thinking creature and convey a variety of emotions. It comes down to very subtle head movements and the use of body language. On the heads we were able to move the eyes, lips, and tongue, which helped a lot."

Breathing was also important in creating the appearance of life. "We had a big air tank inside each whale which would spray air and water out of the vent on the head. We found that compressed air looked too forced and fake, the air that comes out is actually very gentle and wet, so we had to keep our tanks at quite a low pressure. The tanks could be recharged from an air hose that was part of the umbilical cord."

Puppeteering the whales required up to three people to control the subtle mix of movements. "One puppeteer would control the head and tail movement that dictated where the creature went; another would control the action of the fins; and the third would look after the personality aspects of the head, such as the mouth, tongue, and eyes," explains Conti. "When the whales were filmed swimming at the surface of the water, the puppeteers controlled them from a nearby support vessel. When the whales were swimming underwater, however, the puppeteers had to don scuba-gear and submerge themselves and their waterproof control boxes." Careful operation of the head and tail movements could make the creatures swim, dive, or surface. Tail and pectoral movement could create a turn, allowing them to swim in a complete circle. The later models also had a mechanism that shifted internal weights from one side of the body to the other to create a roll. To make the orcas poke their heads up out of the water they were tied down at the tail. A nearby crane could then pull them down into the w ater or release them so they would pop up from below. Conti himself was one of the whale operators.

The nightmares that beset productions such as *Jaws* (1975) and *Waterworld* (1995) are legendary, and so Conti was all too aware that filming at sea with highly complex animatronics could be a recipe for disaster. "Salt water is incredibly corrosive, so at the end of a day's shooting they have to come out of the water and be thoroughly hosed down with fresh water. As well as corroding the mechanics, salt contaminates the urethane skin, making it hard to paint or repair it. Urethane also deteriorates quickly in UV [ultraviolet light], so when they're not in use each whale would have to go under a tent to shade it from the sun. When they're in the water the plasticizers and other components that give the urethane its flexibility also start to leach out, so the skins become increasingly tough."

In addition to the full-size orcas, Conti and his team also built a number of 6ft-long (1.8m), quarter-scale models that were filmed swimming in a large tank. "Filming the models at high speed made them look full-size, so for some shots it was a lot easier to shoot miniatures in the controlled conditions of a tank rather than out at sea."

21

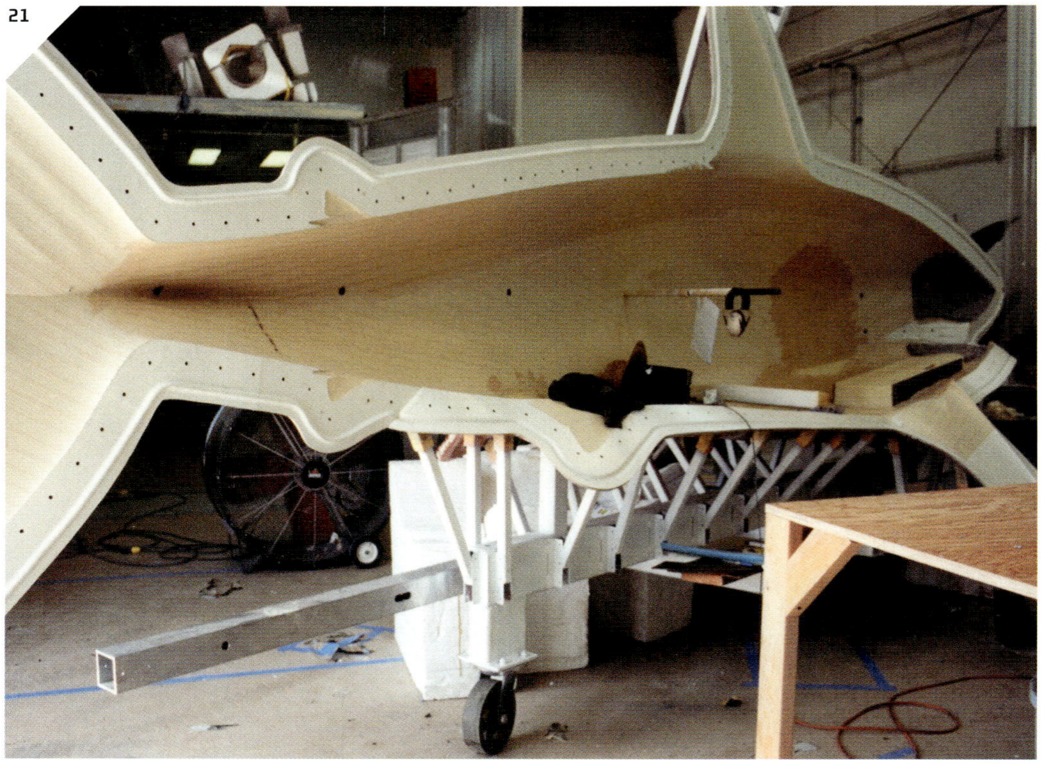

22

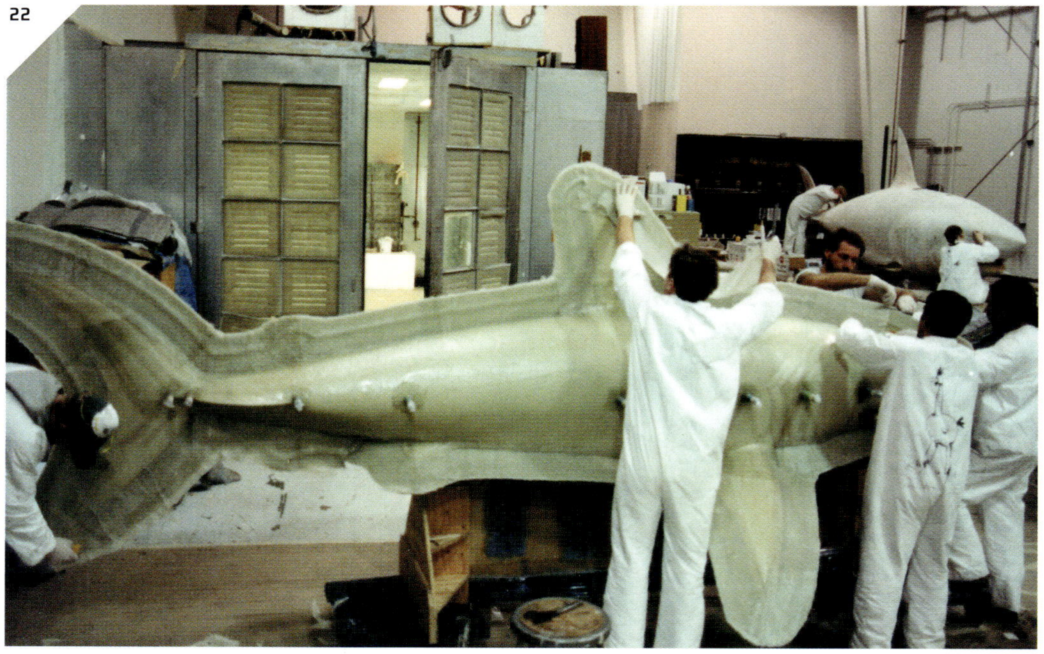

(21) One section of a shark mold for *Deep Blue Sea* (1999) **(22)** Technicians prepare to open a shark mould that has been filled with liquid urethane **(23)** The powerful internal mechanism of an animatronic shark.

(24) A urethane shark emerges from its mold **(25)** Some of the sharks for *Deep Blue Sea* were mounted on hydraulic motion platforms, allowing them to lunge from the water **(26)** Divers maneuver one of the free–floating sharks.

03

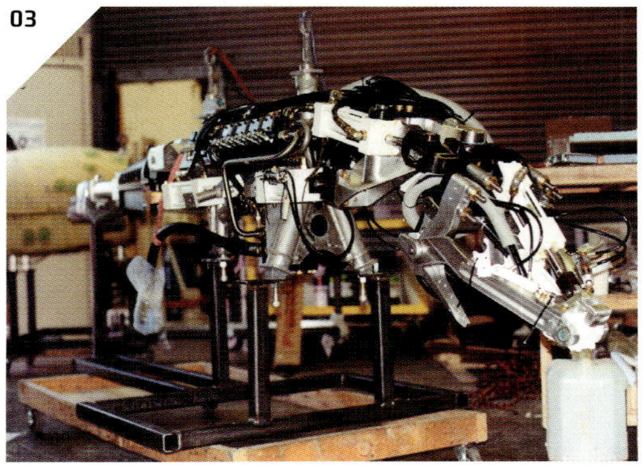

24

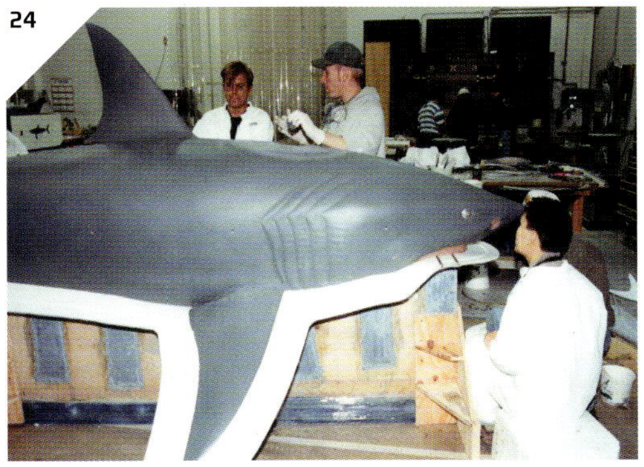

25

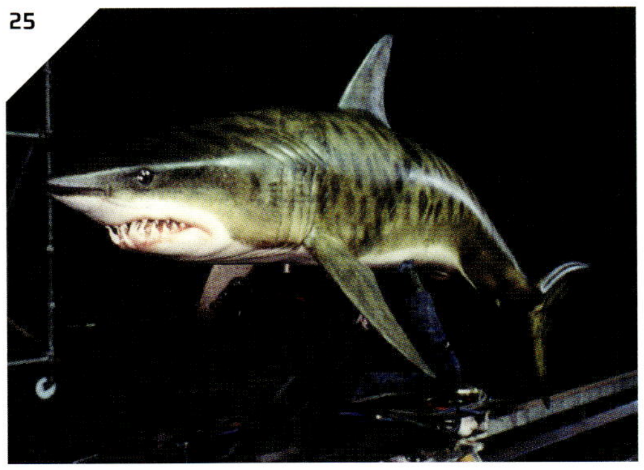

26

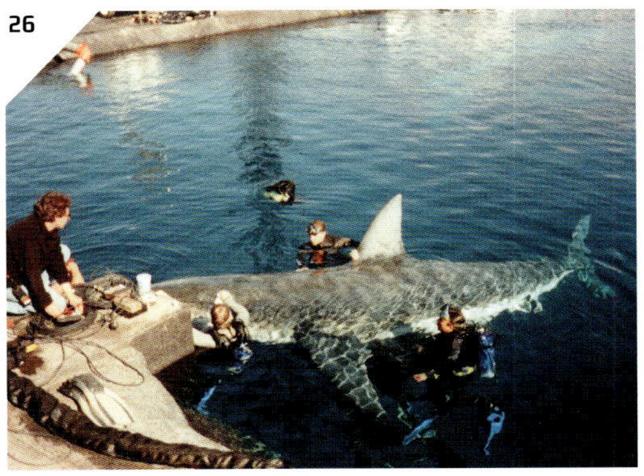

Whether using full-scale orcas at sea or miniatures in a pool, the *Free Willy* whales remain a benchmark in believable animatronic creatures. Following the success of his whales, Conti was asked to create dolphins for a number of productions, including *Flipper* (1996), *White Squall* (1996), and the *SeaQuest DSV* television series (1993–96).

Many people are surprised to learn that dolphins need to be recreated as animatronic creatures, but, as Conti explains, the affable creatures are not the best movie performers. "People always think that dolphins are ideal to film with because they're cute and easy to train," says Conti. "In reality, you can rarely get them to do things exactly the way you want them to. They also get bored really quickly and want to go off and do something else, and there's only a certain number of times you can bribe them with a fish. So, while the productions we worked on did use real dolphins, they could not generally be relied upon to convey story cues. Generally speaking, a dolphin swimming along, interacting with a performer, or doing some kind of expressive move needs to be done with animatronics. The stuff where they jump out of the water or do acrobatics is left to the real thing."

Much of what applied to the construction of Conti's *Free Willy* whales applied equally to his dolphins, although there were some major differences. "The biggest thing with dolphins is getting the energy into them—they're such fast, hyperactive animals. That meant packing a huge amount of power and speed into a fairly small space. We developed our own servos, which are 10–15 times more powerful than anything you can buy. We didn't need the umbilical cord that was necessary when using hydraulic rams. The dolphins could therefore be entirely self contained."

Early dolphins built by Conti had no cord, which meant that potentially they could swim beyond the reach of the puppeteer's radio signal. "If they went too far the radio receiver would automatically stop the swim functions and the creature would glide to a halt. Then we'd have to retrieve it and bring it closer to the puppeteers," Conti says. "But once digital erasing was easier we built them with a very thin umbilical cord to supply the control information and also the electrical power, which meant they could go much further in a single shot and didn't have to carry batteries."

As with all his underwater creations, it was important that the dolphins contained no air within their body once they were taken underwater. Trapped air will cause buoyancy problems, making it hard to control the performance. "We would always 'burp' the dolphins once they were underwater," says Conti. "Divers would go down with them and shake them around at different angles to ensure all the air bubbles were out."

For *Deep Blue Sea* (1999) Conti was asked to create terrifying genetically engineered sharks. A number of variations were built, including independently swimming, radio-controlled sharks, and computer-controlled, motion-platform-mounted sharks— both full-scale and miniature.

"Sharks are very slow moving, stealthy things, but they can suddenly power into awesome strike maneuvers of incredible speed and strength," says Conti. "Much of our work was about creating very fast, powerful moves. The sharks also had to be incredibly flexible. Our dolphins and whales had fairly rigid central torsos, but our sharks were constructed with articulated torsos, enabling them to bend almost in half when they thrashed about. The fairly inflexible torsos of the whales and dolphins had made a convenient container for all our mechanical workings, but the shark's articulated torso flexed around, meaning we had to package up the workings and divide them between the segmented body sections."

To produce fast, powerful attacks, some sharks were mounted on a hydraulic motion platform that was affixed to the bottom of their stomachs. Large animatronic creatures controlled in this

27

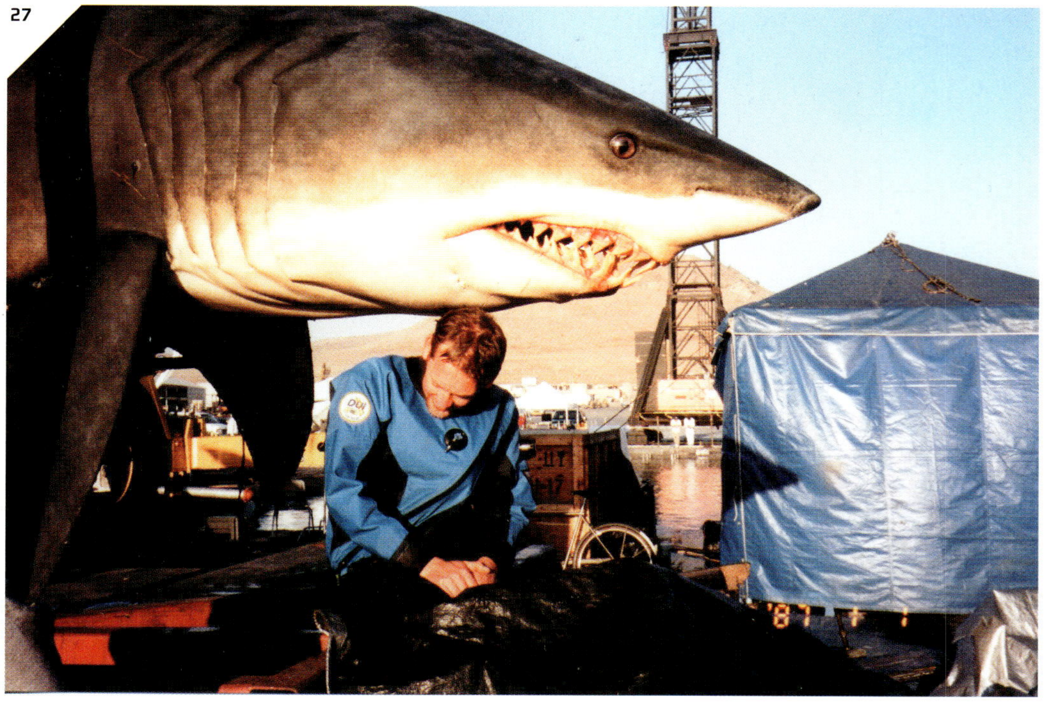

fashion normally make use of adapted platforms originally constructed for use as flight simulators in the aerospace industry. Conti, however, built his own 2,000-horsepower platform that could operate underwater. The computer-controlled, motion-base sharks could be programmed one axis at a time, gradually building up each move. These moves could then be played back slowly at first, enabling performers to rehearse their reactions. The sharks were then sped up for final takes. In one shot a stunt performer had a prosthetic arm ripped from his shoulder in a lightning-fast, motion-controlled precision shark attack.

Perhaps fittingly, Conti and his team spent a lot of time engineering the jaws of their sharks. "Sharks have something called a floating or extendable jaw, meaning that it isn't attached to anything and can be thrust outward, away from the upper mouth," says Conti. "We built a very complex mechanism to give our sharks this ability, and although it looks as if the gums are peeling away from the teeth it is the teeth thrusting forward that achieves the effect."

Another innovation was the quality of the sharks' skin. "The sudden and extreme movements of the sharks meant that their skin needed to be really flexible," Conti says. "In addition, unlike whale and dolphin skin, which is very smooth, sharks are covered in patches of tiny scales. The scales were detailed into the original clay sculpture using a stamp. When the molds were made, we filled the tiny scale indentations, each just a couple of millimeters across, with a thin layer of hard urethane. Then we filled the rest of the mold with our regular urethane mix. The result was a supple skin with many minute, hard scales."

For most of the time sharks remain expressionless, cruising along gracefully, but with very few outward signs of conscience or personality. This lack of expression was initially considered to be a problem when it came to creating an artificial shark performance. "Sharks have these completely dead-looking, black eyes. In fact, they look kind of fake. The production asked us to art direct the eyes to introduce a little more life into the characters. We tried all kinds of eye designs, from subtle to quite extreme, but the more life we gave them the more fake they looked. In the end we just went with the expressionless, glassy, black look and they worked fine."

In the end the shark's believability stemmed from combining an accurate physical likeness with some appropriate puppeteering. "Unlike working with whales or dolphins, when you control the performance of a shark there's no conveyance of personality or subtlety of movement to pull off," Conti says. "They're all about brutal attitude. They're either cruising on autopilot with a dead stare on their face or attacking with high-speed lunges."

Conti's ability to tackle extreme engineering challenges had also been tested for the film *Anaconda* (1997). This time the slippery challenge was to create a lifelike giant snake that could move like the real thing and strike with lightning speed. Conti eventually built two snakes for the film. One was 40ft (12m) long and weighed 4,410 pounds (2,000kg) while a "small" version was just 15ft long (4.5m), weighing 1,540 pounds (700kg).

"The snakes were a real challenge because of the shape—just a long thin sock. There was very little room in which to fit the necessary mechanics," says Conti. "That meant that no 'off-the-shelf' components would fit inside, and so everything had to be engineered especially for the project."

To create the structure of the snake, Conti and his team manufactured 60 vertebrae, each similar in design to the vertebrae of a real snake, and linked to form the flexible inner skeleton. Each vertebra was hydraulically powered and had two axes of movement, up and down, left and right. Wrapped around the vertebrae was a snaking tangle of cables and pipes used to control the movement and to feed oil to and from the hydraulic rams. These cables, around 1,000 in all, exited the snake's belly at the halfway point. With the belly secured to the floor of the studio, the front and back half of the snake could coil and lift with complete freedom.

28

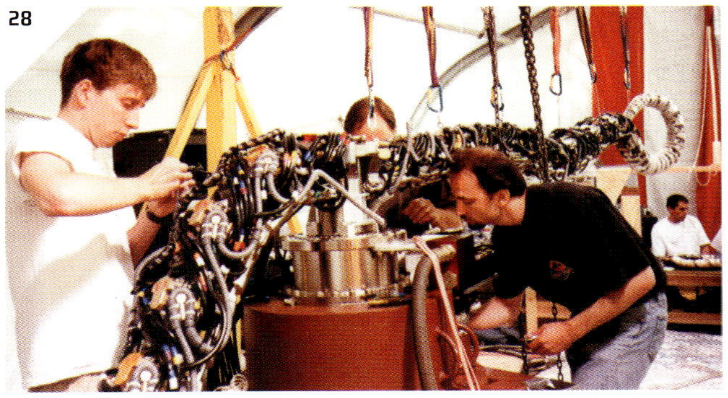

29

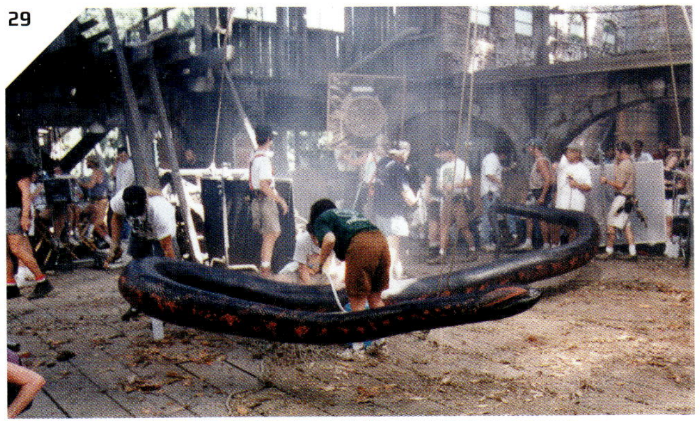

30

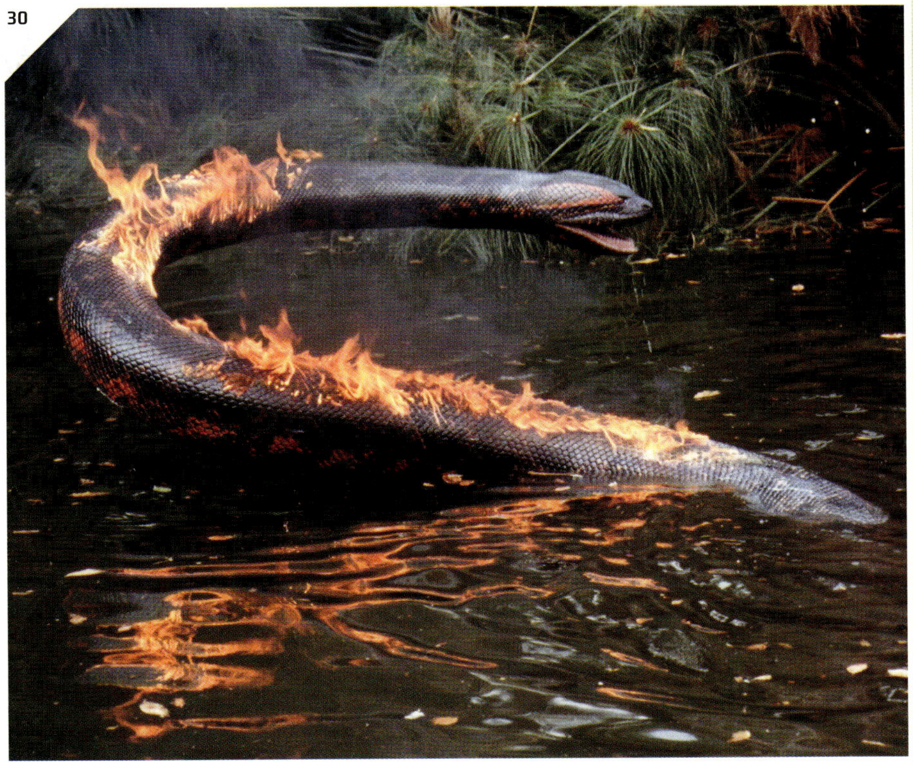

One of the greatest challenges of the project was how to puppeteer 120 axes of movement to produce the necessary writhing motions of a real snake. "Obviously we couldn't have each axis controlled by a puppeteer using joy sticks and radio control," says Conti. "It would also be impossible to coordinate the movement of each axis in order to create a sinuous, snake-like motion." The solution was sought in commercially available computer-animation software. "We built a computer model of the snake, which included each of the 60 vertebrae," says Conti. "That model was then linked to a Waldo, a small model of the snake. The Waldo was manually moved to a new position for every few frames of a sequence. That 'key-frame' position was recorded by the computer which then interpolated those positions to calculate the position of the snake's body for each of the intermediate frames.

"The final animation could be edited and refined and then used to control the performance of the full-size animatronic snake. To control the performance and pacing during filming, we could use a dial to speed up or slow down the prerecorded moves, making the snake interact better with the environment and performers during filming." While the overall movements of the snake were computer controlled, smaller actions, such as eye and mouth movement, were puppeteered live by remote control during filming.

"One of the trickiest effects to achieve was the giant snake's tiny, flicking tongue. This was achieved using two thin strips of sprung steel. When the longer piece of steel was pushed forward it would cause the lower piece to bend. When placed inside the snake's forked tongue, rapidly pushing and pulling the longer piece of metal with a servo would create the flicking action. The simple-looking effect caused Conti and his team a disproportionate amount of effort. "I've built some of the biggest, most sophisticated animatronic characters ever made," he says, "but on all those projects there's always some little detail that ends up taking a lot of work."

(27) On the set of *Deep Blue Sea* **(28)** Conti and his team built a full-sized animatronic snake for *Anaconda*.This image shows the intricate mass of hydraulics and motors needed to control the creature **(29)** The snake was capable of freely moving both head and tail but was controlled by cables exiting beneath its belly at the midway point **(30)** Conti's Anaconda continued to operate perfectly throughout its spectacular, fiery death sequence.

GLOSSARY

ANIMATRONIC
Any remotely controlled system that uses pneumatics, hydraulics, cables, rods, or motors to produce lifelike performances from puppets or models.

ARTICULATION
Any form of artificially produced movement in a puppet or makeup design.

ARCUS SENILIS
A milky ring that forms around the edges of the iris in the eyes of some older people. Often included in old-age makeups by using specially painted contact lenses.

BALD CAP
A rubber cap stretched over a performer's head to create the illusion of baldness, or ensure that a wig fits snugly over real hair.

BLEND LINE
The point at which any prosthetic appliance, such as a nose, tapers off into real skin. Much of the art of sculpting, making, and applying prosthetic appliances lies in ensuring that the blend between reality and trickery is unnoticeable.

CABLE CONTROL
The remote-controlled operation of puppets or models via cables that are pushed and pulled either by hand or by small motors.

COLLODION
A highly flammable, syrupy liquid made from cellulose dissolved in ether and alcohol, which was once used in the production of photographic plates and also painted on to cuts like a form of liquid plaster. It was combined with cotton to sculpt many early makeups, such as Jack Pierce's Frankenstein's Monster.

COMPUTER AIDED DESIGN (CAD)
Specialized engineering or design software used in the planning and construction of mechanisms, props, sets, lighting setups, and complex special-effects equipment.

CORE
If a mold made from a character sculpture were to have foam latex injected into it, the result would be a solid foam representation of that character. Usually only a thin foam skin is required, and so an inner mold, or core, is created. Foam latex is injected into the gap between the outer mold and the inner core to produce the skin. Because the core fits perfectly within the resulting skin it is often used as a shell for the final animatronic creature's body—the skin goes on the outside of the core, the inner mechanisms are housed within it.

CORNEAL BULGE
A small, barely visible bulge on the front of the eye that is noticeable when the eyelid stretches over it during a blink. When incorporated in the most realistic fake eyeballs, a corneal bulge also requires a flexible eyelid, as traditional hard-shell eyelids will hit the bulge when they close.

CORNEAL LENS
A contact lens, such as those used for normal sight correction, that covers only the front, corneal area of the eye.

CYBERSCAN
A method of transcribing a real object into a digital model by accurately measuring its features with a laser. Normally used to create a scan of a performer or maquette in order to produce a 3-D copy for sculpting purposes. Originally developed by the US military as a rapid way of measuring troops for uniforms.

DENTAL ALGINATE
A quick-setting plaster made with seaweed extracts used to make lifecasts of faces and body parts for makeup purposes.

FABRICATION
The creation of a character by using body pieces individually sculpted in various materials to represent flesh, bone, and muscle. When the understructure of pieces is complete, a skin or fur covering is placed over the top. Also used to refer to the build process of any character.

FIBERGLASS
The common term used for a composite of minute glass fibers with various resins to produce a very strong, plastic-like material. Used to create molds and internal body parts, such as skulls.

FLOCKING
Covering any surface with fur using an electrostatic charge to make the fibers stand on end.

FOAM LATEX
A rubbery, sponge-like material that is lightweight and easy to paint and glue. Liquid latex, the milky white sap of the Malaysian rubber tree, is mixed with various additives and then whipped up into a foam. The foam is injected into molds and then baked to produce prosthetic appliances, rubber suits, and the skins of animatronic characters.

FUR TRANSFER
Method of transferring real or synthetic fur from one backing material to another

GELATIN
Gelatin (or gelatine) is made from the boiled bones, skins, and tendons of animals. Used in catering to set foods, in makeup gelatin can be melted and poured into molds to make prosthetic appliances such as scars or eye-bags. Quick and easy to make, but it can start to melt under the heat of studio lights.

HAIR PUNCHING
Creating an artificial coat of hair by using a needle to push individual fibers into the skin of a creature suit or puppet.

HAIR TYING
The creation of wigs, facial-hair appliances, and hair suits by laboriously hand-tying strands of hair to a fabric backing. The traditional term for wig-making using this technique is ventilating.

HOT MELT
A range of synthetic materials with varying qualities that can be melted and, typically, used as glues. In makeup, hot-melt materials can be used to produce various objects or body parts.

HYDRAULICS
The use of high-pressure liquids—typically oil—to produce fast and powerful movement in a large-scale animatronic puppet.

LATEX RUBBER
A liquid produced from the sap of the rubber tree. When combined with fungicides, foaming agents, catalysts, and other chemicals, it is used to create various densities of rubber for prosthetic makeup and animatronics.

LEG EXTENSIONS
Metal devices worn by performers inside costumes to extend their limbs in order to give a character less human proportions.

LIFECAST
A mold bearing the exact features of a performer, used for the creation of prosthetic makeup and costumes to ensure a perfect fit. The process usually involves covering the performer's body and face in quick-drying alginate to produce a negative mold from which a positive cast can be taken. Instead of the traditional method of producing a lifecast, which can be unnerving for the subject, a cyberscan (see above) can now be used to create an accurate replica of a performer's features in a computerized milling process.

MAQUETTE
A small sculpture made to help directors and other artists envisage how a full-size character will appear when built.

MECH
Short for "mechanism." Any mechanical device or arrangement that facilitates the movement of parts of an animatronic creature. For example, an eye mech is the mechanical assemblage that holds a character's artificial eyes, receives radio-controlled signals from puppeteers, and uses servo motors to produce an eye performance.

MILLING
The use of automated machines to carve materials such as rigid foam or polystyrene. A technique more prevalent in makeup since the increase in use of CAD programs and cyberscans. Three-dimensional digital models created using these techniques can be fed to milling machines in order to create a physical model of the desired dimensions.

MOLD
The negative shape of any object which, when filled with a material such as foam latex, will produce an exact copy. The creation of most makeup characters and appliances involves a complicated process of making positive and negative molds based on original clay sculptures.

MOTION CAPTURE
The use of various techniques to record the movement of a human or animal performer. The movement can be edited and redesigned before being used to drive computer-generated or animatronic characters.

MOTION CONTROL
A method of recording or programming the movements of a puppet so that a performance can be achieved exactly as required, and repeated whenever necessary. Also used to control the movement of cameras and other special-effects equipment.

NATIONAL FIBER TECHNOLOGY
Massachusetts-based company used by most makeup studios to supply custom-made synthetic hair and fur.

NOSE PUTTY
A wax-based material that can be softened in the hands and then pressed on to the skin and sculpted to the right shape before having makeup applied over the top. It is most commonly used by stage actors to change the shape of their nose or chin.

PATCHING
Repairing foam-latex costumes damaged during filming by filling small holes and rips with fresh foam latex before curing in an oven, or with a heat gun.

PAX PAINT
A flexible, high-bond color pigment used to paint on a range of prosthetic materials. Created by combining water-based acrylic colors with Pros-Aide adhesive.

PHOTOSHOP
Leading two-dimensional image-creation and editing software used by many artists to create and enhance digital character designs.

PNEUMATICS
The use of compressed air to drive pistons to create movement in a puppet.

PRACTICAL EFFECTS
Any creature or makeup effect—or other form of special effect—that is performed using physical props and models during actual filming.

PROS-AIDE
A flexible acrylic-emulsion adhesive used for many purposes in the makeup industry. Mostly used to fix prosthetic appliance to performers, it can be mixed with cosmetic-grade pigments to create a smudge-proof paint for use on prosthetic appliances (PAX paint). After it dries, Pros-Aide is waterproof and remains tacky until powdered. Also used as a backing for artificial furs.

PROSTHETICS
False limbs, noses, or other appendages normally made from foam latex, silicone, or gelatin, which are seamlessly affixed to the face or body of a performer.

PUPPETEER
Any person who actively generates the performance of a puppet or animatronic character by operating cables, rods, or radio-control consoles. Sometimes also used to refer to a performer who wears a creature suit.

RADIO CONTROL (RC)
The use of radio waves to control remotely the motors that create the performance of a character. Animatronic creatures are typically operated using a handheld radio-control console of the type used by model boat, aircraft, and car hobbyists.

RIGID FOAM
A dense foam that can be carved to create sculptures or body parts for fabricated-suit costumes.

ROD PUPPET
A puppet that is manually controlled using a series of rods connected to its joints and limbs. Such rods are normally used by puppeteers to create a character's performance, although they can be connected to a motion-control device that mechanically moves them according to a preprogrammed pattern. Rods visible in the final shot can now be digitally erased.

SCLERAL LENS
Contact lenses that cover the entire front surface of the eye, including the whites, or sclera.

SERVO
Small radio-controlled motors of varying sizes and specifications that are used to actuate movement within a makeup character.

SILICONE
Flexible silicone-based compounds used to create prosthetic appliances and the skins for creature suits and animatronic characters. Similar to the sealant used around bathroom fixtures, it comes as a thick gel to which a catalyst is added to solidify it. Unlike opaque foam latex, silicone has a translucency similar to skin, so has become favored by some artists over the past decade. It is nevertheless generally more demanding to apply and paint than foam.

SPANDEX
A stretchy fabric, often also called Lycra, used to make various garments, including the all-in-one body suits that form the core of most creature costumes.

TELEMETRY
The use of a mechanical measuring system to record the position and movement of joints and limbs on a human performer or a skeletal puppet in order to use that data to drive the performance of a computer-generated or animatronic character.

WALDO
A simplified telemetric model of an animatronic creature used for puppeteering purposes. Each joint on a Waldo has a potentiometer or other form of sensor that measures movement when the puppet is manipulated by hand. The movement data is stored on a computer and can be edited before being relayed to the full-size puppet to create movement. Full-size Waldos can be worn on a performer's body or face to relay their performance to an animatronic or computer-generated character. The term Waldo is widely used as a generic term for such technology, although the word itself is the trademarked name of the devices built by makeup company The Creature Shop.

WIRE REMOVAL
The removal of wires, rods, cables, and rigs used to support or puppeteer characters or objects during filming, as well as other unwanted elements from a scene. A painstaking task when attempted optically, it is now achieved digitally with relative ease. Also called rig removal.

YAK HAIR
Yak hair can be dyed, punched, flocked, tied, and dressed to create the look of many different types of animal hair and fur. Most commonly used is the soft hair grown on the creature's belly as insulation against harsh mountain winters. If not shaved from the yak this fur is naturally shed in the spring. Most yak hair comes from China.

ZBRUSH
Leading three-dimensional sculpting software that allows designers to shape "digital clay" in 3-D to produce computer-generated characters.

INDEX

THANKS

Images copyright and/or courtesy of

AI: Artificial Intelligence (Dreamworks/ Amblin/Warner Bros/Aaron Sims)

Alien Resurrection (Twentieth Century Fox/ADI)

Alien Vs Predator (T wentieth Century Fox/ADI/The Kobal Collection)

Anaconda (Columbia/Miles Teves/ Walt Conti)

Batman Returns (Warner Bros/ Miles Teves)

Bedazzled (Twentieth Century Fox/ Ocean/ADI/Steve Wang)

Black Sheep (Livestock Films/Ken George/Weta Workshop)

Blade (New Line/Miles Teves)

Blade: Trinity (New Line/ Carlos Huante/Steve Wang/Spectral Motion)

Braindead (Wingnut Films/ Weta workshop)

Buddy (Columbia Pictures/ Jim Henson's Creature Shop)

The Cave (Lakeshore Entertainment/ Screen Gems/Steve Wang/Brian Steele)

The Chronicles of Narnia: The Lion, the Witch and the Wardrobe (Walt Disney Pictures/Walden media/KNB)

Conquest of the Pole (The British Film Institute)

Constantine (Warner Bros/Aaron Sims)

Creature from the Black Lagoon (Universal/The British Film Institute)

Die Niebelungen (UFA/Ronald Grant Archive)

Doctor Jekyll and Mr Hyde (Paramount/ The British Film Institute)

Doom (Di Bona Ventura/Universal/ Aaron Sims/Brian Steele)

The Empire Strikes Back (Twentieth Century Fox/Lucasfilm Ltd/The Kobal Collection)

Fantastic Four (Twentieth Century Fox/ Carlos Huante)

Flipper (Universal/Walt Conti)

The Four Hundred Tricks of the Devil (The British Film Institute)

Free Willy (Warner Bros/Walt Conti)

From Dusk Till Dawn (Los Hooligans/ A Band Apart/KNB)

Godzilla (Columbia Tristar/Steve Wang/Patrick Tatopoulos)

Gremlins 2 (Warner Bros/Aaron Sims/ Steve Wang)

Guyver: Dark Hero (Steve Wang)

Harry and the Hendersons (Universal/ Brian Steele)

Hellboy (Revolution/Columbia Tristar/ Steve Wang/Spectral Motion)

Hook (Columbia Tristar/Mitch DeVane)

Independence Day (Twentieth Century Fox/Patrick Tatopoulos)

I Robot (Twentieth Century Fox/ Patrick Tatopoulos)

King Kong (1933 - RKO/The British Film Institute)

King Kong (2005 – Universal/Weta Workshop/Miles Teves/The Kobal Collection)

Kung Fu Rascals (Steve Wang)

Lord of the Rings (New Line/The Kobal Collection/Ronald Grant Archive)

Lady in the Water (Warner Bros/ Spectral Motion)

Legend (Twentieth Century Fox / Miles Teves/The Kobal Collection)

The Lost World (First National/ The British Film Institute)

Meet the Feebles (Wingnut Films/ Weta Workshop)

Men in Black (Columbia/Aaron Sims/ The Kobal Collection)

Men in Black 2 (Columbia/Carlos Huante)

Metropolis (UFA/The British Film Institute)

Mighty Joe Young (Walt Disney Pictures/Carlos Huante)

Moby Dick (Warner Bros/The Kobal Collection)

Nosferatu (Prana-Film/The Kobal Collection)

The Nutty Professor (Imagine Entertainment/Mitch DeVane)

Phantom of the Opera (Universal/ The Kobal Collection)

Pirates of the Caribbean (Walt Disney Pictures/Jerry Bruckheimer/ Professional VisionCare)

Planet of the Apes (Twentieth Century Fox/The Zanuck Co/Kazuhiro Tsuji)

Predator (Twentieth Century Fox/Steve Wang)

Public Eye (Gibson Group/ Weta Workshop)

The Santa Clause 2 (Walt Disney Pictures/ADI)

Shaggy Dog (Walt Disney Pictures/ Miles Teves)

Stargate (Canal+/Carolco/ Patrick Tatopoulos)

Starship Troopers (Columbia/ADI)

Terminator 3: Rise of the Machines (C-2 Pictures/Warner Bros/Aaron Sims)

Underworld (Lakeshore Entertainment/ Screen Gems/ Patrick Tatopoulos)

Underworld: Evolution (Lakeshore Entertainment/Screen Gems/Steve Wang/Brian Steele/Professional VisionCare)

The Valley of Gwangi (Morningside/ Ray Harryhausen)

Van Helsing (Universal/Miles Teves/ Carlos Huante)

War of the Worlds (Dreamworks/ Paramount/Carlos Huante)

X-Men (Twentieth Century Fox/Marvel Entertainment/ Miles Teves)

X-Men: The Last Stand (Twentieth Century Fox/Marvel Entertainment/ Spectral Motion/Carlos Huante/ Mitch DeVane)

Other images copyright and/or courtesy of: Jim Henson's Creature Shop, Stan Winston, Richard Rickitt, Rick Baker, Jeff Himmell, Mitch DeVane, Kazuhiro Tsuji, Steve Wang, Mike Elizalde, Jon Dawe, ADI, KNB, Brian Steele, Professional VisionCare Associates

Thanks to everyone at Rotovision, in particular Chris Middleton who worked so hard to fit too many words onto too few pages. Thanks also to my agent, Ben Mason, for making sure the wheels were kept well greased. Huge thanks and a big hug to my wife Varsha and to Charlie, our own little monster, for living without me while I locked myself away and scribbled. Above all I would like to thank the following individuals for their various contributions to this book—in particular those who gave willingly of their time, but whose voice didn't make it into the final book for editorial reasons.

Tom Woodruff Jr., AlecGillis (ADI); Ty Boyce; Walt Conti (Edge Innovations); Howard Berger; Tami Lane; Jim Leonard; Beth Hathaway; Jeff Himmel (KNB); Guy Himber; Allison Klein; Patrick Tatopoulos (Patrick Tatopoulos Studio); Roland Blancaflor; Mike Elizalde; Fernando Favila; Mark Setrakian; Brian Walsh (Spectral Motion); Marion Davey, Tania Rodger, Richard Taylor, Jenny Williams (Weta Workshop); Cristina Patterson Ceret (Professional VisionCare Associates); Jon Dawe; Mitch DeVane; Ray Harryhausen; Carlos Huante; Doug Jones; Brendan Lonergan; John Norris; Matt Rose; Brian Steele; Miles Teves; Kazuhiro Tsuji; Aaron Sims; and Steve Wang.

The publishers would like to thank Paul and Jerome at Studio Tonne.